Fodor's

ARGENTINA

7th Edition

Fodor's Travel Publications New York, Toronto, London, Sydney, Auckland

www.fodors.com

Portions of this book appear in *Fodor's Buenos Aires*.

FODOR'S ARGENTINA

Writers: Amanda Barnes, Cathy Brown, Karina Martinez-Carter, Sorrel Moseley-Williams, Victoria Patience, Dan Perlman, Jessica Pollack, Brian Stevenson
Editors: Heidi Leigh Johanssen, Debbie Harmsen, Jess Moss

Production Editor: Carrie Parker
Maps & Illustrations: David Lindroth, *cartographer;* Rebecca Baer, *map editor;* William Wu, *information graphics*
Design: Fabrizio La Rocca, *creative director*; Tina Malaney, Chie Ushio, Jessica Walsh, *designers*; Melanie Marin, *associate director of photography;* Jennifer Romains, *photo research*
Cover Photo: (Tango lesson, Buenos Aires): Javier Pierini/Getty Images
Production Manager: Angela L. McLean

7th Edition

ISBN 978-0-307-92918-1

ISSN 1526–1360

SPECIAL SALES

This book is available at special discounts for bulk purchases for sales promotions or premiums. Special editions, including personalized covers, excerpts of existing books, and corporate imprints, can be created in large quantities for special needs. For more information, write to Special Markets/Premium Sales, 1745 Broadway, MD 3-1, New York, NY 10019, or e-mail specialmarkets@randomhouse.com.

AN IMPORTANT TIP & AN INVITATION

Although all prices, opening times, and other details in this book are based on information supplied to us at press time, changes occur all the time in the travel world, and Fodor's cannot accept responsibility for facts that become outdated or for inadvertent errors or omissions. So **always confirm information when it matters,** especially if you're making a detour to visit a specific place. Your experiences—positive and negative—matter to us. If we have missed or misstated something, **please write to us.** Share your opinion instantly through our online feedback center at fodors.com/contact-us.

PRINTED IN CHINA

10 9 8 7 6 5 4 3 2 1

ABOUT THIS BOOK

Our Ratings

At Fodor's, we spend considerable time choosing the best places in a destination so you don't have to. By default, anything we recommend in this book is worth visiting. But some sights, properties, and experiences are so great that we've recognized them with additional accolades. Orange **Fodor's Choice** stars indicate our top recommendations; black stars highlight places we deem **Highly Recommended**; and **Best Bets** call attention to top properties in various categories. Disagree with any of our choices? Care to nominate a new place? Visit our feedback center at www.fodors.com/contact-us.

For expanded hotel reviews, visit **Fodors.com**

Hotels

Hotels have private bath, phone, TV, and air-conditioning, and do not offer meals unless we specify that in the review. We always list facilities but not whether you'll be charged an extra fee to use them.

Restaurants

Unless we state otherwise, restaurants are open for lunch and dinner daily. We mention dress only when there's a specific requirement and reservations only when they're essential or not accepted—it's always best to book ahead.

Credit Cards

We assume that restaurants and hotels accept credit cards. If not, we'll note it in the review.

Budget Well

Hotel and restaurant price categories from **$** to **$$$$** are defined in the opening pages of the respective chapters. For attractions, we always give standard adult admission fees; reductions are usually available for children, students, and senior citizens.

Listings
- ★ Fodor's Choice
- ★ Highly recommended
- ✉ Physical address
- ✣ Directions or Map coordinates
- Mailing address
- ☎ Telephone
- Fax
- On the Web
- E-mail
- Admission fee
- Open/closed times
- Ⓜ Metro stations
- No credit cards

Hotels & Restaurants
- Hotel
- Number of rooms
- Facilities
- Meal plans
- ✕ Restaurant
- Reservations
- Dress code
- Smoking

Outdoors
- Golf
- Camping

Other
- Family-friendly
- ⇨ See also
- Branch address
- ☞ Take note

Experience Argentina

1

WHAT'S WHERE

Numbers refer to chapters in this book.

2 Buenos Aires. Elegant boulevards and quirky cobbled streets give the capital a European air, but the chaotic traffic and frequent protest marches are distinctly Latin American. The home of tango is *the* place to learn the dance or take in a show. Also visit Argentina's biggest selection of boutiques, restaurants, and museums.

3 Side Trips from Buenos Aires. Vastly varied scenery lies an hour's bus, ferry, or plane ride from Buenos Aires. Traditional estancias (ranches) dot the pampas near San Antonio de Areco, waterways replace roads in the semitropical Tigre delta, and windswept dunes line the Atlantic coast. Gorgeous colonial buildings are the pull at Colonia de Sacramento, Uruguay, but nature built the mind-blowing Iguazú Falls.

4 The Northwest. Rock-strewn mountain passes, deep red gorges, verdant valleys, humid forests, Inca ruins, and the arid landscape of the Puna: the backdrop in the Northwest changes constantly. Rich Andean traditions live on in the region's food and folk music, beautiful Salta city has a colonial feel, and wines from nearby high-altitude vineyards are the latest thing.

5 The Wine Regions. Argentina's vintners use desert sun, mountain snow, and extreme altitudes to craft distinctive wines—especially Malbec. Mendoza's wineries enjoy the greatest reputation, those in the Valle de Uco grow their grapes incredibly high up, and family-owned wineries in tiny San Rafael focus on quality. The Pan-American Highway passes through Mendoza, heading west over spectacular Uspallata Pass to Chile. Along the way are hot springs, Inca ruins, and incomparable views of Mount Aconcagua.

6 The Lake District. Alpine scenery on a gigantic scale is one way to describe this region's pine forests and snowcapped peaks, many protected in national parks. There are breathtaking views of its eponymous lakes on the Camino de los Siete Lagos (Seven Lakes Route), which connects the posh resort towns of San Martín de los Andes and Villa La Angostura. Like the region's hub, Bariloche, these are near some of Argentina's best ski spots. In summer, you can climb, hike, and bike in the region, or indulge in the freshly caught trout, barbecued lamb, handmade chocolate, and craft beer the Lake District is also famous for.

7 Patagonia. Patagonia really is the end of the world: Tierra del Fuego is closer to Antarctica than to Buenos Aires, and Ushuaia is the world's southernmost city. The monumental natural beauty of the Perito Moreno glacier is alone worth the trip south, but on the Chilean side of the Andes, Parque Nacional Torres del Paine competes in grandeur. Both countries are also blessed with eerily still glacial lakes and rugged peaks that climbers love. Penguins, whales, and sea lions are the natural attractions on the windswept, wave-battered Atlantic coast.

BOLIVIA
PARAGUAY
CHILE
BRAZIL
URUGUAY
CHILE
JUJUY
San Salvador de Jujuy
SALTA
Salta
4
Coronel Moldes
San Miguel de Tucumán
CATAMARCA
TUCUMÁN
Santiago del Estero
San Fernando del Valle de Catamarca
La Rioja
Ambargasta
LA RIOJA
SANTIAGO DEL ESTERO
FORMOSA
CHACO
ASUNCIÓN
Iguazú Falls
MISIONES
Corrientes
Posadas
ESTEROS DEL IBERÁ
CORRIENTES
Reconquista
Mercedes
SANTA FÉ
Ceres
SAN JUAN
San José de Jachal
San Juan
Villa de Soto
Córdoba
CÓRDOBA
La Paz
ENTRE RIOS
Chajarí
Concordia
Santa Fé
Paraná
Mendoza City
5
SANTIAGO
San Luís
Villa María
Rosario
3
Gualeguaychu
Río Cuarto
MENDOZA
Colón
Tigre
BUENOS AIRES
San Rafael
SAN LUÍS
Junín
La Plata
2
Trenque Lauquen
Malargüe
Castelli
Santa Isabel
Santa Rosa
BUENOS AIRES
Azul
Maipu
Pinamar
LA PAMPA
Chos Malal
NEUQUÉN
Jacinto Arauz
Necochea
Mar del Plata
Neuquén
Bahía Blanca
Río Colorado
6
Junín de los Andes
San Antonio Oeste
Carmen de Patagones
Bariloche
Villa La Angostura
RÍO NEGRO
La Lobería
Ingeniero Jacobacci
Sierra Grande
El Bolsón
PENÍNSULA VALDÉS
Puerto Madryn
Puerto Pirámides
Esquel
Gaiman
Rawson
CHUBUT
A N D E S
Pacific Ocean
Río Mayo
Sarmiento
Comodore Rivadavía
Caleta Olivia
Las Heras
Perito Moreno
Monumento Natural Bosques Petrificados
CABO TRES PUNTAS
Parque Nacional F. P. Moreno
Puerto Deseado
PATAGONIA
SANTA CRUZ
7
El Chaltén
Puerto San Julián
Atlantic Ocean
Tres Lagos
Parque Nacional los Glaciares
Puerto Santa Cruz
El Calafate
Río Turbio
Río Gallegos
0
200 mi
0
200 km
TIERRA DEL FUEGO
Río Grande
TIERRA DEL FUEGO
Ushuaia
1

ARGENTINA PLANNER

Visitor Info

Travel advice, the lowdown on learning tango, tips on buying property, winery recommendations—you'll probably find it all on the government-run **Argentina** (🌐 *www.argentina.ar*) website. The umbrella organization for all regional tourist offices is the **Secretaría de Turismo** (Secretariat of Tourism; 🌐 *www.turismo.gov.ar*).

Travel Agents

Argentina-based travel agents can help you pack a lot into a short trip. The 24-hour support many offer is particularly good when internal flights are delayed, a common occurrence. Argentina Escapes, Buenos Aires Tours, and Wow! Argentina are reliable local agencies. Limitless Argentina is a U.S.-based company with offices in Argentina.

Argentina Travel Agents Argentina Escapes ☎ *11/5032–2938* 🌐 *www.argentinaescapes.com*. **Buenos Aires Tours** 🌐 *www.buenosaires-tours.com.ar*. **Limitless Argentina** ☎ *202/536–5812 in U.S., 11/4772–8700 in Buenos Aires* 🌐 *www.limitlessargentina.com*. **Wow! Argentina** ☎ *11/5239–3019* 🌐 *www.wowargentina.com*.

Driving

Argentina is a fantastic place for a road trip: the vast distances and unique windswept scenery are some of the most drive-worthy on the planet. If you're heading to the Lake District or Mendoza or Córdoba province, for example, try to spend at least a little time driving around.

If you don't fancy dealing with driving yourself, you can also hire a *remis con chofer* (car and driver) in most cities. You can arrange this through hotels or local taxi companies. For trips to and from a specific destination, you pay a pre-agreed-upon flat fare. Otherwise most companies charge an hourly rate of around 60–100 pesos (usually with a two- or three-hour minimum) to have a driver at your disposal all day. Rental companies also offer this service, but are more expensive.

Some major highways are maintained by private companies, others by provincial governments; surface conditions vary greatly. Many national highways (*rutas*) have only one lane in each direction; you get two or three lanes on an *autopista* (freeway), but these only connect some major cities. Local driving styles range from erratic to downright dangerous, and the road mortality rate is shockingly high. Heavy truck traffic can also make some routes slow, frustrating, and tricky for passing. Don't count on good signage leading to estancias or wineries. Do as the locals do: pull over and ask directions. In towns, intersections without traffic lights or signs function like four-way stops: a car approaching from your right has right of way.

Your rental-car agency should have an emergency help line; the best is usually through the Automóvil Club Argentina (ACA), which can dispatch help to nearly anywhere in the country within a reasonable amount of time. In the event of an accident, stay by your car until the police arrive. To report a stolen car, head to the nearest police station.

Contacts American Automobile Association (*AAA*) ☎ *800/564–6222* 🌐 *www.aaa.com*. **Automóvil Club Argentino** (*ACA*) ☎ *11/4808–4000, 800/777–2894 emergencies* 🌐 *www.aca.org.ar*. **Police** ☎ *101*.

Information Dirección Nacional de Vialidad ☎ *11/4343–8520* 🌐 *www.vialidad.gov.ar*.

Safety

Argentina is safer than many Latin American countries. However, there has been an increase in street crime—mainly pickpocketing, bag-snatching, and occasionally mugging—especially in Buenos Aires. Taking a few precautions when traveling in the region is usually enough to avoid being a target.

Crime. Walk with purpose; if you don't look like a target, you'll likely be left alone. Avoid wearing jewelry, even nice-looking imitation pieces. Keep a grip on your purse or bag, and keep it in your lap if you're sitting (never leave it hanging on the back of a chair or on the floor). Make use of your hotel safe, consider carrying a dummy wallet, or keep your valuables in several different places on your person. Keep enough on hand to have something to hand over if you do get mugged. Nearly all physical attacks on tourists are the direct result of their resisting would-be pickpockets or muggers; comply with demands, hand over your stuff, and try to get the situation over with as quickly as possible—then let your travel insurance take care of it.

Piropos. Women can expect pointed looks, the occasional *piropo* (a flirtatious remark, usually alluding to some physical aspect), and some advances. These catcalls rarely escalate into actual physical harassment—the best reaction is to ignore them; reply only if you're really confident with Spanish.

Protests. Argentines like to speak their minds, and there has been a huge increase in strikes and street protests since the economic crisis of 2001–02. Protesters frequently block streets in downtown Buenos Aires, causing traffic jams. Trigger-happy local police have historically proved themselves more of a worry than the demonstrators; though protests are usually peaceful, exercise caution.

Scams. Beware scams such as a kindly passerby offering to help you clean the mustard/ketchup/cream that has somehow appeared on your clothes: while your attention is occupied, an accomplice picks your pocket or snatches your bag. When taking a taxi, hailing one during the day in big cities is usually safe, but be sure the driver turns the meter on. Have a good idea of where you're headed to avoid being taken on a circuitous route. Some salespeople, especially street vendors, take advantage of confused tourists by charging dollars for goods that are actually priced in pesos. If you're in doubt, ask.

Advisories and Other Information Transportation Security Administration (*TSA*) 🌐 *www.tsa.gov*. **U.S. Department of State** 🌐 *www.travel.state.gov*.

When to Go

Remember: when it's summer in the Northern Hemisphere it's winter in Argentina.

Buenos Aires is least crowded in January and February, when locals beat the heat at resorts along the Atlantic and in Córdoba Province. City sightseeing is most pleasant during the temperate spring and fall. Try to visit Iguazú Falls in August through October, when temperatures are lower, the falls are fuller, and the spring coloring is at its brightest.

If you're heading to the Lake District or Patagonia, visit during the shoulder seasons of December and March. Southern seas batter the Patagonian coast year-round, and winds there often reach gale force. In Tierra del Fuego, fragments of glaciers cave into lakes with a rumble throughout the thaw from October to the end of April.

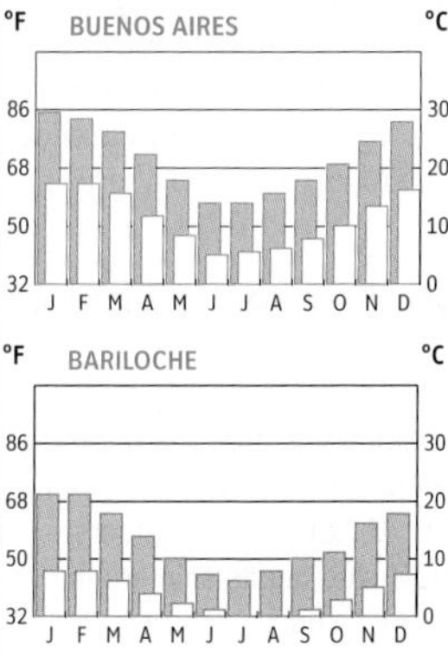

ARGENTINA TODAY

They say the only thing certain in life is change, and no one knows it like Argentinians do. But while the world panics over recession, crashes, and cuts, today Argentinians can smile smugly. After hitting rock bottom in 2001–02, the country said no to austerity measures, and its exponential economic growth suggests that the gamble has paid off. From the ashes of economic burnout, a vibrant, global Argentina is rising.

Today's Argentina . . .

. . . is full of free speech. Forget writing to your representatives when you've got a gripe with the system—in Argentina, you take to the streets. Both city avenues and highways are regularly blocked by drum- and banner-toting crowds chanting in a tuneful unison that can come only from practice. Sometimes they're protesting or petitioning to change laws; at others they're celebrating political or sporting victories, or simply marking an event. Many demonstrators are in their teens and twenties: commitment to causes is cool in Argentina. It's not all on the streets, though. In 2009 independent journalists and media-watchers rejoiced when the congress and senate replaced the country's anachronistic TV and radio licensing laws, a legacy from the last military dictatorship. Previously, one media group controlled the majority of local TV and radio licenses, while the new law benefits educational, community, and non-profit programming.

. . . is going global. Locals can't get over the number of out-of-towners flooding the country. And more and more of the 2.3 million annual foreign visitors are staying on. Tango enthusiasts are snapping up old apartments in Buenos Aires, wine aficionados are investing in vineyards, outdoors enthusiasts are buying chunks of Patagonia. The number of exchange students at universities in Buenos Aires and Córdoba has soared, and there's a thriving expat scene complete with how-to blogs and magazines. Comparatively low property prices and a relatively favorable exchange rate mean that some of these European and North American newcomers can afford not to work: would-be novelists, painters, musicians—and former investment bankers—abound. Quick to see the benefits of visitor dollars, the government is eager to improve Argentina's image. Popular tourist sites are getting the spit-and-polish treatment and tourist-friendly attitudes are being keenly promoted.

WHAT'S HOT IN ARGENTINA NOW

Electric music. Listening to *cumbia* (a local tropical-style rhythm) was once as trashy as it got. But now Argentina's hottest club nights spin around electronic cumbia remixes. Some call it "electrotropical" or "electrocumbia," others "cumbiatrónica"; whatever its name, its trademark "shh-chicki-shh" beat has clubbers hooked. Itinerant Club Night Zizek (🌐 *www.zzkclub.com*) is *the* place to go: it's toured the United States and Europe.

Being out. In 2010 Argentina became the first country in Latin America—and only the ninth in the world—to fully legalize same-sex marriage, sealing Argentina's claim to the title of Latin America's gay capital. It's not just bars and clubs, either, but also tango schools, *milongas* (tango dance halls), hotels, and travel agencies. The annual Marcha

. . . is coming to terms with its past. The military juntas behind Argentina's 1976–83 dictatorship called their reign the National Reorganization Process, a grim euphemism for six years of state-run terror during which 30,000 people "disappeared" and countless more were brutally tortured. Justice has been slow in coming: although some military officials were brought to trial in the 1980s, President Carlos Menem later pardoned them all. But after years of tireless campaigning by victims and human rights groups such as the Madres de Plaza de Mayo (Mothers of Plaza de Mayo), the current government has revoked these pardons and military officers responsible for torture and disappearances are being sentenced for crimes against humanity. Former clandestine detention centers have been transformed into cultural centers, and the anniversary of the start of the dictatorship, March 24, has been made a public day of remembrance marked by thousands each year.

Another organization, Abuelas de Plaza de Mayo (Grandmothers of Plaza de Mayo), continues to search for missing grandchildren, stolen at birth from kidnapped mothers and often raised by the very people who killed the children's parents. The creation of a genetic information bank has meant that 105 children—now in their thirties—have been "found."

. . . is geeking out. Science and technology are center stage in the new Argentina. After decades of fuga de cerébros (brain drain), 850 top Argentinian scientists have been tempted back from abroad by government investment programs. The country is betting on future techies, too: free netbooks have been given to 1.7 million students at public high schools. Half of Argentina's electronics are now made at a specialist industrial park in Tierra del Fuego, and a state-of-the-art research complex is opening in Buenos Aires that will also contain Argentina's first science museum. In 2011 local techie achievements past, present, and future went on display at Tecnópolis, a temporary technology exhibition in Buenos Aires that attracted so many visitors it's being made permanent. The sky's the limit—literally: in 2011 Argentina's space agency launched its first satellite, SAC-D Aquarius, in collaboration with NASA.

del Orgullo Gay (Gay Pride March) attracts tens of thousands of revelers in Buenos Aires and other big cities each November.

Food Culture. There was a time when all Argentine diners cared about was how big their steak was. But serious foodie culture has arrived, and locals value quality over quantity. Celebrity chefs are busy evangelizing enthralled TV audiences, and former table-wine drinkers now vigorously debate grape varietals and name-drop boutique vineyards.

El Bicentenario. Argentinians have always been patriotic, but flags are flying higher and brighter than usual since the 2010 bicentenary of the May Revolution, which led to Argentina's independence.

ARGENTINA TOP ATTRACTIONS

A

B

C

D

Iguazú Falls

(A) On the Argentine–Brazilian border some 1.7 million gallons of the Iguazú River plummet over a precipice each second, forming a 275-meter-wide (900-foot-wide) wall of water. Trails, metal catwalks, and Zodiacs all allow for spray-soaked close-ups.

La Quebrada de Humahuaca

(B) Dramatically colored, craggy rock faces overlook the traditional villages that nestle in this gorge. The most stunning section is the Camino de los Siete Colores (Seven Colors Trail) in Purmamarca, with its red, ocher, and mossy-green rock layers. Music pouring from area *peñas* (folk bars) is the perfect soundtrack.

Laguna de los Pozuelos

Thousands of Andean flamingos form a salmon-pink swath across this remote lake near Argentina's border with Bolivia. The harsh beauty of the Puna region's gritty slopes and scrubby high-altitude plains offsets the birds' extravagant plumage perfectly.

Mendoza Wineries

(C) Malbec is the grape that has made Argentina's name in the wine world, and Mendoza is where they do it best. But getting you tipsy isn't all the 20 or so area wineries do: informative tours, atmospheric accommodations, and top-notch dining are also on offer, all within spitting distance of the Andes.

Plaza de Mayo and San Telmo, Buenos Aires

(D) Revolution, mass protests, Evita's inflammatory speeches: never a dull moment for the square that is the historic heart of Buenos Aires. The past also lives on in the cobbled streets of the San Telmo neighborhood. Its elegant 19th-century mansions once housed brothels, tenements, and tango dens. The tango remains, but these days it's antiques and hip designers that draw crowds.

Perito Moreno Glacier

(E) A translucent blue-green cliff of frosty majesty forms where this glacier reaches Lago Argentino in southern Patagonia. Blocks splinter off the ice face all the time, but they're ice cubes compared to the tons that come crashing down roughly every four years as a result of pressure building from behind.

Camino de los Siete Lagos (Seven Lakes Route)

(F) Between San Martín de los Andes and Villa La Angostura, the partly paved Ruta Nacional 234 winds alongside seven beautiful bodies of water fringed by pine forests and overlooked by the Andes. You can do the trip in a day, or stay on at inns or campsites for the gorgeous sunsets and sunrises.

Península Valdés

(G) Graceful *ballenas francas* (southern right whales) are literally the largest attraction at this Atlantic coast nature reserve. They come for mating season, June through November. Orcas, sea lions, elephant seals, and vast penguin colonies keep the beach busy the rest of the year.

Salta

(H) Stately colonial buildings, hopping nightlife, and fabulous local food and wine make the city of Salta more than just a gateway to the Northwest. When you do decide to get out of town, hiking, rafting, and tours to wineries and salt lakes are all options.

QUINTESSENTIAL ARGENTINA

Beef

Argentina is cow country. The beef is so good that some Argentinians see little reason to eat anything else, though chicken and Patagonian lamb are tasty alternatives, as is *chivito* (kid) in some parts of the country. *Carne asada* (roasted cuts of beef) might be done on a grill over hot coals (*a la parrilla*), roasted in an oven (*al horno*), or slowly roasted on a metal spit stuck in the ground aslant on a bed of hot coals (*al asador*). A family *asado* (barbecue), where men show off their barbecuing skills, is the classic way to spend a Sunday afternoon. The nearest restaurant experience is to order a *parrillada mixta* (mixed grill). Expect different cuts of beef—both on and off the bone and usually roasted in huge pieces—as well as chorizo sausage, roasted sweetbreads, and less bloodthirsty optional accompaniments like provolone cheese and bell peppers.

Vino

Given their high consumption of beef, Argentinians understandably drink a lot of *vino tinto* (red wine). Although much of the wine consumed here is nondescript table wine, the wine industry has boomed, and Argentine vineyards (especially so-called boutique vineyards) are firmly on the map. The most popular grapes are Cabernet Sauvignon, Malbec, and Shiraz (known locally as Syrah), but Tempranillo, Tannat, and Merlot are also popular. If you prefer *vino blanco* (white wine), try a Sauvignon Blanc or Chardonnay from Mendoza, or lesser-known wineries from Salta, where the Torrontés grape, another local specialty, thrives. This varietal produces a dry white with a lovely floral bouquet.

It's easy to enjoy Argentina's daily rituals. Among other things, you can enjoy some fancy footwork—on the playing field or in the ballroom—or savor the rich flavors (and conversation) of a leisurely meal.

Fútbol

In a country where Diego Maradona is revered as a god, nothing unites and divides Argentinians as much as their passion for soccer. Local teams are the subject of fiery dispute and serious rivalry; the national team brings the country together for displays of unrivaled passion and suicidal despair, especially during the World Cup. Argentina's blue-and-white-stripe jerseys have flashed across international TV screens even before it won the 1978 and 1986 World Cups, and nothing can lift—or crush—the spirits of the nation like the result of a soccer match. Every weekend, stadiums fill to bursting with screaming fans toting drums and banners and filling the air with confetti and flares in their team's colors, which—together with the play on the field—makes for a sporting spectacle second to none.

Tango

There's no question as to what the soundtrack of Buenos Aires is: the city and the tango are inseparable. From its beginnings in portside brothels at the turn of the 19th century, tango has marked and reflected the character of Buenos Aires and its inhabitants. Although visitors associate tango with dance, for locals it's more about the music and the lyrics, and you can't help but cross paths with both forms. You may hear strains of tango on the radio while sipping coffee in a boulevard café, see high-kicking sequined dancers in a glitzy dinner show, or listen to musicians in a cabaret. Regardless, you'll experience the best of this broody, melancholic, impassioned, art form.

IF YOU LIKE

Wild, Gorgeous Nature

Argentina's climates range from tropical to subantarctic, and altitudes descend from 22,000 feet to below sea level, so natural environments here vary hugely. Plants, birds, and animals thrive undisturbed in their habitats. Along the south Atlantic coast, sea mammals mate and give birth on empty beaches and in protected bays. To the north, guanaco, rhea, and native deer travel miles over Andean trails and across windswept plains, while birds pass above in clouds of thousands or descend on lagoons like blankets of feathers.

Glaciar Perito Moreno, Patagonia. Tons of ice regularly peel off the 197-foot-tall, 2.5-mile-long front of this advancing glacier and crash into Lago Argentino.

Cataratas de Iguazú, Northeast. Iguazú Falls National Park protects 275 waterfalls and countless species of animals. Trails disappear into a greenhouse of creepers, epiphytes, orchids, and bromeliads.

Península Valdés, Patagonia. Small boats bring you alongside southern right whales as they feed, mate, give birth, and nurse their offspring.

Parque Nacional Nahuel Huapi, Bariloche. Rich forest surrounds the sapphire-blue waters of Lake Nahuel Huapi. Smaller bodies of water nearby make this Argentina's lake district.

Quebrada de Humahuaca. Vibrant pinks, yellows, and greens color the walls of this northwestern canyon like giant swaths of paint.

Reserva Faunistica Punta Tombo, Patagonia. This Atlantic peninsula is home to the world's largest colony of Magellanic penguins.

Adrenaline Rushes

If an eyeful of natural beauty doesn't make your heart race in the way you'd like, why not try an adventure sport? Argentina is great for winter rushes—skiing, snowboarding, and dogsledding among them. When temperatures soar, you can cool down by white-water rafting or leaping (with a parachute) into the breeze.

Ice Trekking on the Perito Moreno Glacier. You can trek over the glacier's 1,000-year-old ice, then celebrate your ascent with cocktails served over cubes of it.

White-water rafting in the Río Mendoza. This river's medium-to-difficult rapids course through Andean foothills. You can combine one- or two-day descents with horseback riding in the mountains.

Skiing and snowboarding at Las Leñas, Catedral, and Chapelco ski areas. Las Leñas near Mendoza, Catedral near Bariloche, and Chapelco near San Martín de los Andes offer groomed runs, open bowls, and trails that follow the fall line to cozy inns or luxurious hotels.

Tierra Mayor, Patagonia. This family-run Nordic center near Ushuaia has such novelties as dogsled rides, snowcat trips, and wind skiing.

Mountain climbing at Aconcagua, Mendoza Province. Close to the Chilean border, this 6,959-meter (22,831-foot) peak is the highest in the Western and Southern hemispheres and is surrounded by a host of other climbable mountains.

Culture and History

Buenos Aires is a city of European-inspired boulevards and historic neighborhoods. Beyond the urban sprawl, gauchos work ranches that reach the horizons. The Andes tower above the age-old vineyards of Mendoza and San Juan, while Salta and Jujuy retain traditions that stretch back to before the arrival of Europeans. The windswept reaches of Patagonia roll on forever and a few miles more.

Museo de Arte Latinoamericana de Buenos Aires (MALBA). One of the world's few museums specializing in Latin American art is in a stunningly simple building.

Festival de Tango, Buenos Aires. The world's most important tango festival is a two-week extravaganza culminating in a huge *milonga* (dance session) along Avenida Corrientes.

Festival de la Vendimia, Mendoza. At the grape-harvest festival, during the first week of March, parades, folk dancing, and fireworks take place. The crowning of a queen marks the grand finale.

Museo de Arqueología de la Alta Montaña, Salta. The rich pre-Columbian heritage of Argentina's Northwest is explored at this modern museum.

Carnaval. Brazilian-style feathers and sequins characterize February parades in Entre Ríos and Corrientes provinces, but pre-Columbian rituals mark celebrations in Salta and Jujuy provinces. In Buenos Aires, neighborhood troupes take to the streets to sing and dance murga.

Museo Paleontológico, Trelew. You can marvel at dinosaur bones and watch archaeologists at work at this impressive paleontology museum.

Shopping

Argentinians love to shop. On weekends town squares become *ferias* (open-air markets); street performers wind their way between stalls of handmade offerings. Big shopping malls stock local and international brands. Wine, chocolate, cookies, and preserves are some of the consumables for sale.

Handmade jewelry and housewares, Buenos Aires. Artisans sell wares for you and your home in alpaca, wood, and leather.

Silver and leather, San Antonio de Areco. Modern-day gauchos can stock up on saddles, bridles, asado knives, belts, and even handbags and jewelry in this town of leatherworkers and silversmiths.

Ceramics and weavings, Salta and Jujuy. Salta is famed for its rich red and black ponchos. Woven wall hangings and alpaca knitwear are ubiquitous in Jujuy. Red-clay figures and cookware abound.

Wine, Mendoza and Salta. Tour the vineyards, sampling Malbecs, Cabernets, and Torrontéses at leisure, before stocking up on those you liked most.

Cutting-edge designer clothing, Buenos Aires. In trendy Palermo Viejo and San Telmo, cobbled streets are lined with the boutiques of up-and-coming designers.

Chocolate and beer, Bariloche. Many of Bariloche's founders were German, hence the thriving trade in craft beer and chocolate in flaky sticks (en rama) or bars filled with locally grown berries.

FLAVORS OF ARGENTINA

Argentina's food traditions combine wild foods native to the region with crops cultivated from pre-Columbian times. Add in techniques brought by the European colonizers: first the wheat and cattle that built the country's reputation as the granary—and slaughterhouse—of the world; then the wines, pastas, and ice creams brought by 20th-century immigrants from Spain and Italy.

Compared with other Latin American fare, Argentinian cuisine is found bland by some. And while there are parts of the country that love their spices, the local food philosophy is more about letting top-notch ingredients speak for themselves. Here are some of the flavors that might cross your plate.

Beef

Admit it: a juicy steak comes to mind when you think of Argentina. Locals proudly boast that the grass-fed cattle of the pampas produce the world's tastiest beef. Although the exponential growth of soy farming is elbowing the cows off the pampas and increasing local beef prices, Argentina's inhabitants still manage to consume 57 kg of carne per capita per year, second only to neighboring Uruguay and well ahead of the U.S.'s 44 kg. Sunday *asados* (barbecues) are a sacred national ritual. Whether they're grilling in the garden or ordering a *parrillada* (mixed grill) at a restaurant, Argentinians typically go for at least two cuts of beef, one on the bone and one off. *Tira de asado* (prime ribs) and *vacío* (flank steak) are the standard selections, and are usually slow-roasted in huge pieces weighing 5–10 lbs. Choicer cuts like *bife de chorizo* (porterhouse) or *lomo* (tenderloin) are more likely to be cooked and ordered as individual steaks.

The preludes to the meat include chorizo, *morcilla* (blood sausage), and grilled offal: crispy curls of *chinchulines* (chitterlings) and rich *mollejas* (sweetbreads) are especially popular.

Cow culture doesn't end at the barbecue. Mildly spiced ground or sliced beef is the most traditional filling for empanadas (a pastry turnover), the country's star snack. Another local favorite is the *milanesa,* a plate-sized breaded beef cutlet served with fries or a salad, in a sandwich, or topped with tomato sauce and melted cheese (*a la napolitana*). Other beef-centered classics include *bifes a la criolla,* thin slices of steak cooked with onions and red peppers; and *carbonada,* a rich beef stew containing corn and dried peaches.

Andean Ingredients

Maize is the backbone of Andean fare and comes in an impressive range of sizes and colors. The most ubiquitous corn-based dishes are *humitas* and tamales, fist-sized balls of maize meal stuffed with cheese or ground beef, respectively, and steamed in corn husks. Sweet corn spiced and mixed with goat's cheese is also a popular filling for the area's tiny but incredibly addictive empanadas. Large, nutty-tasting ears of rehydrated dried white maize are popular additions to salads and stews. You can even drink maize: it's fermented into a dangerously powerful alcoholic beverage called *chicha.* Bucketfuls of the soupy-looking concoction fuel the action during the long nights of carnaval, Pachamama, and other traditional festivals.

The Andes are the spiritual home of the potato. Forget big fluffy brown spuds: Andean potato varieties (of which there are scores) are tiny and dense, and might be purple, crimson, green, or rich yellow. Fresh, they're a common side dish, and

form part of spicy stews. They're also preserved by being left to freeze outside and then dehydrated. The resulting starchy balls (or a flour ground from them) are known as *chuño* and are a common addition to soups and stews.

Once a staple of the Incas, quinoa continues to grow in these parts. This nutty, protein-rich grain was traditionally incorporated into stews, but these days it's just as common to find it served as a risotto. Llama steak is more fibrous than beef and has a sweet, gamey edge to it. *Charqui* (the local word for jerky or dried salted meat) is also commonplace in stews. At dessert, don't pass up a plate of *quesillo* (raw goat cheese or stringy fresh white cheese) with *dulce de cayote* (a sweet cactus preserve). It's usually served with a handful of nuts and dribbled with *arrope* (a thick, dark fruit syrup).

Patagonian Wild Foods

In the southern half of Argentina the cow plays second fiddle to wilder fare. The star catch along the Atlantic coast is *centolla* or king crab, but mussels, clams, octopus, and shrimp are also regional specialties, as are freshly caught sole, salmon, hake, cod, or silverside. Fish is on the menu in Andean Patagonia, too, which is famous for its wild-river trout. Avoid the cheesy sauces local chefs favor and go for something simple that lets you appreciate the star ingredient—*manteca negra* (browned butter) is a fail-safe choice.

If you're feeling game, *jabalí* (wild boar), *ciervo colorado* (red deer), and *liebre* (hare) are the land-lubbing southern specialties. They're usually served roasted or in stews, often accompanied by sauces made from berries or craft beer (or even berry-flavored beer), some of the other products Patagonia is famous for.

Best of all, you can take it all away with you. Boar, venison, hare, trout, and seafood are sold pickled and canned (a product known as *escabeche*), and there's a roaring trade in homemade jams and jellies concocted from *rosa mosqueta* (rosehip), *guinda* (morello cherries), and all manner of berries.

Dulce de leche

Milk, sugar, and not a whole lot else go into this rich brown milk caramel, which is practically a food group in Argentina. Get your first hit each day by spreading some on your toast at breakfast, where you may also find dulce de leche oozing out of cylindrical millefeuille pastries known as *cañoncitos* (little cannons) or long, ridged donuts called *churros.* Midmorning you might encounter it sandwiched between two cookies to form an *alfajor,* the nation's favorite sweet snack.

Dulce de leche is a standard flavor for ice cream; you'll also find chocolate-chip dulce de leche, or dulce de leche with swirls of—you guessed it—extra dulce de leche. Diners think nothing of asking for a dollop of dulce de leche on the side of already sugar-laden desserts like *flan* (crème caramel) or flambéed pancakes. Super-sweet chocolate cakes filled with dulce de leche are a common fixture in bakery windows. Bananas and dulce de leche are a killer combination: imitate local kids and mash the two together for an instant sugar fix.

All the same, connoisseurs insist that the best way to appreciate it is on a spoon straight from the pot. Why not line up some jars of brands like La Salamandra, Chimbote, and Havanna, and do a dulce de leche tasting of your own?

GREAT ITINERARIES

PORTEÑOS AND PAMPAS

Day 1: Arrival

Arrive in Buenos Aires and pick up a city map from the tourist office right before you enter the main airport terminal. Get cash at the ATM before taking a taxi to your hotel. Ignore the drivers asking if you need a cab; head straight for the taxi booth, pay up front for your ticket (about 150 pesos), and let staffers assign you a driver, who will take you straight to a car. Spend your first afternoon in La Recoleta, whose famous cemetery contains Eva Perón's tomb. Make your first meal a memorable one at a grill with a *bife de chorizo* (porterhouse steak).

Day 2: San Telmo and La Boca

Begin with a taxi ride to La Boca, the port neighborhood where tango was born. The main strip is Caminito, which though colorful and iconic, is too touristy to merit more than an hour or two. Lunch at El Obrero is a classic. So is afternoon coffee (or a beer) at Bar Dorrego on San Telmo's Plaza Dorrego, a short taxi ride away. Spend the afternoon wandering through the antiques and clothes shops of this characteristic old neighborhood. Set aside an hour to get up close to its history with a visit to El Zanjón de Granados. Dinner at an innovative restaurant will give you the fortitude to hit the bars.

Day 3: Palermo

After a leisurely breakfast, head for a stroll, skate, or cycle through the Parque 3 de Febrero, and linger at the Jardín Japonés or the Rosedal. Walk or take a short taxi ride to MALBA, which opens at noon, and work up an appetite viewing Latin American art. Hop a cab to the cutting-edge Palermo Hollywood neighborhood, where you can lunch on sushi, Vietnamese, or far-out fusion. Afterward, wander leisurely over to Palermo Soho, browsing the city's coolest clothing and shoe stores. When night falls, have coffee or a cocktail near Plaza Serrano, and finish with dinner at a modern restaurant, say Casa Cruz. If you're up for a nightcap, you're already where all the action is.

Day 4: El Centro and Puerto Madero

Have your morning coffee and croissants at ultra-traditional Gran Café Tortoni. Stroll down Avenida de Mayo to take in Plaza de Mayo and the nearby Museo Etnográfico. Cross over the old docks into Puerto Madero for a light deli lunch or a full-blown grill affair. Get back to nature only yards from the skyscrapers with a quick ramble in the Reserva Ecológica. Finish with an all-out evening wine experience at the Gran Bar Danzón in Retiro.

Day 5: Buenos Aires to the Pampas

After getting a sense of the city, hit the highway for gaucho country. The town of San Antonio de Areco, in the heart of the pampas, is home to several estancias, country houses turned hotels where gauchos tend to the horses. Most estancias include four meals per day in the room price. To get there, arrange ground transportation through your estancia or reserve a rental car downtown, not at the airport. After a late breakfast, take the Acceso Norte to the Panamericana (RN9) to Pilar and then RN8, a slower road, to San Antonio. Browse the silversmiths' and artisans' stores before having lunch at the Almacén de Ramos Generales. Then check out the gaucho museum, wander the sleepy streets, and finish with a beer or coffee at La Esquina de Mertí, an old-fashioned corner bar. Head to your estancia, where you'll have time to relax before dinner.

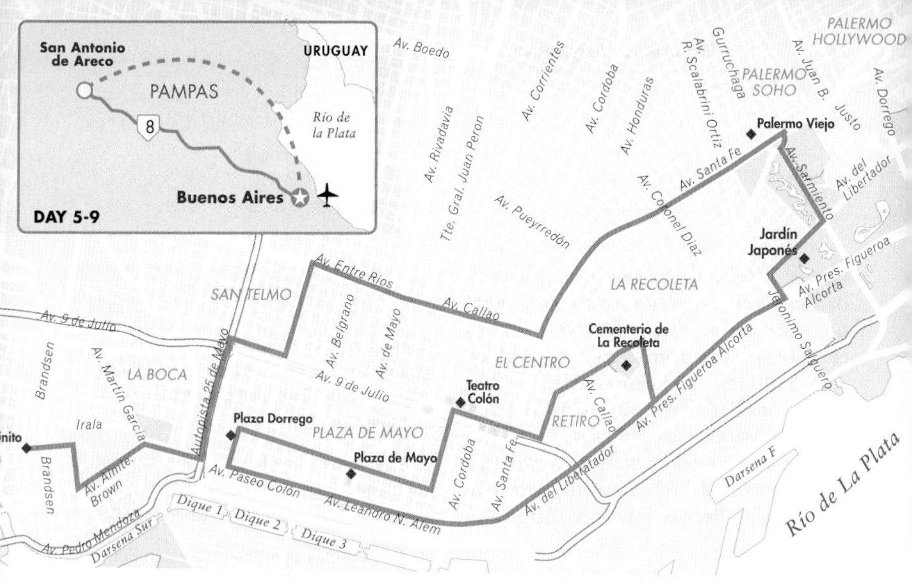

Day 6: San Antonio de Areco

Spend your morning in the pampas on horseback, roaming across the grassland with a resident gaucho. This, like other activities, should be included in the estancia price. Seasoned riders can gallop, while beginners walk, trot, or ride in a buggy. If there's a day-trip group coming in, the midday meal might be accompanied by a musical performance with whooping gauchos—cheesy, but fun. Take an afternoon swim in the pool, and then have dinner at the estancia, perhaps followed by a game of pool or cards with other guests, who by now may be good friends.

Days 7 and 8: To Buenos Aires and Home

Return to Buenos Aires after one last long estancia lunch. Spend the evening revisiting your favorite neighborhood.

You could spend your last day catching up on culture at the Museo Nacional de Bellas Artes or history at the Museo Evita. Later, try out your footwork with a tango class and a visit to a milonga, or see the pros in action at an evening show.

Sportier alternatives include taking a bike tour with La Bicicleta Naranja or hitting the river with Smile on Sea. If you're a soccer fan and Boca Juniors are playing during your stay in Buenos Aires, don't miss it. Getting tickets yourself can be complicated—consider booking with tour company **Tangol** (☏ *11/4312–7276* 🌐 *www.tangol.com*). A visit to the Museo de la Pasión Boquense is the next-best option. Local fans follow up with pizza at nearby Banchero.

If shopping is your idea of an extreme sport, divide your last day between the chain stores on Avenida Santa Fe, top-end mall Paseo Alcorta, and the boutiques in Palermo. Have a blowout final meal: good splurge restaurants are Tomo I, Le Mistral at the Four Seasons, and La Bourgogne.

On Day 8, allow at least an hour to get to Ezeiza for your flight home. If you kept your rental car so that you can drive yourself to the airport, make sure your hotel has a garage, and allow an extra half hour before your flight to return the car.

ALTERNATIVES

You can combine this eight-day itinerary with a trip to Iguazú Falls, in Argentina's northeast corner on the border with Brazil, or go there instead of San Antonio on days 5 and 6. Spend one day on the Argentine side of things, in the Parque Nacional Iguazú, then head into town for dinner at Aqva. Spend the second morning in the

Parque Nacional Foz do Iguaçu, Brazil's national park, then return to the Argentine park for a few hours. (Note that to enter Brazil Americans need a visa, which costs $140 USD. In Puerto Iguazú the Brazilian consulate has a same-day visa service and is open weekdays 8–1, and in Buenos Aires weekdays 9–3.) Aerolíneas Argentinas and LAN have three to five daily flights between Buenos Aires and Iguazú.

Another add-on or replacement side trip is to Uruguay. The port town of Colonia is easily accessible by Colonia Express, a fast ferry, which also has connecting buses to Montevideo. In summer the beach resort of Punta del Este is another option. Spending two or three days in Uruguay isn't just a fun way to get an extra passport stamp—it's a window into a country whose cultural differences from Argentina (their heightened obsession with mate, for instance) are readily apparent.

BARILOCHE TO PATAGONIA

Day 1: Arrival and on to Bariloche

It's a long trip to Patagonia. After you arrive at Buenos Aires' Ezeiza International you need to transfer to the downtown Aeroparque for your flight to Bariloche. Rent a car at the airport, and drive to your hotel (consider a place on the Circuito Chico outside town). If you could use a beer after all that, choose a laid-back downtown pub to enjoy a local craft brew.

Day 2: Bariloche and Circuito Chico

Spend the day exploring the Circuito Chico and Peninsula Llao Llao. Start early so you have time for a boat excursion from the dock at Puerto Pañuelo on the peninsula's edge as well as for some late-afternoon shopping back in Bariloche. Spend the evening devouring Patagonian lamb *a la cruz* (spit-roasted over an open fire).

Day 3: Circuito Grande to Villa La Angostura

Villa La Angostura is a tranquil lakeside retreat that marks the beginning of the legendary Circuito Grande. Driving there is a gorgeous experience, as you hug the shores of Lago Nahuel Huapi on Ruta 237 and Ruta 231. Relax to the full by checking into a hotel in quiet Puerto Manzano, about 10 minutes outside Villa La Angostura—Puerto Sur is a good choice, with its endless water views.

Day 4: Villa La Angostura

Spend your second day in Villa La Angostura skiing at Cerro Bayo if it's winter and that's your thing. In warmer weather, explore the Parque Nacional los

TIPS

1. The Porteños and Pampas itinerary works best if Day 1 (arrival) is on a Friday and Day 8 (to Buenos Aires and Home) is the following Friday.

2. Stay in the same Buenos Aires hotel at the beginning and end of your trip so you can leave extra bags there while traveling.

3. An eight-day apartment rental in Buenos Aires could save you money, even if you aren't spending all your time there.

4. Flights to and from Iguazú use the Aeroparque in Palermo; international flights leave from Ezeiza. If you can't avoid same-day arrival and departure, allow at least four hours between landing at one airport and leaving from the other.

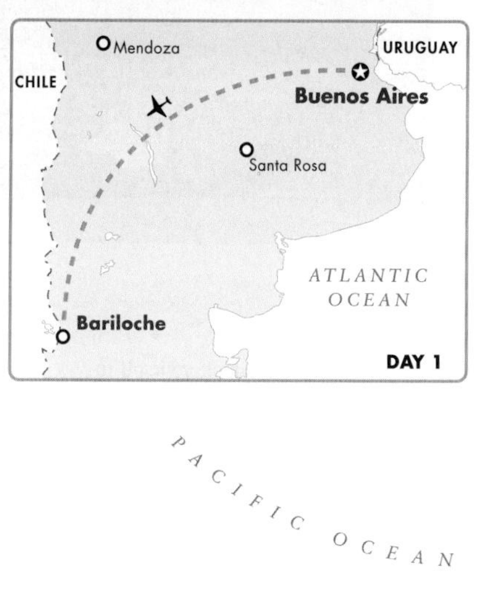

Arrayanes, the only forest of these myrtle trees in the world, or simply relax by the lake—if you're staying at Puerto Sur, this might be the most appealing option.

Day 5: Seven Lakes Route to San Martín de los Andes

Head out of Villa La Angostura onto the unbelievable Seven Lakes Route (Ruta 234), which branches right and along the way passes seven beautiful lakes: Correntoso, Espejo, Pichi Traful, Villarino, Falkner, Hermoso, and Machónico. If you leave early, add the hour-long detour to Lago Traful, where you can stop for lunch. The route brings to you to smart San Martín, where you can spend the late afternoon shopping, trying rainbow trout and other delicacies at the smoke shops, then enjoying them all over again for dinner. Note that the Seven Lakes Route is closed in winter, when you have to go through Junín de los Andes to get to San Martín.

Day 6: San Martín de los Andes

In winter, skiers should plan on at least one full day at Cerro Chapelco, near San Martín. Otherwise, spend the day relaxing on the beach, fishing, horseback riding, rafting, or just strolling the town.

Day 7: Flight to El Calafate

Get an extremely early start from San Martín de los Andes for the five-hour drive back to Bariloche for the nearly four-hour flight to El Calafate, the base for exploring Parque Nacional Los Glaciares. Be sure to take the longer but faster route through Junín from San Martín to Bariloche (Ruta Nacional 234 and Ruta Nacional 237). If you follow the only partly paved Seven Lakes Route, you'll have little chance of making an early afternoon flight.

In El Calafate, grab a taxi to your hotel, have dinner, and get some sleep in preparation for glacier-viewing tomorrow. If money is no object, stay at Hostería Los Notros, the only hotel within the park and in view of the glacier. The sky-high rates include all meals and excursions. Otherwise, stay at a hotel in El Calafate and book your glacier visits through El Calafate tour operators—preferably before 7 pm today.

Day 8: El Calafate and Perito Moreno Glacier

Spend two days taking in Perito Moreno from different angles. Devote today either to the Upsala Glacier tour, which traverses the lakes in view of an impressive series of glaciers, or the hour-long Safari

Nautico on a boat that sails as close as possible to the front of the glacier. Enjoy a well-deserved dinner back in El Calafate. Again, remember to arrange tomorrow's activities by 7 pm: tonight this means organizing an ice trek.

Day 9: El Calafate and Perito Moreno Glacier

Today you don crampons and trek across Perito Moreno's icy surface. The trip is expensive, but worth every penny. You crawl through ice tunnels and hike across ice ridges that seem to glow bright blue. After all this, dinner—and everything else—will seem insignificant.

Day 10: Departure

Board a bus or taxi for El Calafate's renovated airport, and take a flight back through Buenos Aires and home. Note that if you are not connecting to another Aerolíneas flight home, you may have to spend an additional night in Buenos Aires on the way back.

ALTERNATIVES

Sports and outdoors enthusiasts can really customize this itinerary. Skiers, for example, can skip southern Patagonia, spending a day or two in Cerro Catedral, near Bariloche, and a day at Cerro Chapelco. Rafters can work with Bariloche operators to create trips that range from floats down the Río Manso—an eight-hour outing with easy rapids through a unique ecosystem—to 13-hour excursions to the Chilean border. Serious hikers can boat across Lago Mascardi to Pampa Linda, then hike to the black glaciers of Tronador, continuing up above timberline to Refugio Otto Meiling, spending the night, walking along the crest of the Andes with glacier views, then returning to Pampa Linda. Day hikes to the foot of Tronador leave more time for a mountain-bike or horseback ride in the same area.

The most adventurous travelers drive from Bariloche to El Calafate instead of flying. It adds, oh, about a week to the itinerary, but it involves an unforgettable trip down the largely unpaved Ruta Nacional 40. Don't attempt this route without a four-wheel-drive vehicle that has two spares. And pack plenty of extra food and water as well as camping gear. Getting stuck in a place where cars and trucks pass only once every day or two is dangerous.

TIPS

1. In the dead of winter limit yourself to the ski resorts in the Lake District. That said, Bariloche is teeming with kids on high-school vacation trips July through September.

2. Book your flight to Argentina and your round-trip ticket to Bariloche at the same time. Booking a separate flight with another carrier will mean you won't be able to check your luggage through, and you'll have to time things very carefully to avoid missing your connection.

3. It's difficult to tour the Lake District without a rental car. If you don't want to drive, confine your visit to southern Patagonia, spending more time in El Calafate or extending into Tierra del Fuego.

A PASSIONATE HISTORY

by Victoria Patience

If there's one thing Argentinians have learned from their history, it's that there's not a lot you can count on. Fierce—often violent—political, economic, and social instability have been the only constants in the story of a people who seem never to be able to escape that famous Chinese curse, "May you live in interesting times."

Although most accounts of Argentinian history begin 500 years ago with the arrival of the conquistadors, humans have been living in what is now Argentina for around 13,000 years. They created the oldest recorded art in South America—a cave of handprints in Santa Cruz, Patagonia (c. 7500 BC)—and eventually became part of the Inca Empire.

Spanish and Portuguese sailors came in the early 16th century, including Ferdinand Magellan. The Spanish were forced out 300 years later by locals hungry for independence. Though autonomous on paper, in practice the early republic depended heavily on trade with Europe. Conflict and civil war wracked the United Provinces of the South as the region struggled to define its political identity and the economic model it would follow.

Spanish and Italian immigrants arrived in the 20th century, changing Argentina's population profile forever. Unstable politics characterized the rest of the century, which saw the rise and fall of Juan Perón and a series of increasingly bloody military dictatorships. Nearly 30 years of uninterrupted democracy have passed since the last junta fell, an achievement Argentinians value hugely.

(left) Ferdinand Magellan (c. 1480–1521)
(right) Stamp featuring Evita

Magellan sails down Argentinian coast

Juan de Garay founds Buenos Aires

PRE-1500s | INCA INVASION | 1500 | 1600

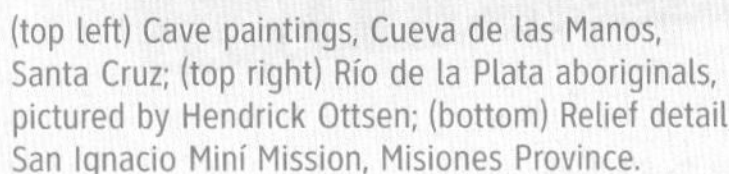

(top left) Cave paintings, Cueva de las Manos, Santa Cruz; (top right) Río de la Plata aboriginals, pictured by Hendrick Ottsen; (bottom) Relief detail, San Ignacio Miní Mission, Misiones Province.

PRE-1500

PRE-CONQUEST/ INCA

Argentina's original inhabitants were a diverse group of indigenous peoples. Their surroundings defined their lifestyles: nomadic hunter-gatherers lived in Patagonia and the Pampas, while the inhabitants of the northeast and northwest were largely farming communities. The first foreign power to invade the region was the Inca Empire, in the 15th century. Its roads and tribute systems extended over the entire northwest, reaching as far south as some parts of modern-day Mendoza.

1500–1809

BIRTH OF THE COLONY

European explorers first began to arrive at the River Plate area in the early 1500s, and in 1520 Ferdinand Magellan sailed right down the coast of what is now Argentina and on into the Pacific. Buenos Aires was founded twice: Pedro de Mendoza's 1536 attempt led to starving colonists turning to cannibalism before running for Asunción; Juan de Garay's attempt in 1580 was successful. Conquistadors of Spanish origin came from what are now Peru, Chile, and Paraguay and founded other cities. The whole area was part of the Viceroyalty of Peru until 1776, when the Spanish king Carlos III decreed present-day Argentina, Uruguay, Paraguay, and most of Bolivia to be the Viceroyalty of the Río de la Plata. Buenos Aires became the main port and the only legal exit point for silver from Potosí. Smuggling grew as fast as the city itself. In 1806–07 English forces tried twice to invade Argentina. Militia from Buenos Aires fought them off with no help from Spain, inciting ideas of independence among *criollos* (Argentinian-born Spaniards, who had fewer rights than those born in Europe).

(left) Julio Roca
(right) Monument to General San Martín;

1810—1860s BIRTH OF THE NATION: INDEPENDENCE AND THE CONSTITUTION

Early-19th-century proto-Argentinians were getting itchy for independence after the American Revolution. On May 25, 1810, Buenos Aires' leading citizens ousted the last Spanish viceroy. A series of elected juntas and triumvirates followed while military heroes José de San Martín and Manuel Belgrano won battles that allowed the Provincias Unidas de América del Sur to declare independence in Tucumán on July 9, 1816. San Martín went on to liberate Chile and Peru.

Political infighting marked the republic's first 40 years. The conflict centered on control of the port. Inhabitants of Buenos Aires wanted a centralist state run from the city, a position known as *unitario*, but landowners and leaders in the provinces wanted a federal state with greater Latin American integration. The federal side won when Juan Manuel de Rosas came to power: he made peace with indigenous leaders and gave rights to marginal social sectors like gauchos, although his increasingly iron-fisted rule later killed or outlawed the opposition. The centralist constitution established on his downfall returned power to the land-owning elite.

1860—1942 RISE OF THE MODERN STATE

Argentina staggered back and forth between political extremes on its rocky road to modern statehood. Relatively liberal leaders alternated with corrupt warlord types. The most infamous of these was Julio Roca, whose military campaigns massacred most of Argentina's remaining indigenous populations in order to seize the land needed to expand the cattle ranching and wheat farming. Roca also sold off services and resources to the English and started the immigration drive that brought millions of Europeans to Argentina between 1870 and 1930.

Coup ends privitization | Perón elected president

1930 · 1940 · 1950

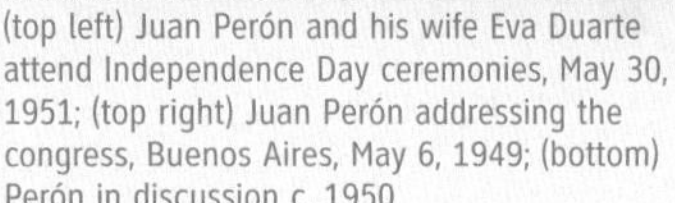

(top left) Juan Perón and his wife Eva Duarte attend Independence Day ceremonies, May 30, 1951; (top right) Juan Perón addressing the congress, Buenos Aires, May 6, 1949; (bottom) Perón in discussion c. 1950

1942–1973

THE RISE AND FALL OF PERONISM

A 1943 coup ended a decade of privatization that had caused the gap between rich and poor to grow exponentially. One of the soldiers involved was a little-known general named Juan Domingo Perón. He rose through the ranks of the government as quickly as he had through those of the army. Uneasy about Perón's growing popularity, other members of the military government imprisoned him, provoking a wave of uprisings that led to his release and swept him to the presidency as head of the newly formed labor party in 1946. Mid-campaign, he quietly married the young B-movie actress he'd been living with, Eva Duarte, soon to be known universally as "Evita." Their idiosyncratic, his'n'hers politics hinged on a massive personality cult. Together, they rallied the masses with their cries for social justice, political sovereignty, economic independence, and Latin American unity. Then, while he was busy improving worker's rights and trying to industrialize Argentina, she set about press-ganging Argentina's landed elite into funding her social aid program. Their tireless efforts to close the gap between rich and poor earned them the slavish devotion of Argentina's working classes and the passionate hatred of the rich. But everything began to go wrong when Evita died of uterine cancer in 1952. By 1955, the Marshall Plan in Europe reduced Argentina's export advantage, and the dwindling economy was grounds for Perón being ousted by another military coup. For the next 18 years, both he and his party were illegal in Argentina—mentioning his name or even whistling the Peronist anthem could land you in prison.

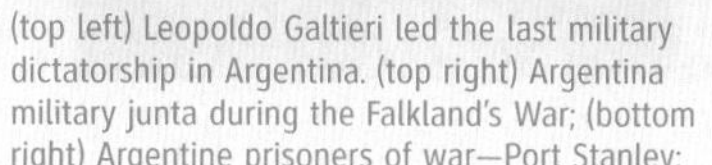

(top left) Leopoldo Galtieri led the last military dictatorship in Argentina. (top right) Argentina military junta during the Falkland's War; (bottom right) Argentine prisoners of war—Port Stanley;

1973—1983

DICTATORSHIP, STATE TERRORISM & THE FALKLANDS

The two civilian presidencies that followed both ended in fresh military coups until Perón was allowed to return in 1973. Despite falling out with left-wing student and guerrilla groups who had campaigned for him in his absence, he still won another election by a landslide. However, one problematic year later, he died in office. His farcical successor was the vice-president, an ex-cabaret dancer known as Isabelita, who was also Perón's third wife. Her chaotic leadership was brought to an end in 1976 by yet another military coup widely supported by civil society. The succession of juntas that ruled the country called their bloody dictatorship a "process of national reorganization"; these days it's referred to as state-led terrorism.

Much of the world seemingly ignored the actions of Argentina's government during its six-year reign of terror. Throughout the country, students, activists, and any other undesirable element were kidnapped and tortured in clandestine detention centers. Many victims' children were stolen and given up for adoption by pro-military families after their parents' bodies had been dumped in the River Plate. More than 30,000 people "disappeared" and thousands more went into exile. Government ministries were handed over to private businessmen. Massive corruption took external debt from $7 million to $66 million. In 1982, desperate for something to distract people with, the junta started war with Britain over the Islas Malvinas, or Falkland Islands. The disastrous campaign lasted just four months and, together with increasing pressure from local and international human rights activitsts, led to the downfall of the dictatorship.

TIMELINE

Falklands War	Menem elected president		State of emergency declared	Economic revival	Bicentenary	Cristina Kirchner re-elected
INFLATION REACHES 3,000%	1990	*ECONOMY IN TATTERS*	2000		2010	

(top) President Carlos Menem mobbed by the public; (top right) a revitalized economy brings new construction. (bottom) Argentine riot police drag away a demonstrator near the Casa Rosada in Buenos Aires.

1982–1999 RETURN OF DEMOCRACY

Celebrations marked the return to democracy. The main players in the dictatorship went on trial, but received relatively small sentences and were eventually pardoned. Inflation reached a terrifying 3,000% in 1988 and only stabilized when Carlos Menem became president the following year. Menem pegged the peso to the dollar, privatized services and resources, and even changed the constitution to extend his mandate. But despite an initial illusion of economic well-being, by the time Menem left office in 1999 poverty had skyrocketed, and the economy was in tatters.

2000–PRESENT CRISIS & THE K YEARS

The longer-term results of Menem's policies came in December 2001, when the government tried to prevent a rush on funds by freezing all private savings accounts. Thousands of people took to the streets in protest; on December 20, the violent police response transformed the demonstrations into riots. President Fernando de la Rúa declared a state of emergency, then resigned, and was followed by four temporary presidents in almost as many days. When things finally settled, the peso had devaluated drastically, many people had lost their savings, and the future looked dark.

However, under the center-leftist government of Argentina's following president, Néstor Kirchner, the economy slowly reactivated. Kirchner reopened trials of high-ranking military officials and championed local industry. In a rather bizarre turn of political events, he was succeeded by his wife, Cristina Fernández. Her fiery speeches have inspired both devotion and derision, but her social and economic policies ensured her landslide re-election in 2011. Times may be better than a few years ago, but Argentinians have lived through so many political ups and downs that they never take anything for granted.

MADE IN ARGENTINA

There's no doubt that Argentinians are an inventive lot. And we're not talking about their skill in arguing their way out of parking tickets: several things you might not be able to imagine life without started out in Argentina.

Una *birome* (ballpoint pen)

BALLPOINT PEN

Although László Jósef Bíró was born in Hungary and first patented the ballpoint pen in Paris, it wasn't until he launched his company in Argentina in 1943 that his invention began to attract attention. As such, Argentinians claim the world's most useful writing instrument as their own.

BLOOD TRANSFUSION

Before ER there was Luis Agote, an Argentinian doctor who, in 1914, was one of the first to perform a blood transfusion using stored blood (rather than doing a patient-to-patient transfusion). The innovation that made the process possible was adding sodium citrate, an anticoagulant, to the blood.

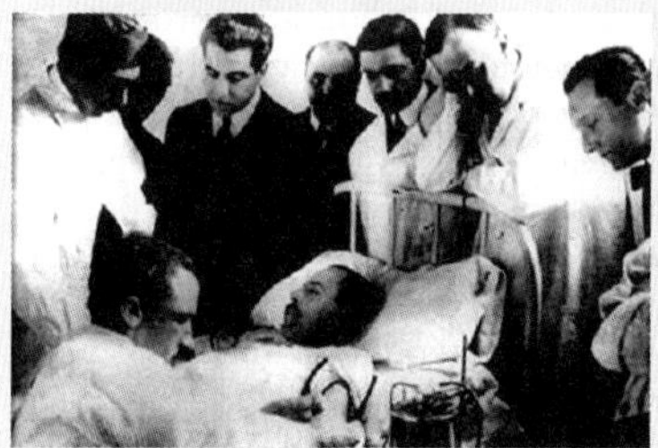

Luis Agote was one of the first to perform a nondirect blood transfusion, in Buenos Aires on November 9, 1914.

FINGERPRINTING

In 1891, Juan Vucetich, a Croatian-born officer of the Buenos Aires police force, came up with a system of classifying fingerprints. He went on to make the first-ever criminal arrest based on fingerprint evidence. Although his method has since been refined, it is still used throughout Latin America.

Huellas digitales (fingerprints)

- Other useful Argentinian claims to fame include the first working helicopter (1916); the first one-piece floor mop (1953); and the first one-use-only hypodermic syringe (1989).

ARGENTINA LODGING PRIMER

Booming visitor numbers have sparked dozens of new accommodation options. There's plenty of variety, whether you're looking for a tried-and-tested international chain, a boutique property, the Old World charm of an estancia, local hospitality at a family-run B&B, or a cheap hostel that's not only clean but stylish, too. Nearly all hotels include breakfast in the room price.

Estancias

For a taste of how Argentina's landed elite live, book a few nights on an estancia (ranch). Most estancia accommodation is in grandiose, European-inspired, century-old country mansions. Rates include activities such as horseback riding and four generous daily meals, usually shared with your hosts and other guests.

Estancias vary greatly: some are still working cattle or sheep farms, but many have switched entirely to tourism. At traditional establishments you'll be hosted by the owners, and stay in rooms that once belonged to family members. Accommodations are usually old-fashioned and tastefully furnished, but rarely luxurious: you might have to share a bathroom, and some rural locations don't have round-the-clock electricity.

Other estancias still belong to their original owners, but a private company runs the accommodation side of things. These properties are hit-and-miss: some are more luxurious and professional than traditional establishments, while others have become bland and generic. Some properties that advertise themselves as estancias are actually redevelopments of old rural houses, which may not have been estancias originally. These emulate traditional estancia style but are generally more luxurious and have modern amenities.

Apartments and Cabins

Self-catering options are plentiful in Argentina and increasingly popular with visitors. The savings are especially significant if you're traveling as a family or group. In Buenos Aires and other big cities you can rent furnished apartments (and sometimes houses) daily, although weekly and monthly rates are usually cheaper. Some properties are in new buildings with pools, gyms, and 24-hour concierges; others are in atmospheric, but less luxurious older buildings.

Cabañas (cabins) often outnumber hotels in destinations popular with Argentinian holiday-makers, such as the Atlantic coast or Bariloche. Some are independent holiday houses, while others form part of vacation complexes and include maid service and breakfast. Being outside busy town centers in natural surroundings is a boon, but you often need your own vehicle to reach properties comfortably.

Bed-and-breakfasts

In many smaller destinations large mid-range hotels tend to be impersonal, institutional setups aimed at passing business travelers. If you're looking for local flavor, consider a smaller hotel or bed-and-breakfast. Some are simple family-run affairs, others are boutique properties; many are housed in recycled old buildings that pack plenty of charm. Friendly, personalized service is another major appeal. Although many now use the term "B&B," you may also find them labeled posada or petit hotel. Hotels with fewer than 10 rooms are very common outside of Buenos Aires—as most hotels in Argentina include breakfast, these properties could be considered B&Bs, even if they don't actively advertise themselves as such.

Buenos Aires

WORD OF MOUTH

"Each day I walked in wider circles, discovering more places in San Telmo I wanted to know better—little theaters, the Spanish film club, hidden markets. I wanted to wake up again in this apartment with the French doors opening to . . . the sun, listening to the sounds of morning, sidewalks being washed, people on the way to work."

—santamonica

WELCOME TO BUENOS AIRES

Feria de San Telmo

TOP REASONS TO GO

★ **Dance the Night Away:** This is the capital of tango, that most passionate of dances. But porteños also dance to samba, salsa, and DJ mixes until the wee hours.

★ **Shop 'Til You Drop:** High-quality silver and leather goods as well as fashionable clothing and accessories are available at world-class boutiques and malls. Open-air markets carry regional and European antiques and provincial handicrafts.

★ **Get Your Culture On:** The architecture, wining-and-dining, and arts activities rival similar offerings in any major capital. But the lifestyle, lower prices, and warm locals are more typical of Latin America.

★ **Meat Your Destiny:** The capital of cow country has more *parrillas* (traditional grill restaurants) than you'll be able to sample.

★ **The Beautiful Game:** Top matches play out in Buenos Aires's colorful stadiums, stuffed to bursting with screaming *fútbol* (soccer) addicts.

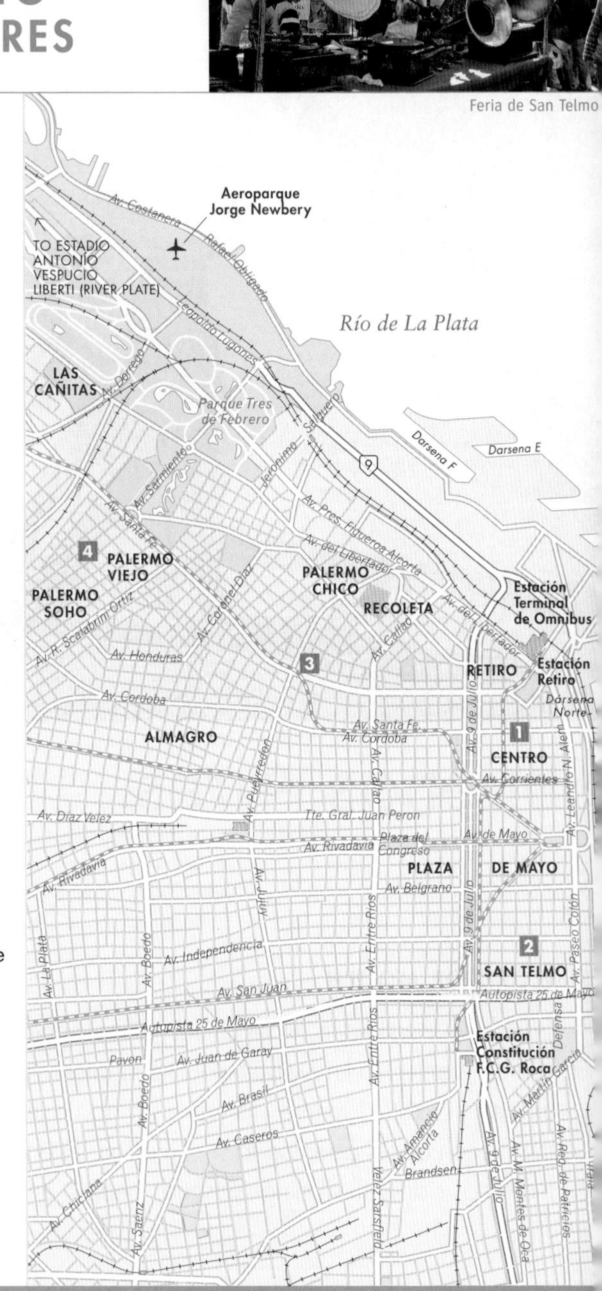

Showing La Boca love

GETTING ORIENTED

Most visitors see only a tiny part of Buenos Aires. It's actually a mammoth megalopolis that stretches more than 200 square km (75 square miles) into the surrounding pampas, Argentina's fertile plains. Around one-third of the country's 40 million inhabitants live in or around the city, making it the center of social as well as economic, political, and cultural life. Venturing out into the city's affluent northern suburbs or grittier west and south give you a very different perspective on Buenos Aires.

1 Centro. Locals use "Centro" as an umbrella term for several action-packed downtown districts. Microcentro, the city's heart, bursts with banks, offices, theaters, bars, cafés, bookstores, and crowds. The area around Plaza and Avenida de Mayo is the hub of political life. Posh hotels, gleaming skyscrapers, and an elegant boardwalk make up Puerto Madero.

2 San Telmo and La Boca. The tango was born in these southern barrios. These days, antiques stores and chic boutiques compete for space along San Telmo's cobbled streets. Just to the south, La Boca was originally settled by Italian immigrants. Now people come from all over for a snapshot of colorful but tacky Caminito or for a soccer match in Boca Juniors stadium.

3 Recoleta and Almagro. Today's elite live, dine, and shop along Recoleta's Paris-inspired streets. They're also often buried in the sumptuous mausoleums of its cemetery. Art galleries and museums are also draws. Gritty, working-class Almagro is known for its fringe theater pickings and tango scene, and the large Abasto shopping mall.

4 Palermo. Large Palermo has many subdistricts. If it's cool and happening, chances are it's in Palermo Viejo: boutiques, bars, restaurants, clubs, galleries, and hotels line the streets surrounding Plaza Serrano. The area across Avenida Juan B. Justo took the name Palermo Hollywood for the film and TV studios based here. There are excellent museums (the MALBA and Museo Evita) in Palermo, also home to parks and the zoo.

Floralis Generica

Updated by Karina Martinez-Carter, Sorrel Moseley-Williams, Victoria Patience, and Dan Perlman

Incredible food, fresh young designers, and a thriving cultural scene—all these Buenos Aires has. Yet the less tangible lies at the heart of the city's sizzle—for one, the spirit of its inhabitants. Here a flirtatious glance can be as passionate as a tango; a heated sports discussion as important as a world-class soccer match. It's this zest for life that makes Buenos Aires one of Latin America's hottest destinations.

The devalued peso is still a draw, although prices are steadily rising. Equally attractive, if you're trying to escape the financial doom and gloom abroad, is the locals' attitude to the financial crisis—they've weathered so many here that this one is barely news.

A booming tango—and tango tourism—revival means dance floors are alive again. And camera crews are now a common sight on street corners: low production costs and "Old World generic" architecture—hinting at many far-off cities but resembling none—are an appealing backdrop for European commercials.

Women are taking more prominent social roles, not least in the form of the first female president, Cristina Kirchner, elected in 2007. (She's technically the second female president, though she's the first woman *elected* to the position. When Perón died, his third wife, Isabelita, took over for a disastrous couple of years.) Marriage and equal rights for same-sex partnerships make Argentina a prime gay destination. And the country is finally seeking to bring the torturers of the 1976–82 dictatorship to justice.

Sadly, there are increasing numbers of homeless people, and protests about the city government's health and education policies are commonplace. Some things stay the same, though. Food, family, and *fútbol* (or fashion) are still the holy trinity for most *porteños* (as city residents are called). Philosophical discussions and psychoanalysis—Buenos Aires has more psychoanalysts per capita than any other city in the world—remain popular pastimes. And in the face of so much change, porteños still approach life with as much dramatic intensity as ever.

BUENOS AIRES PLANNER

WHEN TO GO

Remember that when it's summer in the United States, it's winter in Argentina, and vice versa. Winters (July–September) are chilly. Summer's muggy heat (December–March) can be taxing at midday but makes for warm nights. During these months Argentinians crowd resorts along the Atlantic and in Uruguay.

Spring (September–December) and autumn (April–June), with their mild temperatures—and blossoms or changing leaves—are ideal for urban trekking. It's usually warm enough for just a light jacket, and it's right before or after the peak (and expensive) seasons.

The best time for trips to Iguazú Falls is August–October, when temperatures are lower, the falls are fuller, and the spring coloring is at its brightest.

BUENOS AIRES TEMPERATURES (HIGH/LOW)

JAN.	FEB.	MAR.	APR.	MAY	JUNE
85F 29C/ 63F 17C	83F 28C/ 63F 17C	79F 26C/ 60F 16C	72F 22C/ 53F 12C	64F 18C/ 47F 8C	57F 14C/ 41F 5C
JULY	**AUG.**	**SEPT.**	**OCT.**	**NOV.**	**DEC.**
57F 14C/ 42F 6C	60F 16C/ 43F 6C	64F 18C/ 46F 8C	69F 21C/ 50F 10C	76F 24C/ 56F 13C	82F 28C/ 61F 16C

GETTING HERE AND AROUND

Intriguing architecture, an easy-to-navigate grid layout (a few diagonal transverses aside), and ample window-shopping make Buenos Aires a wonderful place to explore on foot. SUBE, a rechargeable swipe card, can be used on the subway, most city bus lines, and commuter trains.

PUBLIC TRANSIT TRAVEL

Service on the *subte* (subway) is quick, but trains are often packed and strikes are common. Four of the six underground lines (A, B, D, and E) fan out west from downtown; lines C and H (only partly open) connect them. Single-ride tickets cost 1.10 pesos. The subte shuts down around 10:30 pm and reopens at 5 am.

Colectivos (city buses) connect the city's barrios and the greater Buenos Aires area. Ticket machines on board accept coins (fares within the city cost 1.20–1.25 pesos) or the SUBE card. Bus stops are roughly every other block, but you may have to hunt for the small metal route-number signs: they could be stuck on a shelter, lamppost, or even a tree. Stop at a news kiosk and buy the *Guía T*, a route guide.

TAXI TRAVEL

Black-and-yellow taxis fill the streets and take you anywhere in town and short distances into greater Buenos Aires. Fares start at 5.80 pesos with 58¢ per 650 feet. You can hail taxis on the street or ask hotel and restaurant staffers to call for them.

SAFETY

Although Buenos Aires is safer than most Latin American capitals, petty crime is a concern. Pickpocketing and mugging are common, so avoid wearing flashy jewelry, be discreet with money and cameras, and be mindful of bags and wallets. Phone for taxis after dark. Police patrol most areas where you're likely to go, but they do have a reputation for corruption.

Protest marches are a part of life in Buenos Aires: most are peaceful, but some end in confrontations with the police. They often take place in the Plaza de Mayo, in the square outside the Congreso, or along Avenida de Mayo.

TOURS

BA Free Tours. The name says it all: BA Free Tours runs two daily walking tours that won't set you back a penny (tipping the chirpy young guides is a nice gesture, though). To take part, you show up at a designated meeting spot Monday through Saturday. 🌐 *www.bafreetours.com.*

Buenos Aires Bus. Buenos Aires Bus is a hop-on hop-off service run by the city's official tourism body. It's an efficient way to tick off all the main tourist spots in the city. The colorful double-decker buses leave two to three times per hour and have bilingual guides aboard who point out landmarks. ☎ *11/5239–5160* 🌐 *www.buenosairesbus.com.*

Buenos Aires Tours. The service—for tours in town and out—you get from Isabel at Buenos Aires Tours is almost heroic. 🌐 *www.buenosaires-tours.com.ar.*

Cicerones de Buenos Aires. For a local's perspective, contact the Cicerones de Buenos Aires, a free service that pairs you with a porteño to show you parts of town you might not see otherwise. ☎ *11/4330–0800* 🌐 *www.cicerones.org.ar.*

Eternautas. Informed young historians from the University of Buenos Aires lead cultural and historical tours at Eternautas. It offers general city tours, themed private outings (e.g., Evita and Peronism, the literary city, Jewish Buenos Aires), and excursions outside town. ☎ *11/5031–9916* 🌐 *www.eternautas.com.*

Opción Sur. Large onboard screens make the posh minibuses used by Opción Sur part transport and part cinema. Each stop on their tours of the city and the Tigre Delta is introduced by relevant historical footage (e.g., Evita rallying the masses at Plaza de Mayo). ☎ *11/4777–9029* 🌐 *www.opcionsur.com.ar.*

Smile on Sea. See Buenos Aires from the river on a 2½-hour sailboat tour with Smile on Sea. ☎ *11/15–5018–8662* 🌐 *www.smileonsea.com.*

Travel Line. See the major sights and get the lay of the land on the basic three-hour bus tours in English and Spanish run by Travel Line. ☎ *11/4393–9000* 🌐 *www.travelline.com.ar.*

Wow! Argentina. For tailor-made city tours, contact Wow! Argentina well in advance of your arrival in Buenos Aires. Enthusiastic Cintia Stella and her team also arrange excursions all over Argentina. ☎ *11/5239–3019* 🌐 *www.wowargentina.com.*

VISITOR INFORMATION

The website of the city tourist board, **Turismo Buenos Aires** (🌐 *www.bue.gov.ar*) has lively, downloadable MP3 walking tours in English. Information booths at the airports and seven other locations provide maps and have English-speaking staff. Hours can be erratic, but the booth at the intersection of Florida and Marcelo T. de Alvear is usually open during the day.

EXPLORING BUENOS AIRES

Unlike most other Latin American cities, where the architecture reveals a strong Spanish influence, little remains of Buenos Aires's colonial days. This is due in part to the short lifespan of the adobe (mud and straw) used to build the city's first houses, and also to the fact that Buenos Aires's elite have always followed Europe's architectural trends closely. The result is an arresting hodgepodge of building styles that hints at many far-off cities—Rome, Madrid, Paris, Budapest. With their boulevards lined with palatial mansions and spacious parks, Palermo, La Recoleta, and some parts of the downtown area are testament to days of urban planning on a grandiose scale (and budget), whereas San Telmo and La Boca have a more working-class Italian feel.

CENTRO AND ENVIRONS

Office workers, shoppers, and sightseers fill Centro's streets each day. Traffic noise and driving tactics also reach superlative levels. Locals profess to hate the chaos; unrushed visitors get a buzz out of the bustle. Either way, Centro provokes extreme reactions.

This is one of the city's oldest areas. Plaza de Mayo is the original main square, and civic buildings both past and present are clustered between it and Plaza Congreso. Though you probably know Plaza de Mayo best from the balcony scene in the 1996 film *Evita*, many of Argentina's most historic events—including revolutions, demonstrations, and terrorist attacks—took place around it. Bullet-marked facades, sidewalks embedded with plaques, and memorials where buildings once stood are reminders of all this history, and the protesters who fill the streets regularly are history in the making.

More upbeat gatherings—open-air concerts, soccer victory celebrations, post-election reveling—take place around the Obelisco, a scaled-down Washington Monument look-alike that honors the founding of Buenos Aires. Inescapably phallic, it's the butt of local jokes about male insecurity in this oh-so-macho city. It's even dressed in a giant red condom each year on AIDS Awareness Day.

The town's most highbrow cultural events are hosted a few blocks away in the Teatro Colón, and the highest-grossing theatrical productions line Avenida Corrientes, whose sidewalks overflow on weekends with dolled-up locals. Argentina's biggest scandals center—the judicial district—is on nearby Tribunales.

GETTING ORIENTED

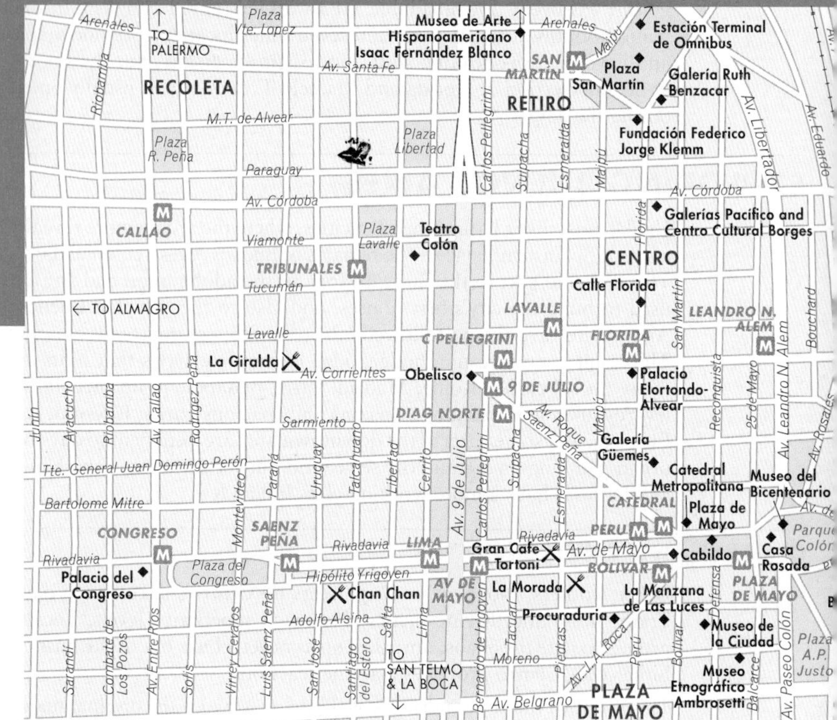

TOP EXPERIENCES

Reflecting: on Argentina's indigenous history at the Museo Etnográfico Juan B. Ambrosetti.

Witnessing: demonstrations in Plaza de Mayo, where Evita waved to crowds.

Descending: into the 17th-century tunnels the Jesuits built at La Manzana de las Luces.

Wandering: along Juana Manuela Gorriti and Pierina Dealessi to see Puerto Madero's "recycled" warehouses; Avenida de Mayo to visit 19th-century Europe; or Calle Florida for hustle, bustle, and souvenirs.

THE TERRITORY

The Microcentro (central business district) runs between Avenidas L. N. Alem and 9 de Julio and north of Avenida de Mayo. There are two axes: Avenida Corrientes (east–west) and pedestrian-only shopping street Calle Florida (north–south). Florida's northern end leads into Plaza San Martín in Retiro. South of the Microcentro lies Plaza de Mayo. From here Avenida de Mayo runs 12 blocks west to Plaza del Congreso. Puerto Madero borders the Centro to the east. Both it and its main thoroughfares, Avenida Alicia M. de Justo and Olga Cossentini, run parallel to the river.

SAFETY AND PRECAUTIONS

Be especially alert for "stain scammers" downtown: they squirt liquid on you surreptitiously, then "helpfully" offer to clean it off (as they pick your pocket). Use ATMs only during bank hours (weekdays 10–3); thieves target them after hours. Stay alert on Lavalle, a pedestrian street peppered with adult entertainment. At night, wander with care.

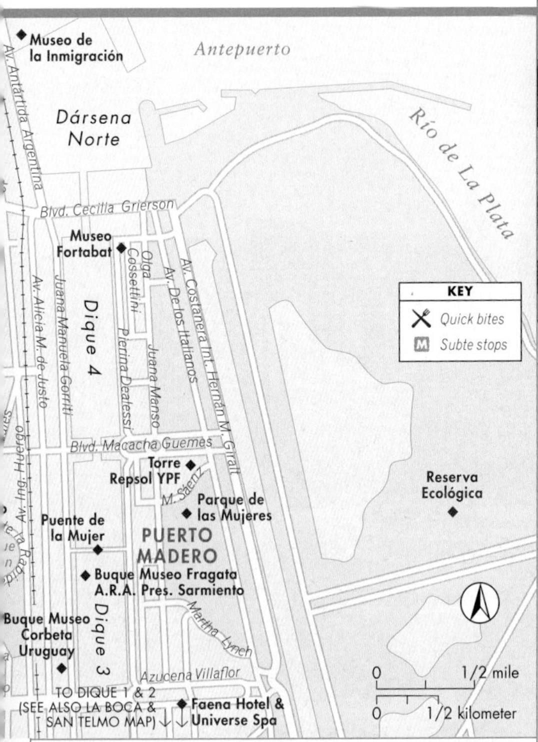

GETTING AROUND

The quickest way into Centro is by subte. For Microcentro, get off at Florida (Línea/Line B) or Lavalle (C). Retiro and Plaza San Martín have eponymous stations on Línea C. Stations Avenida de Mayo (A), Catedral (D), and Bolívar (E) all serve Plaza de Mayo. Línea A has stops along de Mayo, including at Congreso. Líneas B, C, and D intersect at Carlos Pellegrini/Diagonal Norte/9 de Julio. Only change lines here if you're going more than one stop. Otherwise, walking is quicker. Puerto Madero is close to L. N. Alem on Línea A, and is connected by the Tren del Este, a light-rail service running parallel to Avenida Alicia Moreau de Justo.

You can take a taxi or bus to the Microcentro, but walking is the best way to move within it. Bus 17 connects Centro and Recoleta; so do Buses 59 and 93. Bus 130 connects these areas with Puerto Madero. Buses 22 and 24 run between San Telmo and Microcentro.

QUICK BITES

Chan Chan. Among the Peruvian dishes at bargain prices are the spicy ceviches, ideal for stoking your sightseeing fires. ✉ *Hipólito Yrigoyen 1390, Congreso* ☎ *11/4382-8492* ⏲ *Tues.–Sun. 12–4pm and 8pm–12:30am.*

La Morada. Local office workers know that the best empanadas in the Microcentro are made by La Morada. Vintage adverts, 1960s LPs, and photos of late Argentinian celebrities crowd the walls. ✉ *Hipólito Yrigoyen 778, Plaza de Mayo* ☎ *11/4343-3003* 🌐 *www.lamorada.com.ar* ⏲ *Mon.–Thurs. 10–4; Fri.–Sat 10–4 and 6–midnight.*

La Giralda. Beret-wearing intellectuals and perfumed theatergoers love this retro café. Don't let the small tables or surly waiters put you off; its signature *chocolate con churros* (hot chocolate with crisp cigar-shaped donuts) are to die for. ✉ *Av. Corrientes 1453, Centro* ☎ *11/4371-3846* ⏲ *Mon.–Thurs. 7 am–midnight; Fri. and Sat. 7 am–2 am; Sun. 4 pm–midnight.*

DID YOU KNOW?

Plaza del Congreso is great for people-watching, especially during the late-summer carnival (with rides), a saint-day procession, or—for early risers—at the year-round dog run.

Contemporary masterpieces by such world-renowned architects as Sir Norman Foster and César Pelli fill adjacent Puerto Madero, a onetime port area that's now the city's swankiest district, with chic hotels, restaurants, and shops. A promenade along the old docks affords great views of developments across the water in Puerto Madero Este; cross via Santiago Calatrava's Puente de la Mujer, a bridge whose sleek white curves were inspired by tango dancers.

TAKING IT IN

Crowds and traffic can make touring draining: try to do a few short visits rather than one long marathon. You can see most of the sights in the Plaza de Mayo area over the course of a leisurely afternoon; a late-morning wander and lunch in Puerto Madero is one good way to precede this.

Half a day in the Microcentro is enough to take in the sights, though you could spend a lot more time caught up in shops. Office workers on lunch breaks make the Microcentro even more hectic than usual between noon and 2. If you're planning on hard-core shopping, come on a weekend. The area is quiet at night, and a little dangerous in its desolation.

HOW TO SPEND . . .

An Hour or Two: combine a visit to Plaza de Mayo with one nearby museum or some shopping on Calle Florida.

A Half-Day: start with a late-morning wander in Puerto Madero, then visit either the Museo Fortabat or the Museo Etnográfico. Time lunch early enough to get to La Manzana de las Luces for a tour. Finish your afternoon in the shops along Calle Florida or walking along Avenida de Mayo to Plaza del Congreso, refueling at Gran Café Tortoni on the way.

TOP ATTRACTIONS

La Manzana de Las Luces (*The Block of Illumination*). More history is packed into this single block of buildings southwest of Plaza de Mayo than in scores of other city blocks put together. Among other things, it was the enclave for higher learning: the metaphorical *luces* (lights) of its name refer to the "illuminated" scholars who worked within.

The Iglesia de San Ignacio is open to the public, but you can only visit the rest of Manzana de Las Luces on guided tours led by excellent professional historians. Regular departures are in Spanish, but they provide brochures with English summaries of each stage; groups of over 20 people can call ahead to arrange English-language visits.

Procuraduría. The earliest occupant on La Manzana de Las Luces was the controversial Jesuit order, which began construction here in 1661. The only survivor from this first stage is the galleried Procuraduría, the colonial administrative headquarters for the Jesuits' vast land holdings in northeastern Argentina and Paraguay (think: *The Mission*). Historic defense tunnels, still undergoing archaeological excavation, linked the Jesuit headquarters to churches in the area, the Cabildo, and the port. Guided visits here include a glimpse of a specially reinforced section.

After the Jesuits' expulsion from Argentina in 1767 (the Spanish crown saw them as a threat), the simple brick-and-mud structure housed first the city's first school of medicine and then the University of Buenos Aires. Fully restored, it's now home to a school of luthiers and a rather tacky crafts market. ✉ *Corner of Alsina and Perú.*

Iglesia de San Ignacio de Loyola (*Saint Ignatius of Loyola Church*). The Jesuits honored their patron saint at the Iglesia de San Ignacio de Loyola. The first church on the site was built of adobe in 1675; within a few decades it was rebuilt in stone. ✉ *Corner of Alsina and Bolívar.*

Casas Virreinales (*Viceroyal Houses*). Argentina's first congress convened within the Casas Virreinales—ironic, given that it was built to house colonial civil servants. ✉ *Corner of Moreno and Perú.*

Colegio Nacional. The remaining historic building on the La Manzana de Las Luces block is the neoclassical Colegio Nacional, a top-notch public school and a hotbed of political activism that replaced a Jesuit-built structure. The president attends graduation ceremonies, and Einstein gave a lecture here in 1925. ✉ *Entrance and inquiries at Perú 272, Plaza de Mayo* ☎ *11/4342–6973* 🌐 *www.manzanadelasluces.gov.ar* 🎟 *14 pesos* 🕓 *Visits by guided tour only; Spanish-language tours leave weekdays at 3 and at 3, 4:30, and 6 pm on weekends; call two weeks ahead to arrange tours in English* Ⓜ *A to Plaza de Mayo, D to Catedral, E to Bolívar.*

★ **Museo Etnográfico Juan B. Ambrosetti** (*Ethnographic Museum*). Given that the 100-peso bill still honors General Roca, the man responsible for the massacre of most of Patagonia's indigenous population, it's not surprising that information on Argentina's original inhabitants is sparse. This fascinating but little-visited museum is a welcome remedy.

Begun by local scientist Juan Bautista Ambrosetti in 1904, the collection originally focused on so-called exotic art and artifacts, such as the Australasian sculptures and Japanese temple altar showcased in the rust-color introductory room. The real highlights, however, are the Argentine collections: this would be an eye-opening introduction to a visit to Argentina's far north or south.

The ground-floor galleries trace the history of human activity in Patagonia, with an emphasis on the tragic results of the European arrival. Dugout canoes, exquisite Mapuche silver jewelry, and scores of archive photos and illustrations are the main exhibits.

In the upstairs northwestern Argentina gallery the focus is mainly archaeological. Displays briefly chronicle the evolution of Andean civilization, the heyday of the Inca empire, and postcolonial life. Artifacts include ceramics, textiles, jewelry, farming tools, and even food: anyone for some 4,000-year-old corn?

The collection is run by the liberal Philosophy and Letters Faculty of the University of Buenos Aires. Although their insightful labels and explanations are all in Spanish, you can ask for a photocopied sheet with English versions of the texts. It's a pleasure just to wander the quiet, light-filled 19th-century town house that houses both the collection and an anthropological library. The peaceful inner garden is the perfect place for some post-museum reflection. ✉ *Moreno 350, Plaza de Mayo* ☎ *11/4345–8196* 🌐 *www.museoetnografico.filo.uba.ar* 🎟 *3 pesos* ⏲ *Tues.–Fri. 1–7, weekends 3–7* Ⓜ *A to Plaza de Mayo; D to Catedral; E to Bolívar.*

Museo del Bicentenario. Today, the River Plate is nowhere in sight, but the humming traffic circle that overlooks this underground museum behind the Casa Rosada was once on the waterfront. The brick vaults, pillars, and wooden pulley mechanisms are the remains of the 1845 Taylor Customs House and jetty, discovered after being buried for almost a century. In honor of Argentina's 2010 bicentenary celebrations the structure was restored and covered with a glass roof.

Each vault has been assigned a segment of Argentina's political history, told through historic objects—often personal possessions of those who governed from the house overhead—paintings, photographs, film reels, and interactive screens.

Temporary art exhibitions run on the other side of the museum courtyard. However, the large glass structure in the center contains the real star of the show: a 360-degree masterpiece by Mexican muralist David Alfaro Siqueiros which originally covered the walls, floor, and ceiling of a basement room in a client's house. The house was demolished in the early 1990s, and the mural carefully removed in pieces, only to languish in a shipping container for 17 years. Thankfully, Siqueiros's innovative use of industrial paint meant that damage was minimal. Prompted by the campaigns of committed art activists, President Cristina Fernández intervened and the mural has now been fully restored and reassembled here. After donning protective shoes, you cross a small passageway into the work, which represents an underwater scene, against which the feet and faces of swimmers seem to press. The only male figure (swimming upwards on the wall opposite the entrance) is said to represent the artist.

A café at the back of the museum offers coffee, sandwiches, and salads, and a daily set lunch menu. ✉ *Paseo Colón 100, at Hipólito Yrigoyen, Plaza de Mayo* ☎ *11/4344–3802.*

Fodor's Choice ★ **Plaza de Mayo.** Since its construction in 1580, this has been the setting for Argentina's most politically turbulent moments, including the uprising against Spanish colonial rule on May 25, 1810—hence its name. The square was once divided in two by a *recova* (gallery), but this reminder of colonial times was demolished in 1883, and the square's central monument, the Pirámide de Mayo, was later moved to its place. The pyramid you see is actually a 1911 extension of the original, erected in 1811 on the anniversary of the Revolution of May, which is hidden inside. The bronze equestrian statue of General Manuel Belgrano, designer of Argentina's flag, dates from 1873, and stands at the east end of the plaza.

The plaza remains the traditional site for ceremonies, rallies, and protests. Thousands cheered for Perón and Evita here; anti-Peronist planes bombed the gathered crowds in 1955; there were bloody clashes in December 2001 (hence the heavy police presence and crowd-control barriers); but the crowds were jubilant for Argentina's massive bicentenary celebrations in 2010. The white head scarves painted around the Pirámide de Mayo represent the Madres de la Plaza de Mayo (Mothers of May Square) who have marched here every Thursday at 3:30

for more than two decades. Housewives and mothers–turned–militant activists demand justice for *los desaparecidos,* the people who were "disappeared" during the military government's reign from 1976 to 1983, and welcome visitors to join in.

Casa Rosada. The eclectic Casa de Gobierno, better known as the Casa Rosada or Pink House, is at Plaza de Mayo's eastern end, with its back to the river. The building houses the government's executive branch—the president works here but lives elsewhere—and was built in the late 19th century over the foundations of an earlier customhouse and fortress. Swedish, Italian, and French architects have since modified the structure, which accounts for the odd mix of styles. Its curious hue dates from the presidency of Domingo Sarmiento, who ordered it painted pink as a symbol of unification between two warring political factions, the *federales* (whose color was red) and the *unitarios* (represented by white). Local legend has it that the original paint was made by mixing whitewash with bull's blood.

The balcony facing Plaza de Mayo is a presidential podium. From this lofty stage Evita rallied the *descamisados* (the shirtless—meaning the working class), Maradona sang along with soccer fans after winning one World Cup and coming second in another, and Madonna sang her filmed rendition of "Don't Cry for Me Argentina." Check for a small banner hoisted alongside the nation's flag, indicating "the president is in."

On weekends, hour-long guided tours take in some of the presidential offices and the newly opened *Galería de los Patriotas Argentinos del Bicentenario* (Bicentennial Gallery of Patriots), a pictorial who's who of Argentina's national heroes. The country's heroines have a room of their own here, which is often used for presidential press conferences. An impassioned Evita presides over black-and-white photographs of Argentina's other great dames. ✉ *Balcarce 50, Plaza de Mayo* ☎ *11/4344–3714* 🌐 *www.presidencia.gov.ar/visitas-guiadas* 🎫 *Free* 🕑 *Weekends 10–6.*

Museo Histórico Nacional del Cabildo y de la Revolución de Mayo (*Cabildo*). The city council—now based in the ornate building over Avenida de Mayo—originally met in the Cabildo. It dates from 1765, and is the only colonial building on Plaza de Mayo. The epicenter of the May Revolution of 1810, where patriotic citizens gathered to vote against Napleonic rule, the hall is one of Argentina's national shrines. However, this hasn't stopped successive renovations to its detriment, including the demolition of the whole right end of the structure to make way for the new Avenida de Mayo in 1894 and of the left end for Diagonal Julio Roca in 1931. The small museum of artifacts and documents pertaining to the events of the May Revolution is less of an attraction than the building itself. As part of the 2010 bicentenary celebrations, a 3-D video-mapping spectacular was projected onto the facade as an audience of thousands watched from Plaza de Mayo. Thursday and Friday from 11 to 6, an artisan fair takes place on the Patio del Cabildo. ✉ *Bolívar 65, Plaza de Mayo* ☎ *11/4342–6729* 🎫 *4 pesos* 🕑 *Wed.–Fri. 10:30–5, weekends 11:30–6* Ⓜ *A to Plaza de Mayo; D to Catedral; E to Bolívar.*

Fodor's Choice ★ **Teatro Colón.** Its magnitude, magnificent acoustics, and opulence (grander than Milan's La Scala) position the Teatro Colón (Colón Theater) among the world's top five opera theaters. An ever-changing stream of imported talent bolsters the well-regarded local lyric and ballet companies. After an eventful 18-year building process involving the death of one architect and the murder of another, the ornate Italianate structure was finally inaugurated in 1908 with Verdi's *Aïda*. It has hosted the likes of Maria Callas, Richard Strauss, Arturo Toscanini, Igor Stravinsky, Enrico Caruso, and Luciano Pavarotti, who said that the Colón has only one flaw: the acoustics are so good that every mistake can be heard. The theater was closed in 2008 for controversial renovations, which ran way over schedule and budget, but reopened on May 24, 2010, to coincide with Argentina's bicentenary celebrations. Much of the work done was structural, but its stone facade and interior trimmings are now scrubbed and gleaming.

The theater's sumptuous building materials—three kinds of Italian marble, French stained glass, and Venetian mosaics—were imported from Europe to create large-scale lavishness. The seven-tier main theater is breathtaking in size, and has a grand central chandelier with 700 lights to illuminate the 3,000 mere mortals in its red-velvet seats.

Nothing can prepare you for the thrill of seeing an opera or ballet here. The seasons run from April through December, but many seats are reserved for season-ticket holders. Shorter options in the main theater include symphonic cycles by the stable orchestra as well as international orchestral visits. Chamber music concerts are held in the U-shaped Salón Dorado (Golden Room), so named for the 24-karat gold leaf that covers its stucco molding. Underneath the main building is the ultra-minimal Centro Experimental, a tiny theater showcasing avant-garde music, opera, and dramatic performances.

You can see the splendor up close and get in on all the behind-the-scenes action with the theater's extremely popular guided tours. The whirlwind visits take you up and down innumerable staircases to rehearsal rooms and to the costume, shoe, and scenery workshops, before letting you gaze at the stage from a sought-after box. (Arrive at least a half hour before the guided tour you want to take starts, as tours fill up very quickly.)

Buy tickets from the box office on Pasaje Toscanini. If seats are sold out—or beyond your pocket—you can buy 10-peso standing-room tickets on the day of the performance. These are for the lofty upper-tier *paraíso*, from which you can both see and hear perfectly, although three-hour-long operas are hard on the feet. ✉ *Main entrance: Libertad between Tucumán and Viamonte; Box office: Pasaje Toscanini 1180, Centro* ☎ *11/4378–7100 tickets, 11/4378–7127 tours* 🌐 *www.teatrocolon.org.ar* 🎟 *Guided tours 60 pesos* ⏲ *Daily 9–4, guided tours in Spanish every 15 mins., guided tours in English at 11, 12, 1, and 2* Ⓜ *D to Tribunales.*

DID YOU KNOW?

La Puente de la Mujer, or "Bridge of the Woman," connects Microcentro with Puerto Madero. The whole middle section of the bridge, including the skyward-reaching arm, swings like a door on a hinge to let boats pass.

WORTH NOTING

Buque Museo A.R.A. Corbeta Uruguay (*Uruguay Corvette Ship Museum*). The oldest of the Argentine fleet, bought from England in 1874, the ship has been around the world several times and was used in the nation's Antarctic campaigns at the turn of the 20th century. You can see what the captain's cabin and officers' mess looked like at that time; there are also displays of artifacts rescued from shipwrecks. A stroll around the decks affords views of the boat's structure and of Puerto Madero. ✉ *Dique 4, Alicia M. de Justo 500 block, Puerto Madero* ☎ *11/4314–1090* 🌐 *www.ara.mil.ar/pag.asp?idItem=113* 🎫 *2 pesos* ⏲ *Daily 10–7.*

Buque Museo Fragata A.R.A. Presidente Sarmiento (*President Sarmiento Frigate Museum*). The navy commissioned this frigate from England in 1898 to be used as an open-sea training vessel. The 280-foot boat used up to 33 sails and carried more than 300 crew members: the beautifully restored cabins afford a glimpse of what life onboard was like. Surprisingly luxurious officers' quarters include parquet floors, wood paneling, and leather armchairs; cadets had to make do with hammocks. ✉ *Dique 3, Alicia M. de Justo 980, Puerto Madero* ☎ *11/4334–9386* 🌐 *www.ara.mil.ar/pag.asp?idItem=112* 🎫 *2 pesos* ⏲ *Daily 10–7.*

Catedral Metropolitana. The Metropolitan Cathedral's columned neoclassical facade makes it seem more like a temple than a church, and its history follows the pattern of many structures in the Plaza de Mayo area. The first of six buildings on this site was a 16th-century adobe ranch house; the current structure dates from 1822, but has been added to several times. The embalmed remains of General José de San Martín, known as the Liberator of Argentina for his role in the War of Independence, rest here in a marble mausoleum lighted by an eternal flame. Soldiers of the Grenadier Regiment, an elite troop created and trained by San Martín in 1811, permanently guard the tomb. Guided tours (in Spanish) of the mausoleum and crypt leave Monday to Saturday at 11:45 am. ✉ *San Martín 27, at Rivadavía, Plaza de Mayo* ☎ *11/4331–2845* 🌐 *www.catedralbuenosaires.org.ar* 🎫 *Free* ⏲ *Weekdays 7–7, weekends 9–7:30* Ⓜ *A to Plaza de Mayo, D to Catedral, E to Bolívar.*

Museo de Arte Hispanoamericano Isaac Fernández Blanco (*Isaac Fernández Blanco Hispanic-American Art Museum*). The distinctive Peruvian neocolonial-style Palacio Noel serves as the perfect backdrop for this colonial art and craft museum, which was originally built in 1920 as the residence of architect Martín Noel. He and museum founder Fernández Blanco donated most of the exquisite silver items, religious wood carvings, inlaid furnishings, and paintings from the Spanish colonial period that are on display. Guided tours in English can be arranged by calling ahead. Shaded benches in the lush walled gardens provide welcome respite for your feet, and the rustling leaves and birdcalls almost filter out the busy Retiro traffic noises. The museum is an easy five-block walk from Estación San Martín on Línea C: from there go west along Avenida Santa Fe and then turn right into Suipacha and continue four blocks. ✉ *Suipacha 1422, at Av. Libertador, Retiro* ☎ *11/4327–0228* 🌐 *www.museofernandezblanco.buenosaires.gob.ar* 🎫 *1 pesos, free Thurs.* ⏲ *Tues.–Fri. 2–7, weekends 11–7* Ⓜ *C to San Martín.*

Colección de Arte Amalia Lacroze de Fortabat (Museo Fortabat). Argentina's richest woman, Amalia Fortabat, is a cement heiress, so it's not surprising that the building containing her private art collection is made mostly of concrete. It was completed in 2003, but after-effects from Argentina's 2001–02 financial crisis delayed its opening until 2008. Amalita (as she's known locally) was closely involved in the design, and the personal touch continues into the collection, which includes several portraits of her—including a prized Warhol—and many works by her granddaughter, Amalia Amoedo. In general, more money than taste seems to have gone into the project: the highlights are lesser works by big names both local (Berni, Xul Solar, Pettoruti) and international (Brueghel, Dalí, Picasso), hung with little aplomb or explanation in a huge basement gallery that echoes like a high-school gym. The side gallery given over to Carlos Alonso's and Juan Carlos Castagnino's figurative work is a step in the right direction, however. So are the luminous paintings by Soldi in the glass-walled upper gallery. They're rivaled, however, by the view over the docks below—time your visit to end at sunset when pinks and oranges light the redbrick buildings opposite. Views from the dockside café come a close second. ✉ *Olga Cossettini 141, Puerto Madero* ☎ *11/4310–6600* 🌐 *www.coleccionfortabat.org.ar* 🎫 *15 pesos* ⏲ *Tues.–Sun. noon–9.*

Museo de la Ciudad. "Whimsical" is one way to describe the City Museum, which focuses on random aspects of domestic and public life in Buenos Aires in times past. "Eccentric" is probably closer to the mark for the permanent collection: an array of typical porteño doors. Historical toys, embroidery, religion in Buenos Aires, and garden gnomes (yes, really) have been some of the focuses of temporary exhibitions. Still, the peaceful building—which was restored in 2009—is worth a 10-minute wander if you're in the neighborhood. Downstairs, the Farmacia La Estrella sells modern medicine and cosmetics from a perfectly preserved 19th-century shop. ✉ *Alsina 412, Plaza de Mayo* ☎ *11/4331–9855* 🌐 *www.museodelaciudad.buenosaires.gob.ar* 🎫 *1 peso, free Mon. and Wed.* ⏲ *Weekdays 11–7, weekends 10–8* Ⓜ *A to Plaza de Mayo, D to Catedral, E to Bolívar.*

Puente de la Mujer. Tango dancers inspired the sweeping asymmetrical lines of Valencian architect Santiago Calatrava's design for the pedestrian-only Bridge of the Woman. Puerto Madero's street names pay homage to famous Argentine women, hence the bridge's name. (Ironically its most visible part—a soaring 128-foot arm—represents the man of a couple in mid-tango.) The $6 million structure was made in Spain and paid for by local businessmen Alberto L. González, one of the brains behind Puerto Madero's redevelopment; he also built the Hilton Hotel here. Twenty engines rotate the bridge to allow ships to pass through. ✉ *Dique 3, between Pierina Dealessi and Manuela Gorriti, Puerto Madero.*

Reserva Ecológica. The 865-acre Ecological Reserve was built over a landfill, and is home to more than 500 species of birds and a variety of flora and fauna. On weekends thousands of porteños vie for a spot on the grass, so come midweek if you want to bird-watch and sunbathe in peace or use the jogging and cycling tracks. A monthly guided "Walking under the Full Moon" tour in Spanish begins at 7:30 pm April through October and at 8:30 pm November through March. Even if you don't speak Spanish it's still a great way to get back to nature at night; otherwise avoid the area after sunset. It's just a short walk from the south end of Puerto Madero. ✉ *Av. Tristán Achával Rodríguez 1550, Puerto Madero* ☎ *11/4315–4129, 11/4893–1853 tours* 🌐 *www.buenosaires.gov.ar/areas/med_ambiente/reserva* 🎫 *Free* ⏲ *Apr.–Oct., Tues.–Sun. 8–6; Nov.–Mar., Tues.–Sun. 8–7; guided visits in Spanish weekends at 10:30 and 3:30.*

SAN TELMO AND LA BOCA

"The south also exists," quip residents of bohemian neighborhoods like San Telmo and La Boca, which historically played second fiddle to posher northern barrios. No more. The hottest designers have boutiques here, new restaurants are booked out, an art district is burgeoning, and property prices are soaring. The south is also a hotbed for the city's tango revival, appropriate given that the dance was born in these quarters.

San Telmo, Buenos Aires' first suburb, was originally inhabited by sailors, and takes its name from their wandering patron saint. All the same, the mariners' main preoccupations were clearly less than spiritual, and San Telmo became famous for its brothels. That didn't stop the area's first experience of gentrification: wealthy local families built ornate homes here in the early 19th century, but ran for Recoleta when a yellow-fever epidemic struck in 1871. Newly arrived immigrants crammed into their abandoned mansions, known as *conventillos* (tenement houses). Today these same houses are fought over by foreign buyers dying to ride the wave of urban renewal—the *reciclaje* (recycling), as porteños call it—that's sweeping the area.

Neighboring La Boca shares much of San Telmo's gritty history. It sits on the fiercely polluted Riachuelo River, where rusting ships and warehouses remind you that this was once the city's main port. The immigrants who first settled here built their houses from corrugated metal and brightly colored paint left over from the shipyards. Today, imitations of these vibrant buildings form one of Buenos Aires' most emblematic sights, the Caminito. Two quite different colors have made La Boca famous: the blue and gold of the Boca Juniors soccer team, whose massive home stadium is the barrio's unofficial heart.

TAKING IT IN

San Telmo thrives on Sunday, thanks to the art and antiques market in Plaza Dorrego. During the week a leisurely afternoon's visit is ideal. Start with lunch in a café at the northern or southern end of San Telmo, then spend an hour or two wandering the cobbled streets. You still have time for some shopping before winding up with a coffee or a drink. In La Boca, allow two or three hours to explore Caminito and do a museum or two. It's busy all week, but expect extra crowds on weekends.

2

HOW TO SPEND . . .

An hour or two: midweek, combine a brisk walk around San Telmo with a taxi-ride to La Boca for a visit to Fundación Proa and a cursory glance at Caminito. On Sunday, trawl the stalls at the market and do the shortened tour of El Zanjón de Granados.

A full day: ground yourself in history at El Zanjón de Granados, then hit San Telmo's antiques shops before lunch. Do a gallery or some shopping, then catch Bus 53 or a cab to La Boca, where you can go arty at Caminito and Fundación Proa. Finish back in San Telmo for drinks and dinner.

TOP ATTRACTIONS

★ **Calle Museo Camintо.**

See the highlighted listing in this chapter.

Fodor's Choice ★ **El Zanjón de Granados.** All of Buenos Aires' history is packed into this unusual house. The street it's on was once a small river—the *zanjón,* or gorge, of the property's name—where the first, unsuccessful attempt to found Buenos Aires took place in 1536. When the property's current owner—or custodian, as he prefers to be known—decided to develop what was then a run-down conventillo, he began to discover all sorts of things beneath the house: pottery and cutlery, the foundations of past constructions, and a 500-foot network of tunnels that has taken over 20 years to excavate. These were once used to channel water, but like the street itself, they were sealed after San Telmo's yellow-fever outbreaks. With the help of historians and architects, they've now been painstakingly restored, and the entire site has been transformed into a private museum, where the only exhibit is the redbrick building itself. Excellent hour-long guided tours in English and Spanish take you through low-lighted sections of the tunnels. The history lesson then continues aboveground, where you can see the surviving wall of a construction from 1740, the 19th-century mansion built around it, and traces of the conventillo it became. Expect few visitors and plenty of atmosphere on weekdays; cheaper, shorter tours on Sunday draw far more people. If you want to spend even more time here, you can rent the whole place (including an adjacent building reached via the tunnels) for functions. ✉ *Defensa 755, San Telmo* ☎ *11/4361–3002* 🌐 *www.elzanjon.com.ar* 🎟 *Guided tours 60 pesos (1 hr, weekdays only); 40 pesos (30 min, Sun. only)* ⏲ *Tours weekdays 11–3 on the hr; Sun. 1–6 every 30 min. Closed Sat.*

★ **Fundación Proa.** For more than a decade, this thoroughly modern art museum has been nudging traditional La Boca into the present. After major renovation work, its facade alone reads like a manifesto of local urban renewal: part of the original 19th-century Italianate housefront has been cut away, and huge plate-glass windows accented by unfinished steel stand alongside it. The space behind them now includes three adjacent properties. The luminous main gallery retains the building's original Corinthian-style steel columns, artfully rusted, but has sparkling white walls and polished concrete floors. With every flight of stairs you climb, views out over the harbor and cast-iron bridges get better. The first floor contains one of Buenos Aires' best art bookshops,

GETTING ORIENTED

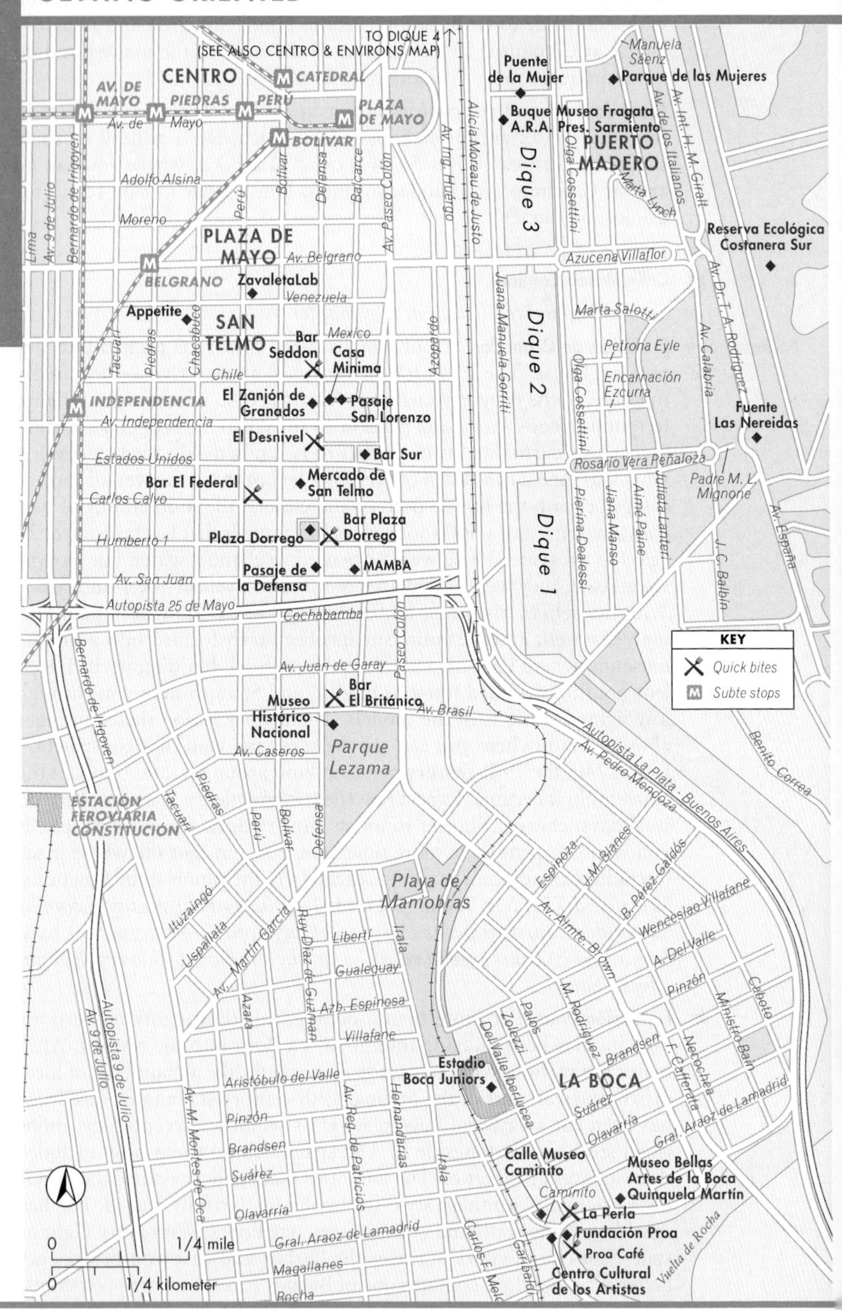

THE TERRITORY

San Telmo, south of the Centro, is bordered by Avenida Madero to the east, Avenidas Brasil and Caseros to the south, Piedras to the west, and—depending on who you ask—Chile or Belgrano to the north. The main drag is north–south Defensa, part of which is pedestrian-only. It forms one side of Plaza Dorrego, the area's tourist hub.

South of Avenida Brasil lies La Boca, whose westernmost edge is Avenida Patricios. The Riachuelo River forms a curving border; Avenida Don Pedro de Mendoza runs beside it.

GETTING AROUND

The subte takes you within about half a mile of San Telmo. The closest stations to the southern end are Independencia (Línea C or E) and San Juan (Línea C). Be prepared to walk nine blocks east along Avenidas Independencia, Estados Unidos, or San Juan to get to Defensa, the main street. To approach San Telmo from the north, get off at Bolívar (Línea E) or Catedral (Línea D) and walk eight blocks south along Bolívar. Buses 22, 24, 26, and 28 connect San Telmo to Centro. The same route by taxi costs 10–12 pesos.

There's no subte to La Boca, so taxi travel is a good bet, especially after dark: expect to pay 18–20 pesos to or from the Centro. Bus 29 runs between La Boca and the Centro; so do Buses 64 and 152, which continue to Palermo. Bus 53 connects La Boca and San Telmo.

SAFETY AND PRECAUTIONS

San Telmo's popularity with visitors has led to increased police presence in the busiest areas (especially near Defensa). Still, instances of petty crime are common. After dark, stick to busy, well-lighted streets close to Defensa.

La Boca is far sketchier, and you'd do best not to stray from the Caminito area. Avoid the neighborhood after dark, and take radio taxis if you must visit then.

TOP EXPERIENCES

Descending: into El Zanjón de Granados's restored tunnels for a different perspective.

Drinking: in the atmosphere—and a *cortado* (coffee with a splash of milk)—at Bar El Federal or La Perla cafés.

Watching: the sun set from Fundación Proa's roof café.

Wandering: Caminito (and adjacent Garibaldi and Magallanes), to tick the sightseeing boxes, or Defensa to cruise antiques stalls (on Sunday) and boutiques.

QUICK BITES

El Desnivel. Trimmings at this classic parrilla (grill) don't go beyond a mixed salad and fries, and surly waiters all but fling food at you—it's part of the experience. ✉ *Defensa 855, San Telmo* ☎ *11/4300–9081* 🌐 *www.parrillaeldesnivel.com.ar* ⏲ *Mon. 7:30 pm–1 am; Tues.–Sun. 12–4:30 pm and 7:30 pm–1 am.*

Proa Café. Gorgeous port views await at the rooftop Proa Café, which does fresh juices and smoothies, salads, quiches, and pastas. ✉ *Fundación Proa, Av. Pedro de Mendoza 1929, La Boca* ☎ *11/4104–1003* ⏲ *Tues.–Sun. 11–7.*

La Perla. Authentic La Perla is *the* spot for a *licuado* (milk shake), or a tostado mixto (a local take on the croque monsieur). ✉ *Av. Pedro de Mendoza 1899, La Boca* ☎ *11/4301–2985* ⏲ *Daily 7 am–8 pm.*

CALLE MUSEO CAMINITO

✉ *Caminito between Av. Pedro de Mendoza (La Vuelta de Rocha promenade) and Olivarría, La Boca* 🎟 *Free* 🕓 *Daily 10–6.*

TIPS

■ "Caminito" comes from a 1926 tango by Juan de Dios Filiberto, who is said to have composed it while thinking of a girl leaning from the balcony of a ramshackle house like those here. It was chosen by local artist Benito Quinquela Martín (Falso Museo de Bellas Artes de La Boca Quinquela Martín), who helped establish the street as an open-air museum.

■ Expect to be canvassed aggressively by rival restaurant owners touting overpriced, touristy menus near the start of Caminito and along every other side street. Each restaurant has its own outdoor stage—competing troupes of stamping gauchos make meals a noisy affair. The best tactic to get by them is to accept their leaflets with a serene smile and "gracias."

■ The Caminito concept spills over into nearby streets Garibaldi and Magallanes, which form a triangle with it. The strange, foot-high sidewalks along streets like Magallanes, designed to prevent flooding, show how the river's proximity has shaped the barrio.

Cobblestones, tango dancers, and haphazardly constructed, colorful conventillos have made Calle Museo Caminito the darling of Buenos Aires' postcard manufacturers since this pedestrian street was created in 1959. Artists fill the block-long street with works depicting port life and tango, which is said to have been born in La Boca. These days it's painfully commercial, and seems more a parody of porteño culture than anything else, but if you're willing to embrace the out-and-out tackiness it can make a fun outing.

HIGHLIGHTS

Conventillos. Many of La Boca's tenements are now souvenir shops. The plastic Che Guevaras and dancing couples make the shops in the Centro Cultural de los Artistas (✉ *Magallanes 861* 🕓 *Mon.–Sat. 10:30–6*) as forgettable as all the others on the street, but the uneven stairs and wrought-iron balcony hint at what a conventillo interior was like. A sculptor owns the turquoise-and-tomato-red Museo Conventillo de Marjan Grum (✉ *Garibaldi 1429* 🎟 *10 pesos* ☎ *11/4302–2472*). The opening hours of this gallery–cultural center are erratic, but even the facade is worth a look.

Local Art. Painters, photographers, and sculptors peddle their creations from stalls along Caminito. Quality varies considerably; if nothing tempts you, focus on the small mosaics set into the walls, such as Luis Perlotti's *Santos Vega*. Another local art form, the brightly colored scrollwork known as *fileteado*, adorns many shop and restaurant fronts near Caminito.

Tangueros. Competition is fierce between the pairs of sultry dancers dressed to the nines in split skirts and fishnets. True, they spend more time trying to entice you into photo ops than actually dancing, but linger long enough (and throw a big enough contribution in the fedora) and you'll see some fancy footwork.

ESTADIO BOCA JUNIORS

Walls exploding with huge, vibrant murals of insurgent workers, famous inhabitants of La Boca, and fútbol greats splashed in blue and gold let you know that the Estadio Boca Juniors is at hand. The stadium that's also known as La Bombonera (meaning "candy box," supposedly because the fans' singing reverberates as it would inside a candy tin) is the home of Argentina's most popular club. Boca Juniors' history is completely tied to the port neighborhood. The nickname, *xeneizes,* is a mangling of *genovés* (Genovese), reflecting the origins of most immigrants to the Boca area. Blue and gold decks the stadium's fiercely banked seating.

2

including a strong collection of local artists' books and photography, which you can browse at trestle tables. On the roof is an airy café serving well-priced salads and sandwiches—bag one of the outdoor sofas around sunset and your photos will rival the work below. English versions of all exhibition information are available. They also run guided tours in English, with two days' notice. ✉ *Av. Pedro de Mendoza 1929, La Boca* ☎ *11/4104–1000* 🌐 *www.proa.org* 🎟 *10 pesos; Tues. free* 🕘 *Tues.–Sun. 11–7.*

Pasaje de la Defensa. Wandering through this well-preserved house affords a glimpse of life in San Telmo's golden era. Behind its elegant but narrow stone facade, the house is built deep into the block around a series of internal courtyards. This type of long, narrow construction is typical of San Telmo, and is known as a *casa chorizo* (sausage house). Once the home of the well-to-do Ezeiza family, it became a conventillo, but is now a picturesque spot for antiques and curio shopping. The stores here are open daily 10 to 6. ✉ *Defensa 1179, San Telmo* ☎ *No phone.*

★ **Plaza Dorrego.** During the week a handful of craftspeople and a few scruffy pigeons are the only ones enjoying the shade from the stately trees in the city's second-oldest square. Sunday couldn't be more different: scores of stalls selling antiques, curios, and just plain old stuff move in to form the Feria de San Pedro Telmo (San Pedro Telmo Fair). Tango dancers take to the cobbles, as do hundreds of shoppers (mostly tourists) browsing the tango memorabilia, antique silver, brass, crystal, and Argentine curios. Note that prices are high at stalls on the square and astronomical in the shops surrounding it, and vendors are immune to bargaining. ⚠ **Pickpockets work as hard as stall owners on Sundays, so keep a firm hold on bags and purses or—wiser still—leave them at home.** More affordable offerings—mostly handicrafts and local artists' work—are on stalls along nearby streets like Defensa. ■ **TIP→ Be on the lookout for antique glass soda siphons that once adorned every bar top in Buenos Aires. Classic colors are green and turquoise.** Be sure to look up as you wander Plaza Dorrego, as the surrounding architecture provides an overview of the influences—Spanish colonial, French classical, and ornate Italian masonry—that shaped the city in the 19th and 20th centuries. ✉ *Defensa and Humberto I.*

WORTH NOTING

Museo de Arte Moderno de Buenos Aires (MAMBA) (*Museum of Modern Art of Buenos Aires*). Some 7000 contemporary artworks make up the permanent collection at this block-long museum. Once the site of a tobacco company, the MAMBA retains the original exposed-brick facade and fabulous wooden doors with wrought-iron fixtures. After being closed for more than five years of renovation work, these doors reopened in late 2010, although only a few galleries are actually up and running. Eventually, most of the wall space will contain a rotating selection of the museum's paintings, sculptures, and new media by 20th- and 21st-century artists both local and international. Since reopening, temporary exhibitions have included engravings by local great Antonio Seguí. Lectures and film screenings will form part of the program. ✉ *Av. San Juan 350, San Telmo* ☎ *11/4341–3001* 🌐 *www.museos.buenosaires.gov.ar/mam.htm* 🎫 *1 peso* ⏲ *Weekdays 12–7, weekends 11–8.*

Museo de Bellas Artes de La Boca Quinquela Martín (*Quinquela Martín Fine Arts Museum of La Boca*). Vibrant port scenes were the trademark of artist and philanthropist Benito Quinquela Martín, the man who first put La Boca on the cultural map. His work and part of his studio are showcased on the third floor of this huge building, which he donated to the state for a cultural center in 1936. Don't be surprised to have to jostle your way in through kids filing into class: downstairs is an elementary school, something that the galleries' bland institutional architecture doesn't let you forget. Quinquela Martín set out to fill the second floor with Argentine art—on the condition that works were figurative and didn't belong to any "ism." Badly lighted rooms and lack of any visible organization make it hard to enjoy the minor paintings by Berni, Sívori, Soldi, and other local masters. Outside is a huge sculpture terrace with great views of the river and old port buildings on one side, with the Boca Juniors stadium and low-rise downtown skyline on the other. ✉ *Av. Pedro de Mendoza 1843, La Boca* ☎ *11/4301–1080* 🎫 *8 pesos* ⏲ *Tues.–Fri. 10–5:30, weekends 11–5:30. Closed on days when Boca Juniors plays at home; call ahead.*

Museo Histórico Nacional. What better place for the National History Museum than overlooking the spot where the city was supposedly founded? The beautiful chestnut-and-white Italianate mansion that houses the museum once belonged to entrepreneur and horticulturalist Gregorio Lezama. It became a quarantine station when cholera and yellow-fever epidemics raged in San Telmo, before opening as this museum in 1897. At this writing, most of the museum is closed for some much-needed renovations, so be sure to check ahead of visiting.

Parque Lezama. The Museo Histórico Nacional sits in the shade of enormous magnolia, palm, cedar, and elm trees on the sloping hillside of Parque Lezama. Bronze statues of Greek heroes, stone urns, and an imposing fountain shipped from Paris hint at former glory. Patchy grass, cracked paths, and unpainted benches are a nod to more recent times. A monument in the northwestern corner celebrates conquistador Pedro de Mendoza, said to have founded Buenos Aires on this spot. Watching over the park are the onion-shaped domes of the Catedral Santísima Trinidad Iglesia Ortodoxa Rusa (Holy Trinity Russian

DID YOU KNOW?

If you're in La Boca at the right time, you might hear thousands of fans cheering from La Bombonera, the home stadium of the Boca Juniors *fútbol* team. Especially along El Caminito and other streets in this neighborhood, kids grow up dreaming of Boca Junior fame. Dreams are forever: 40% of the adult population supports Boca Juniors, the largest percentage for any Argentine team.

Orthodox Church) immortalized by Argentinian writer Ernesto Sabato in his novel *Sobre Heroes y Tumbas* (*Of Heroes and Tombs*). ✉ *Defensa at Brasil, Barracas* ✉ *Calle Defensa 1600, San Telmo* ☎ *11/4307–1182* 🎟 *Free* ⏲ *Wed.–Sun. 11–6.*

RECOLETA AND ALMAGRO

For Buenos Aires' most illustrious families, Recoleta's boundaries are the boundaries of the civilized world. The local equivalents of the Vanderbilts are baptized and married in the Basílica del Pilar, throw parties in the Alvear Palace Hotel, live in spacious 19th-century apartments nearby, and wouldn't dream of shopping anywhere but Avenidas Quintana and Alvear. Ornate mausoleums in the Cementerio de la Recoleta promise an equally stylish afterlife.

Recoleta wasn't always synonymous with elegance. Colonists, including city founder Juan de Garay, farmed here. So did the Franciscan Recoleto friars, whose 1700s settlement here inspired the district's name. Their church, the Basílica del Pilar, was almost on the riverbank then: tanneries grew up around it, and Recoleta became famous for its *pulperías* (taverns) and brothels. Everything changed with the 1871 outbreak of yellow fever in the south of the city. The elite swarmed to Recoleta, building the *palacios* and stately Parisian-style apartment buildings that are now the neighborhood's trademark.

An unofficial subdistrict, Barrio Norte, is one step south of Recoleta proper and one small step down the social ladder. Shopping is the draw: local chains, sportswear flagships, and mini-malls of vintage clothing and clubwear line Avenida Santa Fe between 9 de Julio and Puerreydón.

Almagro lies southwest of Recoleta but is a world apart. Traditionally a gritty, working-class neighborhood, it spawned many tango greats, including the legendary Carlos Gardel. The Abasto subdistrict has long been the heart of the barrio: it centers on the massive art deco building (at Corrientes and Agüero) that was once the city's central market and is now a major mall.

TAKING IT IN

You can blitz Recoleta's main sights in half a day, though you could easily spend a full morning or afternoon in the cemetery or cultural centers alone. Come midweek for quiet exploring, or on the weekend to do the cemetery and Plaza Francia crafts market in one fell swoop.

In Almagro a couple of hours will suffice to see all things Carlos Gardel—tango's greatest hero—and get a feel for the district.

HOW TO SPEND . . .

An Hour or Two: after a quick walk around the cemetery, choose from great painting at the Museo Nacional de Bellas Artes, great furniture at the Museo Nacional de Arte Decorativo, or great clothes along Avenidas Alvear and Santa Fe.

A Half-Day: start with some coffee and people-watching at extortionate but strategic La Biela, then find Evita's grave at the cemetery and look in on the Basílica de Nuestra Señora del Pilar. Take your time over the

Museo Nacional de Bellas Artes, then have lunch or a drink in Barrio Norte. If you've got a full day, add some shopping afterward.

TOP ATTRACTIONS

Basílica de Nuestra Señora del Pilar. This basilica beside the famous Cementerio de la Recoleta on Junín is where Buenos Aires' elite families hold weddings and other ceremonies. It was built by the Recoleto friars in 1732, and is considered a national treasure for its six German Baroque–style altars. The central one is overlaid with Peruvian engraved silver; another contains relics and was sent by Spain's King Carlos III.

Museo de los Claustros del Pilar. In the cloisters, which date from 1716, this small museum contains religious artifacts, pictures, and photographs documenting Recoleta's evolution. Upstairs windows yield excellent views of the cemetery. *5 pesos ⊙ Mon.–Sat. 10:30–6:15, Sun. 2:30–6:15 ✉ Junín 1904, Recoleta ☎ 11/4806–2209 ⊕ www.basilicadelpilar.org.ar Free ⊙ Daily 8 am–10 pm.*

Fodor's Choice ★ **Cementerio de la Recoleta.**
See the highlighted listing in this chapter.

Centro Cultural La Recoleta. Art exhibitions, concerts, fringe theater performances, and workshops are some of the offerings at this major cultural center. The rambling building it's housed in was converted from the cloister patios of the Franciscan monks.

Museo Participativo de Ciencias. Kids love the Museo Participativo de Ciencias, a mini science museum inside the Centro Cultural La Recoleta complex whose motto, *Prohibido No Tocar* (Not Touching Is Forbidden), says it all. ☎ *11/4807–3260 ⊕ www.mpc.org.ar 20 pesos, free for children under 4 ⊙ Jan. and Feb., daily 3:30–7:30; Mar.–Dec., weekdays 10–5, weekends 3:30–7:30; winter school holidays (approx. mid-July–early Aug.), weekdays 12:30–7:30, weekends 3:30–7:30.*

La Feria de Plaza Francia. On weekends artisans' stalls line the small park outside the cultural center and cemetery, forming the open-air market known as La Feria de Plaza Francia. It's usually teeming with shoppers, who come for the quality crafts. Other souvenirs in the area include quirky housewares and designer clothing at the Buenos Aires Design Center, which you reach by following the walkway outside the cultural center into the adjacent Paseo del Pilar shopping mall. *⊕ www.feriaplazafrancia.com ✉ Junín 1930, Recoleta ☎ 11/4803–1040 ⊕ www.centroculturalrecoleta.org ⊙ Mon.–Fri. 2–9, weekends 10–9.*

★ **Floralis Genérica.** The gleaming steel and aluminum petals of this giant flower look very space age, perhaps because they were commissioned from the Lockheed airplane factory by architect Eduardo Catalano, who designed and paid for the monument. The 66-foot-high structure is supposed to open at dawn and close at dusk, when the setting sun turns its mirrored surfaces a glowing pink (sometimes the mechanism is out of order, however). The flower stands in the Plaza Naciones Unidas (behind El Museo Nacional de Bellas Artes over Avenida Figueroa Alcorta), which was remodeled to accommodate it. *✉ Plaza Naciones Unidas at Av. Figueroa Alcorta and J.A. Biblioni, Recoleta ⊙ Dawn–dusk.*

GETTING ORIENTED

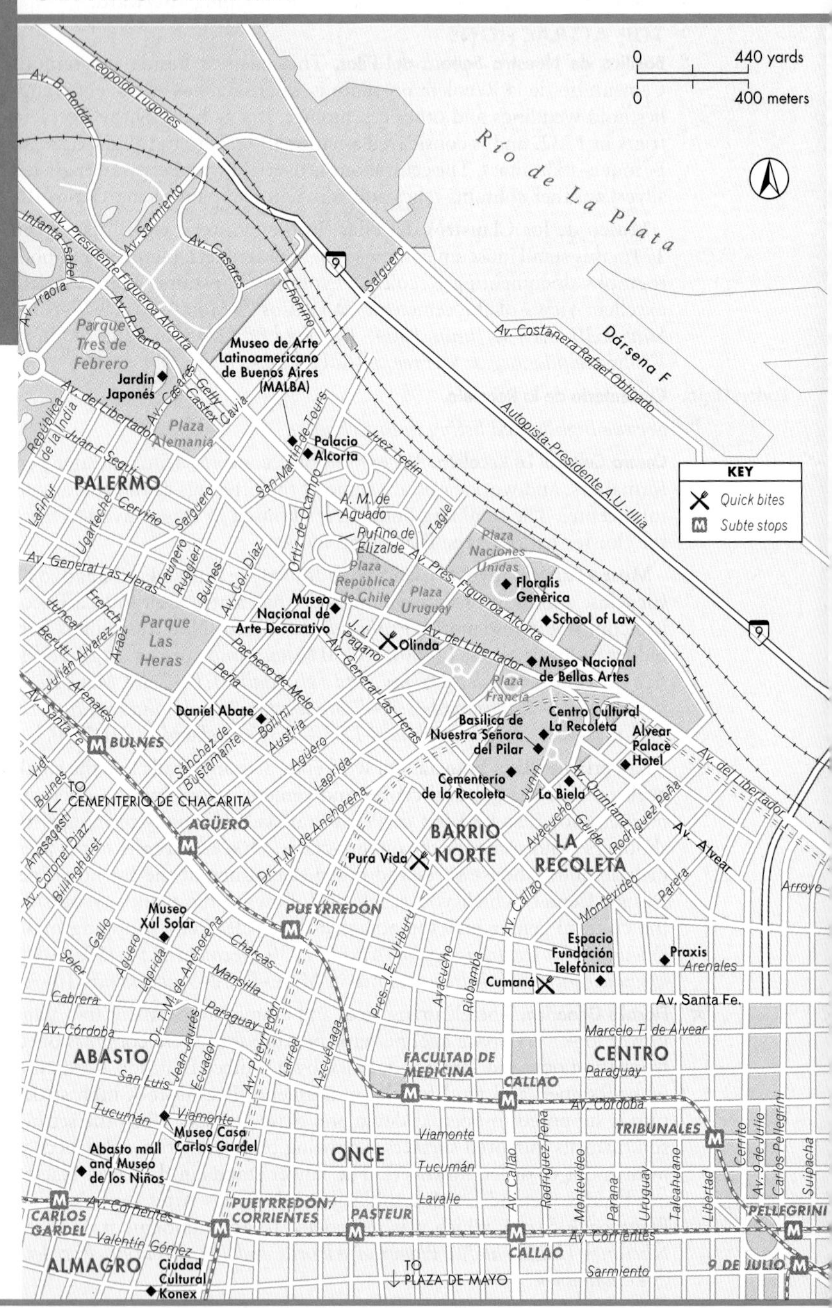

THE TERRITORY

The River Plate borders Recoleta to the north. Uruguay and Montevideo join to form the eastern border; the jagged western edge is made up of Mario Bravo, Coronel Díaz, and Tagle. The area between Juncal and Córdoba—Recoleta's southern boundary—is known as Barrio Norte, whose main thoroughfare is Santa Fe. In Recoleta proper, Avenidas Alvear and Quintana are the key streets.

Almagro is officially bordered by Avenidas Córdoba and Estado de Israel to the north, Río de Janeiro to the west, Independencia to the south, and Sánchez de Bustamente and Gallo to the east. The Abasto subdistrict, which centers on Gallo and Corrientes, stretches a few blocks farther east into neighboring Balvanera.

GETTING AROUND

True to its elite roots, Recoleta has no subway, so taxis are the best option. Expect to pay around 15 pesos from downtown or Palermo. Bus 17 runs from San Telmo and the Centro; the 92 connects Retiro and Recoleta, then continues to central Palermo and Almagro. Traffic can be slow within Recoleta and Barrio Norte—walking is fast and pleasant.

Heavy traffic means Almagro is best reached by subte. Línea B runs along Avenida Corrientes through Almagro; Carlos Gardel station leads right into the Abasto mall. Bus 24 connects Almagro with Centro and San Telmo; the 168 goes west to Palermo Viejo.

SAFETY AND PRECAUTIONS

Recoleta and Barrio Norte are relatively safe in the daytime, but stick to well-lighted streets at night. Bag snatching is opportunist rather than systematic here: keep a firm grip on your purse in the crowded weekend market and in busy restaurants. Although Almagro is on the upswing, many streets near the Abasto mall are still run-down. Wander with caution.

TOP EXPERIENCES

Seeking: unusual statues in Cementerio de la Recoleta.

Window-shopping: on Avenida Quintana for Argentine designs but buying more affordable ones on Avenida Santa Fe or in the Abasto mall.

Comparing: 19th-century Argentine and European art on the first floor of the Museo Nacional de Bellas Artes.

Wandering: Avenida Alvear for the gorgeous late-19th- and early-20th-century mansions.

QUICK BITES

Cumaná. The hearty stews, steaks, and empanadas at chaotic Cumaná are a far cry from Recoleta's European pretensions. Skip dessert (nearby ice-creameries are better). ✉ *Rodríguez Peña 1149, Barrio Norte* ☎ *11/4813–9207* ⏲ *Daily noon–1 am.*

Delicious. It's a hard name to live up to, but there's no doubt this casual café pulls it off. Delicious does super fresh sandwiches, salads, and smoothies, which you can eat in or pack into your picnic basket. An espresso and a portion of their Ultrachocolate cake contains the perfect dose of caffeine and sugar to get you back in the sightseeing saddle. ✉ *Laprida 2015, Recoleta* ☎ *11/4803–1151* 🌐 *www.deliciouscafe.com.ar.*

CEMENTERIO DE LA RECOLETA

☒ *Junín 1760, Recoleta*
☎ *11/4803–1594* 🎟 *Free*
⏲ *Daily 7–6.*

TIPS

■ The city runs free guided visits to the cemetery in English on Tuesday and Thursday at 11; visits in Spanish operate Tuesday through Sunday at 9:30, 11, 2, and 4. Groups gather at the entrance.

■ If you prefer an independent tour, the administrative offices at the entrance can usually provide a free map, and caretakers around the grounds can help you find the more intriguing tombs. These are also labeled on a large map at the entrance.

■ It's easy to get lost in the cemetery: start exploring well before closing time.

■ Look out for such intriguing statues as the life-size likeness of boxer Luis Angel Firpo, who lost the world heavyweight title to Jack Dempsey in 1923. It stands on guard outside his tomb at the back of the cemetery, wearing a robe and boxing boots.

■ The cemetery had its blessing withdrawn by the Catholic Church in 1863, when president Bartolomé Mitre ordered that a suicide be buried there.

★ Fodor's Choice The ominous gates, Doric-columned portico, and labyrinthine paths of the city's oldest cemetery (1822) may leave you with a sense of foreboding. It's the final resting place for the nation's most illustrious figures, and covers 13.5 acres that are rumored to be the most expensive real estate in town. The cemetery has more than 6,400 elaborate vaulted tombs and majestic mausoleums, 70 of which have been declared historic monuments. The mausoleums resemble chapels, Greek temples, pyramids, and miniature mansions.

HIGHLIGHTS

Evita. The embalmed remains of Eva Duarte de Perón, who made it (almost intact) here after 17 years of posthumous wandering, are in the Duarte family vault. Around July 26, the anniversary of her death, flowers pile up here.

Late Greats. If the tomb of brutal *caudillo* (dictator) Facundo Quiroga looks small, it's because he's buried standing—a sign of valor—at his request. Prominent landowner Dorrego Ortíz Basualdo resides in Recoleta's most monumental sepulcher, complete with chandelier. The names of many key players in Argentina's history are chiseled over other sumptuous mausoleums: Alvear, Quintana, Sáenz Peña, Lavalle, Sarmiento.

Spooky Stories. Rufina Cambaceres is known as the girl who died twice. She was thought dead after suffering a cataleptic attack, and was entombed on her 19th birthday in 1902. Rufina awoke inside her casket and clawed the top open but died of a heart attack before she could be rescued. When Alfredo Gath heard of Rufina's story he was appalled and commissioned a special mechanical coffin with an opening device and alarm bell. Gath successfully tested the coffin in situ 12 times, but on the 13th the mechanism failed and he died inside.

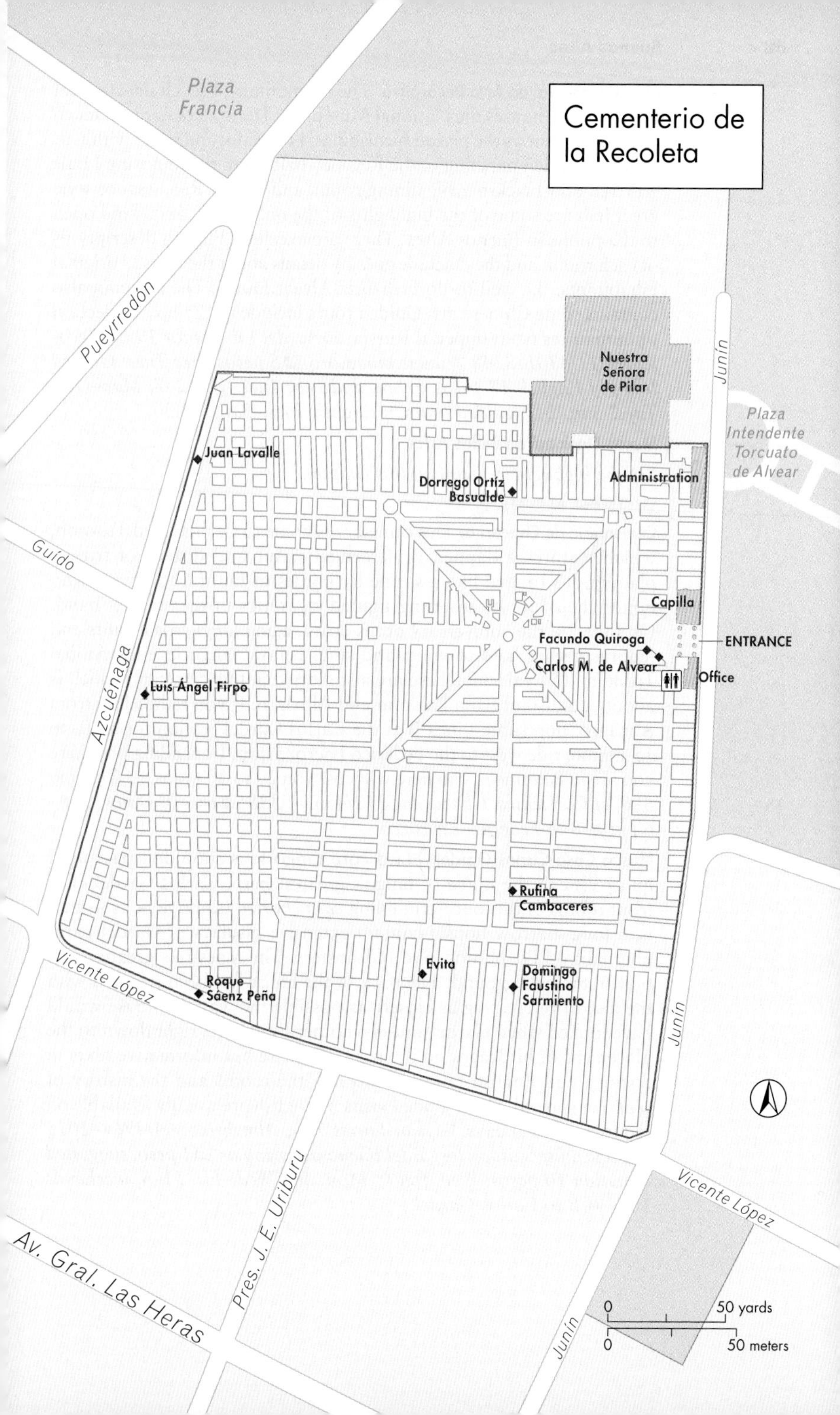

Cementerio de la Recoleta
Plaza Francia
Pueyrredón
Guido
Azcuénaga
Vicente López
Av. Gral. Las Heras
Pres. J. E. Uriburu
Junín
Plaza Intendente Torcuato de Alvear
Nuestra Señora de Pilar
Administration
Capilla
ENTRANCE
Office
Juan Lavalle
Dorrego Ortíz Basualde
Facundo Quiroga
Carlos M. de Alvear
Luis Ángel Firpo
Rufina Cambaceres
Evita
Domingo Faustino Sarmiento
Roque Sáenz Peña
0
50 yards
0
50 meters

Museo Nacional de Arte Decorativo. The harmonious, French neoclassical mansion that houses the National Museum of Decorative Art is as much a reason to visit as the period furnishings, porcelain, and silver within it. Ornate wooden paneling in the Regency ballroom, the imposing Louis XIV red-and-black-marble dining room, and a lofty Renaissance-style great hall are some of the highlights of the only house of its kind open to the public in Buenos Aires. There are excellent English descriptions of each room, and they include gossipy details about the house's original inhabitants, the well-to-do Errázuriz-Alvear family. The museum also contains some Chinese art. Guided tours include the Zubov Collection of miniatures from Imperial Russia. ✉ *Av. del Libertador 1902, Recoleta* ☎ *11/4801–8248* 🌐 *www.mnad.org* 🎫 *5 pesos; free Tues. Guided tours in English 15 pesos* ⏲ *Jan. and Feb. Tues.–Sat. 2–7; Mar.–Dec. Tues.–Sun. 2–7; guided tours in English Tues.–Sat. at 2:30.*

Fodor's Choice ★ **Museo Nacional de Bellas Artes.**

See the highlighted listing in this chapter.

WORTH NOTING

Cementerio de Chacarita. This cemetery is home to Carlos Gardel's tomb, which features a dapper, Brylcreemed statue and dozens of tribute plaques. It's treated like a shrine by hordes of faithful followers who honor their idol by inserting lighted cigarettes in the statue's hand. On June 24, the anniversary of his death, aging *tangueros* in suits and fedoras gather here to weep and sing. Fellow tango legends Aníbal Troilo and Osvaldo Pugliese are also buried in this cemetery, which is about equidistant from Palermo and Almagro. If you're heading from Almagro, hop subte Línea B at the Carlos Gardel Station for a 10- to 15-minute ride west to the Federico Lacroze stop. Depending on where you are in Palermo, a cab here will cost you 20 to 30 pesos. ✉ *Guzmán 680, at Corrientes, Chacarita* ☎ *11/4553–9338* 🎫 *Free* ⏲ *Daily 7 am–6 pm* Ⓜ *B to Federico Lacroze.*

Museo Casa Carlos Gardel. Hard-core tango fans shouldn't pass up a quick visit to the home of tango's greatest hero, Carlos Gardel. The front rooms of this once-crumbling *casa chorizo* (sausage house—that is, a long, narrow house) contain extensive displays of Gardel paraphernalia—LPs, photos, and old posters. The maestro's greatest hits play in the background. The back of the house has been restored with the aim of re-creating as closely as possible the way the house would have looked when Gardel and his mother lived here, right down to the placement of birdcages on the patio. Concise but informative texts in Spanish and English talk you through the rooms and the history of tango in general. Short guided visits in English are usually available on request on weekdays. ✉ *Jean Jaurés 735, Almagro* ☎ *11/4964–2015* 🌐 *www.museocasacarlosgardel.buenosaires.gob.ar* 🎫 *1 peso, suggested donation 10 pesos; Wed. free* ⏲ *Mon. and Wed.–Fri. 11–6, weekends 10–7* Ⓜ *B to Carlos Gardel.*

MUSEO NACIONAL DE BELLAS ARTES

Av. del Libertador 1473, Recoleta 11/5288–9900 www.mnba.org.ar Free Tues.–Fri. 12:30–8:30, weekends 9:30–8:30.

TIPS

- Head straight for the Argentine galleries while you're feeling fresh, and save the European collection for later.
- Information about most works is in Spanish only, as are the excellent themed guided tours. For English information, get one of the MP3 audio guides (35 pesos), or a map (10 pesos) or guide (30 pesos) to the collection.
- The building was once the city's waterworks. Famed local architect Alejandro Bustillo oversaw its conversion into a museum in the early 1930s.
- Cándido López painted the panoramic battle scenes in gallery 23 with his left hand after losing his right arm in the War of the Triple Alliance of the 1870s. His work spearheaded contemporary primitive painting. Local master Eduardo Sívori's tranquil landscapes portray less turbulent times.
- The large modern pavilion behind the museum hosts excellent temporary exhibitions, often showcasing top local artists little known outside Argentina.

Fodor's Choice The world's largest collection of Argentine art is displayed in this huge golden-color stone building. Most of the 24 richly colored ground-floor galleries contain pre-20th century European art. The beautifully curated Argentine circuit starts in Room 22 with works from shortly after the country's independence. The plan is for the upper floor to encompass the museum's 20th-century collection.

HIGHLIGHTS

The Rest of the River Plate. Uruguayan artists like Rafael Barradas and Joaquín Torres García are the focus of the hushed Colección María Luisa Bemberg.

Picturesque Portraits. Gauchos cut evocative figures in Cesáreo Bernaldo de Quirós's oil paintings. The highly colorful depictions of port laborers in *Elevadores a Pleno Sol* are typical of the work of Benito Quinquela Martín, La Boca's unofficial painter laureate.

At the Cutting Edge. The huge final gallery shows the involvement of Argentinian artists in European avant-garde movements before adopting homegrown ideas. Emilio Pettorutti's *El Improvisador* (1937) combines cubist techniques with a Renaissance sense of space, while Lino Enea Spilimbergo's *Terracita* (1932) is an enigmatic urban landscape.

Movers and Shakers. Contemporary Argentine art exhibits include geometric sculptures and the so-called *informalismo* (informalism) of the '60s. Its innovative use of collage is best exemplified in works by Antonio Berni. Psychedelic paintings, op art, and kinetic works from '60s gurus like Jorge de la Vega and Antonio Seguí follow.

PALERMO

Trendy shops, bold restaurants, elegant embassies, acres of parks—Palermo really does have it all. Whether your idea of sightseeing is ticking off museums, flicking through clothing racks, licking your fingers after yet another long lunch, or kicking up a storm on the dance floor, Palermo can oblige. The city's largest barrio is subdivided into various unofficial districts, each with its own distinct flavor.

Elegant boutiques, minimalist lofts, endless bars, and the most fun and daring restaurants in town have made Palermo Viejo (also known as Palermo Soho) the epicenter of Buenos Aires' design revolution. Many are contained in beautifully recycled town houses built in the late 19th century, when Palermo became a popular residential district. Most shops and eateries—not to mention desirable properties—in Palermo Viejo fill the cobbled streets around Plazoleta Cortázar.

In neighboring Palermo Hollywood, quiet barrio houses and the flea market at Dorrego and Niceto Vega sit alongside sharp tapas bars filled with media types from the TV production centers that give the area its nickname.

Some say Palermo takes its name from the surname of a 16th-century Italian immigrant who bought land in the area, others from the abbey honoring Saint Benedict of Palermo. Either way, the area was largely rural until the mid-19th century, when national governor Juan Manuel de Rosas built an estate here. Next, these grounds were turned into the huge patchwork of parks north of Avenida del Libertador. Their official name, Parque Tres de Febrero, is a reference to February 3, 1852, the day Rosas was defeated in battle. The park, which is more commonly known as Los Bosques de Palermo (the Palermo Woods), provides a peaceful escape from the rush of downtown. The zoo and botanical gardens are at its southern end.

Palermo has two mainstream shopping areas. The streets around the intersection of Avenidas Santa Fe and Coronel Díaz are home to the mid-range Alto Palermo mall and many cheap clothing stores. There are more exclusive brands at El Solar de la Abadía mall and the nearby streets of Las Cañitas, Palermo's northwestern outpost. Its thriving bar-and-restaurant scene is the favorite of local models, TV starlets, and others dying to be seen. The quiet residential district around Plaza Güemes brings some relief: it's nicknamed Villa Freud, for the high concentration of psychoanalysts who live and work here.

Plastic surgery and imported everything are the norm in Palermo Chico (between Avenidas Santa Fe and Libertador), whose Parisian-style mansions are shared out between embassies and rich local stars. Higher-brow culture is provided by the gleaming MALBA (Museo de Arte Latinoamericano de Buenos Aires, or the Museum of Latin American Art of Buenos Aires), whose clean stone lines stand out on Avenida Figueroa Alcorta.

2

TAKING IT IN

Palermo is so big that it's best to tackle it in sections. An even-paced ramble through Parque Tres de Febrero should take no more than two hours, though you could easily spend an entire afternoon at the zoo, Japanese Garden, and Botanical Garden. In architectural and geographic terms, Palermo Chico and the MALBA tie in nicely with a visit to Recoleta: allow at least a couple of hours for such an experience.

HOW TO SPEND . . .

An Hour or Two: Palermo is too big to hedge your bets—you're best to pick one major museum (Museo Evita or MALBA) or park.

A Full Day: start with a morning ramble through Parque Tres de Febrero then go arty at the MALBA and Museo Xul Solar, historical at Museo Evita, or back-to-nature at the zoo, Jardín Japonés (Japanese Garden), and Botanical Garden. Shoppers have been known to spend their whole trip in Palermo Viejo, but a couple of hours and a meal are enough to get a feel for it.

TOP ATTRACTIONS

Jardín Japonés (*Japanese Garden*). Like the bonsais in the nursery within it, this park is small but perfectly formed. A slow wander along its arched wooden bridges and walkways is guaranteed to calm frazzled sightseeing nerves during the week; crowds on the weekend make for a less-than-zen experience. A variety of shrubs and flowers frame the ponds, which brim with friendly koi carp that let you pet them should you feel inclined (kids often do). The traditional teahouse, where you can enjoy sushi, adzuki-bean sweets, and tea, overlooks a zen garden. ✉ *Av. Casares at Av. Figueroa Alcorta, Palermo* ☎ *11/4804–4922* 🌐 *www.jardinjapones.org.ar* 🎫 *8 pesos* 🕙 *Daily 10–6.*

★ **Museo Evita.**

See the highlighted listing in this chapter.

Fodor's Choice ★ **Museo de Arte de Latinoamericano de Buenos Aires** *(MALBA, Museum of Latin American Art of Buenos Aires).*

See the highlighted listing in this chapter.

★ **Parque Tres de Febrero.** Known locally as Los Bosques de Palermo (Palermo Woods), this 200-acre green space is really a crazy quilt of smaller parks. Lush grass and shady trees make it an urban oasis, although the busy roads and horn-honking drivers that crisscross the park never let you forget what city you're in. South of Avenida Figueroa Alcorta you can take part in organized tai chi and exercise classes or impromptu soccer matches. You can also jog, bike, or in-line skate here, or take a pedal boat out on the tiny lake. The park gets crowded on sunny weekends, as this is where families come for strolls or picnics. If you'd like to picnic, take advantage of the street vendors who sell refreshments and *choripan* (chorizo sausage in a bread roll) within the park. There are also several posh cafés lining the Paseo de la Infanta (running from Libertador toward Sarmiento in the park).

Museo de Artes Plásticas Eduardo Sívori (*Eduardo Sívori Art Museum*). If you're looking for a sedate activity, try the Museo de Artes Plásticas Eduardo Sívori, which resides in the Parque Tres de

GETTING ORIENTED

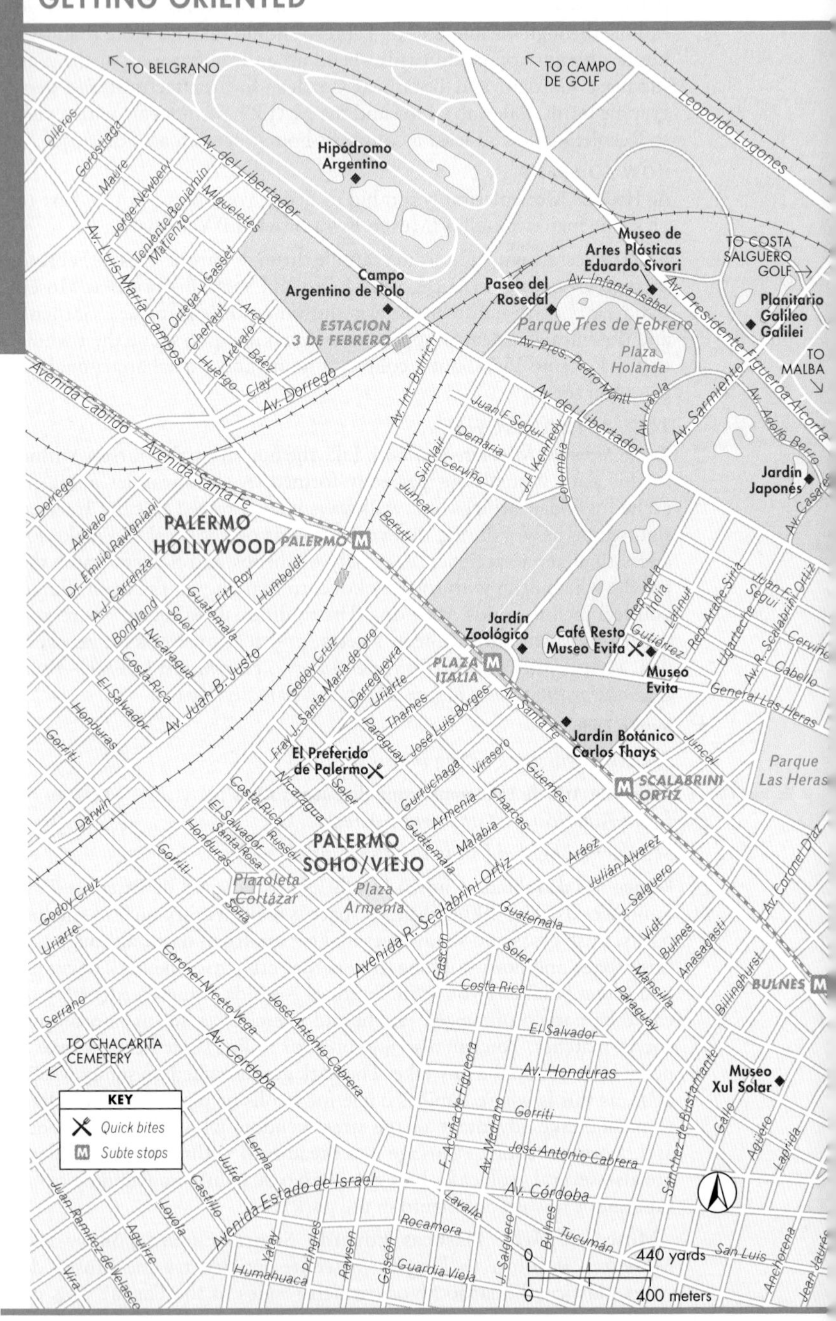

THE TERRITORY

The city's biggest barrio stretches from Avenida Costanera R. Obligado, along the river, to Avenida Córdoba in the south. Its other boundaries are jagged, but include Avenida Coronel Díaz to the east and La Pampa and Dorrego to the west. Avenida Santa Fe cuts the neighborhood roughly in half. Palermo's green spaces and Palermo Chico lie north of it. To the south are Palermo Viejo and Palermo Hollywood, east and west of Avenida Juan B. Justo, respectively.

GETTING AROUND

Subte Línea (Line) D runs along Avenida Santa Fe, but doesn't always bring you to the doorstep of Palermo's attractions, so you may need to combine it with a taxi or some walking. Indeed, weekday traffic makes this combination a better idea than coming all the way from Centro by cab (which costs 20–30 pesos). Get off the subte at Bulnes or Scalabrini Ortíz for Palermo Chico; Plaza Italia for Palermo Viejo and the parks; and Ministro Carranza for Palermo Hollywood.

A more scenic route to Palermo Viejo and Hollywood from Centro is Bus 39 (Route 3, usually with a windshield sign "Palermo Viejo"). It runs along Honduras on the way to Palermo and Gorriti on the way back, and it takes 30–60 minutes. Once you're in Palermo, walking is the best way to get around: much of the district is leafy, and there's little traffic on its smaller streets.

SAFETY AND PRECAUTIONS

Pickpocketing is the biggest threat, especially on crowded streets on weekends. Palermo Viejo's cobbled streets aren't well lighted at night, so avoid walking along any that look lonely. Although locals usually hail cabs on the street, it's safer to ask a restaurant or bar to call one for you. The usual caveats about parks apply to the Palermo woods: don't linger after dark, and avoid remote areas at any time if you're female and alone.

TOP EXPERIENCES

Appreciating: the early works in the permanent collection of the MALBA, featuring painters like Diego Rivera, Xul Solar, and Joaquín Torres García.

Exercising: your arms in Palermo Viejo carrying bags on a boutique crawl.

Visiting: with Evita; understand the phenomenon that she was by taking in the Museo Evita.

Wandering: on the winding paths of Parque Tres de Febrero, to smell the roses, or along Honduras—east of Juan B. Justo for boutiques, west of it for bars and restaurants.

QUICK BITES

El Preferido de Palermo. Trends come and go, but nothing changes at the tall Formica tables of this general-store-meets-snackbar. A plate of cold cuts and pickles or basic (but delicious) sandwiches are the way to go. ✉ *Jorge L. Borges 2108, Palermo Viejo* ☎ *11/4774–6585* ⌚ *Mon.–Sat. 12–4 and 8–12.*

Cafe Resto Museo Evita. The checkered floors and glossy black tables are as stylish as the great lady herself. The Italian-Argentine dishes on the set-price lunch menu change daily. Sticky and flaky, the *medialunas* here are some of the best in town. ✉ *J. M. Gutiérrez 3926, Palermo Botánico* ☎ *11/4800–1599* ⌚ *Mon.–Sat. 9 am–12:30 am, Sun. 9 am–7 pm.*

MUSEO EVITA

Lafinur 2988, 1 block north of Av. Las Heras, Palermo 11/4807–0306 www.museoevita.org 15 pesos; guided tours 35 pesos Tues.–Sun. 11–7 M D to Plaza Italia.

TIPS

- Laminated cards with just-understandable English translations of the exhibits are available in each room and at the ticket booth.
- Plan time for a post-museum coffee (or lunch) at the museum café's outside tables, shaded by classy black umbrellas. There's also a small gift shop.
- The gray-stone mansion dates from 1909. It was purchased in 1948 by the Fundación de Ayuda Social Eva Perón (Eva Perón Social Aid Foundation) and converted into a home for single mothers, to the horror of the rich, conservative families living nearby.
- The Evita myth can be baffling to the uninitiated. The museum's excellent guided visits shed light on the phenomenon and are available in English, but must be arranged by phone in advance.

Eva Duarte de Perón, known universally as Evita, was the wife of populist president Juan Domingo Perón. She was both revered by her working-class followers and despised by the Anglophile oligarchy of the time. The Museo Evita shies from pop culture clichés and conveys facts about Evita's life and works, particularly the social aid programs she instituted and her role in getting women the vote. Knowledgeable staffers answer questions enthusiastically.

HIGHLIGHTS

Photographic Evidence. The route through the collection begins in a darkened room screening footage of hundreds of thousands of mourners lining up to see Evita's body. Family photos and magazine covers document Evita's humble origins and time as a B-list actress. Upstairs there's English-subtitled footage of Evita's incendiary speeches to screaming crowds: her impassioned delivery beats Madonna's hands down.

Death Becomes Her. The final rooms follow Evita's withdrawal from political life and her death from cancer at age 33. A video chronicles the fate of Evita's cadaver: embalmed by Perón, stolen by political opponents, and moved and hidden for 17 years before being returned to Argentina, where it now rests in the Recoleta Cemetery.

Fabulous Clothes. Evita's reputation as fashion plate is reflected in the many designer outfits on display, including her trademark working suits and some gorgeous ball gowns.

Febrero. The focus of this collection is 19th- and 20th-century Argentine art, including paintings by local masters like Emilio Petorutti, Lino Eneo Spilimbergo, Antonio Berni, and the museum's namesake Sívori. The shaded sculpture garden is the perfect combination of art and park. ✉ *Av. Infanta Isabel 555, Palermo* ☎ *11/4774–9452* 🌐 *www.museosivori.org* 🎫 *1 peso, Wed. and Sat. free* ⏲ *Tues.–Fri. noon–8, weekends 10–8.*

Paseo del Rosedal (*Rose Garden*). Close to the Museo de Artes Plásticas Eduardo Sívori (within the Parque Tres Febrero) is the Paseo del Rosedal. About 12,000 rosebushes (more than 1,000 different species) bloom seasonally in this rose garden. A stroll along the paths takes you through the Jardín de los Poetas (Poets' Garden), dotted with statues of literary figures, and to the enchanting Patio Andaluz (Andalusian Patio), whose majolica tiles and Spanish mosaics sit under a vine-covered pergola. ✉ *Avs. Infanta Isabel and Iraola* 🎫 *Free* ⏲ *Apr.–Oct., daily 9–6; Nov.–Mar., daily 8–8.*

Planetario Galileo Galilei (*Galileo Galilei Planetarium*). One of the city's most iconic buildings, the Planetario Galileo Galilei is a great orb positioned on a massive concrete tripod. Built in the early 1960s, it looks like something out of *Close Encounters of the Third Kind,* and it seems as though small green men could descend from its central staircase at any moment. At this writing, the inside was closed for renovation, but the authentic 3,373-pound asteroid remained in place at the entrance. The nearby pond with swans, geese, and ducks is a favorite with kids. ✉ *Avs. Sarmiento and Figueroa Alcorta* ☎ *11/4771–9393* 🌐 *www.planetario.gob.ar* 🎫 *Free* ✉ *Bounded by Avs. del Libertador, Sarmiento, Leopoldo Lugones, and Dorrego* Ⓜ *D to Plaza Italia.*

WORTH NOTING

Jardín Botánico Carlos Thays. With 18 acres of gardens and 5,500 varieties of exotic and local flora, the Carlos Thays Botanical Garden is an unexpected green haven wedged between three busy Palermo streets. Different sections re-create the environments of Asia, Africa, Oceania, Europe, and the Americas. Among the treasures is the Chinese "tree of gold," purportedly the only one of its kind. An organic vegetable garden aims to teach children healthy habits. Winding paths lead to hidden statues, a brook, and past the resident cats and dragonflies. The central area contains a beautiful greenhouse, brought from France in 1900, and the exposed-brick botanical school and library. ✉ *Av. Santa Fe 3951, Palermo* ☎ *11/4832–1552* 🌐 *www.jardinbotanico.buenosaires.gob.ar* 🎫 *Free* ⏲ *Sept.–Mar., weekdays 8–7, weekends 9:30–7; Apr.–Aug., weekdays 8–6, weekends 9:30–6.* Ⓜ *D to Plaza Italia.*

Jardín Zoológico. The grandiose stone pens and mews—many dating from the zoo's opening in 1874—are as much an attraction at the 45-acre city zoo as their inhabitants. Jorge Luis Borges said the recurring presence of tigers in his work was inspired by time spent here. Today, the rare albino tiger may inspire you to pen a few lines of your own. South American animals you may not have seen before include the *aguará guazú* (a sort of fox), the *coatí* (a local raccoon), anteaters, and the black howler monkey. Some smaller animals roam freely, and there

MALBA

Av. Presidente Figueroa Alcorta 3415, Palermo 11/4808-6500 www.malba.org.ar 22 pesos; Wed. 10 pesos Thurs.-Mon. noon-8, Wed. noon-9.

TIPS

- MALBA also has a great art cinema showing restored copies of classics, never-released features, and silent films with live music, as well as local films of note.
- Kids love hands-on kinetic works like Julio Le Parc's Seven Unexpected Movements, a sculpture with gleaming parts that move at the press of a button.
- Leave time to browse the art books and funky design objects of the museum's excellent gift shop.
- Young, enthusiastic guides give great tours of the permanent collection in Spanish on Wednesdays and Sundays at 4 pm.
- Give your feet—and eyes—a rest on the first-floor sculpture deck, with views over Belgrano and Barrio Norte.
- Córdoba-based studio AFT Arquitectos' triangular construction in creamy stone and steel is one of the museum's draws. The main galleries run along a four-story atrium, flooded in natural light from a wall of windows.

The fabulous Museum of Latin American Art of Buenos Aires (MALBA) is one of the cornerstones of the city's cultural life. Its centerpiece is businessman and founder Eduardo Constantini's collection of more than 220 works of 19th- and 20th-century Latin-American art in the main first-floor gallery.

HIGHLIGHTS

Europe vs. Latin America. Early works in the permanent collection reflect the European avant-garde experiences of painters like Diego Rivera, Xul Solar, Roberto Matta, and Joaquín Torres García. Soon the Latin American experience gave rise to works like *Abaporu* (1928) by Tarsila do Amaral, a Brazilian involved in the "cannibalistic" Movimento Antropofágico (rather than eating white Europeans, proponents of the movement proposed devouring European culture and digesting it into something new). Geometric paintings and sculptures from the 1940s represent movements such as Arte Concreto, Constructivism, and Arte Madí.

Argentine Art. Argentina's undisputed modern master is Antonio Berni, represented by a poptastic collage called *The Great Temptation* (1962) and the bizarre sculpture *Voracity or Ramona's Nightmare* (1964), both featuring the eccentric prostitute Ramona, a character Berni created in this series of works criticizing consumer society. Works by local greats Liliana Porter, Marta Minujín, Guillermo Kuitca, and Alejandro Kuropatwa form the end of the permanent collection.

Temporary Exhibitions. World-class temporary exhibitions are held on the second floor two or three times a year, and two small basement galleries show art by cutting-edge locals.

are play areas for children, a petting farm, and a seal show. *Mateos* (traditional, decorated horse-drawn carriages) stand poised at the entrance to whisk you around the nearby parks. ✉ *Avs. General Las Heras and Sarmiento, Palermo* ☎ *11/4011–9900* 🌐 *www.zoobuenosaires.com.ar* 🎫 *32 pesos* ⏲ *Tues.–Sun. 10–5* Ⓜ *D to Plaza Italia.*

Museo Xul Solar. Avant-garde artist, linguist, esoteric philosopher, and close friend of Borges, Xul Solar is best known for his luminous, semi-abstract watercolors. They glow against the low-lighted concrete walls of this hushed museum. Solar's wacky but endearing beliefs in universalism led him to design a pan-language, pan-chess (a set is displayed here), and the Pan Klub, where these ideas were debated. One of its former members, architect Pablo Beitia, masterminded the transformation of the town house where Solar lived and worked. Open stairways crisscross the space, an homage to one of Solar's favorite motifs. ✉ *Laprida 1212, Palermo* ☎ *11/4824–3302* 🌐 *www.xulsolar.org.ar* 🎫 *10 pesos, free Thurs.* ⏲ *Tues.–Fri. noon–7, Sat. noon–6.*

WHERE TO EAT

Visitors may flock to Buenos Aires for the steak and Malbec wine, but the food scene goes far beyond those two attractions. Awakening from decades of political repression, the city over the last dozen or so years has burst onto the international food scene with gusto.

There's a demand for more and more creative food. Here three things have come together to create a truly modern cuisine: diverse cultural influences, high culinary aspirations, and a relentless devotion to aesthetics, from plate garnishes to room decor. Tradition dictates late dining, and the majority of restaurants don't open until 8 or 9 pm for dinner and don't get busy until after 10. Dinner is a leisurely affair, and the sobremesa, or after-dinner chat over coffee or a digestif is near obligatory. Rushing from the table is frowned on—anyway, where would you go? Bars and clubs often don't open until after midnight.

The core of the population is of Italian and Spanish heritage, and pizza, pasta, *puchero* (beef boil), and paella are as common as the *parrilla* (steakhouse). Argentinians have taken the classics and made them their own with different techniques and ingredients, but they're still recognizable to the international traveler. Pizzas and empanadas are the favored local snack food, the former piled high with cheese, the latter typically filled with steak or chicken. And while steak is indisputably king in this town, it's got fierce competition in tender Patagonian lamb, game meats, fish, and shellfish.

Cafés, too, are an important part of the culture, and locals will stop in at their favorite for a *cafecito* at least once a day, not only to knock back a little caffeine, but also to see friends and catch up on the latest news and gossip.

Use the coordinate (✥ 2:C5) at the end of each listing to locate a site on the corresponding Where to Eat and Stay map.

DID YOU KNOW?

Parque Tres de Febrero, in Palermo, is an oasis of calm. Leave the collectivo exhaust behind and come take a paddleboat ride, stroll through the woods, or just laze in the grass to people-watch with your mate in hand.

2

DINING PRICE CATEGORIES (IN ARGENTINE PESOS)				
	$	$$	$$$	$$$$
Restaurants	40 pesos and under	41 pesos–64 pesos	65 pesos–75 pesos	over 75 pesos

Restaurant prices are for a first course (*entrada*), second course (*principal*), and dessert (*postre*).

CENTRO AND ENVIRONS

Centro and its environs offer a bit of everything: old-school porteño hangouts, fast-paced lunch spots, and modern, tourist-friendly locales in Puerto Madero.

CENTRO

$ CAFÉ **Confitería La Ideal.** Part of the charm of this spacious 1912 coffee shop–milonga is its sense of nostalgia: think fleur-de-lis motifs, time-worn European furnishings, and stained glass. No wonder they chose to film the 1998 movie *The Tango Lesson* here. La Ideal is famous for its *palmeritas* (glazed cookies) and tea service and for the scores of locals and foreigners who attend the milongas here. Tango lessons are offered Monday through Saturday at varying times throughout the day and night; evening concerts take place every night except Tuesday and Thursday. Its informality is its best trait; just show up at any hour and chances are you'll hear and see some great tango. *Suipacha 380, at Av. Corrientes, Centro 11/5265–8069 www.confiteriaideal.com No credit cards M C to C. Pellegrini, D to 9 de Julio 1:D4.*

$ PIZZA **El Cuartito.** For nearly 80 years this icon of porteño pizza has been tugging at the heartstrings of locals, who get misty-eyed when they think about the fresh tomato sauce and the mile-high pile of oozing mozzarella on these classics. You'll spot the occasional fellow tourist, but the vast majority of seats will be filled with locals who've been coming here for years. Every square inch of wall space is dedicated to posters, photos, and memorabilia of sports legends, musicians, tango dancers, and actors, and every local has his or her cherished spot in the dining room. The best pizza? A classic *mitad-mitad*, or half and half, one side a straightforward tomato sauce and cheese, the other simply festooned with sauce and anchovies. Don't pass on dessert, with the classic flan leading the pack. *Talcahuano 937, Centro 11/4816–4331 No credit cards M D to Tribunales 1:C3.*

$$ SPANISH **El Globo.** Much like the neighborhood in which it resides, El Globo is touristy but good. Hearty *pucheros* (mixed boiled meat dinners), roast suckling pig, squid, and other Spanish-Argentine fare are served in a large dining area, as they have been since the restaurant opened in 1908. The *cazuela de mariscos* (seafood stew) is another specialty. *Hipólito Yrigoyen 1199, Centro 11/4381–3926 M C to Av. de Mayo, A to Lima 1:C5.*

$ CAFÉ **Gran Café Tortoni.** You'll never again find this much local art, Tiffany lamps, and art nouveau touches in one room. And while you may have to wait in a line outside, depending on the time of day and how the tourist season is doing, it'll be worth it to knock back an espresso or sip a *submarino*, the local version of hot chocolate. Nibble on one of the dozens of sandwich varieties or fork in one of the exquisite pastries and contemplate that you may well be sitting in the same seat that a former president, a tango singer, or a famed artist or writer sat in many a time before. It's a place and time out of the past, and thankfully well preserved. Reservations are a must during the dinner-hour tango show. ✉ *Av. de Mayo 825, Centro* ☎ *11/4342–4328* 🌐 *www.cafetortoni.com.ar* Ⓜ *A to Perú* ⊕ *1:D4.*

$$$ ARGENTINE ✕ **Sabot.** Likely you'll be the only tourist amid scores of older businessmen who've been making this landmark a classic for more than 40 years. Day in and day out, this is the spot where behind-the-scenes negotiations take place over French-influenced local fare. The *centolla* (king crab) or *langostino* (prawn) salad is a throwback to another age, but it's perfectly prepared. Tuck into properly prepared pastas and a house specialty, semolina gnocchi, or slice into a delicious steak—the *entrecote* is king here. Add to the food some of the friendliest and most efficient service you'll find in town, and it's a don't-miss downtown lunch. ✉ *25 de Mayo 756, between Cordoba and Viamonte, Centro* ☎ *11/4313–6587* ✍ *Reservations essential* ⏲ *Closed weekends. No dinner* Ⓜ *B to L.N. Alem* ⊕ *1:E3.*

$$$$ ARGENTINE ✕ **Tomo I.** For a truly sublime dining experience, visit the recently renovated Tomo I, the consistently superb restaurant that's been run by the Concaro sisters since 1971. The inviting beige burlap walls lead to a back-lighted bar fronted by a gorgeous wood table made from an Algarrobo tree. The two dining rooms can be both romantic and functional; perfect for closing a business deal or celebrating an anniversary. The food is extraordinary: chilled carrot soup with orange and ginger, fresh Spanish octopus in pesto and garlic, and mouth-watering suckled pig are all top choices. This is food you won't soon forget. Reservations are recommended. ✉ *Carlos Pellegrini 521, Centro* ☎ *11/4326–6695* 🌐 *www.tomo1.com.ar* ⏲ *Closed Sun. No lunch Sat.* Ⓜ *B to Carlos Pellegrini, D to 9 de Julio* ⊕ *1:C3.*

$$$$ JAPANESE ✕ **Yuki.** Getting in requires a reservation, but once you're through the unmarked facade, you'll find yourself in the closest thing Buenos Aires has to a sushi temple. Japanese businessmen are quietly making deals in semi-hidden salons with tatami mats, while local aficionados are deftly wielding chopsticks at the small tables, or, if they're lucky, seated at the sushi bar in front of sushi-master Kazuo-san. The fish is pristinely fresh and changes daily based on availability, but always goes far beyond the BA standard of salmon and cream cheese (the latter thankfully not offered). For a special experience, order the *omakase* (chef's choice) menu and let the chef do his thing while you knock back a sake or two from the impressive selection. ✉ *Pasco 740, between Independencia and Chile, Congreso* ☎ *11/4942–7510* ✍ *Reservations essential* Ⓜ *E to Pichincha* ⊕ *1:A5.*

PUERTO MADERO

$$$$ STEAKHOUSE ✕ **Cabaña Las Lilas.** This place is a tourist trap, but a good one. It's probably the most famous steak house in all of Argentina, and has become wildly popular with foreigners. Although you'll hear lots of English, German, and French spoken here, if you look around, it's also

populated with lots of locals, at least the ones who can afford it. Las Lilas is best known for its beef that comes directly from its own estancia in the Pampas. The best cuts are the rib eye and *bife de lomo*. Salads and desserts are fantastic, too. Bottom line: if you're pressed for time, and can't leave Puerto Madero, this is your place for steak, even though you'll pay dearly for it. Otherwise, venture out to some better, and cheaper, places outside downtown. ✉ *A. M. de Justo 516, Puerto Madero* ☎ *11/4313–1336* 🌐 *www.laslilas.com* ✣ *1:E3.*

WORD OF MOUTH

"Go to Gran Café Tortoni for the atmosphere and the building itself. It is historic and elegant. Have coffee and dessert or a snack. It's not noted as a great place for dinner, but worth a visit more as part of your sightseeing and general Buenos Aires experience." —raquel_z

2

RETIRO

$$ ARGENTINE ★ ✕ **DaDá.** Poster-art kitsch is the decor in this foodie favorite. With a short but creative menu, this spot serves up some of the most interesting food to be found in the district. Don't miss out on the house specialties: phyllo-wrapped Morbier cheese salad as a starter and the perfectly cooked *ojo de bife* (rib-eye steak). The kitchen also deftly turns out perfectly cooked pastas, particularly those with seafood. Relax, enjoy a glass of wine, read the paper, sit at the bar and chat, and eat well. Hours can be as eclectic as their food, and they may or may not open at posted times, though likely they won't be too far off. ✉ *San Martín 941, Retiro* ☎ *11/4314–4787* ⏲ *Closed Sun.* Ⓜ *C to San Martín* ✣ *1:D3.*

$$ ITALIAN ✕ **Filo.** Crowded and lively, particularly at lunch, this is the hot spot for pizza and pasta in the downtown area. True Neapolitan-style pizzas with smoky, charred crusts direct from the wood-fired oven are among the best in the city. For a real treat, order the *Filo*, a wheel of a pizza with each slice a different topping according to the pizzero's whims. Pastas are served perfectly *al dente*, a rarity in town, and come with both classic and creative sauces. If you're dining solo, the bar is a great spot to grab a stool and dine, and the pizzas are available in individual sizes. One note, no photos allowed: "some of our guests may be dining with someone that they'd prefer their spouse doesn't see." Check out the ever-changing art gallery in the basement. ✉ *San Martín 975, between Alvear and Paraguay, Retiro* ☎ *11/4311–1871* 🌐 *www.filo-ristorante.com* Ⓜ *C to San Martín* ✣ *1:D3.*

$$ SUSHI ★ ✕ **Gran Bar Danzón.** It's a two-story climb up the steep stairs to BA's best wine bar. Go early in the evening, and it's your worst nightmare of a dimly lit lounge with hard-drinking middle-aged businessmen. Wait until dinner hour—after 8—and the crowd changes to the local yuppie and wine-geek set wolfing down some of the best lounge food in town, including great sushi (don't miss the crispy prawn rolls), eclectic appetizers and main courses, and a selection of wines by the glass that can't be beat. It's not too bad on the wallet either, particularly for the neighborhood and quality. Wednesday nights there's live jazz early. ✉ *Libertad 1161, 2nd floor, Retiro* ☎ *11/4811–1108* 🌐 *www.granbardanzon.com.ar* ✍ *Reservations essential* ⏲ *No lunch* Ⓜ *C to San Martín* ✣ *1:C2.*

Gran Café Tortoni, on Avenida de Mayo, is as iconic Argentine as it gets.

SAN TELMO AND LA BOCA

The most historic neighborhoods in the city have a few gems that are well worth visiting. Note that most of the eateries near the pedestrian-only El Caminito thoroughfare are cheesy tourist traps.

SAN TELMO

$ CAFÉ **Bar Dorrego.** Not a place to take a table if you plan to eat a meal, there are far better options pretty much anywhere. But, Bar Dorrego has the unquestioned best view of Plaza Dorrego. Have a coffee, sip a cocktail, order a beer, and get a dish of peanuts. Then sit back and people-watch. It's a place filled with local businessmen grabbing a sandwich or pastry on weekdays, and no one but tourists on the weekends. Given the century-old decor and grime, the nose-in-the-air attitude of the waiters is far misplaced. ✉ *Defensa 1098, at Humberto I, on Plaza Dorrego, San Telmo* ☎ *11/4361–0141* ▭ *No credit cards* Ⓜ *C or E to Independencia* ✣ *1:E6.*

$$ FRENCH **Brasserie Petanque.** Upon entering this classic French brasserie, you're greeted by a long and imposing bar, bookended by white pillars and backed by shelf after enticing shelf of liquor and wine. This festive San Telmo locale has scores of small white-linen tables where you can enjoy great onion soup and local interpretations of French classics, like steak tartare and beef bourguignonne. Surprisingly, the wine list is quite small, with only a few French wines, but they make up for it with an ample spirits selection and friendly bartenders. Get a table by the window to check out the people cruising by outside. Reservations are recommended. ✉ *Defensa 596, San Telmo* ☎ *11/4342–7930* 🌐 *www.brasseriepetanque.com* ⏲ *Closed Mon.* ✣ *1:D5.*

$$$$ ARGENTINE ✕ **La Vineria de Gualterio Bolivar.** The pioneer of molecular cooking spots in Buenos Aires, chef Alejandro Digilio deserves all credit for bringing this style of cooking with foams, gels, and powders to the dining scene in Buenos Aires. Over the last couple of years, however, the restaurant has started to rest on its laurels a bit, with repetitve menus and less attention to detail than in its early days. It's still an eye-opening experience, but one that can now be had at any of a dozen other spots in town, and often at a lower price. Still, it's a charming room, impeccable service, and an opportunity to try something different from the pizzerias and steak houses that surround it in San Telmo. No à la carte menu available, just a multi-course tasting menu. ✉ *Bolivar 865, San Telmo* ☎ *11/4361–4709* 🌐 *www.lavineriadegualteriobolivar.com* ⏲ *Closed Mon.* ✣ *1:D6.*

$$ WINE BAR ✕ **Martiño.** You know wine is going to be important here when you step in and see the gleaming glass wine cave that dominates the back wall, and that's what owner Marcelo Soto intends. A regularly changing selection of some of Argentina's best wines, many available by the glass, are paired up with some of the best Spanish tapas in the city. Don't miss his grandmother's rendition of a *tortilla española* or, if you're feeling adventurous, the sampler plate of delicious offal preparations. Share multiple small plates or order from the equally good dinner menu. ✉ *Bolívar 933, San Telmo* ☎ *11/4300–6897* 🌐 *www.martinio.com.ar* ⏲ *No lunch weekdays* Ⓜ *C or E to Independencía* ✣ *1:D6.*

LA BOCA

$$ STEAKHOUSE ✕ **El Obrero.** You'll half expect sawdust on the floor and a saloon fight to break out when you walk into this old-time steak house just off the docks of La Boca. While the place is filled with locals, it's also a spot for in-the-know tourists, and a regular stop for touring rock stars who seem to have chosen it as "the" spot to go when in town for a performance. Big, juicy steaks cooked right, massive side dishes, and more ambience than you can shake a stick at, El Obrero is a movie director's dream of an Argentine steak house come to life. The neighborhood is a little iffy, particularly at night, and it's down a little side street—take a taxi to and from (they'll call one for you). ✉ *Augustín R. Caffarena 64, La Boca* ☎ *11/4362–9912* ▭ *No credit cards* ⏲ *Closed Sun.* ✣ *1:F6.*

$$$$ ARGENTINE ✕ **Patagonia Sur.** Located just off the picture-postcard tourist trap of El Caminito in La Boca, this was once Francis Mallman's flagship restaurant. Arguably the country's most beloved chef, he's moved most of his attention to his newer ventures in Uruguay. Fame, particularly television fame, have had their price—mostly in raising them. Patagonia Sur is likely the most expensive restaurant in the country, particularly since it serves up rustic steak-house fare, with a flare to be sure, but nothing extraordinary. These days, the only option at either lunch or dinner is a three-course prix fixe at a price that would make a London or New York chef blush with embarrasment. ✉ *Rocha 801, La Boca* ☎ *11/4303–5917* 🌐 *www.restaurantepatagoniasur.com* ⏲ *Closed Sun. and Mon.* ✣ *1:F6.*

RECOLETA

Recoleta is the toniest neighborhood in Buenos Aires, and as such, is home to some of the city's top hotels and restaurants. At the same time, there's something for everyone, and the somewhat touristy Village Recoleta strip along Junín and R.M. Ortíz has a mix of old-time cafés and eateries. More and more ethnic places are popping up all over.

$$ AMERICAN
Buller Brewing Company. Smack in the middle of the touristy Village Recoleta strip, a respite from one steak house after another, Buller (English pronunciation) is the city's first microbrewery. Turning out an impressive seven different styles of beer (don't miss the Oktoberfest or the Porter), they also offer up a sampler tasting of the whole range that's worth a try. Great sandwiches and one of the better burgers in the neighborhood are even more reason to drop in. Service can seem a bit slow, at least until you get your first beer in hand, but it's worth the wait. ✉ *R. M. Ortíz 1827, Recoleta* ☎ *11/4808–9061* ⊕ *1:B1.*

$$$$ MODERN ARGENTINE Fodor's Choice ★
Duhau Restaurante & Vinoteca. An oasis of elegance and grace in the heart of old, wealthy Recoleta, the Duhau is not only a grand hotel, but it also serves up some of the best food of any hotel in the city. While French technique may be the base, the ingredients are pure South America. Particularly favored by the chef are the seafood and meats of Patagonia. Standout dishes include butter-soft Angus tenderloin, crispy sweetbreads, and a decadent molten chocolate cake. If the weather is nice, grab a table on the terrace overlooking the courtyard gardens. Don't miss a pre- or post-dinner visit to the wine and cheese bar with a fantastic array of each, by glass, bottle, and small plate, respectively, and then take an after-meal walk through the hotel's underground art gallery. ✉ *Av. Alvear 1661, Recoleta* ☎ *11/5171–1340* 🌐 *www.buenosaires.park.hyatt.com* ⏲ *No lunch weekends* ⊕ *1:C1.*

$ ARGENTINE Fodor's Choice ★
El Sanjuanino. Mostly tourists from the nearby hotels flock to this Northern Argentine regional spot, but you'll spot some longtime locals, particularly at lunchtime. It's cramped, crowded, and kitschy, and in hot weather the roaring wood-fired ovens can make the main floor a bit too toasty (head downstairs, where it's cooler), but it's worth it for great empanadas, the city's best *locro* (corn, squash, and meat stew), and, if you're feeling adventurous, one of their iconic game dishes. Don't bother with the wine list, the house wine served in pitchers is just as good at half the price. The waiters have fun with the crowd, and generally speak at least basic conversational phrases in a half-dozen or more languages. ✉ *Posadas 1515, at Callao, Recoleta* ☎ *11/4804–2909* ⏲ *Closed Mon.* ⊕ *1:C1.*

$ STEAKHOUSE
Juana M. The minimalist chic decor of this hip basement restaurant stands in stark contrast to the menu: down-to-earth parrilla fare at good prices. Catch a glimpse of meats sizzling on the grill behind the bar, check out the impressive artwork on the walls, and then head to your table to devour your steak and chorizo. This place has the best salad bar in the city, hands down. The homemade pastas aren't bad, either. The staff is young and friendly. It's wildly popular with a lunchtime work crowd during the week and for birthday parties at night. ✉ *Carlos Pellegrini 1535, Recoleta* ☎ *11/4326–0462* Ⓜ *C to San Martín* ⊕ *1:D2.*

WORD OF MOUTH

"If you are foodies, I would recommend [the restaurants] Tomo I or La Bourgogne." —drdawaggy

$ CAFÉ ✕ **La Biela.** Porteños linger at this quintessential sidewalk café opposite the Recoleta Cemetery, sipping espressos, discussing politics, and people-watching—all of which are best done at a table beneath the shade of an ancient rubber tree. Service can be spotty, but if you're just there for a coffee, who cares. Keep your eyes open for actor and tango enthusiast Robert Duvall, who is a regular here. ✉ *Quintana 596, at Junín, Recoleta* ☎ *11/4804–0449* ⊕ *1:B1.*

$$$$ FRENCH Fodor's Choice ★ ✕ **La Bourgogne.** White tablecloths, fresh roses, and slick red-leather chairs emphasize the restaurant's innate elegance, and it is consistently considered to be one of the city's very best restaurants. A sophisticated waitstaff brings you complimentary hors d'oeuvres as you choose from chef Jean-Paul Bondoux's creations, which include foie gras, rabbit, lamb, chateaubriand, *côte de veau* (veal steak), and black hake. The loquacious chef is known to stroll through the vast room and sit down for a chat with patrons. The fixed-price tasting menu is more affordable and more adventurous than à la carte selections and features a different wine with each plate. Arrange to be seated in the mysterious wine cellar for a more intimate experience. The wine list reads like a book, and offers the very best blends from France, Italy, and Argentina. ✉ *Alvear Palace Hotel, Ayacucho 2027, Recoleta* ☎ *11/4805–3857, 11/4808–2100* ⚠ *Reservations essential* ⊗ *Closed Sun. No lunch Sat.* ⊕ *1:B1.*

$$ ITALIAN ✕ **La Parolaccia.** Right off the main shopping strip on Santa Fé, this place feels like a warm, family-run and family-friendly Italian restaurant you could find in any big city. Given the corporate ownership, they serve up surprisingly excellent homemade pastas with a wide variety of sauces and styles at each of their nine locations in town. Particularly good are their hand-rolled *fusilli;* don't overlook the three-course lunch specials. They're happy to make half portions of pasta for your kids as well. You'll be greeted at your table with a complimentary cocktail and sent off with a digestif of limoncello at the end of your meal. ✉ *Riobamba 1046, Recoleta* ☎ *11/4783–0200* ⊕ *www.laparolaccia.com* Ⓜ *C to Congreso, B to Callao* ⊕ *1:B4.*

$$$$ FRENCH ✕ **Nectarine.** Both elegant and quaint, the second-floor dining room of this modern French temple to haute cuisine is a spot for the wealthy, both local and visiting. The regularly changing menu is set up as a one- to five-course prix-fixe (with some supplements) of like-sized courses—nothing is specifically appetizer or entrée, it's entirely up to you to design your dinner. The place generates mixed sentiments from diners, who find some dishes to be exquisite and others overwrought. At lunch it's quiet; at dinner reservations are a must. Expect to shell out a fair amount for a meal, even by international standards. ✉ *Pasaje del Correo, Vicente López 1661, Recoleta* ☎ *11/4813–6993* ⚠ *Reservations essential* ⊗ *Closed Sun. No lunch Sat.* ⊕ *1:B2.*

$$$$ SPANISH Fodor's Choice ★ ✕ **Oviedo.** Soft lighting, white tablecloths, tranquil ambience, and sea-themed artwork adorning the walls will greet you in this elegant Spanish-style establishment in the heart of Recoleta. In a meat-centric

city like Buenos Aires, beautifully cooked seafood is a welcome change, and Oviedo is the best in the city. From classics to modern creative, the kitchen turns out beautifully plated fillets of fish—don't miss their daily catch with pickled baby vegetables and the pristine shellfish. They're no slouches in the meat department either. Top it all off with one of the better wine lists in the area, and you're in for a memorable lunch or dinner. ✉ *Beruti 2602, at Ecuador, Recoleta* ☎ *11/4821–3741* 🌐 *www.oviedoresto.com.ar* ⊗ *Closed Sun.* Ⓜ *D to Pueyrredón* ✣ *1:A2.*

PALERMO AND ENVIRONS

The city's largest neighborhood, Palermo offers something for every taste, style, and budget. It's the city's undisputed culinary hot spot, with enclaves that have their own distinct style and vibe. If you want the tastiest, most cutting-edge, most traditional, most ethnic, most daring, and most fashionable food in Buenos Aires, then you head to Palermo. It's that simple.

$$$$ PERUVIAN ✕ **Astrid & Gaston.** Its opening in early 2009 was marked by much hype by BA foodies, who had longed for famed Peruvian chef Gaston Acurio's cuisine in their city. As a whole, the food and atmosphere inside the beautifully recycled Palermo home is spirited, but in many cases style trumps service. The waitstaff look great in black suits and ties, but they don't offer consistent service, and non-Spanish speakers may have a hard time communicating with them. That said, the food is delicious and imaginative: marinated boneless pork with sweet potatoes and red onions; white salmon with peas and scallop risotto; *arroz con mariscos* (rice and shellfish), and *aji de gallina* (chili chicken) are all top choices. Most of the food lacks the spice normally found in many Peruvian dishes, a regrettable trend that most ethnic restaurants in BA adhere to in order to cater to porteños' weak palates. ✉ *Lafinur 3222, Palermo* ☎ *11/4802–2991* ✍ *Reservations essential* ⊗ *Closed Sun.* ✣ *2:E3.*

$$$$ ARGENTINE ✕ **Casa Cruz.** Trendsetters come and go, but there are few whose food is truly sublime. With its imposing bronze-doored entrance, dim lighting, expanses of mahogany, and cozy banquettes, you'd have to be a bumbling fool not to impress your date here. And yet it's chef Germán Martitegui's kitchen that will really blow your mind, working rabbit medallions into a state of melting tenderness, and pairing delicately crisped *morcilla* (blood sausage) with jammy fruit. The wine list is huge, and wildly overpriced. The cocktails served up by resident bar maiden Inés de los Santos are the best in the city. This is a place you won't soon forget. ✉ *Uriarte 1658, Palermo Soho* ☎ *11/4833–1112* 🌐 *www.casacruz-restaurant.com* ✍ *Reservations essential* ⊗ *Closed Sun. No lunch* ✣ *2:B4.*

$$ STEAKHOUSE Fodor's Choice ★ ✕ **Don Julio.** Behind an unassuming facade, and amid rows and rows of empty wine bottles that festoon every available surface, one of Palermo's best steak houses awaits you. A mixed local and expat crowd packs the place at lunch and dinner, dining on the fantastic *ojo de bife* (rib eye) and *cuadril* (rump steak), plus great chorizo sausages, and pretty much anything else you might want off a grill. One of the city's better curated wine lists adds to the fun—ask for Pablo, the owner, who

PURA TIERRA IN BELGRANO

Fodor's Choice ★ ✕ **Pura Tierra.** Set in a charming, converted Belgrano home, chef Martín Molteni's creative dining room offers up a tribute to the lesser known products of Argentina. Specializing in unusual meats—llama, wild boar, rabbit, and quail are regular offerings—as well as fresh fish, unusual grains and vegetables, and hand-crafted cheeses, he brings his overseas training in France and Australia to bear on his Argentine heritage. The menu changes completely every 2-3 months to reflect the freshest in seasonal ingredients. While the menu doesn't list vegetarian options, give advance notice when you reserve, and the kitchen will turn out equally stunning vegetable plates. A chef's tasting menu is also available. ✉ *3 de Febrero 1167, Belgrano* ☎ *11/4899–2007* 🌐 *www.puratierra.com.ar* ⏲ *Closed Sun.* ✢ *1:A1.*

knows the ins and outs of every bottle on his list. ✉ *Guatemala 4691, at Gurruchaga, Palermo Soho* ☎ *11/4831–9564* ✢ *2:C4.*

$$$$ PERUVIAN Fodor's Choice ★ ✕ **Francesco.** With a privileged elevated view of a quiet residential street in Palermo, Francesco serves the city's finest Peruvian cuisine. Start your evening with what must be the tastiest, frothiest pisco sour in town, then move on to one of the many fresh fish appetizers. Naturally, this restaurant does wonderful ceviche dishes that perfectly blend citrus juices with subtly spicy flavors. The main courses run the gamut from fish to pasta to meat. A highlight is the *piqueo criollo*, a salmon and shrimp platter with fresh tomatoes, onions, and peppers. For dessert, try the *suspiro de limena*, a delicious custard-like dessert topped with meringue and cinnamon. The owners operate two similar namesake restaurants in Lima and Miami, and know how to satisfy an international clientele, which shows in the modern, but welcoming dining room and in the top-notch service. ✉ *Sinclair 3096, Palermo* ☎ *11/5291–1597* 🌐 *www.francesco.com.pe* ⏲ *No lunch Sat. Closed Sun.* ✢ *2:C2.*

$$$ ECLECTIC ✕ **Hernán Gipponi Restaurant.** The long, narrow, cream-colored room leading to the hotel's garden patio may not seem like the "in-spot" for creative cooking, but don't let appearances fool you. The chef is turning out some of the most creative food in Palermo, with a skill honed by years of working in top kitchens in Spain. While you can order from the à la carte menu, local foodies are packing in for the daily changing nine-course chef's tasting menu. Gipponi is particularly deft with his fish dishes. Backing up the kitchen is one of the better wine lists in the city, managed by a team of top sommeliers, and an excellent cocktail selection from the bar. ✉ *Fierro Hotel Boutique, Soler 5862, Palermo* ☎ *11/3220–6820* 🌐 *www.fierrohotel.com* ✍ *Reservations essential* ⏲ *No dinner Sun. and Mon.* Ⓜ *D to Ministro Carranza* ✢ *2:A3.*

$$$ JAPANESE ✕ **Jardín Japonés.** Easily the most impressive setting for sushi in Buenos Aires is inside the Japanese Garden on the northern edge of Palermo. Come for lunch, before or after touring the garden, or come for a romantic dinner. The sushi and sashimi are fresh, especially the salmon, but the hot dishes, such as pork with mushrooms, won't necessarily blow you away. ✉ *Jardín Japonés, Av. Casares 2966, Bosques de Pal-*

ermo ☎ *11/4800–1322* 🌐 *www.jardinjapones.org.ar* ⊗ *Closed Tues. dinner* ⊕ *2:D4.*

$$$ STEAKHOUSE Fodor's Choice ★ ✕ **La Cabrera.** Palermo's best parrilla is on the quiet corner of Cabrera and Thames. Fun paraphernalia hangs everywhere, giving the feel of an old grocery store. La Cabrera is particularly known for its excellent *provoleta de queso de cabra* (grilled goat cheese) and its *chinchulines de cordero* (small lamb intestines). Try also the *cuadril vuelta y vuelta* (rare rump steak) and the *mollejas* (sweetbreads), which are also top-notch. The servings are abundant, as is the noise. What really sets it apart from other parrillas are the complimentary side dishes like pumpkin purée, eggplant salad, and others. ✉ *Cabrera 5099, Palermo Soho* ☎ *11/4831–7002* 🌐 *www.parrillalacabrera.com* ⛭ *Reservations essential* ⊕ *2:B5.*

$$ ECLECTIC Fodor's Choice ★ ✕ **Las Pizarras Bistró.** Quirky and kitschy, this 40-seat hole-in-the-wall looks like any of hundreds of other neighorhood hangouts throughout the city. But stop for a moment and take a look at the chalkboard-covered walls *(las pizarras)* and you'll know instantly this isn't your typical spot for cheap steaks and *milanesas*. Chef Rodrigo Castillo is one of the most unsung chefs in the city. He turns out a constantly changing, market-driven menu of a dozen plates of some of the most interesting, eclectic food you'll find in the area, and the local food *cognoscenti* line up to get in. There's an equally creative wine list spread out on other boards along one wall. Pricing is civil, portions are huge, service can be a trifle slow, but it's worth the wait. ✉ *Thames 2296, at Charcas, Palermo* ☎ *11/4775–0625* ⛭ *Reservations essential* ⊗ *Closed Mon. No lunch.* Ⓜ *D to Plaza Italia* ⊕ *2:C4.*

$$$$ JAPANESE FUSION Fodor's Choice ★ ✕ **Osaka.** Osaka blends tradition with innovation, fusing Peruvian and Asian cuisines for lofty results, making it one of the most exciting restaurants in the city. However, it does attract a pretentious crowd: there are too many people trying too hard to look too cool, but the food all but makes up for it. The snug downstairs dining area has both a sushi bar and a cocktail bar, surrounded by tables of varying sizes. Upstairs, you can dine outside in a more relaxed patio setting. Ceviche is your best bet for starters, followed by rounds of fresh, delicious, and imaginative (by local standards, anyway) sushi. Don't miss spot-on interpretations of Peruvian recipes that were imported directly from the chain's Lima location, like the *Misoudado*, an amazing red-curry grouper. ✉ *Soler 5608, Palermo* ☎ *11/4775–6964* 🌐 *www.osaka.com.pe* ⊗ *Closed Sun.* ⊕ *2:B3.*

$$$ STEAKHOUSE Fodor's Choice ★ ✕ **Rio Alba.** In terms of quality, price, and charm, this is the best parrilla in Buenos Aires. Period. It consistently serves the tastiest and tenderest cuts of beef. The *asado de tira* is particularly good, as is the flavorful *entrana*. Ask for a minigrill at your table to keep your meat warm; you're going to need time to finish the enormous servings. The old-school waiters wear vests and bow ties and refuse to write anything down, but they always get the order right. This place is packed every night of the week with businesspeople and families. If you arrive after 9:30 pm, expect to wait for a table. ✉ *Cervino 4499, Palermo* ☎ *11/4773–5748* ⊕ *2:D3.*

WORD OF MOUTH

"This vegetable display in Palermo sums up the style in Buenos Aires. That is, even the vegetables have style!" —photo by Martin Byrne, Fodors.com member

A
B
C
D
1
2
3
4
5
6
RECOLETA
Pura Tierra
Hotel Bel Air
CEMENTERIO DE LA RECOLETA
La Biela
Buller Brewing Company
La Bourgogne
El Sanjuanino
Alvear Palace Hotel
Park Hyatt Palacio Duhau
Duhau Restaurante & Vinoteca
Oviedo
Nectarine
Algodon Mansion
Four Seasons Hotel Buenos Aires
Juana M
ESTACIÓN TERMINAL DE OMNIBUS
Sofitel Buenos Aries
Art Hotel
Casa Calma
Marriott Plaza Hotel
Gran Bar Danzón
Design cE Hotel de Diseño
RETIRO
El Cuartito
DaDá
Filo
Abasto Hotel
TEATRO COLÓN
Tomo I
CENTRO
Rooney's Boutique Hotel
OBELISCO
Confiteria La Ideal
La Parolaccia
Gran Café Tortoni
PLAZA DE MAYO
El Globo
NH City & Tower
PLAZA DE MAYO
Axel Hotel Buenos Aires
Yuki
Brasserie Petanque
Martiño
Mansion Dandi Royal
La Vineria de Gualterio Bolivar
Gurda Tango Boutique Hotel
SAN TELMO
Av. Gral. Las Heras
Vincent López
Av. Pueyrredon
Junín
Azucuenaga
Beruti
Juncal
Guido
Av. Pte. F. Quintana
Av. Alvear
Posadas
Arenales
Juncal
Av. Callao
Montevideo
M.T. De Alvear
Av. Santa Fe.
Alvear
Uruguay
Paraguay
Av. Cordoba
Viamonte
Tucumán
Levalle
Parana
Talcahuano
Suipacha
Esmeralda
Maipú
Florida
San Martín
Av. Corrientes
Sarmiento
Juan D. Perón
Mitre
Libertad
Cerrito
C. Pellegrini
Diag. N
San Martín
Reconquista
Av. de Mayo
Av. Rivadavia
Plaza del Congreso
Av. H. Yrigoyen
Alsina
Moreno
Av. Belgrano
Venezuela
Mexico
Chile
Matheu
Pichyncha
Pasco
Av. 9 de Julio
Lima
Diag. S
Bolivar
Defensa
Perú
Chacabuco
Piedras
Av. Independencia
Estados Unidos
Carlos Calvo
Humberto
Av. Entre Rios
Av. San Juan

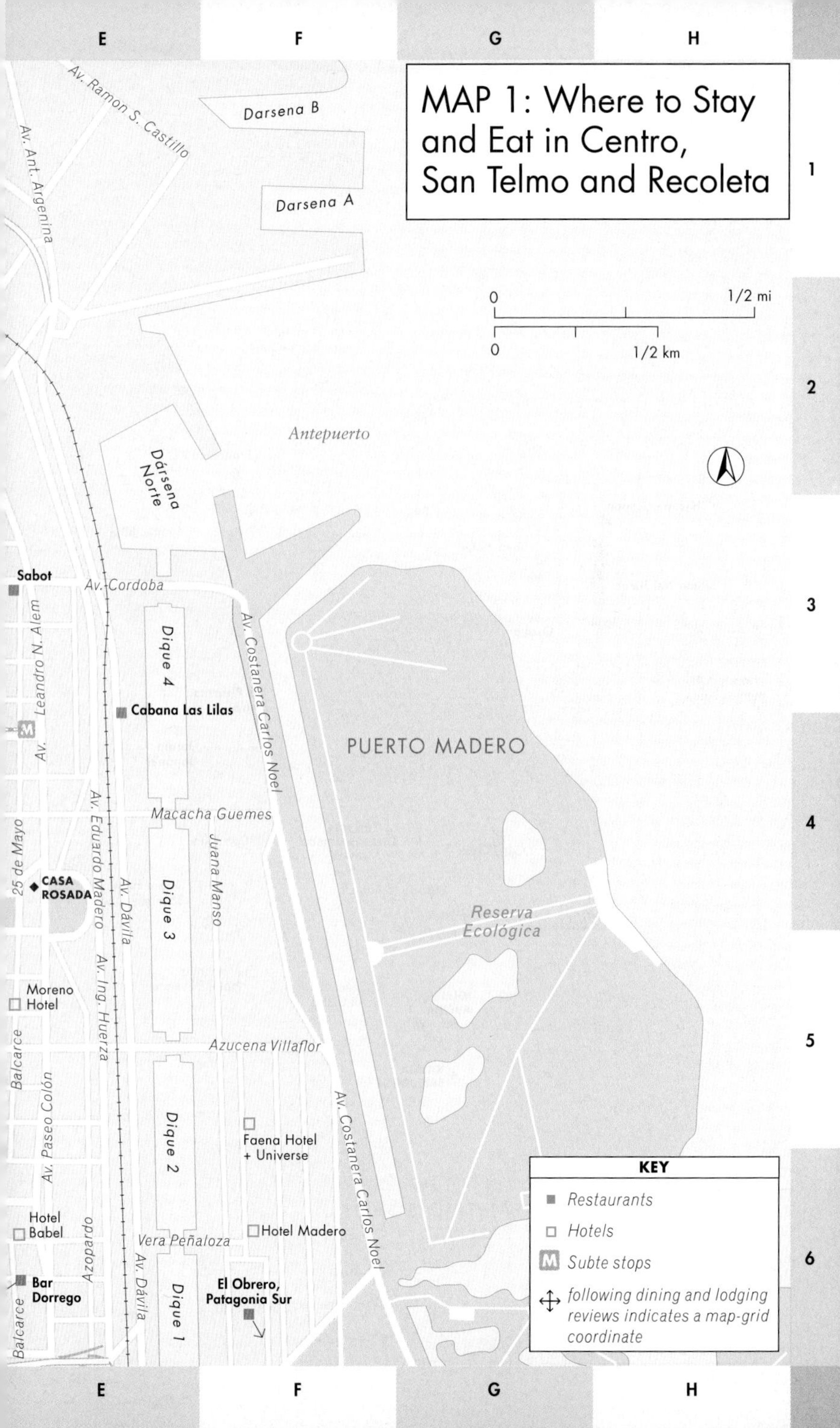

MAP 1: Where to Stay and Eat in Centro, San Telmo and Recoleta
E
F
G
H
1
2
3
4
5
6
0
1/2 mi
0
1/2 km
Av. Ramon S. Castillo
Av. Ant. Argenina
Darsena B
Darsena A
Antepuerto
Dársena Norte
Sabot
Av. Cordoba
Av. Leandro N. Alem
Dique 4
Cabana Las Lilas
Av. Costanera Carlos Noel
PUERTO MADERO
Macacha Guemes
Av. Eduardo Madero
25 de Mayo
CASA ROSADA
Av. Dávila
Dique 3
Juana Manso
Reserva Ecológica
Av. Ing. Huerza
Moreno Hotel
Azucena Villaflor
Balcarce
Av. Paseo Colón
Dique 2
Faena Hotel + Universe
Av. Costanera Carlos Noel
Hotel Babel
Azopardo
Vera Peñaloza
Hotel Madero
Bar Dorrego
Av. Dávila
Dique 1
El Obrero, Patagonia Sur
Balcarce
KEY
Restaurants
Hotels
Subte stops
following dining and lodging reviews indicates a map-grid coordinate
E
F
G
H

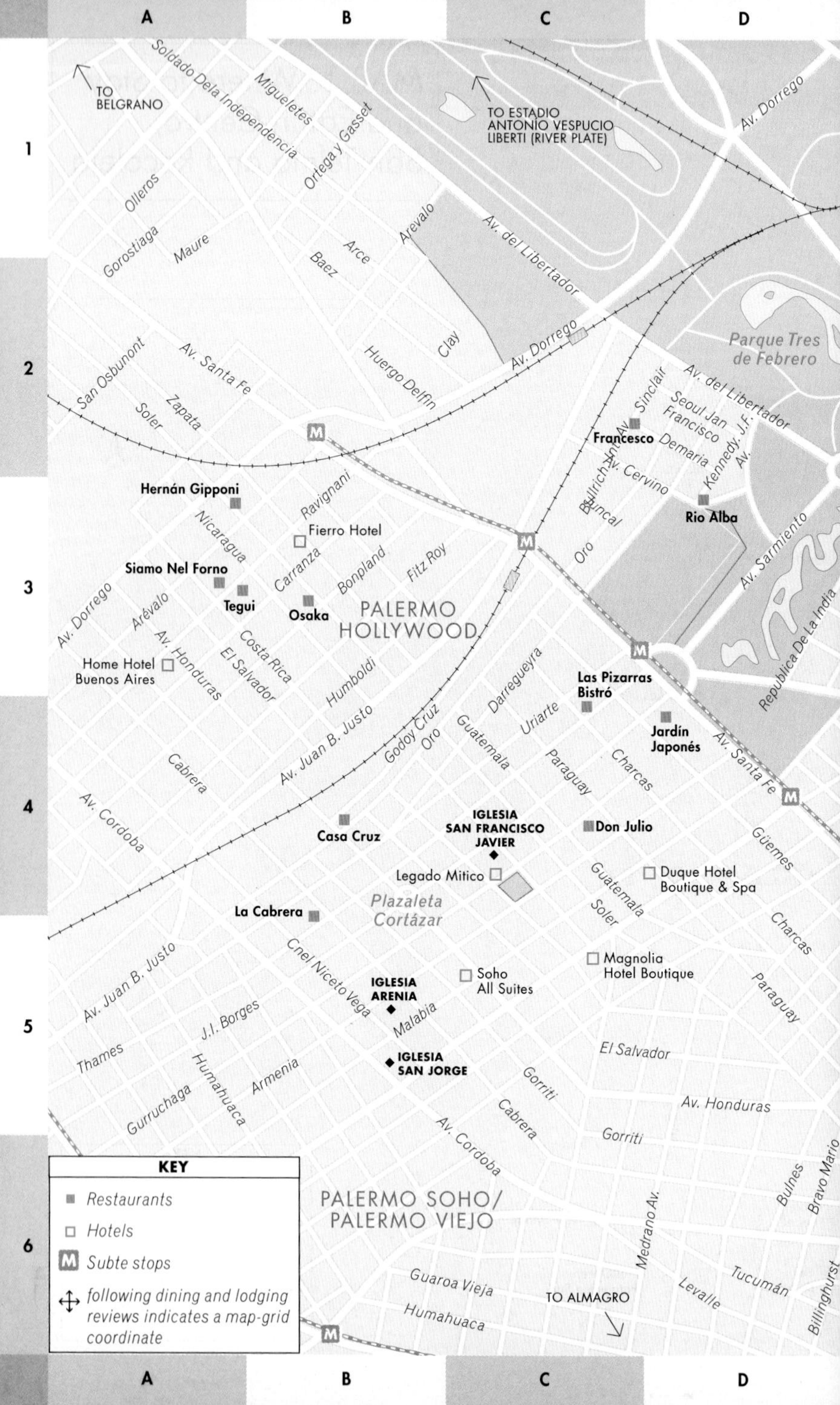

A
B
C
D
1
2
3
4
5
6
TO BELGRANO
TO ESTADIO ANTONIO VESPUCIO LIBERTI (RIVER PLATE)
Parque Tres de Febrero
PALERMO HOLLYWOOD
PALERMO SOHO/ PALERMO VIEJO
Plazaleta Cortázar
TO ALMAGRO
Hernán Gipponi
Fierro Hotel
Siamo Nel Forno
Tegui
Osaka
Home Hotel Buenos Aires
Francesco
Rio Alba
Las Pizarras Bistró
Jardín Japonés
Don Julio
Casa Cruz
IGLESIA SAN FRANCISCO JAVIER
Legado Mitico
Duque Hotel Boutique & Spa
La Cabrera
Magnolia Hotel Boutique
Soho All Suites
IGLESIA ARENIA
IGLESIA SAN JORGE
KEY
Restaurants
Hotels
Subte stops
following dining and lodging reviews indicates a map-grid coordinate

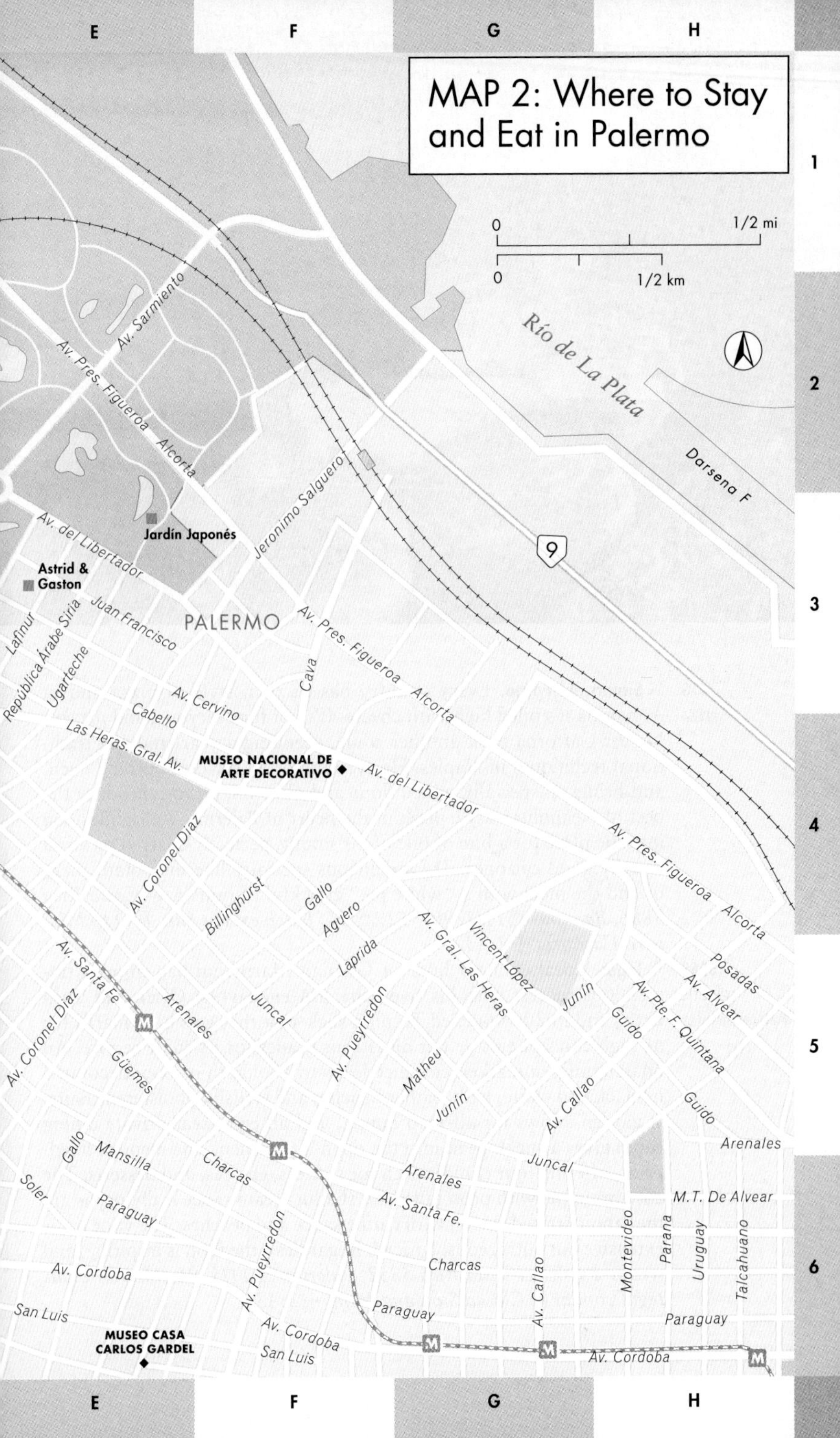
MAP 2: Where to Stay and Eat in Palermo
E
F
G
H
1
2
3
4
5
6
0
1/2 mi
0
1/2 km
Río de La Plata
Darsena F
9
Av. Sarmiento
Av. Pres. Figueroa Alcorta
Jardín Japonés
Av. del Libertador
Astrid & Gaston
Jeronimo Salguero
PALERMO
Juan Francisco
Lafinur
República Árabe Siria
Ugarteche
Av. Pres. Figueroa Alcorta
Cava
Av. Cervino
Cabello
Las Heras. Gral. Av.
MUSEO NACIONAL DE ARTE DECORATIVO
Av. del Libertador
Av. Pres. Figueroa Alcorta
Av. Coronel Diaz
Billinghurst
Gallo
Aguero
Laprida
Av. Gral. Las Heras
Vincent López
Posadas
Av. Alvear
Av. Pte. F. Quintana
Junín
Guido
Av. Santa Fe
Arenales
Juncal
Av. Pueyrredon
Av. Coronel Diaz
Güemes
Matheu
Junín
Av. Callao
Guido
Arenales
Gallo
Mansilla
Charcas
Juncal
Arenales
Soler
Paraguay
Av. Santa Fe.
M.T. De Alvear
Montevideo
Parana
Uruguay
Talcahuano
Av. Cordoba
Av. Pueyrredon
Charcas
Av. Callao
San Luis
Paraguay
Paraguay
Av. Cordoba
MUSEO CASA CARLOS GARDEL
San Luis
Av. Cordoba
M

Restaurant parrillas like this one offer everything from classic *bife de lomo* to all manner of offal.

$ PIZZA

Siamo nel Forno. Every country has its own style of pizza and in Argentina it's piled high with cheese. It's not for everyone, and *pizzero* Nestor Gattorna took another route, spending a year studying traditional techniques in Naples. He even imported a wood-burning oven, and brings in specially milled flour and olive oil, all to reproduce the best of Neapolitan-style pizza in the heart of Palermo. Italophiles jam into the place for a bite of one of his smoky, perfectly charred pies and equally good calzones. Try a delicious specialty like his potato pizza or end the meal with a "white pie" chockful of nutella. ✉ *Costa Rica 5886, Palermo* ☎ *11/5290–9529* ⏲ *No lunch except Sun.* Ⓜ *D to Ministro Carranza* ✣ *2:A3.*

$$$$ ECLECTIC Fodor's Choice ★

Tegui. Local culinary hotshot German Martitegui has enjoyed tremendous success with his two other BA endeavors, Ølsen and Casa Cruz, and in 2009 opened Tegui, a slick spot that gets high marks for its high-concept cuisine but disastrous grades for its snide service. An unassuming, unmarked entrance leads to a long, thin room decorated in black and white, with leather benches and stylish upholstered chairs. A garden allows for alfresco dining, and an eight-seat private dining room gives a sneak peak into the open-air kitchen. The menu is fixed-price, offering four choices each for starters, entrées, and desserts. The cow-brain pie with prosciutto and shallot cream sauce is divine, as are the rabbit-stuffed ravioli with truffle sauce and peaches. The wine list is extensive but outrageously priced. Regardless, the food is inspiring, and worth a visit. ✉ *Costa Rica 5852, Palermo* ☎ *11/5291–3333* 🌐 *www.tegui.com.ar* ⏲ *Closed Sun. and Mon.* ✣ *2:A3.*

WHERE TO STAY

In Buenos Aires, neighborhoods each have their own energy and spirit, and hotels tend to both mimic the identity of their neighborhood and help to shape it. The lodging options here are some of the most impressive of any international, cosmopolitan locale. From luxurious, majestic hotels (many with recognizable chain names) to boutique hotels operating a handful of rooms and injected with local flair, one thing is certain: you're bound to encounter plenty of attractive lodging options.

Though prices have climbed in Argentina in recent years, the city is still highly affordable for international visitors on the dollar, euro, and real. Many visitors, having discovered the intoxicating energy of the city, return again and again. Hotel owners and staff are some of the key players in helping people to fall in love with the city or lure them back.

Downtown—in Centro and Puerto Madero—you'll find sleek, soaring hotel properties; inch toward Recoleta and you can choose from some of the ritziest hotels in town, especially around Avenida Alvear and the Recoleta Cemetery. Boutique hotels are where Buenos Aires' options really shine, and while intimate, stylish spots dot most of the city's neighborhoods, they are found in greatest concentration in the vast, hip barrio of Palermo. Each neighborhood offers visitors the chance to experience one facet of the buzzing, intriguing city of Buenos Aires.

	WHAT IT COSTS IN ARGENTINE PESOS			
	$	$$	$$$	$$$$
Hotels	450 pesos and under	451 pesos–700 pesos	701 pesos–1000 pesos	over 1000 pesos

Hotel prices are for two people in a standard double room in high season.

Use the coordinate (⊕ 2:C5) at the end of each listing to locate a site on the corresponding Where to Eat and Stay map.

For expanded hotel reviews, visit Fodors.com.

CENTRO AND ENVIRONS

CENTRO

$$$ **Casa Calma.** This boutique property and "wellness hotel" in the heart of downtown Buenos Aires has taken the concept of in-house spa to a new level, equipping each of its 17 rooms with a Jacuzzi, and the six deluxe rooms also with saunas. **Pros:** the "honesty bar" allows guests to help themselves to juice, wine, and sweets, and counts on them to pay the tab. **Cons:** situated on a chaotic city street; during the day the movement outside can be suffocating and at night can attract some sketchy characters. ✉ *Suipacha 1015, Centro* ☎ *11/5199–2800* 🌐 *www.casacalma.com.ar* *17 rooms* *In-room: safe, Wi-Fi. In-hotel: restaurant, bar, spa, laundry facilities* ⊕ *1:C2.*

Fodor's Choice ★

$$ **Design cE Hotel de Diseño.** This hotel drips with coolness; rooms feel like pimped-out Tribeca lofts, with rotating flat-screen TVs that let you watch from bed or from one of the leather recliners. **Pros:** supermodern

and spacious suites; great location; breakfast is served 24 hours a day. **Cons:** common areas are on the small side. ✉ *Marcelo T. Alvear 1695, Centro* ☎ *11/5237–3100* 🌐 *www.designce.com* 20 *rooms, 8 suites* *In-room: a/c, safe, kitchen, Internet, Wi-Fi. In-hotel: bar, pool, gym* Ⓜ *D to Callao* ✣ *1:B2.*

$$$ **Marriott Plaza Hotel.** This Buenos Aires landmark brims with old-school style; built in 1909 and renovated in 2003, the hotel sits at the top of pedestrian-only Florida Street and overlooks the leafy Plaza San Martín. **Pros:** elegant lobby; clean rooms; every area of the building offers a unique and fascinating view of the city. **Cons:** the main lobby is small and often gets crowded; check-in can be a lengthy process, especially now that it has become a popular stop for cruise-ship passengers; rooms aren't huge. ✉ *Florida 1005, Centro* ☎ *11/4318–3000, 800/228–9290 in U.S.* 🌐 *www.marriott.com* *270 rooms, 48 suites* *In-room: safe, Internet. In-hotel: restaurant, bar, pool, gym* *Breakfast* Ⓜ *C to San Martín* ✣ *1:D2.*

$$ **NH City & Tower.** This enormous art deco hotel is a throwback to an earlier era; the contemporary rooms have dark-wood floors and color schemes that include bold oranges, reds, and black. **Pros:** old-school feel brings you back to another period in Buenos Aires' history; amazing views from the roof. **Cons:** despite its downtown location, feels isolated from other attractions; area can be sketchy at night. ✉ *Bolívar 160, Centro* ☎ *11/4121–6464* 🌐 *www.nh-hotels.com* *369 rooms* *In-room: safe, Internet, Wi-Fi. In-hotel: restaurant, bar, pool, gym* *Breakfast* Ⓜ *A to Perú, E to Bolívar* ✣ *1:D5.*

$$ Fodor's Choice ★ **Rooney's Boutique Hotel.** The former boarding house on the third floor of a century-old building is evocative of French elegance, such that one would expect to find Marie Antoinette herself lolling about in the teal living area or in one of the guest rooms, all outfitted in unique pieces of antique, refurbished furniture. **Pros:** the hotel clears out one of the parlors for complimentary, nightly tango lessons. **Cons:** the location smack in the Centro near historic sites means forgoing a relaxed, neighborhood feel. ✉ *Sarmiento 1775, Centro* ☎ *11/5252–5060* 🌐 *www.rooneysboutiquehotel.com* *14 rooms* *In-room: a/c, safe, Wi-Fi. In-hotel: bar* *Breakfast* Ⓜ *B to Callao* ✣ *1:B4.*

$$$$ Fodor's Choice ★ **Sofitel Buenos Aires.** Built in 1929 by a Yugoslavian shipping magnate, the tower was the tallest building in the city for some years; left to disrepair, it was restored and renovated by Sofitel in 2003, and is now one of the classiest hotels in Buenos Aires, known for its understated elegance with French flair. **Pros:** on a quiet, swanky street lined with art galleries; lovely beds and amenities. **Cons:** the lobby can get crowded and noisy during receptions and art-gallery exhibition openings. ✉ *Arroyo 841, Centro* ☎ *11/4131–0000* 🌐 *www.sofitelbuenosaires.com.ar* *115 rooms, 28 suites* *In-room: safe, Internet, Wi-Fi. In-hotel: restaurant, bar, pool, gym, spa, parking* Ⓜ *C to San Martin* ✣ *1:D2.*

PUERTO MADERO

$$$$ Fodor's Choice ★ **Faena Hotel + Universe.** Argentine fashion impresario Alan Faena and famed French architect Philippe Starck set out to create a "universe" unto itself, and they have succeeded in spades: Rooms are feng-shui perfect, with rich reds and crisp whites, sporting velvet curtains and

2

WHERE SHOULD I STAY?

NEIGHBORHOOD	VIBE	PROS	CONS
Centro and Environs	The center of it all; you have a little bit of everything here, from history (Retiro and Congreso) to modernity (Puerto Madero). It buzzes by day, but is quiet at night.	Close to all major city sights; good transportation options to other parts of the city. If you're only in town briefly, this is your place.	Certain areas are loud, chaotic, dirty, and deserted at night, which can make them dangerous. Don't walk around alone.
La Boca and San Telmo	The oldest barrios in the city; you can get a real feel for how Buenos Aires has operated for the past 100-plus years.	Old-world charm: cobblestone streets, corner cafés, tango music. You're sure to meet some interesting characters in this area.	Streets are dark and not well policed. Limited public transportation options. Locals have been known to target tourists.
Recoleta/Barrio Norte	The most upscale area of the city, home to Argentina's high society. Certain enclaves will convince you you're in Paris.	Proximity to sights in Centro. It's safe, friendly, and chic. Great eating options; high-end stores and art galleries abound.	Prices are sometimes inflated for foreigners. Streets and sights are often crowded with tourists.
Palermo	The biggest neighborhood in the city; it's a mix of old family homes, soaring new towers, and renovated warehouses.	It's the undisputed hot spot of Buenos Aires' gastronomic scene. The city's biggest park, polo field, horse track, and casino are also here.	The über-cool attitude of some locals is a turn-off. Some quality-of-life issues like clean sidewalks have been ignored in recent property developments.
Almagro/Belgrano/Las Cañitas	Quiet, leafy, family neighborhoods home to universities. Las Cañitas is more of a Palermo vibe; Belgrano and Almagro are more no-frills, working class.	Fantastic restaurants and bars in Las Cañitas. Stately, unique homes in Belgrano. In certain areas it's easy to forget you're in a mega-metropolis.	In other areas, the main thoroughfares are packed with noisy city buses and reckless messengers on motorcycles. You're far from downtown action.

Venetian blinds opening electronically to river and city views. **Pros:** quite simply, one of the most dramatic hotels on the planet; luxury abounds; feng shui galore. **Cons:** an "are you cool enough?" vibe is ever-present. ✉ *Martha Salotti 445, Puerto Madero* ☎ *11/4010–9000* 🌐 *www.faenahotelanduniverse.com* *110 rooms, 16 suites* *In-room: safe, Internet, Wi-Fi. In-hotel: restaurant, bar, pool, gym, parking* *Breakfast* ⊕ *1:G5.*

$$ **Hotel Madero.** This slick hotel is within walking distance of downtown as well as the riverside ecological reserve, and is a favorite for visiting British rock stars and fashion photographers. **Pros:** the lobby bar attracts a cool after-office crowd, and has some of the most original cocktails in the city. **Cons:** the gym and pool are in cramped quarters; extra fee for Internet service; no subte service nearby. ✉ *Rosario*

Vera Peñaloza 360, Dique 2, Puerto Madero ☎ 11/5776–7777 ⊕ www.hotelmadero.com ⇨ 169 rooms, 28 suites ♨ In-room: safe, Internet, Wi-Fi. In-hotel: restaurant, bar, pool, gym ⓘ Breakfast ✦ 1:F6.

SAN TELMO

$$ **Axel Hotel Buenos Aires.** Billed as Latin America's first gay hotel, the Axel Hotel Buenos Aires is modeled after the successful original hotel in Barcelona. **Pros:** gigantic outside pool, bar, and deck area offer an upbeat and festive environment; a respite from the chaotic city streets. **Cons:** rooms are small and very close together; the doors and balconies practically sit on top of each other, so privacy is at a minimum. ✉ *Venezuela 649, San Telmo ☎ 11/4136–9393 ⊕ www.axelhotels.com ⇨ 48 rooms ♨ In-room: safe, Wi-Fi. In-hotel: restaurant, bar, pool, gym, parking* Ⓜ *E to Belgrano ✦ 1:D5.*

$ **Gurda Tango Boutique Hotel.** In the heart of San Telmo, the Gurda will give you a glimpse of what life was like at the turn of the 19th century. **Pros:** the young, friendly staff can organize wine tastings with local sommeliers and tango lessons. **Cons:** the entrance is right on a busy street full of buses; the restaurant and bar are noisy. ✉ *Defensa 1521, San Telmo ☎ 11/4307–0646 ⊕ www.gurdahotel.com ⇨ 7 rooms ♨ In-room: safe, Wi-Fi. In-hotel: restaurant, bar, parking ⓘ Breakfast* Ⓜ *C to Constitucion ✦ 1:C6.*

$ **Hotel Babel.** This 200-year-old former home of late Argentinian president Juan Manuel de Rosas sits on one of the city's most historic streets, exactly nine blocks from the Casa Rosada, in the heart of San Telmo. **Pros:** beautiful and welcoming lobby; only nine rooms, all lovely; guests are greeted with a complimentary glass of Argentine wine upon arrival; local artists display their works throughout the hotel and hold monthly openings. **Cons:** it's an old house: rooms are close together and the open-air patio can mean noise—and sometimes rainwater—outside your door. ✉ *Balcarce 946, San Telmo ☎ 11/4300–8300 ⊕ www.hotelbabel.com.ar ⇨ 9 rooms ♨ In-room: safe, Wi-Fi. In-hotel: bar ⓘ Breakfast ✦ 1:E6.*

Fodor's Choice ★

$$ **La Mansión Dandi Royal.** For a glimpse of early-20th-century high society, look no further than this hotel, where 20 exquisite rooms are decorated with classic wood furnishings and period murals. **Pros:** a tango junkie's heaven; stunning interiors. **Cons:** the surrounding streets are often populated with unsavory characters. ✉ *Piedras 922/936, San Telmo ☎ 11/4361–3537 ⊕ www.mansiondandiroyal.com ⇨ 20 rooms ♨ In-room: safe, Internet, Wi-Fi. In-hotel: bar, pool, gym, spa, parking* Ⓜ *C to San Juan ✦ 1:D6.*

$$ **Moreno Hotel.** A gorgeous art deco building dating back to 1929, the Moreno's architects were posed with the challenge of restoring the 80-year-old site without disturbing its original elements, like mosaic tiling and stained-glass windows; the seven-floor hotel has spacious and sexy rooms, each decorated in a color motif complete with chaise longues, Argentine cowhide rugs, and big fluffy beds. **Pros:** there's a top-notch restaurant and 130-seat theater on-site. **Cons:** some rooms are just steps away from the main lobby and elevator. ✉ *Moreno 376, San Telmo ☎ 11/6091–2003 ⊕ www.morenobuenosaires.com ⇨ 39 rooms*

Fodor's Choice ★

In-room: safe, Internet, Wi-Fi. In-hotel: restaurant, bar, gym, parking *Breakfast* Ⓜ *A to Plaza de Mayo* ⊕ *1:F5.*

RECOLETA AND ALMAGRO

RECOLETA

$$$$ Fodor's Choice ★ **Algodon Mansion.** It is clear in every detail of this hotel, one of the ritziest properties in the city, that a guest's stay was considered through and through: Private concierge services contact each guest ahead of time to begin preparing an itinerary, and, once they arrive, guests are welcomed with a drink, have a butler tend to them throughout their stay, and can request whatever they desire for breakfast. **Pros:** the Algodon brand also operates a vineyard in Mendoza, and each room comes with a complimentary bottle of wine. **Cons:** the draw of the hotel's bars and restaurant means a number of nonguests are in and out. *Montevideo 1647, Recoleta* *11/3535–1367* *www.algodonmansion.com* *10 suites* *In-hotel: restaurant, bar, pool* *Breakfast* Ⓜ *D to Callao* ⊕ *1:C2.*

$$$$ Fodor's Choice ★ **Alvear Palace Hotel.** The Alvear Palace has been the standard-bearer for upscale sophistication since 1932, and is undoubtedly the shining star of Buenos Aires' hotel offerings; scores of dignitaries, celebrities, and VIPs have passed through its doors over the years, and they keep coming back for the world-class service and atmosphere. **Pros:** gorgeously appointed rooms; the beautiful spa features therapeutic wave pools, a sauna, and steam rooms. **Cons:** bathrooms are on the small side, owing to the building's age; one of the country's most expensive hotels. *Av. Alvear 1891, Recoleta* *11/4808–2100, 11/4804–7777, 800/448–8355 in U.S.* *www.alvearpalace.com* *97 rooms, 100 suites* *In-room: safe, Internet, Wi-Fi. In-hotel: restaurant, bar, pool, gym, spa, business center* *Breakfast* ⊕ *1:C1.*

$ **Art Hotel.** The aptly named Art Hotel has an impressive ground-floor gallery where exhibits of paintings, photographs, and sculptures by acclaimed Argentine artists change monthly. **Pros:** its bohemian vibe will make you feel like you've joined an artists' colony. **Cons:** rooms are dark and somewhat antiquated. *Azcuenaga 1268, Recoleta* *11/4821–4744* *www.arthotel.com.ar* *35 rooms* *In-room: safe, Internet. In-hotel: bar, pool* *Breakfast* Ⓜ *D to Pueyrredón* ⊕ *1:A2.*

$$$$ **Four Seasons Hotel Buenos Aires.** This exquisite hotel envelops you in a pampering atmosphere that screams turn-of-the-19th-century Paris. **Pros:** classic elegance; good location. **Cons:** pandemonium breaks out when rock stars stay here. *Posadas 1086, Recoleta* *11/4321–1200* *www.fourseasons.com/buenosaires* *116 rooms, 49 suites* *In-room: a/c, safe, Internet, Wi-Fi. In-hotel: restaurant, bar, pool, gym, spa, parking* *Breakfast* ⊕ *1:C2.*

$$ **Hotel Bel Air.** Given the fancy French-style facade, you could mistake the Bel Air for a neighborhood hotel somewhere in Paris. **Pros:** great price and great location on one of the city's poshest streets. **Cons:** the staff is easily distracted; hallways and common areas are cramped. *Arenales 1462, Recoleta* *11/4021–4000* *www.hotelbelair.com.ar* *77 rooms* *In-room: safe, Wi-Fi. In-hotel: restaurant, bar, gym* *Breakfast* Ⓜ *D to Tribunales* ⊕ *1:B1.*

Faena Hotel + Universe

Algodon Mansion

Alvear Palace Hotel

Park Hyatt Palacio Duhau

Sofitel Buenos Aires

Casa Calma

$$$$ Fodor's Choice ★ **Park Hyatt Palacio Duhau.** This gorgeous hotel has upped the ante for elegance in Buenos Aires: Its two buildings, a restored 1930s-era mansion (the palace) and a 17-story tower, are connected by an underground art gallery and a leafy garden, and the rooms are decorated in rich hues of wood, marble, and Argentine leather. **Pros:** understated elegance; great restaurant; the 3,500 bottle Wine Library and "Cheese Room" are unique attractions. **Cons:** a long walk from one side of the hotel to the other; although elegantly decorated, some of the common areas lack warmth. ✉ *Av. Alvear 1661, Recoleta* ☎ *11/5171–1234* 🌐 *www.buenosaires.park.hyatt.com* *126 rooms, 39 suites* *In-room: a/c, safe, Internet, Wi-Fi. In-hotel: restaurant, bar, pool, gym, spa* ✥ *1:C1.*

ALMAGRO

$$ **Abasto Hotel.** This place is *all* about the tango: Suites each have their own dance floor for private lessons, or you can join other guests for nightly tango lessons and a live show. **Pros:** if you're in Buenos Aires to tango, this is your place; large rooms. **Cons:** tango overload is a very real possibility; the furnishings and bedding are a bit tired. ✉ *Av. Corrientes 3190, Almagro* ☎ *11/6311–4466* 🌐 *www.abastohotel.com* *120 rooms, 6 suites* *In-room: Internet, Wi-Fi. In-hotel: restaurant, bar, pool, gym* *Breakfast* Ⓜ *B to Carlos Gardel* ✥ *1:A3.*

PALERMO

$$ **Duque Hotel Boutique & Spa.** This 1920s French-style hotel is fit for a duke, as the name suggests, or even a president, as the mansion is a late Argentine president's former home. **Pros:** shared common area is spacious and inviting; a dining room, business center, enclosed patio, spa, and outdoor terrace with a pool mean guests often just use rooms for sleeping. **Cons:** some rooms are on the small side. ✉ *Guatemala 4364, Palermo Soho* ☎ *11/4832–0312* 🌐 *www.duquehotel.com* *14 rooms* *In-room: a/c, safe, Wi-Fi. In-hotel: restaurant, pool, spa, business center* *Breakfast* ✥ *2:D4.*

$$$ Fodor's Choice ★ **Fierro Hotel.** "The hotel for the gourmand" opened in late 2010 has quickly become choice lodging for visiting executives, film production teams, and all those looking for a five-star stay in a boutique package. **Pros:** the hotel's rooftop pool, heated in winter months, has skyline views of Palermo and neighboring barrios; iPads for rent at the front desk. **Cons:** while rooms are much larger (at least 42 meters) than the city's average hotel rooms, common areas are small. ✉ *Soler 5862, Palermo Hollywood* ☎ *11/3220–6800* 🌐 *www.fierrohotel.com* *27 rooms* *In-room: a/c, Wi-Fi. In-hotel: restaurant, bar, pool, gym, spa* *Breakfast* ✥ *2:B3.*

$$ **Home Hotel Buenos Aires.** Run by Argentinian Patricia O'Shea and her British husband, Tom Rixton, a well-known music producer, Home Hotel oozes coolness and class. **Pros:** impossibly hip and fun; always interesting people staying here. **Cons:** lots of nonguests come here to hang out, reducing the intimacy factor. ✉ *Honduras 5860, Palermo Hollywood* ☎ *11/4778–1008* 🌐 *www.homebuenosaires.com* *14 rooms, 4 suites, 2 apartments* *In-room: safe, Internet, Wi-Fi. In-*

hotel: restaurant, bar, pool, spa 🍴 *Breakfast* Ⓜ *D to Ministro Carranza* ⊕ *2:A3.*

$$$$ 🏨 **Legado Mitico.** Blessed with the city's most gorgeous sitting room, the Legado Mitico transports guests to another era by evoking the legacy of Argentine icons, after whom the hotel's 11 rooms are named. **Pros:** large, exquisitely decorated rooms provide an authentic and unique Argentine experience; on-site security guard. **Cons:** common areas and hallways are very dark; the upstairs terrace disappoints for a property of this quality. ✉ *Gurruchaga 1848, Palermo* ☎ *11/4833–1300* 🌐 *www.legadomitico.com* 🛏 *11 rooms* 👍 *In-room: safe, Wi-Fi. In-hotel: bar, pool, laundry facilities* 🍴 *Breakfast* ⊕ *2:C4.*

$$$ 🏨 **Magnolia Hotel Boutique.** Magnolia Hotel feels like home—that is if home were a high-ceilinged Palermo townhouse from the 1890s, complete with wrapped staircase. **Pros:** an airy, top-floor terrace with large, plush outdoor couches and a grill; homemade baked goods at breakfast. **Cons:** some rooms require walking outdoors. ✉ *Julián Álvarez 1746, Palermo Soho* ☎ *11/4867–4900* 🌐 *www.magnoliahotel.com.ar* 🛏 *8 rooms* 👍 *In-room: a/c, safe, Wi-Fi* 🍴 *Breakfast* ⊕ *2:C5.*

Fodor's Choice ★

$$$ 🏨 **Soho All Suites.** In the heart of Palermo Soho, this smart hotel offers sneak peaks into the backyards of the neighborhood's many private homes, where some of Argentina's coolest artists reside. **Pros:** massage parlor on-site for those urgent post-shopping sores. **Cons:** not well maintained: walls need painting and wood floors need polishing. ✉ *Honduras 4762, Palermo Soho* ☎ *11/4832–3000* 🌐 *www.sohoallsuites.com* 🛏 *21 suites* 👍 *In-room: a/c, safe, kitchen, Wi-Fi. In-hotel: bar, gym, parking* 🍴 *Breakfast* Ⓜ *D to Plaza Italia* ⊕ *1:E5.*

NIGHTLIFE AND THE ARTS

Preparing for an evening out in Buenos Aires has an element of marathon training to it. Rest up with a siesta, chow down some carbs, and drink plenty of fluids before, during, and after. That's right, the key to nightlife porteño style is longevity, where an early night means hailing a taxi at 6 am. Good times lie ahead at a glossy cocktail bar, an old-school jazz café, a classic tango haunt, or on a packed dance floor. Whatever your preferences are, you'll find a space that suits.

As an increasing number of expatriate-run bars flourish in Palermo and San Telmo, with them come happy hours starting at around 9 pm that often stretch way beyond an hour. Downtown drinking establishments kick off even earlier to lure workers to part with hard-earned pesos, spawning the Wednesday "after-office" across the city, which is now a nightlife fixture.

Hours are relaxed, but there are general guidelines: theater performances begin around 9 pm and the last movie begins after midnight. Lines to get into popular bars start forming by midnight while clubs aren't buzzing until 4 am. If in doubt, turn up later than you consider reasonable if you're meeting a local; being 30 minutes late is the norm. The subte closes by 10:30 pm and opens at 5:30 am, so taking a cab to and from home is generally a good idea. It's also quicker than waiting for a colectivo bus.

Don't forget your best dancing shoes: nightclubs, like this one in Palermo, are a stylish affair.

CENTRO

COCKTAIL BARS

★ **Dadá.** Cozy and colorful, Dadá has a short but sweet cocktail list and an ideal bar to perch at while sipping one of the classics. With its owners doubling up as bar staff, Dadá attracts an eclectic mix of locals and visitors popping in for dinner, a drink, or both. Grab a booth at the back for extra privacy. ✉ *San Martin 941, Centro* ☎ *11/4314–4787.*

The Kilkenny. A popular pub that spawned a whole street of imitators, the Kilkenny serves surprisingly good Irish food and has Guinness on draft. Celtic or rock bands play every night, entertaining the after-work crowd from nearby offices that comes for the extended happy hour and stays into the small hours. ✉ *Marcelo T. De Alvear 399, Centro* ☎ *11/4312–7291* 🌐 *www.thekilkenny.com.ar/* Ⓜ *C to San Martín.*

Le Bar. Le Bar is a stylish stalwart of Centro's drinking scene. Up the stairs from the cocktail lounge is a clever sunken seating arrangement; farther still is a smokers' terrace. Office workers get the evening started; hot DJs spin sounds until late while it's also a great spot to catch cool local indie bands. ✉ *Tucuman 422, Centro* ☎ *11/5219–8580* 🌐 *www.lebarbuenosaires.blogspot.com.*

DANCE CLUBS

Fodor's Choice ★ **Bahrein.** Sheik—er, *chic* and super-stylish, this party palace is in a 100-year-old former bank. Head straight to the ground floor's Funky Room, where beautiful, tightly clothed youth groove to pop, rock, and funk. The downstairs Excess Room has electronic beats and dizzying wall visuals. Consistently good and popular with North American visitors is Tuesday drum-and-bass night run by local vegetarian DJ hero, Bad Boy Orange. ✉ *Lavalle 345, Centro* ☎ *11/4315–2403* 🌐 *www.bahreinba.com* Ⓜ *B to Alem.*

Cocoliche. Cocoliche enjoys cult status in both the straight and gay communities. Upstairs is a diverse art gallery big on young locals; downstairs, underground house and techno drives one of the city's darkest dance floors, while DJs with huge followings line up to take on the decks. ✉ *Rivadavia 878, Centro* ☎ *11/4342–9485* 🌐 *www.cocoliche.net* Ⓜ *A to Piedras.*

GAY AND LESBIAN

Contramano. It's been around since 1984, when it was the city's most popular and pioneering gay disco. Today Contramano operates more as a laid-back small bar with an older, male-only clientele. Occasionally there's live music and male strippers. ✉ *Rodríguez Peña 1082, Centro* ☎ *No phone* 🌐 *www.contramano.com* Ⓜ *D to Callao.*

LATE-NIGHT BARS

La Cigale. After moving two blocks down the road, La Cigale has undergone a serious upgrade, proving that size does matter. Take advantage of happy hour until 10 pm at its curvaceously seductive first-floor bar which leads to the street-side balcony. Another flight of stairs winds up to the stage, ready and waiting for local indie, jazz, and acoustic bands any night of the week. ✉ *25 de Mayo 597, Centro* ☎ *11/4893–2332* Ⓜ *B to L.N. Alem.*

LIVE MUSIC

ND/Ateneo. This spacious theater and cultural space mainly invites mid-level local bands, showmen, and comedians to entertain you. Get tickets from the box office from 12 pm to 8 pm Monday through Saturday, or through Ticketek. ✉ *Paraguay 918, Centro* ☎ *11/4328–2888* 🌐 *www.ndateneo.com.ar.*

★ **Ultra.** The owners of this dynamic space for art and live music have run an independent record label for more than a decade. On weekends they throw big parties until daybreak, and on most weeknights there's a strong line-up of local bands and even small festivals. ✉ *San Martin 678, Centro* ☎ *11/4312–5605* 🌐 *www.ultrapop-ar.blogspot.com.*

PUERTO MADERO

COCKTAIL BARS

Asia de Cuba. Once *the* spot to be seen sipping Champagne and eating sushi, Asia de Cuba still draws local celebrities, though it's now lost some of its white-hot luster. The candlelight and red-and-black Asian decor set the mood for an exotic evening—by local standards. Grab a booth to watch and be watched. ✉ *Pierina Dealessi 750, Puerto Madero* ☎ *11/4894–1329* 🌐 *www.asiadecuba.com.ar.*

DINNER SHOW

Fodor'sChoice ★ **Rojo Tango.** Five-star food, musicians, choreography, and glamour: you wouldn't expect anything less from the Faena Hotel + Universe. Crimson velvet lines everything from the walls to the menu at the Cabaret, and tables often hold celebs both local and global. The implausibly

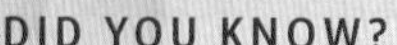

DID YOU KNOW?

The uniquely porteño style of decorative sign art seen here is called *fileteado*. It's generally used in association with well-loved, nostalgia-inducing things, like tango halls, old *collectivos* (city buses), or a realy good *cortado* (coffee).

good-looking troupe puts on a tango-through-the-ages show, which includes jazz-tango, semi-naked numbers, and even the tango version of Roxanne from *Moulin Rouge*. It's worth breaking the piggy bank for. ✉ *Martha Salotti 445, Puerto Madero* ☎ *11/5787–1536* 🌐 *www.rojotango.com.*

SAN TELMO

COCKTAIL BARS

★ **Doppelganger.** With a list of 100 cocktails and an excellent menu to match, this corner bar on the edge of San Telmo is a hidden gem. The music, the choice of books on the shelf, and the quotations in the menu show that the concept has been thought through down to the finest details. But your focus should be on the carefully made martinis, bitters, and vermouth, and having a good time. Take advantage of its happy two hours from 7 to 9 Tuesday through Friday. ✉ *Avenida Juan de Garay 500, San Telmo* ☎ *11/4300–0201* 🌐 *www.doppelganger.com.ar.*

DANCE CLUBS

Rey Castro. Just because this Cuban restaurant-bar gets a little wild on weekends doesn't mean things get out of hand: the bouncers look like NFL players. It's a popular spot for birthday parties and great mojitos. After the nightly live dance show, DJs crank up the Cuban rhythms; you're likely to learn some sexy new moves. ✉ *Perú 342, San Telmo* ☎ *11/4342–9998* 🌐 *www.reycastro.com* Ⓜ *A to Perú.*

GAY AND LESBIAN

Sky Bar. Open to the elements—and the gazes of guests at the hetero-friendly Axel Hotel—the Sky Bar works well by day (Sunday pool parties) and by night (Friday pre-dance sessions) and has quickly become key to the trendy sector of the Buenos Aires gay scene. It's international, very cool, and a six-pack of finely honed abs is a prerequisite in the summer months from October to April. ✉ *Venezuela 649, San Telmo* ☎ *11/4136–9393* 🌐 *www.axelhotels.com.*

LATE-NIGHT BARS

Bar Británico. This traditional corner bar opposite Parque Lezama is one of San Telmo's most iconic spots and still stands more than 90 years after it opened. Day and night it's full of characters and passionate discussions, and serves up drinks and snacks until all hours. Named after the English who helped build the railway lines in nearby Constitución, its original owners were in fact Spanish. ✉ *Brasil 399, San Telmo* ☎ *11/4361–2107.*

La Puerta Roja. Pass through its scarlet entrance and clamber the stairs to this trendy yet friendly bar which often has a decent happy hour. There's a wide selection of spirits and beers on tap, plus a pool table, and a sociable mix of locals and expat regulars. ✉ *Chacabuco 733, San Telmo* ☎ *11/4362–5649.*

Las del BarCo. Get down with the hipsters who spill out onto the San Telmo sidewalk rain or shine when Las del BarCo gets too full. Pull up a love seat and grab a pint, and check out the ever-changing art exhibitions. Fun and frivolous, this hot spot has already attracted a dedicated following and not just for its 300 minutes of happy hour. ✉ *Bolivar 684, San Telmo* 🌐 *www.lasdelbarcobar.blogspot.com.*

LIVE MUSIC

Centro Cultural Torquato Tasso. Here classic trios and quartets share the stage with young musicians performing hip tango and folk sets. There are also milongas on weekends. ✉ *Defensa 1575, San Telmo* ☎ *11/4307–6506* 🌐 *www.torquatotasso.com.ar.*

Gran Café Tortoni. Excellent local musicians put on daily performances of tango classics in the downstairs salon of this famous café, but note that ticket prices can be steep. There's jazz sometimes on weekends, too. ✉ *Av. de Mayo 829, Plaza de Mayo* ☎ *11/4342–4328* 🌐 *www.cafetortoni.com.ar.*

TANGO

Buenos Ayres Club. Rousing live orchestras keep even non-dancers entertained at the nontraditional milongas that are this club's hallmark. La Orquesta Típica El Afronte provides the music for two versions of the same milonga, La Bendita and La Maldita (*11/4560–1514*), on Mondays and Wednesdays, respectively. The vibe is clubby on Sundays for La Milonga Andariega (☎ *11/4362–3296*), while Tuesday's Tango Queer (*11/15–3252–6894, www.tangoqueer.com*) draws both gay and straight dancers looking to escape the confines of more conservative local dance floors. ✉ *Perú 571, San Telmo* ☎ *011/4331–1518* 🌐 *www.buenosayresclub.com.*

★ **La Ideal.** Soaring columns, tarnished mirrors, and ancient chandeliers are part of La Ideal's crumbling Old World glamour, along with a rather pungent musty smell. The classic tearoom hosts milongas organized by different groups in its first-floor dance hall every day of the week. Some are held during the afternoon and evening, others late at night, like the popular Unitango Club (☎ *11/4301–3723*), held on Fridays. Many include live orchestras. ✉ *Suipacha 384, Plaza de Mayo* ☎ *11/4328–7750* 🌐 *www.confiteriaideal.com.*

★ **La Marshall.** A refreshing exception to the sometimes suffocatingly macho world of tango, this is *the* gay milonga. The main night is Wednesday, when a cool set of guys and girls, both gay and straight, look to break with the "he leads, she follows" doctrine. It also runs on Friday at Riobamba 416 (at Av. Corrientes) in the Congreso district. ✉ *Av. Independencia 572, San Telmo* ☎ *11/5458–3423.*

RECOLETA AND ALMAGRO

COCKTAIL BARS

Gran Bar Danzon. If Carrie Bradshaw lived in Buenos Aires, she'd probably frequent this first-floor hot spot where local business sharks and chic internationals sip cocktails and eat sushi by candlelight. It's extremely popular during happy hour, but people stick around for dinner and the occasional live jazz shows, too. The wine list and appetizers are superb, as is the flirting. ✉ *Libertad 1161, Recoleta* ☎ *11/4811–1108* 🌐 *www.granbardanzon.com.ar* Ⓜ *C to Retiro.*

Continued on page 115

The Dance of Buenos Aires

by Victoria Patience

"THE TANGO IS MACHO, THE TANGO IS STRONG. IT SMELLS OF WINE AND TASTES LIKE DEATH."

So goes the famous tango "Why I Sing Like This," whose mix of nostalgia, violence, and sensuality sum up what is truly the dance of Buenos Aires. From its beginnings, tango and its two-four beat marked and reflected the character of Buenos Aires. You may hear strains of tango on the radio while sipping coffee in a café, see high-kicking sequined dancers in a glitzy dinner show, or listen to musicians in a darkened cabaret. But one of the most memorable ways to experience the best of this broody, melancholic, impassioned art form is through dancing it yourself.

DANCING THE TANGO

Many milongas now kick off with group dance classes which usually last an hour or two and cost 15–20 pesos; some lessons are free, though chaotic. These classes are great for getting over nerves and getting you in the mood. However, most *milongueros* (people who dance at *milongas*, or tango dance halls) take tango very seriously and don't look kindly on left-footed beginners crowding the floor. We recommend you take a few private classes first—they can make a huge difference to your technique.

English-speaking private teachers abound in Buenos Aires; classes generally last 1½ hours and prices can range from $20 to $80 a class. Complete beginners should plan on at least three or four classes before hitting a milonga. Many private instructors organize milonga outings with groups of their students (usually for a separate fee). Others even offer a so-called "taxi dance service": you pay for them to dance with you all night. See the end of this feature for a rundown of some of the best options for lessons and milongas.

DANCE STYLES

Tango milonguero, the style danced at milongas and taught in most classes in Buenos Aires, is quite different from the so-called salon or ballroom tango danced in Hollywood movies and in competitions outside Argentina. Ballroom tango is all fixed steps and staccato movements, and dancers' backs arch away from each other in a stiff embrace. Tango milonguero is a highly improvised style built around a variety of typical movements, not fixed steps. Dancers embrace closely, their chests touching. There are other, historical tango styles, but it's

less common to see them on milonga floors. (Confusingly, "milonga" refers both to traditional tango dance halls and to a style of music and dance that predates the tango; though similar to tango, it has a more syncopated beat and faster, simpler steps.)

AT THE MILONGA

Dancers of all ages sit at tables that edge the floor, and men invite women to dance through *cabeceo* (subtle eye contact and head-nodding), a hard art to master. Note that women sitting with male partners won't be asked to the floor by other men.

Dances come in sets of three, four, or five, broken by a *cortina* (obvious divider of non-tango music), and it's common to stay with the same partner for a set. Being discarded in the middle is a sign that your dancing's not up to scratch, but staying for more than two sets with the same partner could be interpreted as a come-on.

To fit in seamlessly, move around the floor counterclockwise without zigzagging, sticking to the inside layers of dancers if you're a beginner. Respect other dancers' space by avoiding collisions and keeping your movements small on crowded floors. Don't spend a long time doing showy moves on the spot: it holds up traffic. Finally, take time to sit some out, catch your breath, and watch the experts.

TANGO TALK

Abrazo: the embrace or stance dancers use; in tango, this varies from hip-touching and loose shoulders to close chests and more fluid hips, depending on style.

Abrazo

Barrida

Barrida: literally, "a sweep"; one partner sweeps the other's foot into a position.

Caminada: a walking step that is the basis of the tango.

Caminada

Canyengue: style of tango dancing with short and restricted steps; from the 1910s and '20s when tight hobble skirts were popular.

Ocho: eight; a criss-crossing walk.

Parada: literally a "stop"; the lead dancer stops the other's foot with his own.

Petitero: measured style of tango developed after the 1955 military coup, when large tango gatherings were banned and the dance relegated to small cafés.

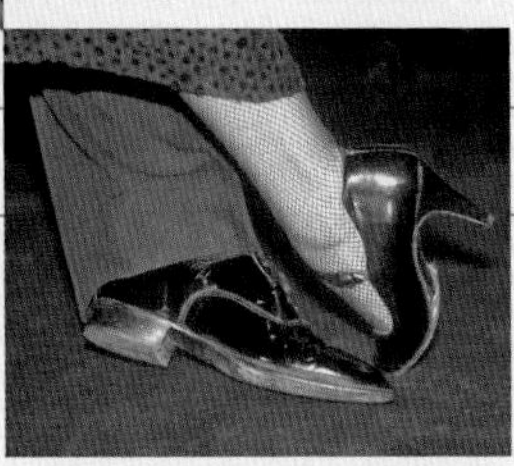
Parada

MILONGA STYLE

Wearing a fedora hat or fishnet stockings is as good as a neon sign reading "beginner." Forget what on-stage tango dancers wear and follow a few basic rules.

Go for comfortable clothes that allow you to move freely; a sure bet are breathable, natural fabrics with a bit of stretch. Be sure it's something that makes you feel sexy. If in doubt, wear black. Avoid showy outfits: it's your footwork that should stand out. It's also smart to steer clear of big buckles, studs, stones, or anything that might catch on your partner. Try not to wear skirts that are too long or too tight. Also a bad idea are jeans or gymwear.

A good example of what to wear for men would be black dress pants and a black shirt; for women, two of many options are a simple halter-neck dress with a loose, calf-length skirt or palazzo pants with a fitted top.

As for your feet: look for dance shoes with flexible leather or suede soles that allow you to glide and pivot. The fit should be snug but comfortable. Note that rubber-soled street shoes or sneakers mark the dance floor and are often forbidden. High heels are a must for women; the most popular style is an open-toed sandal with an ankle strap (which stops them coming off). Black lace-ups are the favorite among men, so leave your two-tone spats at home.

TANGO THROUGH TIME

The tango and modern Buenos Aires were born in the same place: the *conventillos* (tenement houses) of the port neighborhood of La Boca in the late 19th century, where River Plate culture collided with that of European immigrants. The dance eventually swept from the immigrant-quarter brothels and cabarets to the rest of the city; rich playboys took the tango to Paris on their grand tours, and by the 1920s the dance had become respectable enough to fill the salons and drawing rooms of the upper class in Argentina and abroad. In the 1930s, with the advent of singers like Carlos Gardel, tango music became popular in its own right. Accordingly, musical accompaniment started to come from larger bands known as *orquestas típicas*.

Carlos Gardel

By the '40s and '50s, *porteños* (people from Buenos Aires) celebrated tango as the national music of the people, and tango artists lent Evita and Perón their support. The military coup that ousted Perón in 1955 forbade large tango dances, which it saw as potential political gatherings, and (bizarrely) encouraged rock 'n' roll instead. Young people listened, and tango fell out of popular favor.

The '90s saw a huge revival in both traditional *milongas* (dance halls) and a more improvised dance style. Musical offerings now include modern takes on classic tangos and electrotango or *tangofusión*. Even local rock stars are starting to include a tango or two in their repertory. And since 1998, thousands of people from around the world have attended the annual fortnight-long Festival de Tango in Buenos Aires (🌐 *www.tangobuenosaires.gob.ar*), held late winter or spring.

Whether you decide to take in a show or take up dancing yourself, sit down for a classic concert or groove at an electrotango night, there are more ways to experience tango in Buenos Aires than anywhere else on earth.

DID YOU KNOW?

- Tango so horrified Kaiser Wilhelm and Pope Pius X that they banned the dance.
- In 1915, before he was famous, Carlos Gardel was injured in a barroom brawl with Ernesto Guevara Lynch, Che's father.
- One of Gardel's most famous numbers, "Por Una Cabeza," is the tango featured in *Schindler's List, Scent of a Woman*, and *True Lies.*
- The coup of 1930 prompted composers like Enrique Santos Discépolo to write protest tangos.
- Finnish tango has been a distinct musical genre since at least mid-century and is still one of the most popular in Finland; there's even an annual *Tangomarkkinat* (tango festival) in Seinäjoki, complete with the crowning of a Tango King and Queen.

NEXT STEPS

TOURS & HOTELS

If you're serious about the dance of Buenos Aires, get in touch with the Web-based company **Argentina Tango** (🌐 www.argentinatango.com). Run by a British devotee, it offers highly organized, tailor-made tango tours.

SHOPS WITH TANGO GEAR

Head to shoe shop **Comme Il Faut,** for colorful, handcrafted high heels so gorgeous they're worth taking up tango for.

If you'd like high quality and classic designs, check out **Flabella.** At **Tango Brujo,** you'll find a variety of well-made footwear, clothing, how-to DVDs, and other tango merchandise.

Your best bet for milonga-worthy duds is regular casual clothing stores. (For more information, ⇨ see Shoes and Clothing in Shopping.)

SCHOOLS & INSTRUCTORS

Some schools we like are **La Escuela del Tango** (✉ San José 364, Constitución ☎ 11/4383–0466 🌐 www.laescueladeltango.com.ar), **La Academia de Tango Milonguero** (✉ Riobamba 416, Centro ☎ 11/3166–4800 🌐 www.laacademiatango.com), and **Estudio DNI Tango** (✉ Bulnes 1011, Almagro ☎ 11/4866–3663 🌐 www.dni-tango.com).

Private instructors **Ana Schapira** (☎ 11/4962–7922 🌐 http://anamariaschapira.bloog.it), **Claudia Bozzo** of La Escuela de Tango, and **Susana Miller** (🌐 www.susanamiller.com.ar) of La Academia de Tango Milonguero are worth their salt.

The **Academia Nacional de Tango** (🌐 www.anacdeltango.org.ar) runs highbrow seminars on tango culture and history.

MILONGAS

For a novice-friendly floor, try **La Ideal or La Viruta**. **La Nacional** and **Niño Bien** at El Centro Region Leonesa are popular with locals.

The hippest tangueros flock to **La Catedral** and **Parakultural at Salón Canning**.

For breaking the "he leads, she follows" rule, head to **La Marshall**.

For the latest list of milongas, and instructors, look for the English-language publication ***El Tangauta*** at newsstands (you can also download it for free at 🌐 www.eltangauta.com). The website 🌐 www.milmilongas.com has listings of most milongas in town.

(above) Milonga in Buenos Aries.

★ **Milión.** One of the city's most stunning bars spread across three floors, this perfectly restored French-style mansion is packed on weekends for its drinks and cool vibes. The sweet of tooth should try a basil daiquiri. Don't be surprised if the resident black cat drops in for petting. When the back garden fills on balmy summer nights, squeeze onto the marble steps with the beautiful people. ✉ *Paraná 1048, Recoleta* ☎ *11/4815–9925* 🌐 *www.milion.com.ar* Ⓜ *D to Callao.*

DANCE CLUBS

The Basement. This rowdy nightspot downstairs at the Shamrock pub is owned by an Irish father-and-son duo and is popular with expats and young upwardly mobile porteño party people. Stop first for a Guinness at the bar upstairs, where you can yap away in English and easily forget you're in South America. Follow the techno beats to the downstairs dance club, to find Argentina's finest DJs burning up the decks. ✉ *Rodríguez Peña 1220, Recoleta* ☎ *11/4812–3584* Ⓜ *D to Callao.*

GAY AND LESBIAN

Zoom. Half a block from the very cruisey section of Santa Fe, between Avenidas Callao and Coronel Díaz, Zoom offers a good lounge bar, a maze, video cabins, and plenty of dark corners. It can get pretty intense, but there's good security. ✉ *Uriburu 1018, Recoleta* ☎ *11/4827–4828* 🌐 *www.zoombuenosaires.com* Ⓜ *D to Pueyrredón.*

LATE-NIGHT BARS

El Alamo Bar. From the outside, it's only the signs asking patrons to leave quietly that suggest this isn't the demure bar it appears to be. The generous drinks promotions (ladies drink free until midnight Fridays) add substantial rowdiness, and it turns into a proper little party zone on weekends. A sports bar at heart, El Alamo also hosts bikini competitions—just so you know. ✉ *Uruguay 1175, Recoleta* ☎ *11/4813–7324* ⏲ *24 hrs.*

Los Porteños. A traditional Buenos Aires bar with plenty of *fileteado* (colorful, swirly graphic embellishments) and wooden tables, Los Porteños serves coffee and snacks all day and stays open late into the night; it doesn't shut at all on Saturday. It's one block from Recoleta Cemetery and a good option when the dives on Vicente Lopez get to be too much. ✉ *Av. Las Heras 2101, Recoleta* ☎ *11/4809–3548.*

LIVE MUSIC

Clásica y Moderna. It's not just a jazz club but a restaurant and bookshop besides. An older, artsy crowd gathers here for dinner, drinks, philosophy, and live jazz. The program makes good use of their grand piano; singers take on bossa nova, tango, and bolero. ✉ *Av. Callao 892, Recoleta* ☎ *11/4812–8707* 🌐 *www.clasicaymoderna.com* Ⓜ *D to Callao.*

★ **Notorious.** A jazz bar, restaurant, and record shop rolled into one, some of the area's best musicians, such as guitarist Walter Malosetti and vocalist Ibrahim Ferrer Jr., play here often. You can also listen to the club's extensive music collection on the CD players at each table. ✉ *Av. Callao 966, Recoleta* ☎ *11/4813–6888* 🌐 *www.notorious.com.ar* Ⓜ *D to Callao.*

TANGO

La Catedral. Behind its unmarked doors is a hip club where the tango is somehow very rock. There are classes and milongas every evening, although Tuesdays are the most popular. It's a cool night out even if you're not planning to dance. ✉ *Sarmiento 4006, Almagro* ☎ *11/15–5325–1630* 🌐 *www.lacatedralclub.com.*

PALERMO

COCKTAIL BARS

Acabar. This is an offbeat bar in the heart of Palermo Hollywood that's become a big hit, and the lines to get in are only exacerbated by the abundance of board games inside, including giant Jenga. Those who manage to get a table are quickly charmed by the buzz of the place and the easy-going atmosphere. ✉ *Honduras 5733, Palermo Hollywood* ☎ *11/4772–0845* 🌐 *www.acabarnet.com.ar.*

Bar 6. A Palermo Soho institution known for its dangerous happy hour cocktails combo, Bar 6's indifferent waitstaff serve up decent steak sandwiches and an "anti-panic" menu. A central neighborhood meeting point for handsome businessmen and ladies who lunch but not necessarily together thanks to a stylish bar and comfy armchairs, Bar 6 opens for breakfast at 8 am yet morphs into a cool drinking spot by nightfall. ✉ *Armenia 1676, Palermo* ☎ *11/4833–6807* 🌐 *www.barseis.com* ⏲ *Daily 8 am–2 am.*

Isabel. Feel like a star sipping a cocktail under the twinkling ceiling lights, while actually star-spotting if you're up to date with your Argentinian models and polo players. Glamour is the name of Isabel's game, so bling is a must—as is a bottomless wallet. ✉ *Uriarte 1664, Palermo Soho* ☎ *011/4834–6969* 🌐 *www.isabel.bz.*

DANCE CLUBS

Club Aráoz. It may be intimate, but Club Aráoz attracts a serious party crowd. Thursday is block-rocking hip-hop night; Friday and Saturday see DJs spinning rock music and electronic dance music for a relatively laid-back bunch of Buenos Aires youth. ✉ *Aráoz 2424, Palermo* ☎ *11/4833–7775* 🌐 *www.clubaraoz.com.ar.*

★ **Kika.** Right in the heart of Palermo and next door to Congo bar, Kika is much bigger than you'd guess from the outside. Thanks to its funky musical orientation, its two dance floors fill up quickly. The back room sometimes hosts live bands while Tuesdays are all about Hype, an all-in-one electro, hip-hop, indie, and dubstep night that gets students moving till dawn. ✉ *Honduras 5339, Palermo Soho* ☎ *11/4137–5311* 🌐 *www.kikaclub.com.ar.*

Fodor's Choice ★ **Niceto.** One of the city's best venues features everything from demure indie rock to the outrageous and legendary Club 69 on Thursdays (think under-dressed cross-dressers). Check out live bands and dancing in the main room, while something contrasting and chill simultaneously takes place in the back room. ✉ *Cnel. Niceto Vega 5510, Palermo Hollywood* ☎ *11/4779–9396* 🌐 *www.nicetoclub.com.*

GAY AND LESBIAN

Amerika. This enormous gay disco has three floors of high-energy action and shows. Friday and Saturday are fun and frivolous verging on hectic thanks to its one-fee, drink-all-you-can entry. Thursday and Sunday are quieter, with greater emphasis on the music. Amerika remains the city's gay club to check out, and be checked out in, at least once. ✉ *Gascon 1040, Palermo* ☎ *11/4865–4416* 🌐 *www.ameri-k.com.ar.*

LATE-NIGHT BARS

★ **Antares.** Originating in Mar del Plata in 1999, Antares is now a successful national brewer making seven of its own ales, which you can taste in shot-size glasses. The bar attracts a cosmopolitan group of drinkers who keep the spacious bar packed from after-office until the small hours. Service is friendly and efficient; the music's feel-good, and the bar snacks tasty. Also check out a newer establishment in Las Cañitas at Arévalo 2876. ✉ *Armenia 1447, Palermo Soho* ☎ *11/4833–9611* 🌐 *www.cervezaantares.com.*

Bangalore. A pub and curry house in Buenos Aires? Well located, the Bangalore has it all—right down to a blazing log fire in winter. There's limited seating both at the bar and in the tiny restaurant upstairs, but somehow there's hardly ever too much of a wait at the bar. Service is friendly, and there's a wide range of draught beers. Revelers spill out onto the street with their pints in summer. ✉ *Humboldt 1416, Palermo Hollywood* ☎ *11/4779–2621.*

★ **Congo.** Beautiful people—in faded fitted jeans, hipster sneakers, and leather jackets—frequent this hangout post-dinner and pre-club. The back garden is large enough and fun enough to easily convince many would-be clubbers to stick around for another drink or three. Offers up a great cocktail list worth browsing at the lengthy bar. ✉ *Honduras 5329, Palermo Soho* ☎ *11/4833–5857.*

878. One of the original speakeasies that kicked off a spate of followers over the past few years, 878 remains a leader despite now playing it by the book. A fabulous establishment with an extensive drinks list, armchairs to kick back in, and a super-cool clientele, this bar for cocktail lovers remains a classic. ✉ *Thames 878, Palermo Viejo* ☎ *11/4773–1098* 🌐 *www.878bar.com.ar.*

Mundo Bizarro. They've been building their faithful late-night crowd and perfecting cocktails here since 1997, so they've got a magic ingredient or two in terms of B.A. nightlife longevity. Red lights, kitsch artwork, rock-and-roll, and even a pole for dancing provide the backdrop; the rest gets improvised afresh every evening. ✉ *Serrano 1222, Palermo Soho* ☎ *11/4773–1967* 🌐 *www.mundobizarrobar.com.*

Sugar Bar. If cumbia and salsa are becoming a bitter pill to swallow, a trip to Sugar will sweeten up an evening. With an extensive happy hour or three until midnight, this Palermo fixture is run by three expats and attracts a fun-loving crowd of Argentinians and foreigners alike looking for good times and big-game matches under the flattering red lighting. ✉ *Costa Rica 4619, Palermo Viejo* ☎ *11/4831–3276* 🌐 *www.sugarbuenosaires.com.*

LIVE MUSIC

★ **Thelonious Bar.** The best porteño jazz bands (and occasional foreign imports) play at this intimate, upscale spot. Arrive early for a good seat, as it's a long, narrow bar and not all tables have good views; on weekends there are usually two shows per night. ✉ *Salguero 1884, Palermo* ☎ *11/4829–1562* 🌐 *www.theloniousclub.com.ar.*

★ **Virasoro Bar.** This is an intimate art deco venue for local jazz maestros and appreciative audiences. Although the names on the program are only familiar to those on the local circuit, it's a great space and you can get up close and personal with musicians, who draw from a deep well of talent and cover a lot of ground, from improv to standards and experimental. ✉ *Guatemala 4328, Palermo* ☎ *11/4831–8918* 🌐 *www.virasorobar.com.ar* Ⓜ *D to Scalabrini Ortiz.*

TANGO

Fodor's Choice ★ **Salón Canning.** Several milongas call this large dance hall home. The coolest is Parakultural (☎ *11/15–5738–3850* 🌐 *www.parakultural.com.ar*), which takes place late on Monday, Tuesday, and Friday. Reservations are essential on Friday—the dance floor is totally packed by midnight, so get here early, too. Originally an alternative, "underground" milonga, it now attracts large numbers of locals, including longtime expats. ✉ *Av. Scalabrini Ortíz 1331, Palermo* ☎ *11/4832–6753.*

SHOPPING

Whether you're looking for a unique handicraft, a cowhide chair, the latest boutique-vineyard Malbec, a one-off pair of rhodochrosite earrings set in silver, or jeans no one's got back home, you're sure to leave Buenos Aires with your bags full. Ever since Argentina's economic collapse in 2001, designers have had to inject a new level of creativity into their wares in order to survive. Innovation is key, and it can be found on every corner and at every street fair and upmarket boutique.

If you love the hustle and bustle, elbow your way to the stalls at the city's outdoor markets. Many artisans set up around squares such as Plazas Francia, Armenia, and Serrano. On weekends in Palermo Soho, some artisans simply lay out handcrafted leather mate gourds or colorful aguayo hair clips symmetrically on the sidewalk, while Sundays at San Telmo's Plaza Dorrego turn into an outdoor theater show, with living statues and tango dancers jostling for space among the antiques.

CENTRO

CLOTHING FOR MEN AND WOMEN

Ona Saez. The ultrafitted jeans at Ona Saez are designed to be worn with sky-high heels and slinky tops for a sexy night out. The menswear is equally slick, mixing dressed-down denim with cool cotton shirts and tees. ✉ *Florida 789, #203, Centro* ☎ *11/5555–5203* 🌐 *www.onasaez.com* ✉ *Santa Fe 1609, Barrio Norte* ☎ *11/4815–0029.*

Stock Center. The official light-blue-and-white shirts worn by the Argentine soccer team, the Pumas (the national rugby team), and the Leonas (women's hockey team) are bestsellers and make excellent souvenirs from this sporting megastore. Pick up Converse, Nike, Adidas, and Puma clothing and footwear as well as uber-trendy Gola sneakers. ✉ *Corrientes 590, Microcentro* ☎ *11/4326–2131* 🌐 *www.stockcenter.com.ar.*

HANDICRAFTS, SILVER, AND SOUVENIRS

Plata Lappas. Classic silver trays, cutlery sets, tea sets, and ice buckets have been favorites on porteño high-society wedding lists for more than 110 years. Department stores worldwide stock Lappas silverware, but why pay export prices? ✉ *Florida 740, Microcentro* ☎ *11/4325–9568* 🌐 *www.lappas.com* Ⓜ *B to Florida* ✉ *Santa Fe 1381, Barrio Norte* ☎ *11/4811–6866.*

Platería Parodi. This über-traditional store is chockablock with everything a gaucho about town needs to accessorize, all in top-quality silver. There are belt buckles and knives, and the no-nonsense Pampa-style women's jewelry would go great with Gap and Ralph Lauren alike. ✉ *Av. de Mayo 720, Plaza de Mayo* ☎ *11/4342–2207* 🌐 *www.parodijoyas.com.ar* Ⓜ *A to Piedras.*

JEWELRY AND ACCESSORIES

★ **Autoría Bs As.** After browsing the ready-to-wear women's collections by Mariana Dappiano and Vero Ivaldi, head to jewelry and accessories. Necklaces may be made of coiled silver by María Medici or crocheted by Tatiana Pini. Some handbags have been fashioned from car tires, others are crafted from top-quality leather or organic wool. This is one of the few places to pick up a one-of-a-kind Manto Abrigo coat, hand-woven in luminous colors in the north of Argentina. ✉ *Suipacha 1025, Microcentro* ☎ *11/5252–2474* 🌐 *www.autoriabsas.com.ar.*

★ **Plata Nativa.** This tiny shop in an arcade is filled with delights for both boho chicks and collectors of singular ethnic jewelry. Complex, chunky necklaces with turquoise, amber, and malachite—all based on original Araucanian (ethnic Argentine) pieces—and Mapuche-style silver earrings and brooches are some of the offerings. Happy customers include Sharon Stone, Pedro Almodóvar, and the Textile Museum in Washington, D.C. ✉ *Galería del Sol, Shop 41, Florida 860* ☎ *11/4312–1398* 🌐 *www.platanativa.com* Ⓜ *C to San Martín.*

LUGGAGE, LEATHER, AND HANDBAGS

Carpincho. Specializing in stippled *carpincho* leather from the capybara—the world's largest rodent, native to Argentina—which has super-soft skin, the main attraction are the gloves, which come in *carpincho* and kidskin and in many lengths and colors, from classic chocolate brown to tangerine and lime. ✉ *Esmeralda 775, Centro* ☎ *11/4322–9919* 🌐 *www.carpinchonet.com.ar* Ⓜ *C to Lavalle.*

Casa López. Don't let the drab storefront put you off: you're as likely to find a trouser suit in floral-print suede as a staid handbag for grandma. A two-part store: the right-hand shop (Number 658) has totes in chestnut- and chocolate-color leather that looks good enough to eat; there are also classic jackets. More unusual fare include fur sacks with wool fringes, black cowhide baguettes, and tangerine purses next door at Number

640. ✉ *Marcelo T. de Alvear 640 and 658, Centro* ☎ *11/4311–3044* 🌐 *www.casalopez.com.ar* Ⓜ *C to San Martín.*

SAN TELMO

CLOTHING FOR MEN AND WOMEN

Un Lugar en el Mundo. A trailblazer of San Telmo cool, this hip little store has been showcasing young designer streetwear for years. Named after the 1992 Argentine movie, the eminently wearable togs include plain but garishly bright dresses by Muda, quirky print tees for guys and girls, and Manos del Uruguay's exquisite knits from across the River Plate. Bolsas de Viaje's vinyl and canvas creations evoke the golden age of air travel, while Mir's satchels and totes in heavily stitched chestnut leather will convince you school is cool. ✉ *Defensa 891, San Telmo* ☎ *11/4362–3836* Ⓜ *C or E to Independencia (walk 6 blocks along Estados Unidos).*

Fodor's Choice ★ **Pablo Ramírez.** His tiny shop front is unadorned except for "Ramírez" printed on the glass over the door—when you're this big, why say more? Recently voted Argentina's best designer by the fashion blogger Scott Schuman, Ramírez's couture doesn't come cheap, but these perfectly tailored numbers are worth every *centavo*. He favors black or white for both waspishly waisted women's wear and slick gent's suits, though a few other shades are creeping in. ✉ *Perú 587, San Telmo* ☎ *11/4342–7154* 🌐 *www.pabloramirez.com.ar* Ⓜ *E to Belgrano.*

CLOTHING FOR WOMEN

María Rojo. This multibrand boutique takes up an entire traditional 1920s San Telmo *casa chorizo*. Each room opens out onto another to end with a kitsch café; all contain simple racks lined with different small designers' wares. Viotti and Arias Dorado do great-value chic cotton tops to accessorize with a pastel-colored Florencia Herraiz bag. The brighter clothes at the back include reversible T-shirts by Monoreversible, to which you could add far-out feet in multicolored Duvas sneakers and Pebeta Teta's mirrored bird-in-hoop earrings. ✉ *Carlos Calvo 618, San Telmo* ☎ *11/4362–3340* Ⓜ *C to San Juan; C or E to Independencia (walk 6 blocks along Carlos Calvo).*

Vicki Otero. With one recent collection focusing on milkmaids gone sexy, this favorite local designer who regularly shows her wares at Buenos Aires Fashion Week combines black and white with the occasional splash of grey to simple, saucy effect. Always with an eye on the feminine, Otero also holds design workshops. ✉ *Carlos Calvo 516, San Telmo* ☎ *11/4300–8739* 🌐 *www.vickiotero.com.ar.*

HANDICRAFTS, SILVER, AND SOUVENIRS

Artepampa. An artist-and-architect duo is behind these singular works, which are inspired by native Argentine art. They use an unusual papier-mâché technique to create boxes, frames, tapestries, and freestanding sculptures. The primitive-looking pieces, a vision of rich rusts and earthy browns, make highly original gifts. ✉ *Defensa 917 and 832, on Plaza Dorrego, San Telmo* ☎ *11/4362–6406* 🌐 *www.artepampa.com* Ⓜ *C to San Juan (walk 6 blocks along Humberto 1).*

Soda syphons for sale in the San Telmo flea market in Plaza Dorrego.

Juan Carlos Pallarols Orfebre. Argentina's legendary silversmith has made pieces for a mile-long list of celebrities that includes Frank Sinatra, Sharon Stone, Antonio Banderas, Bill Clinton, Nelson Mandela, the king and queen of Spain, and Princess Máxima Zorrequieta—a local export now integrated into the Dutch royal family. A set of ornate silver-handled steak knives is the perfect momento of cow country, although it will set you back a few grand. ✉ *Defensa 1039, San Telmo* ☎ *11/4362–0641* 🌐 *www.pallarols.com.ar* Ⓜ *C or E to Independencia (walk 6 blocks along Estados Unidos).*

Fodor's Choice ★ **Marcelo Toledo.** Sunlight and the smell of solder fill the rooms of this old San Telmo house, which doubles up as a store and open workshop for celebrity silversmith Marcelo Toledo. A huge silver mosaic of Evita gives away who Toledo's main muse is: he has created replicas of her own jewelry (and is the only silversmith authorized by her estate to do so) as well as pieces inspired by her. Eva Duarte Perón isn't the only crowd-pleasing politician Toledo's been associated with: a local magnate commissioned cuff links as an inauguration gift to President Obama. His most recent celebrated gift was a mate designed especially for Prince William and his bride Kate Middleton. ✉ *Humberto I 458, San Telmo* ☎ *11/4362–0841* 🌐 *www.marcelotoledo.net.*

JEWELRY AND ACCESSORIES

Abraxas. "Yes" is pretty much guaranteed if you propose with one of the period engagement rings that dazzle in the window of this antique jewelers. If you're not planning on an "I do" anytime soon, surely you can find a home for some art deco earrings with the tiniest of diamonds or a gossamer-fine bracelet? ✉ *Defensa 1092, San Telmo*

☎ *11/4361–7512* 🌐 *www.abraxasantiques.com* Ⓜ *C to San Juan (walk 6 blocks along Humberto I).*

RECOLETA AND ALMAGRO

CLOTHING FOR MEN AND WOMEN

Giesso. A classic gents' tailor for well over a century, Giesso is pulling a Thomas Pink by adding jewel-color ties and shirts to its range of timeless suits and corduroy jackets. A women's line includes gorgeous linen suits and cashmere overcoats. ✉ *Av. Alvear 1882, Recoleta* ☎ *11/4804–8288* 🌐 *www.giesso.com.ar.*

CLOTHING FOR MEN

★ **La Dolfina.** Being the world's best polo player wasn't enough for Adolfo Cambiaso—he founded his own team in 1995, then started a clothing line which he also models for. If you thought polo is all about knee-high boots and preppy chinos, think again: Cambiaso sells some of the best urban menswear in town. The Italian-cotton shirts, sharp leather jackets, and to-die-for totes are perfect for any occasion. ✉ *Av. Alvear 1751, Recoleta* ☎ *11/4815–2698* 🌐 *www.ladolfina.com.*

CLOTHING FOR WOMEN

Cora Groppo. A queen of the porteño haute-couture scene, Cora Groppo made her name designing flirty cocktail dresses with lots of cleavage and short flared or bell-shaped skirts, the main offerings at the Recoleta branch which have taken her designs to Italy and El Salvador. Her lower-key Palermo store sells skinny pants and shorts best accompanied by draped tops, although the whisper-thin cotton jersey most are made of doesn't do much for those without catwalk figures. ✉ *Uruguay 1296, Recoleta* ☎ *11/4815–8516* 🌐 *www.coragroppo.com.*

Evangelina Bomparola. Evangelina takes her clothes very seriously and it's easy to see why. Top-of-the-line materials and detailed attention to the way they hang means that although simple, her designs are far from boring. This is *the* place to come for a little (or long) black dress, but wilder items such as a '60s-style funnel-neck coat or a raw-silk jumpsuit also line the minimalist boutique's racks. ✉ *Alvear 1920, Recoleta* ☎ *11/4802–8807* 🌐 *www.evangelinabomparola.com.*

Marcelo Senra. Irregular natural linen, hand-knit sweaters, cow-hair boots—it's all about texture at Marcelo Senra, a long-established local designer. Loose, flowing evening dresses come in raw silk or satin, offset by belts or chunky wooden jewelry. Handwoven accessories complement the clothes' earthy palette, and are a reason in themselves to visit Senra's Barrio Norte showroom. ✉ *Talcahuano 1133, Unit 3A, Barrio Norte* ☎ *11/4813–2770* 🌐 *www.marcelosenra.com.*

★ **Tramando, Martín Churba.** This store's name means both "weaving" and "plotting": designer Martín Churba is doing plenty of both. Unique evening tops made of layers of draped and pleated sheer fabric adorned with circular beads and irregular embroidery look fit for an urban mermaid. Asymmetrical shrugs, screen-printed tees, and even vases are some of the other woven wonders in the hushed town-house store where art meets fashion. ✉ *Rodríguez Peña 1973, Recoleta* ☎ *11/4811–0465* 🌐 *www.tramando.com.*

Trosman. Highly unusual beadwork is the only adornment on designer Jessica Trosman's clothes. There's nothing small and sparkling about it: her beads are smooth, inch-wide acrylic orbs that look futuristic yet organic. You might balk at the price tags, considering that most of the clothes are made of T-shirting, but that hasn't stopped Tokyo or Paris from stocking her wares. The Palermo outlet carries jeans and tops from past seasons. ✉ *Patio Bullrich Mall, Av. del Libertador 750, Store 1, Recoleta* ☎ *11/4814–7414* 🌐 *www.trosman.com.*

★ **Varanasi.** The structural perfection of Varanasi's clothes is a clue that the brains behind them trained as architects. Find A-line dresses built from silk patchwork and unadorned bias cuts, some of the night-out joys that local celebs shop for. ✉ *Juncal 1280, Recoleta* ☎ *11/4812–4282* 🌐 *www.varanasi-online.com.*

JEWELRY AND ACCESSORIES

Fodor's Choice ★ **Celedonio.** Local boy Celedonio Lohidoy has designed pieces—often with frothy bunches of natural pearls—for Kenzo and Emanuel Ungaro; his work has even been slung around Sarah Jessica Parker's neck on *Sex in the City*. He favors irregular semiprecious stones, set in asymmetrical, organic-looking designs such as butterflies and daisies. ✉ *Castex 3225, Recoleta* ☎ *11/4803–7598* 🌐 *www.celedonio.com.ar.*

Fahoma. This small boutique has enough accessories to make the rest of your outfit a mere formality. Berry-size beads go into chunky but affordable necklaces, and all manner of handbags line the back wall. ✉ *Libertad 1169, Recoleta* ☎ *11/4813–5103.*

Homero. Bright, playful acrylic and raw-looking black rubber offset diamonds and white gold in Homero's innovative necklaces and rings. Other pieces include cross pendants and silver-and-leather cufflinks. ✉ *Patio Bullrich, Av. Libertador 750, Third floor, Recoleta* ☎ *11/4812–9881* 🌐 *www.homero-joyas.com.ar.*

MALLS

Abasto. The soaring art deco architecture of what was once the city's central market is as much a reason to come here as the three levels of shops. Although Abasto has many top local chains, it's not as exclusive as other malls, so you can find relative bargains at the 250 shops such as Ver, Yagmour, and Markova. You can also dress up at Ayres, Paula Cahen d'Anvers, Akiabara, Rapsodia, or the Spanish chain Zara, famous for its cut-price versions of catwalk looks. Levi's, Billabong, Puma, Gola, and Adidas are among the casual international offerings; for something smarter, there's Yves Saint Laurent. Men can hit such trendy shops as Bensimon and Old Bridge or go for the *estanciero* look with La Martina polo wear. Take a break in the top-floor food court beneath the glass panes and steel supports of the building's original roof. The mall also has 12 movie screens and two 3-D ones and hosts the annual Bafici independent international film festival in April; you can also pick up tickets for live entertainment around town at the Ticketek booth near the food court. ✉ *Av. Corrientes 3247, Almagro* ☎ *11/4959–3400* 🌐 *www.abasto-shopping.com.ar* Ⓜ *B to Carlos Gardel.*

Patio Bullrich. The city's most upscale mall was once the headquarters for the Bullrich family's meat-auction house. Inside, stone cow heads mounted on pillars still watch over the clientele. A colonnaded front, a domed-glass ceiling, and steel supports are reminders of another age. Top local stores are relegated to the lowest level, making way for the likes of Lacroix, Cacharel, and Calvin Klein. Urban leatherware brand Lazaro has a shop here, as does Palermo fashion princess Jessica Trosman, whose spare women's clothes are decorated with unusual heavy beadwork. The enfant terrible of Argentine footwear, Ricky Sarkany, sells dangerously pointed stilettos in colors that walk the line between exciting and kitsch. Named after the polo team, edgy but elegant menswear brand Etiqueta Negra has its first store outside the snooty northern suburbs here, while La Martina is giving them fierce competition. When the bags begin to weigh you down, stop for cake at Nucha, on the Avenida del Libertador side of the building. ✉ *Enter at Posadas 1245, or Av. del Libertador 750, Recoleta* ☎ *11/4814–7400* 🌐 *www.shoppingbullrich.com.ar* Ⓜ *C to Retiro (walk 7 blocks up Av. del Libertador).*

SHOES

Guido. In Argentina loafers mean Guido, whose retro-looking logo has been the hallmark of quality footwear since 1952. Try on timeless handmade Oxfords and wing tips; there are also fun items like a tomato-red handbag or a cow-skin tote. Accessories include simple belts and suede wallets. ✉ *Av. Quintana 333, Recoleta* ☎ *11/4811–4567* 🌐 *www.guidomocasines.com.ar.*

Lonte. There's something naughty-but-oh-so-nice about Lonte's shoes. Chunky gold peep-toe heels are a dream, and the outré animal-print numbers are a favorite of local diva, TV presenter Susana Giménez. For more discreet feet there are patent-leather boots or classic heels in straightforward colors. ✉ *Arenales 1272, Recoleta* ☎ *11/4813–3736* 🌐 *www.lonteshoes.com.*

Zapatos de María. María Conorti was one of the first young designers to set up shop in this area, and she's still going strong. Wedge heels, satin ankle-ties, and abundant use of patent leather in pumps and boots are the trademark touches of her quirky designs. Head to the basement at the back of the store for discounted past seasons. ✉ *Libertad 1665, Recoleta* ☎ *11/4815–5001* 🌐 *www.zapatosdemaria.com.ar.*

WINE

★ **Grand Cru.** Incredibly savvy staff, some trained as sommeliers, will guide you through Grand Cru's peerless selection—high-end wines from small vineyards predominate—and they can FedEx up to 12 bottles anywhere in the world. ✉ *Rodríguez Peña 1886, Recoleta* ☎ *11/4816–3975* 🌐 *www.grandcru.com.ar.*

Ligier. Ligier has a string of shops across town and lots of experience guiding bewildered drinkers through their impressive selection. Although they stock some boutique-vineyard wines, they truly specialize in the big names like Rutini and Luigi Bosca, as well as more modest mass-produced wines. ✉ *Callao 1111, Recoleta* ☎ *11/5353–8050* 🌐 *www.ligier.com.ar* Ⓜ *C to San Martín.*

TANGO TO GO

Flabella. Some of the best tango shoes in town, including classic spats, 1920s T-bar designs, and glitzier numbers for men and women are all made to measure and handmade at Flabella. ✉ *Suipacha 263, Microcentro* ☎ *11/4322–6036* 🌐 *www.flabella.com.*

Comme Il Faut. For foxier-than-thou footwear that's kicking up storms on milonga floors worldwide, head to Comme Il Faut; dedicated dancers love its combination of top-notch quality and gorgeous, show-stopping colors like teal or plum, usually with metallic trims. Animal-print suede, fake snakeskin, and glittering ruby take-me-home-to-Kansas numbers are some of the wilder options. ✉ *Arenales 1239, 3M, Barrio Norte* ☎ *11/4815–5690* 🌐 *www.commeilfaut.com.ar.*

Segunda Generación. For custom-made, haute-couture tango wear and accessories, a trip to the family-run Segunda Generación is worth the effort. Also caters to teens and younger. ✉ *Esmeralda 1249, Microcentro* ☎ *011/4312–7136* 🌐 *www.2gen.com.ar.*

Zivals. Recordings by every tango musician under the sun can be found at Zivals. They stock CDs by classic and modern performers, and electro-tango as well as DVDs, sheet music, books, and T-shirts. ✉ *Av. Callao 395, Congreso* ☎ *11/5128–7500* 🌐 *www.tangostore.com* Ⓜ *B to Callao* ✉ *Serrano 1445, Palermo Viejo* ☎ *11/4833–7948.*

PALERMO

CLOTHING FOR MEN AND WOMEN

Antique Denim. Burberry meets Diesel at Antique Denim, where smart, dark jeans are paired with colorful tweed jackets with leather elbow patches. The denim cuts are sharp and tailored, made for cruising the town. ✉ *Gurruchaga 1692, Palermo Viejo* ☎ *11/4834–6829.*

Nadine Zlotogora. Bring a sense of humor to Nadine Zlotogora when you fight your way through giant knitted cacti to rifle through her way-out designs which are playful yet exquisitely put together. Sheer fabrics are embroidered with organic-looking designs, then worn alone or over thin cotton. Even the menswear gets the tulle treatment: military-look shirts come with a transparent top layer. ✉ *El Salvador 4638, Palermo Viejo* ☎ *11/4831–4203* 🌐 *www.nadinez.com.*

CLOTHING FOR MEN

Félix. Waxed floorboards, worn rugs, exposed brick, and aging cabinets are the backdrop to the shop's cool clothes. Beat-up denim, crisp shirts, and knits that look like a loving granny whipped them up are among the many delights. ✉ *Gurruchaga 1670, Palermo Viejo* ☎ *11/4832–2994* 🌐 *www.felixba.com.ar.*

HANDICRAFTS, SILVER, AND SOUVENIRS

★ **Elementos Argentinos.** A fair-trade agreement links this luminous Palermo town house to a team of craftswomen in northwest Argentina who spin, dye, and weave the exquisite woolen goods sold here. Some of the handmade rugs, blankets, and throws follow traditional patterns

Stop in for a browse at stylish Félix in Palermo.

and use only natural pigments (such as *yerba maté* or beetroot juice); others are contemporary designs using brighter colors. Packable souvenirs include sheep-wool table runners, alpaca scarves, and knitted cacti. Ask about designing your own rug. ✉ *Gurruchaga 1881, Palermo Viejo* ☎ *11/4832–6299*.

Tienda Palacio. The slogan here is "Cool Stuff," and it's spot on. From dress-up refrigerator magnet sets of Evita and Che to traditional penguin-shape wine jugs, Tienda Palacio is full of nifty Argentine paraphernalia with a heavy emphasis on kitsch meeting tongue in cheek. Also check out the San Telmo branch at Defensa 926. ✉ *Honduras 5272, Palermo Viejo* ☎ *11/4833–9456* ✉ *Defensa 926, San Telmo* ☎ *11/4361–4325*.

JEWELRY AND ACCESSORIES

Infinit. Infinit's signature thick acrylic eyeglass frames are favored by graphic designers and models alike. If the classic black rectangular versions are too severe for you, the same style comes in a range of candy colors and two-tones. Bug-eye shades and over-sized '70s-inspired designs are other options. ✉ *Thames 1602, Palermo Viejo* ☎ *11/4831–7070* 🌐 *www.infinit.la*.

★ **Metalistería.** Seriously fun jewelry rules at this multidesigner boutique. As well as the silver, steel, and aluminum the store's name suggests, quirky pieces can include leather, wool, cotton, acrylic, laminated newspaper cuttings, or even papier-mâché. ✉ *Jorge Luis Borges 2021, Palermo Viejo* ☎ *11/3151–2777* 🌐 *www.metalisteria.com.ar*.

LUGGAGE, LEATHER, AND HANDBAGS

Doma. Doma's leather jackets are both hard-wearing and eye-catching. Military-style coats in olive-green suede will keep you snug in winter while cooler summer options include collarless biker jackets in silver, electric blue, or deep red. ✉ *El Salvador 4693, Palermo Viejo* ☎ *11/ 4831–6852* 🌐 *www.doma-leather.com.*

Fodor's Choice ★ **Humawaca.** Their innovative bag shapes and funky colors keep this brand at the top of Buenos Aires design icons. The trendiest leather name in town also makes stylish laptop totes and travel bags, which come with a handy magazine-carrying strap. Cowhide is a favorite here, as are lively combinations like milk-chocolate-brown leather and moss-green suede, or electric blue nobuk with a floral lining. Price tags on the bags may make you gulp, but there are wallets, gloves, and pencil cases, too. ✉ *El Salvador 4692, Palermo Viejo* ☎ *11/4832–2662* 🌐 *www.humawaca.com* ✉ *Posadas 1380* ☎ *11/4811–5995.*

★ **Uma.** Light, butter-soft leather takes very modern forms here, with geometric stitching the only adornment on jackets and asymmetrical bags that might come in rich violet in winter and aqua-blue in summer. The top-quality footwear includes teetering heels and ultrasimple boots and sandals with, mercifully, next to no elevation. Ultra-tight jeans and tops are also on offer. ✉ *Paseo Alcorta Mall, Shop 1005, Jerónimo Salguero 3172, at Av. Figueroa Alcorta, Palermo* ☎ *11/0800–888–8862* 🌐 *www.umacuero.com.ar.*

MALLS

★ **Paseo Alcorta.** If you're a serious shopper with only enough time to visit one mall, make it this one. Local fashionistas favor it for its mix of high-end local chains and boutiques from some of the city's best designers. Trendsetters such as Trosman, Jazmín Chebar, and Allô Martinez make cool clothes for women, while María Cher and Chocolate offer more classic chic. The men can hold their own at Etiqueta Negra and Felix. Both girls and boys can break the bank at Tramando or save at Zara. There's even a personal shopper service if it all gets too overwhelming. The international presence is strong, too, with stores from Swarovski, Lacroix, and Cacharel, as well as the usual sports brands. Free transfers from hotels, a classy food hall, and Wi-Fi round off the reasons to come here. ✉ *Jerónimo Salguero 3172, at Av. Figueroa Alcorta, Palermo* ☎ *11/5777–6500* 🌐 *www.paseoalcorta.com.ar.*

SHOES

28Sport. These leather bowling sneakers and boxing-style boots are the heart and, er, sole of retro. All the models are variations on a classic round-toed lace-up, but come with different-length legs. Plain black or chestnut uppers go with everything, but equally tempting are the two-tone numbers—in chocolate and orange, or black with curving white panels, for example. Even the store is a nod to the past, kitted out like a 1950s living room. ✉ *Gurruchaga 1481, Palermo Viejo* ☎ *11/4833–4287* 🌐 *www.28sport.com.*

Divia. Step out in a pair of limited-edition Divias and it doesn't really matter what else you've got on. Designer Virginia Spagnuolo draws inspiration from travels to India, her own vintage shoe collection, and even her cat. The results are leather collages—suede, textured metallic, or patent leathers—in colors such as teal, ruby, or plum. Order à la carte and commission a custom-made pair. ✉ *Armenia 1489, Palermo Viejo* ☎ *11/4831–9090* 🌐 *www.diviashoes.com.*

Josefina Ferroni. Thickly wedged heels and points that taper beyond reason and are some of Ferroni's trademarks. Stacked heels in dark textured leather with metallic trim look like a contemporary take on something Evita might have worn. If all that height brings on vertigo, fear not: the three-tone boots and ballet pumps are pancake-flat. ✉ *Armenia 1687, Palermo Viejo* ☎ *11/4831–4033* 🌐 *www.josefinaferroni.com.ar.*

★ **Lucila Iotti.** Two or three swathes of shockingly bright citrus patent leather combined with thick tapering heels in another flashy color: these shoes are showstoppers. *Sex and the City* stylists certainly agree: they ordered a dozen pairs. The open-toed but arch-covering sandals Iotti favors have a definite whiff of Carnaby Street about them. ✉ *Malabia 2212, Palermo* ☎ *11/4833–0206* 🌐 *www.lucilaiotti.com.*

Mishka. At this longtime Palermo favorite, your feet will go to the ball in high-heel lace-ups, kick some butt in metallic boots, or feel like a princess sporting ballet pumps. Footwear comes in leather as well as in fabrics like brocade; most styles run narrow. Check out the new store in San Telmo (Balcarce 1011). ✉ *El Salvador 4673, Palermo Viejo* ☎ *11/4833–6566* 🌐 *www.mishkashoes.com.ar.*

WINE

Fodor's Choice ★ **Terroir.** A wine-lover's heaven is tucked away in this white stone Palermo town house. Expert English-speaking staffers are on hand to help you make sense of the massive selection of Argentine wine, which includes collector's gems such as the 1999 Angélica Zapata Cabernet Sauvignon. They even arrange private wine-tasting courses to get you up to speed on local vintages: call a week or two before you arrive. Terroir ships all over the world. ✉ *Buschiazzo 3040, Palermo* ☎ *11/4778–3443* 🌐 *www.terroir.com.ar.*

Rogelio Wine Store & Art. Spacious yet not cavernous, this new addition on the Palermo wine scene takes pride in boutique and more commercial labels, offers private tastings, and has a wide range of Champagne on hand for special occasions. ✉ *Gorriti 4966, Palermo* ☎ *11/4897–2186* 🌐 *www.rogeliowinestore.com.ar.*

3

Side Trips

TRIPS TO URUGUAY, BUENOS AIRES PROVINCE, THE COAST, AND IGUAZÚ FALLS

WORD OF MOUTH

"The zodiac plows right into the falls and we became totally drenched. It was over 100 degrees, so it felt great. This ride made the 'Maid of the Mist' at Niagara Falls seem like child's play. "

—jstoll

WELCOME TO BUENOS AIRES' ENVIRONS

Iguazu Fal

TOP REASONS TO GO

★ **The Wall of Water:** Nothing can prepare you for the roaring, thunderous Cataratas del Iguazú (Iguazú Falls). We think you'll agree.

★ **Cowboy Culture:** No visit to the *pampas* (grasslands) is complete without a stay at an *estancia*, a stately ranch house, like those around San Antonio de Areco. Sleep in an old-fashioned bedroom and share meals with the owners for a true taste of the lifestyle.

★ **Colonial Days:** Gorgeous 18th- and 19th-century stone buildings line Colonia del Sacramento's cobbled streets. Many now contain the stylish bed-and-breakfasts favored by porteños looking to escape the big city.

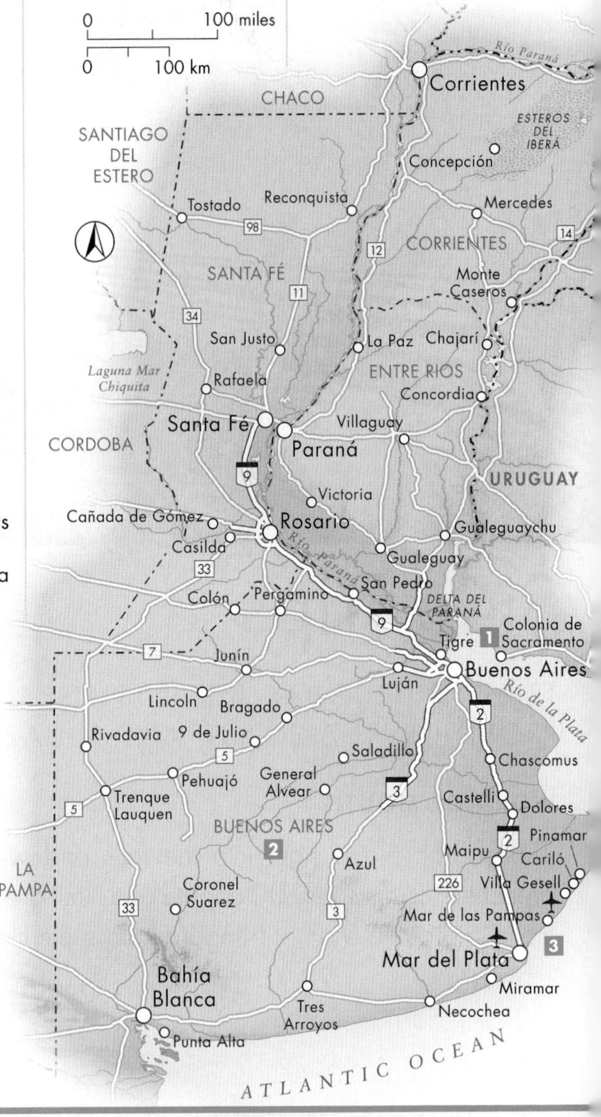

Colonia del Sacramento

3

GETTING ORIENTED

Argentina's famous pampas begin in Buenos Aires Province—an unending sea of crops and cattle-studded grass that occupies nearly one-quarter of the country's landscapes. Here are the region's most traditional towns, including San Antonio de Areco. In southern Buenos Aires Province the pampas stretch to the Atlantic coast, which is dotted with resort towns that spring to life in summer. From Buenos Aires ferries cross the massive Río de la Plata (River Plate) estuary to the small Uruguayan town of Colonia del Sacramento. Suburban trains connect Buenos Aires to Tigre, close to the labyrinthine waterways of the Paraná Delta, explorable only by boat. The delta feeds the Esteros del Iberá, an immense wetland reserve hundreds of kilometers north, in Corrientes Province. On Argentina's northeastern tip, readily accessible by plane, are the jaw-dropping Cataratas del Iguazú.

1 Colonia del Sacramento, Uruguay. It's hard not to fall in love with Colonia. The picturesque town has a six-by-six-block old city with wonderfully preserved architecture, rough cobblestone streets, and a sleepy grace. Tranquility reigns here—bicycles and golf carts outnumber cars.

2 Buenos Aires Province. An hour's drive from Buenos Aires leads to varied sights. The gaucho town of San Antonio de Areco lies northwest of other sites such as the semitropical delta of the Paraná River, near the town of Tigre, and the provincial capital La Plata.

3 The Atlantic Coast. Rolling dunes and coastal pine woods make windy Atlantic beaches peaceful places for some sea air in the low season; in summer, though, they're among Argentina's top party spots. Although they're a good escape from the city's stifle, don't expect sugary sand or crystal-clear waters.

4 Iguazú Falls (Cataratas del Iguazú). The grandeur of this vast sheet of white water cascading in constant cymbal-banging cacophony makes Niagara Falls and Victoria Falls seem sedate. Allow at least two full days to take in this magnificent sight.

Capybara

Updated by Victoria Patience and Jessica Pollack

To hear *porteños* (inhabitants of Buenos Aires) talk of their city, you'd think Argentina stops where Buenos Aires ends. Not far beyond it, however, the skies open up and the pampas—Argentina's huge flat grasslands—begin. Pampean traditions are alive and well in farming communities that still dot the plains that make up Buenos Aires Province.

The best-known is San Antonio de Areco, a well-preserved provincial town that's making a name for itself as gaucho central. You can ride across the pampas and get a taste of country life (and lots of grass-fed beef) by visiting—or staying at—a traditional estancia (ranch).

If you like your natural wonders supersized, take a short flight or a long bus-ride to Iguazú Falls, northeast of Buenos Aires in semitropical Misiones Province. Here, straddling the border between Argentina and Brazil, two natural parks contain and protect hundreds of roaring falls and a delicate jungle ecosystem. The spectacle caused Eleanor Roosevelt to exclaim "Poor Niagara!", but most people are simply left speechless by the sheer size and force of the Garganta del Diablo, the grandest falls of them all.

The sand and sea of the Atlantic coast begin just a few hours south from the capital. It might not be the Caribbean, but there's something charmingly retro about resorts like Mar del Plata. In the summer months, when temperatures in Buenos Aires soar, hordes of porteños seek relief here, and the capital's music and theater scene decamps with them, making these *the* places to see and be seen.

One of South America's most beautiful towns, Colonia del Sacramento, Uruguay, juts out on a small peninsula into the Río de la Plata and is only an hour from Buenos Aires. Here sleepy cobbled streets and colonial buildings are a reminder of days gone by.

PLANNING

WHEN TO GO

Temperatures in Buenos Aires Province rarely reach extremes. Note that some hotels and restaurants in areas popular with local tourists open *only* on weekends outside of peak season—this coincides with school holidays in summer (January and February), winter (July), and the Easter weekend. You'll get great discounts at those that open midweek in winter.

Early November's a good time to visit San Antonio de Areco, which holds its annual gaucho festival then. Like Buenos Aires, it feels curiously empty in January, when everyone decamps to the coast. December through March is peak seaside season, and beach-town establishments are usually booked up; make advance reservations. Beaches get cold and windy in winter (June–September).

Though the falls are thrilling year-round, seasonal rainfall and upstream Brazilian barrages (minidams) can affect the falls' water volume. If you visit between November and March, booking a hotel with air-conditioning and a swimming pool is as essential as taking mosquito repellent.

BORDER CROSSINGS

U.S., Canadian, and British citizens need only a valid passport for stays of up to 90 days in Uruguay. Crossing into Brazil at Iguazú is a thorny issue. In theory, *all* U.S. citizens need a visa to enter Brazil. Visas are issued in about three hours from the Brazilian consulate in Puerto Iguazú (as opposed to the three days they take in Buenos Aires) and cost the peso equivalent of $140 USD. The Buenos Aires consulate also has a reputation for refusing visas to travelers who don't have onward tickets from Brazil.

If you stay in Foz do Iguaçu, travel on to other Brazilian cities, or do a day trip to Brazil by public bus or through an Argentine company, you'll need a visa. There have been reports of getting around this by using a Brazilian travel agent or by using local taxis (both Argentine and Brazilian) that have "arrangements" with border control. Though the practice is well established (most hotels and travel agents in Puerto Iguazú have deals with Brazilian companies and can arrange a visa-less visit), it *is* illegal. Enforcement of the law is generally lax, but sudden crackdowns and on-the-spot fines of hundreds of dollars have been reported.

BRAZILIAN CONSULATES

In Buenos Aires. ✉ *Carlos Pellegrini 1363, 5th fl.* ☎ *11/4515–6500* 🌐 *www.conbrasil.org.ar*.

In Puerto Iguazú. ✉ *Av. Córdoba 264, Puerto Iguazú* ☎ *3757/421–348*.

CAR TRAVEL

Driving is the most convenient—though rarely the cheapest—option for getting around the province. Avis, Alamo, and Hertz have branches in many large towns and cities. At this writing, gas—known as *nafta*—costs around 5.20 pesos a liter, and if you plan to drive extensively, it's worth looking into renting a vehicle running on diesel, which will reduce fuel costs significantly. There are plenty of gas stations in cities and on major highways, but they can be few and far between on rural roads. A useful website when planning road trips is 🌐 *www.ruta0.com*, which calculates distances and tolls between two places and offers several route options.

Be careful on the road. Argentina has one of the world's worst records for traffic accidents, and the busy highways of Buenos Aires Province are often where they happen. January and February are the worst times, when drivers anxious to get to and from their holiday destination speed, tailgate, and exercise illegal maneuvers even more alarmingly than usual. If you're driving, do so very defensively and avoid traveling on Friday and Sunday, when traffic is worst.

Expressways and interprovincial routes tend to be atrociously signposted, so take a map. Getting a GPS-equipped rental car costs an extra 35 pesos or so per day: devices usually work well in cities, but the calibration is often a couple of hundred yards off in rural areas. Major routes are usually privately owned, which means frequent tolls. There are sometimes alternative roads to use, but they're generally smaller, slower, and in poor condition. On main roads the speed limit is 80 kph (50 mph), while on highways it's 130 kph (80 mph), though Argentinean drivers rarely pay heed to this.

SAFETY

Provincial towns like San Antonio de Areco and Colonia del Sacramento in Uruguay are usually extremely safe, and the areas visited by tourists are well patrolled.

Puerto Iguazú is fairly quiet in itself, but mugging and theft are common in nearby Foz do Iguaçu in Brazil, especially at night, when its streets are deserted. Worse yet is neighboring Ciudad del Este in Paraguay, where gun crime is a problem. Avoid the area near the border.

Taxi drivers are usually honest, and are less likely to rip you off than the transport services arranged by top hotels. All the same, locals recommend that unaccompanied women phone for taxis late at night rather than hailing them on the street. The police in the provinces have an iffy reputation: at worst, horribly corrupt, and at best, rather inefficient. Don't count on support, sympathy, or much else from them if you're the victim of a crime.

Argentina Emergency Services Ambulance ☎ *107.* **Fire** ☎ *100.* **Police** ☎ *101.*

Brazil Emergency Services General Emergencies ☎ *199.* **Ambulance** ☎ *192.* **Fire** ☎ *193.* **Police** ☎ *194.*

Uruguay Emergency Services General Emergencies ☎ *911.* **Ambulance** ☎ *105.* **Fire** ☎ *104.* **Police** ☎ *109.* **Policía Caminera (Highway Patrol)** ☎ *108.*

MONEY MATTERS

Argentine currency is accepted everywhere in Colonia, Uruguay—have an idea of the exchange rate to avoid overcharging. Not changing money? Use Argentine pesos for small transactions; hotels give better rates for dollars. Avoid exchanging at the ferry terminal, as the commission's often high.

Uruguayan bills come in denominations of 20, 50, 100, 200, 500, 1,000, and 2,000 pesos uruguayos. Coins are available in 1, 2, 5, and 10 pesos. At this writing, there are 4.50 Uruguayan pesos to the Argentine peso, and 19.50 Uruguayan pesos to the U.S. dollar.

Brazil's currency is the real (R$; plural: *reais* or *reals*). One real is 100 centavos. There are 1, 5, 10, 20, 50, and 100 real notes and 1, 5, 10, 25, and 50 centavo and 1 real coins. At this writing, there are 0.41 reais to the Argentine peso, and 1.75 reais to the U.S. dollar.

HOTEL AND RESTAURANT COSTS

Hotels and restaurants in Colonia list prices in U.S. dollars.

WHAT IT COSTS IN U.S. DOLLARS				
	$	$$	$$$	$$$$
Restaurants	$8 and under	$9–$12	$13–16	over $16
Hotels	$80 and under	$81–$130	$131–$200	over $200

Restaurant prices are based on the median main course price at dinner. Hotel prices are for two people in a standard double room in high season.

COLONIA DEL SACRAMENTO, URUGUAY

The peaceful cobbled streets of Colonia are just over the Río de la Plata from Buenos Aires, but they seem a world away. Founded in 1680, the city was subject to a long series of wars and pacts between Spain and Portugal, which eventually gave up its claim. Its many tiny museums are dedicated to the story of its tumultuous history.

The best activity in Colonia, however, is walking through its *Barrio Histórico* (Old Town), a UNESCO World Heritage Site. Porteños come to Colonia for romantic getaways or a break from the city. If you like to keep busy on your travels, a late-morning arrival and early-evening departure gives you plenty of time to see the sights and wander at will. To really relax or see the city at its own pace, consider spending the night in one of its many colonial-style bed-and-breakfasts: this offsets travel costs and time and makes a visit here far more rewarding.

GETTING HERE AND AROUND

Hydrofoils and ferries cross the Río de la Plata between Buenos Aires and Uruguay several times a day. Boats often sell out, particularly on summer weekends, so book tickets at least a few days ahead. The two competing companies that operate services—Buquebus and Colonia Express—often wage a reduced rates war in the low season.

Buquebus provides two kinds of service for passengers and cars: the quickest crossing takes an hour by hydrofoil (190 pesos one-way, three daily services in each direction), and the slower ferry takes around three hours (130 pesos, two daily services). The Buquebus terminal is at the northern end of Puerto Madero at the intersection of Avenida Alicia M. de Justo and Avenida Córdoba (which changes its name here to Bulevar Cecilia Grierson). It's accessible by taxi or by walking seven blocks from Leandro N. Alem subte station along Trinidad Guevara.

Cobblestones abound in the Old Town section of Colonia del Sacramento, Uruguay.

Colonia Express operates the cheapest and fastest services to Colonia but has only three daily services in each direction. The 50-minute catamaran trip costs 173 pesos one-way or 268 pesos for a same-day return, but there are often huge discounts if you buy tickets in advance. The Colonia Express terminal is south of Puerto Madero on Avenida Pedro de Mendoza, the extension of Avenida Huergo. It's best reached by taxi, but Bus 130 from Avenidas Libertador and L.M. Alem also stops outside it.

The shortest way to the Barrio Histórico is to turn left out of the port parking lot onto Florida—it's a six-block walk. Walking is the perfect way to get around this part of town; equally practical—and lots of fun—are golf carts and sand buggies that you can rent from Thrifty.

ESSENTIALS

Bank Banco República ✉ *Av. Gral. Flores 151.*

Ferry Contacts Buquebus ✉ *Av. Antartida Argentina 821, Puerto Madero* ☎ *11/4316–6500* 🌐 *www.buquebus.com* ✉ *Av. Córdoba 867, Centro.* **Colonia Express** ✉ *Av. Pedro de Mendoza 330, La Boca* ☎ *11/4317–4100 in Buenos Aires, 52/29676 in Colonia* 🌐 *www.coloniaexpress.com* ✉ *Av. Córdoba 753, Centro.*

Medical Assistance Hospital de Colonia ✉ *18 de Julio 462* ☎ *52/22994.*

Rental Cars Thrifty ✉ *Av. Gral. Flores 172* ☎ *52/22939* 🌐 *www.thrifty.com.uy.*

Taxi Taxis Colonia ☎ *52/22920.*

Visitor Info Colonia del Sacramento Tourist Board ✉ *General Flores and Rivera* ☎ *52/23700* 🌐 *www.coloniaturismo.com* ⏲ *Daily 9 am–7 pm* ✉ *Manuel Lobo between Ituzaingó and Paseo San Antonio.*

EXPLORING

Begin your tour at the reconstructed Portón de Campo or city gate, where remnants of the old bastion walls lead to the river. A block farther is Calle de los Suspiros, the aptly named Street of Sighs, a cobblestone stretch of one-story colonials that can rival any street in Latin America for sheer romantic effect. It runs between a lookout point on the river, called the Bastión de San Miguel, and the Plaza Mayor, a lovely square filled with Spanish moss, palms, and spiky, flowering *palo borracho* trees. The many cafés around the square are ideal places to take it all in. Clusters of bougainvillea flow over the walls here and in the other quiet streets of the Barrio Histórico, many of which are lined with art galleries and antiques shops.

Another great place to watch daily life is the Plaza de Armas Manoel Lobo, where you can find the Iglesia Matriz, the oldest church in Uruguay. The square itself is crisscrossed with wooden catwalks over the ruins of a house dating to the founding of the town. The tables from the square's small eateries spill from the sidewalk right onto the cobblestones: they're all rather touristy, but give you an excellent view of the drum-toting *candombe* (a style of music from Uruguay) squads that beat their way around the Old Town each afternoon.

You can visit all of Colonia's museums with the same ticket, which you buy from the Museo Portugués or the Museo Municipal for about $2.50. Most take only a few minutes to visit, but you can use the ticket on two consecutive days.

Casa Nacarello. A colonial Portuguese residence has been lovingly recreated inside this 17th-century structure. The simple bedroom and kitchen furnishings are period pieces, but the real attraction is the house itself, with its thick whitewashed walls and low ceilings. ✉ *Plaza Mayor at Henríquez de la Peña* ⏲ *Closed Thurs.*

Faro. Towering above the Plaza Mayor is the lighthouse, which was built in 1857 on top of a tower that was part of the ruined San Xavier convent. The whole structure was engulfed in flames in 1873 after a lighthouse keeper had an accident with the oil used in the lamp at the time. Your reward for climbing it are great views over the Barrio Histórico and the River Plate. ✉ *Plaza Mayor* ⏲ *Weekdays 1 pm–sunset; weekends 11 am–sunset.*

Museo del Azulejo. A small collection of the beautiful handmade French majolica tiles that adorn fountains all over Colonia are on display at the tile museum, housed in a small 18th-century building near the river. ✉ *Misiones de los Tapies at Paseo San Gabriel* ⏲ *Fri.–Wed. 11:15–4:45.*

Museo Municipal. A sundry collection of objects related to the city's history is housed here. ✉ *Plaza Mayor at Misiones de los Tapies* ⏲ *Closed Tues.*

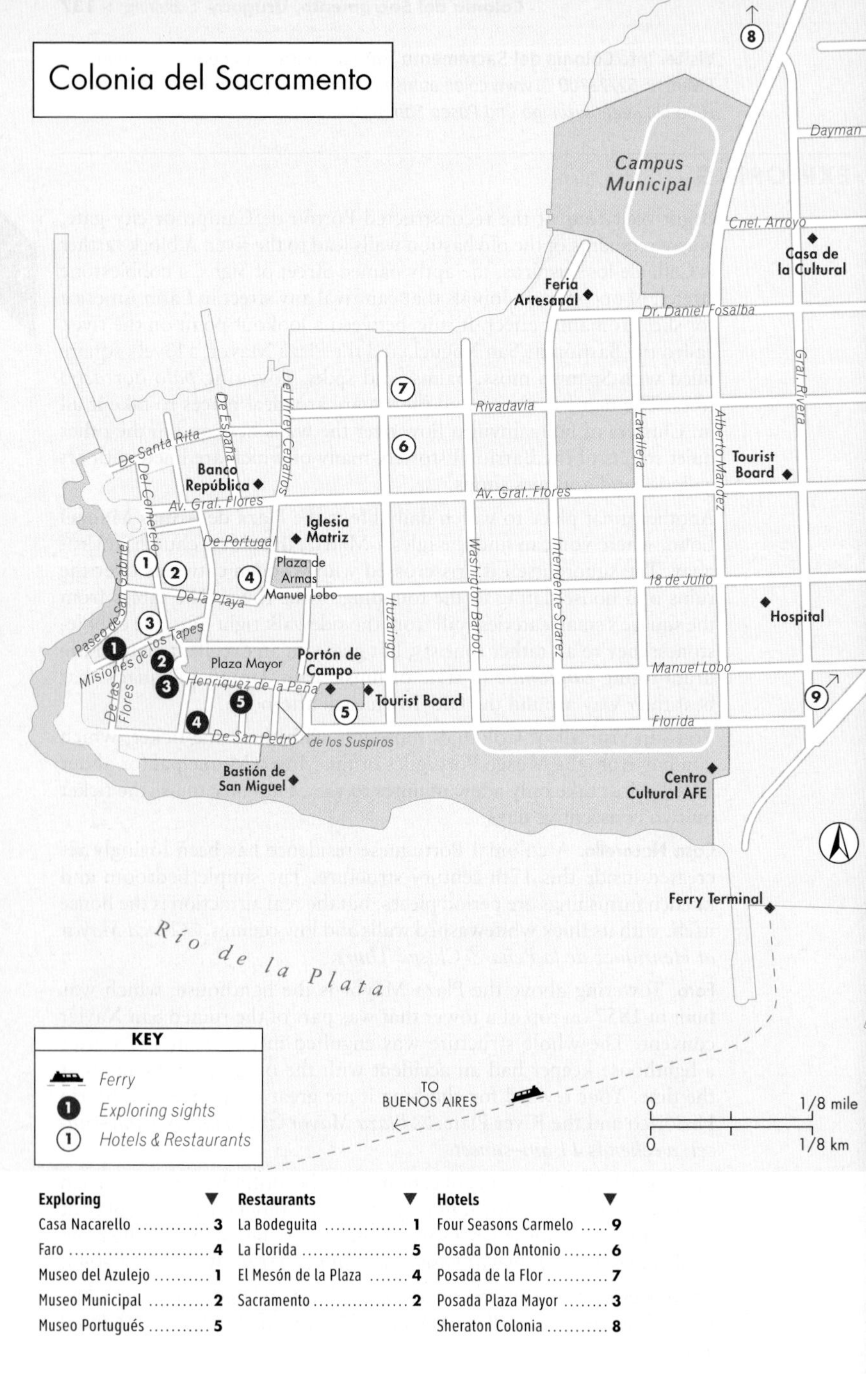

Exploring

Casa Nacarello 3
Faro 4
Museo del Azulejo 1
Museo Municipal 2
Museo Portugués 5

Restaurants

La Bodeguita 1
La Florida 5
El Mesón de la Plaza 4
Sacramento 2

Hotels

Four Seasons Carmelo 9
Posada Don Antonio 6
Posada de la Flor 7
Posada Plaza Mayor 3
Sheraton Colonia 8

Museo Portugués. The museum that's most worth a visit is this one, which documents the city's ties to Portugal. It's most notable for its collection of old map reproductions based on Portuguese naval expeditions. A small selection of period furnishings, clothes, and jewelry from Colonia's days as a Portuguese colony complete the offerings. Exhibits are well labeled, but in Spanish only. ✉ *Plaza Mayor between Calle de los Suspiros and De Solís* ⌚ *Thurs.–Tues. 11:15–4:45.*

WHERE TO EAT

In Colonia prices are displayed in dollars at all hotels and many restaurants. Uruguayan food is as beef-based as Argentine fare, and also has a notable Italian influence. The standout national dish is *chivito,* a well-stuffed steak sandwich that typically contains bacon, fried egg, cheese, onion, lettuce, olives, and anything else you care to throw into it, heavily laced with ketchup and mayonnaise.

$$ SOUTH AMERICAN **El Mesón de la Plaza.** Simple dishes—many steak-based—made with good-quality ingredients have made this traditional restaurant a favorite with porteño visitors to Colonia. The comprehensive wine list showcases Uruguayan vineyards hard to sample anywhere outside the country. Try to get one of the outside tables that sit right on the peaceful Plaza de Armas. ✉ *Vasconcellos 153* ☎ *52/24807* ⌚ *No dinner Mon.*

$$ PIZZA **La Bodeguita.** This hip restaurant serves incredibly delicious, crispy pizza, sliced into bite-size rectangles. The backyard tables overlook the river, and inside is cozy, with warm walls. ✉ *Calle del Comercio 167* ☎ *52/25329* ▭ *No credit cards* ⌚ *Closed Mon., no lunch Tues.–Fri.*

$$$$ ECLECTIC **La Florida.** The black-and-white photos, lace tablecloths, and quaint knickknacks that clutter this long, low house belie the fact that it was once a brothel. It still has private rooms, but it's dining that politicians and the occasional celeb rent them for these days. You, too, can ask to be seated in one, but consider the airy back dining room, which has views over the river. It's hard to say if it's the flamboyant French-Argentinian owner's tall tales that keep regulars returning, or his excellent cooking. Specialties include kingfish, sole, and salmon cooked to order: you can suggest sauces of your own or go with house suggestions like orange-infused cream. ✉ *Florida 215* ☎ *94/293–036* ▭ *No credit cards* ⌚ *Closed Wed., Apr.–Nov. dinner by reservation only.*

WHERE TO STAY

For expanded hotel reviews, visit Fodors.com.

$$ ★ **Four Seasons Carmelo.** Serenity pervades this harmoniously decorated resort an hour west of Colonia del Sacramento, reachable by car, boat, or a 25-minute flight from Buenos Aires. **Pros:** all rooms are spacious bungalows; fabulous, personalized service; on-site activities compensate for distance to sights and restaurants. **Cons:** despite copious netting and bug spray, the mosquitoes can get out of hand; food quality is erratic; noisy families can infringe on romantic getaways. ✉ *Ruta 21, Km 262, Carmelo* ☎ *54/29000* 🌐 *www.fourseasons.com/carmelo* ⇨ 20

bungalows, 24 duplex suites ♿ *In-room: safe. In-hotel: restaurant, golf course, pool, tennis court, gym, spa, children's programs* 🍽 *Breakfast.*

$ ★ **Posada de la Flor.** This colonial-style hotel is on a quiet street leading to the river and is arranged around a sunny courtyard. **Pros:** peaceful location near river and the Barrio Histórico; gorgeous breakfast area and roof terrace; great value. **Cons:** standard rooms are cramped; damp spots on some ceilings; ground-floor rooms open onto the courtyard and can be noisy. ✉ *Calle Ituzaingó 268* ☎ *52/30794* 🌐 *www.posada-delaflor.com* *14 rooms* *In-room: safe* *No credit cards* 🍽 *Breakfast.*

$ **Posada Don Antonio.** Rooms open onto long galleries that overlook an enormous split-level courtyard at Posada Don Antonio, the latest incarnation of a large, elegant building that has housed one hotel or another for over a century. **Pros:** sparkling turquoise pool, surrounded by loungers; two blocks from the Barrio Histórico; rates are low but there are proper hotel perks like poolside snacks. **Cons:** staff are sometimes indifferent; plain, characterless rooms; ill-fitting doors let in courtyard noise. ✉ *Ituzaingó 232* ☎ *52/25344* 🌐 *www.posadadonantonio.com* *38 rooms* *In-room: Wi-Fi. In-hotel: pool, laundry facilities, business center* 🍽 *Breakfast.*

$ **Posada Plaza Mayor.** A faint scent of jasmine fills the air at this lovely old hotel. **Pros:** beautiful green spaces; on a quiet street of the Barrio Histórico; cheerful, accommodating staff. **Cons:** cramped bathrooms; the three cheapest rooms are small and lack the atmosphere of the regular standard rooms; high price of deluxe rooms isn't justified by the amenities. ✉ *Calle del Comercio 111* ☎ *52/23193* 🌐 *www.posadaplazamayor.com* *14 rooms* *In-room: Wi-Fi* 🍽 *Breakfast.*

$$$$ ★ **Sheraton Colonia.** This riverside hotel and spa is a favorite with porteños on weekend escapes. **Pros:** peaceful location with river views from many rooms; great spa; rooms are often discounted mid-week. **Cons:** it's a 15-minute drive or taxi ride north of the Barrio Histórico; lots of noisy kids on weekends; staff sometimes unhelpful. ✉ *Cont. Rambla de las Américas s/n* ☎ *54/29000* 🌐 *www.sheraton.com* *88 rooms, 4 suites* *In-room: safe, Internet. In-hotel: restaurant, bar, golf course, pool, gym, spa* 🍽 *Breakfast.*

BUENOS AIRES PROVINCE

Plains fan out where the city of Buenos Aires ends: this is the beginning of the pampas, which derive their name from the native Quechua word for "flat field." All over this fertile earth are signs of active ranch life, from the grazing cattle to the modern-day gauchos. The region is also noted for its crops, although these days the traditional alfalfa, sunflowers, wheat, and corn have largely been replaced by soy.

While Argentina was still a Spanish colony, settlers gradually began to force indigenous tribes away from the pampas near Buenos Aires, making extensive agriculture and cattle breeding possible. (In 1880, during the bloody Campaign of the Desert, the southern pampas were also "cleared" of indigenous tribes.) By the latter half of the 19th century the region had become known as the grain supplier for the world. From

1850 to 1950 more than 400 important estancias were built in Buenos Aires Province alone. Some of these have been modified for use as guest ranches and provide the best glimpse of the fabled Pampean lifestyle.

SAN ANTONIO DE ARECO

110 km (68 miles) west of Buenos Aires.

There's no better place to experience traditional provincial life in the pampas than this well-to-do farming town off Ruta Nacional 8. Grand estancias dot the land in and around San Antonio. Many of the families that own them, which form a sort of local aristocracy, mix lucrative soy farming with estancia tourism. The gauchos who were once ranch hands now cook up huge *asados* (barbecues) and lead horseback expeditions for the ever-growing numbers of foreign tourists. You can visit one for a day—*un día de campo*—or immerse yourself with an overnight visit.

Porteño visitors tend to base themselves in the town itself, which is becoming known for its B&Bs. The fiercely conservative inhabitants have done a good job of preserving the turn-of-the-20th-century Italianate buildings that fill the sleepy *casco histórico* (historic center). Many contain bars and general stores, which maintain their original fittings; others are the workshops of some of the best craftspeople in the country.

In summer the banks of the Río Areco (Areco River), which runs through town, are teeming with picnickers—especially near the center of town, at the Puente Viejo (Old Bridge), which is overlooked by the open-air tables of various riverside parrillas. Nearby is the Museo Gauchesco y Parque Criollo Ricardo Güiraldes, which celebrates historical gaucho life. During the week surrounding November 10, the *Día de la Tradición* (Day of Tradition) celebrates the gaucho with shows, community barbecues, riding competitions, and a huge crafts fair. It's more fun to visit San Antonio on weekends, as many restaurants are closed Monday–Thursday.

GETTING HERE AND AROUND

To drive to San Antonio de Areco, leave Buenos Aires on Ruta Nacional 9, crossing to Ruta Nacional 8 when it intersects at Km 35 (total tolls of 15.6 pesos). There are more than 20 daily buses from Buenos Aires' Retiro Station to San Antonio; most are run by Nueva Chevallier, and some by Pullman General Belgrano. Each company operates from its own bus stop in San Antonio. Once you've arrived, the best way to get around is on foot, but you'll need a *remis* (radio taxi) to get to most estancias, though some have their own shuttle service.

ESSENTIALS

Bank **Banco de la Nación Argentina** ✉ *Alsina 250, at San Martín, San Antonio de Areco* ☎ *2326/452150* 🌐 *www.bna.com.ar.*

Bus Contacts **Chevallier** ☎ *2326/453–904 in San Antonio de Areco, 11/4311–0033 in Buenos Aires* 🌐 *www.nuevachevallier.com.* **Pullman General Belgrano** ☎ *2326/454–059 in San Antonio de Areco, 11/4315–6522 in Buenos Aires* 🌐 *www.gralbelgrano.com.ar.* **Terminal de Ómnibus Retiro** ☎ *11/4310–0700* 🌐 *www.tebasa.com.ar.*

Medical Assistance **Farmacia Risolino** ✉ *Arellano at San Martín, San Antonio de Areco* ☎ *2326/455–200.* **Hospital Emilio Zerboni** ✉ *Moreno at Lavalle, San Antonio de Areco* ☎ *2326/452–759.*

Taxi **Remis Centro** ☎ *2326/456–225.*

Visitor Info **San Antonio de Areco Tourist Board** ✉ *Bul. Zerboni at Arellano, San Antonio de Areco* ☎ *2326/453–165* 🌐 *www.pagosdeareco.com.ar* ⏲ *Weekdays 8–7, weekends 8–8.*

EXPLORING

Museo Gauchesco y Parque Criollo Ricardo Güiraldes. Gaucho life of the past is celebrated—and idealized—at this quiet museum on a small estate just outside town. Start at the 150-year-old *pulpería* (the gaucho version of the saloon), complete with dressed-up wax figures ready for a drink. Then head for the museum proper, an early-20th-century replica of a stately 18th-century *casco de estancia* (estancia house). Here, polished wooden cases contain a collection of traditional gaucho gear: mates, elaborately decorated knives, ponchos, and all manner of elaborate saddlery and bridlery. The museum is named for local writer Ricardo Güiraldes (1886–1927), whose romantic gaucho novels captured the imagination of the Argentinean people. Several rooms document his life in San Antonio de Areco and the real-life gauchos who

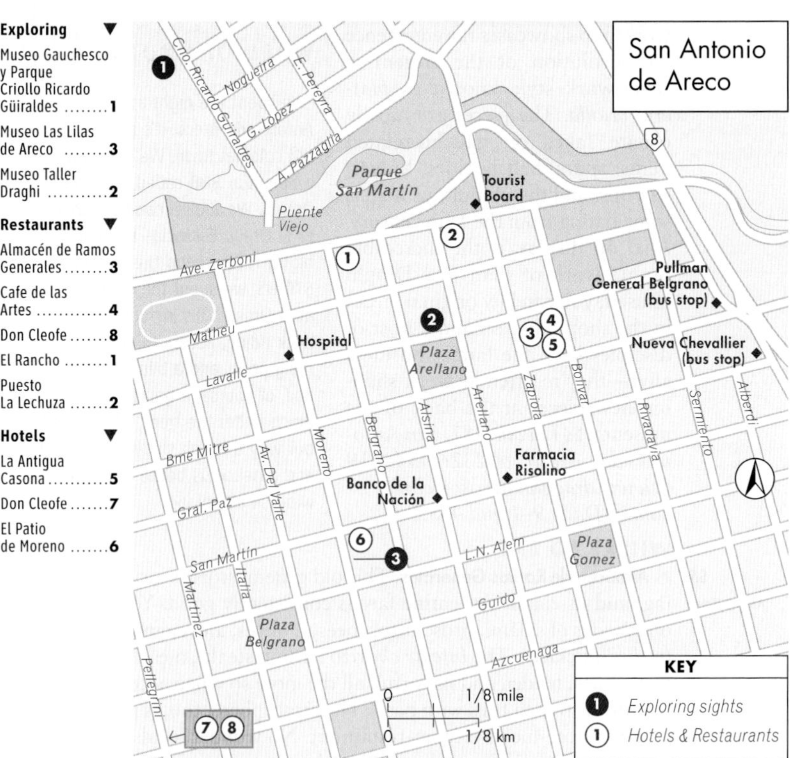

inspired his work. ✉ *Camino Ricardo Güiraldes, San Antonio de Areco* ☎ *2326/455–839* ⏲ *Wed.–Mon. 11–5.*

Museo Las Lilas de Areco. Although iconic Argentinean painter Florencio Molina Campos was not from San Antonio de Areco, the foundation behind this museum felt that this was the most appropriate home for his humorous paintings of traditional pampas life. The works usually depict red-nosed, pigeon-toed gauchos astride comical steeds, staggering drunkenly outside pulperías, engaged in cockfighting or folk dancing, and taming bucking broncos. The collection is fun and beautifully set out but too small to justify the unreasonably high entrance price, which seems more to reflect the no-expenses-spared renovation of the traditional house that contains the museum. Still, your ticket includes coffee and croissants in the jarringly modern café, which also does great empanadas and sandwiches. Behind its curtained walls lie huge theme park–style 3-D recreations of three paintings, periodically revealed. The lively and insightful voice-over explaining them is in Spanish only. ✉ *Moreno 279, San Antonio de Areco* ☎ *2326/456–425* 🌐 *www.museolaslilas.org* 🎫 *20 pesos* ⏲ *June–Sept., Fri.–Sun. 10–6; Oct.–May, Fri.–Sun. 10–8.*

Museo Taller Draghi. San Antonio is famed for its silversmiths, and the late Juan José Draghi was the best in town. This small museum adjoining his workshop showcases the emergence and evolution of the Argentine silver-work style known as *platería criolla*. The pieces are mostly ornate takes on gaucho-related items: spurs, belt buckles, knives, stirrups, and the ubiquitous mates, some dating from the 18th century. Also on display is the incredibly ornate work of Juan José Draghi himself; you can buy original pieces in the shop. His son and a host of disciples keep the family business alive—they're often at work shaping new pieces at the back of the museum. ✉ *Lavalle 387, San Antonio de Areco* ☎ *2326/454–219* 🌐 *www.draghiplaterosorfebres.com* ⏲ *Daily 9–1 and 4–8.*

> **WORD OF MOUTH**
>
> "We spent the night at San Antonio de Areco. It's a lovely old colonial town. We stayed at a beautiful B&B called Paradores Draghi. We took a cab from there to El Ombu Estancia—I would highly recommend this outing. For $70 US, we spent the entire day at El Ombu. This included horseback riding, access to two swimming pools and a billiard table, and, of course, a great parilla lunch under the trees. We worked our way through six types of meat and a delicious bottle of Malbec wine." —alitablanc

WHERE TO EAT

$$ ARGENTINE ✕ **Almacen de Ramos Generales.** This old general store is airy and charming, and its classic Argentine fare is consistently good. You can snack on *picadas* of salami, prosciutto, cheeses, olives, and eggplant "*en escabeche*" (pickled). The *bife de chorizo* (sirloin steak), meanwhile, is perfectly juicy, tender, and flavorful, all the more so when accompanied by wondrous french fries with basil. The atmosphere, too, is just right: it's country-store-meets-elegant-restaurant. No wonder locals and visiting porteños alike vie for tables—on weekends, reservations are essential. ✉ *Zapiola 143, between Lavalle and Sdo. Sombra, San Antonio de Areco* ☎ *2326/456–376* 🌐 *www.ramosgeneralesareco.com.ar* ⏲ *Open daily for lunch and dinner.*

$$ CONTEMPORARY ✕ **Café de las Artes.** The charismatic owner of this intimate restaurant clearly gets a kick out of breaking the rules. Instead of the country style most San Antonio eateries go for, the walls here are painted bordello red and are cluttered with art, crafts, photos, and souvenirs from all over the world. Pasta dishes are the specialty: expect unusual combinations like duck ravioli in a saffron and walnut sauce or tenderloin and carrot ravioli in spiced tomato. Only the wine list comes up short—literally so—though the few options on it are very reasonably priced, as is the food. ✉ *Bolívar 70, San Antonio de Areco* ☎ *2326/456–398* 💳 *No credit cards* ⏲ *Closed Mon.–Thurs.*

$$ CONTEMPORARY ★ ✕ **Don Cleofe.** Three things set Don Cleofe apart: a peaceful location just outside of town; a setting inside a century-old adobe house with buttercup-yellow walls hung with weavings and pottery from northwestern Argentina, where the chef is from; and the food. Forget about asado and *milanesas:* here the stars are *lomo* (tenderloin) in a Malbec reduction and rabbit stew with *papines* (small potatoes native to the Andes). Locals make the 10-block trek here on weekend nights, but consider coming at lunch for the fabulous views over surrounding fields. Note that this restaurant is officially only open Friday through Sunday, but

as it's in a hotel (that's always open), the management has been known to open during off-hours (even for only two people); just call ahead. ✉ *Guido s/n, west of town over old train tracks, San Antonio de Areco* ☎ *2326/455–858* 🌐 *www.doncleofe.com* ▭ *No credit cards* ⏲ *Closed Mon.–Thurs. except by reservation.*

$$ ARGENTINE ✕ **Puesto La Lechuza.** Your first difficult decision is where to sit: the breezy outside tables overlook the river, and the rustic yellow-painted interior is hung with historic pictures of gauchos. Let gaucho-diet principles guide your order—go for the asado or *vacío* (beef on and off the bone, respectively), slow-cooked over hot coals. The little stage where folky guitar players perform in the evenings might look touristy, but locals love the sing-song here as much as visitors. Weekend reservations are essential. ✉ *Arrellano (at the river), San Antonio de Areco* ☎ *2326/452–351.*

3

WHERE TO STAY

For expanded hotel reviews, visit Fodors.com.

$ **Don Cleofe.** Rolling farmland spreads out before this family-run establishment, which is a bit out of town but feels a million miles from everywhere. **Pros:** fabulous home cooking; fresh air and serious peace and quiet within walking distance of the main drag; friendly but nonintrusive owners. **Cons:** small rooms; only the best room has views of the fields; cold in winter. ✉ *Guido s/n, west of town over old train tracks, San Antonio de Areco* ☎ *2326/455–858* 🌐 *www.doncleofe.com* *7 rooms* *In-room: no a/c, no TV. In-hotel: restaurant* ▭ *No credit cards* *Breakfast.*

$$$ ★ **El Patio de Moreno.** You might be in gauchoville, but that doesn't mean you have to renounce creature comforts or slick design: hip hotel chain New Age has turned this 1910 town house into the coolest digs in town. **Pros:** two blocks from main street; beautifully designed rooms and lobby; most bathrooms have double sinks and shower heads. **Cons:** rooms overlooking street can be noisy; kids might be uncomfortable with very adult vibe; service is professional but not personal. ✉ *Moreno 251, at San Martín, San Antonio de Areco* ☎ *2326/455–197* 🌐 *www.patiodemoreno.com* *11 rooms* *In-room: safe, no TV, Wi-Fi. In-hotel: bar, pool, business center* *Breakfast.*

$ **La Antigua Casona.** The dusky pink walls, brass bedsteads, antique wardrobes, and embroidered linens of this small B&B make you feel like you're staying in a Merchant-Ivory film. **Pros:** vintage furnishings; sunny, sheltered patio; two blocks from the main square. **Cons:** high ceilings make some rooms drafty in winter; getting to the bathroom of one room involves crossing the (admittedly pretty) kitchen. ✉ *Segundo Sombra 495, at Bolívar, San Antonio de Areco* ☎ *2326/456–600* 🌐 *www.antiguacasona.com* *5 rooms* *In-room: no TV* ▭ *No credit cards* *Breakfast.*

Continued on page 153

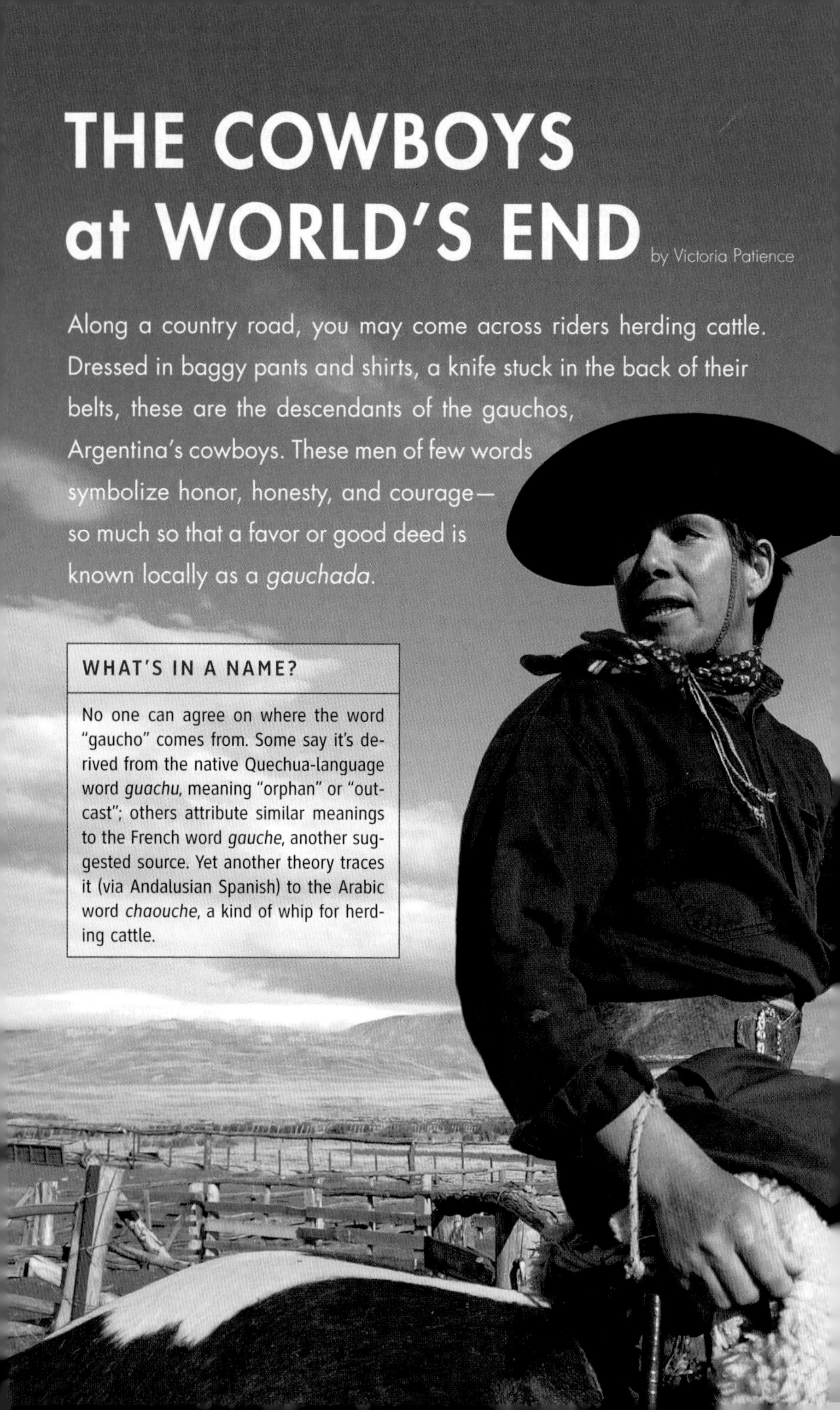

THE COWBOYS at WORLD'S END

by Victoria Patience

Along a country road, you may come across riders herding cattle. Dressed in baggy pants and shirts, a knife stuck in the back of their belts, these are the descendants of the gauchos, Argentina's cowboys. These men of few words symbolize honor, honesty, and courage—so much so that a favor or good deed is known locally as a *gauchada*.

WHAT'S IN A NAME?

No one can agree on where the word "gaucho" comes from. Some say it's derived from the native Quechua-language word *guachu*, meaning "orphan" or "outcast"; others attribute similar meanings to the French word *gauche*, another suggested source. Yet another theory traces it (via Andalusian Spanish) to the Arabic word *chaouche*, a kind of whip for herding cattle.

Gauchos were the cattle-herding settlers of the pampas (grasslands), renowned for their prowess as horsemen. Most were criollos (Argentina-born descendants of Spanish immigrants) or mestizos (of mixed Spanish and native Argentine descent). They lived in villages but spent much of their time riding the plains, much like North American cowboys.

With the establishment of big estancias (ranches) in the early- and mid-19th century, landowners began taking on gauchos as hired hands. The sheer size of these ranches meant that the gaucho's nomadic lifestyle remained largely unchanged, however.

In the 1860s Argentina's president Domingo Faustino Sarmiento encouraged massive settlement of the pampas, and branded gauchos as barbaric, potentially criminal elements. (Despite being of humble origins, Sarmiento as a snob about anything he saw as uncivilized.) Laws requiring travelers to carry passes ended the gaucho's right to roam. Many more than ever signed on as permanent ranch hands; others were drafted into military service, at times becoming deserters and outlaws.

Vindication came in the late-19th and early-20th century, when a wave of literary works like José Hernández's Martín Fierro and Ricardo Güiraldes's Don Segundo Sombra captured the national imagination with their dramatic, romantic descriptions of gauchos and their nomadic lifestyle. The gaucho—proud, brave, and melancholy—has been a national icon ever since.

Gaucho on an estancia near El Calafate, Patagonia, Argentina

GAUCHO GEAR

SOMBRERO
Although a sombrero (flat-crowned, wide-brimmed hat) is the most typical style, conical felt hats (shown), berets, flat caps, and even top hats are also worn.

CAMISA
Traditionally smocked shirt with baggy sleeves. Modern gauchos wear regular long-sleeved cotton shirts.

BOMBACHA
Baggy pants cinched at the ankle; the story goes that after the Crimean War, surplus Turkish-style army pants were sold to Argentina by Britain and France. The fashion caught on: no gaucho is seen without these.

BOTAS
Early gauchos wore rough, rawhide boots with open toes or a flip-flop-style thong. Today, gauchos in colder parts of Argentina wear flat-soled, tapered boots, usually with a baggy pirate-style leg.

PAÑUELO
Large, brightly colored kerchief, worn knotted around the neck; some gauchos drape them under their hats to protect their necks from the sun or cold.

CHAQUETA
Jacket; often kept for special occasions, and usually worn short and unbuttoned, to better display the shirt and waistcoat underneath.

CHIRIPÁ
Before bombachas arrived, gauchos used to wind a large swathe of woven fabric (like an oversize loincloth) over thin, long underpants.

FAJA
A long strip of colorful woven fabric once worn to hold the pants up, now mainly decorative and often replaced by a leather belt. Either way, gauchos stick their knives in the back.

ESPUELAS
Spurs; most gauchos favor those with spiked wheel-like designs.

Gaucho traditionally dressed

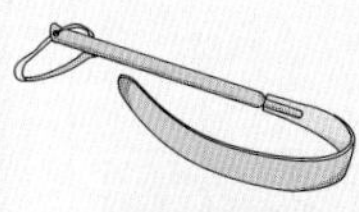

REBENQUE
A short rawhide crop, often with a decorative metal handle.

PONCHO
Woven from sheep's or llama's wool, usually long and often vertically striped. Some colors denote certain provinces.

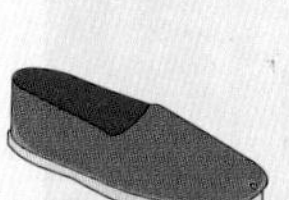

ALPARGATAS
Spanish immigrants in the 18th century popularized flat, rope-soled espadrilles in warmer parts of Argentina. Today, rubber-soled versions are more common.

BOLEADORAS
Gauchos adopted this native Argentinian device for catching animals. It's made of two or three stones wrapped in cowhide and mounted at the end of a cowhide cord. You whirl the boleadora then release it at the animal's legs.

LAZO
A braided rawhide lasso used for roping cattle.

CUCHILLO OR FACÓN
No gaucho leaves home without his knife. Indeed, most Argentine men have one to use at barbecues (early gauchos used theirs for fighting, too). Handles are made of wood or horn, blades are triangular.

SUPER GAUCHOS

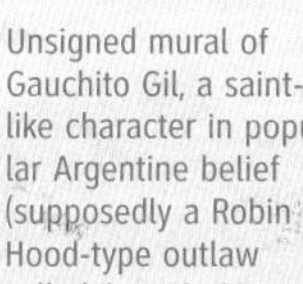

Unsigned mural of Gauchito Gil, a saint-like character in popular Argentine belief (supposedly a Robin Hood-type outlaw called Antonio Mamerto Gil Núñez).

EL GAUCHITO GIL: legend has it that this gaucho from Corrientes Province was hunted down by a sheriff over a woman. He was hung by his feet from a tree but, just before his throat was cut, he predicted that the sheriff would find his son at home mortally ill and only able to recover if the sheriff prayed to Gil. The prediction came true, and the repentant sheriff spread the word. Today, roadsides all over Argentina are dotted with red-painted shrines to this folk saint. Superstitious locals leave offerings, hoping for help with their problems.

MARTÍN FIERRO: the fictional hero of an eponymous 19th-century epic poem written by José Hernández. Fierro is a poor but noble gaucho who's drafted into the army. He deserts and becomes an outlaw. His pride, independence, and love of the land embody the national ideal of what a man should be. Writer Jorge Luis Borges so loved the poem that he started a literary magazine with the same name.

JUAN MOREIRA: a real-life gaucho who married the daughter of a wealthy landowner, provoking the wrath of a jealous local judge. Wrongly accused of various crimes, Moreira became a fugitive and a famed knife-fighter, killing 16 men before eventually dying in a police ambush in 1874 in the town of Lobos in Buenos Aires Province. A 1973 biographical film by arty local director Leonardo Favio was a box-office smash.

UN DIA DE CAMPO

In the late 19th century, well-to-do European families bought huge blocks of pampas land on which to build estancias, often with luxurious houses reminiscent of the old country. The advent of industrial agriculture has led many estancias to turn to tourism for income; others combine tourism with small-scale farming.

The gauchos who once herded cows now have a new sideline shepherding visitors, putting on riding shows or preparing large-scale *asados* (barbecues). You can visit an estancia for a *día de campo* (day in the country) or to stay overnight or for a weekend. There are estancias for most budgets: some are ultraluxurious bed-and-breakfasts, others are homey, family-run farms.

A day at an estancia typically involves a late breakfast; horseback riding or a long walk; a full-blown asado accompanied by Argentine red wine; and afternoon tea. Longer stays at upscale establishments might also include golf or other sports; at working farms you can feed animals or help with the milking. Estancia accommodation generally includes all meals, and although some estancias are close to towns, it's rare to leave the grounds during a stay.

Gaucho on an estancia near El Calafate, Patagonia, Argentina

HORSEMANSHIP

During a visit to an estancia, you may see gauchos demonstrating traditional skills and games such as:

Zapateo Criollo: a complicated, rhythmic, foot-stomping dance.

Jineteada or Doma: rodeo, gaucho-style.

La Carrera de Sortija: riders gallop under a bar from which metal rings are hung, trying to spear a ring on a stick as they pass.

Carrera Cuadrera: a short horseback sprint that riders start from a standstill.

Boleadas and Pialadas: catching an animal using boleadoras or a lasso, respectively.

La Maroma: participants hang from a bar or rope and jump onto a horse that gallops beneath them.

GAUCHO GRUB

When gauchos were out on the pampas for weeks, even months, at a time, their diet revolved around one food—beef—and one drink—mate (a type of tea). Times may have changed, but most Argentinians still consume a lot of both.

MAKING THE MOST OF AN ASADO

Whether you're just at someone's home or out on an estancia, a traditional Argentinian asado is a drawn-out affair. All sorts of meats go on the grill initially, including chorizo sausage, black pudding, and sweetbreads. These are grilled and served before the larger cuts. You'll probably also be served a picada (cheese, salami, and other snacks). Follow the local example and go easy on these starters: there's lots more to come.

The main event is, of course, the beef. Huge, grass-fed chunks of it, roasted for at least two hours over hot coals and flavored with little more than salt. While the asador (barbecuer) does his stuff, it's traditional to admire his or her skills; interfering (criticism, touching the meat, or the like) is not part of this tradition. The first meat to be served is often thick-cut ribs, accompanied simply by a mixed salad and bread. Then there will be a pause for digestion, and the asador will serve the choicest cuts: flank or tenderloin, usually. All this is washed down with a robust red wine and, not surprisingly, followed by a siesta.

Gaucho *asado* (barbecue), Argentina

MATE FOR BEGINNERS

Mate (mah-tay) is a strong tea made from the dried leaves of *Ilex paraguariensis*, known as yerba. It's drunk from a gourd (also called a mate) through a metal straw with a filter on the end (the *bombilla*).

A gaucho drinking mate, at the estancia La Cina, Buenos Aires Provence

Mate has long been a traditional drink for the Guaraní people native to Argentina's northeast. They introduced it to Jesuit missionaries, who learned to cultivate it, and today, most yerba mate is still grown in Misiones and Corrientes provinces. The drink eventually became popular throughout Argentina, Uruguay, and southern Brazil.

Much like tea in England, mate serves as the basis of social interaction: people drink it at any hour of the day. Several drinkers share the same gourd, which is refilled and passed round the group. It's often extended to strangers as a welcoming gesture. If you're shown this hospitality be sure to wait your turn, drink all the mate in the gourd fairly quickly, and hand the gourd directly back to the *cebador* (server). Don't pour yourself a mate if someone else is the cebador, and avoid wiping or wiggling the straw around. Also, you don't say "gracias" until you've had your fill.

WHAT'S IN A MATE?

Caffeine: 30 mg per 8-oz serving (versus 47 mg in tea and 100 mg in coffee)

Vitamins:
A, C, E, B1, B2, B3, B5, B complex

Minerals:
Calcium, manganese, iron, selenium, potassium, magnesium, phosphorus, zinc

Antioxidant properties:
similar to green tea

SERVING MATE

1) Heat a kettle of water to just before boiling (176°F/80°C)—boiling water ruins yerba.

2) Fill ⅔ of the gourd with yerba.

3) Without the bombilla in place, cover the gourd with your hand, and turn it quickly upside down (to get rid of any fine yerba dust that can block the bombilla).

4) For some reason, yerba never sits flat in the gourd; pour some hot water in the empty space left by the slightly slanting yerba leaves. Let the yerba swell a little, cover the top of the bombilla with your thumb, and drive it firmly into the leaves.

5) Finish filling the gourd with water, pouring it in slowly near the bombilla's base. (Some people also add sugar at this point.)

6) Drink all the mate in the gourd (the cebador traditionally drinks first, so the mate isn't so bitter when brewed for others) and repeat Step 5, passing the gourd to the next drinker—and so on—until the yerba mate loses its flavor.

THE ATLANTIC COAST

Southern Buenos Aires Province is synonymous with one thing—*la playa* (the beach). Every summer Argentineans flock to resort towns along the coast, many of which were originally large estates. Now they all hinge around a long *peatonal* (a pedestrians-only street) or central avenue. It can be hard to see the sand in the summer months. However, by walking (or driving) a little farther, you can get some beach action in more agreeable surroundings even in peak season. Locals prefer to be in the thick of things by renting a canvas tent at a *balneario* or *paraje* (beach club); weekly rents are extortionate, but include access to toilets and showers, otherwise nonexistent on Argentine beaches. Happily, buying a drink at their snack bars earns you the same privilege.

Although the weather is usually hot and sunny December through February, the sea is usually bracing, and temperatures drop in the evenings, when the wind picks up. Off-peak, the beaches tend to be deserted, and luxury accommodations are half price or cheaper. Though the weather can get chilly, walks along the windswept sands—when followed by an evening in front of a warm log fire—can be very romantic. Bear in mind, though, that many hotels and restaurants open only on weekends April through November.

GETTING HERE AND AROUND

Comfortable long-distance buses connect Buenos Aires with the Atlantic Coast. Although extra buses are added in January and February, tickets sell out fast. The best service to Mar del Plata is with Flechabus and Nueva Chevallier; there are 10–20 daily departures, and the five-hour trip costs 145–180 pesos. There are numerous daily services to Villa Gesell, the closest town to Mar de las Pampas, with Expreso Alberino and Nueva Chevallier; the five-hour trip costs 125–150 pesos. Local company El Último Querandí runs buses every hour from Villa Gesell to Mar de las Pampas.

Ferrobaires runs comfortable daily trains between Buenos Aires' Estación Constitución and Mar del Plata (150–200 pesos; six hours). Services leave Buenos Aires at 8 am and Mar del Plata at 4 pm, and have three classes: primera, pullman, and super-pullman (the most luxurious).

The Aeropuerto Internacional Mar del Plata (Km 398 on AU2, about five minutes outside the city) is the beach region's main airport. There are two daily flights (around 500 pesos one-way) year-round to and from Buenos Aires on Aerolíneas Argentinas. Note that this is a coveted route in summer, so make reservations early.

Having your own wheels is a great boon on the coast. You can rent cars locally, or drive from Buenos Aires via Autopista La Plata and AU2, a two-lane highway that continues straight to Mar del Plata (tolls of 18 pesos). The four- to five-hour drive is just one long straight highway, though that highway does get very busy in summer. To reach the northern coast, come off AU2 at Dolores, continue 30 km (20 miles) on Ruta Provincial 63 to Esquina de Crotto, then turn onto Ruta Provincial 56. This takes you the 110 km (70 miles) to Pinamar. The Pinamar turn-off also intersects with Ruta Provincial 11, also known as the Interbalnearia, a two-lane coast road that connects Pinamar with Mar de las Pampas.

ESSENTIALS

Airline Contact Aerolíneas Argentinas ☎ *0810/2228-6527* 🌐 *www.aerolineas.com.ar.*

Bus Contacts El Rápido Argentino ☎ *0800/333-1970* 🌐 *www.rapido-argentino.com.* **Expreso Alberino** ☎ *11/4576-7940* 🌐 *www.expresoalberino.com.* **Flechabus** ☎ *11/4000-5200* 🌐 *www.flechabus.com.ar.* **Nueva Chevallier** ☎ *11/4000-5255 in Buenos Aires* 🌐 *www.nuevachevallier.com.* **Plusmar** ☎ *0810/999-1111* 🌐 *www.plusmar.com.ar.* **Montemar** ☎ *2254/404-501.* **Terminal de Ómnibus de Retiro** ☎ *11/4310-0700* 🌐 *www.tebasa.com.ar.*

Train Contact Ferrobaires ☎ *0810/666-8736* 🌐 *www.ferrobaires.gba.gov.ar.*

MAR DE LAS PAMPAS

21 km (13 miles) south of Pinamar on RN11.

The secret is out: this tiny town, once known only to campers and backpackers, has suddenly become the most sought-after vacation spot on the northern coast. Those willing to fork out the immense summer rents are generally rich, nature-loving porteños. They come for the quiet sandy streets, heavily wooded lots, and stylish stone-and-wood cabins that have become Mar de las Pampas' trademark. Most of these are really glorified hotels and include breakfast and maid service.

Huge dunes separate the town from the beach, and despite the fleets of new four-wheel drives that pack the few blocks around Avenida Cruz del Sur and El Lucero, the commercial center, the sands are wide and peaceful. Two smaller towns, Las Gaviotas and Mar Azul, lie south of Mar de las Pampas and maintain an equally peaceful—if less-exclusive—back-to-nature vibe.

GETTING HERE AND AROUND

The nearest long-distance bus station to Mar de las Pampas is in Villa Gesell, a crowded, unattractive resort town 6 km (4 miles) north of Mar de las Pampas. Taxis depart from an official stand in the Villa Gesell terminal and cost around 35 pesos to Mar de las Pampas. Local bus company El Ultimo Querandí also connects the two: their groaning, sand-filled buses leave Avenida 3 in Villa Gesell every hour on the half hour, and return from Mar de las Pampas' main square on the hour.

As Mar de las Pampas has no supermarket or bank (only an ATM), a car is useful for stays of more than a day or two. If you don't fancy the drive from Buenos Aires, you can rent a car in Pinamar or Villa Gesell, then continue along Ruta Nacional 11 until you reach the clearly labeled left-hand turnoff to Mar de las Pampas.

ESSENTIALS

Bank (ATM only) Red Link ✉ *Miguel Cané, between Av. Lucero y El Ceibo, Mar de las Pampas* 🌐 *www.redlink.com.ar.*

Medical Assistance Farmacia Pujol ✉ *In Paseo Sendas del Encuentro shopping center, Santa María between El Lucero and El Ceibo, Mar de las Pampas* ☎ *2255/451–827.* **Hospital General de Agudos** ✉ *Av. 8 at Paseo 124, Villa Gesell* ☎ *2255/462–618.*

Taxi Remises Sol ✉ *Villa Gesell* ☎ *2255/464–377.*

Visitor Info Mar de las Pampas Tourist Board ✉ *Av. Antonio Vazquez at Av. Del Plata, Mar de las Pampas* ☎ *2255/470–324* 🌐 *www.mardelaspampas.info* ⏲ *Dec.–Mar., daily 10–8.*

WHERE TO EAT AND STAY

Mar de las Pampas has several campsites, which the tourist office can direct you to. Be warned that in summer they're often packed to bursting with noisy teenagers. Most other accommodations here are cabins and apart-hotels (a cross between a furnished apartment and a hotel—breakfast is usually offered, as is maid service, and each room has a private kitchen and living room). In January and February, the minimum stay is often one week.

For expanded hotel reviews, visit Fodors.com.

$$ ITALIAN **Amorinda.** Mom and dad are in the kitchen, and their grown-up daughters wait tables, but the real secret to this family-run restaurant are the killer pasta recipes grandma brought with her from Italy. The creamy whiskey-and-tomato sauce packs a punch, but it's not just flavors that knock you over here. Portions of pancetta-and-broccoli or ricotta ravioli easily serve two, while the mammoth lasagna, scattered with tiny meatballs, might fill even more. Their dense tiramisu might be too much to contemplate; the trembling panna cotta in marmalade sauce is easier to deal with. ✉ *Av. Lucero at Cerchunoff, Mar de las Pampas* ☎ *2255/479–750* *Reservations essential* *No credit cards* ⏲ *Closed Mon.–Thurs., no dinner Sun. Apr.–June and Aug.–Nov.*

$ CAFÉ **Viejos Tiempos.** Teahouses abound in this area, but none have more tranquil surroundings than this one, which sits in a beautifully kept garden. In summer hummingbirds hover over the flowers, while tea and cakes are served at heavy wooden tables set with floral-patterned china. Inside, the chintz-and-lace drapes and cloying red cloths look like something your great-grandma would love, but at least the open fireplace keeps things toasty in winter. After years of making some of the best cakes in town, Viejos Tiempos has added (bizarrely) Mexican dishes to the menu, but it's the sweets that remain the main draw here. ✉ *Leoncio Paiva at Cruz del Sur, Mar de las Pampas* ☎ *2255/479–524* *No credit cards* ⏲ *Closed weekdays Apr.–Oct.*

$$$ **Abedul.** Solid stone walls, oak fixtures, and handwoven drapes make the split-level cabins at Abedul very earthy. **Pros:** close to the beach and even closer to restaurants in the town center; lovely wooded grounds; low-key and laid-back but staff still try hard to please. **Cons:** in summer, four-wheel drives roar up and down the road outside; limited nearby grocery stores make the kitchen redundant; beds are on the hard side. ✉ *Santa María between El Lucero and El Ceibo, Mar de las Pampas* ☎ *2255/455–819* 🌐 *www.abedulmardelaspampas.com* *7 cabins*

Mar del Plata isn't just surf and sand; explore some of the unique architecture.

In-room: no a/c, kitchen, Wi-Fi. In-hotel: pool ▭ *No credit cards* ⏲ *Closed weekdays Apr.–June and Aug.–Nov.* 🍽 *Breakfast.*

$$$ ★ **Heiwa.** The sea breezes that ruffle the cotton drapes at this beachfront hotel are almost as calming as the owners' Zenned-out approach. **Pros:** any closer to the sea and you're in it; breakfast is served on the beach; incredible sushi restaurant by the same name and beach bar on-site. **Cons:** far from other restaurants and the center of Mar de las Pampas; dead zone after midnight, aside from the in-house bar; tiny bedrooms. ✉ *Calle 34 at beachfront, Las Gaviotas* ✣ *3 km (2 miles) from Mar de las Pampas* ☎ *2255/453–674* 🌐 *www.heiwa.com.ar* *5 apartments* *In-room: no a/c, kitchen. In-hotel: restaurant, bar, beach* ▭ *No credit cards* ⏲ *No lunch, closed weekdays Apr.–June and Aug.–Nov.* 🍽 *Multiple meal plans.*

MAR DEL PLATA

400 km (248 miles) south of Buenos Aires via AU2.

Come summer, Argentina becomes obsessed with Mar del Plata. The city of 600,000 residents is the country's most popular beach resort—and at least five times as big as any runners-up. Dull gray sand and chilly water may not make for the best beach experience, but in Mar del Plata activities like people-watching, eating, shopping, and clubbing are just as important. The sands are comically crowded in January and February, when there's a carnival-like atmosphere day and night.

The tourist infrastructure hums, with more than 700 hotels and countless eateries. Off-season can get a bit lonely, though the windy sands and almost deserted boulevards feel cinematic. The city becomes literally cinematic each November, when it hosts the Festival Internacional de Cine de Mar del Plata, Argentina's biggest film festival.

Although most hotels are within walking distance of a beach, and the city center is navigable on foot, you'll need a taxi or bus to get to other parts of town, like the port. There are several downtown-area beaches; the summertime action revolves around Playa Bristol. The trendiest strip of sand is south of the lighthouse, but you need a car to get here comfortably.

ESSENTIALS

Bank Banco de la Nación Argentina ✉ *San Martin 2594, Mar del Plata* ☎ *223/491–5477* 🌐 *www.bna.com.ar.*

Medical Assistance Hospital Español de Mar del Plata ✉ *San Luis 2562, Mar del Plata* ☎ *223/410–8810.*

Taxi Tele Taxi Mar del Plata ☎ *223/475–8888.*

Visitor Info Mar del Plata Tourist Board ✉ *Blvd. Marítimo P. Peralta Ramos 2270, Local 51, Mar del Plata* ☎ *223/495–1777* 🌐 *www.turismomardelplata.gov.ar* ⏲ *Jan.–Mar., daily 8 am–10 pm; Apr.–Nov., Mon.–Sat. 8–8, Sun. 10–5.*

EXPLORING

Aquarium Mar del Plata. More of a sea-theme amusement park than a true aquarium, this slick set-up has performing dolphins and sea lions, waterskiing shows, and a 3-D movie theater. Penguins, crocodiles, tortoises, and, yes, some fish, are also present. The place also has its own beach (open December through March) with beach chairs, umbrellas, and a bar. ✉ *Av. Martínez de Hoz 5600, Mar del Plata* ☎ *223/467–0000* 🌐 *www.mdpaquarium.com.ar* 🎫 *85 pesos* ⏲ *Check "horarios" on website before your visit.*

El Puerto. Beaches aside, Mar del Plata's tourist action hinges around the port area, 7 km (4 miles) south of the city center. A cluster of tacky but fun seafood restaurants form the **Complejo Comercial Puerto**. A half-mile walk toward the sea along 12 de Octubre brings you to a stretch of souvenir shops and fishmongers, beyond which lies the **Barranca de Lobos**. This is the port proper, home to hundreds of brightly painted fishing vessels and a colony of lobos marinos (sea lions)—their powerful stench announces their presence well before you sight them. The huge creatures often haul themselves out of the water to sun themselves on the breakwater as happy crowds of holiday makers snap photos. ✉ *Av. Martínez de Hoz at 12 de Octubre, Mar del Plata.*

Museo del Mar. More than 30,000 seashells are the main exhibit at this attractive, modern museum. The four-story complex has numerous sea-related exhibits, including a petting pool and explanations of marine life and rock formations. You can also check out the café, library, movie theater, and gift shop. The rooftop lookout provides panoramic city views. Puppet shows and kiddie-oriented theater are common during school vacations. ✉ *Av. Colón 1114, Mar del Plata* ☎ *223/451–9779* 🌐 *www.museodelmar.com* 🎫 *18 pesos* ⏲ *Jan.–Mar., daily 10–9; Apr.–*

June and Aug.–Nov., Tues.–Thurs. 10–8, Fri.–Sun. 10–9; July and Dec., daily 10–8.

WHERE TO EAT AND STAY

For expanded hotel reviews, visit Fodors.com.

$ SEAFOOD ✕ **Chichilo.** Fancy, it ain't: you line up cafeteria style to be served, then elbow your way to a Formica table, scattering the seagulls that peck at scraps from the floor. But the plates are piled with calamari and fries, and the huge portions of hake and sole are cooked on griddles as you watch. This friendly seafood joint has been a local favorite for more than 40 years. ✉ *Complejo Comercial del Puerto Local 17, Av. Martínez de Hoz at 12 de Octubre, Mar del Plata* ☎ *223/489–6317* ▭ *No credit cards* ⏲ *Closed weekdays Apr.–June and Aug.–Nov.*

$$$ CONTEMPORARY ✕ **Sarasanegro.** The menu and portions might be small, but each dish is packed with enough flavor—and enough ingredients—to make variety moot. Mar del Plata staples like fried prawns and sole come in a lettuce sauce or bathed in clam juice. The *mollejas* (sweetbreads) are crisply caramelized in sherry. The two young chefs behind the restaurant are so intent on the food that they've left the restaurant rather bare. Still, by the time you're through your scallops with tomato couscous and are on to the apple millefeuille, you probably won't care. The eight-course tasting menu is a great way to sample everything. ✉ *San Martín 3458, Mar del Plata* ☎ *223/473–0808* 🌐 *www.sarasanegro.com.ar* ▭ *No credit cards* ⏲ *No lunch. Closed Mon. and Sun. Apr.–Nov.*

$$$ SEAFOOD ✕ **Viento en Popa.** Word of mouth is the only advertising this restaurant seems to need: it doesn't even have a sign outside yet its tables are always full. Owner Ñeco Gioffi is a pioneer of so-called south Atlantic cuisine, aiming to show off the quality of ultra-fresh local fish and seafood, rather than bathe them in sauces. Dishes such as the *burriqueta en oliva* (burriqueta fish in olive oil and tarragon) or *lenguado con alcaparras* (sole with capers) are testament to the success of his formula. ✉ *Av. Martínez de Hoz 257, Mar del Plata* ☎ *223/489–0220* ✍ *Reservations essential* ▭ *No credit cards* ⏲ *Closed Mon.*

$$$$ 🏨 **Hotel Costa Galana.** This may be Argentina's most popular seaside resort, but the look at Costa Galana is anything but beachy: rooms are richly decorated with thick wool carpets, mahogany furniture, and heavy drapes. **Pros:** large pool protected from the wind; direct access to a (relatively) quiet beach through a small underpass; great service. **Cons:** far from the center of town; despite high prices, they charge for extras like Internet; standard rooms are a bit small. ✉ *Blvd. Marítimo P. Peralta Ramos 5725, Mar del Plata* ☎ *223/410–5000* 🌐 *www.hotelcostagalana.com* ⇆ *186 rooms* ☝ *In-room: safe, Internet. In-hotel: restaurant, bar, pool, gym, spa, beach* 🍽 *Breakfast.*

IGUAZÚ FALLS

1,358 km (843 miles) north of Buenos Aires; 637 km (396 miles) west of Curitiba, 544 (338 miles) west of Vila Velha.

Iguazú consists of some 275 separate waterfalls—in the rainy season there are as many as 350—that plunge more than 200 feet onto the rocks below. They cascade in a deafening roar at a bend in the Iguazú

River (Río Iguazú/Rio Iguaçu) where the borders of Argentina, Brazil, and Paraguay meet. Dense, lush jungle surrounds the falls: here the tropical sun and the omnipresent moisture produce a towering pine tree in two decades instead of the seven it takes in, say, Scandinavia. By the falls and along the roadside, rainbows and butterflies are set off against vast walls of red earth, which is so ubiquitous that eventually even paper currency in the area turns red from exposure to the stuff.

DOOR-TO-DOOR

Argentine travel agency **Sol Iguazú Turismo** (☎ *3757/421-008* 🌐 *www.soliguazu.com.ar*) organizes door-to-door transport to both sides of the falls, and can reserve places on the Iguazú Jungle Explorer trips. It also runs day trips to the Jesuit ruins in San Ignacio, the Itaipú Dam, and to other areas of Misiones Province.

The falls and the lands around them are protected by Argentina's Parque Nacional Iguazú (where the falls are referred to by their Spanish name, the Cataratas de Iguazú) and by Brazil's Parque Nacional do Iguaçu (where the falls go by the Portuguese name of Cataratas do Iguaçu). The Argentine town of Puerto Iguazú and the Brazilian city of Foz do Iguaçu are the hubs for exploring the falls (the Paraguayan city of Ciudad del Este is also nearby).

GETTING HERE AND AROUND

ARGENTINA INFO

Aerolíneas Argentinas flies four to five times daily between Aeroparque Jorge Newbery in Buenos Aires and the Aeropuerto Internacional de Puerto Iguazú (20 km/12 miles southeast of Puerto Iguazú); the trip takes 1¾ hours. LAN does the same trip two or three times daily. Normal rates start at about 800 pesos each way. Four Tourist Travel runs shuttle buses from the airport to hotels in Puerto Iguazú. They leave after every flight lands and cost 25 pesos. Taxis to Puerto Iguazú cost 100 pesos.

Vía Bariloche operates several daily buses between the Retiro bus station in Buenos Aires and the Puerto Iguazú Terminal de Omnibus in the center of town. The trip takes 16–18 hours, so it's worth paying the little extra for *coche cama* (sleeper) or *cama ejecutivo* (deluxe sleeper) services, which cost about 470 pesos one-way (regular semi-cama services cost around 410 pesos). You can travel direct to Rio de Janeiro (22 hours) and São Paolo (15 hours) with Crucero del Norte; the trips cost 545 and 476 pesos, respectively.

From Puerto Iguazú to the falls or the hotels along Ruta Nacional 12, take El Práctico from the terminal or along Avenida Victoria Aguirre. Buses leave every 15 minutes 7–7 and cost 20 pesos round-trip.

There's little point in renting a car around Puerto Iguazú: daily rentals start at 260–300 pesos, more than twice what you pay for a taxi between the town and the falls. A hire car is useful for visiting the Jesuit ruins at San Ignacio, 256 km (165 miles) south of Puerto Iguazú on Ruta Nacional 12, a two-lane highway in excellent condition.

ARGENTINA ESSENTIALS

Airline Contacts **Aerolíneas Argentinas** ☎ *0810/2228-6527* 🌐 *www.aerolineas.com.ar.* **LAN** ☎ *0810/999-9526* 🌐 *www.lan.com.*

Banks and Currency Exchange **Argencam** ✉ *Av. Victoria Aguirre 1162, Puerto Iguazú, Misiones.* **Banco de la Nación** ✉ *Av. Victoria Aguirre 179, Puerto Iguazú, Misiones* 🌐 *www.bna.com.ar.*

Bus Contacts **Crucero del Norte** ☎ *11/4315-1652 in Buenos Aires, 3757/421-916 in Puerto Iguazú* 🌐 *www.crucerodelnorte.com.ar.* **Four Tourist Travel** ☎ *3757/422-962 at airport, 3757/420-681 in Puerto Iguazú.* **Vía Bariloche** ☎ *0810/333-7575 in Buenos Aires, 3757/420-854 in Puerto Iguazú* 🌐 *www.viabariloche.com.ar.*

CROSS-BORDER BUS

Crucero del Norte. This company runs an hourly cross-border public bus service (8 pesos) between the bus stations of Puerto Iguazú and Foz do Iguaçu. Locals don't have to get on and off for immigration, but be sure you do so. To reach the Argentine falls, change to local minibus service El Práctico at the intersection with Ruta Nacional 12 on the Argentine side. For the Brazilian park, change to a local bus at the Avenida Cataratas roundabout. ☎ *3757/421-916 in Puerto Iguazú* 🌐 *www.crucerodelnorte.com.ar.*

Internet **Telecentro** ✉ *Av. Victoria Aguirre Norte 294, Puerto Iguazú, Misiones* ☎ *3757/422-454.*

Medical Assistance **Farmacia Bravo** ✉ *Av. Victoria Aguirre 423, Puerto Iguazú, Misiones* ☎ *3757/420-479.* **Hospital Samic** ✉ *Av. Victoria Aguirre 131, Puerto Iguazú* ☎ *3757/420-288.*

Taxis **Remises Iguazú** ✉ *Puerto Iguazú* ☎ *3757/422-008.*

Visitor Info **Cataratas del Iguazú Visitors Center** ✉ *Park entrance, Puerto Iguazú, Misiones* ☎ *3757/420-180* 🌐 *www.iguazuargentina.com* ⏲ *Mar.–Aug., daily 8 am–6 pm; Sept.–Feb., daily 8 am–8 pm.* **Puerto Iguazú Tourist Office** ✉ *Av. Victoria Aguirre 311, Puerto Iguazú* ☎ *3757/420-800* ⏲ *Daily 7–1 and 2–9.*

BRAZIL INFO

There are direct flights between Foz do Iguaçu and São Paulo (1½ hours; $230), Rio de Janeiro (2 hours; $260), and Curitiba (1 hour; $280) on TAM, which also has connecting flights to Salvador, Recife, Brasilia, other Brazilian cities, and Buenos Aires. Low-cost airline GOL operates slightly cheaper direct flights on the same three routes.

The Aeroporto Internacional Foz do Iguaçu is 13 km (8 mi) southeast of downtown Foz. The 20-minute taxi ride should cost R$40–50; the 45-minute regular bus ride about R$2.60. Note that several major hotels are on the highway to downtown, so a cab ride from the airport to these may be less than R$30. A cab ride from downtown hotels directly to the Parque Nacional in Brazil costs about R$70.

Via bus, the trip between São Paolo and Foz do Iguaçu takes 15 hours (R$153). The Terminal Rodoviário in Foz do Iguaçu is 5 km (3 miles) northeast of downtown. There are regular buses into town; they stop at the Terminal de Transportes Urbano (local bus station, often shortened

Exploring ▼

Itaipú Dam and Hydroelectric Power Plant **1**

Parque das Aves **2**

Restaurants ▼

Búfalo Branco ... **1**

Tempero da Bahia **3**

Zaragoza **2**

Hotels ▼

Hotel das Cataratas **4**

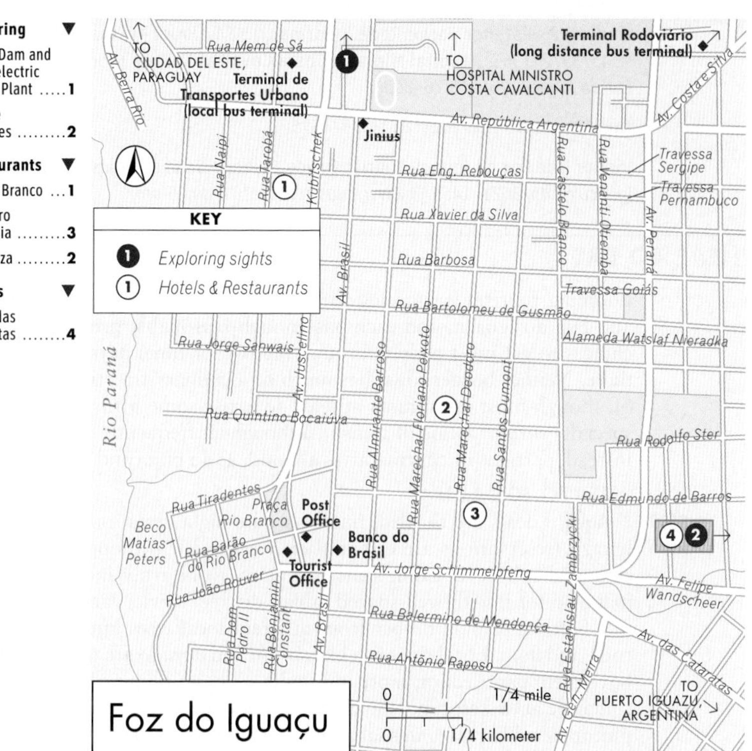

to TTU) at Avenida Juscelino Kubitschek and Rua Mem de Sá. From platform 2, Bus 120 (labeled "Parque Nacional") also departs every 15 minutes (7–7) to the visitor center at the park entrance; the fare is R$2.60. The buses run along Avenida Juscelino Kubitschek and Avenida Jorge Schimmelpfeng, where you can also flag them down.

There's no real reason to rent a car in Foz do Iguaçu: it's cheaper and easier to use taxis or local tour companies to visit the falls, especially as you can't cross the border in a rental car. There are taxi stands (*pontos de taxi*) at intersections all over town, each with its own phone number. Hotels and restaurants can call you a cab, but you can also hail them on the street.

BRAZIL ESSENTIALS

Airline Contacts GOL ☎ *300/115–2121 toll-free, 45/3521–4230 in Foz do Iguaçu* 🌐 *www.voegol.com.br.* **TAM** ☎ *800/570–5700 toll-free, 45/3521–7500 in Foz do Iguaçu* 🌐 *www.tam.com.br.*

Bus Contacts Pluma ☎ *0800/646–0300 toll-free, 045/3522–2515 in Foz do Iguaçu* 🌐 *www.pluma.com.br.*

Banks and Currency Exchange Banco do Brasil ✉ *Av. Brasil 1377, Foz do Iguaçu* 🌐 *www.bb.com.br.*

Medical Assistance FarmaRede (pharmacy) ✉ *Av. Brasil 46, Foz do Iguaçu* ☎ *45/3572–1363.* **Hospital Ministro Costa Cavalcanti** ✉ *Av. Gramado 580, Foz do Iguaçu* ☎ *45/3576–8000.*

Taxis Ponto de Taxi 20 ☎ *45/3523–4625.*

Visitor Info Foz do Iguaçu Tourist Office ✉ *Praça Getúlio Vargas 69, Foz do Iguaçu* ☎ *45/3521–1455* 🌐 *www.iguassu.tur.br* ⏲ *8 am–6 pm.*

WHERE TO EAT

Booming tourism is kindling the restaurant scenes of Puerto Iguazú and Foz do Iguaçu, and each has enough reasonably priced, reliable choices to get most people through the two or three days they spend there. Neither border town has much of a culinary tradition to speak of, though most restaurants at least advertise some form of the local specialty *surubí* (a kind of catfish), although it's frequently out of stock. Instead, parrillas or churrascarias abound, as do pizza and pasta joints.

PUERTO IGUAZÚ

$$$$ SEAFOOD ✕ **Aqva.** Locals are thrilled: finally, a date-night restaurant in Puerto Iguazú (reservations are essential on weekends). Although the high-ceilinged split-level cabin seats too many to be truly intimate, they make up for it with well-spaced tables, discreet service, and low lighting. Softly gleaming timber from different local trees lines the walls, roof, and floor. Local river fish like *surubí* and *dorado* are the specialty: have them panfried, or, more unusually, as pasta fillings. Forget being romantic at dessert time: the chef's signature dessert, fresh mango and pineapple with a *torrontés* sabayon, is definitely worth keeping to yourself. ✉ *Av. Córdoba at Carlos Thays, Puerto Iguazú, Misiones, Argentina* ☎ *3757/422–064.*

$$$$ ARGENTINE ✕ **La Rueda.** This parrilla is so popular with visitors that they start serving dinner as early as 7:30 pm—teatime by Argentine standards. The local beef isn't quite up to Buenos Aires standards, but La Rueda's *bife de chorizo* is one of the best in town. Surubí is another house specialty, but skip the traditional Roquefort sauce, which overwhelms the fish's flavor. The surroundings stay true to the restaurant's rustic roots: hefty tree trunks hold up the bamboo-lined roof, and the walls are adorned by a curious wooden frieze carved by a local artist. ✉ *Av. Córdoba 28, Puerto Iguazú, Misiones, Argentina* ☎ *3757/422–531* ✍ *Reservations essential* ⏲ *No lunch Mon.–Tues.*

FOZ DO IGUAÇU

$$$$ BRAZILIAN ✕ **Búfalo Branco.** The city's finest and largest churrascaria does a killer *rodizio* (all-you-can-eat meat buffet). The *picanha* stands out from the 25 meat choices, but pork, lamb, chicken, and even—yum—bull testicles find their way onto the metal skewers they use to grill the meat. The salad bar is well stocked, a boon for vegetarians. ✉ *Av. Rebouças 530, Foz do Iguaçu, Brazil* ☎ *45/3523–9744.*

$$$$ SEAFOOD ✕ **Tempero da Bahia.** If you're not going as far as Bahia on your trip, you can at least check out its flavors at this busy tangerine-painted restaurant. It specializes in northeastern fare like *moquecas* (a rich seafood

Continued on page 170

By Victoria Patience

IGUAZÚ FALLS

Big water. That's what *y-guasu*—the name given to the falls by the indigenous Guaraní people—means. As you approach, a thundering fills the air and steam rises above the trees. Then the jungle parts. Spray-soaked and speechless, you face the Devil's Throat, and it's clear that "big" doesn't come close to describing this wall of water.

Taller than Niagara, wider than Victoria, Iguazú's raging, monumental beauty is one of nature's most awe-inspiring sights. The Iguazú River, on the border between Argentina and Brazil, plummets 200 feet to form the Cataratas de Iguazú (as the falls are known in Spanish) or Foz do Iguaçu (their Portuguese name). Considered to be one waterfall, Iguazú is actually made up of around 275 individual drops, that stretch along 2.7 km (1.7 mi) of cliff-face. Ranging from picturesque cascades to immense cataracts, this incredible variety is what makes Iguazú so special. National parks in Brazil and Argentina protect the falls and the flora and fauna that surround them. Exploring their jungle-fringed trails can take two or three days: you get right alongside some falls, gaze down dizzily into others, and can take in the whole spectacle from afar. You're sure to come across lizards, emerald- and sapphire-colored hummingbirds, clouds of butterflies, and scavenging raccoonlike coatis. You'll also glimpse monkeys and toucans, if you're lucky.

GEOLOGY 101

Over 100 million years ago, lava surged up through cracks in the earth's crust near Iguazú. It spread out over the surrounding area, forming three layers of basalt (a dark, fine-grained rock) tens of meters high. The Iguazú River, which starts 1,200 km (745 mi) east, flowed over this. Later, the movement of tectonic plates raised parts of the surface, which became stepped. As the river flowed over these steps it eroded the rock surface it fell on even more, and over the next few million years, the waters carved out what are now the falls.

WHEN TO GO

Time of year	Advantages	Disadvantages
Nov.–Feb.	High rainfall in December and January, so expect lots of water.	Hot and sticky. December and January are popular with local visitors. High water levels stop Zodiac rides.
Mar.–Jun.	Increasingly cooler weather. Fewer local tourists. Water levels are usually good.	Too cold for some people, especially when you get wet. Occasional freak water shortages.
Jul.–Oct.	Cool weather.	Low rainfall in July and August—water levels can be low. July is peak season for local visitors.

WHERE TO GO: ARGENTINA VS. BRAZIL

Argentines and Brazilians can fight all day about who has the best angle on the falls. But the two sides are so different that comparisons are academic. To really say you've done Iguazú (*or* Iguaçu), you need to visit both. If you twist our arm, we'll say the Argentine side is a better experience with lots more to do, but (and this is a big "but") the Brazilian side gives you a tick in the box and the best been-there-done-that photos. It's also got more non-falls-related activities (but you have to pay extra for them).

	ARGENTINA	BRAZIL
Park Name	Parque Nacional Iguazú	Parque Nacional do Iguaçu
The experience	Up close and personal (you're going to get wet).	What a view!
The falls	Two-thirds are in Argentina including Garganta del Diablo, the star attraction.	The fabulous panoramic perspective of the Garganta do Diablo is what people really come for.
Timing	One day to blitz the main attractions. Two days to explore fully.	Half a day to see the falls; all day if you do other activities.
Other activities	Extensive self-guided hiking and Zodiac rides.	Organized hikes, Zodiac rides, boat rides, helicopter rides, rafting, abseiling.
Park size	67,620 hectares (167,092 acres)	182,262 hectares (450,379 acres)
Animal species	80 mammals/450 birds	50 mammals/200 birds

VITAL STATISTICS

Number of falls: 160–275*	**Total length:** 2.7 km (1.7 mi)	**Average Flow:** 396,258 gallons per second **Peak Flow:** 1,717,118 gallons per second
Major falls: 19	**Height of Garganta del Diablo:** 82 m (270 feet)	**Age:** 120–150 million years

*Depending on water levels

IGUAZÚ ITINERARIES

LIGHTNING VISIT. If you only have one day, limit your visit to the Argentine park. Arrive when it opens, and get your first look at the falls aboard one of Iguazú Jungle Explorer's Zodiacs. The rides finish at the Circuito Inferior: take a couple of hours to explore this. (Longer summer opening hours give you time to squeeze in the **Isla San Martín**.) Grab a quick lunch at the Dos Hermanas snack bar, then blitz the shorter Circuito Superior. You've kept the best for last: catch the train from **Estación Cataratas** to **Estación Garganta del Diablo**, where the trail to the viewing platform starts (allow at least two hours for this).

Tren Ecologico de la Selva

BEST OF BOTH SIDES. Two days gives you enough time to see both sides of the falls. Visit the Brazilian park on your second day to get the panoramic take on what you've experienced up-close in Argentina. If you arrive at 9 AM, you've got time to walk the entire trail, take photos, have lunch in the Porto Canoas service area, and be back at the park entrance by 1 PM. You could spend the afternoon doing excursions and activities from Macuco Safari and Ma-

KEY

Wheelchair-accessible
Restaurant
Scenic Viewpoint
Walking/Hiking Trails
Ferry Lines
Rail Lines

Estación Garganta del Diablo
Garganta del Diablo
Garganta del Diablo
ARGENTINA
Parque Nacional do Iguaçu
BRAZIL
Isla San Martín
Río Iguazú

Walkway view at Garganta del Diablo

cuco EcoAventura, or visiting the Itaipú dam. Alternatively, you could keep the visit to Brazil for the afternoon of the second day, and start off with a lightning return visit to the Argentine park and see the **Garganta del Diablo** (left) with the sun rising behind it.

SEE IT ALL. With three days you can explore both parks at a leisurely pace. Follow the one-day itinerary, then return to the Argentine park on your second day. Make a beeline for the Garganta del Diablo, which looks different in the mornings, then spend the afternoon exploring the **Sendero Macuco** (and Isla San Martín, if you didn't have time on the first day). You'll also have time to visit Güira Oga bird sanctuary or La Aripuca (both on RN 12) afterwards. You could spend all of your third day in the Brazilian park, or just the morning, giving you time to catch an afternoon flight or bus.

Estación Central
Estación Cataratas
Circuito Superior
Parque Nacional Iguazú
Circuito Inferior
Dos Hermanas

VISITING THE PARKS

Visitors gaze at the falls in Parque Nacional Iguazú.

Argentina's side of the falls is in the **Parque Nacional Iguazú,** which was founded in 1934 and declared a World Heritage Site in 1984. The park is divided into two areas, each of which is organized around a train station: Estación Cataratas or the Estación Garganta del Diablo. (A third, Estación Central, is near the park entrance.)

Paved walkways lead from the main entrance past the **Visitor Center,** called *Yvyrá Retá*—"country of the trees" in Guaraní (☎ 3757/49-1469 🌐 www.iguazuargentina.com 🎫 60 pesos 🕒 Mar.–Aug. 8–6; Sept.–Feb. 8–8). Colorful visual displays provide a good explanation of the region's ecology and human history. To reach the park proper, you cross through a small plaza containing a food court, gift shops, and ATM. From the nearby Estación Central, the gas-propelled Tren de la Selva (Jungle Train) departs every 20 minutes.

In Brazil, the falls can be seen from the **Parque Nacional Foz do Iguaçu** (☎ 45/3521–4400 🌐 www.cataratasdoiguacu.com.br 🎫 R$21.15 🕒 Apr.–Sep 9–5; Oct.–Mar. 9–6). Much of the park is protected rain forest—off-limits to visitors and home to the last viable populations of panthers as well as rare flora. Buses and taxis drop you off at a vast, plaza alongside the park entrance building. As well as ticket booths, there's an ATM, a snack bar, gift shop, and information and currency exchange. Next to the entrance turnstiles is the small **Visitor Center,** where helpful geological models explain how the falls were formed. Double-decker buses run every 15 minutes between the entrance and the trailhead to the falls, 11 km (7 mi) away; the buses stop at the entrances to excursions run by private operators Macuco Safari and Macuco Ecoaventura (these aren't included in your ticket). The trail ends in the **Porto Canoas** service area. There's a posh linen-service restaurant with river views, and two fast-food counters the with tables overlooking the rapids leading to the falls.

VISAS

U.S. citizens don't need a visa to visit Argentina as tourists, but the situation is more complicated in Brazil. ⇨ See the planning section at the beginning of the chapter.

EXCURSIONS IN AND AROUND THE PARKS

A Zodiac trip to the falls.

Iguazú Jungle Explorer (☎ 3757/42–1696 🌐 www.iguazujungleexplorer.com) runs trips within the Argentine park. Their standard trip, the Gran Aventura, costs 150 pesos and includes a truck ride through the forest and a Zodiac ride to San Martín, Bossetti, and the Salto Tres Mosqueteros (be ready to get soaked). The truck carries so many people that most animals are scared away: you're better off buying the 75-peso boat trip—Aventura Nautica—separately.

You can take to the water on the Brazilian side with **Macuco Safari** (☎ 045/3574–4244 🌐 www.macucosafari.com.br). Their signature trip is a Zodiac ride around (and under) the Salto Tres Mosqueteros. You get a more sedate ride on the Iguaçu Explorer, a 3½ hour trip up the river.

It's all about adrenaline with **Iguazú Forest** (☎ 3757/42–1140 🌐 www.iguazuforest.com). Their full day expedition involves kayaking, abseiling, waterfall-climbing, mountain-biking, and canopying all within the Argentine park.

In Brazil, **Cânion Iguaçu** (☎ 045/3529–6040 🌐 www.campodedesafios.com.br) offers rafting and canopying, as well as abseiling over the river from the Salto San Martín. They also offer wheelchair-compatible equipment.

Argentine park ranger Daniel Somay organizes two-hour Jeep tours with an ecological focus through his Puerto Iguazú–based **Explorador Expediciones** (☎ 3757/42–1632 🌐 www.rainforestevt.com.ar). The tours cost 120 pesos and include detailed explanations of the Iguazú ecosystem and lots of photo ops. A specialist leads the birdwatching trips, which cost US$100 and include the use of binoculars and hotel pick-up and drop-off.

Macuco Ecoaventura (☎ 045/3529–6927 🌐 www.macucoecoaventura.com.br) is one of the official tour operators within the Brazilian park. Their Trilha do Pozo Negro combines a 9-km guided hike or bike ride with a scary boat trip along the upper river (the bit before the falls). The aptly-named Floating trip is more leisurely; shorter jungle hikes are also offered.

ON THE CATWALK

You spend most of your visit to the falls walking the many trails and catwalks, so be sure to wear comfortable shoes.

stew made with coconut milk and palm oil); their delicious versions are unusual for mixing prawns with local river fish. Spicy panfried sole and salmon are lighter options. The flavors aren't quite so subtle at the all-out seafood (and river food) buffets they hold several times a week, but at R$40 for all you can eat, they certainly pull in crowds. ✉ *Rua Marechal Deodoro 1228, Foz do Iguaçu, Brazil* ☎ *45/3025–1144* ⊙ *Mon.–Sat. open from 6, Sun. from noon* ⊙ *No dinner Sun.*

$$$$ SPANISH ✕ **Zaragoza.** On a tree-lined street in a quiet neighborhood, this traditional restaurant's Spanish owner is an expert at matching Iguaçu's fresh river fish to authentic Spanish seafood recipes. Brazilian ingredients sneak into some dishes—the *surubi à Goya* (catfish in a tomato-and-coconut-milk sauce) definitely merits a try. ✉ *Rua Quintino Bocaiúva 882, Foz do Iguaçu, Brazil* ☎ *45/3028–8084.*

WHERE TO STAY

Once you've decided which country to base yourself in, the next big decision is whether to stay in town or at the five-star hotel inside each park. If you're on a lightning one-night visit and you only want to see one side of the falls, the convenience of staying inside the park might offset the otherwise unreasonably high prices for mediocre levels of luxury. Otherwise, you get much better value for money at the establishments in town or on highways BR489 (Rodavia das Cataratas) in Brazil or Ruta Nacional 12 in Argentina. During the day you're a 20-minute bus ride from the falls and the border, and at night you're closer to restaurants and nightlife (buses stop running to the park after 7 or 8; after that, it's a 100-peso taxi ride into town from the park).

Hotels in Argentina are generally cheaper than in Brazil. During low season (late September–early November and February–May, excluding Easter) rooms are often heavily discounted. ⚠ **Staying on the Brazilian side (apart from at the Hotel das Cataratas in the park) is not recommended. It's dangerous, especially after dark, more expensive, and the hotels are worse.**

PUERTO IGUAZÚ

For expanded hotel reviews, visit Fodors.com.

$$$ **Hostel-Inn Iguazú.** An enormous turquoise pool surrounded by classy wooden loungers and well-kept gardens lets you know this hostel is far from typical. **Pros:** beautiful pool area; rooms are simple but clean and well designed; location between town and the falls gives you the best of both worlds. **Cons:** impersonal service from indifferent staff; lounge and kitchen are run-down; very basic breakfast. ✉ *Ruta 12, Km 5, Puerto Iguazú, Misiones, Argentina* ☎ *3757/421–823* 🌐 *www.hostel-inn.com* *52 rooms* *In-room: Wi-Fi. In-hotel: restaurant, bar, pool* *No credit cards* *Breakfast.*

$$$$ ★ **Panoramic Hotel Iguazú.** The falls aren't the only good views in Iguazú: half the rooms of this chic hotel look onto the churning, jungle-framed waters of the Iguazú and Paraná rivers. **Pros:** river views; great attention to detail in the beautifully designed rooms; the gorgeous pool. **Cons:** the in-house casino can make the lobby noisy; indifferent staff aren't up to the price tag; it's a short taxi ride to the town center, and

in-house transport is overpriced. ✉ *Paraguay 372, Puerto Iguazú, Misiones, Argentina* ☎ *3757/498–100, 3757/498–050* 🌐 *www.panoramic-hoteliguazu.com* *91 rooms* *In-room: safe, Wi-Fi. In-hotel: restaurant, bar, pool* *Breakfast.*

$$$ ★ **Río Tropic.** Friendly owners Rémy and Romina give you a warm welcome at this rootsy B&B, which is surrounded by a lush garden. **Pros:** the wonderfully helpful and attentive owners; peaceful surroundings; abundant homemade breakfasts served on a terrace in the garden. **Cons:** too far from the town center to walk to; low on luxury. ✉ *Montecarlo s/n, at Km 5, RN12, Puerto Iguazú, Misiones, Argentina* ☎ *5493757/571–403* 🌐 *www.riotropic.com.ar* *10 rooms* *In-room: no TV, Wi-Fi. In-hotel: bar, pool* *No credit cards* *Breakfast.*

$$ **Secret Garden Iguazú.** Dense tropical vegetation overhangs the wooden walkway that leads to this tiny guesthouse's three rooms, tucked away in a pale-blue clapboard house. **Pros:** wooden deck overlooking the back-to-nature garden; knowledgeable owner John's charm and expert mixology; home-away-from-home vibe. **Cons:** the three rooms book up fast; no pool; comfortable but not luxurious. ✉ *Los Lapachos 623, Puerto Iguazú, Misiones, Argentina* ☎ *3757/423–099* 🌐 *www.secretgardeniguazu.com* *3 rooms* *In-room: no TV, Wi-Fi* *No credit cards* *Breakfast.*

$$$$ **Sheraton International Iguazú.** That thundering you can hear in the distance lets you know how close this hotel is to the falls. **Pros:** the falls are on your doorstep; great buffet breakfasts; well-designed spa. **Cons:** rooms are in need of a complete makeover; mediocre food and service at dinner; other restaurants are an expensive taxi-ride away. ✉ *Parque Nacional Iguazú, Argentina* ☎ *3757/491–800* 🌐 *www.sheraton.com* *176 rooms, 4 suites* *In-room: safe, Internet. In-hotel: restaurant, bar, pool, tennis court, gym, spa* *Breakfast.*

FOZ DO IGUAÇU

$$$$ ★ **Hotel das Cataratas.** Not only is this stately hotel *in* the national park, with views of the smaller falls from the front-side suites, but it also provides the traditional comforts of a colonial-style establishment: large rooms, terraces, vintage furniture, and hammocks. **Pros:** right inside the park, a short walk from the falls; serious colonial-style charm; friendly, helpful staff. **Cons:** rooms aren't as luxurious as the price promises; far from Foz do Iguaçu so you're limited to the on-site restaurants; only the most-expensive suites have views of the falls. ✉ *Km 28, Rodovia das Cataratas, Foz do Iguaçu, Brazil* ☎ *045/2102–7000, 0800/726–4545* 🌐 *www.hoteldascataratas.com.br* *198 rooms, 5 suites* *In-room: safe, Wi-Fi. In-hotel: restaurant, pool, tennis court, gym, business center* *Breakfast.*

[illegible]

$$$ [illegible]

★ [illegible]

$$ Secret Garden Iguazú. [illegible]

$$ Marcopolo Inn Iguazú. [illegible]

FOZ DO IGUAÇU

$$$$ Hotel das Cataratas. [illegible]

★ [illegible]

4

The Northwest

WORD OF MOUTH

"[In the vicinity of Salta/Purmamarca/Cachi/Cafayate], there are plenty of hiking trails all over—all are very scenic, with thousands of stunning views."

—flintstones

WELCOME TO THE NORTHWEST

ceramics, Salta Province

TOP REASONS TO GO

★ **The Quebrada:** In this vast, mountainous, color-splashed landscape, gaze up at an eternity of stars or the other-worldly carved walls of the gorge.

★ **Sports and the Outdoors:** Rivers deep, mountains high, valleys, lakes, and plains all play their part in tempting the adventurous into hiking, horseback riding, rafting, fishing, and rock climbing. Take a spin in a kite buggy on the Salinas Grandes or go trekking with a llama.

★ **Folk Music:** Simply the best places to dive into Argentina's folk-music scene, a night out at one of Salta's peñas (halls of food, music, and dancing) is essential. Wind instruments, diverse percussion, and soaring harmonies define the high-Andean soundtrack.

★ **Wine:** Now part of Argentina's Wine Trail, wines from the north, especially in the Cafayate region of Salta, are gaining worldwide recognition for their cépages grown at great heights.

Salta city center

1 Jujuy. A province of varied histories and geographies, Jujuy was once the battleground of South America's struggle for independence. It's still home to the peoples who lived here before colonization by the Incas and the Spanish.

2 Salta. This colonial city is the perfect base for exploring the wonders of the eponymous province. Chief of these is the Calchaqui Valley, which follows the Inca Trail and Ruta 40 through improbably charming towns in a dusty, cactus-studded wilderness. And in the midst of this are the world's highest vineyards.

GETTING ORIENTED

The landscape in Argentina's northwestern reaches is incredibly varied—from 22,000-foot-high Andean peaks to the high, barren plateau known as the Puna, from subtropical jungles to narrow sandstone canyons. Much of the area is desert, cut and eroded by raging brown rivers that wash away everything in sight during summer rains. The region's inhabitants have a tough, resilient quality. Here you'll find some of the country's most vibrant cities—but even they grind to a halt each afternoon for a siesta.

iglesia (church) in Molinos

TREN A LAS NUBES

With a bird's-eye view of its passage over the 210-foot-high Viaducto La Polvorilla, the Tren a las Nubes (Train to the Clouds) is probably the Northwest's most famous attraction. This train ride of a lifetime takes you on a 16-hour journey to the high, desolate Puna and back.

(above) Approaching the tracks for the Tren a las Nubes, Salta Province (top right) Car and engine, Tren a las Nubes (bottom right) Famous La Polvorilla Viaduct, a highlight of the journey

The trip begins at 4,336 feet as the train climbs out of the Lerma Valley from Salta into the mountains. It rattles over steel bridges that span wild rivers, winding ever upward through many turns and tunnels to reach the viaduct (13,770 feet) just beyond San Antonio de los Cobres, the only town of any size in the Puna. Here, you can disembark to test the thin air and visit a train-side market set up by locals for just this occasion.

The 217-km (135-mile) round-trip takes in 29 bridges, 21 tunnels, 13 viaducts, and a couple of hairpin bends and spirals, all of which are interpreted by the bilingual guides on board. Medical assistants take the ride with you to help with altitude sickness. Stop in at the dining car; breakfast and an afternoon snack are included in the fare.

WHEN TO GO

The heavy rains of summer mean the train stops running completely between the end of November through March, and in wintertime those that mind the cold might want to think twice about committing to 15 hours' travel in the mountains. On August 1 the Festival of the Pachamama is celebrated in San Antonio de los Cobres.

WHAT'S OUT THE WINDOW

The infrastructure alone makes the trip incredible, as the rack-and-pinionless train uses all the tricks in the book to gain altitude while avoiding steep grades. The trip isn't only for railway enthusiasts, though: an otherworldly landscape offers view after spectacular view as the train twists and turns along the route. For the parts where the train is accompanied by a road, or as it passes through infrequent villages, there are people to wave to. In San Antonio de los Cobres and on the lookout at the Viaducto la Polvorilla, locals gather round the train for a chat—and to sell handicrafts and trinkets. The guides in each carriage provide lots of information for each stage of the journey; when there's nothing more to be seen out the window, or once the sun's gone down on the return journey, they double as entertainers.

SAN ANTONIO DE LOS COBRES

San Antonio is as slow-moving as many small towns in rural Argentina; it's also heavily battered by sun and wind. It's also really difficult to get to and has very little oxygen in the air. Essential accessories for visitors are sunscreen, extra clothes for warmth at night, and coca leaves—they're chewed as an aide to digestion (which helps with altitude sickness). All that saliva production promotes swallowing, too, which will pop your ears (like sucking hard candies on a plane). Only since the last couple of years have there been lodging options: the basic **Hostal del Cielo** (✉ *Belgrano at Comandante Goulu* ☎ *387/490–9912* 🌐 *www.vivirenloscobres.com.ar*) and the smarter **Hosteria de las Nubes** (✉ *RN51 s/n* ☎ *387/490–9059* 🌐 *www.hoteldelasnubes.com*) are the best right now, although more accommodations are being built. Renting a room in someone's house is an option, too. A small ethnographic and archaeological museum, ANTAPU, fills in some detail on the town's background, but it's still very young and needs more work. The main business is making artesanías—handmade goods that can be sold to tourists.

RESERVATIONS

Reservations can be made at many agencies in Salta or with **Les Amis** (✉ *Cerrito 844* ☎ *11/5246–6670*) in Buenos Aires, and cost $169 USD. ✉ *Salta Station, Ameghino and Balcarce, Salta* ☎ *0800/888–6823* 🌐 www.trenalasnubes.com.ar.

EXTENDING YOUR TRIP

Though you can only buy return tickets, there's nothing to stop you getting off in San Antonio and continuing north to the salinas (salt flats) and on to Purmamarca in Jujuy. Bear in mind, however, that there's no public transport, though for the right price drivers will take you in their own cars. Going south to Cachi isn't as easy; the road is narrow and dangerous. Make sure to tell the gendarmeria (border guards) in San Antonio if you're going to attempt this route.

4

Updated by Sorrel Moseley-Williams

The provinces of Jujuy and Salta take center stage with regard to the history of Argentina, and the setting is along the ancient road of the Inca. Its first characters, the Incan people, traveled south from Peru along this route to conquer the tribes of northern Argentina and Chile in the late 1470s and were followed a few hundred years later by the Spaniards, who took that same route in search of gold and silver.

By 1535 the Royal Road of the Inca was a well-established trade route through the Andes between the mines in the north and Argentina's agricultural riches as far south as Mendoza. Even today, evidence of both the pre-Columbian and colonial cultures can be seen in the area's architecture, music, language, dress, and craftsmanship. Gastronomy-wise, many staple ingredients, such as beans and grains, remain the same. White adobe churches built by the Jesuits in the 17th century dot the landscape; Incan settlements lie half-buried in remote valleys and high plateaus; and pre-Inca mummies, often children, continue to be unearthed in the highest peaks of the Andes near Salta.

Neighboring Bolivia calls the high-altitude Andean desert of this region by its Spanish name, the altiplano, but Argentina prefers to use the ancient Quechua Indian term: the Puna. This desert covers an area of 90,000 square km (34,750 square miles) from Catamarca north across the Andes into Bolivia, Peru, and Chile. Llamas, alpacas, guanacos, goats, and vicuñas are the only animals hardy enough to exist on this terrain; dry grasses and thorny shrubs with deep roots seeking out moisture are the only plants in this oft-barren landscape. The wind is relentless. The sun beats down. Who could live here? Just as you've asked yourself this question, the colorful red poncho of a *coya* (native woman of this region) momentarily brightens the barren landscape as she appears out of nowhere, herding goats into an unseen ravine. Many people can't breathe at this altitude, let alone walk or sleep: luckily, ordinary mortals can experience a taste of the Puna from the Tren a las Nubes (Train to the Clouds) in Salta, or by car driving north from Humahuaca to La Quiaca on the Bolivian border.

Farther south, the colonial villages of Cafayate and Cachi bask in the warm, sunny Calchaquí Valley, which borders Tucumán and Salta provinces. Wherever you travel in the Northwest, you are never far from spectacular canyons, the Quebrada de Las Conchas between Salta and Cafayate, and the Quebrada de Humahuaca in Jujuy Province, impressive natural constructions due to their peculiar rock formations. The peaks of the Andes run down the border with Chile, and subtropical jungle bursts out in Jujuy, which also has some of the most productive agricultural land in the country.

THE NORTHWEST PLANNER

WHEN TO GO

January and February are Argentina's summer vacation months, meaning hotels get booked up and prices rise. Ironically, these two months coincide with rainy season, when flooding and/or landslides can block mountain roads. (The Salta–Cachi route is notorious for this.) Other busy times are winter break (July), Easter week, and movable feasts such as Carnaval in the Quebrada de Humahuaca. Most facilities remain open year-round.

GETTING HERE AND AROUND

AIR TRAVEL

Aerolíneas Argentinas/Austral (🌐 *www.aerolineas.com.ar*) has direct flights from Buenos Aires to San Salvador de Jujuy, Salta, La Rioja, and Tucumán, but is plagued by delays and cancellations. LAN Chile (🌐 *www.lan.com*) and Andes (🌐 *www.andesonline.com*) fly from Buenos Aires to Salta. There are connecting flights between Salta and Iguazú and Mendoza with Aerolíneas Argentinas. All flights between Buenos Aires and the Northwest use the capital's Aeroparque Jorge Newbery, about 15 minutes north of downtown.

BUS TRAVEL

Buses are reliable, affordable, and well used, though certain routes require a little advance planning. Some companies offer roadside pickup; others have luxury double-decker buses offering overnight services and maybe even a glass of sparkling wine. Tourist offices can advise which companies go where. In peak season, buy tickets a day or two in advance.

CAR TRAVEL

Traveling outside of cities is often easiest by car. However, picking up a car in one city and dropping it off in another incurs significant extra costs, so rent cars for only parts of your journey or commit to a round-trip. Roads are generally good and not very crowded, but be prepared for paved roads turning *ripio* (unpaved) and bumpy for long stretches. Very few routes require a 4x4 (apart from in wet weather). A Volkswagen Gol costs about 300 pesos per day; 4x4s start at 400 pesos per day.

Two main roads cross the area: the legendary Ruta 40, winding its unpaved way through small towns nearly 3,000 miles to the country's southern tip, and Ruta 9, the ancient road of the Incas, which takes you from Bolivia through San Salvador de Jujuy, Salta, Tucumán, Santiago del Estero, and on toward Córdoba. Before you set out, visit an ACA (🌐 *www.aca.org.ar*) office for maps and information, especially during the January–March rainy season.

REMIS TRAVEL

For short trips (e.g., Salta to Cafayate), consider hiring a *remis* (fixed-price taxi). Some routes have shared services, where you split the cost with others making the same journey. You can find a remis at airports, bus stations, and on main plazas—or your hotel can call one for you. Be sure to agree on a price before setting off, however.

HEALTH AND SAFETY

Newcomers to traveling at a great height may be susceptible to soroche, or altitude sickness, resulting in shortness of breath and headaches. Walk slowly, eat carbohydrates, and drink plenty of fluids (but avoid alcohol). Locals swear by the coqueando remedy: sucking on coca leaves (sold at corner groceries and street vendors for a few pesos). Tear off the stems and stuff several leaves into the space between your teeth and cheek; leave them in for an hour or so, neither chewing nor spitting, but swallowing when you salivate.

Aside from being sold an overpriced tour (recommended rates are listed in Salta's tourism office), you're unlikely to encounter crime, and local people are happy and curious to receive visitors. Many hotels pride themselves on not needing safety deposit boxes.

The many roadside shrines marking car accidents, especially on winding mountain routes, are a reminder to check your speed. Also take care on the many bumpy, unpaved roads. And wear your seatbelt, as it is the law.

MONEY

Although this should be standard procedure around the country, avoid people on the street who offer to change your currency to pesos; head to a bank or casa de cambio instead. Banks are generally open weekdays 7–2. For ATMs, look for the maroon-and-white "Banelco" sign of Argentina's largest ATM network. You can use your Plus or Cirrus card to withdraw pesos. Traveler's checks aren't recommended in the Northwest. Few places accept them, and with ATMs so easy to find, especially in larger towns, there's little need for them. Outside the major cities many businesses don't accept credit cards, meaning cash is the only option.

RESTAURANTS

The Northwest's indigenous heritage still influences its cuisine: corn, grains, beans, and potatoes are common ingredients stemming back to the days of the Inca. Dishes worth trying include *locro*, a spicy soup with corn, beans, and red peppers which becomes a rich stew when meat is added; *tamales*, ground corn baked with potatoes and meat and tied up in a corn husk; and *humitas*, grated corn with melted cheese cooked in a corn husk. Grilled *cabrito* (goat) is also a regional specialty. For dessert you may come across *cayote*, an interesting concoction of green-squash marmalade served with nuts and local goat cheese.

HOTELS

Hotels in the Northwest's major cities tend to be modern and comfortable. Most accept credit cards, although if you are paying in cash, do ask whether a discount is offered. Many *estancias* (ranches) in the foothills accept guests and are listed with local tourist offices. Although the whole region has really started to open up to local and foreign tourism, chain hotels are few and far between. Instead, take advantage of a dazzling array of boutique hotels and estancias built—or reinvented—to reflect history and ever mindful of their location.

ACA (Automóvil Club Argentino) maintains simple hotels and good campgrounds featuring numerous amenities. Note that as you travel farther north into smaller towns, English is increasingly less common.

WHAT IT COSTS IN PESOS

	$	$$	$$$	$$$$
Restaurants	30 pesos and under	31 pesos–50 pesos	51 pesos–75 pesos	over 75 pesos
Hotels	300 pesos and under	301 pesos–500 pesos	501 pesos–800 pesos	over 800 pesos

Restaurant prices are for one main course at dinner. Hotel prices are for two people in a standard double room in high season.

SAN SALVADOR DE JUJUY

1,643 km (1,020 miles) northwest of Buenos Aires; 97 km (60 miles) north of Salta on RN9.

Founded by Spaniards in 1593, San Salvador de Jujuy (known as Jujuy to most Argentinians, and "S.S. de Jujuy" on signs) was the northernmost town on the military and trade route between the Spanish garrisons in Peru, Bolivia's silver mines, and the northern cities of Argentina.

Today the quarter-million inhabitants—including a large indigenous population—of this city busy themselves with administrating the province's main sources of income (tobacco, mining, and sugarcane), although a few are beginning to deal with tourism. Jujuy may lack nearby Salta's colonial dreaminess (and hotel selection), but it has a laid-back, unadulterated local culture, with a touch of frontier-town charm, and makes a great stop-off point and base. Just outside town you can ride horses along mountain paths in the jungle or go boating in valley waterways.

GETTING HERE AND AROUND

Aerolíneas Argentinas flies once a day from Buenos Aires. The trip takes just over two hours. Jujuy's Aeropuerto Dr. Horacio Guzmán is 30 km (19 miles) southeast of town. Andesmar, Balut, and Panamericano run from Salta to Jujuy. The latter two also run north to Purmamarca, Tilcara, Humahuaca, and La Quiaca at the Bolivian border—a route also served by La Quiaqueño, which has nine departures a day.

Jujuy's one-way grid system is easy to navigate by rental car or in cabs, which are cheap and bright red in color, although traffic builds up a

bit around the beginning and end of the siesta. That said, Jujuy is flat despite the altitude: most sights, restaurants, and hotels are within easy walking distance of Plaza Belgrano, in the city center between the Río Grande and Río Xibi Xibi. The exception is the Alto de la Viña district, which is worth the 10-peso taxi fare to reach.

You can arrange airport pickups, city tours, and excursions outside town through NASA, a family-owned and -operated travel office with two generations of experience, or with the very efficient and friendly Tawantinsuyo agency, which can arrange custom tours.

ESSENTIALS

Bus Contacts **Andesmar** ☎ *388/4243–733.* **Atahualpa** ☎ *388/155–815–298.* **Balut** ☎ *388/422–2134.* **La Estrella** ☎ *388/424–2318.* **Panamericano** ☎ *388/423–7330.* **Terminal de Omnibus** ✉ *R9 and R66, Acceso Sur, San Salvador de Jujuy* ☎ *388/422–1374.*

Banks and Currency Exchange **Banco Macro** ✉ *San Martín 785, San Salvador de Jujuy.* **Horus** ✉ *Belgrano 722, San Salvador de Jujuy.* **HSBC** ✉ *Alvear 970, San Salvador de Jujuy.*

Internet **Ciber Zone** ✉ *Lavalle 388, San Salvador de Jujuy.*

Medical Assistance Farmacia Siufi ✉ *Alvear 1058, San Salvador de Jujuy* ☎ *388/422–3623, 0800/222–5810.* **Hospital Pablo Soria** ✉ *Av. General Güemes 1345, San Salvador de Jujuy* ☎ *388/422–1228, 388/422–1256.*

Rental Cars Hertz ✉ *Jujuy airport, San Salvador de Jujuy* ☎ *388/491–1505.*

Taxis Parada Uno ☎ *388/425–6500.*

Visitor and Tour Info NASA ✉ *Av. Senador Pérez 154, San Salvador de Jujuy* ☎ *388/422–3938* 🌐 *www.turismonorte.com.ar.* **Secretaría de Turismo y Cultura de la Provincia de Jujuy** ✉ *Gorriti 295, San Salvador de Jujuy* ☎ *388/422–1325* 🌐 *www.turismo.jujuy.gov.ar.* **Tawantinsuyo** ✉ *Belgrano 566, San Salvador de Jujuy* ☎ *388/424–4658* 🌐 *www.evttawantinsuyo.com.ar.*

4

EXPLORING

TOP ATTRACTIONS

Catedral de Jujuy. The city cathedral dates from 1765, and was the first building constructed in S.S. de Jujuy, but it has been augmented and remodeled so many times that it's now a hodgepodge of architectural styles. The interior contains an ornately carved, gold-plated pulpit, said to be the finest in South America. A close look reveals an intricate population of carved figures, biblical and otherwise. It was inspired by the Cusqueña school of art from Cuzco, Peru, as were the building's ornate doors and confessionals. ✉ *West side of Plaza General Belgrano, San Salvador de Jujuy* ☎ *388/423–5333* 🎫 *Free* ⏲ *Weekdays 10–noon and 5–10, weekends 7–noon and 5–10.*

Centro Cultural y Museo Pasquini López. Elevated on a natural balcony overlooking the city and with its own small patch of regenerated jungle, this mansion has a little museum of centuries-old ceramics and other artifacts found locally. Better still, botanists have been developing a mile-long nature trail that buzzes with cicadas. Knowledgeable guides can enlighten you on the flora. Call ahead to organize tours in English. ✉ *Victor Hugo 45, Alto la Viña, San Salvador de Jujuy* ☎ *388/154–047–509* 🎫 *10 pesos* ⏲ *Mon.–Sat. 10–12, 4–7.*

Iglesia de San Francisco. An ornate 18th-century wooden pulpit with dozens of figures of monks is the centerpiece of the Church of St. Francis, two blocks west of Plaza General Belgrano. There's some debate about who carved the pulpit: it may have been local artisans, or the pulpit may have been transported from Bolivia. Although the church and bell tower look colonial, they date from 1930. ✉ *Belgrano and Lavalle, San Salvador de Jujuy* 🎫 *Free* ⏲ *Daily 10–1 and 5–9.*

Museo Arqueológico Provincial. The Provincial Archaeological Museum houses such treasures as a 2,600-year-old ceramic goddess and the mummy of a two-year-old child dating back 1,000 years. Ceramic pots painted with geometric designs from Yavi and Humahuaca are constantly being added to the collection, and there are ancient bone exhibits, too. A diorama shows what life was like here 9,000 years ago. ✉ *Belgrano 677, San Salvador de Jujuy* ☎ *388/422–3344* 🎫 *10 pesos* ⏲ *Mon.–Sat. 8–2, 5–9.*

Plaza General Belgrano. Orange trees and vendors populate the central square, which is surrounded by colonial buildings—including the imposing government palace. It's empty by day, but starts to fill with gossiping Jujeños, old and young, by late afternoon.

> **WORD OF MOUTH**
>
> "We meandered our way through the villages, taking plenty of time to explore the markets of Purmamarca and Humahuaca." —colibri

Casa de Gobierno. The 1907 Casa de Gobierno (Government House) fronts the plaza on San Martín and contains the provincial government offices. A first-floor hall, the Salón de la Bandera, displays the original Argentine flag donated by General Belgrano in 1813, a gift to the city after it cooperated with the Belgrano-headed Exodus of Jujuy during the War of Independence. Entry is on Sarmiento street. The flag was replaced a few years later by the current white and sky-blue stripe version, and the one here is now used as the national coat of arms. ✉ *San Martín 450, San Salvador de Jujuy* ☎ *388/423–9400* 🎫 *Free* ⏲ *Daily 8–12, 5–8* ✉ *San Salvador de Jujuy.*

WORTH NOTING

Museo Histórico Provincial Juan Lavalle. Arms, trophies, and memorabilia from military campaigns collected from the 25 years of fighting for independence are on display at the Juan Lavalle Provincial History Museum. In this adobe building General Juan Lavalle, a hero of the wars of independence and an enemy of the dictator Juan Manuel de Rosas, was assassinated. A replica of the door through which Lavalle was shot in 1746 is part of the exhibit, as is the oldest flag in the country. ✉ *Lavalle 256, San Salvador de Jujuy* ☎ *388/422–1355* 🎫 *2 pesos* ⏲ *Weekdays 8–8, Saturdays 9–1 and 4–8, Sundays 4–8.*

Museo y Centro Cultural Culturarte. For a change in scenery and a quick dip into contemporary art and photography, hop into Culturarte for a modern immersion. A good spot for a coffee, pull up a breezy balcony seat for a different side-on view of the Government House. ✉ *Sarmiento and San Martín, San Salvador de Jujuy* ☎ *388/424–9548* 🎫 *Free* ⏲ *Weekdays 8–10, Saturdays 10–1, 5–10, Sundays 5–8.*

WHERE TO EAT

$$ ARGENTINE

✕ **Carena Resto Bar.** The muted lighting and slick furniture give this bar-restaurant a 1980s New York bond-trader look and feel. The clientele here is clearly the local bourgeoisie. It's a good spot for an afternoon coffee. ✉ *Belgrano and Balcarce, San Salvador de Jujuy* ☎ *388/154–761–676* 💳 *No credit cards.*

$$ ARGENTINE ★

✕ **Manos Jujeñas.** Ponchos on the walls, old paintings, native artifacts, stucco archways, and Andean background music are clues that this might be one of the best places to sample authentic Northwestern cuisine. Try the *locro*: a stew of maize, white beans, beef, chorizo, pancetta, and a wonderful red pepper–oil glaze, all of which come together in a mélange of savory, starchy flavors. Ask for a table at the back for a more

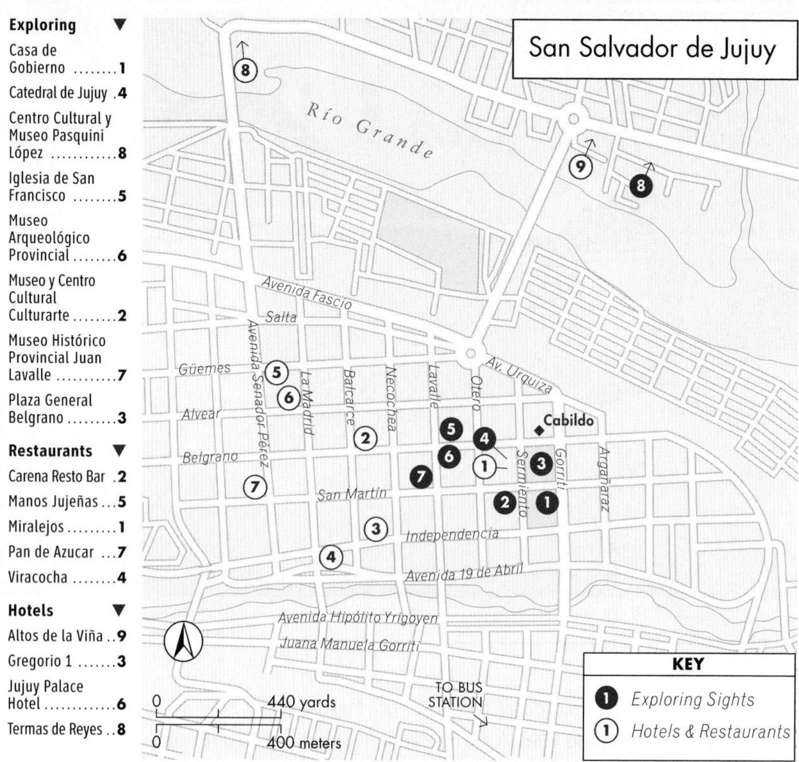

authentic and less hurried dining experience. ✉ *Senador Pérez 379, San Salvador de Jujuy* ☎ *388/424–3270* ▭ *No credit cards* ⏲ *Closed Mon.*

$$ ARGENTINE ✕ **Miralejos.** With a great location on the main square nestling between the cathedral and the handicrafts market, Miralejos serves both Argentine standards and regional dishes with a view of the bustling activity. Enjoy them with a home-brewed beer. ✉ *Sarmiento 268, San Salvador de Jujuy* ☎ *388/422–4911.*

$$$ ARGENTINE ✕ **Pan de Azucár.** For Jujeña classics with an eclectic twist, head to Pan de Azucár, where an ample menu offers original conoctions of the local staple, llama—think curry, carpaccio, grilled fillet, or stuffed in ravioli. House specialities also include quinoa, pork, and pasta. ✉ *Senador Perez 110, San Salvador de Jujuy* ☎ *388/423–2275* ▭ *No credit cards.*

$$ ARGENTINE Fodor's Choice ★ ✕ **Viracocha.** The menu at this unassuming *picanteria* (restaurant specializing in spicy foods) has everything from trout to rabbit, but llama or quinoa are the dishes to try: give them a go as an empanada starter. Less adventurous eaters can have one of the pasta dishes. Named after an Andean god, Viracocha's staff is helpful, and the atmosphere amid the yellow walls and arches is happily relaxed. ✉ *Independencia 994, corner of Lamadrid, San Salvador de Jujuy* ☎ *0388/423–3554* ▭ *No credit cards* ⏲ *Closed Tues. No dinner Sun.*

Head to Jujuy Province to see Puna architecture—like this church in Tafna—as stark as the landscape.

WHERE TO STAY

For expanded hotel reviews, visit Fodors.com.

$$$ Fodor's Choice ★ **Altos de la Viña.** A former state-owned hotel a short ride out of town is now one of the best reasons for spending time in San Salvador de Jujuy: The view from the swimming pool takes in most of the city and the mountains beyond, and the facilities span across five hectares, including a spa and a very good and reasonably priced restaurant. **Pros:** great pool; good for families; helipad. **Cons:** very little within walking distance. ✉ *Pasquini López 50, Alto la Viña, San Salvador de Jujuy* ☎ *388/426–2626* 🌐 *www.altosdelavina.com.ar* *60 rooms* *In-room: safe, Wi-Fi. In-hotel: restaurant, bar, pool, tennis court, gym, spa, business center, parking.*

$$ **Gregorio 1.** This downtown boutique hotel has sober rooms with parquet floors and all the modern conveniences. **Pros:** close to everything; attentive service; clean and simple. **Cons:** few in-hotel services. ✉ *Independencia 829, San Salvador de Jujuy* ☎ *388/424–4747* 🌐 *www.gregoriohotel.com* *18 rooms, 1 suite* *In-room: Wi-Fi* *Breakfast.*

$$ **Jujuy Palace Hotel.** Large rooms with impeccable facilities and balconies overlooking the street, a rooftop gym, a gated parking lot, and a formal second-floor dining room with first-class service are among the things that make this hotel stand out. **Pros:** comfortable; bilingual service, top-floor views. **Cons:** primarily a business hotel. ✉ *Belgrano 1060, San Salvador de Jujuy* ☎ *388/423–0433* 🌐 *www.jujuypalacehotel.com* *54 rooms, 5 suites* *In-room: safe, Wi-Fi. In-hotel: restaurant, bar, gym, laundry facilities, parking.*

$$$ **Termas de Reyes.** This countryside complex (which was once run by Evita Perón's charity and twice hosted the famed first lady who stayed in the current room 100), with natural thermal baths, indoor and out, bubbling up from underground hot springs, is on the edge of a spectacular river valley. **Pros:** the chance to take the cure and find inner peace; great views. **Cons:** a location 19 km (12 miles) outside Jujuy on a partially paved road. ✉ *R4, Km 19, San Salvador de Jujuy* ☎ *388/492–2522* 🌐 *www.termasdereyes.com* *60 rooms* *In-hotel: restaurant, bar, pool, gym, spa, laundry facilities, some age restrictions.*

4

NIGHTLIFE

El Bodegón. This popular spot covered with hundreds of vinyl records on the walls calls itself "the cathedral of Jujuy folklore." This downtown peña is predominantly filled with a young crowd of locals who have no qualms about taking to the small stage. ✉ *Güemes, corner of Ramirez de Velazco, San Salvador de Jujuy* ☎ *388/423–0802.*

Punta Norte. Check out the relatively new peña Punta Norte on the main plaza for regional live music and local bands. ✉ *Bolivar and Belgrano, Tilcara.*

Urquiza Bar. Pop into this buzzing downtown bar for live music and happy hours most nights of the week except Sundays. ✉ *Alvear 441, corner of Gral. Urquiza, San Salvador de Jujuy* ☎ *388/155–705–829.*

SHOPPING

Annuar Shopping. The shiny new Annuar Shopping mall may stock regular high-street fare, but it's worth popping into for two reasons: first, to cool off with an ice-cream and some AC on a hot summer's day, and, second, for a different perspective of the Cathedral's steeple from the mall's top floor. ✉ *Belgrano 563, San Salvador de Jujuy* ☎ *388/423–6178* 🌐 *www.annuarshopping.com.ar.*

La Hilanderia. Specializing in high-end textiles, La Hilanderia has bedspreads, scarves, throws, bags, and other woven artifacts from hand-selected sheep and llama wool brought down from the Puna to La Hilanderia's factory just outside of town. ✉ *Belgrano 592, San Salvador de Jujuy* ☎ *388/424–2875* 🌐 *www.decotextil.com.ar.*

Paseo de los Artesanos. The modest Paseo de los Artesanos on Plaza General Belgrano has reasonable prices on all kinds of woven and handcrafted souvenirs. And those coca tea bags, imported from Bolivia, are a curiosity that's hard to resist. ✉ *Sarmiento 240, San Salvador de Jujuy* ☎ *No phone* ⏲ *9 am–9:30 pm.*

SPORTS AND THE OUTDOORS

With its jungles, lakes, waterfalls, and wild rivers, the area around San Salvador de Jujuy is great for hiking and horseback riding.

There are a number of operators offering excursions, but only a handful have an online presence, which makes things hard, as most trips must be booked a few days in advance. One notable exception is **Paisajes del**

Noroeste (✉ *San Martin 132* ☎ *388/423–7565* 🌐 *www.noroestevirtual.com.ar*). The staff can arrange treks and horseback rides as well as paragliding and sand-boarding (think snowboarding but on sand dunes) outings. Check the Jujuy tourism board's website for a complete list of operators.

JUJUY PROVINCE

Although San Salvador de Jujuy is the provincial capital and the region's gateway, the star attraction of Jujuy (pronounced "hoo-hoo-wee"), Argentina's northernmost province, is the 161-km (100-mile) Quebrada de Humahuaca. Located in this breathtaking gorge, which has been used as a trade route for more than 10,000 years, are the three towns of Purmamarca, Tilcara, and Humahuaca, each with a unique feel. Most of the region's attractions on day trips are within easy reach of these bases, and in fact, there are few visitor facilities elsewhere.

By far the largest part of Jujuy is the area known as the Puna: vast, high-altitude desert plains that merge into the Andes. Except for some villages built around exquisite adobe churches (most notably in the town of Yavi, near the Bolivian border), this area is pristine and tough, baked by day and chilly at night. The easiest way to experience it is on a trip to the Salinas Grandes (Great Salt Plains) from Purmamarca, a two-hour drive offering spectacular views as you scale the Cuesta de Lipan range.

For an otherworldly adventure, head to Laguna de los Pozuelos, with its exotic year-round colony of pink flamingos. Note, though, that it's a long way from the nearest hotel. The best approach is via Abra Pampa, the town where Ruta 9 and Ruta 40 meet, a 97-km (60-mi) drive from Humahuaca.

PURMAMARCA

65 km (40 miles) north of San Salvador de Jujuy.

Nestled in the shadow of craggy rocks and multicolored, cactus-studded hills—with the occasional low-flying cloud happening by—the colonial village of Purmamarca (altitude 7,200 feet/2,195 meters) is one of the best bases from which to explore the Quebrada. Its few lights and dry air also make it a great spot for stargazing.

Here blazing red adobe replaces the white stucco used in architecture elsewhere, and the simple, square buildings play off the matching red rock. Come quick, before it's completely transformed from a one-horse town with basic stores and a few artisans selling their wares in the pleasant, tree-shaded plaza into a more exclusive destination.

GETTING HERE AND AROUND

You arrive here via a clearly marked 3-km (2-mile) detour off Ruta 9 onto Ruta 52. Any of the many buses running from Jujuy to Humahuaca and beyond will drop you at the junction where you can wait for a local bus to take you the final 3 km (2 miles) into town. Evelina

SA runs about 10 buses a day through here, to and from both Jujuy and Humahuaca.

Almost no place has its own street number (they're marked "s/n" or *sin numero* [no number] in addresses), but the town is so small that everything is either on or within one block of the main square, Plaza 9 de Julio. There's no bank or hospital, but there is a cash machine next to the tourist information office.

ESSENTIALS

Transportation Contacts Evelina SA buses ☎ *388/423–6975.* **Taxi** ☎ *388/490–8030.*

Visitor and Tour Info Tourist Office ✉ *Florida casi Rivadavia, Purmamarca* ☎ *388/490–8443.*

EXPLORING

Bodega Fernando Dupont. If the river floods, it makes arriving at this winery rather tricky. Five km (3 miles) from Purmamarca, with La Paleta del Pintor mountain range as its stunning backdrop, Bodego Fernando Dupont's grounds are lovely: cardon cacti mingle with Malbec, Cabernet Sauvignon, and Syrah vines which do well at 2,500 meters (8,200 feet) thanks to the long autumns. Call ahead for a brief yet interesting tasting. ✉ *Maimará* ☎ *388/154–731–918* 🌐 *www.bodegafernandodupont.com* ⏲ *Mon.–Sat. 9–6.*

★ **Cerro de Siete Colores.** Looming above Purmamarca is the Cerro de Siete Colores, Hill of Seven Colors, with its lavenders, oranges, and yellows. Look closely and see if you can find all seven—most people can pick out only four. ■ **TIP→ The colors are most clearly visible in the morning.** The best way to see the hill is by walking a 3-km (2-mile) loop called the **Paseo de Siete Colores,** which starts to the left of the church on the main square. This one-lane gravel road winds through bizarre, human-like formations of bright, craggy, red rock, before passing a series of stark, sweeping, Mars-like vistas with stands of trees in the river valley. The road then passes a few family farms and ends with a striking view of the Cerro itself before bringing you back to the center of Purmamarca. The tourist office has a map showing the best points for photos. ✉ *Purmamarca.*

Iglesia de Santa Rosa de Lima. The most notable feature downtown on the central plaza is the landmark 1648 Iglesia de Santa Rosa de Lima, which was constructed from adobe and thistle wood. ✉ *Purmamarca.*

Salinas Grandes. One of the more surreal sights to see near Purmamarca is the Salinas Grandes, more than 200 square km (80 square miles) of dazzling salt flats at the top of a mountain. Take the sinuous Ruta 52 for 64 km (40 miles) over the majestic Cuesta de Lipan (Lipan Rise)—which tops out at 4,170 meters (13,700 feet) above sea level—and cross Ruta 40. The salty landscape is surreal, and it's made even more so by a building constructed entirely out of slabs of salt turned a brownish color and salt furniture set up like church pews, complete with lectern. A series of small pools have been cut out of the salt flats' surface, revealing a layer of water and freshly forming crystals underneath. Take a camera, a hat, and sunblock. ✉ *Purmamarca.*

Continued on page 199

TOURING THE QUEBRADA DE HUMAHUACA

by Andy Footner, updated by Sorrel Moseley-Williams

This rugged, windswept canyon connects Argentina's desert-like Puna near Bolivia with the city of San Salvador de Jujuy 150 km (93 mi) further south. It's a natural passage through the surrounding mountains, so it's no surprise that thousands of years of history have played out between its sandstone walls. For many, those very walls are the main attraction: colorful minerals, seismic activity, and a powerful river continue to shape one of Argentina's most fascinating geological formations.

Cardones, or cacti, and sandstone formations are a major part of the landscape in Argentina's northwest

HISTORY OF THE QUEBRADA

Jujuy Province, Quebrada de Humahuaca landscape near Purmamarca village

The Quebrada de Humahuaca continues to be carved into existence by the ever-changing Rio Grande. A roaring, splashing force in summer, the river in winter reduces to barely a trickle in its wide, dry riverbed. You'll have a good view wherever you are in the main canyon of the Quebrada; Route 9, the main north-south road through here, runs parallel to it. Like the river, people have come through this canyon in both trickles and torrents over the centuries—but unlike the river, the sense of history is strong whenever you visit.

PEÑAS

Clubs, restaurants, and *peñas* attract both locals and tourists, who come to hear regional folk bands give it their all on small, cramped stages. Adding to the rowdy, dinner-theater atmosphere are the local dancers who entice (and often entrap) foreigners into strutting their stuff on stage; it's always a good laugh, no matter what language you speak.

PRE-INCAN TO THE CAMINO INCA

Ten thousand years ago, the first humans to inhabit the Southern Cone came from the north through this very canyon. Some stayed, becoming this area's original indigenous peoples. In the 15th and 16th centuries, the Incan Empire left its mark on the valley and the culture; the single road through this protected canyon became part of the hugely important Camino Inca—the Inca Trail, a system of roads used to travel through the empire which eventually spanned much of the Andes. Because of this unique Andean history, the culture here can seem to share more with those of Bolivia and Peru than with other parts of Argentina; keep your ears open in town squares: in this part of Argentina you can still hear people speaking Quechua and Aymara, two of the main languages of the Incas.

Tilcara, Children's carnival, Quebrada de Humauaca

JESUITS AND VICEROYALTIES

The Incans weren't the only conquering force that found the protected valley appealing: in the 17th century, Jesuit priests used Aymara and Quechua to convert the locals to Catholocism, which helped the Spanish eventually use the Quebrada to connect the Viceroyalties (administration center) of Peru in Lima and La Plata in what would later become Buenos Aires. Today, the local mix of pre-Incan, Incan, and Christian traditions and symbols are reflected in everything from dress to architecture to the kinds of items you'll find for sale.

WORLD HERITAGE

Traditions and festivals celebrated along the Quebrada include a unique combination of ancient Andean rites and European religious celebrations. In 2003, UNESCO added the Quebrada to its World Heritage list for its continued legacy of pre-Hispanic and pre-Incan settlements in the area.

SHOPPING CULTURE

The best shopping is in Humahuaca. Numerous small shops sell tourist trinkets, and there's a daily handicrafts market on the steps leading up the hill to the monument. Most of the items for sale will be familiar to anyone who has traveled in the central Andean region, and there are a few artisans making jewelery and other items in more modern Argentine styles.

GEOLOGICAL COLORS: A TIMELINE

The hills in the Quebrada de Humahuaca are famous for their colors—caused by mineral deposits formed from 1 to 400 million years ago. The two best places to see the colors are the Paleta del Pintur (Painter's Palette, pictured) and the Cerro de los Siete Colores (Hill of Seven Colors).

red composed of clay and iron oxide	light orange composed of red clay, mud, and sand	green colored by copper oxides	brown colored by manganese oxides and hydroxides
3–4 MILLION YEARS			1–2 MILLION YEARS

ITINERARY

Salinas Grandes

DAY ONE

MORNING: Purmamarca

The smallest and most picturesque town in the Quebrada, Purmamarca is about two hours north of Salta or over an hour north of San Salvador de Jujuy on R9. The turnoff (left side) onto RA52 is well marked. Arrive as early as possible for the morning light. Get your bearings with a view of the Cerro de Los Siete Colores (Hill of Seven Colors) from a popular viewpoint on the north side of RA52; the trailhead is on your right as you approach town. You can also walk along Paseo de los Colorados, a dirt road (watch for vehicles) that winds around the base of hill itself; to get to it from Plaza 9 de Julio, head west on Florida for 3 blocks.

AFTERNOON: Siesta or Salinas Grandes

Purmamarca goes from quiet to dead during the afternoon siesta; take a siesta yourself, or head out on a half-day side trip. Drive further west on RA52 as it winds its way up the **Cuesta de Lipan** (the Lipan Slope, the Quebrada's mountainous western barrier) and on to the **Salinas Grandes** (Big Salt Flats). If you're without your own transport, there are plenty of taxis, remises, or guides to take you. Technically, the Salinas Grandes themselves are outside of the Quebrada, but the drive there takes you through a dramatic mountain pass—and the highest driveable point in the Quebrada; look for a sign marking your altitude of 4170 m (13,681 ft). After an hour or two (depending on your vehicle's horsepower and photo stops), you'll take unpaved EX-RN40 south to the turnoff (right side) for the Salinas Grandes. Drive until you're on the salt flats themselves—this is the parking lot. This is a working salt flat; don't miss gazing into the clear blue harvesting pools.

NIGHT: Purmamarca

Once back in Purmamarca, explore some nouveau Andean cuisine at **Los Morteros**. After dinner, head to **El Rincon de Claudia Vilte**, a friendly peña where the musicians like to find out where the audience is from in between renditions of folk songs about the Quebrada.

DAY TWO

MORNING: Tilcara

Set out early and take R9 north to Tilcara; head straight to the **Pucará de Tilcara**. This partially reconstructed pre-Columbian fort shows one of the most complex ruins in Argentina. Make time to visit the botanical garden next door. Wander through the central square's market, one of the best in the region. Leave to arrive in Humahuaca before noon.

AFTERNOON: Humahuaca to Maimara

Every day at noon at San Francisco Solano church, a statue of the church's namesake pops out of the clock tower and, as the story goes, delivers a blessing. Catch this if you can, then have lunch and explore the market near the monument steps. Stop in at the small yet atmospheric folklore museum. On your way back to Salta or Jujuy, make brief photo stops at the **Tropic of Capricorn** at Huacalera, the church at Uquia (known for its Cuzco School angel paintings), and the photogenic cemetery of the town of Maimara. If sunset is approaching, however, simply head straight for Maimara—visible behind the cemetary is the Painter's Palette. This flat segment of the east canyon wall contains colored layers of mineral deposits that attain stunningly rich hues as the light shines in from the west.

Pucará de Tilcara

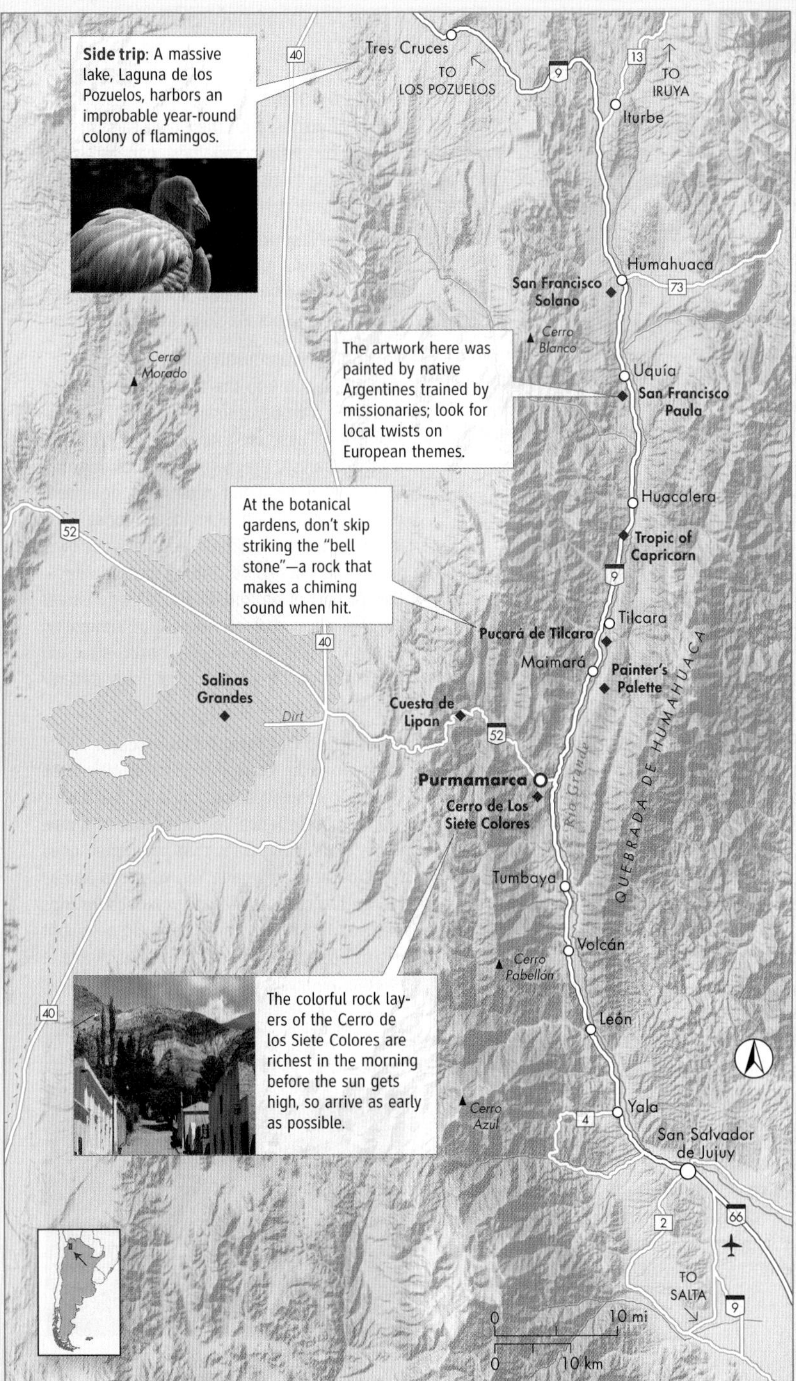
Side trip: A massive lake, Laguna de los Pozuelos, harbors an improbable year-round colony of flamingos.
Tres Cruces
TO LOS POZUELOS
TO IRUYA
Iturbe
Humahuaca
San Francisco Solano
Cerro Blanco
Cerro Morado
The artwork here was painted by native Argentines trained by missionaries; look for local twists on European themes.
Uquía
San Francisco Paula
Huacalera
Tropic of Capricorn
At the botanical gardens, don't skip striking the "bell stone"—a rock that makes a chiming sound when hit.
Pucará de Tilcara
Tilcara
Maimará
Painter's Palette
Salinas Grandes
Dirt
Cuesta de Lipan
Purmamarca
Cerro de Los Siete Colores
Río Grande
QUEBRADA DE HUMAHUACA
Tumbaya
Volcán
Cerro Pabellón
The colorful rock layers of the Cerro de los Siete Colores are richest in the morning before the sun gets high, so arrive as early as possible.
León
Cerro Azul
Yala
San Salvador de Jujuy
TO SALTA
0
10 mi
0
10 km

PLANNING YOUR VISIT

PUBLIC TRANSIT

A good and frequent bus system and shared taxis between the main towns mean hitchhiking isn't common or necessary. However, although buses reach all destinations described, renting a car or going with a guide mean you can stop at any point to explore, take pictures, and admire the views.

SELF-DRIVE LOGISTICS

Cars can be rented in Salta and Jujuy. Check the conditions for off-road driving and the options for crossing a pass into Chile—these are not automatically included in the rental.

Good to Know:

- Car hire agencies like to calculate the price on the spot and there's little transparency in their calculations. Many destinations from Salta and San Salvador de Jujuy involve unpaved roads that are punishing on cars, so it might help to let them know your itinerary if you're only visiting the Quebrada (where all the roads are paved). Pricing systems favor round trips (i.e. there's a big surcharge for dropping off a car in another city).
- Gas stations can be found in most of the towns, but they don't all take credit cards. Except for in Humahuaca (ACA—the Automovil Club Argentino) and San Salvador de Jujuy, plan for cash only. As well as providing gas and good maps, ACA is the Argentine equivalent of the AAA and can help you out if your car breaks down somewhere.
- The roads in the Quebrada are better than most in the area—they're well marked and have clear passing lanes—but during the rainy season (between October and February), falling rocks or mudslides can block the roads.

Car Rental Agencies: In Salta, **Hertz** (✉ Caseros 374 4400 ☎ 387/421-6785) and **Localiza** (☎ 387/431-4045; 0800/999-2999 central reservations) are reputable companies. In Jujuy, contact **Hertz** (✉ Hotel Agustus Belgrano 715 ☎ 388/422-9582).

GUIDED TOURS

Personal guides, with their own cars or ones owned by their companies, can be found through the tourism offices of Salta and Jujuy. From Salta in particular, a sure bet is:

Angélica Vasquez de Zaleski (☎ 387/4964-0658 ✉ langie_guide@hotmail.com). There are also many, many bus trips from Salta or Jujuy, taking in the Quebrada sights in a day or longer.

For Indigenous Culture:

When you pull into the town of Humahuaca, you'll see a group of locals waiting under the main sign. These are tour guides; if you know a little Spanish, they're a wealth of information on how Wichí and other indigenous peoples live and work in Humahuaca today. Even if you're here with a tour guide of your own, he or she might hire one of these guides—they're part of an initiative to provide career alternatives in a place where drug smuggling (Bolivia is just a few clicks north, after all) has in the past been one of the only decent-paying jobs available.

For Getting Out Into the Landscape:

Caravana de Llamas (☎ 0388/495-5326 🌐 www.caravanadellamas.com.ar), out of Tilcara, offers an experience you won't get at home: llama treks along trails that have been used for thousands of years. You lead the llamas along; they carry everything you need for trips that can last from 1 to 10 days. On overnight excursions, you're hosted by the inhabitants of remote mountain huts.

Crias, or baby llamas, Jujuy Province

WHERE TO EAT

$$ ARGENTINE Fodor's Choice ★ **El Churqui.** For a more sophisticated take on regional delicacies, such as llama in Malbec, or grilled trout from the local Yala river, El Churqui has got it. A restaurant and vinoteca with a cellar worth checking out, it only stocks wines made at great height. This busy spot, which takes advantage of a modern use of ingredients, cooks up a succulent goat stew and a sizzling barbecue worth ordering for its smell alone. Reservations are a good idea. *Salta s/n, Purmamarca 388/490–8063 No credit cards 12–3:30, 7:30–10:30.*

$$ ARGENTINE **La Posta de Purmamarca.** Empanadas, llama dishes, and other regional specialties dominate the menu at this eatery on the main square. Take a seat by the window and watch the scene at the market stalls outside while enjoying Jujeño staples such as *picante de pollo* (spicy chicken). *Rivadavia s/n, on Plaza 9 de Julio, Purmamarca 388/490–8040 No credit cards Closed Mon.*

WHERE TO STAY

For expanded hotel reviews, visit Fodors.com.

$ **El Cardon.** It's small and no-frills, but if you're just looking for a place to sleep in between excursions, this friendly lodging a short walk from the main square is a good bet. **Pros:** a reliable, in-town option. **Cons:** few facilities; often booked in high season. *Belgrano s/n, Purmamarca 388/490–8672 7 rooms In-room: no a/c, no TV No credit cards.*

$$$ ★ **El Manantial del Silencio.** At this tranquil retreat, weeping willows, red rocks, and gardens filled with birdsong are hemmed in by the craggy Quebrada and its utter calm; inside the colonial-style stucco mansion, local artifacts and earth tones make things warm and harmonious throughout. **Pros:** the grandest lodging in the Quebrada; great gardens, restaurant, and pool. **Cons:** the most expensive lodging in the Quebrada. *RN52, Km 3.5, Purmamarca 388/490–8080 www.hotelmanantialdesilencio.com.ar 18 rooms, 1 suite, one house In-room: no a/c, safe, no TV, Wi-Fi. In-hotel: restaurant, bar, pool, parking.*

$$$ **La Comarca.** The various rooms, cabins, and houses (which can sleep up to six people) surround a garden of flowers and cacti; all accommodations are built with traditional local materials—adobe, cane, wood—and are decorated with a contemporary eye. **Pros:** quiet; well decorated; good restaurant. **Cons:** showers not designed for tall people. *RN52, Km 3.8, Purmamarca 388/490–8098 www.lacomarcahotel.com.ar 12 rooms, 2 houses, 2 cabins, 1 suite In-room: no a/c, kitchen, no TV, Wi-Fi. In-hotel: restaurant, bar, pool, gym, spa, parking.*

$$ **Los Colorados.** All the reddish adobe walls of the cabins here, on the Cerro de Siete Colores, have rounded corners, giving the whole place a look of having been sculpted straight from the earth; this is a perfect spot for kicking back, whether you're curled up by the fireplace in your room, or on the common terrace stargazing. **Pros:** quiet retreat; a six-person Jacuzzi. **Cons:** small bathrooms. *El Chapacal 511, Purmamarca 388/490–8182 www.loscoloradosjujuy.com.ar 7 rooms/cabins In-room: no a/c, safe, kitchen, no TV. In-hotel: parking.*

4

"Rectangles have been dug out [of Salinas Grandes] to allow the water to seep through and salt to crystallize for the miners to harvest. The clearest water and the whitest salt I have ever seen." —Clive Ellston, Fodors.com member

NIGHTLIFE

El Heriberto. At the town's only late-night bar, El Heriberto, you get a good mix of locals and visitors eager for drinks and dinner. In high season it's open from 10 pm until the last customer leaves or until 5 am, whichever comes first. ✉ *Sarmiento s/n, close to corner of Libertad, Purmamarca* ☎ *388/490–8026.*

El Rincon de Claudia Vilte. At El Rincon de Claudia Vilte, named after a singer from Salta, the crowd is fairly cosmopolitan, but on the small stage of this intimate peña it's pure Jujeño, with pan pipes, drums, and guitars as well as the occasional storytelling session with tales about local traditions and happenings. ✉ *Libertad s/n, close to corner of Belgrano, Purmamarca* ☎ *388/490–8088.*

TILCARA

85 km (53 miles) north of San Salvador; 18 km (11 miles) northeast of Purmamarca via RN9.

The town of Tilcara (altitude 8,100 feet), founded in 1600 and witness to many battles during the War of Independence, is on the eastern side of the Río Grande at its confluence with the Río Huasamayo. Purveyors of local crafts crowd the main plaza, and artists and musicians escaping the big cities fill the cafés and bars. There are several reasons to stop off in this sleepy Quebrada town: an interesting museum; nearby Inca ruins, caves, and waterfalls; and a good selection of accommodations and restaurants.

GETTING HERE AND AROUND

You get here along Ruta 9, which is well served by buses running between San Salvador de Jujuy and Humahuaca or La Quiaca. Arriving from the south, look out for the surprisingly large cemetery of Maimará, which sprawls on either side of the road outside town. If you're heading to San Salvador de Jujuy from Tilcara, consider taking one of the shared taxis that are available at the bus terminal; they cost about the same as buses.

ESSENTIALS

Bank Banco Macro ✉ *Lavalle s/n, at Marcelino Vargas, Tilcara.*

Bus Contacts Atahualpa ☎ *387/155–815–298.* **Evelia SA** ☎ *388/495–5216.*

Medical Assistance Hospital ✉ *Lavalle 552, Tilcara* ☎ *388/495–5001.*

Visitor Info Tourist Office ✉ *Belgrano s/n, at Padilla, Tilcara* ☎ *No phone.*

EXPLORING

La Garganta del Diablo. Seven kilometers (4 miles) west of town is La Garganta del Diablo (The Devil's Throat), a red-rock gorge with waterfalls (the number depends on the season). The tourist office in Tilcara can point you in the right direction; ask about the path that knocks about half the distance off the journey. Ask, too, for directions to the wind-eroded caves that are a similar distance east of town. ✉ *Tilcara.*

Museo Arqueológico. Exhibitions at the Museo Arqueológico, run by the University of Buenos Aires, can be a little confusing due to a lack of labels on artifacts. The two mummies on display are considerably less well explained and cared for than those in Salta's Museum of High Altitude Archaeology, but no less fascinating. The clothes, hair, and skin of the first, which was found in San Pedro de Atacama in Chile, are well preserved. Other rooms show Nazca, Inca, Moche, and other remains from the past 2,000 years. Keep your ticket stubs, as they'll get you in to the nearby Pucará de Tilcara ruins, where some of this museum's artifacts were found. ✉ *Belgrano 445, Tilcara* ☎ *388/495–5006* 🌐 *tilcara.filo.uba.ar/* 🎫 *30 pesos* ⏲ *Daily 9–6.*

★ **Pucará de Tilcara.** These ruins are located on a hill above the left bank of the Río Grande about a mile south of town. This fortified, pre-Inca settlement (*pucará*) is the best-preserved of several in the Quebrada de Humahuaca, and the only one that can be visited. The different areas of the village (some have been rebuilt) nestling among the hundreds of cardon cacti on the hill are obvious. Allow at least 90 minutes to walk around where around 2,000 Omaguaca lived, worshipped, and kept their animals. On your way out, turn right at the entrance to the fort for the Jardin Botanico (Botanical Garden), with a large array of cacti among its plantings. Don't turn down the invitation on a sign to strike the Piedra Campana with a mallet disguised as a stick—true to its name (Bell Stone) it rings like a bell. Note that ticket stubs from a visit to the Museo Arqueológico in town get you free entrance to both the ruins and the botanical garden. ✉ *Tilcara* 🎫 *30 pesos* ⏲ *Daily 9–12:30 and 2–6.*

PARTY TIME, QUEBRADA-STYLE

If you time your trip to Salta and Jujuy provinces right, you'll get to see some of the most unique partying this side of the Paraná Delta.

CARNAVAL

Where? All over the province, but especially in Humahuaca.

When? The week before Lent.

Go if you like . . . dancing with a lot of strangers and dressed-up devils.

The north of Argentina and neighboring Brazil have a few good options for Carnaval, but the Quebrada de Humahuaca's take on the festival is a treat to witness. Local papers carry lists of performance times and places for carnival bands, and people get dressed up and dance all day and night, encouraged by plentiful *chicha* (a potent spirit made from fermented corn or peanuts).

PACHAMAMA

Where? All over the Quebrada.

When? August 1.

Go if you like . . . ecological awareness and age-old tradition.

The Pachamama is the Northwest's Thanksgiving festival, when people show their appreciation of *Madre Tierra* (Mother Earth). The best meats, corn, potatoes, and other vegetables are dried and stored in preparation for August 1st, when they are prepared in a *tijtincha* (stew) and "fed" to the earth—they're buried under stones in a hole in the ground—along with other food, cigarettes, coca leaves, alcohol, and trinkets. During the rest of the year the Pachamama is honored through the gradual construction of *apachetas* (piles of stones) by the side of the road or on tops of hills, to which passersby add one stone at a time.

INTI RAYMI

Where? Huacalera.

When? June 20–21.

Go if you like . . . sunshine in the winter.

On the eve of the winter solstice at the monument and sundial in Hualcalera marking the Tropic of Capricorn, they light fires for the Festival of the Sun, standing round big fires sharing hot alcoholic drinks and trying to keep warm. One of the most important Inca festivals, this is a huge party in Peru, which was reintroduced to the Quebrada in the '90s and gets bigger each year.

EXODO JUJEÑO

Where? All over the province.

When? August 22 and 23.

Go if you like . . . history and celebrating strategic retreats.

In commemoration of General Belgrano's decision to evacuate Jujuy in 1812 in the face of a large Spanish advance, a drastic step which served to disorient the enemy and ultimately gain vital ground. It's now become the focal point of the province's pride and is celebrated with parades in the streets and reenactments.

FIESTA DE LA VIRGEN DE LA CANDELARIA

Where? Humahuaca.

When? February 2.

Go if you like . . . low-key processions, traditional music.

The patron saint of Humahuaca is honored on February 2, with preparations building up in the days before. Bands of young men play *sikuris* and *cajas* (Andean flutes and drums) while a statue of the Virgin is carried through the streets.

WHERE TO EAT

$$$ ARGENTINE Fodor's Choice ★ **El Nuevo Progreso.** The food is superb; the wine list is good and fairly priced; and the wooden floors, whimsical lights, and artwork make the space appealing. What's more, every evening around 9:30 there's live music, generally performed by friends of the owners. It's right in the center of town, with windows looking out across the small plaza. *Lavalle 351, Tilcara 388/495–5237.*

$$ ARGENTINE **El Patio.** With three dining rooms, a patio out back, a location just yards from the central plaza, and well-priced regional cuisine, El Patio is one of Tilcara's most recommended restaurants. The menu is an unpretentious yet delectable mix of regional specialties and standard Argentine fare, and service is friendly. *Lavalle 352, Tilcara 388/495–5044 Closed Tues.*

$$ ARGENTINE **Los Puestos.** A poetic narrative in the menu describes this place as "a haven for parched travelers," along the lines of the watering holes used for centuries by area shepherds. As well as water and wine, they offer bread and empanadas baked in the oven right by the entrance and delicate cuts of meat. Try the fillet of llama with orange sauce and Andean new potatoes. *Belgrano, corner of Padilla, Tilcara 388/495–5100 Closed Mon.*

$$ ARGENTINE **Yacón.** The friendly service, wooden tables and chairs, cane roof, and stone walls all suggest tradition. Yet the kitchen shows some innovation by serving up llama meat on skewers and a shepherd's pie made with quinoa. It's just a block from the main square. *Rivadavia 222, Tilcara 388/495–5611 No dinner Sun.*

WHERE TO STAY

For expanded hotel reviews, visit Fodors.com.

$$ **Las Terrazas.** A few blocks from the square in a quieter area, Las Terrazas has nine spacious rooms, each with its own balcony. **Pros:** good-size rooms and spacious bathrooms; great views; great breakfast. **Cons:** not very central. *Calle de la Sorpresa s/n, at San Martín, Tilcara 388/495–5589 www.lasterrazastilcara.com.ar 9 rooms In-room: no a/c, safe, Wi-Fi. In-hotel: bar, parking.*

$$ **Refugio del Pintor.** The building that houses this hotel (look carefully for the sign, or you'll miss it) was formerly used by the painter Medardo Pantoja from Jujuy, hence the name and the local artworks on the walls; the garden and the sweeping views have been here a while—everything else has been redone with style and imagination. **Pros:** attentive staff; great views; plenty of common spaces; good breakfast with homemade bread. **Cons:** small rooms. *Alverro s/n, between Jujuy and Ambroseti, Tilcara 388/427–1432 www.elrefugiodelpintor.com 13 rooms In-room: no a/c, Wi-Fi. In-hotel: restaurant, bar.*

$ **Uwa Wasi.** The name means "a house with grapes," and it does, indeed, have a few vines in its rambling back garden, where there's also space to relax and get to know your hosts, whose grandparents built the house, and one of whom works for the tourism office. **Pros:** good location; friendly service; nice garden. **Cons:** small rooms; few facilities. *Lavalle 564, Tilcara 388/495–5368 www.uwawasi.com.ar 6 rooms In-room: no a/c, Internet Breakfast.*

4

Cardones (cacti) grow amid the ruins of the Pucará de Tilcara in Jujuy Province.

$$ **Viento Norte.** This long, thin, adobe boutique hotel overlooks a decent-size swimming pool; inside, rooms have simple decorations and low lighting. **Pros:** central yet quiet; a good breakfast; great bathrooms. **Cons:** pool is visible from the street. ✉ *Jujuy 536, Tilcara* ☎ *388/495–5605* 🌐 *www.hotelvientonorte.com.ar* *11 rooms* *In-room: no a/c, safe, Wi-Fi. In-hotel: bar, pool.*

SHOPPING

The central plaza fills with stalls selling Andean-type souvenirs and gifts, some handcrafted by the stallholder, some imported from Bolivia. The best of the local stuff includes knitted hats and scarves. On a Saturday afternoon there are also carts selling *chicha*—an alcoholic drink made from fermented corn. You won't want a lot, but it's a rare opportunity to try it.

SPORTS AND THE OUTDOORS

Caravana de Llamas. For a memorable trekking experience, hook up with Caravana de Llamas. You'll lead the llamas along trails that have been used for thousands of years; they carry everything you need for trips that can last from one to ten days. On overnight excursions you're hosted by the inhabitants of remote mountain huts. ✉ *Tilcara* ☎ *0388/495–5326* 🌐 *www.caravanadellamas.com.ar.*

HUMAHUACA

126 km (78 miles) north of San Salvador de Jujuy; 42 km (26 miles) north of Tilcara on RN9.

Humahuaca (9,700 feet) is the gateway to the Puna. Its narrow stone streets hark back to pre-Hispanic civilizations, when aboriginals fought the Incas who came marauding from the north. The struggle for survival continued into the 16th century, when the Spanish arrived.

Given its location, Humahuaca is a bit touristy, flooded with vendors hawking artisan wares. Things are busiest at midday, when an automated carving of Saint Francisco Solano emerges like a cuckoo from a clock to bless visitors in the main plaza with his mechanized arm. The town is slowly coming out of its shell in terms of providing for tourism, and more visitor amenities are slowly becoming available: however, the tourist board is less than organized (if you find it open) and lodgings are predominantly hostels.

A wiser decision might be to stay in Tilcara, which has more accommodations and restaurants. And, indeed, most people visit Humahuaca on a day trip from there, Purmamarca, or San Salvador de Jujuy, or as a stop en route to Iruya. That said, if you're nearby around the time of Carnaval (40 days before Easter), it's worth putting up with whatever lodgings you can find to participate in the wonderful festivities that are a complicated mix of Catholicism and paganism.

GETTING HERE AND AROUND

You can easily visit the town and nearby gorge as a day trip from San Salvador de Jujuy or Salta, either with a car or with a tour group. Ruta Nacional 9 leads straight here on its way from San Salvador to La Quiaca, and Balut, Panamericano, and other lines have buses going each way almost every hour during the day.

ESSENTIALS

Bank Banco Macro ⊠ *Jujuy 327, Humahuaca.*

Medical Assistance Farmacia ⊠ *Cabildo, central plaza, Humahuaca.*

Visitor Info Tourist Office ⊠ *Cabildo, central plaza, Humahuaca* ☎ *388/421–375.*

EXPLORING

Cabildo. Humahuaca's picturesque *cabildo* (town hall), on the main square, is the most striking building in the village, with a beautifully colored and detailed clock tower. Each day at about noon crowds fill the small plaza to watch a life-size mechanized statue of San Francisco Solano pop out of the tower—it's kitschy fun and one of the world's few clock performances. You can't enter the cabildo, but you can peer into the courtyard. ⊠ *Central plaza, Humahuaca.*

Iglesia de la Candelaria. The 1631 Iglesia de la Candelaria contains fine examples of Cusqueño art, most notably paintings depicting elongated figures of Old Testament prophets by 18th-century artist Marcos Zapaca. ⊠ *Calle Buenos Aires, west side of central plaza, Humahuaca.*

★ **Museo Folklórico Regional.** At first sight the Museo Folklórico Regional appears to be a dusty collection of stones and strange objects, but allow a guide to show you around (arrange in advance for one who speaks English), and you'll learn a lot about the indigenous population. The museum was founded by Sixto Vázquez Zuleta, who has invested a huge amount of passion and imagination, and each exhibit—from dolls made of dried apricots to musical instruments made from armadillos—provides a new insight into the carnival spirit of the area. ✉ *Buenos Aires 435, Humahuaca* ☎ *388/421–064* 🎫 *10 pesos* 🕒 *Daily 8–8.*

OFF THE BEATEN PATH

Iruya. If you can endure a harrowing five-hour, 50-km (31-mile) ride east from Humahuaca on an unpaved cliffside road, you'll be rewarded with one of Argentina's most stunning settings. (Take the bus from Humahuaca rather than driving yourself; you really have to know the road, as the bus drivers do, to negotiate it safely.) This cobblestoned town, which clings to sheer rock, is becoming an increasingly popular stop. It has just one 15-room hotel, the **Hosteria de Iruya** (☎ *3887/482–002*), but many villagers offer rooms for rent. The busiest times to visit are during the first and second weekends in October, when the village celebrates its festival, and at Easter. There are some good hikes from Iruya to even more remote towns like San Isidro, three hours away through the mountains. For more information and guide recommendations, call Arminda Monteyano at the **Tourist Office** (☎ *3887/482–001*). ✉ *Humahuaca.*

WHERE TO EAT

$$ ARGENTINE

✕ **Hostel El Portillo.** This restaurant-café, which also offers seven modest double rooms to rent for 150 pesos a night, caters to the Quebrada- or Puna-bound travelers. That said, it retains a rustic, local feel. Friendly service puts you at ease, and an attractive adobe courtyard allows for a lazy lunch in the midday sun. You can get a llama steak or a hearty version of the classic regional dish *locro* (here it's made with yellow squash, pureed beans and corn, and various types of pork). There's even a short wine list. ✉ *Tucumán 69, Humahuaca* ☎ *3887/421–288* 🌐 *www.elportillohumahuaca.com.ar.*

$$ ARGENTINE ★

✕ **K'allapurca.** At lunch the best tables are taken by groups of tourists being serenaded by a band of minstrels, but don't let that put you off. The food is well-presented, simple Andean fare, and the prices are very reasonable. The kitchen can cater to vegetarians, too. ✉ *Belgrano 210, Humahuaca* ☎ *3887/421–318.*

SHOPPING

The shops just east of the plaza are full of the same ponchos, bags, hats, and shirts sold elsewhere in the Quebrada. Though things are reasonably priced, they're more expensive than they would be in Bolivia, which is where most of the stock originates. There are also some interesting original articles on sale in the main plaza.

SALTA

92 km (57 miles) south of San Salvador de Jujuy on RN9 or 311 km (193 miles) south of San Salvador de Jujuy on R34 (La Cornisa Rd.).

> **WORD OF MOUTH**
>
> "For me the NW region around Salta was by far my favourite experience in Argentina, if not the whole of South America. The scenery is just amazing, the food and wine great, and the people really welcoming." —crellston

It's not just "Salta" to most Argentinians, but "Salta la Linda" (Salta the Beautiful). That nickname is actually redundant: "Salta" already comes from an indigenous Aymara word meaning "beautiful." But for the country's finest colonial city, it's worth stating twice. Walking among its well-preserved 18th- and 19th-century buildings, single-story houses, and narrow streets, you could easily forget that this is a city of more than half a million people. But the ever-increasing traffic, the youthful population, and the growing contingent of international itinerants also give the city a cosmopolitan edge. All in all, it's a hard place to leave. For its friendliness, its facilities, its connections, and its central location, Salta is also the best base for a thorough exploration of the Northwest. Do make good use of the tourist office, which has a very helpful staff armed with a wealth of maps and useful information.

Salta is hardly an urban jungle, but some visitors opt to stay in the quieter hillside suburb of San Lorenzo, 10 km (6 miles) to the northwest and a cooler 980 feet higher. It's a great place if you have a car or can adhere to the every-30-minute bus service to and from Salta.

GETTING HERE AND AROUND

Flights take two hours between Salta and Buenos Aires. Aerolíneas Argentinas flies four times a day; LAN three times a day; and Andes once a day. From Aeropuerto El Aybal it's a 10-km (6-mile) drive southeast into Salta, 30 pesos by taxi or 10 pesos by bus.

Balut buses (15 trips daily) connect Salta to San Salvador de Jujuy, Humahuaca (six trips daily), and Tucumán (once a day). El Indio has two buses a day to Cafayate (four hours). Marco Rueda has one or two buses daily to Cachi (4½ hours); buy a ticket the day before, as most leave early in the morning.

In the city most sights are within walking distance of one another, and taxis are cheap and easy to find. However, renting a car does make exploring the province much easier. That said, many roads are unpaved and can be dangerous in bad weather, so the price of cars is rather high, approaching 300 pesos per day.

MoviTrack offers excursions around Salta, but is best known for its Bus to the Clouds, an oxygen-equipped vehicle that follows the same route as the Tren a las Nubes. Trips last 15-plus hours, and depart daily in winter and nearly every day in summer. Check the MoviTrack website for schedules and prices. A very active member of the Fodors.com forums (known as "Flintstones"), Angélica Vasquez de Zaleski is

Sights

Cabildo 4
Casa de Hernández 5
Catedral Basilica de Salta 2
Convento de San Bernardo 11
Convento San Francisco 8
Museo de Arqueología (MAAM) 3
Museo de Arte Contemporáneo 9
Museo de Arte Etnico 13
Museo de Bellas Artes 6
Museo Folclórico 10
Museo Presidente Uriburu 7
Plaza 9 de Julio 1
Teleférico 12

Restaurants

Casa Moderna 4
Doña Salta 1
José Balcarce 11
Jovi Dos 9
La Posta 5
Lo de Andrés 13

Hotels

Ayres de Salta 7
Hotel del Antiguo Convento 6
Hotel El Lagar 12
Hotel Salta 2
Hotel Solar de la Plaza 8
Legado Mitico 10
Provincial Plaza 3

an independent tour guide with years of experience, a passion for the region, and loads of good recommendations.

ESSENTIALS

Bus Contacts Balut ☎ *388/424–2883.* **El Indio** ☎ *387/432–0846.* **Marcos Rueda** ☎ *387/421–4447.* **Panamericano** ☎ *387/431–1957.* **Terminal de Omnibus** ✉ *Av. Hipólito Yrigoyen 339, Salta* ☎ *387/401–1143.*

Banks and Currency Exchange Banco de la Nación ✉ *Mitre 151 at Belgrano, Salta.* **Cambio Dinar** ✉ *Mitre 101, on Plaza 9 de Julio, Salta.*

Medical Assistance Farmacia Avenida Belgrano ✉ *Belgrano and Dean Funes, Salta* ☎ *387/421–3962.* **Hospital San Bernardo** ✉ *Tobís 69, Salta* ☎ *0800/444–0401.*

Post Office Post Office ✉ *Dean Funes 160, Salta.*

Rental Cars Hertz ✉ *Caseros 374, Salta* ☎ *387/421–6785.* **Perfil Rent a Car** ✉ *Buenos Aires 189, Albania* ☎ *387/422–7855,* 🌐 *www.perfilrentacar.com.*

Taxis Taxi Car ☎ *387/439–0530.*

Visitor and Tour Info Angélica Vasquez de Zaleski ☎ *387/4964–0658* ✉ *angie_guide@hotmail.com.* **MoviTrack** ✉ *Buenos Aires 68, Salta* ☎ *387/431–1223* 🌐 *www.movitrack.com.ar.* **Salta Tourist Office** ✉ *Buenos Aires 93, Salta* ☎ *0800/222–3752* 🌐 *www.turismosalta.gov.ar.*

EXPLORING

TOP ATTRACTIONS

Cabildo. The whitewashed town hall, first constructed in 1582 and rebuilt many times since, used to house Salta's municipal government. Not only a colonial gem in itself, the Cabildo is also home to the Museo Histórico del Norte, which includes a relevant collection of pre-Hispanic stone sculptures as well as religious artifacts and a rather obscure selection of vintage cars in the back garden. ✉ *Caseros 549, Salta* ☎ *387/421–5340* 🌐 *www.museonor.gov.ar* 🎫 *5 pesos* ⊙ *Weekdays 9–7, weekends 9–1:30.*

Catedral Basílica de Salta. The city's 1882 neoclassical cathedral fronts the central plaza, and is notable for the enormous frescoes portraying the four gospel writers on the portico around the altar and its impressive stained glass windows. Inside the entrance is the Panteón de las Glorias del Norte, enclosing the tombs of General Martín Miguel de Güemes and other heroes from the War of Independence. Wander to the back of the cathedral for a peek at the beautiful, jasmine-infused garden. ✉ *España 558, Salta* ☎ *387/431–8206* 🌐 *www.catedralsalta.org* 🎫 *Free* ⊙ *Mon.–Sat. 6:30–12:15 and 4:30–8:15, Sun. 7:30–12:15 and 5–8:15, Sun. winter holidays 7:30–12:15 and 5–8:15.*

Convento de San Bernardo. The Convent of St. Bernard, Salta's oldest religious building, served as a chapel first, then a hospital. Today a cloistered order of Carmelite nuns lives here, so the convent is closed to the public except for morning Mass. The wooden rococo-style door, carved by indigenous craftsmen in 1762, contrasts markedly with the

DID YOU KNOW?

Iruya, a tiny hillside town tucked in a valley northeast of the Quebrada de Humahuaca, is literally the end of the road. To explore beyond, you'll need to leave your vehicle behind.

otherwise stark exterior of this 1625 structure. ✉ *Caseros 73, Salta* ☎ *387/431–0092* 🎫 *Free* ⏲ *Mass Mon.–Sat. at 7:45 am, Sun. at 8 am and 10 am.*

★ **Convento San Francisco.** Every Salteño's heart and soul belongs to the town's landmark St. Francis Church and convent, with its white pillars and bright terra-cotta-and-gold facade. The first temple and convent were built in 1625; the second, erected in 1674, was destroyed by fire; the present church was completed in 1882. The 173-foot-high belfry houses the Campaña de la Patria, a bell made from the bronze cannons used in the War of Independence which sounds once a day at 7:30 pm. In the sacristy, the Museo Convento San Francisco displays religious art. ✉ *Córdoba 33, Salta* ☎ *387/432–1445* 🎫 *Church free, museum 4 pesos* ⏲ *Church daily 8–noon and 5–9, museum daily 10:30–noon and 5–7.*

Fodor's Choice ★ **Museo de Árqueología de Alta Montaña.** The fascinating Museum of High Mountain Archaeology (MAAM) holds the mummified remains of three children born into nobility—ages 6, 7, and 15—and the 146 objects buried with them in Incan sacrificial services almost 600 years ago. They were discovered at the summit of the 6, 723-meter (22,058-foot) Volcán Llullaillaco, on the Argentine–Chilean border, in 1999. The high altitude and freezing temperatures kept their skin, hair, hands, and clothes in impeccable condition, although the face of one was damaged by lightning. The museum also contains an exhibition about the Qhapaq Ñan Inca trading route from southern Colombia to Mendoza and another mummy, the Reina del Cerro (Queen of the Mountain), which for decades was illegally in the hands of private collectors. ✉ *Mitre 77, Salta* ☎ *387/437–0499* 🌐 *maam.culturasalta.gov.ar/* 🎫 *30 pesos* ⏲ *Tues.–Sun. 11–7:30.*

Museo de Arte Etnico Americano Pajcha. The small, private Museum of Ethnic American Art Pajcha has artifacts and illustrations from the pre-Columbian world and later. Enthusiastic guided tours explain exhibits, from religion to furniture to the Mapuche culture. A new addition to the museum, which moved premises in order to accommodate its growing collection, is an impeccable textile anthology. There's enough reason to linger for hours, and when you're done, relax with a coffee on the back terrace. ✉ *20 de Febrero 831, Salta* ☎ *387/422–9417* 🎫 *20 pesos, plus 10 pesos for a tour guide* ⏲ *Mon.–Sat. 9–8.*

★ **Museo Folclórico Pajarito Velarde.** The two rooms of this museum are stuffed with curiosities and background information on the cultural and artistic elite that were the constant companions of Guillermo "Pajarito" Velarde Mors, the consummate bohemian who brought tango to Salta and lived here from 1930 to 1965. The space is brimming with the trinkets, art, and possessions belonging to this eccentric. Take a look at the hat that Carlos Gardel gave him and the rosewood bed that folk singer Atahualpa Yupanki slept on. Even if you're not au fait with Argentine culture from half a century ago, this museum is a delightful tribute to a real character who owned one of the finest tango record collections in Salta. ✉ *Pueyrredón 106, Salta* ☎ *387/421–2921* 🎫 *10 pesos* ⏲ *Weekdays 10:30–2, 3:30–6.*

Plaza 9 de Julio. The heart of Salta is quintessential Latin America: a leafy central plaza named after the date of independence. Arcaded buildings, many housing cafés, line the streets surrounding the square (commemorating the founding of the city in 1582), providing perfect spots to while away a warm afternoon. Popular with families who take shade under the palm and jacaranda trees, the square is dotted with craftsmen and teens canoodling by the bandstand. ✉ *Salta* ☎ *387/401–1002.*

NEED A BREAK?

Van Gogh. The Parisian-style Van Gogh café, with reproductions of works by its namesake master, is a great spot on Plaza 9 de Julio to leisurely take in a coffee and a piece of cake while writing postcards to folks back home. ✉ ***España 502, Salta*** ☎ ***387/431-4659.***

Teleférico a Cerro San Bernardo. The Cerro San Bernardo rises east of downtown Salta, a cool 880 feet higher than the city center. This cable car takes you up the hill from a station across from Parque San Martín in less than 10 minutes. Views of the entire Lerma Valley reward you at the top, and you can also wander the garden with its cool breezes and pond. If you're in the mood for a little light exercise, take the staircase back down. ✉ *San Martín and H. Yrigoyen, Salta* ☎ *387/431–0641* *30 pesos* *Daily 10–7.*

WORTH NOTING

Casa de Hernández/Museo de la Ciudad. Inside an 1879 neocolonial house is the City Museum, the ground floor displays an exceptional collection of musical instruments. Rooms upstairs document the history of Salta through paintings and photographs. ✉ *La Florida 97, Salta* ☎ *387/437–3352* *Voluntary donation* *Mon.–Sat. 9–1 and 4–8:30.*

Museo de Arte Contemporáneo. In a privileged position on a corner of Plaza 9 de Julio, the Contemporary Art Museum has a "Museum of the Year" award from the Association of Argentine Art Critics under its belt. It rotates the shows on both floors; expect photography, installations, and traveling exhibitions from other Argentine galleries. ✉ *Zuviria 90, Salta* ☎ *387/437–0498* *2 pesos* *Tues.–Sat. 9–8, Sun. and holidays 4–8.*

Museo de Bellas Artes. The Fine Arts Museum's collection of colonial-era religious art includes figures from Argentina's Jesuit missions as well as Cuzco-style paintings from Peru and Bolivia. Another part of the museum highlights 20th-century works by Salteño artists. ✉ *Belgrano 992, Salta* ☎ *387/431–8562* *5 pesos* *Weekdays 9–7, Sat., holidays 11–7.*

Museo Presidente José Evaristo Uriburu. Fine examples of late-colonial architecture—an interior courtyard, thick adobe walls, a reed-and-tile roof—abound in this simple building, the 19th- and 20th-century home of the Uriburu family, which gave Argentina two presidents. Furniture, costumes, paintings, and family documents are on display across six rooms. ✉ *Caseros 417, Salta* ☎ *387/421–5310* *5 pesos* *Tues.–Fri. 9–12 and 2–7, Sat. 9–1:30.*

WHERE TO EAT

SALTA

$$ ARGENTINE **Casa Moderna.** For a cured-meat cut above the rest, head to this delicatessen and winebar, which also owns a small winery, selling hearty reds under the Los Morros brand. *Picadas* are the stars of the show, a selection of choice local cheese and hams accompanied by bread baked in-store. The Camembert is a winner, and do try the smoked boar and trout. The restaurant does get busy, but staff are generally friendly. Sit out on the back terrace away from the hustle and bustle. ✉ *España 674, Salta* ☎ *387/422–0066* ▭ *No credit cards.*

$$ ARGENTINE **Doña Salta.** This warm, festive, family-friendly locale serves dishes quite typical of Salta and the Northwest. You'll dine in a room steeped in local tradition, amid wine jugs and old wooden implements. Try classics like *humita* (steamed corn husks filled with cheese) or the local *locro* stew, with beans and hunks of beef. Empanadas and meats are also reliable; the pastas are unremarkable, though. The location, across from Iglesia San Francisco, couldn't be more central. ✉ *Córdoba 46, Salta* ☎ *387/432–1921* ▭ *No credit cards.*

$$$ ARGENTINE **José Balcarce.** A group of chefs launched a restaurant and catering service with high Andean cuisine as its goal—"high" referring to both the altitude and the gourmet techniques. The result is José Balcarce, in a brick-and-wood building with large windows just two blocks from bustling Balcarce Street. The menu is short, and the service can be slow, but the food is fresh and delicious. ✉ *Necochea 590, Salta* ☎ *387/421–1628* ⏲ *No lunch. Closed Sun.*

$$ ARGENTINE **Jovi Dos.** It's an eclectic, great-value restaurant on a quiet downtown corner. The big, high-ceilinged room, with wood beams and plate-glass windows, is crammed with local businesspeople at lunch. Noteworthy starters include marinated eggplant and baked meat empanadas. Grilled meats, seafood, pizza, and pasta have equal billing on the ridiculously long menu. Dishes such as the *ravioles mixtas* (ravioli filled with spinach and cheese and topped with a creamy sauce) are big enough for two people. The waitstaff is attentive, and the wine list is solid. ✉ *Balcarce 601, Salta* ☎ *387/432–9438* ▭ *No credit cards.*

$$$ ARGENTINE **La Posta.** A crimson-and-cream color scheme and a checkerboard floor lend personality to this bright, cavernous downtown eatery. Start with a salad from the bar and one of the outstanding cheese empanadas, and then move on to *cabrito al asador* (goat grilled over an open fire)—a luscious, salty indulgence. Pair it with a local Cabernet. For dessert there's the unique *dulce de cayote,* a molasseslike marmalade served with walnuts atop local goat cheese. ✉ *España 456, Salta* ☎ *387/421–7091* ▭ *No credit cards.*

SAN LORENZO

$$$ ARGENTINE **Lo de Andrés.** Folks from Salta and San Lorenzo favor this bright, airy semi-enclosed brick-and-glass building with a vaulted ceiling for weekend dining. Andrés prepares a lightly spiced Argentine-style parrillada, but if you're not up for such a feast, there are empanadas and *milanesas* (breaded steak) as well as regional dishes such as tamales and humita.

⌧*Juan Carlos Dávalos and Gorriti, San Lorenzo* ☎*387/492–1600* ⌚*No lunch Mon.*

WHERE TO STAY

For expanded hotel reviews, visit Fodors.com.

SALTA

$$ **Ayres de Salta.** Conveniently located between the main plaza and Balcarce Street, Ayres de Salta has a small pool and fitness center on the roof and a good little restaurant on the ground floor; rooms are large and well equipped. **Pros:** efficient, professional staff; good location; buffet breakfast. **Cons:** some rooms look into the windows of other rooms. ⌧*General Güemes 650, Salta* ☎*387/422–1616* *www.ayresdesalta.com.ar* *40 rooms* *In-room: safe, Wi-Fi. In-hotel: restaurant, bar, pool, parking.*

$$ **Hotel del Antiguo Convento.** This charming property is in a former convent and run by a cheerful and attentive young staff; rooms are clean, bright, and well priced. **Pros:** staffers go out of their way to be helpful; convenient location. **Cons:** small courtyard and pool. ⌧*Caseros 113, Salta* ☎*387/422–7267* *www.hoteldelconvento.com.ar* *15 rooms* *In-room: safe, kitchen. In-hotel: bar, pool, parking* *No credit cards.*

$$ ★ **Hotel El Lagar.** The wrought-iron door is always locked, and there's no sign to indicate there's a hotel here on this quiet street a few blocks north of the city center, but inside you'll find Salta's most exclusive—though not at all stuffy—bed-and-breakfast. **Pros:** attentive staff; charming garden with swimming pool; large breakfast. **Cons:** a few blocks from the main plaza; a wine cellar crying out to be used for tastings. ⌧*20 de Febrero 877, Salta* ☎*387/431–9439* *10 rooms* *In-room: a/c, safe, Wi-Fi. In-hotel: pool, parking.*

$$$ ★ **Hotel Salta.** The Salta is in a handsome neocolonial building, a National Historic Monument, in the heart of the city; antique furniture and views of either the plaza or the surrounding mountains make every room attractive. **Pros:** ideal location; access to Salta Polo Club; spa; breakfast buffet. **Cons:** rooms facing the plaza can be noisy. ⌧*Buenos Aires 1, Salta* ☎*387/426–7500* *www.hotelsalta.com* *99 rooms* *In-room: a/c, safe, Wi-Fi. In-hotel: restaurant, bar, pool, gym, spa, parking.*

$$$ ★ **Hotel Solar de la Plaza.** The exterior of this beautiful old house belies the modern comforts within; inside, an elegant lobby leads to a beautifully appointed sitting room, airy courtyard spaces, and a good (though expensive) restaurant. **Pros:** high comfort; rooftop pool; buffet breakfast. **Cons:** rather pricey. ⌧*Leguizamón 669, Salta* ☎*387/431–5111* *www.solardelaplaza.com.ar* *28 rooms, 2 suites* *In-room: safe, Wi-Fi. In-hotel: restaurant, bar, pool, gym.*

$$$ **Legado Mitico.** Sister to the Buenos Aires hotel of the same name, the family-run Legado Mitico has attention to detail down to a science, making it second to none, down to the welcome glass of wine of your choice. **Pros:** warm and welcoming spaces; the living room and terrace are comfy spots for a moment of relaxation; interesting rooms and artwork. **Cons:** located on a rather busy main drag; street-facing rooms

DID YOU KNOW?

The Iglesia de San Francisco in Salta is perhaps the most unusual colonial structure in town; watch visitors' reactions as they realize the heavy white drapes over the front entrances are actually carved stone.

can be noisy. ✉ *Bartolomé Mitre 647, Salta* ☎ *387/422–8786* 🌐 *www.legadomitico.com* ➡ *11 rooms* ♨ *In-room: a/c, safe, Wi-Fi.*

$ **Provincial Plaza.** This hotel is on a corner just blocks from Plaza 9 de Julio; only a few of the standard rooms have not been renovated—superior and executive floors are spruced up and have good facilities. **Pros:** central location; full buffet breakfast. **Cons:** lower floors get street noise. ✉ *Caseros 786, Salta* ☎ *387/432–2000* 🌐 *www.provincialplaza.com.ar* ➡ *88 rooms* ♨ *In-room: Wi-Fi. In-hotel: restaurant, bar, pool, children's programs, parking.*

SAN LORENZO

$$ **Eaton Place.** Despite appearances, this elegant Georgian-style mansion and its beautiful gardens date only from the 1980s, when it was built as a home; it still feels like a private house, with bright and airy rooms in the main house and guesthouse with huge windows, hardwood floors, and period furniture. **Pros:** well appointed; large breakfast. **Cons:** a long way from the center of town. ✉ *San Martín 2457, San Lorenzo* ☎ *387/492–1347* 🌐 *www.eatonplacesalta.com.ar* ➡ *8 rooms, 1 suite* ♨ *In-room: no a/c, kitchen, no TV. In-hotel: pool* ▭ *No credit cards.*

NIGHTLIFE

Salta is a young and lively city, with a bar district along a few blocks of Balcarce Street that can get quite busy. Clubs, restaurants, and peñas attract both locals and tourists, who come to hear regional folk bands give it their all on small, cramped stages. Adding to the rowdy, dinner-theater atmosphere are the local gaucho dancers who entice (and often entrap) foreigners into strutting their stuff on stage; it's always a good laugh, no matter what language you speak.

La Casona del Molino. Twenty-odd blocks down Caseros Street from the main plaza, La Casona del Molino is renowned for its nightly folk performances and its good regional food including locro and tamales. ✉ *Luis Burela 1, Salta* ☎ *387/434–2835.*

La Vieja Estacion. A top spot for music, gaucho dancers, and the like is self-proclaimed "home of folkore" La Vieja Estacion, which hosts nightly shows. ✉ *Balcarce 885, Salta* ☎ *387/421–7727* 🌐 *www.la-viejaestacion.com.ar.*

Macondo. At Macondo, a raucous pub where blues and beer are always on tap, you're as likely to meet backpacking Aussies as you are local law students. ✉ *Balcarce 980, Salta* ☎ *387/431–7191.*

Peña Gauchos de Guemes. With more than 50 years hosting folk music nights, this peña retains a gaucho spirit, hosting regional dancers and groups at one of the most traditional venues in the city. ✉ *Uruguay 750, Salta* ☎ *387/421–7007* 🌐 *www.gauchosdesalta.com.ar.*

SHOPPING

En lo de Carmén. Although it stocks a far smaller selection of products than the Mercado Artesanal, artist Carmén Clerici de Dominguez's store does house a workshop for craftsmen. Pick up reasonably priced ceramic dishes, hand-knitted alpaca socks and gloves, and paintings by local artists. ✉ *Balcarce 725, Salta* ☎ *387/421–3207.*

Feria de la Balcarce. Every Sunday, on Balcarce street between Entre Ríos and Ameghino, around 200 local artisans get together for this weekly handicrafts street market, considered the most important in the north. Pick up ceramics, knitwear, rugs, shawls, and even furry llama toys. ✉ *Balcarce 700 between Entre Ríos and Ameghino, Salta* ⏲ *Sundays 10 am–10:30 pm.*

Mercado Artesanal. Salta has all the usual main high-street shops where you can stock up on sundries, but for souvenirs and regional products, provincial villages are a better bet. However, there are a few proud exceptions to that rule, including the huge 1882 Jesuit monastery that holds the Mercado Artesanal and the open stalls across the street. Look for red-and-black Salteño ponchos, alpaca knitwear and weavings, leather goods, wooden animal masks, and fine silver. Everything is open daily 9–9. ✉ *Av. San Martín 2555, Salta* ☎ *387/434–2808.*

4

SPORTS AND THE OUTDOORS

Salta has just a few outfitters, but the options they offer feel fresh and exciting. Horseback riding is an activity growing in popularity, as are rafting, paragliding, and mountain biking.

Finca Lesser. Fifteen km (10 miles) west of Salta, Finca Lesser provides horseback-riding tours on a huge private estate. Trips can last anywhere from a few hours to two days. They can also organize a folk-music performance and a tour showing gauchos at work. ✉ *4 km [2½ miles] past Castellanos, San Lorenzo, Salta* ☎ *387/155–827–321* 🌐 *www.redsalta.com/fincalesser.*

MacDermott's Argentina. Despite being told by local gauchos that he and his horse Pancho wouldn't make it crossing the Andes, Hugh MacDermott proved the cynics wrong, and he now shares his expertise by leading horse-riding holidays across the northwest. ✉ *Salta* ☎ *387/155–395–820* 🌐 *www.macdermottsargentina.com.*

Salta Rafting. Salta Rafting operates from a base 35 km (21 miles) south of Salta by the Cabra Corral dam, and offers much more than just getting wet in exciting circumstances in a kayak. They also offer tandem paragliding jumps and have a "death slide"—a network of zip-line cables for a breathtaking canopy surfing experience that crosses high above the Río Juramento. ✉ *Caseros 117, Salta* ☎ *387/421–3216* 🌐 *www.saltarafting.com.*

Sayta. Sayta offers stays out at a ranch in Chicoana, 40 km (24 miles) south of Salta, and horseback treks lasting from one to 10 days for riders of all levels. The estancia offers meals and accommodation. ✉ *Chicoana, Salta* ☎ *387/156–836–565* 🌐 *www.saltacabalgatas.com.ar.*

EN ROUTE

When the road to Cachi starts ascending toward Piedra de Molina—a lookout point at 11,000 feet above sea level—it winds up the spectacular Cuesta del Obispo (Bishop's Rise) and, shortly before the top, reaches the **Parque Nacional Los Cardones.** Almost nothing other than thousands of *cardones* (the cardon cacti, for which the park is named) can thrive here, and even they've been threatened. (People were chopping them down for use as "wood" at a faster rate than they could grow back; they're now protected). Try to make the journey in the morning, as clouds descend in the afternoon and the road becomes difficult to navigate; never drive the route at night, and seek advice before setting out in the rainy season. Halfway through the park the road splits: the quicker route is via Payogasta to the north, but Ruta 42 takes you on a fantastic but unpaved road through red mountains nicknamed Los Colorados.

SALTA PROVINCE

Unofficial capital of the Argentine north, the city of Salta is known for its colonial architecture and its unassuming provincial appeal. It's also a hot spot for international visitors, and compared with its neighbors it's really got its tourism act together. That said, much of the province of Salta has yet to be discovered by outsiders. Even the main circuit, the Valles Calchaquíes (Calchaqui Valley), involves long drives on unpaved roads with few other vehicles in sight.

Only the central third of the province has much in the way of population (the east and the west being vast, uninhabitable wilderness) but within that there's plenty of variety. Although new circuits are being opened up that take in the Cabra Corral dam and thermal waters of Rosario de la Frontera, the main destinations outside the city of Salta are Cafayate for its wine, Cachi for its landscape and archaeological sites, and San Antonio de las Cobres—the destination of the Tren a las Nubes (Train to the Clouds).

CACHI

157 km (97 miles) southwest of Salta.

Cachi is a small village on Ruta 40 that's fast becoming a base for exploring the north of Calchaqui Valley. The town also has a charming church, a small archaeological museum, and a couple of decent hotels and restaurants, although there is nothing in the way of nightlife. Watching over it all is the 6,340-meter (20,800-foot) Nevado de Cachi, a few miles away.

The surrounding area is loaded with archaeological sites that have scarcely been explored. El Tero is a site of pre-colonial dwellings, and within 15 km (10 miles) are two more important sites: Puerta La Paya to the southwest and Las Pailas to the north (at the foot of the Nevado de Cachi). A little farther north, en route to La Poma, are the Graneros Incaicos (Incan Graneries), a cave in a stunning setting used by the Inca for storing grain.

GETTING HERE AND AROUND

Just one bus company, Marcos Rueda, serves Cachi from Salta. You're advised to buy tickets the day before for the journey that takes just over four hours on a good day. For more flexibility, Remis San José runs a fixed-price taxi service four times a day. The cost is about 200 pesos.

THE NORTHWEST SHOPPING EXPERIENCE

Throughout the Northwest, almost every town has a main area where vendors sell *artesenías*—emblematic crafts using local materials and incorporating the culture. Spending time at these markets, which may simply be set up around the main plaza, isn't just a great way to find the perfect souvenir; it's also a real opportunity to interact with locals.

Andean *artesanías* come in two forms: mass-produced products (generally imported from Bolivia) and locally produced handmade items. Often, stall owners will sell a mix of the two; ask which are locally made and opt for them, as they do more to support the local community. Bolivian goods get cheaper the farther north you go. Some towns such as Humahuaca and Tilcara have shops that are exclusively fair trade, so look out for the signs saying "comercio justo."

Also, you'll see lots of dimpled *cardon* (cactus) wood carved into all manner of souvenirs, but there's no system right now for verifying the origin of the wood (only souvenirs carved from already-dead cardones are legal). We encourage you to ask your guide or another local for vendor recommendations.

Alpaca knits. Alpacas look like a cross between a llama and a sheep with a glossy, silky fleece. Textiles from them feel lovely and are unmistakably Andean, with the traditional designs.

Coca. Freely available, coca here is a medicine rather than a narcotic. Coca tea is neatly packaged and doesn't taste too bad. But don't try taking it home without checking customs regulations first.

Leather. Unless there's an item that particularly catches your eye, save your leather purchases for the pampas. They do use cows and leather in the Quebrada, but not in the decorative ways of elsewhere in the country.

Masks. If you don't experience Humahuaca at carnival time, you might be surprised by the number of masks—of humans and animals, made of wood or pottery—among the souvenir stalls. If you do go in carnival time, it'll make more sense.

Musical instruments. Panpipes are easy to play for anyone (though harder to play well) and instantly evocative of the windswept Quebrada. There are more intricate instruments available for musicians or the curious. For some tips on how to play, take it to a peña in the evening and corner one of the performers.

Ponchos. They go with everything, are useful against the cool cloudless nights in the Quebrada, and make a great regional gift. Ponchos are made from sheep or llama wool; you can also pick up hats and gloves in matching patterns. Don't wear your poncho out in Buenos Aires if you want to blend in.

Silver. It was its position on the road to the Potosí silver mines that made the Quebrada so important in colonial days, but don't count on the silver on sale now being locally sourced. What you do have, though, are traditional motifs and symbols cast into silver as jewelry and, borrowing traditions from elsewhere, tableware.

Iglesia San Pedro de Nolasco, Molinos

They also offer transfers to Cafayate and the villages in between and sightseeing tours of the area.

ESSENTIALS

Bus Contacts Marcos Rueda ☎ *387/421–4447.*

Banks Banco Macro ✉ *Ruiz de los Llanos, at the plaza, Cachi.*

Medical Assistance Hospital Dr Arne Hoygard ✉ *Benjamín Zorrilla s/n, Cachi* ☎ *3868/491–038.*

Taxis Remis San José ✉ *Cachi* ☎ *3868/491–907.* **Remisería Cachi** ✉ *Cachi* ☎ *3868/491–163.*

Visitor and Tour Info Tourist office ✉ *General Güemes s/n, Cachi* ☎ *3868/491–902.* **Turismo Urkupiña** ✉ *Benjamin Zorrilla s/n, Cachi* ☎ *3868/491–317.*

WHERE TO STAY

For expanded hotel reviews, visit Fodors.com.

$$$ **ACA Hosteria.** For most of the past 40 years this Argentine Automobile Club hosteria was the only decent place to stay in Cachi, but it's now facing some stiff competition from more boutique offerings; still, it has a pool, a good restaurant, facilities for kids, and a nice garden. **Pros:** good facilities; buffet breakfast; children's play area. **Cons:** small rooms. ✉ *Av. Automóvil Club Argentino s/n, Cachi* ☎ *3868/491–105* 🌐 *www.soldelvalle.com.ar* *33 rooms* *In-room: safe, Wi-Fi. In-hotel: restaurant, bar, pool, parking.*

$$ **El Cortijo.** This rustic boutique hotel was converted from an old house; it stands out for its friendly service, a great view from the balcony of its courtyard, a wine cellar, a restaurant, and well-decorated rooms. **Pros:** good service; artistic decoration; buffet breakfast. **Cons:** construction work is slated to continue indefinitely—ask when you book. ✉ *Av. Automóvil Club Argentino s/n, Cachi* ☎ *3868/491–034* 🌐 *www.elcortijohotel.com* *12 rooms* *In-room: Wi-Fi. In-hotel: bar, parking.*

$$$ **La Merced del Alto.** Although this stately white-adobe building looks like it's been here forever, it was in fact built in 2006; inside, rooms are huge and comfortable with tasteful wood and iron furniture. **Pros:** expansive grounds with great views; attention to detail; accessible for people with disabilities; buffet breakfast. **Cons:** 3 km (2 miles) from Cachi; echoing corridors. ✉ *Fuerte Alto s/n, Cachi* ☎ *3868/490–030* 🌐 *www.lamerceddelalto.com* *13 rooms, 1 suite* *In-room: no a/c, safe, no TV, Wi-Fi. In-hotel: restaurant, bar, pool, spa.*

Fodor's Choice ★

4

MOLINOS

206 km (128 miles) southwest of Salta (via Cachi); 50 km (31 miles) south of Cachi.

Molinos has a photogenic church and a small farm breeding vicuñas, an animal similar to a llama but one whose fur makes a much finer (and more expensive) wool. Its main draw, however, is its location on the way to Cafayate, with its many *bodegas* (wineries), and to Colomé, Argentina's oldest bodega, with one of the world's highest vineyards and some luxury facilities, including tastings, horse riding, and a fabulous restaurant.

Molinos is also just a few miles from the Camino de Artesanos (Road of the Artisans) of Seclantás, who weave ponchos and scarves by the roadside on contraptions improvised from wood and old bicycle parts. The Laguna de Brealito, 10 km (6 miles) due west of Seclantás, is a picturesque lake in the middle of nowhere. Eight kilometers (5 miles) east of Molinos are the pre-Columbian ruins of Chicoana.

EXPLORING

★ **Estancia Colomé.** Remote wineries are one thing; Colomé, set up by Swiss winemaker Donald Hess and his wife, is quite something else. Arriving puts the miles of driving along bumpy, unpaved roads firmly into perspective: Colomé, a world-class winery that dates from 1831, offers tastings, a delectable restaurant with a vineyard view, horse-riding expeditions, and an art gallery out in the relative wilderness 20 km (13 miles) from Molinos. Formerly operating as a luxury hotel with all the perks imaginable, the estancia is now open only for group bookings. Since 2009 Colomé has also been home to the James Turrell Museum, showcasing five decades of the artist's works with light and space, and including a fun tunnel of color. It's open between 2 pm and 6 pm daily, although you're advised to make a reservation in advance. ✉ *RP53 Km 20, Molinos* ☎ *387/439–4009* 🌐 *www.estanciacolome.com.*

WHERE TO EAT

$$ ARGENTINE **Inti Ray.** It's an honest little restaurant in Seclantás, with some fine old photos on the walls and good, oven-baked empanadas. Other attractions are a delicious goat stew, locro, regional breads and jams, and a warm welcome from your host, Alejandro Diaz. *Cornejo s/n, Seclantás 3868/498–009 No credit cards.*

CAFAYATE

185 km (115 miles) southwest of Salta via RN68; 340 km (211 miles) southwest of Salta via R40; 230 km (143 miles) northwest of San Miguel de Tucumán.

Thanks to a microclimate and fertile soil, Cafayate and the surrounding area is one of Argentina's booming wine-growing regions. The town itself is very civilized and orderly, with various bodegas offering free tours and tastings, lots of good restaurants, and some exquisite hotels. But wander a couple of blocks from the central plaza and you're back on unpaved roads. Take a bit of a hike, and you're in the mountains—probably enjoying a wine-tasting session at a tiny *finca* and trying hard to get your camera to do justice to the view. There are also some authentic handicrafts to buy, a five-aisle cathedral, and a world-famous ice-cream man.

GETTING HERE AND AROUND

El Indio runs three bus services a day from Salta (four hours). It's best to buy your ticket the day before, especially in summer. In town, many agencies and hotels offer bicycle rental, and there are some good bodegas and sights to visit within a few miles of town. There are also plenty of opportunities to explore the countryside on horseback or go on a hike, either organized or by yourself.

ESSENTIALS

Bank Banco de la Nacion *Nuestra Señora del Rosario 103, Cafayate 3868/421–215.*

Medical Assistance Laboratorio del Sol *San Martín 37, Cafayate 3868/421–008.*

Visitor Info Tourist Office *Plaza 20 de Febrero, Cafayate 3868/422–224 www.turismosalta.gov.ar.*

EXPLORING

Museo de la Vid y del Vino. This museum, located in a warehouse dating from 1881, has undergone an extensive refurbishment to include more flash and 3-D exhibitions. You can learn about wine-making in the Calchquíes valleys. Machinery, agricultural implements, and old photographs also tell the history of wine-making in this area. *Guemes Sur and Fermín Perdiguero, Cafayate 3868/422–322 www.museodelavidyelvino.gov.ar 30 pesos Tues.–Sun. 10–7:30.*

Museo Regional y Arqueológico Rodolfo Bravo. For 66 years, Rodolfo Bravo collected and catalogued funerary and religious objects from local excavations. These objects, made of clay, ceramic, metal, and textiles, are on display at the private Museo Regional y Arqueológico Rodolfo Bravo

(Rudolfo Bravo Regional and Archaeological Museum). Artifacts from the Incas (15th century) and Diaguitas of the Calchaqui Valley also form part of the collection. ✉ *Colón 191, Cafayate* ☎ *3868/421–054* 🎫 *Voluntary contribution* ⏲ *Weekdays 11:30–9, Sat. 11:30–3.*

NEED A BREAK?

Helados Miranda. Helados Miranda is an essential stop in Cafayate for wine-tasting with a difference. In 1994, at the age of 60, Ricardo Miranda decided that he wasn't going to make it as a painter and that he could only make a living out of something he wasn't passionate about. It took him two years to perfect his creation: wine sorbets. Sweet Torrontés arguably makes sense as a sorbet; the Cabernet makes a good match for it and his fruit-flavored ice creams. All are made organically on the premises. ✉ ***Av. Güemes Norte 170, Cafayate*** ☎ ***3868/421-106.***

4

Quebrada de las Conchas. The first 50 km (30 miles) of the direct road to Salta (or the last stretch if you don't come via Cachi and Molinos), known as the Gorge of the Shells, encompasses such breathtaking scenery that the Quebrada is now rightfully its own attraction. Various rock formations have been eroded into wildly different shapes that have been nicknamed the Windows, the Castles, the Frog, the Friar—each name seems truly fanciful, that is until the road winds around the corner and you're actually confronted by the formation itself. The climax is the Amphitheater, sometimes used as a venue for proper orchestras thanks to its outstanding natural acoustics; wandering minstrels offer impromptu performances. ✉ *RN68, Km 6–Km 46, Cafayate.*

BODEGAS

Although Salta makes only 1% of Argentina's wines, the province accounts for 15% of the country's exports. Most of the production is in or around Cafayate, which has a dozen bodegas, ranging from small family businesses to small branches of multinational concerns.

Bodega Nanni. Nanni has been in the same family and in the same building—just a block from the main square—since 1897. It has the only organic certification in Cafayate, and nearly a third of its small production of Torrontés, Malbec, Cabernet Sauvignon, and Tannat is exported to the United States. Tour and a tasting cost 10 pesos. ✉ *Silverio Chavarria 151, Cafayate* ☎ *3868/421–527* 🌐 *www.bodegananni.com* 🎫 *10 pesos* ⏲ *Daily 9:30–1 and 2:30–6.*

Domingo Molina. A few miles northwest of Cafayate is Domingo Molina, which has been making Torrontés, a 90-point Malbec, and various blends since 2000. A drive takes you high up into the hills, and offers stunning views of the wine lands to the east. Book in advance for a *picada* or an *asado* at the winery and take a look at their oldest vine, a 100-year-old Malbec, still providing drinkable grapes. Sister winery located in town, Domingo Hermanos, is one of Cafayate's biggest operations, producing three million liters a year. ✉ *Km 6, Yacochuya Norte, 2 km north of Cafayate on RN40, Cafayate* ☎ *3868/452–887* 🌐 *www.domingomolina.com.ar* 🎫 *20 pesos* ⏲ *Wed.–Fri. 10–5, Mon. 10–1.*

El Esteco. Producers of several lines of well-received wines such as Ciclos and Altimus, El Esteco is just as famous for being the home of the Patios de

Cafayate Hotel & Spa. The bodega is 3 km (2 miles) from the center of Cafayate, so it's easy to drop in for a comprehensive tour and/or tasting, but book ahead to try out the hotel's fine restaurant. ✉ *RN40 at RN68, Cafayate* ☎ *3868/1556–6019* 🌐 *www.elesteco.com.ar* 🎫 *20 pesos* ⏲ *Tours weekdays at 10, 11, noon, 2:30, 3:30, 4:30, 5:30 and 6:30, weekends at 10, 11, and noon.*

El Transito. Inside a blocky modern building in the center of town is the family-run El Transito's bodega and visitor center. Drop in for a tour and the chance to sample Malbec, Cabernet Sauvignon, and Torrontés. ✉ *Belgrano 102, Cafayate* ☎ *3868/422–385* 🌐 *www.bodegaeltransito.com* 🎫 *Free* ⏲ *Mon.–Sat. 9–1 and 3–7, Sun. 10–1 and 3–6.*

Etchart. Founded in 1850, the Etchart Bodega is a large estate 10 km (6 miles) south of town. As well as the chance to take a tour, a visit is an opportunity to taste some of the area's most successful wines. ✉ *RN40, Km 1,043, Cafayate* ☎ *3868/421–310* 🌐 *www.bodegasetchart.com* 🎫 *Free* ⏲ *Weekdays 1:15, 2:15, 4:15.*

Finca de las Nubes. Built up on the land of the Bodega José Luis Mounier in El Divisadero, 4 km (2 miles) out of town, this is one of Salta's best boutique wineries. Almost half of its small line of reds, whites, rosés, and sparklings is sold in the bodega itself. The small fee for tours is discounted against any purchases, and they also offer lunch if you book ahead. ✉ *El Divisadero, Km 4, Cafayate* ☎ *3868/422–129* 🌐 *www.bodegamounier.com.ar* 🎫 *15 pesos* ⏲ *Mon.–Sat 9:30–5.*

La Última Pulpería. For a time-warp trip, pop into this store, which has barely changed since opening in 1923. An Aladdin's Cave selling dozens of loose herbs and spices, animal hides, and produce, La Última Pulpería is a historical little gem. If you can pry owner, Miguel Dioli, away from his regular Salta brand beer-drinking customers at the makeshift bar, he's good for a chat in Spanish. ✉ *Mitre 20, Cafayate* ☎ *3868/421–629.*

Peña Veyrat Durbex. Off the beaten track, this delightful getaway for the bon vivant has eight guest rooms (510 pesos with garden view, 670 pesos with vineyard view), a wine cellar, a restaurant, and an organic winery. It offers wine tours and tastings to day visitors. It's 18 km (11 miles) from the center of Cafayate and on the way to the Quebrada de las Conchas. ✉ *RN68, Km 18.5, Cafayate* ☎ *3868/492–056* 🌐 *www.lacasadelabodega.com.ar* 🎫 *35 pesos* ⏲ *Daily 10:30–5 with reservation.*

HOME STAYS

Red de Turismo Communitario (*Network of Community Tourism*). Ruta 40 continues unpaved most of the way to Cafayate, with a public transport gap between Molinos and Angastaco. If you're traveling this way, look into the Red de Turismo Communitario, an unusual scheme that inserts visitors into communities, not only staying with families but joining in their daily tasks, such as baking bread. There are places to stay in Angastaco, Cachi, Santa Rosa, San Carlos, Animaná, and Divisadero. It helps to know some Spanish. ✉ *San Martín Mediador 560, San Carlos* ☎ *3868/154–55127* 🌐 *www.turismocampesino.org.*

Drying chilies near Cachi, Calchaquí Valley

San Pedro de Yacochuya. Head 8 km (5 miles) northwest out of town toward the hills to find Arnaldo Etchart's boutique, small-scale winery, a fledgling in the area whose reputation preceeds it for its three award-winning wines (it enlisted the help of Michel Rolland in the early days). Tastings are available if you book ahead for a meal (300 pesos with wine) at the estancia, from which you can enjoy the views over the valley. ✉ *Yacochuya, RN40, km 6, Cafayate* ☎ *3868/421–487* 🌐 *www.sanpedrodeyacochuya.com.ar* 🎫 *Free* ⏲ *Weekdays 10–6, Sat. 10–1.*

Vasija Secreta. On the northern edge of town, Bodega La Banda is in a grand 154-year-old building with a small museum displaying imported oak barrels and machinery for pumping and bottling wine. Short tours fill in some history and show how production methods have changed. There are also 10 beautiful but facility-free guest rooms (650 pesos) and a simple restaurant serving local dishes (50 pesos for lunch). ✉ *RN40 s/n, Cafayate* ☎ *3868/421–850* 🌐 *www.vasijasecreta.com* 🎫 *30 pesos with tasting and museum tour* ⏲ *Daily 9–1 and 2:30–7.*

WHERE TO EAT

$$$ ARGENTINE ✕ **El Rancho.** This big barn of a restaurant faces the main plaza, and offers big portions of regional specialties such as baked rabbit and classic Argentinian steaks and pastas. Expect a bustling atmosphere, live folk music, and wines from Bodega Río Colorado, just a block away. ✉ *Vicario Toscano 4, Cafayate* ☎ *3868/421–256* 🌐 *www.elranchocafayate.com.ar* 💳 *No credit cards* ⏲ *Closed Mon.*

$$ ARGENTINE ✕ **Peña y Parrillada de la Plaza.** This place makes the list for its music rather than its food—though the barbecued meats and empanadas are good deals. Singers, musicians, and sometimes dancers bring the

place to life each night. ✉ *Nuestra Señora de Rosario 96, Cafayate* ☎ *3868/421–043.*

$$$ ARGENTINE ★ ✕ **Macacha Gourmet.** The three dining rooms are themed after the local Nanni, Domingo Hermanos, and Etchart bodegas, with wine displays and special cutlery. The decoration is from all around the world, but the food is strictly local, with llama, quinoa, rabbit, kid, and Andean potatoes prominent on the menu. The convivial wine bar stays open late to serve its wines from every bodega in town. Live music and dancing goes on some weekends. ✉ *Av. Güemes Norte 28, Cafayate* ☎ *3868/422–319* ▭ *No credit cards* ◷ *Closed Sun.*

WHERE TO STAY

For expanded hotel reviews, visit Fodors.com.

$$$ **Altalaluna Hotel Boutique & Spa.** In the village of Tolombón 14 km (9 miles) south of Cafayate is Altalaluna, a wonderful 1892 colonial mansion that is now a boutique hotel; there's a wine bar and cellar, an excellent restaurant, a reading room complete with fireplace, and a peaceful spa overlooking endless vines. **Pros:** great facilities; perfect for star-spotting. **Cons:** the pitter-patter of small feet running past rooms can sound very loud. ✉ *RN40, km 4326, Cafayate* ☎ *3868/422–501* 🌐 *www.altalaluna.com* *20 rooms* *In-room: a/c, safe, Wi-Fi. In-hotel: restaurant, pool, gym, spa, business center, parking.*

$$$ **Cafayate Wine Resort.** Three kilometers (2 miles) from the plaza on a straight dusty road lined with vineyards and in the shadow of San Isidro is a large white adobe building with 12 rooms built around a wide courtyard. **Pros:** spacious shared areas and access to veranda from all rooms; vineyards right up to the hotel; buffet breakfast. **Cons:** a little isolated from the town. ✉ *25 de Mayo s/n, Camino Al Divisadero, Cafayate* ☎ *3868/422–272* 🌐 *www.cafayatewineresort.com* *12 rooms* *In-room: a/c, safe, Wi-Fi. In-hotel: restaurant, bar, pool, parking.*

$ **El Hospedaje.** This century-old building used to be a youth hostel until the owner got tired of the noise and chaos. Rooms are basic, but they're set around a pleasant courtyard or the swimming pool. **Pros:** quiet and close to center; Continental breakfast in a large dining room. **Cons:** few facilities; bigger breakfasts elsewhere. ✉ *Camila Quintana de Niño s/n, at Salta 13, Cafayate* ☎ *3868/421–680* *12 rooms* *In-room: a/c, Wi-Fi. In-hotel: bar, pool, parking* ▭ *No credit cards.*

$$$ **Hotel Asturias.** The swimming pool is terrific, the garden is ample, and this, the biggest and oldest hotel in town, is quite comfortable. **Pros:** great garden and pool; two art galleries; close to the center; buffet breakfast. **Cons:** superior rooms more expensive; restaurant open only in high season. ✉ *Av. Güemes Sur 154, Cafayate* ☎ *3868/421–328* 🌐 *www.cafayateasturias.com* *63 rooms* *In-room: no a/c, safe, Wi-Fi. In-hotel: restaurant, bar, pool, parking.*

$$$$ **Patios de Cafayate Hotel & Spa.** Creature comforts and a fine restaurant make this luxury Starwood property a top choice, where rustic rooms are decorated in rich red and green tones and overlook vineyards. **Pros:** very exclusive; afternoon tea and breakfast included; fabulous facilities. **Cons:** very expensive. ✉ *R40 at RN68, Cafayate* ☎ *3868/422–229* 🌐 *www.patiosdecafayate.com* *30 rooms* *In-room: safe, Wi-Fi. In-hotel: restaurant, bar, pool, parking.*

$$$ ★ **Portal del Santo.** Just two blocks from the plaza but already on the edge of town, this place feels like a hideaway; behind the large colonial-style building, with its big guest rooms and its fireplace-warmed common area, is a garden with a blue-and-white swimming pool and great views. **Pros:** both central and quiet; good bathrooms; big breakfast. **Cons:** many guests are families, which tends to disturb the peace. ✉ *Silvero Chavarria 250, Cafayate* ☎ *3868/422–500* 🌐 *www.portaldelsanto.com.ar* *13 rooms* *In-room: safe, Wi-Fi. In-hotel: bar, pool, parking.*

SHOPPING

Cesteria (weaving with cane), *tejidos* (weaving with fabric), and *cerámica* (pottery) are the local specialties. Find these goods in the Paseo de Artesanos on the main plaza or in individual workshops. The tourist office opposite the Paseo de Artesanos has details.

Calchaquitos. Calchaquitos, just next to the plaza, sells cookies and chocolates, local jams, wine, and clothes. ✉ *Güemes Sur 118, Cafayate* ☎ *3868/421–799.*

SPORTS AND THE OUTDOORS

Getting active in Cafayate involves the gentler end of adventure tourism: there are lots of opportunities for hikes, horseback rides, and bike excursions, but nothing too extreme. The waterfalls in the Río Colorado make a good excursion on a bike or on foot.

Turismo Cordillerano. This outfit rents mountain bikes and offers half-day to five-day treks and horseback rides. ✉ *Camila Quintana de Niño 59, Cafayate* ☎ *3868/422–137* 🌐 *www.turismocordillerano.com.ar.*

Wine Regions

MENDOZA AND SAN JUAN: THE HEART OF WINE COUNTRY

WORD OF MOUTH

"And what a wine day it was! We visited four wineries, had an unbelievable gourmet lunch, and came away with 10 bottles of holy-crap-this-is-amazing wine."

—BostonGal

WELCOME TO WINE REGIONS

TOP REASONS TO GO

★ **Scenic Wonders:** Wherever you go—over the pass to Chile, north to San Juan, south to San Rafael—the sight of those towering white Andean peaks never ceases to amaze.

★ **Fun in the Sun:** This sun-soaked land will delight, whether you pedal a bike along flat vineyard roads, ride a horse along Andean trails, or go skiing.

★ **Bed and Bodega:** Country inns with gourmet restaurants, vineyard visits and tastings, cooking classes, and discussions with oenologists make wine touring a pure pleasure.

★ **Food and Wine:** Some of Argentina's premier chefs have left resorts on the coast and the bistros of Buenos Aires for wine-country inns and wineries.

★ **Unique Terroir:** All the big-name wineries have planted in the high-altitude region of the Valle de Uco, where grapes ripen slowly and varieties show tremendous fruitiness.

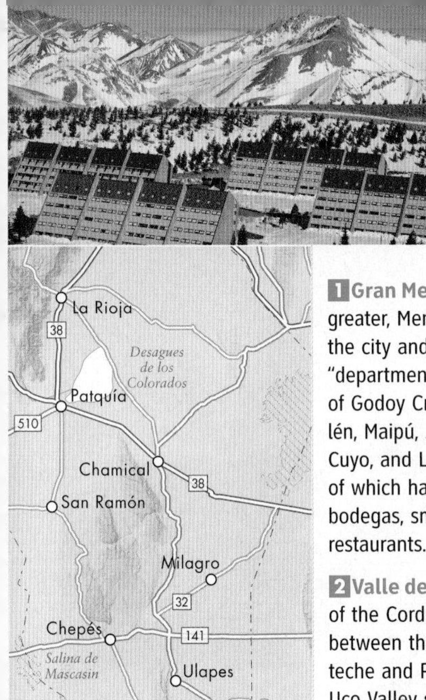

Top left: Familia Zuccardi Winery
Top right: Las Lenas, Mendoza

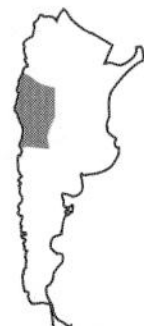

GETTING ORIENTED

The provinces of Mendoza and San Juan, in the central-west portion of Argentina, lie at the foot of the highest Andean ranges along the border with Chile. The city of Mendoza and its surrounding departments are in Mendoza Province's northern portion, 1,040 km (646 miles) from Buenos Aires but only 360 km (224 miles) from Santiago, Chile. The east–west Ruta Nacional 7 (RN7 Pan Americano or Panamerican Highway) crosses the Andes from Mendoza to Chile and links Argentina and neighboring countries (Brazil, Uruguay, Paraguay) with Pacific ports. Ruta Nacional 40 runs north–south the length of the country, passing through San Juan and down to Mendoza, the Valle de Uco, and San Rafael.

1 Gran Mendoza. Gran, or greater, Mendoza refers to the city and the surrounding "departments" (urban areas) of Godoy Cruz, Guaymallén, Maipú, Junín, Luján de Cuyo, and Las Heras—all of which have vineyards, bodegas, small hotels, and restaurants.

2 Valle de Uco. At the foot of the Cordón del Plata, between the towns of Ugarteche and Pareditas, the Uco Valley spreads its green mantle of vineyards and fruit orchards for 125 km (78 miles). The Río Tunuyán and its many arroyos (streams) create an oasis in this otherwise dry, desert region.

3 San Rafael. The vineyards and olive groves that surround this growing agricultural town in the southern portion of Mendoza Province are irrigated by the Ríos Atuel and Diamante, which flow from the nearby Andes.

4 San Juan. From this historic town surrounded by three important wine-producing valleys—Tulum, Ullum, and Zonda—you can travel west up the Río San Juan into a landscape of mountains, valleys, and desert.

lunch at Cava de Cano, Mendoza

5

CERRO ACONCAGUA VIA THE USPALLATA PASS

At 6,957 meters (22,825 feet), it's the highest mountain in the Americas and in the southern hemisphere. It towers over the Andes with its five glaciers gleaming in the sun. Every year, from late November through March, hundreds try to conquer the so-called Giant of America.

(above) Sunset on Aconcagua from Plaza de Mulas base camp (top right) Poplar trees en route to the pass (bottom right) Look up: condor sightings are common in this area.

However, you don't have to be a mountaineer to enjoy the wild beauty here. Although guided climbing expeditions require two weeks of hiking and acclimating, a worthy alternative is to park at the rangers' cabin right off Ruta Nacional 7 just beyond the Puente del Inca, pay the park fee, and hike three hours from the Río Horcones to a lagoon. If this seems like a short hike for such a drive out, relax knowing that the journey to this place is as breathtaking as Aconcagua itself.

While fauna isn't thick, sight lines are unobstructed, and you might see foxes or shy guanacos; look up for condors, too. Alpine meadows bloom in the spring, and lichen are up to 500 years old.

DRIVE SAFELY

Ruta Nacional 7 is the only road that connects the Pacific ports of Chile with Argentina, Brazil, and Uruguay. Be prepared for heavy truck traffic.

Note that roads become icy in winter and can close for days due to snow. The altitude jumps from 762 meters (2,500 feet) in Mendoza to 3,184 meters (10,446 feet) at the top of the pass; winds can sometimes be brutal.

ALONG THE USPALLATA PASS (RN7, THE PANAMERICAN HIGHWAY)

Leaving Mendoza, green vineyards give way to barren hills and scrub brush as you follow the river for 30 km (19 miles). If you find yourself engulfed in fog and drizzle, don't despair: you'll likely find brilliant sunshine when you reach the Potrerillos Valley 39 km (24 miles) along. The road passes a long dam and then follows the Río Mendoza for 105 km (65 miles) to Uspallata, the last town before the Chilean frontier.

Along the way, the Ríos Blanco and Tambillos rush down from the mountains into the Río Mendoza, and remnants of Inca *tambos* (resting places) marked by signs along the way remind you that this was once an Inca route; if you're traveling with a guide, she or he will stop for you to check them out. At Punta de Vacas, corrals that held cattle on their way to Chile lie abandoned alongside defunct railway tracks. Two kilometers (1 mile) beyond the army barracks and customs office three valleys converge. Looking south, the region's third-highest mountain, Cerro Tupungato, an inactive volcano (6,800 meters/22,310 feet), reigns above the Valle de Uco.

After passing the ski area at Los Penitentes, you arrive at Puente del Inca (2,950 meters/9,680 feet). Legend has it that long before the Spaniards arrived an Inca chief traveled here to cure his paralysis in the thermal waters. Today, in addition to the thermal springs, you'll see a natural bridge of red rocks encrusted with yellow sulfur that spans the Río Cuevas; what's left of a spa hotel, built in the 1920s and destroyed in a 1965 flood, is covered in copper and gold sediment below the bridge. A few miles farther west, past the Argentine customs check, are the entrance to the park and the ranger's cabin. Fifteen kilometers (9 miles) farther along, the highway passes Las Cuevas, a settlement where the road forks right to Chile or left to the statue of Cristo Redentor (Christ the Redeemer) on the Chilean border (at 4,206 meters/13,800 feet), commemorating the 1902 peace pact between the two countries.

HIKING GUIDES AND LOGISTICS

Aim for November–March for two- or three-day guided treks to the Plaza de Mulas base camp at 4,325 meters (14,190 feet), where there's a *refugio* (cabin with bunk beds; ☎ *261/423–1571* in Mendoza for reservations).

Inka Expeditions. Inka Expeditions has 10 years of experience leading tours to base camp. ☎ *261/425–0871* 🌐 *www.inka.com.ar.*

Purchase a permit at **Cuba House** on San Martin Park in Mendoza City (✉ *Las Tipas at Los Robles* 🎫 *Trekking permits $50–$110 USD, depending on season and permit level; Ascent permits $160–$500* 🕓 *Weekdays 8–6, weekends 9–1*).

INTO CHILE

Some tours and independent travelers continue on through to Chile to explore the vintages there. Visas, required of U.S. citizens, can be obtained at the border. (⇨ *See the Crossing the Andes section of the "Wines of Chile and Argentina" feature in this chapter.*)

5

Updated by Cathy Brown

In the center of Argentina, in the provinces of Mendoza and San Juan, melting snow from the Andes flows into rivers, streams, and underground aquifers, and transforms this semi-arid region into the largest area under irrigation in Argentina. Eighty percent of the country's wine is produced here, as are olive oil, garlic, and a cornucopia of fruits and vegetables.

Argentina is the world's fifth-largest wine producer; in Mendoza alone more than 200,000 hectares (494,200 acres) of vineyards bask in the sun from the suburbs of Mendoza City south through the Valle de Uco (Uco Valley) to San Rafael. The grapes are protected from the humid winds of the Pacific by the Andes, and grow at altitudes between 609 and 1,524 meters (2,000 to 5,000 feet), where they ripen slowly during long, hot summer days, while cool nights maintain acidity for long-lasting taste. Indeed, many vineyards could be classified as organic, as chemicals are seldom used or needed. Because irrigation is controlled and there is little to no rainfall in the growing season, pests are minimal and Argentina doesn't tend to have "good years" or "bad years" for wine. There is much more consistency here than in other wine-growing areas of the world.

This wine-growing region is often referred to as the Cuyo—a name passed down from the early indigenous Huarpe people, who called it Cuyum Mapu (Land of Sand). *Acéquias* (canals) built by the Huarpes and improved upon by the conquering Incas and Spaniards, as well as by modern engineers, continue to capture the flow of the region's great rivers and channel it along the shady streets of the region's major cities: Mendoza, San Juan, and San Rafael.

Jesuit missionaries crossed the Andes from Chile to plant the first grape vines in 1556, followed by Spanish settlers who founded the city of Mendoza in 1561 and San Juan a year later. At that time the Cuyo was part of the Spanish Viceroyalty of Peru. Most of the area was cattle country, and ranchers drove their herds over the Andes to markets in

Santiago. Although the Cuyo became part of the eastern Viceroyalty of the Río de la Plata in 1776, the long, hard journey across the country by horse cart to Buenos Aires kept the region economically and more culturally tied to Chile until 1884, when the railroad from Buenos Aires reached Mendoza.

The area is known not only for its wine but also for its outdoor activities. River rafting, horseback riding, and hiking in the highest range of the Andes, including Aconcagua, soaking in thermal baths, and skiing at Las Leñas and Penitentes—all these activities attract people year-round. In addition, one of the world's richest paleontological areas—the Parque Provincial Ischigualasto in San Juan Province—is a UNESCO World Heritage Site.

WINE REGIONS PLANNER

WHEN TO GO

The wine harvest ends in autumn and is celebrated with a week of festivities that culminate in the *vendimia* (wine festival). In Mendoza this takes place during the last days of February and first week of March. A parade circles the Plaza Independencia and ends in the soccer stadium in San Martín Park with a grand finale of music, dancing, and religious ceremonies to ensure a good harvest. People shop and graze at food stands in the parks and plazas.

Winter is time for pruning and tying vines. Ski season begins in July, the month with the best weather and the one most favored by Argentineans and Brazilians. August usually has plenty of snow, and September offers spring conditions. Weather in the Andes is unpredictable; pack clothes for all conditions, and get reports from ski areas. Springtime in the Valle de Uco brings trees covered in pink and white blossoms and new life in the vineyards. The snowcapped Andes form a spectacular backdrop, so bring your wide-angle lens.

GETTING HERE AND AROUND

Mendoza, San Juan, and San Rafael all have bus stations, car-rental agencies, cheap taxis, and *remises* (hired cars with drivers). If you're combining a ski vacation in Las Leñas with wine tours, fly from Buenos Aires to San Rafael, then travel north through the Valle de Uco to Mendoza. If you're skiing in Chile, fly from Santiago (or take a bus) to Mendoza.

Hiring a remis for an hour or a day is a good use of money, as frequent detours, road construction, or washed-out roads, and misleading (or nonexistent) signs can make driving yourself frustrating. Further, finding wineries on your own requires not only a good map but also a working knowledge of Spanish. That said, if you have the time and the temperament for it, exploring on your own—stopping for photos and to chat with locals—has its rewards. Driving to Andean villages and the border with Chile is a particularly remarkable experience.

RESTAURANTS

Most of the region follows national culinary trends—beef, lamb, chicken, and pork *a la parrilla* (grilled). Second- and third-generation Italian restaurants serve family recipes with fresh ingredients like wild asparagus and mushrooms. Olive oil, garlic, melons (ripe February–March), and many other fruits (such as plums, apricots, peaches, and quince) and vegetables are grown locally. Hearty Spanish soups and casseroles are a connection to the region's past, as is *clérico*, a white-wine version of sangria. You may also have the opportunity to attend an *asado* (a traditional outdoor barbecue). Malargüe, southwest of San Rafael, is famous for its *chivito* (goat)—cooked a la parrilla or *al asador* (skewered on a metal cross stuck in the ground aslant a bed of hot coals).

HOTELS

Tourist offices can recommend all kinds of *hospedajes* (lodgings), apart-hotels (rooms with cooking facilities and sometimes a sitting area), *cabañas* (cabins), hostels, and *residenciales* (bed-and-breakfasts), all of which are generally well maintained and offer good bargains. In the countryside you'll find everything from campgrounds to *hosterías* (inns), *estancias* (ranches), and even a spa hotel. *Posadas* (country inns) can be cozy and old-fashioned, sprawling and ranchlike, or sleek and modern. Some have first-rate restaurants and an extensive wine list. Afternoon tea, wine tastings, custom tours, and horseback rides are all possible activities.

Mendoza City has lively hostels, many medium-size hotels and apart-hotels, and the Hyatt and the Diplomat for luxury. San Rafael has two modern hotels, a few smaller ones, a golf and tennis resort, bodega and hotel, and Finca Los Alamos—a historic country mansion family-owned since 1890.

WHAT IT COSTS IN PESOS

	$	$$	$$$	$$$$
Restaurants	30 pesos and under	31 pesos–50 pesos	51 pesos–75 pesos	over 75 pesos
Hotels	300 pesos and under	301 pesos–500 pesos	501 pesos–800 pesos	over 800 pesos

Restaurant prices are for one main course at dinner. Hotel prices are for two people in a standard double room in high season.

WINE TOURS

Most wineries require reservations. It's even better to arrange tours to vineyards through your hotel, a tourist office, or a local tour operator. Tours are particularly good if there's a specific bodega you wish to visit or if you're traveling with a group and/or during the harvest. If you do head out yourself, don't be put off by security precautions such as a locked gate or a uniformed guard. Many wineries charge for tastings, so make sure to ask when you make your reservation.

TOURS

Aventura and Wine (Bacchus Tours). Private, very personalized wine tours include a visit with the owner or winemaker. ✉ *Granaderos 1307* ☎ *261/429–3014 in Mendoza* 🌐 *www.aventurawine.com.*

Aymará Turismo. With 20 years in the business, Aymará offers a large variety of wine tours. ✉ *9 de Julio 1023* ☎ *261/420–2064 in Mendoza* 🌐 *www.aymaramendoza.com.ar.*

Hon Travel. Directed by Marcelo Navarro, this agency is the cream of the crop. ✉ *Amigorena 56* ☎ *261/420–2134* 🌐 *www.hontravel.com.*

Malbec Symphony. Directed by a sommelier, this agency offers wine tours from Mendoza to the San Juan region. ☎ *261/543–3292* 🌐 *www.malbecsymphony.com.*

Mendoza Viajes. Wine tours, rafting, and horseback riding are offered here. ✉ *Sarmiento 129* ☎ *261/461–0210 in Mendoza* 🌐 *www.mendozaviajes.com.*

Mendoza Wine Camp. Offering more hands-on tours, including one where you create your own personal blend. ☎ *261/630–0026* 🌐 *www.mendozawinecamp.com.*

San Rafael Wine Tours. Custom itineraries to get to know the best of San Rafael. ☎ *2627/1553–2759* 🌐 *www.sanrafaelwinetours.com.ar.*

Trout & Wine Tours. Both private and group tours to top bodegas in Mendoza and the Valle de Uco. ☎ *261/425–5613, 261/15–541–3892 cell* 🌐 *www.troutandwine.com.*

SELF-GUIDED WINE TOURS

Each area has its own unique *caminos del vino* (wine routes). San Juan wineries have pooled their resources to print a booklet, *Ruta del Vino,* with maps, photos, and information in Spanish. In San Rafael, pick up information in your hotel or at the tourist office. Mendoza's caminos del vino are featured on several maps. The WINEMAP, available at bookstores and wineries, consists of four maps and a guidebook (in Spanish).

EMERGENCY CONTACTS

Ambulance–Medical Emergencies ☎ *107.*

Fire ☎ *100.*

Police ☎ *101.*

GRAN MENDOZA

Mendoza Province, its eponymous capital, and the capital's environs (departments) are home to about 1,700,000 people, roughly 130,000 of whom live in Mendoza City. Most of the major vineyards and bodegas are in departments south of the city (Maipú, Godoy Cruz, Luján de Cuyo) and farther south across the Río Mendoza, in the regions of Agrelo and Perdriel. Still more vineyards are farther south in the Valle de Uco. Each department has its own commercial areas, with shopping centers, hotels, and restaurants.

MENDOZA CITY

1,060 km (659 miles) southwest of Buenos Aires; 250 km (155 miles) east of Santiago, Chile.

Mendoza's streets are shaded from the summer sun by a canopy of poplars, elms, and sycamores. Water runs along its sidewalks in *acéquias*, disappears at intersections, then bursts from fountains in the city's 74 parks and squares. Many acéquias were built by the Huarpe Indians and improved upon by the Incas long before the city was founded in 1561 by Pedro del Castillo.

Thanks to the booming wine and tourism industries, Mendoza bustles with innovative restaurants and lodgings that range from slick high-rises with conference rooms for serious wine tasting to low-key inns and B&Bs for serious relaxing. Low-rise colonial buildings with their lofty ceilings, narrow doorways, and tile floors house restaurants and shops. In the afternoon shops close, streets empty, and siesta-time rules—until around 5, when the city comes back to life and goes back to work.

GETTING HERE AND AROUND

Mendoza's Aeropuerto Internacional Francisco Gabrielli is 6 km (4 miles) north of town on Ruta Nacional 40. Aerolíneas Argentinas has flights (about two hours) from Buenos Aires. LAN Chile has 55-minute flights from Santiago, Chile.

Bus Terminal del Sol is in Guaymallén, an eastern suburb about a 10-minute cab ride to or from town. From here buses travel to every major Argentine city and to Santiago, Chile. Transport companies include Andesmar and La Cumbre, with service to San Juan (3 hours); Chevallier, with daily service to Buenos Aires (14 hours); El Rápido, with daily buses to Buenos Aires and Santiago, Chile (8 hours). You should never cut it close on timing when it comes to bus connections or flights. If the bus company says that the trip will take 10 hours, unfortunately sometimes it takes 12 or 13. So plan on a decent amount of time for extenuating circumstances, just in case.

Driving from Buenos Aires (along lonely but paved Ruta Nacional 7, aka Ruta Pan Americano or the Panamerican Highway) or Santiago (again, on Ruta Nacional 7, which is sometimes closed along this stretch in winter) is an option, provided you have plenty of time and speak some Spanish. There's little need for a car in town, and it's hard to find wineries in outlying areas on your own—even when you *do* speak Spanish. Further, Mendocinos are known for their cavalier attitude toward traffic rules. Pay attention to weather and road information. If you fear getting lost or breaking down in remote areas, hire a remis (a car with a driver) or arrange a tour. ⚠ **Downtown streets have ankle-breaking holes, steps, and unexpected obstacles, so watch where you're going.**

Air Contacts Aerolíneas Argentinas ✉ *Paseo Sarmiento 82* ☎ *261/420–4100.* **LAN** ✉ *Rivadavia 256* ☎ *261/448–4411 in Mendoza, 0810/9999–526 elsewhere* 🌐 *www.lan.com.*

Bus Contacts Andesmar ☎ *261/429–9501* 🌐 *www.andesmar.com.* **Chevallier** ☎ *261/431–0235* 🌐 *www.nuevachevallier.com.* **El Rápido** ☎ *261/405–4344* 🌐 *www.elrapidoint.com.ar.* **Terminal de Ómnibus** ✉ *Av. Gobernador Videla at Av. Acceso Oeste* ☎ *261/431–5000.*

Car Rentals Avis ✉ *Primitivo de la Reta 914* ☎ *261/420–3178* 🌐 *www.avis.com.* **Hertz** ✉ *Espejo 391* ☎ *2627/423–0225.* **Localiza** ✉ *Primitivo de la Reta 936* ☎ *261/429–6800* 🌐 *www.localiza.com.ar.* **MDZ Rent a Car** ✉ *Avenida España 23* ☎ *261/424–6442* 🌐 *www.mdzrentacar.com.*

Taxis La Veloz del Este ✉ *Alem 439* ☎ *261/429–9999.*

ESSENTIALS

Banks Banco de la Nación ✉ *Av. San Martín at Gutiérrez.* **Banelco** ✉ *Av. San Martín at San Lorenzo* ✉ *San Martín at Sarmiento.* **Citibank** ✉ *Av. San Martín 1098.*

Internet Locutorio Internet ✉ *Av. Villanueva 570.* **WH Internet** ✉ *Av. Las Heras 61.*

Medical Assistance Farmacia del Puente ✉ *Av. Las Heras 201* ☎ *261/423–8800.* **Hospital Central** ✉ *Alem 10, near bus station* ☎ *261/449–0500.*

Visitor Info Mendoza Tourist Board ✉ *Av. San Martín 1143, at Garibaldi* ☎ *261/413–2101,* 🌐 *www.turismo.mendoza.gov.ar* ⏲ *Weekdays 9–1 and 4–8, Sat. 9–1.*

EXPLORING

In 1861 an earthquake destroyed the city, killing 11,000 people. Mendoza was reconstructed on a grid, making it easy to explore on foot. Four small squares (Chile, San Martín, Italia, and España) radiate from the four corners of Plaza Independencia, the main square. Their Spanish tiles, exuberant fountains, shaded walkways, and myriad trees and flowers lend peace and beauty. Avenida San Martín, the town's major thoroughfare, runs north–south out into the southern departments and wine districts. Calle Sarmiento intersects San Martín at the tourist office and becomes a *peatonal* (pedestrian mall) with cafés, shops, offices, and bars. It crosses the Plaza Independencia, stops in front of the Hyatt Plaza, then continues on the other side of the hotel.

NEED A BREAK?

Bonafide Expresso. For a fresh cup of coffee, stop in at Bonafide Expresso. The Bonafide brand was the first to bring a coffee roasting machine to Argentina in 1917. On the corner of Sarmiento and 9 de Julio near the central plaza, enjoy a steaming cup of joe with *medialunas* (sweet croissants) and *alfajores* (cookies with dulce de leche, sweet carmelized milk). ✉ ***Peatonal Sarmiento 102*** ☎ ***261/423–7915.***

TOP ATTRACTIONS

Plaza Independencia. In Mendoza's main square you can sit on a bench in the shade of a sycamore tree and watch children playing in the fountains, browse the stands at a weekend art fair, or take a stroll after lunch to the adjacent historic Plaza Hotel (now a Hyatt) on your way to the

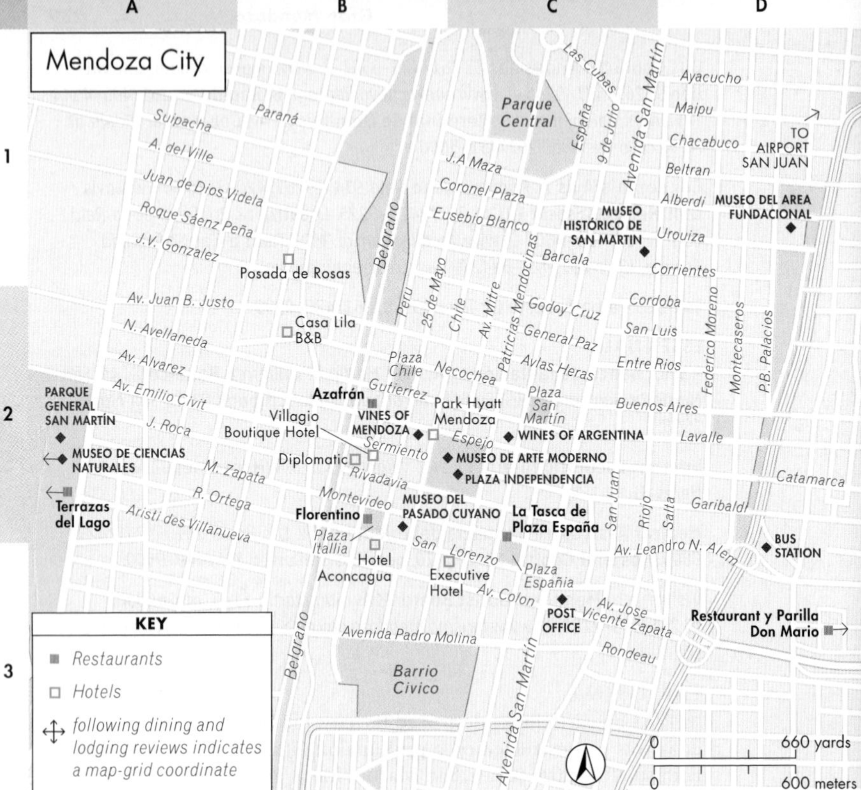

shops and outdoor cafés on the pedestrian-only Calle Sarmiento, which bisects the square.

Museo Arte Moderno. Right in Plaza Independencia, this museum exhibits more than 450 paintings, ceramics, sculptures, and drawings by Mendocino artists from 1930 to the present. ✉ *Plaza Independencia* ☎ *261/425–7279* 🎫 *8 pesos, Wed. free* ⏲ *Mon.–Sat. 9–1 and 4–9, Sun. 5–9* ✉ *Mendoza.*

Parque General San Martín. This 971-acre park dates back to 1896, and has more than 50,000 trees from all over the world. Fifteen kilometers (9 miles) of paths meander through the park, and the gorgeous rose garden has about 500 varieties. You can observe aquatic competitions from the rowing club's balcony restaurant, visit the zoo that has monkeys running loose, or play tennis or golf. Scenes of the 1817 Andes crossing by José de San Martín and his army during the campaign to liberate Argentina are depicted on a monument atop Cerro de la Gloria (Glory Hill) in the park's center. The stadium hosts popular soccer games, and was built for the 1978 World Cup (which Argentina won). The Amphitheater (capacity 22,500) fills to the brim during Vendimia, the annual wine-harvest festival. ✉ *Mendoza.*

WORTH NOTING

Arena Maipu Casino Resort. Brand new in 2011, this huge complex features more than 480 slots, 40 electronic roulette tables, five traditional roulette tables, and six card tables. There are often shows at the on-site stadium, in addition to a dance club and a cinema. It's outside of town center, but easily accesible by a quick cab or bus ride. ✉ *Emilio Civit y Maza, Maipu* ☎ *261/481–9800.*

> **TOURING TIPS**
>
> In winter a *bus turístico* (tourist bus) departs at 9:30 am and 2:30 pm from the tourist office and travels along a tour route, letting you on and off at designated stops. Also, you can pick up a free walking-tour map (the Circuitos Peatonales) at hotels or the tourist office.

Museo de Ciencias Naturales. Lose yourself in an interesting and varied collection of more than 40,000 examples of anthropology, minerology, paleontology, archeology, and zoology. ✉ *Parque General San Martin, at Av. de las Tipas and Av. de Circunvalacion* ☎ *261/428–7666* 🎫 *2 pesos* ⏲ *Weekdays 8–1 and 2–7, weekends 3–7.*

Museo del Area Fundacional. On the site of the original *cabildo* (town hall), the Foundation Museum explains the region's social and historical development. Of note is the display of a mummified child found on Aconcagua, with photos of his burial treasures. Excavations, made visible by a glass-covered viewing area, reveal layers of pre-Hispanic and Spanish remains. ✉ *Beltrán and Videla Castillo* ☎ *261/425–6927* 🎫 *8 pesos* ⏲ *Tues.–Sat. 8–8, Sun. 3–8.*

Museo del Pasado Cuyano. This 26-bedroom, 1873 mansion, the home of former governor and senator Emilio Civit, was the gathering place of the Belle Epoque elite. Today it's the Museum of the Cuyo's Past, a gallery with paintings, antiques, a library with over 5,000 volumes devoted to the history of Mendoza, and a gallery of weaponry used in the Independence of Argentina. ✉ *Montevideo 544* ☎ *261/423–6031* 🎫 *Donation suggested* ⏲ *Weekdays 9–1.*

Museo Histórico de San Martín. The San Martín Historical Museum has a decent library and a token collection of artifacts, including uniforms and journal entries from campaigns of the Great Liberator. ✉ *Remedios de Escalada de San Martin 1843* ☎ *261/425–7947* 🎫 *3 pesos* ⏲ *Weekdays 8–8, Sat. 8–12:30.*

NEED A BREAK?

Soppelsa. More than 40 ice-cream flavors, including traditional Argentine staples such as *dulce de leche* (sweet caramelized milk) with *granizado* (chocolate chip) and many fresh berry and chocolate concoctions, merit a visit (or two) to Soppelsa. ✉ *Emilio Civit 2 at Belgrano.*

WINERIES

The department of Maipú, south and slightly east of Mendoza City, has some 12 wineries in the districts of General Gutierrez, Coquimbito, and Cruz de Piedra. To the south, the department of Luján de Cuyo borders both banks of the Mendoza River and has 27 wineries in the districts of Agrelo, Carodilla, Chacras de Coria, Drummond, Perdriel,

INSIDER INFO

Vines of Mendoza. Before heading out to the wineries, stop by the Vines of Mendoza's Tasting Room and Blending Lab, located at Espejo 567 right by the Park Hyatt. Their website is a great place to get travel and wine info before you even leave home. The Vines is owned by an American entrepreneur, Michael Evans, and Pablo Gimenez-Riili, a third-generation winemaker from Mendoza. Their intention was to create a gathering place where English-speaking visitors can explore the region's wineries with an insider's perspective.

In addition to offering more than 100 boutique wines by the glass and flight, they offer wines from bodegas that are not open to the public. They also offer weekly events, such as chats and tastings with local winemakers. You can also have the chance to play winemaker by blending your own wine to take home at their Blending Lab. Or, if you are feeling extravagant, you can purchase your own custom barrel filled with wine that you can blend, bottle, and have labeled for shipment to the US.

You can continue your Mendoza wine experience even after you return home by joining their Acequia Wine Club. You will receive shipments, four times per year, of four to six bottles of boutique Argentine wine rarely found outside of Argentina.

If you're a super-serious wine lover, you can purchase a 3–10 acre Private Vineyard Estate in Valle de Uco from Vines of Mendoza. As an owner, you consult with their top-notch team of winemakers and vineyard managers, participating in everything from choosing what to plant to designing your own label. It's the ultimate way to be a Mendoza insider. ✉ *Espejo 567, between Chile and 25 de Mayo* ☎ *0261/438–1031* 🌐 *www.vinesofmendoza.com* ⏲ *Daily 3–10 pm.*

Ugarteche, and Vistalba. ■ **TIP→ Aceso Sur (Ruta Nacional 40), the main highway south, is the fastest way to get to the area. Ruta Provincial 15 runs parallel to 40, and most of the wineries are on this route.**

MAIPÚ

Bodega la Rural. In 1855, Felipe Rutini left the hills of Italy to found a winery in the raw land of Coquimbito, Argentina. His descendants planted the first grapes (Chardonnay and Merlot) in the now-popular Tupungato District of the Valle de Uco. Today, Bodega la Rural is still family-owned and -operated. The winery's well-known San Felipe label was created by Alejandro Sirio, a famous Spanish artist. Inside the original adobe barns the Museo del Vino (Wine Museum) displays leather hoppers, antique pressing machines, vintage carriages; 100-year-old leather, wood, and copper tools; and even an amazing mousetrap. ✉ *Montecaseros 2625, Coquimbito, Maipu* ☎ *261/497–2013* 🌐 *www.bodegalarural.com.ar* ⏲ *Tours every 30 mins Mon.–Sat. 9–1 and 2–5; Sun. 10–1 with reservations.*

Bodegas y Viñedos López. Wines up to 60 years old are stored in the main cellar of this traditional winery, established in 1898 and still owned by the same family. After a winery tour, tastings take place in

Bodega Catena Zapata, Lujan de Cuyo

the cave, where lunches can be arranged with a two-day notice. Also on tap are more extensive programs and tours; in March, you can sign up for hands-on learning about the harvest. ✉ *Ozamis 375, Maipu* ☎ *261/497–2406* 🌐 *www.bodegaslopez.com.ar* ⏲ *Weekdays tours hourly 9–5; Sat. tours at 9:30, 10:30, 12:30; Sun. open only by appt.*

Di Tomasso. A family business in a gorgeous 1869 building, Di Tomasso maintains the best of old and new in their bodega. Although the roof is made of mud and cane, the machinery inside is only the best from France and Italy. This is one of the few bodegas that does not require advance reservations. The casual restaurant on site, La Chiase, offers salads, sandwiches, and Italian-influenced foods, with tables outside overlooking the vines. ✉ *Carril Urquiza 8136, Maipu* ☎ *261/524–1829* 🌐 *www.familiaditommaso.com* ⏲ *Mon.–Sat. 10–6.*

Fodor's Choice ★ **Familia Zuccardi.** In 1950 Don Alberto Zuccardi, a civil engineer, developed a more modern system of irrigation for his vineyards in Maipú and later in Santa Rosa. He and his son Sebastian continue to push boundaries and play with new approaches to viniculture, and have been called by Decanter magazine among the top 5 most influential personalities in Argentine wine. Their newest innovation, the Cava de Turísmo, is an air-conditioned cave where you can join tours of the bodega led by family members or an oenologist. A soft, soothing light glows on cobblestone floors, concrete walls, and warm woodwork in the tasting room and gift shop. Outside, walk through the neatly labeled vineyards to the garden restaurant for a wine-tasting lunch or tea. During harvest time (February and March), Vení a Cosechar (Come and Harvest) is a program for wannabe grape-pickers that includes an early-morning pickup at your hotel, breakfast, and a morning of hard work in the vineyards (guided by agronomists and oenologists). This is followed by a wine tasting and lunch. From June to August a similar program teaches the art of pruning. Cooking classes, music, balloon rides, and art exhibits are also offered. ✉ *RP33, Km 7.5, Maipu* ☎ *261/441–0000* 🌐 *www.familiazuccardi.com* ⏲ *Mon.–Sat. 9–5:30.*

Finca Flichman. In 1873 Don Sami Flichman, a Jewish immigrant, planted the first vines in the stony soil of a former riverbed in the *barrancas* (ravines) next to the Mendoza River. His son Isaac acquired the property during the 1930s Depression and had the foresight to produce only high-quality grapes. In 1983 the Wertheim family bought the winery, introduced new technology, and added another winery, installing stainless-steel tanks and computerized temperature controls in the underground cellars. ✉ *Munives 800, Maipu* ☎ *261/497–2039* 🌐 *www.flichman.com.ar* ⏲ *Mon.–Sat. 10–12 and 1–4.*

LUJÁN DE CUYO AND ENVIRONS

★ **Achával Ferrer.** With a past score of 97 from *Wine Spectator* for their Malbec, Santiago Achaval's winery on the banks of the Mendoza River continues to consistently score high points for its red wines. The top-quality wines coming out of this winery get huge respect from fellow winemakers. Guided visits include prepaid barrel and bottle tastings. Quimera is a delicious blend of red grapes (Malbec, Merlot, Cabernet Sauvignon, and Cabernet Franc) grown on three different *fincas*, including one in the Valle de Uco. Quantities of each grape are adjusted to the quality of the grapes. The tasting fee is discounted from any wine purchase. ✉ *Calle Cobos 2601, Perdriel, Lujan de Cuyo* ☎ *261/448–1131* 🌐 *www.achaval-ferrer.com* ⏲ *Weekdays tours 9:30, 11:00, 12:30, and 3, with reservation.*

★ **Bodega Catena Zapata.** A faux Mayan pyramid rising from the vineyards fronts the towering Andes at this landmark winery where the architecture rivals the wine. You descend from a crystal cupola through concentric spaces to the tasting room, which is surrounded by 400 oak barrels. Founding father Nicola Catena arrived in 1898 and planted his first vineyard of Malbec grapes in 1902. Sons Domingo and Nicolás manage the vineyards planted at varying altitudes, blending varietals from these different microclimates to create complex, distinctive wines. Special tastings with meals can be arranged for groups with prior notice. ✉ *Calle J. Cobos s/n, Agrelo* ☎ *261/490–0214* 🌐 *www.catenawines.com.*

Bodega Lagarde. Built in 1897, Lagarde is one of the oldest and most traditional wineries in Mendoza. The third generation of the Pescarmona family now cultivates the grapes, producing limited quantities of quality wine and searching for ways to improve while avoiding fleeting trends. A five-course tasting lunch is served in the 19th-century *casona* (farm house). ✉ *San Martín 1745, Mayor Drummond, Luján de Cuyo* ☎ *261/498–0011* 🌐 *www.lagarde.com.ar* ⏲ *Weekdays 9–5:30 with reservations, Sat. 9:30–2.*

Bodega Norton. In 1895 English engineer Sir Edmund Norton built the first winery in the valley south of the Mendoza River. Part of the old adobe house and a wing of the winery demonstrate the traditional construction of beamed ceilings with bamboo reeds under a zinc roof. In 1989 an Austrian businessman purchased the already huge company, and his son continues to modernize and expand the production of the 100-year-old vineyards. La Vid, their restaurant, has a six-plate tasting menu, picnics, and even a children's menu. ✉ *RP15, Km 23.5, Perdriel, Luján de Cuyo* ☎ *261/490–9700* 🌐 *www.norton.com.ar* ⏲ *Hourly tours daily 9–noon and 3–4:30.*

WORD OF MOUTH

"The day after our arrival, we did wine tastings in the area. We had our own car and found that we could get around just fine, as most of the wineries we wanted to go to were all within 20 minutes of the resort." —Mary5

Fodor's Choice ★ **Bodega Vistalba.** During his seven years as president of Salentein, a Dutch company with three bodegas, Carlos Pulenta increased the number of European varietals, installed the latest technology, and put Salentein wine on the tables of the world. He left in 2004 and returned to his family's land in Vistalba. Surrounded by vineyards, the courtyard entrance frames a perfect view of the 4,900-meter (16,000-foot) Cordón de Plata mountain range. Underground in the bodega, a wall exposes the tumbled rocks and dirt to show you the soil structure that Malbec thrives in. Pulenta and his team of family advisers and oenologists have created three blends using Malbec, Cabernet, Merlot, and Bonarda, plus a delicate Sauvignon Blanc and a Torrontés from their vineyard in Salta, and a Semillon that begs to be tried. Day tours include lunch at La Bourgogne, the award-winning restaurant. The light stone and polished concrete complex houses two comfortable rooms for overnight guests. ✉ *Roque Saenz Peña 3531, Vistalba, Luján de Cuyo* ☎ *261/498–9400* 🌐 *www.carlospulentawines.com.*

Bodegas Nieto y Senetiner S.A. White adobe walls, tile roofs, flower-bed-lined walkways, and huge shade trees welcome you to this bodega. From mid-March to mid-April volunteer pickers arrive for breakfast, a brief explanation of harvest technique, and an introduction to their foreman. Then, with tools in hand, it's off to the vineyards with the agronomist until baskets are inspected to see who wins the prize for the best pick. From mid-August until the end of September pruning (*podar*) takes place, and you can join the experts in cutting, tying, and modifying vines. Perhaps the most unusual tour is a three-hour, 2-km (1-mile) horseback ride to a hilltop for a view of the mountains and vineyards. During a mate and muffin break, an oenologist explains the varietals growing around you. All of these activities include lunch at the bodega, tasting, and a tour, and all require reservations. ✉ *Guaradia Viaje, between RN7 and Rosque Sáenz Peña s/n, Vistalba, Luján de Cuyo* ☎ *261/498–0315* 🌐 *www.nietosenetiner.com.ar* ⏲ *Summer: tours weekdays at 10, 11, 12:30, and 4; Other seasons: tours weekdays at 10, 11, 12:30, and 3.*

Bodegas Tapíz. When the Ortiz family bought this modern bodega from Kendall Jackson in 2003, CEO Patricia Ortiz and oenologist Fabián Valenzuela decided to make "happier wines" that are easier to drink

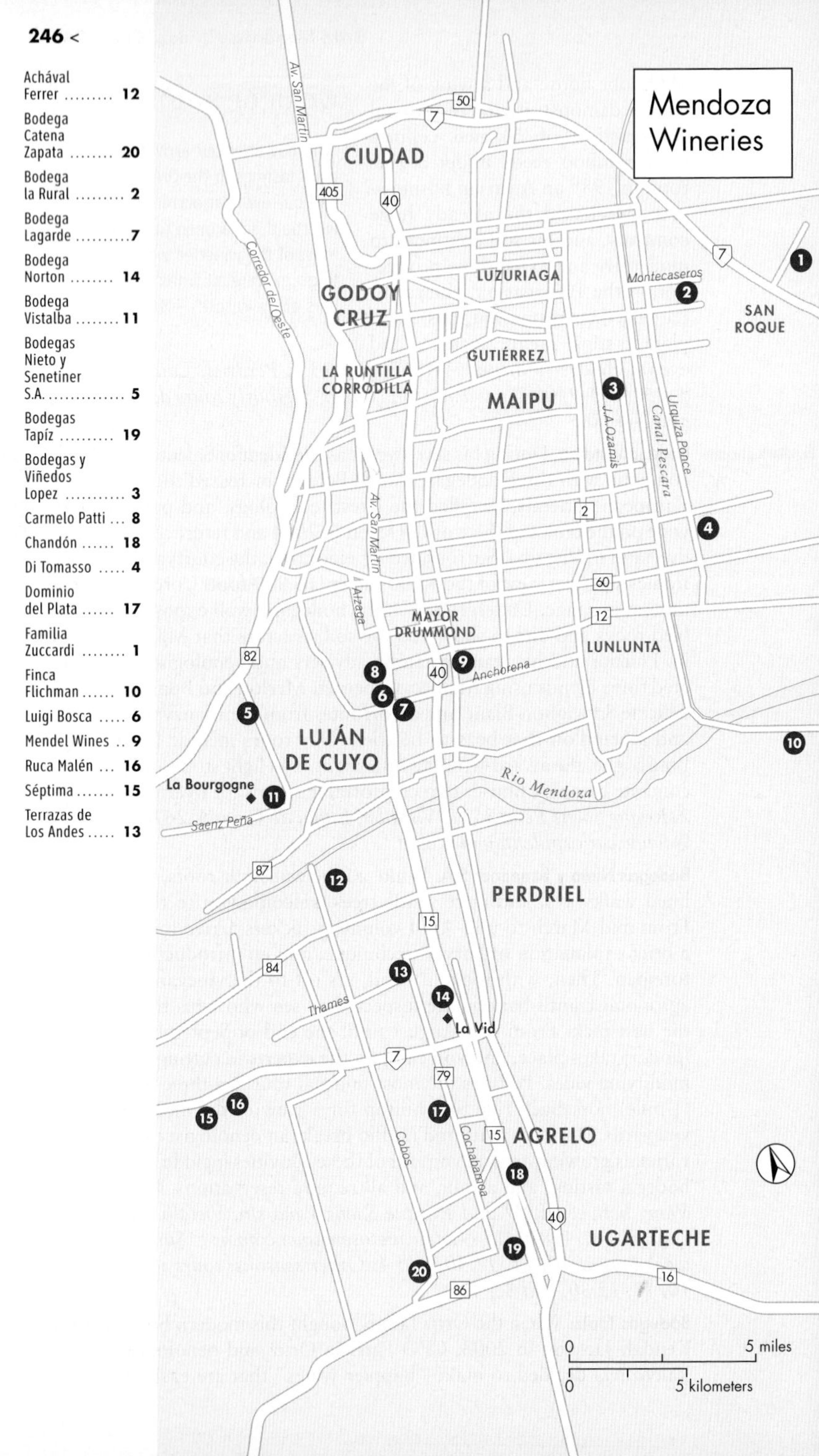
Mendoza Wineries
Achával Ferrer 12
Bodega Catena Zapata 20
Bodega la Rural 2
Bodega Lagarde 7
Bodega Norton 14
Bodega Vistalba 11
Bodegas Nieto y Senetiner S.A. 5
Bodegas Tapíz 19
Bodegas y Viñedos Lopez 3
Carmelo Patti ... 8
Chandón 18
Di Tomasso 4
Dominio del Plata 17
Familia Zuccardi 1
Finca Flichman 10
Luigi Bosca 6
Mendel Wines .. 9
Ruca Malén ... 16
Séptima 15
Terrazas de Los Andes 13
CIUDAD
GODOY CRUZ
LUZURIAGA
GUTIÉRREZ
LA RUNTILLA CORRODILLA
MAIPU
SAN ROQUE
MAYOR DRUMMOND
LUNLUNTA
LUJÁN DE CUYO
PERDRIEL
AGRELO
UGARTECHE
La Bourgogne
La Vid
Av. San Martín
Corredor del Oeste
Montecaseros
J.A.Ozamis
Canal Pescara
Urquiza Ponce
Arizeta
Anchorena
Rio Mendoza
Saenz Peña
Thames
Cobos
Cochabamba
50
7
405
40
2
60
12
82
87
15
84
79
16
86
0
5 miles
0
5 kilometers

and more food-friendly. Inside the bodega, walls of loose river rocks held in place by wire mesh contrast with the slick granite walls and long corridors. Tours begin in the vineyard, followed by tank, barrel, and bottle tastings. In summer a two-horse carriage driven by a local gaucho takes you on a learning tour of the vineyard. Club Tapiz, a seven-room inn with a spa and the restaurant Terruño, is only 20 minutes away. ✉ *RP15, Km 32, Agrelo, Luján de Cuyo* ☎ *261/490–0202* 🌐 *www.tapiz.com* ⏲ *Weekdays 9–4, Sat. 10–12.*

Carmelo Patti. Carmelo, the friendly and passionate owner and winemaker behind this operation, answers the phone, greets you at the door, and personally conducts tours (in Spanish only), drawing wine from the barrel and entertaining guests with anecdotes and entertaining facts about everything from growing grapes to making wine and how to drink it, to the preservation of corks. He is a legendary winemaker of the old school, and is famous for his Cabernet Sauvignon. Producing only 10,000 bottles at a time, he notes the harvest and bottling dates on the label. He has an extraordinary reputation and has accumulated a cultlike following for his top-quality wines. The bodega is nothing fancy, but as Carmelo likes to point out, he puts all of his energy into where he feels it needs to go: into making incredible wines, not into the pomp and flash of maintaining a fancy bodega building. ✉ *San Martín 2614, Mayor Drummond* ☎ *261/498–1379* ⏲ *By appointment.*

5

Chandon. The president of Moët & Chandon was so impressed by the *terroir* (soil, climate, and topography that contribute to making each wine unique) in Agrelo that he decided to build the first foreign branch of his family's company here. Today the winery is producing *vino spumante* (sparkling wine) in great quantities. During harvest (February, March, and April) an agronomist takes groups to work in the vineyard with modern equipment; lunch is included. Special workshops can be arranged for business groups, wine clubs, and wannabe winemakers. ✉ *RN40, Km 29, Agrelo, Luján de Cuyo* ☎ *261/490–9968* 🌐 *www.chandon.com.ar* ⏲ *Hourly tours weekdays; winter weekday tours at 11:30, 2, 3:30, and 5. Sat. tours require reservation.*

Dominio del Plata. Since 2001 Susana Balbo and her husband, viticulturalist Pedro Marchevsky, have combined their formidable skills with the newest technology and a passion for the care and cultivation of their land. Balbo, Argentina's first licensed woman oenologist and an internationally known winemaking consultant, can look out her living room window across a sea of vineyards to the sparkling Cordón de Plata mountain range. From her dining-room window she can see the stainless-steel tanks and pipes of the bodega she designed. ✉ *Cochebamba 7801, Agrelo, Luján de Cuyo* ☎ *261/498–6572* 🌐 *www.dominiodelplata.com* ✍ *Reservations essential* ⏲ *Weekdays 10, 12, and 3:30.*

Luigi Bosca. Alberto, Raul, and Roberto Arizú—descendants of Leoncio Arizú, who brought the original vines from Spain in 1890—believe that a winemaker's job is to preserve what nature has delivered. Here nature is on their side. The terroir has much to do with the unique character of Luigi Bosca's wine. This bodega is an architectural gem, with 14 carved reliefs depicting the history of winemaking in Argentina, tile floors, inlaid wood ceilings, and painted arches. ✉ *San Martín 2044, Mayor Drummond, Luján de Cuyo* ☎ *261/498–1974* 🌐 *www.luigibosca.com.ar* 🕑 *Daily tours at 10, 11, 12:30.*

Mendel Wines. Mendel regularly receives scores exceeding 90 from both *Wine Spectator* and Robert Parker's *Wine Advocate* for their Malbec as well as for their Malbec–Cabernet Sauvignon blend (Unus). This is testimony to the expert wine-making of one of Argentina's best known winemakers, Roberto de la Mota, and to the dedicated owners of this limited-production winery, where quality, not quantity, is their mantra. In this unassuming 80-year-old adobe building, informal tours point out the loving care grapes receive—from hand-picking to hand-crushing to storage. Reservations are essential. ✉ *Terrada 1863, Luján de Cuyo* ☎ *261/524–1621* 🌐 *www.mendel.com.ar.*

Ruca Malén. Jon Pierre Thibaud brings more than a decade of experience as president of neighboring Chandón vineyards to this modern, compact boutique winery situated just back from Ruta Nacional 7. Thibaud and his French partner, Jacques Louis de Montalembert, have dedicated their collective skills and passion to selecting the finest grapes for quality wines. Wine tours, tastings, and blending seminars can be followed by a gourmet lunch and wine tasting, after which a quick siesta on the balcony looking up at the Andes revives visitors before continuing on to the next bodega. ✉ *RN7, Km 1059, Agrelo, Luján de Cuyo* ☎ *261/410–6214* 🌐 *www.bodegarucamalen.com* 🕑 *Weekdays 10–5, Sat. 10–1.*

★ **Séptima.** When the Spanish wine group Codorniú decided that Argentina would be their seventh great wine investment, they constructed their winery in the *pirca* style, in which natural stones are piled one atop the other. The Huarpe natives used this technique to build walls, dwellings, and sacred places. Inside theses massive walls is a state-of-the-art winery with sleek wood and glass corridors. Visitors climb over hoses and machinery while they follow the grapes from vineyard to bottle in a natural working atmosphere. A rooftop terrace is available for private lunches, weddings, or sunset wine tastings, and a restaurant, María, uses local ingredients infused with Arabic, Jewish, Greek, and African culinary traditions. ✉ *RN7, Km 6.5, Agrelo, Luján de Cuyo* ☎ *261/498–5164* 🌐 *www.bodegaseptima.com.ar* ✍ *Reservations essential* 🕑 *Weekdays 10–5.*

Terrazas de Los Andes. Four vineyards situated at different heights (terraces)—Syrah at 800 meters (2,600 feet), Cabernet Sauvignon at 980 meters (3,200 feet), Malbec slightly higher, and Chardonnay at 1,200 meters (3,900 feet)—take advantage of different microclimates, allowing each varietal to develop to its maximum potential. Bare brick walls, high ceilings, and a labyrinth of soaring arches shelter premium wines in stainless-steel tanks and oak barrels. Built in 1898 and restored in the mid-1990s, everything in the tasting room—from the bar to the tables to the leather chairs—is made with recycled barrels. A six-room guesthouse and a dining room are available for family or business gatherings with reservations one day in advance by phone or email. ✉ *Thames* *and Cochebamba, Perdriel, Luján de Cuyo* ☎ *261/448–0058* 🌐 *www.terrazasdelosandes.com* ⏲ *Weekdays 9:30, 11, 12:30, 3 and 4. Reservations required.*

WHERE TO EAT

MENDOZA CITY

$$$$ WINE BAR Fodor's Choice ★ ✕ **Azafrán.** It's as much a gourmet grocery and wineshop as it is an incredible restaurant with tons of character—and one that offers a welcome break from parrilla fare. Shelves are stocked with local olive oils, dried herbs and spices, smoked meats, and olives and homemade jams. Eighty wineries are represented by more than 400 labels in the wine bar, where an old wine press has been converted into a tasting table. There is no wine list, but you can explore the wine room and look at the shelves of wine while working with a sommelier to find the perfect pairing for your food order. The food is super fresh, traditionally Argentine yet with creative flair, and gorgeously presented (try the empanada selection with the accompanying wine flight or the pork tenderloin cooked with blueberries in a Malbec sauce). This is a versatile place that works well whether you need to have a business meeting, dine with your family, or have a romantic dinner for two. ✉ *Sarmiento 765* ☎ *261/429–4200* 📧 *Villanueva 287* ✥ *B2.*

$$ MODERN ARGENTINE ★ ✕ **Florentino.** This intimate bistro in a converted house right off of Plaza Italia oozes casual charm. The small courtyard patio is perfect for a romantic dinner. Choice local produce is used by the chef, Sebastian Flores, so the menu often changes depending on what's in season. This is non-pretentious gourmet comfort food: think pumpkin-and-almond ravioli, mushrooms au gratin, asparagus and sun-dried tomato foccacia, and a great selection of meats, all perfectly prepared. The wine list is decent, and the dessert selection is inventive (depending on the season, try to end with the strawberry-black pepper-mint soup with cream gelato). ✉ *Montevideo 675* ☎ *261/464–9077* ⏲ *Closed Sun.* ✥ *B2.*

$$ MEDITERRANEAN ✕ **La Tasca de Plaza España.** If the bright red walls, the strange faces painted above the entrance, and the eclectic art inside don't grab you, the tapas and Mediterranean dishes probably will. Seafood tapas, veal-and-artichoke stew, and a casserole of zucchini, onions, and peppers in a cheese sauce are a few of the tempting dishes served in this intimite old house with tons of character. ✉ *Montevideo 117* ☎ *261/423–1403* ✥ *C3.*

$$$ ARGENTINE ✕ **Restaurant y Parilla Don Mario.** Mendocinos have been coming here for years for their basic beef fix. *Bife de lomo* and *bife de chorizo* are grilled to perfection at this comfortable country-style restaurant with pastas, grilled vegetables, and a good wine list. ✉ *25 de Mayo 1324, Mendoza, Guyaymallén* ☎ *261/431–0801* ✥ *D3.*

$$ ARGENTINE ✕ **Terrazas del Lago.** It's only a 15-minute taxi ride from downtown to this restaurant in Parque General San Martín. The long wood-and-glass building overlooks a lake and two pools that are part of an aquatic club (open for day use by nonmembers). A buffet fills one room. The master of the pasta bar waits to help you—first with choosing from four kinds of ravioli and eight types of noodles, then with selecting a sauce from a simmering pot, and finally with piling your plate with all kinds of other treats. Seating is outdoors on a deck or indoors with air-conditioning

5

DID YOU KNOW?

There are two main pruning methods for grape vines. Spur (or head) pruning involves allowing only two shoots per branch to bear grapes; this is most common in older vineyards or in the warmest growing climates. Cane pruning trains up to four shoots per branch along a trellis so that up to sixteen new shoots will bear fruit along the trellis the next season.

(essential for summer lunches). Reservations are a good idea. ✉ *Av. Las Palmeras s/n, on Parque Gral San Martín* ☎ *261/428–8815* ⏲ *No dinner Sun.; no lunch Mon.* ✣ *A2.*

GODOY CRUZ

$$$$ ARGENTINE ★ ✕ **1884 Restaurante Francis Mallman.** The soft glow of candles on the patio at the 100-year-old Bodega Escorihuela sets the tone for superchef, Francis Mallman, whose version of farm-fresh Patagonian cuisine has won him many awards and international acclaim. You can dine on the patio, where empanadas and traditional meats, including goat, are baked in mud ovens, a custom derived from the Incas. The 36-page wine list has detailed information on grapes and bodegas. ✉ *Belgrano 1188, Godoy Cruz* ☎ *261/424–2698.*

MAIPÚ

$$$$ ARGENTINE ★ ✕ **Terruño.** Light from a whimsical chandelier high in the timbered ceiling highlights the Malbec-color walls and worn floors of this 1890 vintner's elegant residence. Seasonal dishes marrying beef, pork, or veal with Mediterranean and Asian influences create unforgettable meals that have won many awards for chef Max Casá. An experienced staff knows how to pair local wine with each course, including dessert. ✉ *Club Tapiz, Pedro Molina (RP60) s/n, Maipu* ☎ *261/496–0131* 🌐 *www.club-tapiz.com.ar* ✍ *Reservations essential.*

LUJÁN DE CUYO

$$$$ FRENCH Fodor's Choice ★ ✕ **La Bourgogne.** "Cooking comes from regional traditions. My cuisine is tied to the land," says Jean-Paul Bondoux, Argentina's Relais Gourmand chef, who oversees this restaurant along with two others by the same name. He applies his formidable French culinary skills to local produce in this casually elegant restaurant overlooking the vineyards at Carlos Pulenta's winery (Vistalba). Take a tour and select your own herbs from the garden to complement the menu, which is paired with some amazing Pulenta wines. ✉ *Roque Sáenz Peña 3531, Vistalba, Luján de Cuyo* ☎ *261/498–9400* 🌐 *www.carlospulentawines.com* ✍ *Reservations essential* ⏲ *Lunch only (1–3). Closed Sun.*

$$$ ARGENTINE ✕ **La Vid.** At the Norton winery, this restaurant, with its pleasing contemporary design, welcomes guests from all over Mendoza—with or without the wine tour. You can spend the afternoon tasting wines with a six-course tasting menu, or opt for the daily special with a glass of wine, or sample a cheese and charcuterie plate. There is also à-la-carte fare, with unusual dishes like rabbit lasagna and salmon ravioli. They even have a kids' menu and pack-up picnics. ✉ *RP15, Km 23, Perdirel, Lujan de Cuyo* ☎ *260/490–9790* 🌐 *www.norton.com.ar* ✍ *Reservations essential* ⏲ *Open Mon.–Sat. 10–6.*

WHERE TO STAY

For expanded hotel reviews, visit Fodors.com.

MENDOZA CITY

$$ **Casa Lila Bed and Breakfast.** With only four rooms, this charming inn has personalized service within walking distance to the city center, lots of restaurants, and General San Martin park. **Pros:** charming and quiet home base; relaxing oasis amid bustling city. **Cons:** meals upon request, but no on-site restauraunt. ✉ *Nicolás Avellaneda 262* ☎ *261/429–634, 261/467–9272* 🌐 *www.casalila.com.ar* *4 rooms* ✣ *B2.*

Difficult choices at Mendoza City's Mercado Central

$$$ **Diplomatic.** This is the city's big luxury hotel, with plenty of rooms for meetings, parties, wine tastings, and events, plus a famous restaurant (La Bourgogne) and an inviting wine bar. **Pros:** everything you could possibly want in luxury, design, comfort, amenities; big picture windows in rooms. **Cons:** price; artwork or rugs in rooms would make them a little friendlier. ✉ *Belgrano 1014* ☎ *261/405–1900, 0810/122–5000 reservations* ⊕ *www.diplomatic.parksuites.com.ar* *116 rooms* *In-room: a/c, safe, Wi-Fi. In-hotel: restaurant, bar, pool, gym, spa, parking* *Breakfast* ✣ *B2.*

$$ **Executive Hotel.** The tall, elegant tower of this slick, friendly downtown hotel looks out on the Plaza Italia in a quiet residential area just blocks from shops and restaurants. **Pros:** sauna; tasting rooms with free wine from local vinters. **Cons:** windowless bar-restaurant. ✉ *San Lorenzo 660* ☎ *261/524–5000* ⊕ *www.executive.parksuites.com.ar* *49 rooms, 32 suites* *In-room: safe, Wi-Fi. In-hotel: restaurant, pool, gym, parking* *Breakfast* ✣ *C3.*

$$ **Hotel Aconcagua.** The service is friendly and efficient at this popular modern hotel on a quiet street near shops and restaurants. **Pros:** central location; business suites with attendant on top floor. **Cons:** public areas often crowded with wine-business and tour groups. ✉ *San Lorenzo 545* ☎ *261/520–0500* ⊕ *www.hotelaconcagua.com* *159 rooms, 9 suites* *In-room: Wi-Fi. In-hotel: restaurant, pool, parking* *Breakfast* ✣ *B3.*

$$$$ Fodor's Choice ★ **Park Hyatt Mendoza.** Inside may be all modern comforts, but the Hyatt has preserved the landmark Plaza Hotel's 19th-century Spanish colonial facade: a grand pillared entrance and a wide veranda that extends to either side of the street. **Pros:** great central location; staff that is used to

accommodating foreigners; wine and tapas nights at The Vines (Thursday), and special wine-tasting dinners. **Cons:** pool area can get a lot of noise from the street. ✉ *Calle Chile 1124* ☎ *261/441–1234* 🌐 *mendoza.park.hyatt.com* *171 rooms, 15 suites* *In-room: safe, Internet. In-hotel: restaurant, bar, pool, gym, spa, parking* *Breakfast* ✥ *B2.*

$$$ **Posada de Rosas.** Don't be fooled by this ordinary house on an ordinary street—inside, bright rooms are decorated with modern art and ancient Andean weavings, and have just the places to enjoy breakfast (inside or out on the patio) or tea or to curl up with a *New Yorker* or one of the English-language wine magazines that are set out. **Pros:** nice neighborhood with good shops and restaurants; helpful English-speaking owners who know the territory. **Cons:** long walk to town; three-night minimum stay (four in high-season). ✉ *Martínez de Rozas 1641* ☎ *261/423–3629* 🌐 *www.posadaderosas.com* *8 rooms* *In-room: Wi-Fi. In-hotel: pool* *Breakfast* ✥ *B1.*

$$$ **Villaggio Boutique Hotel.** If you want to stay right in the city but prefer to sidestep the big hotel chains, the modern Villaggio offers up an Italian feel and arty interiors one block from the main plaza and shopping street. **Pros:** good location; artful design; sauna; Jacuzzi with a mountain view. **Cons:** some guests complain of thin walls and noise from neighbors; some rooms have views of air shaft. ✉ *25 de Mayo 1010* ☎ *261/524–5200* 🌐 *hotelvillaggio.com.ar* *26 rooms* *In-room: Wi-Fi. In-hotel: restaurant, bar, pool, gym* *Breakfast* ✥ *B2.*

MAIPÚ

$$$ ★ **Club Tapiz.** This 1890 governor's mansion has 11 rooms, and is surrounded by vineyards, making it feel like a private villa, where you can stroll through the old winery, lounge on the enclosed patio, or gaze at the Andes from the outdoor pool or indoor Jacuzzi. **Pros:** great on-site restaurant, Terruño; close to vineyards. **Cons:** far from shops or town. ✉ *Pedro Molina (RP60) s/n, Maipu* ☎ *261/496–3433* 🌐 *www.clubtapiz.com.ar* *11 rooms* *In-hotel: restaurant, bar, spa.*

LUJÁN DE CUYO

$$$$ Fodor's Choice ★ **Cavas Wine Lodge.** Inside a gracious colonial villa surrounded by mountains and vineyards, a reception hall is washed in sunlight from high windows, and common areas are decorated in a luxurious bohemian style—making it easy to imagine yourself in one of the private white-adobe guesthouses, with your own patio and plunge pool in the middle of the vineyards, and your own rooftop deck with a fireplace. **Pros:** luxurious; private; spacious; great personalized service. **Cons:** expensive; far from shops, restaurants, and other urban activities (although you are in the heart of wine country, within biking distance of many of the best bodegas). ✉ *Luján de Cuyo* ✥ *RN40 south, west on RN7, turn off onto Cosa Flores just before Ruca Malen Winery. Follow signs for 2.2 km (1.4 miles)* ☎ *261/410–6927* 🌐 *www.cavaswinelodge.com* *14 cottages* *In-room: safe, Internet. In-hotel: restaurant, bar, pool, gym, spa* *Breakfast.*

$$$$ ★ **La Posada de Vistalba (Carlos Pulenta).** There are two rooms here: one on the second floor of this Tuscan terra-cotta building faces east, where the sun rises over the vineyards; the other faces west, where it sets behind the Andes. Both have cream-colored tile floors, dark wicker

furniture, and taupe-and-café-au-lait-covered furnishings complement the refined architecture. **Pros:** great views; lunch, wine tour, minibar food, and airport pickup included in rate. **Cons:** only double rooms (no king-sized beds); no pool. ✉ *Roque Sáenz Peña 3531, Vistalba, Luján de Cuyo* ☎ *261/498–9400* 🌐 *www.carlospulentawines.com* *2 rooms* *In-room: Wi-Fi. In-hotel: restaurant, bar* *Some meals.*

$$$ **Postales Boutique Wine Hotel (Chacras de Coria).** A stay at this intimate and friendly lodge—where you can enjoy outdoor *asados* (barbecues) and candlelit dinners on the veranda—puts you in an upscale residential area 15 minutes from Mendoza and close to wineries in Maipú and Luján de Cuyo. **Pros:** personalized tours; close to vineyards; good restaurant. **Cons:** in a residential suburb. ✉ *Viamonte 4762, Chacras de Coria, Luján de Cuyo* ☎ *261/496–1888* 🌐 *www.postalesarg.com* *6 rooms, 1 apartment* *In-hotel: restaurant, bar, pool* *Breakfast.*

NIGHTLIFE

Avenida Arístedes Villanueva. Full of bars and cafés, this avenida begins to wake up around 11 pm (don't even bother going any earlier). As the evening progresses, crowds get bigger, and the music—rock, tango, salsa—gets louder. Action peaks after midnight. ✉ *Mendoza.*

Believe Irish Pub. Sick of wine? Get your whiskey and beer fix at this popular Irish pub that is open until 2 am every day. ✉ *Av. Colon 241* ☎ *261/429–5567.*

El Bar del José. The casual El Bar del José was the first gathering place in the trendy Villanueva neighborhood. ✉ *Arístedes Villanueva 740* ☎ *No phone.*

Por Acá. This two-story bar/pizzeria attracts both locals and tourists. Sometimes featuring live music or DJs, this place can get packed after about 1 am. ✉ *Arístedes Villanueva 557* ☎ *261/420–0346.*

Regency Casino. The Regency Casino at the Park Hyatt Mendoza has blackjack, stud poker, roulette tables, slot machines, and an exclusive bar. ✉ *25 de Mayo and Sarmiento* ☎ *261/441–2844.*

SHOPPING

Pick up leather goods, shoes, and clothing along the pedestrian part of Sarmiento and its cross streets, or on Avenida Las Heras, where you'll find regional products to eat, drink, wear, or decorate your house with. On weekends Plaza Independencia becomes an artists' market, with stands selling jewelry, handmade sweaters, ponchos, mate gourds, olive oil, and other regional wares.

CLOTHES AND ACCESSORIES

Talabarterías sell fine leather goods and everything equestrian, from saddles and handmade tack to hats and other gaucho-inspired items.

Cardón. On the peatonal, Cardón carries gaucho clothing and accessories: *bombachas* (baggy, pleated pants), leather jackets and vests, boots, belts, scarves, ponchos, and knives. ✉ *Sarmiento 224.*

La Matera. Mendocinos shop at La Matera for boots, vests, belts, scarves, and riding gear. ✉ *Villanueva 314* ☎ *261/425–3332.*

FOOD AND WINE

Azafrán. This spot is a wine bar, café, wineshop, and delicatessen with regional olive oil, jams, meats, and cheeses. ✉ *Sarmiento 765* ☎ *261/429–4200.*

Historias & Sabores (*Histories and Flavors*). In a beautiful old country house, Historias & Sabores conducts guided tours and tastings of fruits, olives, chocolates, and liquors. Learn how chocolate-covered cordials are made, and grab some goodies to take home as souveniers. ✉ *Carril Gómez 3064, Coquimbito-Maipú* ☎ *261/155–744–614 reservations* ⌚ *Mon.–Sat. 11–6.*

Juan Cedrón. Before your picnic, grab a bottle of Malbec at Juan Cedrón. ✉ *Sarmiento 278.*

La Casa del Vino. There's a huge selection of wine and olive oil at La Casa del Vino. ✉ *Aristedes Villanueva 160* ☎ *261/425–0659.*

Pura Cepa. Pura Cepa conducts in-store wine tastings. ✉ *Sarmiento 664.*

MALLS

Mendoza Plaza Shopping Center. For all the things you forgot to pack, the Mendoza Plaza Shopping Center just 10 minutes outside of town has over 160 stores, including Falabella, an American-style department store, Lacoste, Levi's, and Adidas, plus cafés, and a bookstore (Yenny) with English titles. If shopping isn't your thing, there is a movie theater, bowling, and an indoor amusement park that has a roller coaster, carousel, rides, and games. ✉ *Lateral Accesso Este 3280, Guaymallén.*

Palmares Shopping Mall. A 15-minute taxi ride south of Mendoza, Palmares Shopping Mall has 120 stores, lots of restaurant options, to-die-for Freddo ice cream, and 10 movie theaters (including one in 3-D). While there is a lack of big-name North American brands, check out Eva Miller, Kill, Cheeky, and La Martina. ✉ *Panamericano 2650.*

MARKET

Mercado Central. For more than 120 years the Mercado Central has been selling local foods and handcrafts. Stock up on souvenirs such as ponchos, jewelry, or Indian weavings, spices, olive oil, and jams, while you fill your stomach with dried fruits, homemade empanadas, and fresh cheeses. Stalls are open daily from 9 to 1:30 and 4:30 to 9. ✉ *Av. Las Heras and Patricias Mendocinas.*

SPORTS AND THE OUTDOORS

The high peaks of the Andes provide a natural playground of ski slopes in winter, mountains to climb in summer, and miles of trails to hike, bike, or ride on horseback. Rivers roar out of the mountains in spring, inviting rafters and kayakers to test the water. Country roads in and around the vineyards make great bike paths.

Some of the wildest and most remote mountain areas are made accessible by the Ruta Nacional 7, which crosses the Andes right by Parque Provincial Aconcagua. Uspallata offers lodging and a base close to the action.

Tour operators in Mendoza City offer a variety of adventures.

Argentina Ski Tours. Whether you are a beginner or a back-country expert, this small and highly personalized agency can help plan your ski trip to Las Leñas, or, if you want to stay a little closer to downtown Mendoza, to Penitentes. ✉ *Darrageuira 558, Chacras de Coria* ☎ *261/630–0026* 🌐 *www.argentinaskitours.com.*

AymaraTurismo. AymaraTurismo handles guided horseback rides, trekking, mountain climbing on Aconcagua, and river rafting on the Mendoza River. ✉ *9 de Julio 1023* ☎ *261/420–2064* 🌐 *www.aymaramendoza.com.ar.*

Turismo TrasAndino. Turismo TrasAndino has operations in Mendoza City and in the mountains. They offer trekking to a base camp at Aconcagua as well as 15-day ascents. They also offer mountain biking, rock climbing and rappelling, paragliding, rafting, and horseback trips. ✉ *Av. Las Heras 341 Loc. 3* ☎ *261/425–6726, 261/423–7993* 🌐 *www.trasandinoturismo.com.ar* ✉ *R82, Km 38, Cacheuta* ☎ *262/449–0159.*

5

HORSEBACK RIDING

Cabalgata (horseback riding) is an enjoyable and natural way to explore the mountains west of Mendoza. You can ride to the foot of Aconcagua or Tupungato, or follow the hoofprints of San Martín on a seven-day trip over the Andes.

Trekking Travel. Offering one-day excursions to 11-day trips that will take you across the Andes, this outfitter can accommodate both beginner and expert riders alike. ✉ *Adolfo Calle 4171 Planta Alta, Villa Nueva, Guaymallén* ☎ *261/421–0450, 261/15–306–870 cell* 🌐 *www.horseriding.com.ar.*

MOUNTAIN BIKING

Many of Mendoza's back roads lead through the suburbs and vineyards into the Andean foothills and upward to mountain villages—or all the way to Chile.

Bikes and Wines. Bikes and Wines rents motorbikes and three kinds of mountain bikes for full- or half-day self-guided tours in the wine district of Maipú. Trips include a map, water bottle, a glass of Malbec to get the trip started off right, lunch, and medical and mechanical assistance. You begin at La Rural winery and museum and along the way visit three wineries, a chocolate and liquor factory, and an olive oil company. The lunch stop is at a deli, where you can eat on a patio. ✉ *Urquiza 1606, Maipu* ☎ *261/410–6686* 🌐 *www.bikesandwines.com.*

WHITE-WATER RAFTING

Mendoza-based adventure-tour companies offer half- to two-day Class II to Class IV rafting and kayaking trips on the Río Mendoza near Potrerillos *(⇨ Parque Provincial Anconcagua, below).*

Argentina Rafting. With Argentina Rafting you can raft the Río Mendoza for a half day or full day, take a kayak class, or combine rafting, horseback riding, and mountain biking in a two-day multi-sport outing, spending the night in a mountain refugio. ✉ *Office: Primitivo de la Reta 992, Loc. 4* ☎ *262/429–6325* 🌐 *www.argentinarafting.com.*

Betancourt Rafting. Betancourt Rafting offers rafting and adventure packages that include trekking, rappelling, and horseback riding. They have

Hikers traverse a low portion of the south face of Cerro Aconcagua.

three small cabins and a lodge at the Cacheuta Hot Springs. ✉ *Lavalle 36, Galería Independencia, Loc. 8* ☎ *261/429–9665* 🌐 *www.betancourt.com.ar* ✉ *Ruta Panamericana, Km 26, Luján de Cuyo* ☎ *261/15–559–1329.*

USPALLATA

125 km (78 miles) west of Mendoza City.

At the crossroads of three important routes—Ruta Nacional 7 from Mendoza across the Andes to Ruta 57 from Mendoza via Villavicencio, and Ruta 39 from San Juan via Barreal—this small mountain town lies in the Calingasta Valley between the foothills and the front range of the Andes. It's a good base for excursions into the mountains by 4x4 or on horseback to abandoned mines, a desert ghost town, and spectacular mountain scenery where the 1997 movie *Seven Years in Tibet* was filmed. Metals have been forged at **Las Bóvedas,** the pointed adobe cupolas a few miles north of town, since pre-Columbian times. Arms and cannons for San Martín's army were made here.

GETTING HERE AND AROUND

Head south from Mendoza on Avenida San Martín to the Ruta Nacional 7 and turn west. You can make this 195-km (121-mile) trip from Mendoza by bus (long, with many stops), on a guided tour (advised), or by rental car. You can make it an all-day drive, or break it up with an overnight in Uspallata.

SAFETY

An adventurous way to explore the dramatic landscape around Uspallata is by driving yourself. There are things to keep in mind, though, if you want to have a safe, stress-free time. Always leave town with a full tank of gas, as there are no services available, and traffic is minimal. Carry a flashlight if you leave late in the day, and be aware of weather conditions (not recommended in winter snow storms). Good maps are available at ACA (the automobile club in Mendoza) and at the tourist office.

WORD OF MOUTH

"[Mendoza to Aconcagua] is an amazing drive, and if you drive yourself you can stop where and when you what. It is approximately 4–5 hours each way. Go for the drive, it is awesome. It was the first time I saw purple mountains, yellow mountains, green mountains, and snow-covered mountains together." —sandiej

5

EXPLORING

Fodor's Choice ★ **Parque Provincial Aconcagua.** This provincial park extends for 66,733 hectares (164,900 acres) over wild, high country with few trails other than those used by expeditions climbing the impressive Cerro Aconcagua (Aconcagua Mountain), the main attraction. Stop at the Visitor's Center near Parque San Martin before you leave Mendoza City to fill out the required paperwork to secure permits. ✉ *Visitor's Center, San Martin 1143, Mendoza* 🎫 *Trekking permits US$95–$200, depending on season, permit level, and how many days you plan on hiking; ascent permits $300–$780.* ⏲ *Weekdays 8–6, weekends and holidays 9–1.*

SCENIC DRIVES AND LOOKOUTS

★ **Camino del Año.** From Mendoza traveling 47 km (29 miles) north on Ruta Provincial 52, passing through Canota, you arrive at Villavicencio, the source of mineral water sold throughout Argentina. The nearby Hostaria Villavicencio serves lunch and dinner.

Farther up the road, the Camino del Año begins its ascent around 365 turns to El Balcón atop the pass at Cruz de Paramillo (3,000 meters/9,840 feet). Look for the ruins of a Jesuit mine, the Arucarias de Darwin (petrified trees found by Darwin in 1835), and the 1,000-year-old petroglyphs on Tunderqueral Hill. From the top of the pass you can see three of the highest mountains outside of Asia, all over 6,000 meters (20,000 feet): Aconcagua to the west, Tupungato to the south, and Mercedario (6,770 meters/22,211 feet) to the north.

At Km 67, the road straightens and descends into Uspallata, where you can continue west on Ruta Nacional 7 to Chile or take the lonely road north on Ruta 39 to Barreal in San Juan Province (108 km/67 miles). The road to Barreal crosses a high desert valley, where the only sign of life is an occasional ranch obscured by a grove of alamo trees.

At Los Tambillos, about 40 km (25 miles) north of Uspallata, the route is intersected by the Inca road that ran from Cusco, Peru, through Bolivia and into northern Argentina. The site is surrounded by a fence that protects traces of the original road and remains of an Inca *tambo* (resting place). A map shows the route of the Incas.

The mountains to the west get higher and more spectacular as you approach Barreal. At the San Juan Province border, the road becomes Ruta 412, and is paved the remaining 50 km (31 miles) to Barreal. ✉ *Mendoza.*

Uspallata Pass on Ruta Nacional 7 (*Panamerican Highway*). This route heads west on Ruta 13 and then Ruta Nacional 7 (also known as the Panamerican Highway) and takes you straight into the mountains. You'll go from vineyards to barren hills until you reach the Potrerillos Valley, then head farther west on Ruta 7 into the heart of the Andes. This was a major Inca route, so keep your eyes peeled for Inca tambos. You'll pass ancient thermal springs and the ruins of a spa from the 1920s. This is the only route between Chile and Argentina for miles and miles, so if you're self-driving be ready to share the road with cargo trucks. ✉ *Mendoza.*

WHERE TO EAT

$ ARGENTINE ✕ **Lo de Pato.** This casual roadside spot serves cafeteria-style lunches and grilled meat and pasta dinners; get yourself a cold drink from the refrigerator. The souvenir shop sells candy bars, postcards, T-shirts, and other mementos. ✉ *RN7, Uspallata* ☎ *264/420–249.*

WHERE TO STAY

For expanded hotel reviews, visit Fodors.com.

$ **Hostería Puente del Inca.** Vintage photos in the dining room document this hostel's history as a mountaineering outpost. **Pros:** the only place to sleep atop the pass; close to hot springs. **Cons:** more a shelter for climbers than an actual hotel; preoccupied staff; no amenities. ✉ *RN7, Km 175, Puente del Inca* ☎ *261/470–3706* 🌐 *www.hosteriapdelinca.com.ar* *20 (choice of double, 4, and 6 person) rooms with private baths.* *In-hotel: restaurant.*

$$$ **Hotel Termas Cacheuta.** Hot mineral springs have been bubbling forth at this historic spa next to the Mendoza River since 1885, when visitors arrived by train from Buenos Aires; today, hotel guests and day-trippers begin their day with a steamy sauna in the grotto, followed by a high-powered hot shower, and then a Jacuzzi. **Pros:** scenic surroundings; delicious and nutritious food. **Cons:** watch your head in the grotto; water park can get crowded and noisy. ✉ *RP82, Km 38, Luján de Cuyo* ☎ *2624/490–152* 🌐 *www.termascacheuta.com* *16 rooms* *In-hotel: restaurant, pool, spa, business center* *All meals.*

$$$ **Hotel Uspallata.** In spite of the cavernous hallways, minimal decor, barren walls, and dim lighting (legacies of the Perón era, when the government built hotels for its employees), this grand old hotel offers comfortable refuge en route to Aconcagua, Chile, or Barreal in the opposite direction. **Pros:** large rooms; proximity to outdoor activities including skiing. **Cons:** impersonal decor. ✉ *RN7, Km 1149, Uspallata* ☎ *2624/420–066* 🌐 *www.granhoteluspallata.com.ar* *74 rooms* *In-hotel: restaurant, bar, swimming* *Breakfast.*

$$ **Hotel Valle Andino.** As you approach Uspallata on Ruta Nacional 7, this brick building with a pitched tile roof and wood trim sits beside the road surrounded by scenic vistas in all directions; inside, rooms are modern; some have bunk beds, and all have brick walls and minimalist

furniture. **Pros:** family-friendly (kids under 4 stay free; 20% discount for those ages 4–10). **Cons:** facilities are spread out; need a car to visit nearby sights and town. ✉ *RN7, Uspallata* ☎ *2624/420–095, 261/425–8434 in Mendoza* 🌐 *www.hotelvalleandino.com* 26 rooms *In-hotel: restaurant, bar, pool* 🍴 *Breakfast.*

SPORTS AND THE OUTDOORS

HORSEBACK RIDING

El Rincón de los Oscuros. With gentle horses and experienced guides at their ranch outside of Potrerillos, El Rincón de los Oscuros offers two-hour or all-day rides take you to panoramic vistas, waterfalls, and high-altitude sites where condors and guanacos are often seen. ✉ *Av. Los Cóndores s/n, Potrerillos* ☎ *2624/483–030* 🌐 *www.rincondelososcuros.com.*

HIKING AND MOUNTAINEERING

November through March is the best time for hiking and climbing. You can arrange day hikes with area tour operators. Of the longer treks, the most popular lasts four to seven days and begins at Puente del Inca, at 2,950 meters (9,680 feet), where you spend a night to get acclimated, and then set out for Aconcagua's base camp. On the first day, a steady climb takes you to Confluencia, where most people spend two nights and enjoy a day hike to the south wall and its incredible glacier. The hike continues to the Plaza de Mulas (4,260 meters/13,976 feet) and ends at the base camp for climbers making a final ascent on Cerro Aconcagua.

Centro de Visitantes. You can get permits for climbing Aconcagua through your tour operator or on your own in Mendoza at Centro de Visitantes, in Parque San Martín near the entrance. The center is open weekdays 8–6 and weekends 9–1. ✉ *Av. de Los Robles and Rotondo de Rosedal, Mendoza.*

Fernando Grajales. Guiding since 1976, Fernando Grajales is a veteran of many Aconcagua summits. His company leads 18-day excursions to the summit of Aconcagua, weather permitting, December 1–February 12. ✉ *Mendoza* ☎ *261/15–658–8855 cell, 800/516–6962* 🌐 *www.grajales.net.*

Inka Expeditions. These guides have more than 10 years of experience and hundreds of tours to Aconcagua base camp under their belt (and to the summit, if you are so ambitious). ✉ *Av. Juan B. Justo 345, Mendoza* ☎ *261/425–0871* 🌐 *www.inka.com.ar.*

Termas Cacheuta. Spend a day with your kids at this hot (65–102 degrees F) thermal water park, within walking distance of its namesake hotel. Slide into the wave pool, swim along the 270-meter canal through a tunnel and under a waterfall, or just loll about in the myriad indoor and outdoor pools. Even toddlers will enjoy the shallow pools with small slides. Picnic tables and covered eating areas are located along the river. You can grill your own *bife* in the many parrillas provided or visit the restaurant. This park accommodates over 1,000 visitors on holidays. ✉ *RP82, Km 38, Cacheuta* ☎ *2624/490–139, 261/429–9133* 🌐 *www.termascacheuta.com* *35 pesos* ⏲ *Daily 10–6:30.*

SKIING

Skiers bound for Mendoza's resorts arrive from early July through September at the airports of Mendoza or San Rafael (the latter for Las Leñas only). Los Penitentes is a medium-size ski area that attracts mostly Argentinians, particularly Mendocinos who can drive up for a day. Vallecitos, the province's oldest ski center, is where most Mendocinos made their first turns.

Los Penitentes. Popular as a day destination for Argentinian skiers, this uncrowded ski area, 153 km (95 miles) northwest of Mendoza on Ruta Nacional 7, is named for the rock formations that resemble penitent monks. Despite the elevation of 2,580 meters (8,465 feet) at the base and 3,194 meters (10,479 feet) at the top, the snow here is often thin. When it does snow, the danger of avalanches is severe. The base village has hotels, restaurants, bars, discos, medical services, a ski school, and guides.

Facilities: 700-meter (2,300-foot) vertical drop; 300 hectares (741 acres); 20% beginner, 30% intermediate, 50% advanced; two double chairs, one T-bar, five surface lifts. Cross-country ski trails, extreme and off-piste snowcat skiing, sledding, and *pato* (snow polo).

Lessons and Programs: Ski school, mountain guides, and a children's school and day care.

Lift Tickets: Adults 135 pesos a day.

Rentals: Rental shops at the base area. ✉ *Mendoza* ☎ *261/429–9953* ⏲ *Daily mid-June to late August.*

Vallecitos. Situated at 2,900 meters (9,514 feet) in a glacial valley of the Cordón de Plata range, 80 km (50 miles) from Mendoza and 26 km (16 miles) from Potrerillos, this small ski area owned and operated by Ski Club Mendoza has great off-piste skiing.

Facilities: 400-meter (1,312-foot) vertical drop; 100 hectares (247 acres) of skiable terrain plus unlimited out-of-bounds skiing; 20% beginner, 50% intermediate, 30% advanced; three double chairs, one single chair, three surface lifts.

Rentals: Equipment rental and sales at base lodge. ✉ *Av. Acceso Este 650, Luján del Cuyo* ☎ *261/312–799* ⏲ *Daily July 1–Sept. 30.*

VALLE DE UCO

The Valle de Uco extends southwest of Mendoza along the foothills of the Cordón de Plata and the Andes, whose two highest peaks, Tupungato Volcano and El Plata, rise over 580 meters (19,000 feet) on the western horizon. The Ríos Tunuyán in the north and Las Tunas in the south bring mineral-rich melted snow from the glaciers to the potato fields, apple and cherry orchards, olive groves, and vineyards planted across this immense valley. Old family ranches that once extended all the way to Chile are being sold off or converted to vineyards in what is now the country's fastest-growing wine area.

It's also one of the world's highest wine-growing regions, with approximately 81,000 hectares (200,000 acres) planted at altitudes between

900 and 1,200 meters (3,000–3,900 feet). Cool nights and warm days allow grapes to ripen slowly while developing excellent fruit flavor, good acidity in white wines, and the formation of strong tannins in reds.

Wineries vary from traditional family-run operations to ultramodern facilities, and many names long associated with Argentina's wine industry are building innovative ventures here. Wineries tend to be scattered about in infrequently traveled areas, making reservations highly recommended. The easiest way to see the area is to take a tour or stay in a local lodge that offers tours. ■ **TIP→ If you're on your own, be sure to get the WINEMAP at local wineries or before you leave Mendoza.**

TUPUNGATO

78 km (48 miles) south of Mendoza.

Tupungato is a sleepy agricultural town most of the year. During the wine harvest (February and March), though, the roads in and around it overflow with carts and tractors loaded with grapes from the 24 area wineries. The population doubles from its official number of nearly 30,000 as pickers arrive. Tupungato Volcano rises above the valley in snowbound splendor.

5

GETTING HERE AND AROUND

The most direct route from Mendoza to the Valle de Uco is south on Ruta Nacional 40 for 37 km (23 miles) to Ugarteche, where you turn west onto Ruta 86 for another 37 km (23 miles), passing through the village of San José just before arriving in Tupungato. Although buses arrive several times a day from Mendoza, the best way to get around the area is to join a tour or rent a car. If you're driving north, turn off Ruta Nacional 40 onto Ruta Provincial 88 at Zapata. Ruta Provincial 86 runs north; Ruta Provincial 89 runs south along the foot of the mountains, and most of the important bodegas are on or near these routes. O. Fournier in San Carlos is the southernmost bodega in the Valle de Uco.

If you have some time and aren't put off by driving on a dirt road, a scenic way here is south on Ruta Nacional 40 from Mendoza and west on to Ruta Nacional 7 to the dam at Potrerillos, where you exit and take Ruta Provincial 89 (a dirt road) south through the villages of Las Vegas and El Salto, where clusters of vacation cottages brim with flowers in summer and are covered with snow in winter. The road climbs steeply out of the canyon and over a pass, then crosses a high valley with a magnificent view of the Andes. Soon the great expanse of the Valle de Uco lies before you, with its miles of vineyards and orchards of peaches, almonds, and chestnuts, adding wide swaths of pink and white blossoms in spring (late September–October). This drive is equally impressive in reverse.

ESSENTIALS

Bank Banco de La Nación ✉ *Belgano 1397, Tupungato.*

Medical Assistance Hospital General Las Heras ✉ *General Las Heras and M. Fernandez, Tupungato* ☎ *2622/422–325, 2622/488–293.*

Visitor Info Oficina de Turismo de Tupungato ✉ *Av. Belgrano 348, Tupungato* ☎ *2622/488–016* 🌐 *www.tupungato.mendoza.gov.ar.*

Continued on page 276

Wines of Chile & Argentina

by Margaret Shook

The wine regions of both Chile and Argentina are set against the backdrop of the Andes. And while these mountains do play an important role in the making of wine in both countries, Chile and Argentina have very different traditions and strengths.

Although wine-loving Spaniards settled both countries in the 16th century, only Chile's wine industry developed quickly, largely because the land around Santiago was particularly good for growing grapes. Buenos Aires, on the warm and humid Atlantic coast, however, was hardly an ideal place for viticulture. Mendoza, Argentina's present-day wine wonderland, was impossibly far away to be a reliable supplier of wine to the capital until the railroad united it with the coast in the mid-19th century.

Chile also experienced a boom in the 19th century as new, French-inspired wineries sprang up. Both countries continued without significant change for more than 100 years, until the 1990s international wine boom sparked new interest in South American wines. Big investments from France, Spain, Italy, the United States, and elsewhere—plus some extraordinary winemakers—have made this an exciting place for oenophiles to visit.

(left) Bottle of Maradona red wine; (above) Errazuriz Winery, Chile

NEIGHBORS ACROSS THE ANDES

CHILE

In the early days, the emphasis was on growing cheap wine to consume domestically. Then, in the middle of the 20th century, Chile's political turmoil caused the business to stagnate. It wasn't until the 1980s that wine exports became a major business, and today Chile exports more than it imports.

Chile's appellation system names its valleys from north to south, but today's winegrowers stress that the climatic and geological differences between east and west are more significant. The easternmost valleys closest to the Andes tend to have less fog, more hours of sunlight, and greater daily temperature variations, which help red grapes develop deep color and rich tannins while maintaining bright acidity and fresh fruit characteristics. On the other hand, if you're after crisp whites and bright Pinots, head to the coast, where cool fog creeps inland from the sea each morning and Pacific breezes keep the vines cool all day.

Interior areas in the Central Valley are less prone to extremes and favor varieties that require more balanced conditions, such as Merlot, and Chile's own rich and spicy Carmenère. Syrah, a relatively new grape in Chile, does well in both cold and warm climates.

Vina Cousino Macul, Santiago, Chile

Miguel Torres, Chile

BE SURE TO TASTE:

Sauvignon Blanc: Cool-climate vineyards from Elqui to Bío Bío are producing very exciting Sauvignon with fresh green fruit, crisp acidity, and often an enticing mineral edge.

Carmenère: Chile's signature grape arrived in Chile during the mid-19th century from France, where it was usually a blending grape in Bordeaux. Over time Chileans forgot about it, mistaking it for Merlot, but during the Chilean boom times of the 1990s they realized that they had a very unique grape hidden amongst the other vines in their vineyards.

Cabernet Sauvignon: The king of reds grows well almost anywhere it's planted, but Cabernets from the Alto Maipo are particularly well balanced, displaying elegance and structure.

Syrah: Chile produces two distinct styles of this grape. Be sure to try both: luscious and juicy from Colchagua or enticingly spicy from coastal areas, such as Elqui or San Antonio.

Malbec: True, this is Argentina's grape, but Chile produces award-winning bottlings that have appealing elegance and balance.

Bodega Tres Erres, Chile

ARGENTINA

Unlike Chile, Argentina exports far less wine than it consumes, and much of its wine is produced in accordance with local tastes and wallets. The 1990s wine boom sparked a greater emphasis on export, and following new investments, the country is now widely recognized for the quality of its red wines, particularly its signature Malbec.

Broad-shouldered Argentina looks west to the Andes for a life-giving force. Its wine regions receive no cooling maritime influence, as Chile's do, and its vineyards rely on the mountain altitudes not only to irrigate its lands, but also to attenuate the effects of the blazing sun. The climate here is capricious, so producers must be ever-prepared for untimely downpours, devastating hailstorms, and scorching, dehydrating Zonda winds.

Monteviejo Winery, Clos de los Siete, Mendoza

Estancia San Pablo Tupungato

BE SURE TO TASTE:

Malbec: Just one sip of Argentina's most widely known wine evokes gauchos and tangos. Deep, dark, and handsomely concentrated, this is a must-try on its home turf.

Cabernet Sauvignon: Argentine Cabs are big, bold, and brawny, as is typical of warmer climates. They're perfect with one of those legendary Argentine grilled steaks.

Red Blends: The red blends here may be mixtures of classic Bordeaux varietals with decidedly Argentine results, or audacious combinations that are only possible in the New World.

Torrontés: Argentina's favorite white has floral overtones, grown most often in Cafayate, in the northwestern province of Salta.

Colome Winery, Molinos, Salta

TASTING TIPS ON BOTH SIDES OF THE BORDER

1. Make reservations! Unlike wineries in the U.S., most wineries are not equipped to receive drop-in visitors.

2. Don't expect wineries to be open on Sunday. Winery workers need a day off too.

3. The distances between wineries can be much longer than they look on the map. Be sure to allot plenty of travel time, and plan on no more than three or four wineries per day.

4. Do contact the wine route offices in the region you're visiting. They can be extremely helpful in coordinating visits to wineries and other local attractions.

5. Hire a driver, or choose a designated driver.

6. Know what you are walking into. Some wineries offer free tours and tasting,s others can charge upwards of 100 pesos per person.

GREAT WINE ITINERARIES

SEE CHAPTER FOR WINERY CONTACT INFORMATION

Chile's wine industry was affected by the 8.8-magnitude earthquake that hit the country on February 27, 2010. Early estimates put the total loss at 125 million liters (14 million cases); equal to roughly 12% of the nation's wine output for 2009. Although older adobe structures didn't fair well, most cellars and bottling lines in modern, more quake-resistant buildings were able to be repaired. Vineyards reported little damage to the vines themselves; the grape harvest began on schedule, though damaged roads initially slowed transport. Wine regions most affected were Cachapoal, Colchagua, Curicó and Maule; Maipo (closest to Santiago) faired comparatively well, and areas farther north sustained little to no damage. Call ahead; at this writing, details had not yet been released for which facilities would be temporarily unavailable to the public.

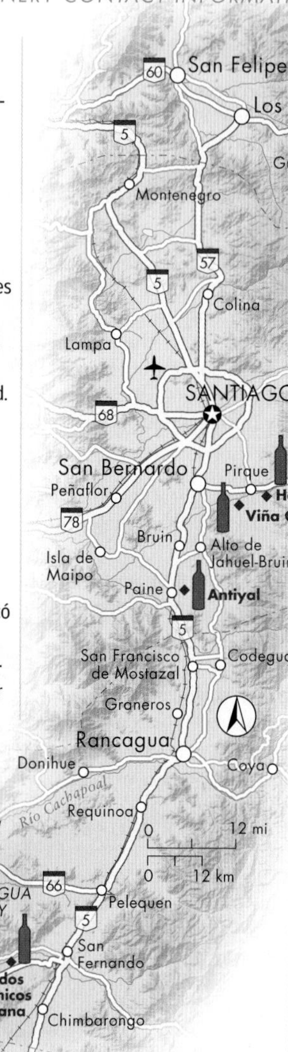

Crossing the Andes will be one of the highlights of your trip, especially the series of switchbacks that wind into the mountains just before the border crossing.

ALTO MAIPO ITINERARY

Plenty of wineries are a day trip from Santiago. You can go solo and hire a taxi ($70 for a half day), but for around US$160 (full day) a guide provides better access.

Concha y Toro. Start the day at one of Chile's oldest and best known wineries, located just outside of the capital in Pirque.

Antiyal. One of Chile's first boutique-garage wineries, Antiyal only makes two red blends, both of which are organic and biodynamic.

Haras de Pirque. Horses are the owners' first love. You'll pass the breeding farm and the race track on the way to this horseshoe-shaped winery tucked up into the Andean hills.

COLCHAGUA ITINERARY

If it's Saturday, book a ride on the Wine Train, which travels from San Fernando to the heart of the Colchagua Valley in Santa Cruz.

Viña Bisquertt. This family-run winery houses several 15-foot-tall wooden casks from the 1940s.

Clos Apalta. Viña Casa Lapostolle built this gravity-flow wonder exclusively for their red blend, Clos Apalta.

Viña Santa Cruz. More than just a winery, this is an entire wine complex. Take the a cable car to the "indigenous village."

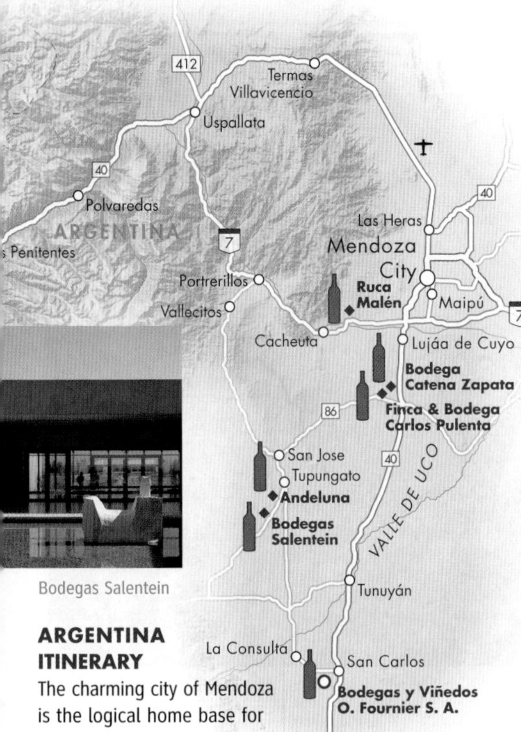

Bodegas Salentein

ARGENTINA ITINERARY

The charming city of Mendoza is the logical home base for exploring Argentine wine country, and the country's finest wineries surround the city.

Ruca Malén. This smallish winery is less than 10 years old and offers a friendly, personalized tour with tastings of its Malbec, Cabernet, and Chardonnay wines. The restaurant is a good place to stop for lunch.

Bodegas Vistalba de Carlos Pulenta. Owned by one of Argentina's most renowned winemakers, Carlos Pulenta, this elegantly modern winery has walls that expose the vineyard's soil profiles.

Bodega Catena Zapata. Rising like a Mayan temple from the fertile soil, this winery produces some of Argentina's most memorable blended wines.

Familia Zuccardi, Mendoza

Harvest time at Andeluna

WINERY-ARCHITECTURE ITINERARY

Fans of spectacular architecture will enjoy visiting Argentina's wineries. Big, modern, sometimes whimsical, and often surprising, many of these enormous high-tech facilities have restaurants and even lodgings to make the long distances between them bearable. Plan for a long day in the beautiful Valle de Uco visiting some striking examples.

Salentein. A perfect example of the "winery-plus" experience in South American wine tourism, this property is a work of art set against a natural backdrop of the Andes, complete with cultural center, restaurant, chapel, and award-winning wines.

Andeluna. The Rutini family has long made wine in Argentina, and its newest endeavor is at the relatively high altitude of 1,300 meters (4,265 feet). Check out the house wines at the wine bar or one of the other tasting centers, or chat in the kitchen as the chef prepares your meal.

O. Fournier. End your day at this highly unusual building that looks, from a distance, like a city of Oz for the new millennium. An enormous, flat roof seems to hover over the building, and the large U-shaped ramp accommodates gravity-flow winemaking.

CROSSING THE ANDES

Mendoza, Argentina; Andean foothills, wine harvest.

■ If you're coming all the way to South America to taste wine, be sure to visit both sides of the Andes. There are frequent hour-long jet flights between Santiago and Mendoza for US$200–$300 that provide a spectacular condor's-eye view of the craggily snow-covered peaks below.

■ If you are visiting in the summer months and have time for the day-long 250 km (155 mi) overland route, by all means take it. Know that you will most likely have to get a roundtrip car rental. Most companies will not allow one-way international crossings. Better to rent a car in Santiago or Buenos Aires to see the wineries in each country, then fly or catch a bus to cross the border. On the Argentina side, a flight from Buenos Aires to Mendoza can save time.

■ Roads are well-maintained and reasonably marked. Take Ruta 57 north from Santiago to the small city of Los Andes, then head east on Ruta 60 toward the mountains and the Argentine border, where the highway's name changes to Ruta 7, to Mendoza.

■ Crossing the Andes will be one of the highlights of your trip, especially the series of switchbacks that wind into the mountains just before the border crossing some 8,200 feet above sea level. Be aware that the Libertadores Pass is often closed for days at a time during the winter months, so don't risk it unless you're willing to spend several days sleeping in your car while you wait for things to clear up. Be sure to bring a jacket any time of year, as it can be very chilly at that altitude.

■ Plan a couple of stops along the way; make the Portillo Ski Resort your last stop on the Chilean side, where you can visit the Laguna del Inca at nearly 10,000 feet. The ski resort is a great place to stop for lunch. On the Argentine side, stop for gas and a bite to eat in Upsallata, about 100 km (65 miles) before reaching Mendoza.

WINE TASTING PRIMER

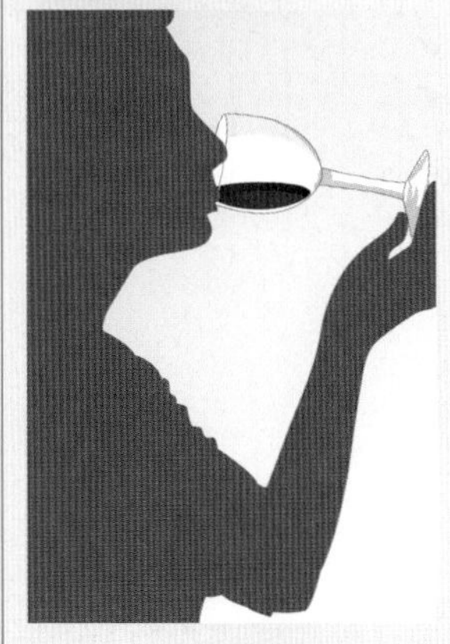

Ordering and tasting wine—whether at a winery, bar, or restaurant—is easy once you master a few simple steps.

LOOK AND NOTE

Hold your glass by the stem and look at the wine in the glass. Note its color, depth, and clarity.

For whites, is it greenish, yellow, or gold? For reds, is it purplish, ruby, or garnet? Is the wine's color pale or deep? Is the liquid clear or cloudy?

SWIRL AND SNIFF

Swirl the wine gently in the glass to intensify the scents, then sniff over the rim of the glass. What do you smell? Try to identify aromas like:

- **Fruits**—citrus, peaches, berries, figs, melon
- **Flowers**—orange blossoms, honey, perfume
- **Spices**—baking spices, pungent, herbal notes
- **Vegetables**—fresh or cooked, herbal notes
- **Minerals**—earth, steely notes, wet stones
- **Dairy**—butter, cream, cheese, yogurt
- **Oak**—toast, vanilla, coconut, tobacco
- **Animal**—leathery, meaty notes

Are there any unpleasant notes, like mildew or wet dog that might indicate that the wine is "off?"

SIP AND SAVOR

Prime your palate with a sip, swishing the wine in your mouth. Then spit in a bucket or swallow.

Take another sip and think about the wine's attributes. Sweetness is detected on the tip of the tongue, acidity on the sides of the tongue, and tannins (a mouth-drying sensation) on the gums. Consider the body—does the wine feel light in the mouth, or is there a rich sensation? Are the flavors consistent with the aromas? If you like the wine, try to pinpoint what you like about it, and vice versa if you don't like it.

Take time to savor the wine as you're sipping it—the tasting experience may seem a bit scientific, but the end goal is your enjoyment.

WINERY CHART

Winery	Reservations	Restaurant	Hotel	Cabernet Franc	Cabernet Sauvignon	Gamay	Italian Varietals	Malbec	Merlot	Petit Verdot	Pinot Noir	Syrah	Tannat	Tempranillo
				REDS										
Mendoza														
★ 12 Achával Ferrer	✔			✔	✔			✔	✔					
★ 20 Bodega Catena Zapata	✔	✔			✔			✔						
2 Bodega La Rural	✔				✔		✔	✔	✔		✔	✔	✔	
7 Bodega Lagarde				✔	✔			✔	✔	✔	✔	✔		✔
14 Bodega Norton	✔				✔		✔	✔	✔			✔		✔
11 Bodega Vistalba	✔	✔	✔		✔		✔	✔	✔	✔				
★ 5 Bodegas Nieto y Senetiner S.A.	✔				✔			✔						
19 Bodegas Tapíz	✔	✔	✔		✔			✔	✔			✔		
3 Bodegas y Viñedos López	✔				✔		✔	✔			✔	✔		
18 Chandón	✔				✔			✔	✔		✔	✔		
18 Di Tommasso		✔			✔			✔						
17 Dominio del Plata	✔				✔		✔	✔				✔		
8 Carmelo Patti	✔				✔									
★ 1 Familia Zuccardi	✔	✔			✔		✔	✔	✔		✔	✔		✔
10 Finca Flichman					✔			✔				✔		
6 Luigi Bosca	✔				✔			✔	✔		✔	✔		✔
9 Mendel Wines	✔				✔			✔						
16 Ruca Malén	✔	✔			✔			✔						
★ 15 Séptima	✔				✔		✔	✔						✔
13 Terrazas de Los Andes	✔		✔		✔			✔						

★ = Fodor's Choice

Rose	Chardonnay	Chenin Blanc	Gewurztraminer	Muscat	Pinot Grigio	Riesling	Sauvignon Blanc	Semillion	Tocai Friulano	Torrontes	Viognier	Labels
	WHITES											
												Altamira, Quimera (blends)
	✔											Nicolás Catena Zapata, Catena, Catena Alta, Álamos
	✔	✔	✔			✔						San Felipe, Trumpeter, Felipe Rutini
	✔			✔			✔	✔			✔	Henry, Lagarde, Altas Cumbres, Sémillon 1942
	✔						✔	✔		✔		Privada, Reserva, Barrel Select, Espumante Extra Brut
							✔					Corte A, Corte B, Corte C
	✔											Cadus, Don Nicanor, Santa Isabel, Reserva Nieto
	✔						✔			✔		Tapíz, Zolo
	✔	✔					✔	✔				Montchenot, Chateaux Vieux, Rincón Famoso, López, Vasco Viejo, Traful
	✔						✔	✔				Valmont, Latitud 33°, Beltour, Clos du Moulin, Castel, Insignia, O2, Dos Voces
	✔						✔			✔		Familia De Tommasso
	✔					✔						BenMarco, Susana Balbo, Crios de Susana Balbo
												Carmelo Patti
	✔						✔			✔	✔	Santa Julia, Vida Orgánica, Malamado, Zeta, "Q"
	✔	✔				✔	✔					Dedicado, Caballero de la Cepa, Viña Plata, Paisaje de Tupungato, Paisaje de Barrancas
	✔		✔			✔	✔				✔	Reserva, Alta Gama, La Linda, Finca Los Nobles, Boheme
												Finca Remota, UNUS
	✔											Kinien, Ruca Malén, Yauquén, Terruño
												Séptima
	✔											Terrazas, Afincado, Reserva

WINERY CHART

Winery	Reservations	Restaurant	Hotel	Cabernet Franc	Cabernet Sauvignon	Gamay	Italian Varietals	Malbec	Merlot	Petit Verdot	Pinot Noir	Syrah	Tannat	Tempranillo
				REDS										
Valle de Uco														
3 Andeluna					✔				✔					
2 Atamisque	✔	✔						✔	✔		✔			
4 La Azúl S.A.		✔						✔	✔					
8 Bodega Aconquija	✔											✔		✔
1 Bodega Bombal	✔		✔				✔	✔						
6 J&F Lurton	✔				✔		✔	✔				✔		
10 Bodega y Viñedos O. Fournier S.A.	✔	✔						✔	✔			✔		✔
5 Salentein	✔	✔	✔		✔			✔	✔		✔	✔		
★ 7 Clos de Los Siete	✔							✔						
9 Finca La Celia				✔	✔			✔	✔			✔		
San Rafael														
6 Algodón Wine Estates	✔	✔	✔		✔		✔	✔		✔				
3 Balbi					✔			✔				✔		
5 Suter					✔			✔	✔		✔			
★ 1 La Champañera Valentín Bianchi	✔				✔			✔	✔		✔	✔		
★ 7 Goyenechea	✔				✔			✔	✔			✔		
4 Jean Rivier	✔				✔			✔						
2 Jorge Simonassi Lyon	✔				✔		✔	✔	✔			✔		
8 Lavaque	✔				✔			✔			✔			
San Juan														
1 Bodegas Santiago Graffigna S.A					✔		✔	✔	✔					
5 Viñas de Segisa					✔			✔			✔			
8 Callia	✔				✔		✔	✔						
9 Casa Montes Bodegas y Viñedos	✔			✔	✔			✔	✔			✔		✔
★ 3 Cavas de Zonda S.A					✔			✔	✔		✔			
7 Champañera Miguel Ángel Mas					✔						✔			
6 Fabril Alto Verde					✔			✔			✔			
4 Las Marianas					✔				✔		✔		✔	✔
2 Museo Antigua Bodega de San Juan					✔						✔			

Rosé	Chardonnay	Chenin Blanc	Gewürztraminer	Muscat	Pinot Grigio	Riesling	Sauvignon Blanc	Sémillion	Tocai Friulano	Torrontés	Viognier	Labels
	WHITES											
	✔											Andeluna
✔	✔								✔			Catalpa, Atamisque, Picaflor
												Azul, Reserva, Gran Vino
✔	✔											Aconquija, Alberto Furque, Furque
	✔						✔					Estancia Ancón, Bombal
✔	✔				✔					✔	✔	Lurton, Finca Las Higueras
												Acrux, Bcrux, Urban Uco
												Salentein, Primus, Finca El Portillo
	✔											Clos de Los Siete, Lindaflor, Petite Fleur, Festivo, Val de Flor
	✔				✔		✔	✔				Reserva, La Consulta, Furia, Magallanes, Angaro
												Viñas Del Golf
	✔											Calvet, Balbi
	✔	✔										Rojo, Etiqueta Marrón, Fritzwein
	✔	✔				✔	✔		✔	✔	✔	Famiglia Bianchi, Enzo Bianchi, Elsa, Elsa's Vineyard, 1887, Don Valentín Lacrado
✔	✔						✔		✔			Marquez de Nevado, Vasconia, Centenario, Quinta Generación
✔		✔										Jean Rivier, Inti Valley
												Andrea's Cavas, Tempo, Finca Simonassi
		✔										Rincón Privado, Lavaque Roble
		✔			✔		✔				✔	Graffigna, Colón, Santa Silvia, Casa de Cubas, Centenario, Tío Paco
	✔									✔		Premium, Fronda
												Magna, Alta, Signos
✔	✔										✔	Alzamora, Don Baltazár, Ampakama
	✔											Gran Cava
	✔									✔		Miguel Mas, Maria Martín
	✔											Buenas Ondas, Nuestra Escencia, Montgallard
												Fray Justo
	✔						✔	✔				Viñas de Chirino, Ensamblache, Antigua Bodega 1929

WINERIES

> **WORD OF MOUTH**
>
> "Don't attempt driving to the wineries in the Uco Valley. Salentien seems right off the highway but O'Fournier was several unmarked turns off the main road on a gravel road. I heard the drive to Andeluna was similar." —julieod

Fodor's Choice ★ **Andeluna.** Surrounded by miles of vineyards, with the majestic Andes as a backdrop, the red brick bodega blends comfortably into the scenery and the vineyards that climb the foothills of the Andes from 1,097 to 1,300 meters (3,600 to 4,265 feet). Inside, the large reception and tasting room—with its stone and slate, leather furnishings, and high ceiling of reeds and open beams—evokes an old Mendocino mansion. The open kitchen at one end serves meals and conducts cooking classes with two days' notice. Winery tours (reservations required) are extensive and detailed, and end with a tasting of the label's intense wines. ✉ *R89, Km 11, Tupungato* ☎ *2622/423–226* 🌐 *www.andeluna.com.ar* ⏲ *Tours daily at 10:30, 12:30, and 3:30.*

Atamisque. The grey adobe building with its uneven slate roof, reminiscent of houses in Spain and France, almost disappears against the background of bushes and mountains. But once inside this boutique winery, visitors quickly see the dedication to detail and the creation of fine wines that is the mission of the French owners who discovered this estancia that dates back to 1658, when the Jesuits owned it. They fell in love with the land, and named it after a native tree. Lunches and tastings are conducted at the nearby restaurant Rincón Atamisque. ✉ *RP86, Km 30, Tupungato* ☎ *261/15–685–5184* 🌐 *www.atamisque.com* ⏲ *Daily 9:30–4:30, by reservation.*

Bodega Bombal. The first generation of Bombals arrived in Tupungato in 1760, and the family built its first bodega in 1914, where Lucila Barrionuevo de Bombal produced the family's first wines. Her son Domingo developed the vineyards and built a new bodega next to the Château d'Ancón, the family's summer home. Today his daughter, Lucila Bombal, produces high-quality wine and hosts the château's many visitors when she's in town. ✉ *R89, 2 km (1 mile) west of San José village and R86, Tupungato* ☎ *2622/488–245* 🌐 *www.estanciancon.com* ⏲ *Tues., Thurs., and Fri. 11–5, weekends 11–6, with reservations.*

La Azul. Exporters of wine as well as peaches, plums, cherries, and apples, this agro-wine complex's vineyard tours demonstrate the different vine-growing methods used over the centuries. Careful attention is paid to grape selection, winemaking, and visitors at this boutique winery, which also features nice lunch options at the restaurant. ✉ *R89, Tupungato* ☎ *2622/423–593* ⏲ *Weekdays 9–5, by reservation.*

WHERE TO EAT

$$ ARGENTINE ✕ **Restaurante Valle de Tupungato.** Traditional grilled meats, homemade pastas, and appetizers featuring locally made cold cuts are hearty fare at this friendly family-style restaurant. On Friday you can help yourself to steak, lamb, chicken, and goat at the open grill. Crowds of locals show up on weekends, overflowing onto the Astroturf lawn. ✉ *Belgrano 542, Tupungato* ☎ *2622/488–421.*

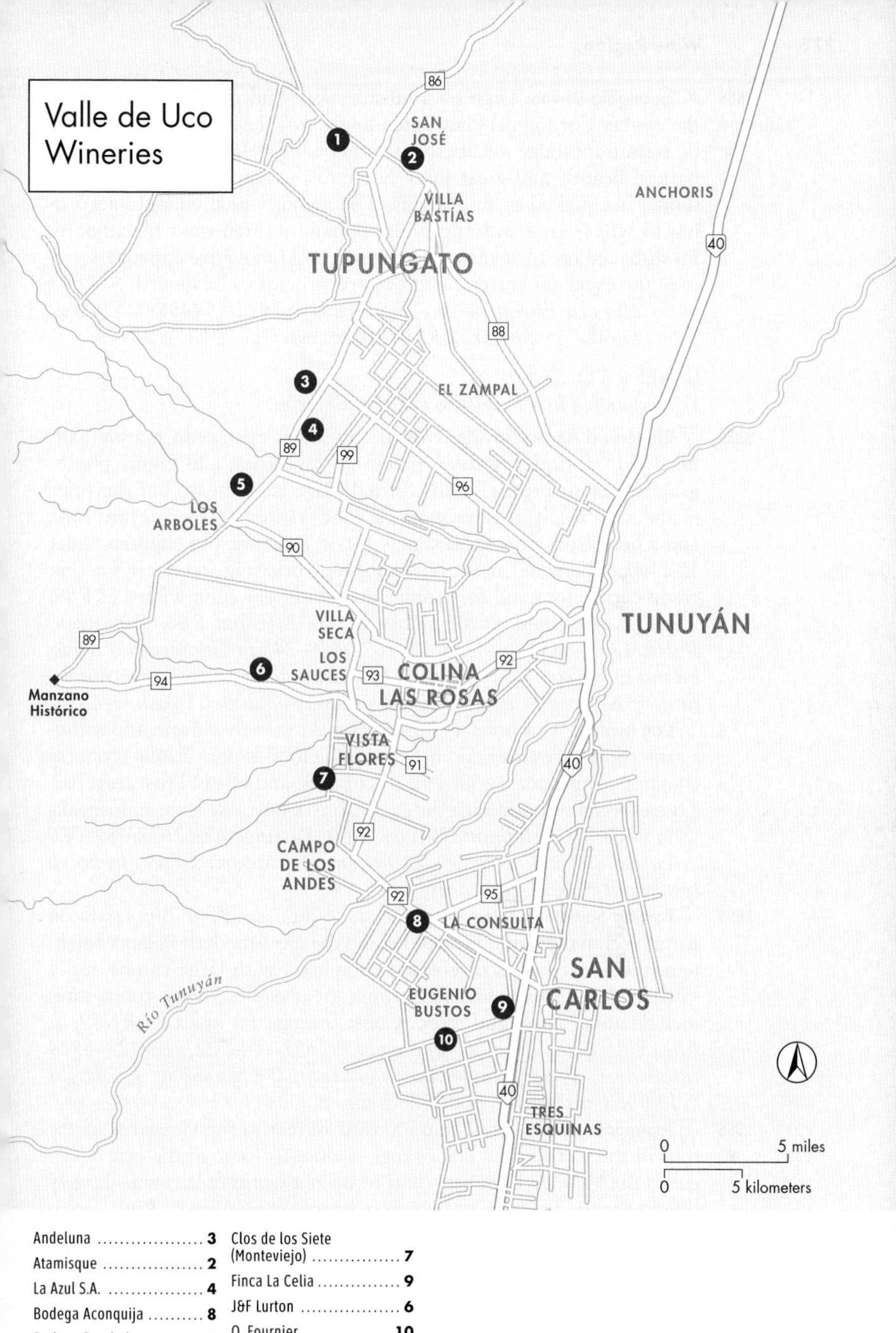

Andeluna **3**
Atamisque **2**
La Azul S.A. **4**
Bodega Aconquija **8**
Bodega Bombal **1**
Clos de los Siete (Monteviejo) **7**
Finca La Celia **9**
J&F Lurton **6**
O. Fournier **10**
Salentein **5**

$$$ ARGENTINE ★ **Tupungato Divino.** High on a hillside, surrounded by vineyards, with the mighty Cordón del Plata extending across the horizon, this romantic restaurant/lodge awaits the determined traveler looking for peace, natural beauty, and great food. Some of the ingredients for lunch or dinner are picked from gardens. The menu, which changes according to what's ripe and appealing, is hand-written on a blackboard. Fresh-baked bread, a variety of cheeses, and innovative appetizers precede the excellent entrées, and desserts are not to be denied. *RP89 and Calle Los Europeos s/n, Tupungato 2622/15448948 www.tupungatodivino.com.ar Reservations essential Closed Tues.*

WHERE TO STAY

For expanded hotel reviews, visit Fodors.com.

$$$$ **Château d'Ancón.** Inside, curved oak doors open onto marble halls filled with antiques, statues, paintings, tapestries, and family photographs; not surprisingly, this formal place isn't cheap, but the price includes all meals, tea, cocktails, a wine tasting, a 4x4 vineyard tour, and a horseback ride. **Pros:** stately decor; romantic (no children under 10); lots of personal attention. **Cons:** high price tag, yet doesn't accept credit cards; not good for families with kids; closed in winter. *R89, 2 km (1 mile) west of the village of San José and R86, Tupungato 261/4235–8455 in Mendoza, 2622/488–245 in Tupungato www.estanciancon.com 6 rooms In-hotel: bar, pool, some age restrictions No credit cards Closed mid-May–mid-Oct. All meals.*

$ **Don Romulo.** This hotel and restaurant is run with warmth and enthusiasm; rooms are clean and basic; and the food is pure *criollo* (country cooking): empanadas, grilled meat, sausages, and salads. **Pros:** great bargain, especially considering the excursions. **Cons:** low-tech; staff speaks little English. *Almirante Brown 1200, Tupungato 2622/489–020 www.donromulo.com.ar 10 rooms In-room: no a/c. In-hotel: restaurant No credit cards.*

$$$$ **Posada Salentein.** Fifteen kilometers (9 mile) south of Tupungato on Ruta Nacional 89, and located behind the ultra-modern Bodega Salentein, this inn consists of cottage complexes with large rooms and a kitchen. **Pros:** lovely hillside setting; great Andes views; room rates include good meals and more. **Cons:** cottages far apart. *RN89, at Elias Videla, Los Arboles, Tupungato 2622/424–722, 261/423–8514 reservations www.bodegasalentein.com 8 rooms in 3 cottages In-hotel: restaurant, pool All meals.*

$$$ ★ **Tupungato Divino.** This mountainside retreat in the vineyards at the foot of the Cordón del Plata range is close to some of the best bodegas in the Valle de Uco, yet seems to be in a world of its own—largely due to the architecture of owner/architect Sergio Viegas. **Pros:** serenity; mountain views; super restaurant; attentive owners; only 2 rooms. **Cons:** remote location; only 2 rooms. *RP89 and Calle Los Europeos s/n, Tupungato 2622/1544–8948 www.tupungatodivino.com.ar 2 rooms In-room: safe, kitchen. In-hotel: restaurant, bar, pool No credit cards Breakfast.*

SHOPPING

KDS Hecho a Mano. At KDS Hecho a Mano, five members of the da Silva family have been designing and selling handmade knives and leather cases since the 1970s. You can watch the process and choose the right knife for your next asado from many designs in their showroom or on their website. ✉ *South of town on RP92, Km 5, Tupungato* ☎ *2622/488–852* 🌐 *www.kdscuchillos.com.ar.*

SPORTS AND THE OUTDOORS

Tupungato Volcano. Snowcapped Tupungato Volcano (6,800 meters/9,200 feet) looms above the high peaks that march along the border between Chile and Mendoza Province. Tupungato Provincial Park covers 110,000 hectares (272,000 acres) in the wesern portion of the departments of Luján de Cuyo, Tupungato, and Tunuyán. There are no roads into the park, but local tour companies lead horseback rides and hikes into the area. Some offer six-day horseback rides to the Chilean border. Mules can be hired to climb to South Glacier at 2,000 meters (6,562 feet). ✉ *Tupungato.*

Make arrangements for horseback riding, hiking, and fishing through area ranches and hotels.

Estancia Rancho 'e Cuero. Near Tupungato, this estancia offers ranch stays with riding, hiking, fishing, and excursions into the mountains to view condors and guanacos. ✉ *Tupungato* ☎ *261/496–1491, 261/15–569–2364* 🌐 *www.ranchoecuero.com.ar.*

5

TUNUYÁN

81 km (50 miles) south of Mendoza.

Tunuyán is twice the size of Tupungato, and makes a good base for touring the Valle de Uco wineries. Downtown consists of two traffic circles on either side of two blocks, where most of the shops cater to the needs of local agricultural pursuits. Along with grape growing, said pursuits include growing cherries, pears, and apples, and making apple cider.

GETTING HERE AND AROUND

There's bus service here from Mendoza, but you'll have a hard time getting around without a car unless you're on a tour. From Mendoza City you can take Ruta Nacional 40 directly to Tunuyán, then use Ruta 88, 89, 90, or 96 to reach Tupungato (your choice will depend on which wineries you want to visit). Consult the WINEMAP before heading out on your own.

Bodega Lurton is on the road to Manzano Histórico, and Clos de los Siete, Monteviejo, and Doña Elvira are south and east of Tunuyán, in the districts of Los Sauces and Vista Flores. Although San Carlos, a dusty agricultural town 25 km (15 miles) south of Tunuyán, isn't yet on the tourist map, it does have several noteworthy wineries near it.

ESSENTIALS

Medical Assistance **Farmacia Galencia** ✉ *San Martín 650, Tunuyán* ☎ *2622/422–826.*

Bodegas in Argentina's wine region often have restaurants with dedicated chefs and stellar cuisine. Some prepare food using traditional methods, like this charcoal grill.

Tourist Information Oficina de Turísmo ✉ *San Martín at Dalmau, Tunuyán* ☎ *2622/425–810* 🌐 *www.tunuyan.mendoza.gov.ar.*

WINERIES

TUNUYÁN VICINITY

★ **Clos de los Siete: Monteviejo, Flecha de Los Andes, Cuvelier de Los Andes.** It's been called "the most ambitious winery project ever attempted." Five wineries owned by seven partners, under the expert supervision of Michel Rolland, share these vineyards, each choosing his particular grape variety. Each makes his own wine, then contributes grapes to make a blend of all of the partners' grapes, bringing together the best grapes of some of the world's best winemakers. The grapes mature at different times because they're planted at different altitudes (this prolongs the harvest over five weeks). These five wineries, notable for their architecture as much as for their impressive and well-respected wine, all receive visitors, and lunch is available at Flecha de Los Andes. ✉ *Clodomiro Silva s/n, Vistaflores, Tunuyán* ☎ *2622/422–054 Monteviejo, 261/405–5640 Flecha de Los Andes, 261/405–5610 Cuvelier de los Andes* ✉ *turismo@clos7.com.ar* 🌐 *www.monteviejo.com* ⏲ *Weekdays 8–4 with reservations 48 hrs in advance.*

J&F Lurton. Jacques and François Lurton began searching for an Argentine vineyard in 1992. Three years later they planted their grapes in Vista Flores, where low yields and a wide temperature range would ensure premium wines with a defined varietal identity. The arched doorways of the wood-and-stucco colonial-style winery lead into three functional areas—one for winemaking, one for storage, and one for sales and tastings. Grapes are harvested by hand and carefully selected by experts—including Marco Toriano, who also leads wine tours and directs tastings. Horseback rides in the vineyards are an added attraction. ✉ *Camino al Manzano, RP94, Km 21, Tunuyán* ☎ *261/441–1100 for tastings and lunch* 🌐 *www.francoislurton.com* ⏲ *Weekdays 10–5 with reservations.*

★ **Salentein.** On a knoll with an Andean backdrop, this ultramodern winery is built in the shape of a cross. Each of its four arms operates as a separate winery with two divisions: one at ground level housing stainless-steel tanks and one belowground where wine matures in oak barrels. These four wineries meet at a circular atrium where visitors are greeted and tastings, sales, and large events are held. Bottling and labeling take place underground. Also on the complex is an art museum, wine bar, and restaurant, making it easy to spend an leisurely afternoon here. ✉ *R89 at Videla, Tunuyán* ☎ *2622/429–000* 🌐 *www.bodegasalentein.com* ⏲ *Daily 10–4.*

5

SAN CARLOS VICINITY

Bodega Aconquija. Handmade labels and dedication to quality mark this boutique winery, where only 80,000 bottles are produced annually. Aconquija means "snow near the moon"—an apt description, given the location. Blessed with sandy soil and wide temperature variation, grapes ripen slowly on the meticulously pruned 30-year-old vines. The Syrah and Rosé blend is fruity. ✉ *España 1094, La Consulta* ☎ *2622/470–379* 🌐 *www.aconquija.com* ⏲ *Weekdays 9–noon, 4–6 with email reservations.*

Finca La Celia. One of the valley's oldest wine projects, Finca La Celia was built by Eugenio Bustos in 1890. It flourished under his daughter Celia's leadership, producing an excellent Malbec. CCU, a Chilean company, now owns the winery and has invested in the latest technology and machinery from France and Italy. ✉ *Circunvalación Celia Bustos de Quiroga 374, San Carlos* ☎ *2622/451–010* 🌐 *www.fincalacelia.com.ar* ⏲ *Weekdays 9–4 (by reservation only).*

O. Fournier. As you approach this ultra-modern winery on a lonely dirt road it looks like a flying saucer has landed in the middle of a vineyard. When you take the tour through the bodega, your guide will explain that every part of the futuristic building is functional, whether it be to make best use of gravity or direct the sometimes brutal winds that can can whip through. Grapes are delivered by truck to rolling vats on the roof, are hand sorted, then slide down to the first floor, where they are gently crushed, then down to the next floor into fermenting tanks and finally to the basement to age in oak barrels. Using both local and international expertise, the Spanish Ortega Gil-Fournier family aims to produce the highest-quality wines. Grapes are planted in rocky, sandy soil on three estates at an altitude of 1,200 meters (3,940 feet), producing red wines that consistently score in the 90s in *Wine Spectator* magazine. ✉ *Los Indios s/n, La Consulta* ☎ *2622/451–579, 261/15–467–1021 cell* 🌐 *www.ofournier.com* ⏲ *Daily 9:30–4:30 (by reservation only).*

WHERE TO EAT AND STAY

For expanded hotel reviews, visit Fodors.com.

$$$ ECLECTIC Fodor'sChoice ★ **Posada del Jamon.** It doesn't matter if you are a world-famous winemaker (many are hugely loyal fans of this place and show up often), a local, or a tourist who speaks no Spanish, you will get the same incredibly warm and personalized service at this casual, family-run place that offers ham cooked up every way imaginable (and some ways you have probably never imagined). There are a surprising number of healthful vegetarian options available, and all of the wines offered are from the neighborhood wineries (a great way to get to know the local wine and the stories behind them). A little shop on-site sells gorgeous artisanal crafts such as hand-knit sweaters, blankets, and artwork. If you like the place so much you don't want to leave, there are very reasonably priced cabañas for rent behind the restaurant. ✉ *Ruta 92 Km 14, Tunuyán* ☎ *2622/492–053* 🌐 *www.laposadadeljamon.com.ar.*

$$$$ SOUTH AMERICAN ★ **URBAN at O. Fournier.** Though she won an award for best restaurant in a winery back in 2007, chef Nadia de Ortega hasn't rested on her laurels; she's still creating innovative entrées that pair gracefully with the many wines served at the wine-tasting lunch. "Wine by the bite" describes this epicurean odyssey—from delicate appetizers to simply gorgeous, perfect mains (think pastas, risottos, or grilled steak with imaginative garnish). Torrontés sherbet with chocolate chips is on offer, as are the likes of coffee ice cream or the chocolate mousse volcano erupting with almonds. Big glass windows frame the mountains, and frogs serenade from the pond in the evening. ✉ *Los Indios s/n, at O. Fournier bodega, La Consulta* ☎ *2622/451–579, 261/15–467–1021* 🌐 *www.ofournier.com* *Reservations essential.*

$$$ **Postales (Valle de Uco Lodge).** If wine touring is all about good wine, good food, beautiful surroundings, and like-minded people, then this cozy lodge has it all. **Pros:** engaged staff can help you arrange activities; lovely country setting; comfy rooms. **Cons:** far from any kind of action and can be difficult to find if you are driving yourself. ✉ *Calle Tabanera, near Corredor Productivo, Colonia de Las Rosas, Tunuyán* ☎ *2622/490–024* 🌐 *www.postalesarg.com* *9 rooms* *In-room: safe. In-hotel: restaurant, bar, pool* *Breakfast.*

TRIUMPHAL MARCH

Manzano Histórico. The Manzano Histórico, 40 km (25 miles) west of Tunuyán, is the site of an apple tree under which General San Martín camped during his return from liberating Chile in 1823. Several local outfitters offer horseback rides that follow the hoofprints of San Martín's triumphal march across the Andes. ✉ *Tunuyán.*

SPORTS AND THE OUTDOORS

HORSEBACK RIDING

You can ride in the foothills of the Andes for a day or cross the Andes to Chile in a six-day adventure that takes you into a treeless landscape of rocky trails, roaring rivers, tiny green meadows, and lofty peaks. Argentine horses aren't allowed in Chile, so you'll have to either change horses at the border or return.

Estancia El Puesto. A large ranch with five bedrooms, Estancia El Puesto is near Manzano Histórico, where you're pampered with food, wine, river swimming, and day rides. Raul Labat, the owner and veteran of more than 30 crossings to Chile, still finds each trip rewarding. He offers three six-day journeys a year in January and February. ✉ *Los Árboles, Tunuyán* ☎ *261/439–3533* 🌐 *www.estanciaelpuesto.com.ar.*

SAN RAFAEL REGION

Numerous dams and acres of irrigated land have created a vigorous agro-industrial oasis in the departments of San Rafael and General Alvear (90 km/56 miles southeast of San Rafael). San Rafael is one of the country's smallest regions to claim a Denominación de Origen (DOC). This is a point of pride for local vintners, and the quality of wine produced in this area speaks for itself.

San Rafael has a nearly perfect climate for growing grapes: low humidity, cold and dry winters, ample temperature variation, just enough rainfall, and plenty of water from the Ríos Diamante and Ateul. But into every vineyard a little rain must fall—and when it comes in the form of hail (*granizo*), it can be devastating, destroying one year's crop and the next year's tiny buds in one short shower. Most vineyards now protect their crops with expensive heavy netting that lets the water drip through and shades the grapes, aiding ripening.

5

SAN RAFAEL

240 km (150 miles) south of Mendoza.

Southern Mendoza would be vast arid plains were it not for the Ríos Atuel and Diamante, which flow from the Andes and irrigate the fine alluvial soil that attracted the first inhabitants, who came from Chile in 1594. As they attempted to farm in the Diamante River Valley, Indian raids made it necessary to build a fort in 1805.

After the area was made safe from raids in 1879, immigrants from Italy, Switzerland, and France brought their advanced viticulture skills and new grape varieties to this frontier region. When the railroad arrived in 1903 the fledgling wine industry was connected to Buenos Aires and the rest of the world. With nearly 100 wineries and a population of 175,000, San Rafael is the second-largest city in Mendoza Province. Wide avenues lined with leafy sycamores and tall poplars fed by streetside canals give this city a bucolic charm.

GETTING HERE AND AROUND

Take Ruta Nacional 40 south from Mendoza to Pareditas, where you pick up Ruta Nacional 143 to San Rafael. There are three flights a week to San Rafael from Buenos Aires, but since Mendoza has daily flights, many visitors fly there first, then drive or take a bus through the Valle de Uco to San Rafael. Locals drive or take overnight buses to and from Buenos Aires (1,000 km/621 miles), as the bus fare is less expensive than flying. The airport is about 15 minutes west of downtown San

Algodón 6
Balbi 3
La Champañera Valentín Bianchi 1
Goyenechea 7
Jean Rivier 4
Jorge Simonassi Lyon 2
Lavaque 8
Suter 5

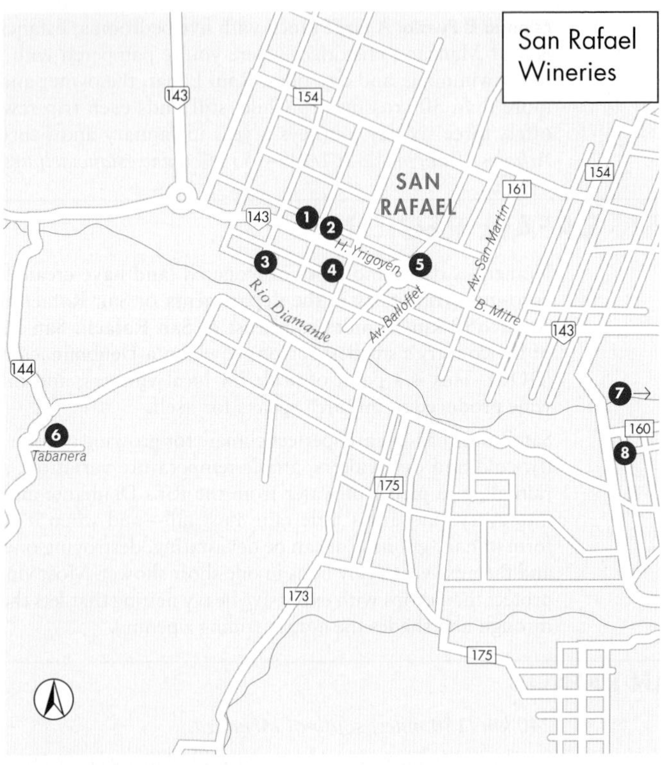

Rafael on Ruta 150, and the bus station is a block south of Avenida Yrigoyen at Avellaneda.

San Rafael is flat and laid out on a grid, which makes it easy to tour on foot. At Km 0, Avenida Yrigoyen crosses the downtown area (north–south) and becomes Bartolome Mitre. At this same intersection (east–west), Avenida El Libertador becomes San Martín—the main shopping street. Hotels are scattered about on the edge of residential areas but still close enough to walk or take a short cab ride to downtown or the tourist office. Note that siesta time lasts from lunch at 1 or 2 pm until 5 or 5:30. Also, beware of the *acéquias*—canals between the sidewalks and streets. At night people riding bicycles with no lights or reflectors on narrow dirt roads can be a hazard.

Joker Viajes offers city tours, wine tours, and excursions into the surrounding mountains and lakes. Rafting, horseback riding, and hiking are some of the active sports they arrange nearby or in the vicinity of Las Leñas ski resort.

Air Contact Aerolíneas Argentinas ☎ *2627/438–808 in San Rafael, 2627/435–156 at the airport* 🌐 *www.aerolineas.com.ar.*

Bus Contacts Andesmar ☎ *2627/427–720* 🌐 *www.andesmar.com.* **TAC** ☎ *2627/422–209* 🌐 *www.viatac.com.ar.* **Terminal de Ómnibus** ✉ *Colonel Suarez and Avellaneda, San Rafael.*

Car Rentals Alamo ✉ *H. Yrigoyen 1240, San Rafael* ☎ *2627/445–656 office, 2627/15–604–158 cell.* **Hertz** ✉ *25 de Mayo 450, San Rafael* ☎ *2627/400–569.*

Taxi Fono-taxi/Remises del Sur ✉ *Rivadavia 31* ☎ *2627/420–200.*

ESSENTIALS

Banks Banco de la Nación (*Link*). ✉ *El Libertador 30, San Rafael* ☎ *2627/423–854* ✉ *H. Yrigoyen 113, San Rafael* ☎ *2627/422–252.* **Banco Galicia** (*Banelco*). ✉ *H. Yrigoyen 28, San Rafael.*

Internet Locutorio Moreno I ✉ *Av. M. Moreno 60, San Rafael* ☎ *2627/43321.* **Locutorio TELEFAX** ✉ *Avellaneda 76, San Rafael* ☎ *2627/433–321.*

Medical Assistance Farmacia 16 Horas ✉ *Libertador 206, San Rafael* ☎ *2627/430–214.* **Hospital Schestakow** ✉ *Cte. Torres 150, San Rafael* ☎ *2627/424–291.*

5

Visitor and Tour Info Joker Viajes ✉ *San Martín 234, San Rafael* ☎ *2627/436–982* 🌐 *www.jokerviajes.com.ar.* **San Rafael Tourist Board** ✉ *Av. H. Yrigoyen 745, at Balloffet, San Rafael* ☎ *2627/424–217* 🌐 *www.sanrafaelturismo.gov.ar.*

WINERIES

Most of the wineries in this region are family-owned; consequently, the owners are busy in the vineyard, working in the bodega, testing wine with the oenologist, or tending to customers. As a courtesy, it's best to make an appointment. Road signs are scarce in the region, although the municipality is working to correct that.

Fodor's Choice ★ **Algodón Wine Estates Lodge.** This resort, about 20 minutes from downtown San Rafael, is a tranquil refuge that offers wine tastings from their on-site bodega, golf, world-class tennis courts (clay, grass, and hard-court), and a great restaurant. There are eight bedrooms, five within the lodge, and three in a remodeled villa built in 1920. Each room either has a fireplace or a woodstove, and all rooms have their own patio. Take a siesta under ancient olive trees, or relax with a glass of wine by the lovely pool. Service is friendly and super-personalized, and the staff can help you plan other wine tours, bicycling, rafting, or even extensive excursions deep into the nearby Andes if you are feeling adventurous. If you fall in love with it there, you can always purchase your own vineyard lot towards the back of the property. For now the lodge is closed in the winter months, but that may change in the near future. ✉ *RN144, Km 674, Cuadro Benegas, San Rafael* ☎ *2627/429–020* 🌐 *www.algodonwineestates.com.*

Balbi. Founded in 1930 by Juan Balbi and now owned by Allied Domecq, this winery has a reputation for making a French-influenced wine, as they bring in wine consultants from Bordeaux every season. Changes in winemaking techniques seem to be moving their wine toward a more readily drinkable style, as they blend grapes from the Valle de Uco and San Rafael. ✉ *BA, Jensen & Sarmiento, Las Paredes, San Rafael* ☎ *2627/430–027* ⏲ *By reservation only.*

★ **Goyenechea.** One of the country's oldest wineries, Goyenechea was founded in 1868 by a Basque immigrant family who had the foresight to build not only a solid brick winery, but also 60 houses for the working families, a school for their children, a repair shop, and a chapel. Today fifth-generation families live in the houses, and the school still rings with the laughter of their children. As you pass through the arched caves where wine ages in bottles, you can see the *piletas,* huge concrete vats that held 8,976 gallons of wine when the industry was focused on quantity, not quality. English-speaking family members often lead tours (if you need a tour led in English, call ahead to make a reservation), and visitors are sometimes invited for wine tastings and snacks next door on the family's patio. ✉ *Sotero Arizú s/n, Villa Atuel, San Rafael* ☎ *2627/470–005, 2627/15–617–294 cell* 🌐 *www.goyenechea.com* ⏲ *Mon.–Sat. 10:30–5:45, tours every 45 minutes.*

Jean Rivier. The Swiss-French brothers who own this winery produce a limited quantity of quality wines from their own grapes. Tours of their spotless winery include crushing, fermentation, and tasting. ✉ *Hipólito Yrigoyen 2385, Rama Caída, San Rafael* ☎ *2627/432–676* 🌐 *www.jeanrivier.com* ⏲ *Weekdays 9–11 and 3–6, Sat. 9–11.*

Jorge Simonassi Lyon. This old-fashioned bodega warmly guides you through winemaking, from grape to glass. A lovely house on the premises can occasionally be rented. Jorge's knowledge of growing grapes and blending wines was passed down from his Asti ancestors in northern Italy. ✉ *RN143, Km 657, Rama Caída, San Rafael* ☎ *2627/436–076* 🌐 *www.bodegasimonassi.com.ar* ⏲ *Weekdays 9–11 and 3–6.*

★ **La Champañera Valentín Bianchi.** After a variety of entrepreneurial endeavors, Valentin Bianchi realized in 1928 that he wanted to do nothing else except make great wine. He struggled until 1934, when one of his wines won a gold medal in Mendoza and high praise in Buenos Aires. His legacy of hard work continues at this bodega, known as *La Champañera,* which is different from other wineries in the area because it is focused solely on the production and tasting of champagne. This is one of the most organized and commercial bodegas in the area, receiving more than 100,000 visitors per year to its lush, garden setting, which is just a little over 3 miles from the center of San Rafael. The wine shop sells all of Bianchi's other lines of wines if champagne isn't what you are looking for. Free tours are run often throughout the day, and end with a champagne tasting. ✉ *R143 at Calle El Salto, Las Paredes, San Rafael* ☎ *2627/435–600* 🌐 *www.vbianchi.com* ⏲ *Daily 9–12:30 and 3–6.*

Lavaque. The Italo-French Lavaque family planted their first vineyards in Cafayate, Salta, in 1870. Their sons and grandsons carry on the tradition in San Rafael; their long white stucco and terra-cotta Spanish winery houses an aesthetically designed interior with Spanish tiles and adobe walls. ✉ *R165, Cañada Seca, San Rafael* ☎📠 *2627/497–044* 🌐 *www.vinasdealtura.com* ⏲ *Weekdays 7:30–4:30 by appointment only. Reservations by email or fax only.*

Suter. In 1900 the Suter family journeyed to Argentina from Switzerland and planted the first Riesling variety in the country. Today the fourth generation of the family continues to produce fine white wines, Malbec,

Cabernet Sauvignon, and Spumante. A tour through this spotless winery leads you through a labyrinth of underground caves filled with huge oak casks—used more to evoke atmosphere than to store wine. ✉ *Hipólito Yrigoyen 2850, near the airport, El Toledano, San Rafael* ☎ *2627/421–076* 🌐 *www.sutersa.com.ar* ⏲ *Mon.–Sat. 9–6 with reservation.*

WHERE TO EAT

$ MIDDLE EASTERN ✕ **Al-Zahir.** Casual Middle Eastern, Morrocan, and Turkish food for dine-in or take-out, which can be a very welcome change from the steak, steak, and more steak culture of Argentina. They offer lots of vegetarian options here, too, and are usually open for lunch and dinner, but hours can be flexible, so it is best to call ahead. ✉ *Av. Ballofet 173, San Rafael* ☎ *2627/423–264.*

$ ARGENTINE ✕ **Bonafide.** A popular gathering place for both locals and visitors just one block from Km 0 (the very center of town), Bonafide serves up freshly ground coffees, a wide range of sandwiches, and lots of chocolates and other goodies to buy for the road. Grab one of the window seats with leather couches and take advantage of the Wi-Fi. ✉ *San Martín 102, San Rafael* ☎ *2627/437–331* ⏲ *Closed Sun.*

$$ ARGENTINE ✕ **Chez Gaston at Algodon.** This charming restaurant, nestled between a golf green and tennis courts, is the center of culinary activity in this luxury golf, tennis, and wine resort about 20 minutes' drive from the center of town. Surrounded by ancient olive groves and vineyards, you can sit outside on the brick patio where pine-log tables are surrounded by comfy couches with puffy white cushions. Here you listen to birds singing while you sip Algodon wine and dine on high-quality (but never pretentious) regional dishes such as goat from nearby Malargüe (spring and summer) with quinoa. Many of the products used, such as the olives, fruits, and walnuts, are harvested right on the property, and bread is baked daily in a clay oven. Reservations are a good idea. ✉ *Cuadro Benegas, San Rafael* ☎ *2627/429–020.*

$ ARGENTINE ✕ **El Restauro.** Two tall doors open into this colonial building owned by the Spanish Club since 1910. There's nothing old-fashioned, however, about the menu. The owners are committed to regional cuisine, using fresh ingredients in recipes handed down from local families. *Tomatican,* for instance, is a blend of fresh tomatoes and spices pureed over toast with melted cheeses. Roasted goat from nearby Malargüe, trout from the Río Atuel, and quinoa are used creatively. ✉ *Comandante Salas at Colonel Day, San Rafael* ☎ *2627/445–482.*

$$$ ARGENTINE ★ ✕ **L'Obrador-Casa de Campo.** About 20 minutes from town, at a typical ranch house, Daniel Ancina, his wife Graciela, and a team of cooks are waiting to greet you, fill your wineglass, introduce you to the other guests, and seat you family-style at a long table. Little pots of spreads and sauces for dipping or spreading on *pan casero* (homemade bread) line the center of the table. Out of the mud-brick oven comes a platter of crisp baked empanadas and then some type of meat—goat, lamb, beef, chicken, or chorizo. Everything is cooked on the spot, and couldn't be a better or warmer introduction to traditional cuisine of the region. Don't even try to find this place on your own. Call to be picked up or inquire at the tourist office for directions and reservations. ✉ *Camino Bentos*

50, San Rafael ☎ *2627/4322–723, 2627/1560–1347* *Reservations essential* ▭ *No credit cards* *Tues., Thurs., Fri., or by appointment.*

$$ ARGENTINE **Malbec.** There's a lot more than just beef on the menu of this small restaurant next to the Hotel San Martín. Crepes with sautéed vegetables and giant ravioli are two tasty entrées. There's also a good selection of salads and brochettes. Don't confuse this restaurant with the Parrilla Malbec. ✉ *Av. San Martín 433, San Rafael* ☎ *2627/445–495, 2627/15–692–484 cell* ▭ *No credit cards.*

$ ARGENTINE **Nina.** At this casual café/bar one block from town center, in an appealing colonial building, the menu is mostly sandwiches, snacks, pizza, and *milanesas* (breaded steak). Beware the giant barrolucos—one order is sufficient for two hungry people. Live music picks up the beat each Wednesday at 11 pm. ✉ *Av. San Martín 98, San Rafael* ☎ *2627/438–883* ▭ *No credit cards.*

WHERE TO STAY

For expanded hotel reviews, visit Fodors.com.

$$$$ Fodor's Choice ★ **Algodón Wine Resort.** This is the sister property to the gorgeous Algodón Mansion in Buenos Aires; you can choose between one of the three charming rooms (all of which have their own fireplace) in the remodeled 1920s farmhouse, or one of the five rooms in the more modern lodge. **Pros:** between the amazing sunset views, birds singing, and availability of Algodón wine around every corner, it's hard not to feel profoundly relaxed here. **Cons:** about 20 minutes outside of town center, and for now it closes in the winter months (although there is talk of changing that in the future). ✉ *RN144, Km 674–Cuadro Benegas, San Rafael* ☎ *2627/429–020* 🌐 *www.algodonwineestates.com* *8 rooms* *In-room: safe, Wi-Fi. In-hotel: golf course, pool, tennis court, parking* 🍽 *Breakfast.*

$$$$ ★ **Finca los Alamos.** When this 150-year-old estancia was established by the great-grandparents of César and Camilo Aldao Bombal in 1830, San Rafael was still a fort. The ranch house (really a gorgeous mansion) today is filled with objects from around the world, and many of Argentina's foremost writers (including Jorge Luis Borges) and artists have stayed here; they left their paintings on walls and their poetry scattered around the premises. **Pros:** eclectic furnishings; Old World surroundings; intimate family experience; a great, hands-on way to learn about Argentine history. **Cons:** 15 minutes outside of town center (although you could see that as a pro, not a con, with the tranquillity it provides). ✉ *Bombal (R146), 10 km (6 miles) from town, San Rafael* *Box 125, San Rafael 5600* ☎ *2627/442–350* 🌐 *www.fincalosalamos.com* *7 rooms* *In-hotel: bar, pool* ▭ *No credit cards* 🍽 *All meals.*

$$$ ★ **Hotel Tower Inn and Suites.** Across the street from the tourist office, this modern hotel offers spacious accommodations with big picture windows that fill the rooms with natural light and come with a view of the main street and mountains in the distance. **Pros:** spacious rooms with plenty of places to stow your stuff; helpful staff who are very used to dealing with foreigners. **Cons:** on a busy street at the edge of town. ✉ *H. Irigoyen 744, San Rafael* ☎ *2627/427–190* 🌐 *www.towersanrafael.com* *89 rooms, 11 suites* *In-room: Wi-Fi. In-hotel: restaurant, bar, pool, gym, spa, business center.*

PRIVATE TOURS

Antu y Lucero. Antu y Lucero is a high-end expedition agency that offers ultra-personalized, private tours and can fulfill almost any Andean-related travel idea you can come up with. Whether it be fly fishing a pristine and hidden lagoon, camping at the top of a mountain to watch the sunrise in the morning, studying the volcanoes of Payunia with scientists, going on a photographic safari, learning handcrafts from indigenous people, horseback riding through vast sand dunes, or extreme back country skiing, they have you covered. This agency is run by an American who goes along on every trip, so English is not a problem. ✉ *San Rafael* ☎ *2627/537–000* 🌐 *www.antuylucero.com.*

5

$$ **Microtel Inn & Suites, Malargüe.** A large lobby with casual furniture, a fireplace, and a sitting room lend a homey feel; the modern rooms have yellow walls and large windows. **Pros:** good restaurant; they often offer promotions for discounts on lift tickets at Las Leñas. **Cons:** long walk to town; pool isn't heated. ✉ *RN40 Norte, Malargüe* ☎ *2627/472–300* 🌐 *www.microyel-malargue.com.ar* *29 rooms, 4 suites* *In-hotel: restaurant, bar, pool* *Breakfast.*

$ **San Martín Hotel & Spa.** At the quiet end of downtown's main street and next to Malbec restaurant, this hotel caters to wine-business travelers. **Pros:** owner-manager makes you feel welcome; good restaurant. **Cons:** small rooms. ✉ *San Martín 435, San Rafael* ☎ *2627/420–400, 2627/433–363* 🌐 *www.sanmartinhotelspa.com* *32 rooms, 2 apartments* *In-hotel: restaurant, spa* *Breakfast.*

$$ **Tierra Mora.** This newer apart-hotel is a compact five-story building overlooking a large park; it's about 14 blocks from downtown but within walking distance of an up-and-coming area with restaurants and shops. **Pros:** large rooms; in a nice part of town with park. **Cons:** not a ton of amenities. ✉ *Ameghino 350, San Rafael* ☎ *2627/447–222* 🌐 *www.tierramora.com* *17 apartments, 2 rooms* *In-room: Wi-Fi. In-hotel: restaurant, parking* *Breakfast.*

SHOPPING

Ketobac. Ketobac sells homemade goodies (such as chocolate-covered figs, raisins, and dried apricots from the region), jams, wines, and alfajores. ✉ *San Martín 175* ☎ *2627/422–082.*

Toca Madera. This is one of many shops on San Martín selling *artesanías*—pottery, weavings, carved wooden items, shoes, and cotton clothing. Local wines and olive oils are available on the same street. ✉ *San Martín 170, San Rafael* ☎ *2627/1567–4604.*

LAS LEÑAS

200 km (124 miles) south of San Rafael.

Las Leñas is the largest ski area served by lifts in the Western Hemisphere—bigger than Whistler/Blackcomb in British Columbia, and

CLOSE UP

A Recreational Drive

Cañón del Atuel (Atuel Canyon). This canyon has been called the world's second Grand Canyon, as they were both formed at the same time, and their coloring is quite similar. The best way to dive into this very photogenic, 160-km (99-miles) canyon with its four hydroelectric stations along the Atuel River is to start at the top of the canyon in the village of El Nihuel, 75 km (47 miles) west of San Rafael. Take Ruta Provincial 144 from San Rafael in the direction of Malargüe, turning south at El Desvío onto 180. At the dam, Ruta 173 descends into a labyrinth of red, brown, and gray sandstone rock formations. Unfortunately, the river disappears into underground pipes—supplying energy for the growing population and the vineyards of Mendoza Province. At Valle Grande the water is collected behind a large dam, after which the river runs freely between sandstone cliffs, beneath shady willows and poplar trees. Swimming holes, sheltered picnic spots, and rafting adventures offer escape from the city on hot summer days. Small hotels, cottages, campsites, and shops renting rafting and kayaking equipment line the road before it returns across the desert to San Rafael.

larger than Vail and Snowbird combined. Although it should be thriving, the area has suffered bankruptcies, absentee owners, and several management teams. You must go through tour operators and travel agents to book into area hotels, all of which require a minimum stay of one week. Accommodations range from dorm-style houses and apart-hotels—some in disrepair—to hotels with indoor/outdoor pools, decent restaurants, bars, and a ski concierge. Travel offices in Buenos Aires, Mendoza, and San Rafael sell ski packages with lift tickets, equipment, and, in some cases, transportation—which may involve a combination of bus rides and charter flights.

The ski season runs from June through October. Most South Americans take their vacation in July, the month to avoid if you don't like crowds and high prices, although the weather is more benign. August has the most reliable snow conditions, September the most varied. Prices for lifts and lodging are lowest from mid-June to early July and from mid-September to early October; rates are highest from mid- to late July.

GETTING HERE AND AROUND

It takes 1½ hours to fly from Buenos Aires to San Rafael, then a 3-hour drive to Las Leñas. During high season (July–August) there are two charter flights a day from Buenos Aires to Malargüe, a town 80 km (50 miles) from the resort. There are no commercial flights to Malargüe. Some ski packages include the 1½-hour flight from Buenos Aires.

From San Rafael, take Ruta Provincial 144 for 141 km (88 miles) to El Sosneado, then pick up Ruta Nacional 40 to the turnoff onto Ruta Provincial 222 that passes through Los Molles, 20 km (12 miles) from Las Leñas.

The town of Malargüe is 45 km (28 miles) south of the turnoff at Ruta 144 on Ruta Nacional 40, roughly 80 km (50 miles) from Las Leñas.

DID YOU KNOW?

The first incarnation of Las Leñas ski resort was built in a mere four months; construction began January 20, 1983, and by June 16 they were welcoming 400 beds' worth of guests. It's since expanded to over 3,000 beds, and has become one of the most popular resort complexes in Latin America.

Carry chains and be aware of weather conditions. This is a dramatically beautiful drive.

You can sleep the whole 11 hours from Buenos Aires in a "Coche-cama" bus—not a bad option if you want to save your pesos for lift tickets and good accommodations.

ESSENTIALS

Visitor Info Malargüe Tourism Office ✉ *Hipólito Yrigoyen 774, San Rafael* ☎ *2627/471–659* 🌐 *www.malargue.gov.ar* ✉ *Inalicán 94, Malargüe.*

SKIING

Las Leñas Ski Resort. From the top (3,429 meters/11,250 feet), a treeless lunar landscape of white peaks extends in every direction. There are steep, scary, 610-meter (2,000-foot) vertical chutes for experts; machine-packed routes for beginners; and plenty of intermediate terrain. A terrain park for snowboarders has jumps and a half pipe. There's also a free-style slope. Off-piste skiing can be arranged through the ski school.

Facilities: 3,300 hectares (8,154 acres) skiable terrain; 1,230-meter (4,035-foot) vertical drop; 64 km (40 miles) of groomed runs, the longest is 8 km (5 miles); 15% beginner, 40% intermediate, 45% expert; 1 quad, 6 double chairs, 5 surface lifts. There are no detachable quad chairs or high-speed lifts.

Seasonal Rate Information: Low: June 13–26. Medium: July 4–10, August 8–September 4. High: July 11–August 7. Special: June 27–July 3, September 5–closing.

Lessons and Programs: Multilingual ski and snowboard instructors give 2½-hour classes or two-hour private lessons for all levels. Good intermediate skiers to experts can experience untracked slopes with heli-ski and off-piste skiing accompanied by trained guides and avalanche experts.

One-Day Adult Lift Tickets: Low: 206 pesos, Medium: 272 pesos, High: 315 pesos

Rentals: The following one-day rental packages are for three types of skis or snowboards, boots, and poles. The price depends on the quality. Low: 96–176, Medium: 124–228, High: 148–270. To rent just one of these items, you must inquire at the shop. "Fat skis" for deep-powder and off-piste skiing are scarce, so bring your own. ✉ *Las Leñas* ☎ *11/4819–6000 in Buenos Aires, 2627/471–100 in Mendoza* 🌐 *www.laslenas.com* ⏲ *Weekdays 9–6, June–late September, depending on snow.*

WHERE TO STAY

For expanded hotel reviews, visit Fodors.com.

$$$ 🏨 **Aries.** This slope-side luxury hotel has plenty of diversions for stormy days: a space for children's games and activities, a piano bar in the lobby, a wine bar serving cheese and regional smoked meats, and a movie theater. **Pros:** proximity to slopes and non-ski alternatives. **Cons:** no direct reservation service and three-day minimum stay. ✉ *Las Leñas Ski Resort, Las Leñas* ☎ *11/4819–6099 in Buenos Aires (off-season),*

2627/471–1000 in Mendoza (ski season) 🌐 www.laslenas.com 97 rooms, 5 suites In-hotel: restaurant, bar, pool, spa, children's programs Multiple meal plans.

$$$ **Escorpio.** This small, intimate ski lodge is right on the slopes; you can watch the action from the terrace while having lunch, or hit the cozy piano bar for après-ski board games with tea or cocktails. **Pros:** proximity to slopes. **Cons:** difficult to make reservations directly at times. ✉ *Las Leñas Ski Resort, Las Leñas ☎ 11/4819–6099 in Buenos Aires (off-season), 2627/471–1000 in Mendoza (ski season) 🌐 www.laslenas.com 47 rooms, 1 suite, 2 apartments In-hotel: restaurant, bar Some meals.*

$$$$ **Piscis.** This deluxe hotel pampers its guests with spa services, ski-equipment delivery, and an indoor-outdoor pool. **Pros:** loads of services. **Cons:** difficult to make direct reservations for less than a five-night minimum stay. ✉ *Las Leñas Ski Resort, Las Leñas ☎ 11/4819–6099 in Buenos Aires (off-season), 2627/471–1000 in Mendoza (ski season) 🌐 www.laslenas.com 90 rooms In-hotel: restaurant, bar, pool, gym, business center Some meals.*

5

SAN JUAN REGION

In the Tulum Valley in the foothills of the Andes, the city of San Juan lies in an oasis of orchards and vineyards, surrounded by the Andes to the west and monotonous desert in every other direction. People here work hard in the fields during the day, take long siestas in the afternoon, and head back to the fields until sundown.

Although San Juan wineries have been slow to make the shift from quantity to quality, some 160 wineries have converted (or are converting) from producing bulk wine, and a new generation of oenologists and vintners is taking the lead. The province produces more wine than Napa and Sonoma combined, and you'll likely find the fine Cabernets, Bonardas, and Syrahs—as well as the whites and sparkling wines—of San Juan on the world's wine lists in short order.

SAN JUAN

167 km (104 miles) northwest of Mendoza.

San Juan was founded in 1562 as part of the Chilean viceroyalty. On January 18, 1817, General José de San Martín gathered his army of 16,000 men in the town's plaza and set out on his historic 21-day march over the Andes to Chile, where he defeated the royalist army at the battles of Chacabuco and Maipú.

San Juan has been producing wine since 1569, though it wasn't until the 1890s, when Graffigna and other major wineries put down roots here, that production increased. At that point wineries began offering varieties other than the sweet white table wines, sherries, and ports that the area had been known for.

A 1944 earthquake destroyed San Juan (but helped to establish Juan Perón as a national figure through his relief efforts, which won him

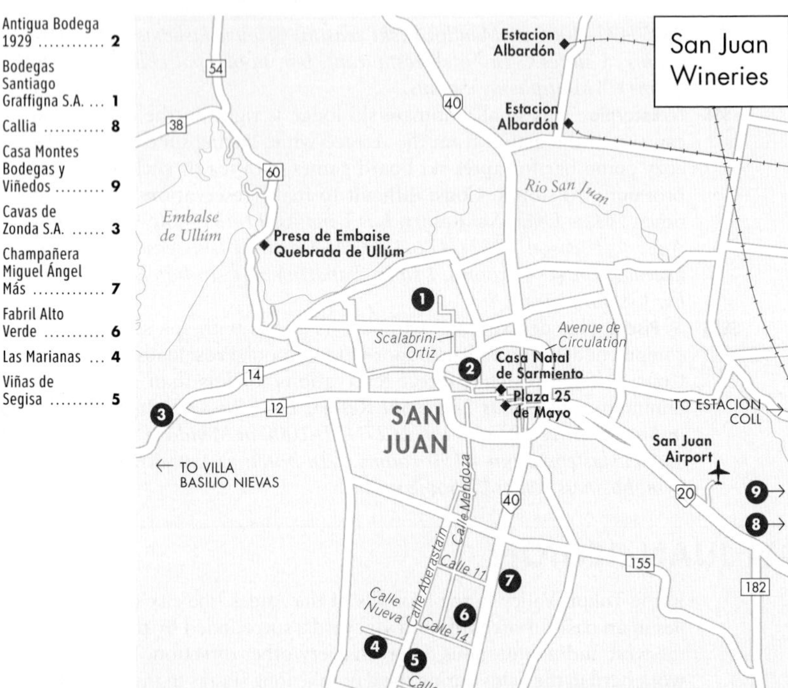

much popularity). A second earthquake in 1977 was just as devastating. The low-rise buildings, tree-lined plazas, and pedestrian walkways you see today are the results of reconstruction. The streets and plazas of this agricultural town are shaded and easygoing, and the city is further cooled by Spanish-built canals that still run beneath the streets.

San Juaninos enjoy sharing their knowledge with visitors. In fact, you're often greeted at bodegas by the owner or a member of the family. In 2004 the tourist office and guide association formed a commission to evaluate wineries for membership in the Ruta del Vino de San Juan. Members guarantee knowledgeable personnel, tasting rooms, public restrooms, and reasonable hours. Eight wineries joined, and their booklet with maps is available at the tourist office.

GETTING HERE AND AROUND

There are daily flights to San Juan from Buenos Aires (1¾ hours), which is 10 hours away by car, slightly longer by bus. The Chacritas Airport is 11 km (7 miles) southeast of town. The 15-minute ride in a taxi or remis costs about 100 pesos. The drive from Mendoza is 1½ hours on Ruta Nacional 40.

It's easy to get around San Juan. There's one main shopping area in a three-block radius around the Plaza 25 de Mayo, from which most hotels are within walking distance or a quick cab ride.

Anna Maria de Montes and her partners at Dante Montes Turismo are experienced local agents with a full-service agency for lodging and transportation. They offer guided tours to bodegas, Valle Fertí (where they own their own cabins), Ischigualasto Park, and beyond. Moneytur conducts local tours of bodegas, including lunch; tours to Ischigualasto, Talampaya, Las Quijades, and Jachal, as well as rafting trips on the Río San Juan and horseback trips in the Calingasta Valley.

Air Contacts **Aerolíneas Argentinas** ✉ *Av. Libertador San Martín Oeste* ☎ *264/427–4444* 🌐 *www.aerolineas.com.ar.*

Bus Contacts **Autotransportes** ✉ *San Juan* ☎ *264/431–1000 San Juan office, 264/422–1105 in terminal* 🌐 *www.atsj.com.ar.* **CATA** ✉ *San Juan* ☎ *264/421–4125* 🌐 *www.catainternacional.com.* **Chevallier** ✉ *San Juan* ☎ *264/422–2871* 🌐 *www.nuevachevallier.com.* **Terminal de Ómnibus** ✉ *Estados Unidos 492, between Santa Fe and España 985* ☎ *264/422–1604.*

Car Rentals **Avis** ✉ *Domingo Sarmiento Sur 164* ☎ *264/420–0571, 264/15–499–1472* 🌐 *www.avis.com.ar* ⏲ *Closed every afternoon 12:30–4, closed Sat. after 12:30, closed Sun.* **Hertz** ✉ *Sarmiento 164 (sur)* ☎ *261/423–0225, 264/422–6798* 🌐 *www.milletrentacar.com.ar.*

Taxis **Argentina Remise** ✉ *Gral. Mariano Acha Norte 989* ☎ *264/422–5522, 264/421–3837.* **Radio Taxi** ✉ *Tucumán 1220* ☎ *264/422–3561, 264/426–5555.*

ESSENTIALS

Banks **Banco de Galícia** ✉ *Rivadavia 102* ☎ *264/421–2490.* **Citibank** ✉ *Av. J.I. de la Roza 211 Oeste* ☎ *264/427–7000.* **Lloyd's Bank** ✉ *General Acha 127 Sur* ☎ *264/420–6480.*

Internet **Casino Cyber Café** ✉ *Rivadavía 12 Este* ☎ *264/420–1397.* **Telefónica** ✉ *Laprida 180 Oeste.* **Upe** ✉ *Mendoza Sur 21* ☎ *264/421–1333.*

Medical Assistance **Farmacia Echague** ✉ *Pedro Echague Este, Esq. Sarmiento* ☎ *264/421–3353.* **Hospital Dr. G. Rawson** ✉ *Av. Rawson Sur 494* ☎ *264/422–2272, 264/422–4005.*

Visitor Info **Dante Montes Turismo** ✉ *Santa Fe 58 Este, Galeria Estornell, Loc 31* ☎ *264/422–9019, 264/421–5198* 🌐 *www.agenciamontes.com.ar.* **Moneytur** ✉ *Santa Fe 202* ☎ *264/420–1010* 🌐 *www.moneytur.com.ar.* **San Juan Secretaria de Turismo** ✉ *Sarmiento 24 Sur* ☎ *264/421–0004, 264/427–5946* 🌐 *www.sanjuan.gov.ar.*

EXPLORING

Casa Natal de Sarmiento (*Sarmiento's Birthplace*). The Casa Natal de Sarmiento is where Domingo Faustino Sarmiento (1811–88) was born. Known in Argentina as the Father of Education (he believed that public education was the right of every citizen), he was a prolific writer and a skilled diplomat. He served as senator of San Juan province in 1857, as governor in 1862, and eventually became president of the nation from 1869 to 1874. During this time he passed laws establishing public education in Argentina. (Just be cautious bringing up Sarmiento's ideas for ceding sections of Patagonia to Chile if you're around any serious Sarmiento enthusiasts). This house was the first National Historic Landmark declared in Argentina. Hours vary by season, so call ahead of your visit. ✉ *Sarmiento 21 Sur* ☎ *264/421–0004* 🌐 *www.casanatalsarmiento.com.ar* 🎫 *5 pesos, free Sun.*

Presa de Embalse Quebrada de Ullum (*Ullum Valley Dam Reservoir*). The Presa de Embalse Quebrada de Ullum, 15 km (9 miles) west of San Juan, is a huge hydroelectric complex with grand views of the Río San Juan. Windsurfing, sailing, swimming, rowing, fishing, and diving keep San Juaninos cool on hot summer days. You can rent boating equipment at the Bahía Las Tablas sports complex, just beyond the dam, where there are a café and change cabins. There's a public beach at the Embarcadero turnoff. You can white-water raft and kayak on the San Juan, Los Patos, and Jachal rivers. Fishing in Las Hornillas River can be arranged through local tour companies. ✉ *San Juan.*

WINERIES

The Ullum, Tullum, and Zonda valleys are the principal wine-growing areas close to the city, and the Río San Juan flows from the mountains into 2,000 km (1,243 miles) of canals to irrigate about 48,500 hectares (120,000 acres) of vineyards. Other growing areas include El Perdenal, southeast near the Mendoza border, and Jachal, to the north.

Antigua Bodega 1929. At this landmark bodega and museum, great concrete wine-storage tubs are exposed in a cavernous old building that survived three earthquakes and now functions as part of the museum. Wine and Spumante are served in the lovely garden or at a wine bar in the front room. ✉ *Salta 782 Norte, Capital, San Juan* ☎ *264/421–2722* 🌐 *www.antiguabodega.com* ⏲ *Mon.–Sat. 11–1 and 6–9.*

Bodegas Santiago Graffigna S.A. Italian wine expert Don Santiago Graffigna founded this winery in 1870 and planted Tulum Valley's first vines. You can learn the history of his family and their vineyard in the excellent museum on the premises. Today the company is owned by Allied Domecq, and grapes arrive at the winery from vineyards in many valleys. An enormous barrel serves as a sitting area in the tasting room. ✉ *Colón 1342 Norte, Desamparados, San Juan* ☎ *264/421–4227* 🌐 *www.graffignawines.com* ⏲ *Mon.–Sat. 9–6, Sun. 10–8.*

Callia. In a hot, dry, wide open valley 35 km (22 miles) from town and with vineyards planted in every direction, this winery produces some of Argentina's best Syrah. It looks modern, but inside its superstructure is the old bodega (albeit with all new equipment). It's owned by Salentein, a formidable Dutch company that also makes wine in the Valle de Uco. Callia is open by appointment only on weekedays. ✉ *Calle de los Ríos s/n, Caucete, San Juan* ☎ *264/496–0000* 🌐 *www.bodegascallia.com.*

Casa Montes Bodegas Y Viñedos. Across the road from Callia, in a white cube surrounded by vineyards, Don Francisco Montes cultivates high quality grapes, and his Ampakama label is widely distributed in Argentina and abroad, including the U.S. Tours are by appointment two days in advance. ✉ *Pozo de los Algarrobos, Calle Colón y Caseros Caucete, San Juan* ☎ *264/423–6632* 🌐 *www.casamontes.com.ar.*

★ **Cavas de Zonda S.A.** This winery isn't on the Caminos del Vino, but it should be; it is a temple. As you enter, Gregorian chant echoes through the whitewashed chambers, creating a sense of drama. Storage, winemaking, bottling, and tasting all take place in a labyrinth of caves, allegedly carved out of the mountain by Yugoslav prisoners in 1932. Outside, a large park is an ideal place to enjoy a picnic lunch with a newly purchased bottle—a good idea, since it's the farthest winery from town. In addition to the typical Argentine wines such as Malbec and Cabernet Sauvignon, Cavas also works with the varietals Viognier and Chenin. ✉ *RP12, Km 15, Rivadavía, San Juan* ☎ *264/494–5144* 🌐 *www.cavasdezonda.com.ar* ⏲ *Daily 9–1 and 3–7.*

Champañera Miguel Ángel Más. There's a lot going on at this small, unassuming little winery. There isn't a fancy tour, but workers will stop to show you how they make sparkling wine, turning the bottles slowly on the many racks. Everything is certified organic—from the wine to the champagne to the garlic and tomatoes that grow out back. ✉ *Calle 11 s/n, 300 meters (328 yards) east of RN40, San Juan* ☎ *264/422–5807* ⏲ *Daily 10–5.*

Fabril Alto Verde. Grapes from this spotless winery are grown organically, and the wine and Spumante are stabilized without preservatives or additives. Internationally certified as organic, the wines are made in small quantities, and a great deal of care and control go into producing the best product. ✉ *RN40, between Calles 13 and 14, San Juan* ☎ *264/492–1905* 🌐 *www.fabril-altoverde.com.ar* ⏲ *Weekdays 9–1 and 3:30–7:30, Sat. 9–1, Sun. by appointment.*

Las Marianas. Founded in 1922, this winery is a fusion of tradition and technology. Gold adobe walls, arched doorways, and wine casks filled with flowers give it an Old Spanish air, but inside everything is state-of-the-art. Lots of care goes into irrigation, growing the grapes on *espalderas altos* (espaliers) or *parrales* (trellises), selecting grapes on the vine, hand harvesting, and hand crushing. The owner leads some of the tours. ✉ *Calle Nueva s/n, La Rinconada, Pocito, San Juan* ☎ *264/423–1191* 🌐 *bodegalasmarianas.com.ar* ⏲ *Daily 10–12:30 and 4–8.*

Viñas de Segisa. Segisa claims to be the first boutique winery in San Juan. In 1925 Don Vicente Perez Ganga settled in San Juan and quickly became one of the best winemakers in the region. Earthquakes ensued, destroying most of the original buildings, but in 1995 new owners resurrected what they could and built a new, anti-seismic facility, using the traditional high ceiling of bamboo canes held in place by crossed timbers and thick brick walls and floors. They offer a Torrontes-Chardonnay blend that stands out as something different. ✉ *Aberastain at Calle 15, La Rinconada, Pocito, San Juan* ☎ *264/492–2000* 🌐 *www.saxsegisa.com.ar* ⏲ *Mon.–Sat. 10–8, Sun. 10–2.*

WHERE TO EAT

$$ ECLECTIC ✕ **de Sanchez Libros y Discos.** What fun to find a gourmet restaurant with good books (*libros*) and old CDs (*discos*) lining one wall, larger-than-life photos of Rita Moreno on the other, and beaded chandeliers lighting the open booths. The menu's unlikely yet delicious fusions include lots of seafood and fresh vegetables like asparagus, artichoke hearts, and green beans—a welcome relief in this country of carnivores. The vibe is hip and healthy; wine glasses (and pours) are large. You can browse and/or buy the books and CDs. ✉ *Rivadavia 61 Oeste, San Juan* ☎ *264/420–3670* 🌐 *www.desanchezrestoran.com.ar* ⏲ *Closed Sun.*

Taking a rest at Cerro Aconcagua's Camp Two.

$$ ARGENTINE ✕ **Las Leñas.** This large, popular grill can serve up to 200 people under its high wooden roof and spinning fans. *Chivito* (goat) is the specialty (it's best in March and April). Otherwise, enjoy a *bife de chorizo* (sirloin), sausages, and chicken, which arrive at your table sizzling on their own grill. If you don't like the music, ask them to play Argentine folklore. On Sunday afternoon families fill the long tables; live musicians often play Friday night. ✉ *Av. Libertador 1670 Oeste, San Juan* ☎ *264/423–5040.*

$$ ARGENTINE ✕ **Remolacha.** Delicious smells from the outdoor grill lure locals off the streets and into this popular smoke-free restaurant in the center of town. Saffron-yellow tablecloths throughout brighten the low-ceilinged dining room and add a splash of color to the outdoor patio. A variety of typical dishes—grilled goat, beef, chicken, and vegetables, pasta, and crepes—are served for lunch and dinner. ✉ *Av. J.I. de la Roza 199 Oeste, at Sarmiento, San Juan* ☎ *264/422–7070.*

$ ARGENTINE ✕ **Restaurante Palito—Club Sirio Libanés.** Tiled walls that look straight out of the Middle East mark the entrance to this popular eatery; in fact, you pass through a small mosque to enter the restaurant. Don't be dismayed by the bright lights and TV showing soccer games; just order a bottle of Malbec, head for the table of appetizers, and fill your plate with crab brochettes, pickled eggplant, fresh tomatoes, and sliced tongue. Entrées include pastas, chicken, and beef prepared with a Mediterranean touch. ✉ *Entre Ríos 33, San Juan* ☎ *264/422–3841* 🌐 *www.hostaldepalito.com.ar* ⏲ *No dinner Sun.*

$ VEGETARIAN ✕ **Soychu.** This is a restaurant dedicated to natural foods, with lots of vegetarian and even vegan options. It's laid back and buffet-style, and you can take food to go or eat it there. Make sure to try the fresh-squeezed fruit and vegetable juices. ✉ *Av. José de la Roza 223, San Juan* ☎ *264/422–1939* ▭ *No credit cards.*

WHERE TO STAY

For expanded hotel reviews, visit Fodors.com.

$ **Albertina.** Bright white walls with colorful art, glass partitions, and slick modern furniture have rejuvenated this venerable four-story hotel on the main square in the center of town. **Pros:** convenient location; basic and comfortable. **Cons:** tiny windows; stairway down to entrance is inconvenient, although elevator access from street to second floor is available. ✉ *Mitre 31/41 Este, San Juan* ☎ *264/421–4222* 🌐 *www.hotelalbertina.com* *35 rooms* *In-hotel: restaurant, bar* *Breakfast.*

$$ **Alkazar.** Polished granite floors, chrome, and glass lend this hotel's lobby a businesslike air. **Pros:** professional staff; good location and business amenities. **Cons:** rooftop pool is small; floral bedroom decor a bit dated. ✉ *Laprida 82 Este, San Juan* ☎ *264/421–4965* 🌐 *www.alkazarhotel.com.ar* *104 rooms, 8 suites* *In-room: safe, Wi-Fi. In-hotel: restaurant, bar, pool, parking* *Breakfast.*

$$$ **Del Bono Park.** Light shines from a skylight four stories above the registration area, lobby, bar, and gathering spaces, and a third-floor glass bridge connects rooms by spanning the atrium, with a circular staircase winding around a glass cylinder down into the basement bar, restaurant, and casino. **Pros:** San Juan's newest, sleekest ultra-modern hotel. **Cons:** just off the Circunvalación (Ring Road). ✉ *Av. J. I. de La Roza 1946, San Juan* ☎ *0800/333–5266, 264/426–2300* *101 rooms* *In-room: safe, Wi-Fi. In-hotel: restaurant, bar, pool, gym, spa, business center, parking* *Breakfast.*

$$ **Gran Hotel Provincial.** Soft sand colors, dark wood floors and trim, and contemporary lighting have transformed this conventional building into a modern, businesss-oriented hotel just steps from shops, restaurants, and the green plaza. **Pros:** location off main plaza in city center; some city views. **Cons:** institutional dining room/bar; simple rooms. ✉ *Av. Ignacio de la Roza 132 Este, San Juan* ☎ *264/422–7501* 🌐 *www.granhotelprovincial.com* *99 rooms, 2 suites* *In-room: a/c, safe, Wi-Fi. In-hotel: restaurant, bar, pool, parking.*

$ **La Deolinda.** The helpful owners of this newer apart-hotel, outside of the ring road (Av. De Circunvalación),have created a friendly complex of cabins with outdoor patios, backyard grills, and a swimming pool. **Pros:** friendly and helpful owners; spacious grounds with open-air pool; nice for families. **Cons:** 15 minutes by car or taxi to town; no public transportation. ✉ *25 de Mayo and Lateral Oeste, San Juan* ☎ *264/422–2923* 🌐 *www.ladeolinda.com.ar* *8 apartments (for 2–6), 4 rooms* *In-room: safe, kitchen, Wi-Fi. In-hotel: pool, parking.*

$ **Villa Don Tomás.** If you're tired of downtown streets with traffic, crowds, and noise, and if you have active children who need to get out and play, consider this resort-like hotel on the outskirts of town. **Pros:** huge lawn; pool; dedicated staff. **Cons:** 15-minute ride in taxi or rental car to town; no nearby shops or restaurants. ✉ *Comandante Cabot 568 Oeste, 5400, San Juan* ☎ *264/428–3842* 🌐 *www.villadontomas.com.ar* *32 rooms, 11 cottages, 8 apts* *In-room: safe, Internet, Wi-Fi. In-hotel: restaurant, bar, pool, gym, business center, parking.*

BARREAL

136 km (85 miles) northwest of San Juan.

Beyond the streets of Barreal, hiding in the shade of *sauce llorones* (weeping willows) and alamos, lie apple orchards, vineyards, and fields of mint, lavender, and anise. Using this tranquil village as your headquarters, you can mountain bike, horseback ride, hike, climb, or drive a 4x4 east into the Sierra Tontal, where at 3,999 meters (13,120 feet) you can see the highest ranges of the Andes, including Aconcagua (6,957 meters/22,825 feet) and Mercedario (6,768 meters/22,205 feet).

GETTING HERE AND AROUND

You can reach Barreal by bus or car in about three hours. Leave San Juan on Ruta Nacional 40 driving north, then veer west on 436 to Talacasto, which becomes 149 to the Calingasta Valley then continues south to Barreal.

Another option is the long, lonely, but scenic drive from Uspallata (⇨ *Scenic Drives in Uspallata*) on north–south Ruta 414 all the way to Barreal. The best way to explore Barreal, the Calingasta Valley, and the surrounding area is by car, using a 4x4 for forays into the mountains, or by joining a tour and letting them drive.

ESSENTIALS

Medical Assistance Hospital Calingasta ✉ *Av Argentina, Barreal* ☎ *264/842–1022.*

Visitor Info Tourist Office ✉ *Municipalidad, Presidente Roca, Barreal* ☎ *264/844–1066.*

EXPLORING

Twenty-two kilometers (14 miles) south of Barreal on Ruta 412 toward Uspallata, a dirt road turns off into **Reserva Natural El Leoncito** (Little Lion Natural Reserve), a vast, rocky area with little vegetation. You can continue on this road for 17 km (11 miles) to the CASLEO observatory, known for its exceptional stargazing. Overnight visits are available through Territorios Andinos. ✉ *Marioano Moreno s/n* ☎ *264/503–2008* 🌐 *www.territoriosandinos.com.ar.*

Near the turnoff, on the western side of Ruta 412 at Pampa Leoncito, the sport of *carrovelismo* (land-sailing) is practiced during summer months in wheeled sand cars called wind yachts that can sail up to 150 kph (93 mph) across a cracked clay lake bed.

An all-day drive (160 km/100 miles round trip) in a 4x4 to Las Hornillas at 3,300 meters (9,500 feet) takes you along the Río Los Patos into a red rock-walled canyon. The road narrows, clinging to the canyon walls, as it winds around closed curves, eventually opening into a small valley where, in 1817, General San Martín's troops gathered before crossing the Andes over the Los Patos Pass on one of his historic liberation campaigns.

A brief glimpse of Aconcagua looming in solitary splendor about 100 miles south is a preview of coming attractions: four peaks over 6,000 meters (20,000 feet) are visible in the Ramada Range to the northwest: Polaco, 6000 meters; Alma Negra, 6,180 meters; La Ramada,

6,460 meters; and Mercaderio, 6,770 meters (fourth highest peak in the Americas). As the road winds ever higher, herds of guanacos graze on the steep slopes, pumas prowl in the bush, and condors soar above.

WHERE TO STAY

For expanded hotel reviews, visit Fodors.com.

$ **El Mercedario.** The young owner (Luís) of this 1928 adobe farmhouse right on the main street is determined to create a gathering place for like-minded lovers of all that Barreal has to offer, as his passion is taking guests in his 4x4 to mountains, rivers, and local sights. **Pros:** friendly, enthusiastic owner/guide Luís speaks English. **Cons:** yard is a work in progress. ✉ *Av. Presidente Roca and Calle Los Enamorados, Barreal* ☎ *264/15–509–0907, 011/15–3241–5886* 🌐 *www.elmercedario.com.ar* *7 rooms* *In-room: no TV. In-hotel: parking* *No credit cards* *Breakfast.*

$$ **La Querencia.** Situated just beyond the south end of town, this Southwest-style inn looks west to the Andes and east to the pre-Cordillera, washed in red tones at sunset; Adela and Carlos, the attentive owners, help plan day trips, suggest restaurants, and serve a farm-fresh breakfast (homemade yogurt, bread, jams) in the casual dining room. **Pros:** big back yard; Andes view with sunset. **Cons:** need car, bike, or horse. ✉ *Florida s/n, Barreal* ☎ *264/15–436–4699* 🌐 *www.laquerenciaposada.com* *6 rooms* *In-room: no TV. In-hotel: parking* *No credit cards* *Breakfast.*

$$ **Posada San Eduardo.** A yellow adobe house with closed green shutters sits on the shady corner of Calle Los Enamorados (Lover's Lane); inside, spacious rooms decorated with local weavings and rustic pine furniture open on to a colonial patio. **Pros:** peaceful setting; attentive staff and owners; good base for mountain forays. **Cons:** rooms are dark. ✉ *Av. San Martín at Los Enamorados, Barreal* ☎ *2648/441–046 in Barreal, 264/423–0192 in San Juan* *14 rooms* *In-hotel: restaurant, bar, pool* *No credit cards* *Breakfast.*

Fodor's Choice ★

SPORTS AND THE OUTDOORS

HIKING AND MOUNTAINEERING

Tour offices in San Juan, Barreal, and as far away as Mendoza offer day hikes and rides or weeklong treks and horseback rides in the Parque Nacional El Leoncito or the high mountain ranges of the Cordillera Ansilta, where seven peaks from 5,160 to 6,035 meters (16,929–19,800 feet) challenge hikers and horseback riders. You can ride for four days to the Paso de Los Patos (Ducks Pass), as San Martín did with 3,200 men in 1817 on his way to liberate Chile.

Fortuna Viajes. Fortuna Viajes has 30 years of experience in outdoor adventure tourism. They offer horseback trips from one to nine days, including hiking and/or riding to Valle Colorado, where you can climb (or admire from your saddle) six peaks over 6,000 meters (20,000 feet). Hiking, mountaineering, rafting, fishing, sand-surfing, and 4x4 excursions are other offerings. ✉ *Mariano Moreno s/n, Barreal* ☎ *264/15–404–0913 cell, 264/404–0913* 🌐 *fortunaviajes.com.ar.*

6

The Lake District

WORD OF MOUTH

"We found that although the flights to Argentina are [expensive], once we arrived, costs were reasonable, especially in restaurants. If you head to Bariloche, consider taking the lakes crossing to Puerto Varas, Chile, beautiful place."

—HappyTrvlr

WELCOME TO THE LAKE DISTRICT

Lanín Volcano

TOP REASONS TO GO

★ **Savage Beauty:** One day a lake is silent, a mirror of its surrounding mountains. Another day waves are crashing on its shores, with wind tearing limbs from trees.

★ **The Great Outdoors:** Well-marked trails in the national parks lead into a world of strange forests, leaping waterfalls, and magnificent vistas. Commercial river rafting or kayaking might carry you to Chile.

★ **Water, Water Everywhere:** 40 different lakes, seven major rivers flowing into two oceans, and you can spend days just staring at Nahuel Huapi Lake with its shoreline disappearing under distant peaks and volcanoes.

★ **Ski in Summer:** In the northern Lake District of Patagonia, June through September is ski season on the slopes of Cerro Catedral, near Bariloche, and Cerro Chapelco, near San Martín de los Andes.

Ashy-headed Goose

1 Bariloche. Full of shops, shoppers, and skiers in winter, this unashamedly touristy city on the southeastern shore of Nahuel Huapi Lake welcomes the world with all levels of hostelry, restaurants, and tour offices. The best part of Bariloche is beyond the city limits.

2 In and Around San Martín. This Andean town is a good base for exploring Parque Nacional Lanín and its nearby rivers and streams. A good variety of accommodations makes this a logical stopover on the Seven Lakes Route.

3 Route of the Seven Lakes (Ruta de los Siete Lagos). The best part of this 105-km (65-mile) drive is between Villa La Angostura and San Martín de los Andes, where the road winds up and around lake after lake—all of them different in shape, size, and setting. Note that the massive Puyehue volcano, just across the Chilean border from Villa La Angostura, erupted in June 2011, so check the region's conditions in advance.

4 Parque Nacional Nahuel Huapi. It's the oldest (founded in 1934), the biggest (272 square miles), and the most popular national park in Patagonia. Buses, boats, and private vehicles transport visitors to its far-flung corners to explore high mountain glaciers, hundreds of lakes, and trails.

5 In and Around El Bolsón. Known to some as a refuge for hippies and ex-urbanites, this amiable little town in a wide valley between two high mountain ranges straddles Ruta Nacional 40 just north of Parque Nacional Lago Puelo on the Chilean border. Acres of hops and berry farms thrive in the microclimate along the Río Azul.

house on the shore of Lago Nahuel Huapi

cozy cabin lodging

GETTING ORIENTED

The Lake District lies in the folds of the Andes along the Chilean border in the provinces of Neuquén, Río Negro, and Chubut, where myriad glacial lakes lap at the forest's edge beneath snowcapped peaks. The area includes four national parks, with towns in each. Bariloche is the base for exploring Parque Nacional Nahuel Huapi, and the departure point for the lake crossing to Chile. North of Bariloche is Parque Nacional Lanín, with the towns of San Martín de los Andes and Junín de los Andes. South of Bariloche and El Bolsón on Ruta Nacional 40 is Parque Nacional Lago Puelo in the Pacific watershed.

Lake Traful, submerged forest

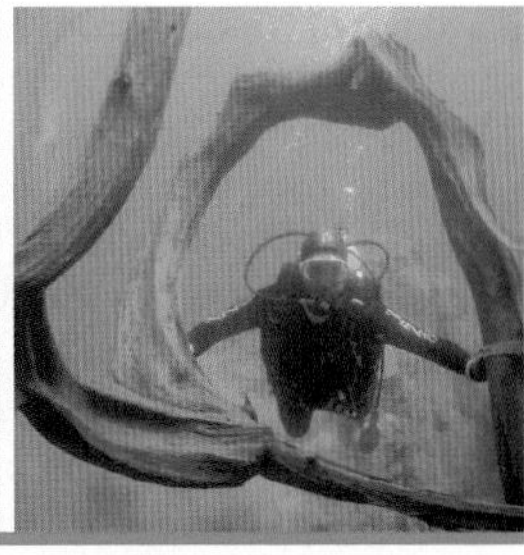

RUTA DE LOS SIETE LAGOS

To fully experience the Lake District, head north of Bariloche past Nahuel Huapi Lake to the Ruta de Los Siete Lagos (Seven Lakes Route). This excursion has it all: lake after lake, mountains, wildflowers, waterfalls, hiking trails, and small towns along the way.

(above) You'll pass lots of big-leaf lupine, or *Lupus polyphyllus*—an invasive species here. (top right) Rainbow trout (bottom right) One of many stunning views along the way

The route itself links Bariloche and San Martín de los Andes. Start in Bariloche and follow the Circuito Grande along Ruta 237 and Ruta 231 to Villa La Angostura, then pass Lagos Espejo and Correntoso on Ruta 231 to get to mostly unpaved Ruta 234; take this north to San Martín.

For a day trip, return from San Martin de Los Andes through Junín de Los Andes and Alicura (Rutas 234, 40, and 237) on 260 km (161miles) of paved road. If you have the time, though, overnight in San Martín de los Andes then take Ruta Provincial 63 to Confluéncia, and then join Ruta 237 south along the Río Limay to Bariloche.

Renting a car is best, but even on a group tour it's spectacular. Buses are available from Bariloche or Villa La Angostura; you can also rent bicycles in these towns and take to the road on two wheels instead of four.

TIPS

Ask about road conditions before you leave Villa La Angostura; The route's unpaved portion north of there is often closed during heavy rains, winter storms, or construction.
Best bets for picnic spots or campsites are the beaches of lakes Villarino, Falkner, and Hermoso.
For maps, pick up *Guía Busch* and *Viajar Hoy* (tour pamphlets in English and Spanish), both available at car-rental agencies, kiosks, and hotels in Bariloche.

HIGHLIGHTS OF THE DRIVE

Rivers. Just past Villa La Angostura, the **Río Correntoso**—one of the world's shortest rivers at 300 meters (984 feet)—flows from the lake of the same name into Nahuel Huapi. This is a classic mouth-of-the-river fishing spot; you can watch the action from the glassed-in deck at the Hotel Correntoso or from the old fishing lodge on the shore of Nahuel Huapi Lake. To join in, contact **Patagon Fly** (✉ *Av. Arrayanes 282* ☎ *2944/494-634* 🌐 *www.patagonfly.com*) at the Banana Fly Shop in Villa La Angostura.

Lakes. Traveling north from Villa Angostura to San Martín de Los Andes is the most scenic part of the drive, and it's no coincidence that this is where you'll find the region's most scenic namesake natural features—lakes. **Lago Correntoso** (Rapid Water Lake) is the first one you'll pass, and you'll do so immediately after you cross over the Río Correntoso. Drive along its northern shore to arrive at an abandoned hotel site; from here you'll see a road that leads to **Lago Espejo Chico** (*Little Mirror Lake*), with a beach, a campground, and trails. Return to the main road and you'll come to **Lago Espejo** (Mirror Lake)—head to the viewpoint for a good lunch spot, or use the camping area's tables. **Lago Falkner** (east side of the road) has sandy beaches and a popular campground. It is linked by a stream and an isthmus, which you will cross to **Lago Villarino** (west side of the road). **Lago Hermoso** (*Beautiful Lake*) is a small sheltered lake. A sunny beach faces west, with nearby camping and a few cabins. Finally, before you reach San Martín de los Andes, enjoy **Lago Machónico**'s dry landscape via the scenic overlook, or take the short walk to the shore.

Waterfalls. Between Lakes Villarino and Falkner, **Cascada Vulignanco,** a 20-meter (66-foot) waterfall, is visible on the left-hand side of the road, where you can pull off at the *mirador* (overlook).

DETOURS

Four km (2.5 miles) south of Lago Villarino, jade-green **Lago Escondido** (*Hidden Lake*) lies veiled in a thick forest of coihue, *ñire*, and *radale* trees. You'll need to park and walk in. At Pichi Traful, turn east on to a bumpy road for 2 km (1 mile) and walk to the sandy beach at **Pichi Traful Lake** (aka Brazo Norte of Lago Traful). Fishermen, mountain bikers, and hikers enjoy camping or picnicking here.

About 30 km (18 miles) north of the junction of Ruta Provincial 234 and Ruta Provincial 65, look on your left for a sign indicating the trail to **Casacada Ñivinenco** (*Whispering Falls*). The 2-km trail crosses a river (though in November and December the river is high; check conditions ahead of time), then follows the river into a silent forest of *caña colihue, ñire*, and coihue.

If you pass through **Confluéncia,** take Ruta Provincial 65 along the Traful River west a few km to **Cuyín Manzano,** a dirt road that continues along the river into a world of strange limestone rock formations, caves, and maybe even a condor sighting.

6

CIRCUITO CHICO Y CIRCUITO GRANDE

If you're in Bariloche, get out of town to take in some of the spectacular scenery and old-school resort feel of the area on either the Circuito Chico (small circuit) or Circuito Grande (large circuit) by rental car, hired driver, or tour group.

(above) "We drove the Circuito Chico and stopped at this overlook." —HappyTrvlr (top right) "With flowers in full bloom it couldn't get much better." —Josh Roe (bottom right) Peninsula Llao Llao.

The Circuito Chico is a 70-km (43½ mile) half-day round-trip from Bariloche along the southern shore of Lago Nahuel Huapi. Visitors head out to the Llao Llao Peninsula to ski or take in the lake views and waterfalls without ever being too far from a cup of tea.

The Circuito Grande covers 250 km (155 miles) and is an all-day excursion across the lake from Bariloche. This drive is more about wooded hikes and hidden lakes, and includes two towns where you could spend a night.

You can do the Circuito Chico on one tank of gas. Circuit Grande, however, has longer unpopulated spans. Leave Bariloche with a full tank and re-fuel at Confluéncia or Villa La Angostura.

WEATHER TIPS

The Circuito Chico has lots of traffic but is otherwise an easy drive whatever the weather. The Circuito Grande is another story. The roads to Villa La Angostura and Confluéncia are good, but Ruta Provincial 65 past Lago Traful is unpaved and can be treacherous in bad weather. Always check road conditions with ACA (Automobil Club Argentina), the park office, or your hotel.

CIRCUITO CHICO

From Bariloche's Centro Cívico (Km 0), follow the shore of Lago Nahuel Huapi west on Ruta 237. At Km 7, stop at **Playa Bonita**'s sandy beach. At km 10, take the chairlift to the top of **Cerro Campanario**. When you reach the Península Llao Llao (Km 25.5), bear right to **Puerto Pañuelo**, where boats embark on lake excursions to Isla Victoria, Puerto Blest, and the boat crossing to Chile. Across from the Puerto Pañuelo, **Hotel Llao Llao** sits on a lakeside knoll with a backdrop of sheer cliffs and snow-covered mountains. Admire it from afar or make a lunch reservation. Continue following Ruta 77 to **Bahía Lopez;** you'll approach through a forest of ghostly, leafless lenga trees. After Bahía Lopez, the road crosses **Arroyo Lopez** (Lopez Creek); stop to hike to the waterfall or continue on Ruta 77 to **Punto Panoramico**, one of the most scenic overlooks on the peninsula. Just before you cross the Moreno Bridge (which separates Lago Moreno east and west), an unmarked dirt road off to the right leads to the rustic village of Colonia Suiza, a perfect stop for tea or lunch. Backtrack to cross Moreno Bridge, then leave Ruta 77 for Ruta 237 back to Bariloche.

CIRCUITO GRANDE

Leaving Bariloche on Ruta 237 heading east, follow the Río Limay into the **Valle Encantado** (*Enchanted Valley*), with its magical red rocks. Before crossing the bridge at Confluéncia (where the Río Traful joins the Limay), turn left onto Ruta 65 to Lago Traful. Five kilometers (3 miles) beyond the turnoff, a dirt road to Cuyín Manzano leads to **astounding sandstone formations**. Return to Ruta 65 and follow Lago Traful's shore. When you see the sign indicating a *mirador* (lookout), stop and climb the wooden stairs to one of the loveliest views in the region. Descend to Villa Traful, follow the lakeshore, then dive into a dense forest of *caña colihue* and lenga trees. At the intersection with Ruta 237, turn left and follow the shore of Lago Correntoso to the paved road down to Villa La Angostura. The road skirts Lago Nahuel Huapi back into Bariloche.

NEED A BREAK?

Circuito Chico: Chiado (✉ *Av. Bustillo (R237), Km 25* ☎ *2944/448–152* ⏲ *Closed Tues.*) is a little log house with a corrugated metal roof, a stone terrace, and red umbrellas hanging out over the lake. Views are through the gnarly branches of a giant coihué tree to blue water and distant mountains. The trout sorrentinos in pesto sauce are as good as the view.

Circuito Grande: If you chose to visit Lago Traful in the morning, chances are you'll arrive in the Villa Traful in time for lunch at Nancu Lahuen, a casual spot in the middle of town with home cooking—a place you can depend upon to be open and ready for tourists. If you've had the foresight to bring a picnic, continue on past the town to the beach, where the road leaves the lake for Ruta 234 and Villa La Angostura. In Villa La Angostura, head to La Casita de la Oma (✉ *Cerro Inacayal 303* ☎ *2544/494–602*), which serves homemade cakes, pies, and scones. Any dulce de leche item is a sure bet.

Updated by Brian Stevenson

Hundreds of sapphire lakes lie hidden amid the snow-covered peaks of the Andes on the western frontier with Chile, in what has become the most popular tourist area in Patagonia—the northern Lake District. Despite its growing popularity and accessibility from developed towns like San Martín de los Andes and Bariloche, visitors are constantly amazed at how easy it is to lose yourself in a silent forest, or by a still lake with no houses, no boats, no piers—just you and the natural surroundings.

Parque Nacional Lanín, in Neuquén Province, and the neighboring Parque Nacional Nahuel Huapi, in Río Negro Province, add up to 2.5 million acres of natural preserve—about the size of New England. South of Bariloche and the Cholila Valley and northwest of Esquel, the Parque Nacional los Alerces, named for its 2,000-year-old *alerce* trees, covers 1,610 square km (1,000 square miles) of mountains, forests, and lakes, with only one dirt road leading into it. Lago Puelo National Park near El Bolsón also has only one access road in Argentina, with a trail out the other side into Chile.

Outdoor activities and a wide variety of lodgings in extraordinary settings attract visitors year-round. In winter skiers come to Cerro Catedral for its size and terrain, its superb setting overlooking Nahuel Huapi Lake, and its proximity to Bariloche. Smaller areas such as Chapelco in San Martín de los Andes and Cerro Bayo in Villa La Angostura attract mostly Argentineans, lots of Brazilians, and a few other foreigners.

THE LAKE DISTRICT PLANNER

WHEN TO GO

From June through September the weather is typical of any ski region—blowing snowstorms, rain, and fog punctuated by days of brilliant sunshine. August and September are the best months for skiing, as the slopes are crowded with vacationers in July.

In December the weather can be cool, breezy, overcast, or rainy, but the rewards for bringing an extra sweater and raingear are great: an abundance of wildflowers and few tourists. January and February are the peak summer months, with long (sunsets at 10 pm) warm days. March and April are good months to visit, although rainy, cloudy days and cold nights can curtail some activities.

GETTING HERE AND AROUND

The most efficient way to get here is by air from Buenos Aires or Calafate. The most scenic way to arrive is from Puerto Montt, Chile, by boat through the lakes. Buses are the new trains—fast, inexpensive, with varying degrees of luxury, including beds, meals, and attendants. A car or bus is the best way to travel between cities in the Lake District, and once you've settled in a destination, you can use local tours, taxis, or a *remis* (car with driver).

AIR TRAVEL

Aerolíneas Argentinas (🌐 *www.aerolineas.com.ar*) flies from Buenos Aires to Bariloche, Esquel, San Martín de los Andes, and Neuqúen; it also connects Bariloche and Calafate. LAN (🌐 *www.lan.com*) also flies to Bariloche from Buenos Aires, as well as from Santiago, Chile.

BOAT TRAVEL

Traveling between Bariloche and Puerto Montt, Chile, by boat is one of the most popular excursions in Argentina. It requires three lake crossings and various buses, and can be done in a day or overnight. Travel agents and tour operators in Bariloche and Buenos Aires can arrange this trip.

BUS TRAVEL

Buses arrive in Bariloche from every corner of Argentina—from Jujuy in the north, Ushuaia in the south, and everywhere in between.

CAR TRAVEL

Driving to the Lake District from Buenos Aires is a long haul (more than 1,500 km [930 miles] and at least three days) of interminable stretches with few hotels, gas stations, or restaurants. In Bariloche, unless you're on a tour or a ski-only vacation, renting a car gives you the freedom to stop when and where you want. The Seven Lakes Route closes when weather is bad; for winter travel, rent a 4x4. Hiring a remis is another option.

RESTAURANTS

Restaurant reservations are seldom needed except during school, Easter, and summer holidays (July, January, and February). Attire is informal, and tipping is the same as in the rest of the country (about 10%).

HOTELS

Idyllic lake-view lodges, cozy *cabañas* (cabins), vast *estancias* (ranches), and inexpensive *hospedajes* or *residenciales* (bed-and-breakfasts) are found in towns and in the countryside throughout northern Patagonia. Super-luxurious hotels in Bariloche and Villa La Angostura attract outdoor enthusiasts from all over the world, as do small family-run hostels where backpackers squeeze five to a room. Fishing lodges near San Martín de los Andes, Junín de los Andes, and in the Cholila Valley are not only for anglers; they make great headquarters for hiking, boating, or just getting away. Most of them include all meals and cocktails. Guides are extra. *Apart-hotels* have small, furnished apartments with kitchenettes. Local tourist offices are helpful in finding anything from a room in a residence to a country inn or a downtown hotel. Advance reservations are highly recommended if you're traveling during peak times (December–March; July–August for the ski resorts). Note: lodging prices include tax (IVA—which is 21%) unless otherwise noted.

WHAT IT COSTS IN PESOS

	$	$$	$$$	$$$$
Restaurants	30 pesos and under	31 pesos–50 pesos	51 pesos–75 pesos	over 75 pesos
Hotels	300 pesos and under	301 pesos–500 pesos	501 pesos–800 pesos	over 800 pesos

Restaurant prices are for one main course at dinner. Hotel prices are for two people in a standard double room in high season.

HEALTH AND SAFETY

There are good doctors and clinics in Bariloche and San Martín de los Andes.

Emergency Services Coast Guard ☎ *106.* **Fire** ☎ *100.* **Forest Fire** ☎ *103.* **Hospital** ☎ *107.* **Police** ☎ *101.*

MONEY

There are ATMs in all towns and cities—even villages. Many hotels and shops give a discount when you're paying in cash (*efectivo*), and give good exchange rates for U.S. dollars.

TOURS

Alunco Turismo specializes in trips around Bariloche for individuals and groups, and can help with reservations. Causana Viajes does custom tours for groups or individuals all over Argentina.

In San Martín, the companies Turismo Messidor, El Claro Turismo, and Siete Lagos run horseback-riding, river-rafting, mountain-biking, lake, and land excursions around San Martín and to Lanín Volcano. In El Bolsón, Huara Viajes y Turismo offers guided fishing, rafting, and horseback-riding trips and excursions to Lago Puelo.

Tour Operators Alunco ✉ *Moreno 187, 1st fl.* ☎ *2944/422–283* 🌐 *www.aluncoturismo.com.ar.* **Causana Viajes** ✉ *Mathews 1325, Puerto Madryn* ☎ *2965/452–769* 🌐 *www.causanaviajes.com.ar.* **El Claro Turismo** ✉ *Colonel Diaz 751* ☎📠 *2972/428–876, 2972/425–876* ✉ *consultas@elclaroturismo.*

com.ar 🌐 *www.elclaroturismo.com.ar.* **Huara Viajes y Turismo** ✉ *Dorrego 410, El Bolsón* ☎ *2944/455-000* 🌐 *www.huaraviajesyturismo.com.ar.* **Siete Lagos Turismo** ✉ *Villegas 313, San Martín de los Andes, Neuquén* ☎📠 *2972/427-877* ✉ *sietelagostmo@smandes.com.ar.* **Turismo Messidor** ✉ *Av. Arrayanes 21, piso 2, Villa La Angostura* ☎ *2944/495-265* 🌐 *www.turismomessidor.com.ar.*

VISITOR INFORMATION

The comprehensive Inter Patagonia website (🌐 *www.interpatagonia.com*) is an excellent resource for tourist information for every city and region in Patagonia. Local tourist offices (Direcciónes de Turismo) are helpful, easy to find, and usually open late every day.

BARILOCHE

1,615 km (1,001 mi) southwest of Buenos Aires (2 hrs by plane); 432 km (268 miles) south of Neuquén on Ruta 237; 1,639 km (1,016 miles) north of Río Gallegos; 876 km (543 miles) northwest of Trelew; 357 km (221 miles) east of Puerto Montt, Chile, via lake crossing.

Bariloche is the gateway to all the recreational and scenic splendors of the northern Lake District and headquarters for 2-million-acre Nahuel Huapi National Park. Although planes, boats, and buses arrive daily, you can escape on land or water—or just by looking out a window—into a dazzling wilderness of lakes, waterfalls, mountain glaciers, forests, and meadows.

The town of Bariloche hugs the southeastern shore of Nahuel Huapi Lake, expanding rapidly east toward the airport and west along the lake toward Llao Llao, as Argentineans and foreigners buy and build without any apparent zoning plan. Being the most popular vacation destination in Patagonia has not been kind to the town once called the "Switzerland of the Andes." Traffic barely moves on streets and sidewalks during holidays and the busy months of January–March, July, and August.

Nevertheless, the Centro Cívico (Civic Center), with its gray-green stone-and-log buildings, has not lost its architectural integrity. Designed by Alejandro Bustillo, this landmark square, with its view of the lake and mountains, is a good place to begin exploring Bariloche.

GETTING HERE AND AROUND

For long excursions, such as the Seven Lakes Route, Circuito Grande, or Tronadór, sign up for a tour through your hotel or with a local tour agency. If you prefer the independence of figuring out maps and driving yourself, rent a car. Tour operators for fishing, rafting, and bike trips will pick you up and transport you to your destination. For good maps and a list of tour operators, look for *Guía Busch* at local bookstores, car-rental agencies, and kiosks. A local bus picks up skiers in Bariloche, and many hotels have their own shuttle.

Bus Contacts Andesmar ✉ *Bus terminal, Bariloche, Río Negro* ☎ *0261/405-0600.* **Bariloche Bus Terminal** ✉ *Av. 12 de Octubre, Bariloche, Río Negro* ☎ *2944/430-211.* **Don Otto** ✉ *At the bus terminal in Bariloche, Av. 12 de Octubre, Bariloche, Río Negro* ☎ *2944/437-699* 🌐 *www.donotto.com.ar.*

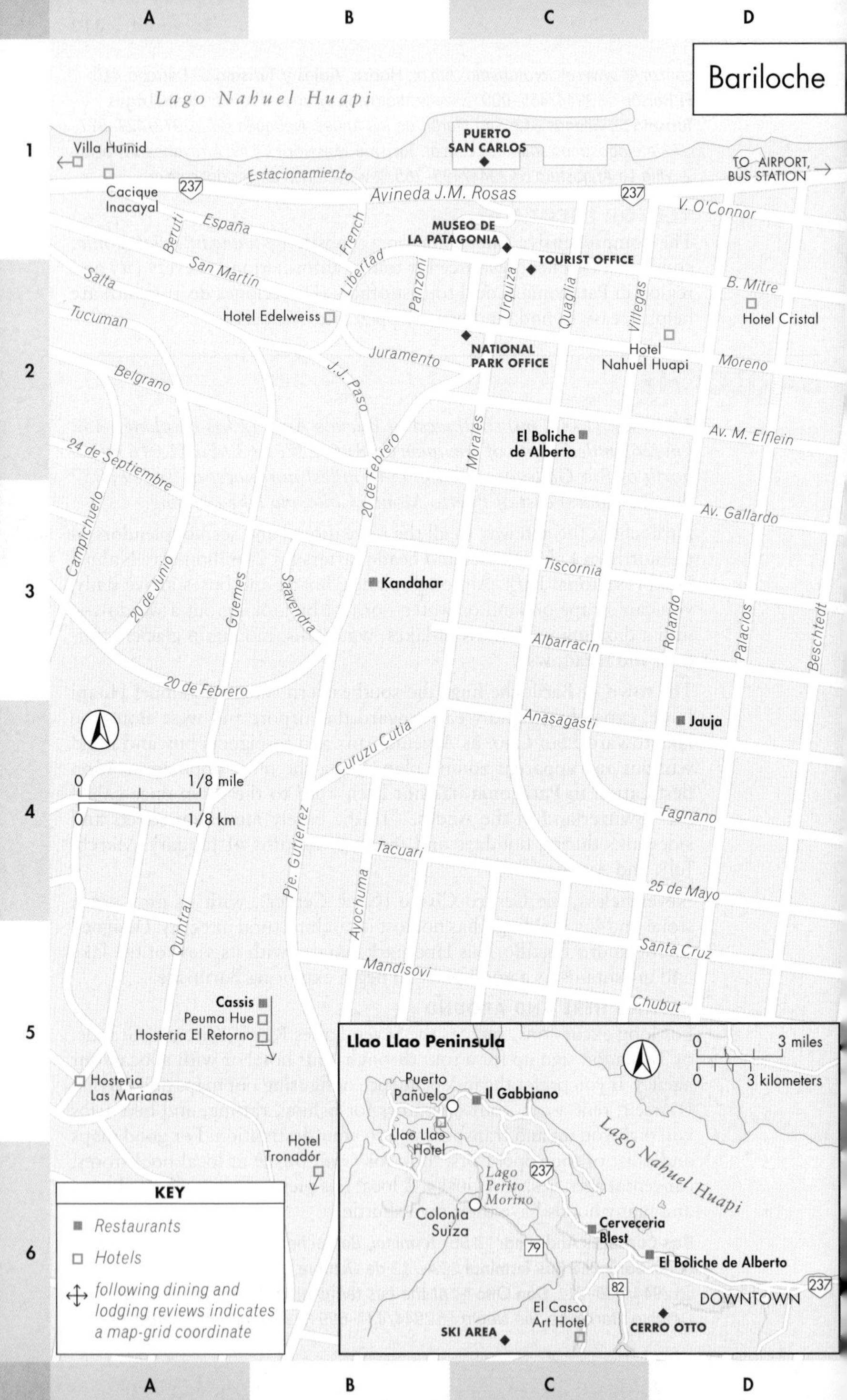
Bariloche
A
B
C
D
1
2
3
4
5
6
Lago Nahuel Huapi
Villa Huinid
Cacique Inacayal
PUERTO SAN CARLOS
TO AIRPORT, BUS STATION
Estacionamiento
Avineda J.M. Rosas
237
V. O'Connor
España
Beruti
French
MUSEO DE LA PATAGONIA
TOURIST OFFICE
San Martín
Libertad
Panzoni
Urquiza
Quaglia
Villegas
B. Mitre
Salta
Tucuman
Hotel Edelweiss
Hotel Cristal
NATIONAL PARK OFFICE
Hotel Nahuel Huapi
Juramento
Moreno
Belgrano
J.J. Paso
Av. M. Elflein
El Boliche de Alberto
Morales
24 de Septiembre
20 de Febrero
Av. Gallardo
Campichuelo
20 de Junio
Guemes
Saavendra
Kandahar
Tiscornia
Rolando
Palacios
Beschtedt
Albarracin
20 de Febrero
Anasagasti
Jauja
Curuzu Cutia
0
1/8 mile
0
1/8 km
Pje. Gutierrez
Fagnano
Tacuari
Ayochuma
25 de Mayo
Quintral
Santa Cruz
Mandisovi
Chubut
Cassis
Peuma Hue
Hosteria El Retorno
Hosteria Las Marianas
Hotel Tronadór
KEY
Restaurants
Hotels
following dining and lodging reviews indicates a map-grid coordinate
Llao Llao Peninsula
0
3 miles
0
3 kilometers
Puerto Pañuelo
Il Gabbiano
Llao Llao Hotel
Lago Nahuel Huapi
Lago Perito Morino
237
Colonia Suiza
Cerveceria Blest
79
El Boliche de Alberto
82
237
DOWNTOWN
El Casco Art Hotel
SKI AREA
CERRO OTTO

El Valle ✉ *Av. 12 de Octubre 1884, Bariloche, Río Negro* ☎ *2944/431–444.* **Via Bariloche** ✉ *Terminal de Buses, Av. 12 de Octubre, Bariloche, Río Negro* ☎ *2944/432–444* 🌐 *www.viabariloche.com.ar.* **VIATAC** ✉ *Terminal de Buses, Av. 12 de Octubre, Bariloche, Río Negro* ☎ *2944/421–235* 🌐 *www.viatac.com.ar.*

Rental Cars **Baricoche** ✉ *Moreno 115, Bariloche, Río Negro* ☎ *2944/427–638* 🌐 *www.baricoche.com.ar.*

SAFETY AND PRECAUTIONS

Driving in Bariloche requires total attention to blind corners, one-way streets, and stop signs where no one stops. Never leave anything in your car. Bariloche's challenging sidewalks are riddled with uneven steps, broken pavement, and unexpected holes—all potential ankle-breakers. When students hit Bariloche during holidays, they party until 5 or 6 in the morning, resulting in serious drunk-driving auto accidents.

ESSENTIALS

Currency Exchange **Banco Frances** ✉ *Av. San Martín 336, Bariloche, Río Negro* ☎ *2944/430–325.* **Bansud** ✉ *Mitre 433, Bariloche, Río Negro* ☎ *2944/421–054.*

Medical Assistance **Angel Gallardo** ✉ *Gallardo 701, Bariloche, Río Negro* ☎ *2944/427–023.* **Farmacia Detina** ✉ *Bustillo 12,500, Bariloche, Río Negro* ☎ *2944/525–900.* **Hospital Sanatorio del Sol** ✉ *20 de Febrero 598, Bariloche, Río Negro* ☎ *2944/525–000.* **Hospital Zonal Ramón Carillo** ✉ *Moreno 601, Bariloche, Río Negro* ☎ *2944/426–100.*

Post Office **Bariloche** ✉ *Perito Moreno 175, Bariloche, Río Negro.*

Remis (Car & Driver) **Patagonia Remises** ✉ *Av. Pioneros 4400, Bariloche, Río Negro* ☎ *2944/443–700.*

Visitor and Tour Info **Oficina Municipal de Turismo.** Open daily 8:30 am–9 pm. ✉ *Centro Cívico, across from clock tower, Bariloche, Río Negro* ☎ *2944/422–484* ✉ *secturismo@bariloche.com.ar* 🌐 *www.barilochepatagonia.info.*

EXPLORING

Cerro Otto. For an aerial view of the area around Bariloche, don't miss Cerro Otto (Mt. Otto; 4,608 feet). The ride to the top in a little red gondola takes about 12 minutes. The cable car is owned by **Teleférico Cerro Otto**, and all proceeds go to local hospitals. The mountain is 5 km (3 miles) west of town; a free shuttle bus leaves from the corner of Mitre and Villegas, and Perito Moreno and Independencia. You can also hike or mountain bike to the top, or drive 8 km (5 miles) up a gravel road from Bariloche. In winter, cross-country skis and sleds are for rent at the cafeteria. In summer, hiking and mountain biking are the main activities. There is a revolving restaurant on the summit. For a real thrill, try soaring in a paraplane out over the lake with the condors. Call for information (☎ *2944/441–035*) on schedules and sled or ski rentals. ✉ *Av. de los Pioneros, Bariloche, Río Negro* 🌐 *www.telefericobariloche.com.ar* 🎫 *30 pesos* ⏲ *Daily 10–5.*

Museo de la Patagonia. This museum tells the social and geological history of northern Patagonia with displays of Indian and gaucho artifacts and exhibits on regional flora and fauna. The histories of the Mapuche and the Conquista del Desierto (Conquest of the Desert) are explained in detail. ✉ *Centro Cívico, next to arch over Bartolomé Mitre, Bariloche, Río Negro* ☎ *2944/422–309* 🌐 *www.bariloche.com.ar/museo* 🎫 *15 pesos* ⏲ *Sat. 10–5, Tues.–Fri. 10–12:30 and 2–7. Closed Sun. and Mon.*

WHERE TO EAT

$$$$ ARGENTINE Fodor's Choice ★ ✕ **Cassis.** Chef Mariana Wolf combines the freshest seasonal ingredients, many from her own rural garden, in dishes that are both elegant and comforting. Meat eaters will love dishes like rib eye in shortcrust pâté brisée pastry, loaded with its own juices and port wine, and served with baked edible lilies and wild pine mushrooms. Mariana's husband Ernesto can recommend the perfect wine pairing from the restaurant's impressively stocked cellar. Desserts here are art. Try the Fruits of the Forest with Cointreau and cardomom ice cream served with oranges. Cassis's forest location near the shores of Lago Gutierrez is worth the drive. ✉ *Ruta 82, Km 5.5, Lago Gutiérrez, Bariloche, Río Negro* ☎ *2944/467–747* 🌐 *www.cassis.com.ar* ⚠ *Reservations essential* 💳 *No credit cards* ✢ *B5.*

$$ ARGENTINE ✕ **Cerveceria Blest.** This lively spot claims that it was the first brewpub in Argentina, and its relaxed bustle hits the spot after a day on the slopes. Don't miss the excellent bock beer, with a toasty coffee flavor, or if you prefer hard cider, the Fruto Prohibido. You can come in just for an après-ski beer sampler or stay for dinner, which might include *costillitas de cerdo ahumadas con chucrut* (smoked pork chops with sauerkraut—is there a more classic beer food than that?). Pizzas, steak potpies, and other Anglophile options round out the menu. ✉ *Av. Bustillo, Km 11.6, Bariloche, Río Negro* ☎ *2944/461–026* 💳 *No credit cards* ✢ *C6.*

$$$ ARGENTINE ✕ **El Boliche de Alberto.** Leather place mats, calfskin menus, and the smell of beef all hint heavily at steak house. Alberto has the best beef in Bariloche. Grilled beef, chicken, lamb, and chorizos all arrive sizzling on a wooden platter, accompanied by empanadas, *provoleta* (fried provolone cheese), salad, fried potatoes, and chimichurri sauce (slather it on the bread). Three locations: ✉ *Elflein 158, Bariloche, Río Negro* ☎ *2944/43–4564* 🌐 *www.elbolichedealberto.com* ✉ *Villegas 347, Bariloche, Río Negro* ☎ *2944/43–1433* ✉ *Bustillo 8.800, Bariloche, Río Negro* ☎ *2944/462–285* ✢ *D6.*

$$$ ITALIAN ✕ **Il Gabbiano.** "We don't serve lunch," the folks at this cozy, candlelit house on the Circuito Chico near Llao Llao boast, "because preparing dinner takes all day." It's hard to argue with that after you sample the exquisite pastas, which change daily. Look for *tortelli* stuffed with wild boar, or pumpkin ravioli; they also have a way with fresh trout. A beautiful wine cellar is open to guests. ✉ *Av. Bustillo, Km 24.300, Bariloche, Río Negro* ☎ *2944/448–346* ⚠ *Reservations essential* 💳 *No credit cards* ⏲ *Closed Tues. No lunch* ✢ *C5.*

$$$$ ARGENTINE ✕ **Jauja.** Locals and families come to this friendly restaurant for its outstanding pastas and variety of entrées listed on an eight-page menu: meats from Patagonia to the pampas, fish from both oceans, local game, fresh vegetables including local mushrooms. An upstairs dining

CLOSE UP

Fishing The Lakes

Fishing season runs November 15–May 1. In some areas catch-and-release is allowed year-round; catch-and-release is usually compulsory, but in some places catches may be kept. Guides are available by the day or the week. Nahuel Huapi, Gutiérrez, Mascardi, Correntoso, and Traful are the most accessible lakes in the Lake District.

If you're seeking the perfect pool or secret stream for fly-fishing, you may have to do some hiking, particularly along the banks of the Chimehuín, Limay, Traful, and Correntoso rivers. Near Junín de los Andes the Malleo and Currihué rivers, and Lakes Huechulafquen, Paimún, and Lácar are good fishing grounds.

Baruzzi Deportes. Oscar Baruzzi at Baruzzi Deportes is a good local fishing guide. ✉ *Urquiza 250, Bariloche, Río Negro* ☎ *2944/424–922* 🌐 *www.barilochefishing.com.*

Direcciones Provinciales de Pesca. Fishing licenses allowing you to catch brown, rainbow, and brook trout as well as perch and *salar sebago* (landlocked salmon) are obtainable in Bariloche at the Direcciones Provinciales de Pesca. You can also get licenses at the Nahuel Huapi National Park office and at most tackle shops. Nonresident license fees are $120/day, $360/week, $480/season. ✉ *Elflein 10, Bariloche, Río Negro* ☎ *2944/425–160.*

Martín Pescador. Martín Pescador has a shop with fishing and hunting equipment. ✉ *Rolando 257, Bariloche, Río Negro* ☎ *2944/422–275* ✉ *martinpescador@bariloche.com.ar.*

Patagonia Fly Shop. Ricardo Almeijeiras, also a guide, owns the Patagonia Fly Shop. ✉ *Quinchahuala 200, Av. Bustillo, Km 6.7, Bariloche, Río Negro* ☎ *2944/441–944* ✉ *flyshop@bariloche.com.ar.*

6

room is available for special events. Empanadas and take-out items can be ordered at the entrance. ✉ *Elflein 148, Bariloche, Río Negro* ☎ *2944/422–952* ⊕ *D4.*

$$$ ARGENTINE **Kandahar.** A rustic wood building with a woodstove and cozy windowseats provide the perfect setting for sipping a pisco sour and savoring a plate of smoked trout or salmon and guacamole. Start with the *tarteleta de hongos* (mushroom tart) and *rosa mosqueta* (rose hip) soup, followed by wild game and profiteroles with hot chocolate sauce. ✉ *20 de Febrero 698, Bariloche, Río Negro* ☎ *2944/424–702* *Reservations essential* ⊕ *B3.*

WHERE TO STAY

If you don't have a car, it's better to stay in town. If you're looking for serenity, consider a lake-view hotel or cabins along the route to the Llao Llao Peninsula. Locations of out-of-town dining and lodging properties are measured in kilometers from the Bariloche Civic Center.

For expanded hotel reviews, visit Fodors.com.

$$$ ★ **Cacique Inacayal.** Looking out from your bedroom window when the wind whips up the waves on Nahuel Huapi Lake, you'll be glad you're on land; perched on a cliff overlooking the lake, Cacique Inacayal has a

CLOSE UP

Chilean Lakes Crossing

Cruce a Chile por Los Lagos (Chilean Lakes Crossing). This unique excursion by land and lakes can be done in one or two days in either direction.

Board the boat at Puerto Pañuelo west of Bariloche, stop for lunch in Puerto Blest, then travel by bus up to Laguna Frías. After crossing that lake to Puerto Fríos, you pass Argentine customs, then board another bus that climbs through lush rain forest over a pass before descending to Peulla. Clear Chilean customs just before a lodge by Lago Todos los Santos. You may spend the night here (recommended) or head straight to Chile by catamaran from Peulla, with volcano views. An overnight stay is mandatory in winter. The boat trip ends at the port of Petrohué. Your final bus ride skirts Lago Llanquihue, stopping at the Petrohué waterfalls, passing the town of Puerto Varas, and arriving, at last, at Puerto Montt. Guides on the Argentina side speak little English; if your Spanish is shaky, do this trip with a tour group. ✉ *In Argentina: Puerto Blest S.A., Mitre 219, Bariloche, Río Negro* ☎ *2944/426–228* 🌐 *www.cruceandino.com* ⏲ *Daily 8:30–3* ✉ *In Chile: Puerto Varas/Turistur, Salvador 72, Puerto Varas, Chile* ☎ *65/228–440.*

If you're pressed for time, return to Bariloche by paved road via Osorno, crossing at Cardenal Samoré (aka Paso Puyehue) to Villa La Angostura (125 km [78 miles] from the border to Bariloche on Ruta Nacional 231).

OTHER CROSSINGS

Paso Hua Hum is the only crossing open year-round. It may be the shortest route—only 47 km (29 miles) from San Martín de los Andes on Ruta Provincial 48—as the condor flies, but it's the longest journey by road, after factoring in the 1½-hour ferry ride across Lake Pirehueico on the Chilean side. There are three ferries daily, and buses leave regularly from San Martín de los Andes. You can also make this crossing by raft on the river Hua Hum.

Farther north, and accessible via Junín de los Andes, are two passes that require a longer excursion. Mamuil Malal (aka Paso Tromen) is 67 km (41½ miles) northwest of Junín de los Andes on Ruta Provincial 60. This dirt road crosses Lanín National Park and passes through a forest of ancient araucaria trees as it heads for the foot of Lanín Volcano. Just before the park office, a road leads to good picnic spots and campsites on Lago Tromen. If you continue on to Chile, you'll see the Villarrica and Quetupillán volcanoes to the south and Pucón to the north.

Paso Icalma is 132 km (82 miles) west of Zapala on Ruta Nacional 13. Villa Pehuenia, 10 km (6 miles) before the pass, is a small village on the shore of Lake Alluminé with modern accommodations and restaurants. Rafting, fishing, or horse, bike, and raft rentals might tempt you to stay awhile.

No fresh fruits, meats, dairy products, or vegetables are allowed across the border, so bring a power bar for long stretches without food. Lake crossings are not fun in driving rain and high waves. Snow may close some passes in winter. If driving, double-check with your rental agent that you have all the necessary paperwork. It's also good to have some Chilean pesos with you; it can be expensive to change them at the border.

—Eddy Ancinas

Whether it's sunbathing weather or ski season, the Lake District delivers.

reception area, bar, and an outdoor patio on the top floor; a fine dining room for hotel guests down one floor; and lakeview rooms on the three floors below. **Pros:** the maître d' makes every dinner seem like a party; dinner's included in the room rate. **Cons:** five rooms on the east side of the building, next to the disco, throb to the beat until late at night during holidays. ✉ *Juan Manuel de Rosas 625, Bariloche, Río Negro* ☎ *2944/433–888* 🌐 *www.hotelinacayal.com.ar* *67 rooms* *In-room: Wi-Fi. In-hotel: bar, pool, spa, parking* *Some meals* ✣ *A1.*

$$$$ Fodor's Choice ★ **El Casco Art Hotel.** Intriguing sculptures perched on marble stands, wooden ledges, or freestanding in the garden are part of a collection of over 200 artworks displayed throughout the hotel, where all public spaces—halls, wine bar, gourmet restaurant—even the downstairs gym, indoor-out swimming pool, and large Jacuzzi—face the lake, where the hotel's private launch is docked at the pier. **Pros:** art everywhere; activities galore; self-contained luxury; close to activities. **Cons:** perhaps too much extravagance for some. ✉ *Av. Bustillo, Km 11.5, Bariloche, Río Negro* ☎ *2944/463–131* 🌐 *www.hotelelcasco.com* *57 suites* *In-hotel: restaurant, bar, pool, gym* *All meals* ✣ *C6.*

$$$ **Hosteria El Retorno.** Just 20 minutes from Bariloche, on the west shore of lovely Lago Gutiérrez, this venerable old lodge has been spruced up inside and out, where a profusion of flowers fills its vast lawns and woods—perhaps that's why guests tend to stay on the premises, enjoying the many activities as well as the quiet and solitude at this country lodge. **Pros:** lots of room for kids to play; stargazing is tough to beat. **Cons:** no nightlife, outside of town. ✉ *Western end of RP82 on Lago Gutiérrez, near Villa Arelauken, Bariloche, Río Negro* ☎ *2944/467–333* 🌐 *www.hosteriaelretorno* *24 rooms, 5 apartments* *In-hotel:*

restaurant, bar, golf course, tennis court, water sports, parking, some pets allowed ⏲ *Closed May* 🍽 *Breakfast* ✥ *B5.*

$$ **Hosteria Las Marianas.** A perfectly proportioned Tyrolean villa, this B&B on a sunny hillside in Barrio Belgrano, the nicest neighborhood in town, is only four blocks from the city center, but it's in a world of its own on a quiet street surrounded by well-tended gardens. **Pros:** away from the crowds. **Cons:** uphill haul from city center. ✉ *24 de Septiembre 218, Bariloche, Río Negro* ☎📠 *2944/439–876* 🌐 *www.hosterialasmarianas.com.ar* ⇨ *16 rooms* 🍽 *Breakfast* ✥ *A5.*

$$ **Hotel Cristal.** A basic businesslike downtown hotel, this recycled old standby in the center of Bariloche has been greatly improved with modern furnishings and better facilities, as tour groups and independent travelers discover the flavor of being on the street with all the chocolate shops. **Pros:** central downtown location; good value. **Cons:** small bathrooms; desultory reception; popular with tour groups. ✉ *Mitre 355, Bariloche, Río Negro* ☎📠 *2944/422–442* 🌐 *www.hotel-cristal.com.ar* ⇨ *50 rooms* ☝ *In-hotel: restaurant, bar* 🍽 *Breakfast* ✥ *D2.*

$$ **Hotel Edelweiss.** Fresh flowers from the owner's nursery are a tradition throughout this medium-size hotel, which is within walking distance of everything in town; rooms on the upper floors have lake views from bay windows. **Pros:** great location; helpful staff. **Cons:** bar has no windows; so-so street-side restaurant. ✉ *Av. San Martín 202, Bariloche, Río Negro* ☎ *2944/445–500* 🌐 *www.edelweiss.com.ar* ⇨ *94 rooms, 6 suites* ☝ *In-room: safe. In-hotel: restaurant, bar, pool, gym, spa, parking* 🍽 *Breakfast* ✥ *B2.*

$$ **Hotel Nahuel Huapi.** This slick city hotel on a busy downtown street in Bariloche has a spacious lobby with a wine bar in one corner and a sit-around fireplace in another; textured beige wallpaper in the large bedrooms show off the deep reds and browns of the woven bedspreads and upholstered chairs. **Pros:** central location; good accessibility for people with disabilities. **Cons:** rooms overlooking street might be noisy. ✉ *Moreno 252, Bariloche, Río Negro* ☎📠 *2944/433–635* 🌐 *www.hotelnahuelhuapi.com.ar* ⇨ *80 rooms* ☝ *In-room: Wi-Fi. In-hotel: restaurant, bar, parking* 🍽 *Breakfast* ✥ *D2.*

$$$ **Hotel Tronadór.** Named for the mountain that towers above the wild landscape of lakes and forests only 25 km (15½ miles) up the road, this stone and log lodge overlooking Lago Mascardi and surrounded by a profusion of flowers has been owned and cared for by the Vereertbrugghen family since 1929. **Pros:** practically in the lap of the region's highest mountain glacier; airport transfers available for a fee; organic garden; game and video room. **Cons:** the road here is one-way heading towards the hotel 10:30 am–2 pm, one-way heading away from 4 pm–7:30 pm, and two-way from 7:30 pm–10:30 am only. Open only from mid-November to mid-April. ✉ *RN40 west from Bariloche 66 km, past Villa Masacardi, turn right on dirt road to west end of Lago Mascardi, Bariloche, Río Negro* ☎ *2944/490–550* 🌐 *www.hoteltronador.com* ⇨ *30 rooms, 7 apartments* ☝ *In-hotel: restaurant, bar, beach, parking* ⏲ *Closed mid-Apr.–mid-Nov.* 🍽 *All meals* ✥ *B6.*

$$$$ **Llao Llao Hotel & Resort.** This masterpiece by architect Alejandro Bustillo sits on a grassy knoll surrounded by three lakes with a backdrop

Evening shoppers on Avenida Bartolomé Mitre, Bariloche

of rock cliffs and snow-covered mountains; rooms in the historic main building are tastefully appointed, and a recent addition to the hotel tastefully incorporates a more modern aesthetic. **Pros:** gorgeous setting; helpful staff; lots of activities; variety of rooms. **Cons:** the public is allowed to visit this landmark hotel only on a guided tour on Wednesday at 3 pm. ✉ *Av. Ezequiel Bustillo, 25 km (15½ miles) west of Bariloche, Bariloche, Río Negro* ☎ *2944/448–530* 🌐 *www.llaollao.com* *153 rooms, 12 suites, 1 cabin* *In-room: safe. In-hotel: restaurant, bar, golf course, pool, gym, spa, water sports, children's programs* *Breakfast* ✣ *B6.*

$$$ **Peuma Hue.** Inside, it's pine beams overhead, kilim rugs on wood floors, a lace table cloth on the dining table, guests gathered around the stone fireplace—a sense of rustic luxury prevails; outside, Lago Gutiérrez shimmers through the trees across the lawn. **Pros:** lovely grounds; massage, yoga, and wine tastings are just the tip of the activities iceberg. **Cons:** remote location. ✉ *Ruta 40, Km 2014, Enter dirt road, 1½ miles to Lago Gutiérrez, Bariloche, Bariloche, Río Negro* ☎ *2944/501–030* 🌐 *www.peuma-hue.com* *10 rooms* *In-room: safe, Wi-Fi. In-hotel: restaurant, bar, beach, parking* *Closed June* *All meals* ✣ *B5.*

$$ **Villa Huinid.** This peaceful complex consists of a grand hotel with a lake-view pool and spa and older two-story log-and-stucco cottages (one-, two-, or three-bedroom) on the lawns below. **Pros:** like renting a cabin with all the amenities of a hotel; view of the lake. **Cons:** outdoor hike to breakfast in hotel. ✉ *Av. Bustillo, Km 2.6, Bariloche, Río Negro* ☎ *2944/523–523* 🌐 *www.villahuinid.com.ar* *46 rooms, 17 cabins* *In-room: kitchen. In-hotel: restaurant, bar, pool, gym* ✣ *A1.*

SHOPPING

Along Bariloche's main streets, Calles Mitre and Moreno, and the cross streets from Quaglia to Rolando, you can find shops selling sports equipment, leather goods, hand-knit sweaters, and gourmet food like homemade jams, dried meats, and chocolate.

Ahumadero Familia Weiss. Come here to buy delicious pâtés, cheeses, smoked fish, and wild game. ✉ *Mitre 131, Bariloche, Río Negro* ☎ *2944/435–874* 🌐 *www.ahumaderoweiss.com* ✉ *Vice Alte. and Palacios, Bariloche, Río Negro* ☎ *2944/421–988.*

Talabarterís sell items for the discerning equestrian or modern gaucho.

El Establo. At El Establo, look for shoes, handbags, belts, wallets, and wall coverings with distinctive black-and-white Mapuche designs. ✉ *Mitre 22, Bariloche, Río Negro* ☎ *2944/426–208.*

SPORTS AND THE OUTDOORS

HORSEBACK RIDING

Argentine horses are sturdy and well trained, much like American quarter horses. *Tábanas* (horseflies) attack humans and animals in summer months, so wear long sleeves on *cabalgatas* (horseback outings).

Carol Jones. The granddaughter of an early pioneering family, Carol Jones's ranch north of town does day rides and overnights from the Patagonian steppes into the mountains. ✉ *Modesta Victoria 5600, Bariloche, Río Negro* ☎ *2944/426–508* 🌐 *www.caroljones.com.ar.*

El Manso. This outfitter combines riding and rafting over the border to Chile. ✉ *Bariloche, Río Negro* ☎ *2944/441–378* 🌐 *www.bastiondelmanso.com.*

Tom Wesley. Located at the Club Hípico Bariloche, Tom Wesley offers rides lasting from one hour to several days. ✉ *Av. Bustillo, Km 15.5, Bariloche, Río Negro* ☎📠 *2944/448–193* 🌐 *www.cabalgatastomwesley.com.*

SKIING

Cerro Catedral (*Mount Cathedral*). Cerro Catedral, named for its Gothic-looking spires, is the largest and oldest ski area in South America, with 38 lifts, 4,500 acres of mostly intermediate terrain, and a comfortable altitude of 6,725 feet. The runs are long, varied, and scenic. One side of the mountain has a vertical drop of 3,000 feet, mostly in the fall line. Near the top of the highest chairlift at 7,385 feet is Refugio Lynch, a small restaurant on the edge of an abyss with a stupendous 360-degree view of Nahuel Huapi Lake. To the southwest, Monte Tronadór, a 12,000-foot extinct volcano, straddles the border with Chile, towering above lesser peaks that surround the lake. August and September are the best months to ski. A terrain park, Nordic skiing in a forest of lenga trees, and online ticket purchasing are the most recent additions. Avoid the first three weeks of July (school vacation).

Villa Catedral, at the base of the mountain, has numerous ski retail and rental shops, information and ticket sales, ski-school offices, restaurants, and even a disco. Frequent buses transport skiers from Bariloche to the ski area. For information and trail maps, contact **La Secretaría de Turismo de Río Negro** (*12 de Octubre 605* ☎ *2944/429–896*). **Club Andino Bariloche** (*20 de Febrero 30* ☎ *2944/422–266*) also has information and trail maps. ✉ *Bariloche, Río Negro* ✣ *46 km (28½ miles) west of town on Av. Bustillo (R237); turn left at Km 8.5 just past Playa Bonita* ☎ *2944/409–000* 🌐 *www.catedralaltapatagonia.com.*

IN AND AROUND SAN MARTÍN DE LOS ANDES

260 km (161 miles) north of Bariloche on Ruta 237, Ruta 40, and Ruta 234 via Junín de los Andes (a 4-hr drive); 158 km (98 miles) north of Bariloche on Ruta 237 and Ruta 63 over the Córdoba Pass (69 km [42 miles] is paved); 90 km (56 miles) northeast of Villa La Angostura on Ruta 234 (Seven Lakes Rd., partly unpaved and closed for much of winter).

In the southeastern corner of Parque Nacional Lanín (Lanín National Park), San Martín de los Andes is the largest town within the park, with roads leading south to Bariloche on the Seven Lakes Route, north on a good paved road to Junín de los Andes (41 km [29 miles]), and west on a dirt road to the Hua Hum crossing into Chile (47 km).

6

Although Junín doesn't have the tourist infrastructure that San Martín has, and it's on the flat Patagonian steppe with no lake in sight, dirt roads leading west take you up the Chimehuin River to Lakes Curruhue, Huechulaufquen, and Paimún—all well known to sports fishermen. As you drive west, the perfect white cone of Lanín Volcano towers in the distance at 12,474 feet. Northwest of Junín, Ruta Provincial 60 takes you north of Lanín Volcano to Paso Tromen (67 km [41½ miles]).

SAN MARTÍN DE LOS ANDES

Surrounded by lakes, dense forests, and mountains, San Martín de los Andes lies in a natural basin at the foot of Lago Lácar. It's a small, easygoing town, much like Bariloche was many decades ago, with small hotels and houses reflecting the distinctive Andean alpine architecture of Bustillo. Wide, flat streets lined with rosebushes run from the town pier on the eastern shore of Lago Lácar to the main square, Plaza San Martín, where two parallel streets—San Martín and General Villegas—teem with block after block of ski and fishing shops, chocolatiers, trinket shops, clothing boutiques, and cafés.

The Mapuche lived in the area long before immigrants of Chilean, French, Dutch, and Italian descent founded the town in 1898. Because all of the water from this area runs into the Pacific, the territory was disputed by Chile, which claimed it as its own until 1902, when it was legally declared Argentine.

After Lanín National Park was established in 1937 and the ski area at Chapelco developed in the 1970s, tourism replaced forestry as the main source of income. Today San Martín is the major tourist center in Neuquén Province—the midpoint in the Seven Lakes Route, and the gateway for exploring the Parque Nacional Lanín.

Restaurants ▼
Fondue Betty **3**
Kú **2**
La Tasca **1**

Hotels ▼
Hostería Anay ... **3**
Hotel la Cheminée **1**
Patagonia Plaza Hotel **2**

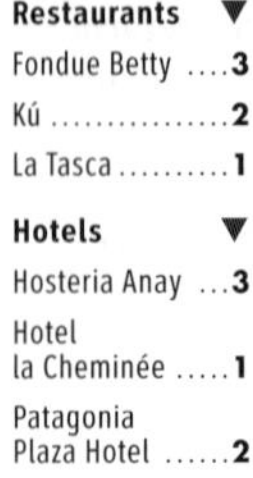

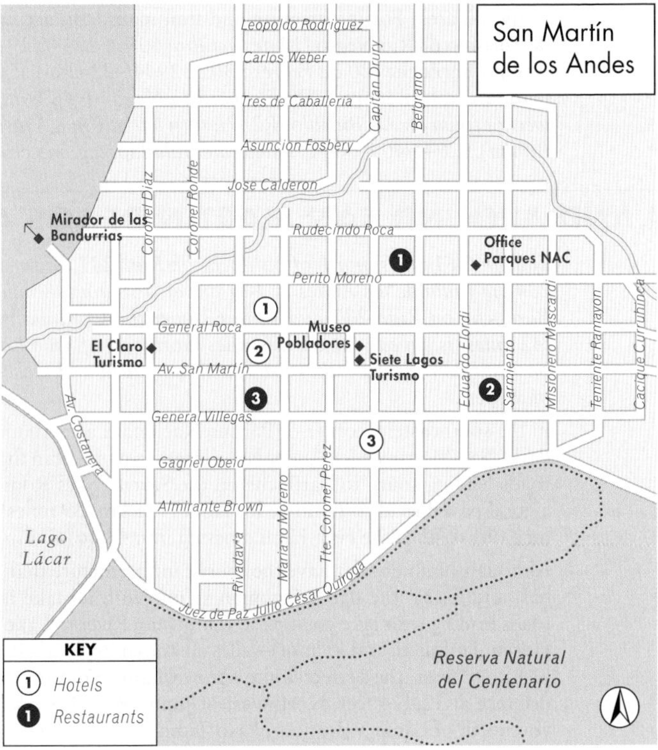

GETTING HERE AND AROUND

Aerolíneas Argentinas and LADE have flights from Buenos Aires, but most people arrive from Bariloche via Junín de los Andes or along the Seven Lakes Route. Buses from Bariloche are frequent and dependable. San Martín is a pleasant walking town, as it's flat. To access nearby beaches, hiking trails, or the ski area in winter, you need to rent a car, join a tour, or be an energetic cyclist. Taxis are inexpensive, and remises can be arranged through your hotel. There are no gas stations on the Seven Lakes Route.

Bus Contacts San Martín de los Andes Bus Terminal ✉ *Villegas 251, San Martín de los Andes, Neuquén* ☎ *2972/427–044.*

ESSENTIALS

Currency Exchange Banco Macro Bansud ✉ *Av. San Martín 836, San Martín de los Andes, Neuquén* ☎ *2972/423–962.* **Banco de la Nación Argentina** ✉ *Av. San Martín 687, San Martín de los Andes, Neuquén* ☎ *2972/427–292.*

Medical Assistance Farmacia del Centro ✉ *San Martín 896, at Belgrano, San Martín de los Andes, Neuquén* ☎ *2972/428–999.* **Hospital Ramón Carillo** ✉ *Av. Moreno 601, San Martín de los Andes, Neuquén* ☎ *2944/426–100.*

Post Office San Martín de los Andes ✉ *At the Civic Center, General Roca at Pérez, San Martín de los Andes, Neuquén.*

Remis (Car and Driver) **Del Oscar** ✉ *Av. San Martín 1254, San Martín de los Andes, Neuquén* ☎ *2972/428–774.*

Visitor and Tour Info Dirección Municipal de Turismo. Open daily 8 am–9 pm ✉ *J.M. Rosas 790, at Av. San Martín, San Martín de los Andes, Neuquén* ☎ *2972/427–347* 🌐 *www.sanmartindelosandes.gov.ar.*

EXPLORING

Mirador de las Bandurrias (*Bandurrias Overlook*). From town you can walk, mountain bike, or drive to the Mirador de las Bandurrias. It's a half-day hike round-trip (5 km [3 miles]) up a steep hill through a dense forest of cypress and oak. The reward is a view of town and the lake and a visit to a Mapuche village (**Paraje Trompul**) of about 40 families, most of whom work in town. You can visit the village for a few pesos, buy refreshments in the *quincho* (café), and see weavings and wood carvings (also for sale). If you're walking, take Avenida San Martín to the lake, turn right, cross the bridge behind the waterworks plant over Puahullo Creek, and then head uphill on a path around the mountain. By car, leave town on Ruta Provincial 48 and drive about 4 km (2½ miles) to a turnoff (no sign) on your left. Take the turn and continue 3 km (2 miles) to the Curruhuinca Community, where you pay a fee to arrive at the lookout (about two hours round-trip). ✉ *San Martín de los Andes, Neuquén.*

6

Museo Pobladores (*Pioneer Museum*). The Museo Pobladores is a tiny building next to the tourist office that was the original city council lodge. It is mainly dedicated to Mapuche ceramics and weavings, and a collection of 13,000-year-old tools and fossils gives an idea of ancient life in the region. Admission is free. ✉ *J.M. de Rosas 700, San Martín de los Andes, Neuquén* ☎ *2972/428–676* ⏲ *Mon., Wed.–Sat. 2–6. Closed Tues., Sun.*

WHERE TO EAT

$$ ARGENTINE ✕ **Fondue Betty.** It wouldn't be a ski town without a fondue restaurant. The cheese fondue is smooth and rich, while the meat fondue comes with cubes of Argentine beef in assorted cuts and up to 12 condiments. Vegetable fondues are a bit limp. The wine list is fantastic. The two rooms are cozy and intimate, equally well suited to children and honeymooners; and there's warm, familiar service from a genial older couple. ✉ *Villegas 586, San Martín de los Andes, Neuquén* ☎ *2972/422–522* 💳 *No credit cards.*

$$$ ARGENTINE ★ ✕ **Kú.** Dark-wood tables and booths, a friendly staff, and a chalkboard—good building blocks for a restaurant. The smoked-meat plate with venison, boar, trout, salmon, and cheese is a good starter. Patagonian lamb *al asador* (on the open fire) and a good assortment of parrilla classics are paired with a fine wine list. ✉ *Av. San Martín 1053, San Martín de los Andes, Neuquén* ☎ *2972/427–039* ✍ *Reservations essential.*

$$$ ARGENTINE ✕ **La Tasca.** This is one of the traditional top-end choices in town for locals and tourists. With tables scattered about the black-stone floor, and wine barrels, shelves, and every other imaginable surface stacked with pickled vegetables, smoked meats, cheese rounds, dried mushrooms and herbs, olive oils in cans and bottles, and wine bottles, you

might think you're in a Patagonian deli. Diners should try local wild game dishes; especially good is the "La Tasca" appetizer platter of smoked salmon, venison, boar, and trout pâté. ✉ *Moreno 886, San Martín de los Andes, Neuquén* ☎ *2972/428–663* *Reservations essential.*

WHERE TO STAY

For expanded hotel reviews, visit Fodors.com.

$$ **Hosteria Anay.** The well-kept grounds and pleasant facade of this small guesthouse belie the unremarkable, somewhat tired rooms inside. **Pros:** quiet location. **Cons:** small, tired rooms. ✉ *Cap. Drury 841, San Martín de los Andes, Neuquén* ☎ *2972/427–514* 🌐 *www.interpatagonia.com/anay* *15 rooms* *In-hotel: parking* *No credit cards* *Breakfast.*

$$$$ ★ **Hotel la Cheminée.** Two blocks from the main street is this comfortable inn with finely carved wooden staircases, a small art gallery, and warm, familiar service; all rooms have been renovated and turned into suites. **Pros:** great breakfast; convenient location; attentive service. **Cons:** on a somewhat busy street. ✉ *M. Moreno at General Roca, San Martín de los Andes, Neuquén* ☎ *2972/427–617* *reservas@lachemineehotel.com* 🌐 *www.lachemineehotel.com* *11 suites, 1 cottage* *In-room: Wi-Fi. In-hotel: bar, pool, spa, parking* *Breakfast.*

$$$$ **Patagonia Plaza Hotel.** Good-bye genteel rusticity, hello modern downtown hotel with all the amenities. **Pros:** central location; big rooms with modern bathrooms. **Cons:** comparatively expensive; atmosphere deficient in restaurant. ✉ *Av. San Martín at Rivadavia, San Martín de los Andes, Neuquén* ☎ *2972/422–280* 🌐 *www.hotelpatagoniaplaza.com.ar* *90 rooms* *In-hotel: restaurant, bar, pool, parking* *Breakfast.*

SPORTS AND THE OUTDOORS

The tour agencies listed below can arrange rafting trips on the Hua Hum or Aluminé rivers, guided mountain-biking, horseback-riding, and fishing tours, visits to Mapuche communities, and excursions to lakes near and far in both Lanín and Nahuel Huapi national parks. An all-day excursion to **Lago Huechulafquen** (✉ *General Roca 826* ☎ *2972/427–877*) with an extension to the hot-springs spa at **Epulaufquen** is also on offer. Fernando Aguirre, a lifelong resident of the area, offers two- to four-day camping trips with combinations of hiking, riding, rafting, biking, and kayaking.

El Refugio. El Refugio is a full service tour company and travel agency. Active travelers can join them for rafting, trekking, mountain biking, fly-fishing, and skiing excursions. Overland road tours are available for the less intrepid. El Refugio can also book airline tickets and accommodations. ✉ *Villegas 698, San Martín de los Andes, Neuquén* ☎ *2972/425–140* 🌐 *www.elrefugioturismo.com.ar.*

BEACHES

Playa Catrite. Four km (2½ miles) from San Martín on Ruta 234, on the south side of Lago Lácar, this sandy beach has a campground, a store with picnic supplies, and a café. ✉ *San Martín de los Andes, Neuquén.*

Playa Quila Quina. 18 km (11 miles) from San Martín, Playa Quila Quina is reached by turning off Ruta 234 2 km (1 mile) before the road to Catrite and then getting on Ruta 108. ✉ *San Martín de los Andes, Neuquén.*

BOATING

Lacar Nonthue. You can rent small boats, canoes, and kayaks at the pier from Lacar Nonthue. You can also rent a bicycle and take an all-day excursion to the other side of Lake Lácar, where there is a nice beach and woods to explore. Another option is the boat tour to Hua Hum at the western end of the lake, where the river of the same name runs to the Chilean border. ⇨ *White-Water Rafting, below.* ✉ *Av. Costanera, San Martín de los Andes, Neuquén* ☎ *2972/427–380.*

FISHING

During the fishing season (November 15–April 15, extended to the end of May in certain areas) local guides take you to their favorite spots on Lakes Lácar, Lolog, Villarino, and Falkner and on the Caleufu, Quiquihue, Malleo, and Hermoso rivers, or farther afield to the Chimehuín River and Lakes Huechulafquen and Paimún.

Parque Nacional Intendencia. Permits are available at the Parque Nacional Intendencia or any licensed fishing stores along Avenida San Martín. Most stores and tour operators can suggest guides. ✉ *Emilio Frey 749, Bariloche, Río Negro* ☎ *2972/427–233.*

HORSEBACK RIDING (CABALGATAS)

Hour-, day-, and week-long organized and guided rides, often with an *asado* (barbecue) included, can be arranged through local tour offices.

Cabalgatas Abuelo Enrique. These folks offer rides with a guide for two hours or all day, asado included. To get there, take Avenida Dr. Koessler (Ruta 234) toward Zapala, turn left at the polo field, and head toward Lago Lolog, then take a right past the military barracks to Callejón Ginsgins. ✉ *Callejón Ginsgins, Campo 9, San Martín de los Andes, Neuquén* ☎ *2972/426–465.*

MOUNTAIN BIKING

San Martín itself is flat, but from there everything goes up. Dirt and paved roads and trails lead through forests to lakes and waterfalls.

HG Rodados. In town, you can rent bikes at HG Rodados. ✉ *Av. San Martín 1061, San Martín de los Andes, Neuquén* ☎ *2972/427–345.*

SKIING

Cerro Chapelco (Chapelco Ski Area). The ski area and summer resort of Cerro Chapelco is 23 km (14 miles) from town—18 km paved and 5 km of dirt road. Ideal for families and beginner-to-intermediate skiers, the area has modern facilities and lifts, including a high-speed *telecabina* (gondola) from the base. On a clear day almost all the runs are visible from the top (6,534 feet), and Lanín Volcano dominates the horizon. Lift tickets run from 170 pesos per day in low season to 285 pesos in high season. Equipment rental facilities are available at the base camp (95 pesos–150 pesos per day for skis, boots, and poles). On some days cars need chains to get up to the mountain, so call and check the latest conditions before driving up. Taxis can also take you up or down for about 45 pesos each way. The summer Adventure Center has mountain biking for experts and classes for beginners, horseback rides, hiking, archery, a swimming pool, an alpine slide, and children's activities. ✉ *Information Office:, San Martín at Elordi, San Martín de los Andes, Neuquén* ☎📠 *2972/427–845* 🌐 *www.cerrochapelco.com.*

WORD OF MOUTH

"Visitors can marvel at the magnificent views of the Andes and Nahuel Huapi Lake from the top of Campanario Hill, accessed by a breathtaking cable car ride." —hdcaplan, Fodors.com member

WHITE-WATER RAFTING

El Claro Turismo. El Claro Turismo is a good rafting outfit offering short and long trips in the area. ✉ *Col. Diaz 751, San Martín de los Andes, Neuquén* ☎📠 *2972/428–876, 2972/425–876* ✉ *consultas@elclaroturismo.com.ar* 🌐 *www.elclaroturismo.com.ar.*

Siete Lagos Turismo. An all-day rafting trip that crosses into Chile on either Río Aluminé or Río Hua Hum can be arranged by Siete Lagos Turismo. ✉ *Villegas 313, San Martín de los Andes, Neuquén* ☎📠 *2972/427–877* ✉ *sietelagostmo@smandes.com.ar* 🌐 *www.sietelagosturismo.com.ar.*

PARQUE NACIONAL LANÍN

Parque Nacional Lanín. The dramatically beautiful Parque Nacional Lanín has 35 mountain lakes, countless rivers, ancient forests, and the Lanín Volcano. Tucked into the folds of the Andes along the Chilean border, it stretches 150 km (93 miles) north–south, covering 3,920 square km (1,508 square miles), and is the third-largest national park in Argentina. The area is home to the Mapuche, and you can learn about their history and buy their handicrafts in one of the 50 communities throughout the park. ✉ *Neuquén* 🌐 *www.parquenacionallanin.gov.ar/.*

GETTING HERE AND AROUND

Three towns have access to the park. The northernmost section is reached from the town of Aluminé (145 km [90 miles] west of Zapala on Ruta Provincial 46), a typical Andean town with no paved streets but an abundance of nearby lakes (Aluminé, Quillén, and Mohquehue being the most accessible). The resort town of Pehuenia is a good base for exploring. Junín de los Andes, in the middle section, is at the end of the paved roads from either San Martín or Bariloche. San Martín, the major town in the park, is in the southern portion. All three of these towns have roads leading to the border with Chile (⇨ *See* Chilean Lakes *Crossing box).*

Intendencia de Parques Nacionales (*National Park Office*). For information on the park, go to the Intendencia de Parques Nacionales in San Martín. They have maps and information on all the parks and trails in the region, as well as fishing permits and information on big-game hunting. ✉ *E. Frey 749, Neuquén* ☎ *2972/427–233* 🕘 *Weekdays 8–1:30.*

EXPLORING

Araucaria Araucana. Found only in this part of the Andes, the ancient Araucaria Araucana tree grows to 100 feet, and has long spiny branches. Cones the size of bowling balls full of pinon nuts provided nourishment to the Mapuche, who call these trees *pehuenes.* The northern portion of the park near Lago Huechulaufquen and Aluminé is one of the best places to view these peculiar giants. ✉ *Neuquén.*

Volcán Lanín. Volcán Lanín rises 3,773 meters (12,378 feet) in solitary snow-clad splendor on the western horizon, towering over the entire park and visible from every direction. It sits on the border with Chile, with Lanín National Park on one side and Chile's Villarica National Park on the other. The closest Argentine access is from Junín, but the northern route to Paso Tromen also offers endless photo ops through the tangled branches of the araucaria trees. You can climb Lanín in three to four days round-trip with a guide—or fly over it with **Aero Club de Los Andes** (*Chapelco in San Martín de los Andes* ☎ *2972/426–254*). ✉ *Neuquén* 🌐 *www.parquenacionallanin.gov.ar/.*

SPORTS AND THE OUTDOORS

BOATING

You'll only find piers or marinas at designated resorts. At Puerto Canoa on Lake Huechulafquen a catamaran takes about 50 passengers on a three-hour excursion to Lake Epulafquen, where you can view huge deposits of lava covered with vegetation at the end of the lake. The culprit, a large volcano minus its cone, looms in the distance. The fishing lodge at Paimún Lake has a dock, and in Villa Pehuenia you can rent boats and kayaks. It's best to organize an excursion at the dock (arrive early) or through a tour operator.

FISHING

Professional fishing guides in San Martín de los Andes, Junín, and Aluminé have their favorite fishing spots, and they offer excursions for a day or a week. To contact a guide, go to 🌐 *www.neuquentur.gov.ar.* Fishing lodges lie concealed along the Chimihín River near Junín de los Andes and deeper into the lakes at Paimún. Smaller rivers such as the Malleo, Quillén, Meliquina, and Hua Hum are ideal for wading. In larger rivers like the Aluminé, Chimihuín, and Caleufu, guides provide rubber float boats.

HIKING

Besides climbing Lanín Volcano, trails throughout the park wind around lakes and streams, mostly at lower elevations. Signs are intermittent, so hiking with a guide is recommended. The best hikes are out of Lago Paimún to a waterfall, Lago Quillén near Aluminé, and Lácar near San Martín. For information, check out 🌐 *www.sendasybosques.com.ar.*

RAFTING

From San Martín you can run the Caleufu River from October through November, then move on to the Hua Hum in December through March. Both are Class II rivers. *Aluminé* in the Mapuche language means "clear," and this wide river in the northern section of the park provides a thrilling descent through dense vegetation and a deep canyon.

6

VILLA TRAFUL

60 km (37 miles) north of Villa La Angostura on Ruta 231 and Ruta 65; 39 km (23 miles) from Confluéncia on Ruta 65; 100 km (60 miles) northwest of Bariloche on Ruta 237 and Ruta 65.

If there were a prize for the most beautiful lake in the region, Lago Traful would win for its clarity, serenity, and wild surroundings. Small log houses peek through the cypress forest along the way to Villa Traful, a village of about 500 inhabitants. The town consists of log cabins, horse corrals, two fishing lodges, shops for picnic and fishing supplies, a school, a post office, and a park ranger's office. Well-maintained campgrounds border the lake, and ranches and private fishing lodges are hidden in the surrounding mountains. By day swimmers play on rocky beaches on the lake, kayaks cut the still blue water, and divers

Continued on page 338

FLY FISHING

by Jack Trout; updated by Jimmy Langman

Chile and Argentina are the final frontier of fly fishing. With so many unexplored rivers, lakes, and spring creeks—most of which are undammed and free flowing to the ocean—every type of fishing is available for all levels of experience. You'll find many species of fish, including rainbow trout, browns, sea-run browns, brooks, sea trout, and steelhead.

Above: Flyfishing in Torres del Paine National Park, Patagonia, Chile

The Southern Cone has endless—and endlessly evolving—rivers, streams, and lakes, which is why they're so good for fly fishing. These waterways formed millions of years ago, as volcanic eruptions and receding glaciers carved out the paths for riverbeds and lakes that feed into the Pacific or Atlantic Oceans. With more than 2,006 volcanoes in Chile alone (including South America's most active mountain, Volcano Llaima, outside of Temuco), the Lake Districts of both countries are still evolving, creating raw and pristine fishing grounds.

Why choose Chile or Argentina for your next fly fishing adventure? If you're only after huge fish, stick to California. What these two South American countries offer is a chance to combine fishing, culture, and food in a unique package during the northern hemisphere's off season. With the right guide, you just might find yourself two hours down a dirt road, fishing turquoise water in the shadow of a glacial peak, with not a soul in sight but the occasional gaucho or huaso. It's an experience you will find nowhere else.

WHAT TO EXPECT ON THE GROUND

Fishing, Chile

LOGISTICS

You'll probably fly into Bariloche, Argentina, or Puerto Montt, Chile. You won't need more than two weeks for a good trip, and hiring a guide can make a big difference in the quality of your experience. Since most rivers are un-dammed, you'll need the extra help managing your drift boat or locating foot access for wading that stream you've spotted around the bend.

If you're fishing in Chile, be aware that the February 2010 earthquake affected some of the region's guides and lodges; call ahead to prevent planning a trip around a river or lodge that might be temporarily unavailable.

GUIDES VS. LODGES

You can purchase your trip package (usually between US $2,900 and US $5,500) through either an independent guide or a specific lodge property. In both cases, packages usually last one week to 10 days, and include breakfast, lunch, and dinner. If you opt to purchase through a lodge, you have the benefit of property-specific guides who know every nook and cranny of stream surrounding the lodge. On the other hand, hiring an independent guide will give you more power to customize your trip and go farther afield.

TIMING

Contact your guide or lodge in October or November, during the southern hemisphere's spring; the upcoming season's peak fishing times depend on snow melt. Plan on traveling in February or March.

CHOOSING YOUR GUIDE

What type of fishing suits you best? Do you like to fish from a boat, or do you prefer wading the river as it rushes by? Ask guides these questions to find the best one for you.

WHAT TO ASK A GUIDE

- How early do you start in the morning?
- Do you mainly spin cast or fly fish?
- How long have you been in business?
- Do you always catch and release?
- Will I fish with you or another guide?
- Can I see pictures of your raft or drift boat?
- Do you supply the flies?
- Where do you get your flies?
- Can we fish a river twice if we like it?
- Which rivers and lakes do you float?
- Can we set an itinerary before I arrive?

WHAT TO BRING

5 to 7 Weight Rod: at least 9 foot (consider bringing 9½ foot for larger rivers, windy days, lakes, and sink-tip streamer fishing).

Floating Lines: for dry fly fishing and nymphing.

Streamers: for use while wading to or from the drift boat.

Lines: 15 to 20 foot sink-tip lines with a sink rate of 5.5 to 8 inches per second. It's good to carry two to four different sink rate lines.

Intermediate sink lines: for lakes and shallow depth fishing.

Line Cleaner: because low-ozone areas (the hole in the ozone is close to Antarctica) will eat up lines if you don't treat and clean the lines daily.

Hook sharpener: most guides don't have this very important item.

Small gifts: for the people you meet. Gift-giving can help you gain access to private rivers and lakes. Chocolates, such as Hershey Kisses, or some unique fly pattern, such as a dragon fly, always go over well.

Good map: Turistel, in Chile, puts out the best maps and internal information for that country (www.turistel.cl). Check Argentina Tourism (www.turismo.gov.ar) for help with that country.

Coffee: Chile has Nescafé instant coffee just about everywhere you go. So if you like a good cup of joe, bring a filter and your favorite coffee. That way all you need is a cup and hot water, and you're all set for your morning fishing.

FLIES

- Ask your guide where he or she gets flies. Those bought at a discount in countries outside of the United States are often sub-par, so get good guidance on this.
- If you can, get a list of flies for the time of year you're scheduled to arrive and buy them in the United States before you go. Pay particular attention to the size as well type of insect.
- The big fish and the quality catches are fooled by the flies that are tied by the guides themselves, because the guides know the hatches and the times they occur.
- Flies are divided up into similar categories in Chile and Argentina since South America has many of the same insects as we do in North America. Check and see what time each insect is hatching. Note their sizes and colors. **You'll need both dry and nymph versions of the following, in a variety of sizes, colors, and patterns:**

Royal Wulff

Bead Head Pheasant Tail

Mudder Minnow

Living Damsel

Bitch Creek

Adams

ARGENTINA FLY-FISHING GUIDES AND RIVERS

Region, Trip Length, Season & Lake or Stream	Guides, Lodges, and Hostel Names	Phone	Web
SAN MARTIN DE LOS ANDES 5 to 7 days December–February Río Filo Huaum/ Parque y Reserva Nacional Lanin Río Careufu Río Collon Cura Río Quiquihue	Alejandro Bucannan	2972/424-767	www.flyfishing-sma.com
	Jorge Trucco	2972/427-561 or 429-561	www.jorgetrucco.com
	Pablo Zaleski / San Huberto Lodge	2972/422-921	www.chimehuinsp.com
	Estancia Tipiliuke	2972/429-466	www.tipiliuke.com
	La Cheminee	2972/427-617	n/a
JUNIN DE LOS ANDES 5 to 7 days December–February Río Malleo Río Chimehuin Río Alumine	Alejandro Bucannan	2972/424-767 or 2944/1530-9469	www.flyfishing-sma.com
	Estancia Quemquemtreu	2972/424-410	www.quemquemtreu.com
	Redding Fly Shop Travel	800/669-3474 (in US)	www.flyfishingtravel.com
BARILOCHE 4 to 6 days December–February Río Limay Río Manso Río Traful Lago Fonk Parque y Reserva Nacional Nahuel Huapi	Martin Rebora / Mountain Cabins	2944/525-314	www.patagoniasinfronteras.com
	Río Manso Lodge	2944/490-546	www.Ríomansolodge.com
	Estancia Peuma Hue	2944/15-501-030	www.peuma-hue.com
	Estancia Arroyo Verde	5411/4801-7448	www.estanciaarroyoverde.com.ar
ESQUEL 5 to 7 days December–February Río Rivadavia Arroyo Pescado Río Carrileufu Río Pico – Lago Senquer Parque Argentino Los Alerces	Esquel Outfitters	2945/15-695-164 or 406/581-1760 (in US)	www.esqueloutfitters.com
	Guided Connections	307/734-2448 (in US)	www.guidedconnections.com
	Patagonia River Guides	2945/457-020 (in Argentina) or 208/520-3034 (in US)	www.patagoniariverguides.com

NOT NATIVE

Patagonian brown trout caught on a surface fly

Trout, salmon, and other common species aren't indigenous to South America. These fish were introduced during the late 19th century, mostly as a result of demand from European settlers. Germans, Scots, and others needed trout-filled rivers to survive, so they stocked the New World streams in the image of those in the Old World. For more information, consult *Fly Fishing in Chilean Patagonia* by Gonzalo Cortes and Nicolas Piwonka or *Fly Fishing the Best Rivers of Patagonia Argentina* by Francisco Bedeschi.

CHILE FLY-FISHING GUIDES AND RIVERS

Region, Trip length, Season & Lake or Stream	Guides, Lodges, and Hostel Names	Phone	Web
PALENA AREA 5 to 7 days December–April Río Palena Río Rosselott Río Yelcho Río Futaleufu Lago Yelcho Parque y Reserva Nacional Palena Parque y Reserva Nacional Corcovado	Jack Trout	530/926-4540 (in US) 65/511-673 (in Chile)	www.jacktrout.com
	Chucao Lodge	2/201-8571	www.chucaolodge.com
	Yelcho Lodge	65/576-005	www.yelcho.cl
	Tres Piedras / Francisco Castano	65/330-157 or 9/7618-7526	www.trespiedras.cl
	Martin Pescador Lodge	207/350-8178 (in US)	martinpescadorfishing.com
PUERTO VARAS AREA 4 to 6 days December–March Río Petrohue Río Puelo Río Maullin Parque y Reserva Saltos de Petrohue	Jack Trout	530/926-4540 (in US) 65/511-673 (in Chile)	www.jacktrout.com
	Tres Piedras / Francisco Castano	65/330-157 or 9/7618-7526	www.trespiedras.cl
	Fundo Santa Ines	9/9430-1030 or 9/9235-5648	www.fundosantaines.cl
	Hotel Licarayen Puerto Varas	65/232-305	www.hotelicarayen.cl
	Hotel Puerto Pilar	65/335-378	www.hotelpuertopilar.cl
COYHAIQUE AREA 4 to 7 days December–April Río Simpson Río Nirehuoa Río Paloma Río Azul Río Manihuales Lago Pollux Parque y Reserva Nacional Simpson Parque y Reserva Nacional Cerro Castillo	La Pasarela Lodge & Cabins	9/981-87390	www.lapasarela.cl
	Heart of Patagonia Lodge		www.patagonia-fly-fishing.com
	Rex Bryngelson	67/236-402	www.chilepatagonia.com
	Alex Príor	98/920-9132	www.flyfishingcoyhaique.com
	El Saltamontes Lodge	67/232-779 or 67/211-111	www.flyfishingcoyhaique.com
	Troy Cowles	99/992-3199	www.patagoniananglers.com
RÍO BAKER & COCHRANE AREAS 4 to 6 days Janurary–April Río Baker Río Cochrane Parque Reserva Nacional Cerro Castillo	David Frederick	406/842-7158 (in US) 98/138-3530 (in Chile)	www.southernlatitudes.com
	Alex Príor	98/920-9132	www.flyfishingcoyhaique.com
	Green Baker Lodge – Río Baker	2/196-0409	www.greenlodgebaker.com
LAKES DISTRICT: PUCON & VILLARRICA 2 to 4 days Nov–Dec., then Mar.–May Río Trancura, Parque Villarrica Lago Quillen, Parque Nacional Lanin Río Quillen, Parque Nacional Lanin	Marío's Fishing Zone	99/760-7280	www.flyfishingpucon.com
	Off Limits	99/492-841	www.offlimits..cl

go under to explore the mysteries of a submerged forest. Night brings silence, stars, and the glow of lakeside campfires. ⚠ **Note that the Puyehue volcano, just across the Chilean border from Villa La Angostura (60 km south of Villa Traful), erupted in June 2011, sending ash several kilometers into the air and prevailing winds carried the plume eastward. Check ahead regarding closures and conditions.**

ESSENTIALS

Visitor Info Oficina Municipal de Turismo ✉ *Across from municipal pier, Ruta Provincial 65, Villa Traful, Neuquén* ☎ *2944/479–099* 🌐 *www.villatraful.gov.ar.*

WHERE TO STAY

For expanded hotel reviews, visit Fodors.com.

$$ **Marinas Puerto Traful.** Across the road from the lake is this bright-blue lodge with wooden decks and views of the water; inside, the refurbished rooms have quiet beige carpeting, white walls and linens, and a bright-orange Mapuche blanket folded across the bed for a splash of color. **Pros:** lake views. **Cons:** closed in winter. ✉ *R65, Villa Traful, Neuquén* ☎ *2944/479–117* 🌐 *www.marinaspuertotraful.com.ar* *15 rooms, 2 suites* *Closed May–Oct.*

SPORTS AND THE OUTDOORS

HIKING

Arroyo Blanco and Arroyo Coa Có. Drive, walk, or pedal about 3 km (2 miles) up from the village to the trailhead at Pampa de los Alamos, a clearing where the trail to Arroyo Blanco descends into a forest of 1,000-year-old *coihué* trees with their ghostly naked trunks, gigantic *lenga* (deciduous beech), and *ñires* that grow only at high altitudes. The trail leads to a wooden walkway along a steep cliff—the only way one could possibly view the waterfall tumbling 66 feet into a dark chasm. Follow the wooden trail along the cliff for increasingly amazing glimpses of this wild gorge, then return up the same route. Arroyo Coa Có is in the opposite direction, with a view of both the waterfall and Lago Traful. ✉ *Villa Traful, Neuquén.*

Casacada Co Lemú. Casacada Co Lemú thunders with a deafening roar down 20 meters at the end of an arduous trail (19 km [12 miles] round-trip). Drive 8 km (5 miles) west toward the Seven Lakes Route to the bridge over Arroyo Cataratas. Before you cross the stream, on your left, the trail climbs slowly at first, then straight up 1,500 meters to the falls. ✉ *Villa Traful, Neuquén.*

Cerro Negro. A strenuous hike (seven hours) from the village to Cerro Negro climbs up through forests of cypress, coihués, lenga, and ñires, passing strange rock formations, then it reaches the summit at 6,000 feet, with a splendid view of Lago Traful and across the Andes all the way to Lanín. ✉ *Villa Traful, Neuquén.*

Laguna Las Mellizas y Pinturas Rupestres (*The Twins Lagoon and Cave paintings*). A 15-minute boat trip across the lake from the wharf takes you to a sandy beach on the northern shore. A two-hour walk down a trail into a steep gully leads to the pools. Nearby caves with 600-year-old Tehuelche cave paintings are worth exploring. The area is protected and registration with national park officials is required. ✉ *Villa Traful, Neuquén.*

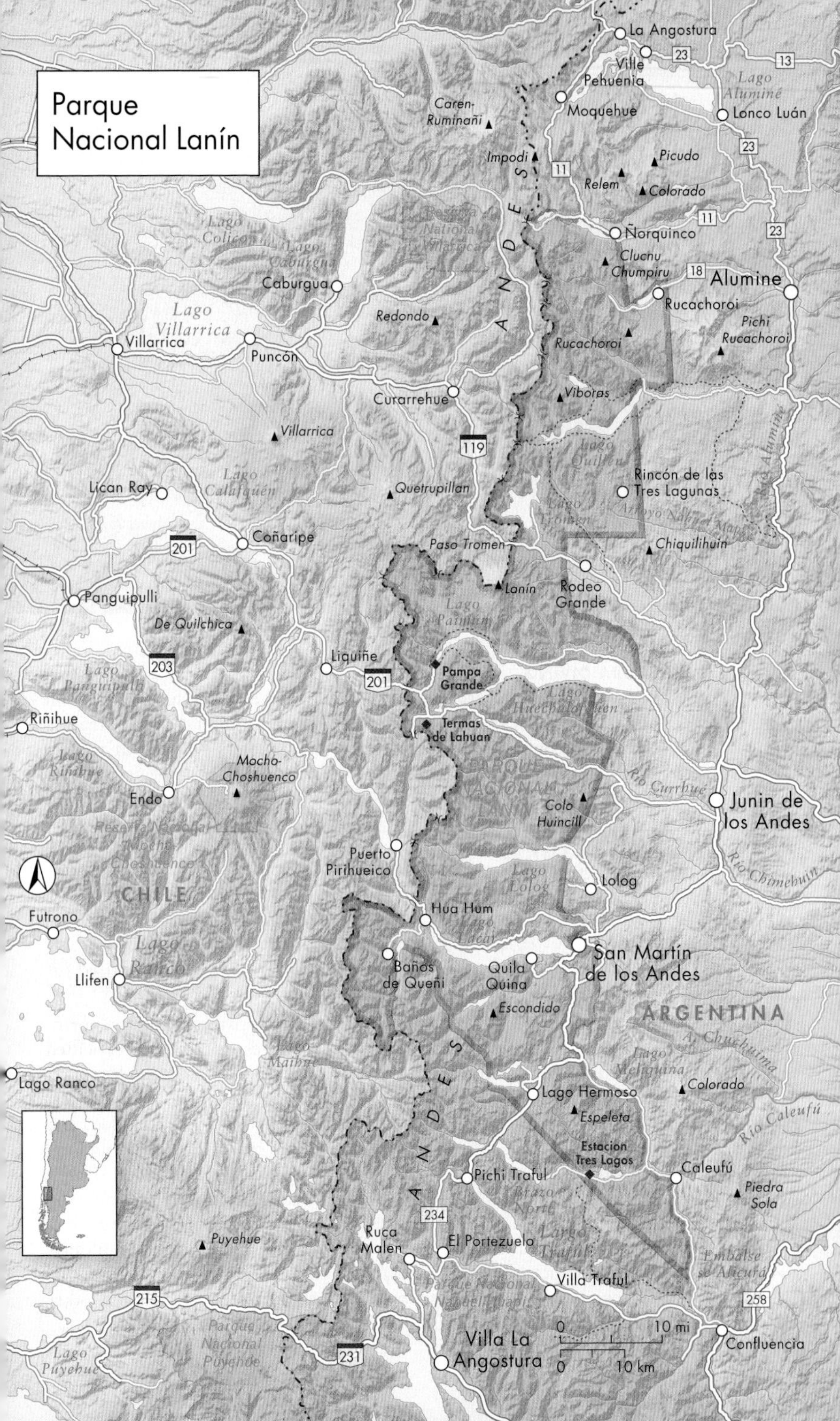

Parque
Nacional Lanín
La Angostura
Ville
Pehuenia
23
13
Lago
Aluminé
Moquehue
Lonco Luán
Caren-
Ruminañi
Impodi
11
Picudo
Relem
Colorado
ANDES
11
23
Ñorquinco
Clucnu
Chumpiru
18
Alumine
Caburgua
Rucachoroi
Lago
Villarrica
Redondo
Pichi
Rucachoroi
Villarrica
Puncón
Rucachoroi
Curarrehue
Viboras
Villarrica
119
Lago
Quillén
Rincón de las
Tres Lagunas
Lican Ray
Lago
Calafquén
Quetrupillan
Lago
Tromen
Arroyo Nahuel Mapa
Coñaripe
201
Paso Tromen
Chiquilihuin
Panguipulli
Lanín
Rodeo
Grande
Lago
Paimún
De Quilchica
203
Liquiñe
201
Pampa
Grande
Lago
Panguipulli
Lago
Huechulafquen
Riñihue
Termas
de Lahuan
Lago
Riñihue
Mocho-
Choshuenco
Parque
Nacional
Lanín
Río Curruhue
Endo
Colo
Huincill
Junin de
los Andes
Puerto
Pirihueico
Lago
Lolog
Río Chimehuín
CHILE
Lolog
Futrono
Hua Hum
Lago
Lácar
Lago
Ranco
San Martín
de los Andes
Baños
de Queñi
Quila
Quina
Llifen
Escondido
ARGENTINA
A. Chuchuima
Lago
Maihue
ANDES
Lago
Meliquina
Lago Ranco
Lago Hermoso
Colorado
Espeleta
Río Caleufú
Estacion
Tres Lagos
Caleufú
Pichi Traful
Brazo
Norte
Piedra
Sola
234
Lago
Traful
Puyehue
Ruca
Malen
El Portezuelo
Embalse
de Alicurá
Villa Traful
Parque Nacional
Nahuel Huapi
215
258
Parque
Nacional
Puyehue
Villa La
Angostura
0
10 mi
0
10 km
Confluencia
Lago
Puyehue
231

Lanín Volcano, an ice-clad, cone-shaped stratovolcano, in Parque Nacional Lanín

SCUBA DIVING

Bosque Sumergido. In 1975 a violent earthquake caused half a mountain and its forest of cypress trees to slide to the bottom of the lake, creating the Bosque Sumergido. You can dive to 30 meters (98 feet) in crystalline water and explore this sunken forest. Boat trips can be arranged at **Cabañas Aiken** (☎ *2944/479–048*). ✉ *Villa Traful, Neuquén.*

VILLA LA ANGOSTURA

81 km (50 miles) northwest of Bariloche (an hour's drive on R231 around the east end of Lago Nahuel Huapi; also accessible by boat from Bariloche); 90 km (56 miles) southwest of San Martín de los Andes on R234 (the Seven Lakes Rte., partly unpaved and closed for much of winter).

Once a lakeside hamlet on a narrow *angostura* (isthmus) on the northern shore of Lake Nahuel Huapi, this small resort town has benefited from thoughtful planning and strict adherence to business codes, making it the second most popular tourist area in the Lake District. Its first hotel was built in 1923, ten years before the town was founded, and today some of the most luxurious hotels and resorts in Patagonia look out on the lake from discreet hiding places along its wooded shores. Shops and restaurants line the Avenida Arrayanes, where you can stop for homemade ice cream or cakes while window-shopping in the three-block-long commercial area. The tourist office and municipal buildings are at El Cruce (the Crossroads), where Ruta 231 from Bariloche to the Chilean border intersects with the road to the port and the Seven Lakes Route, Ruta 234, to San Martín de los Andes.

⚠ Note that the massive Puyehue volcano, just across the Chilean border from Villa La Angostura, erupted in June 2011. It sent clouds of ash several kilometers into the air and prevailing winds carried the plume eastward. Eruptions continued for weeks, and charming Villa La Angostura and surrounding lakes and forest became covered in a meter or more of fine, gray polvo. Intermittent eruptions are ongoing. Townspeople have done a remarkable job of removing ash from their streets, parks, and buildings, but tourist numbers have declined dramatically. Some restaurants and hotels have closed, at least temporarily, and most others are struggling. For travelers interested in geology or episodic natural phenomena, it's well worth spending a couple of days visiting the town and surrounding area. For those not interested in hiking with a dust mask, check in with hotels before booking a trip here for now.

LOCAL SHOPS

En El Bosque. One of the best of the many chocolate shops is En El Bosque, a delicious artisanal producer where the smells of homemade sweets waft out onto the sidewalk; this one also doubles as a little teahouse. ✉ *Av. Arrayanes 218, Villa La Angostura, Neuquén* ☎ *2944/495–738.*

Tanino. The best selection of furs and leather goods—boots, belts, jackets, bags, and purses—in town can be found here. ✉ *Av. Arrayanes 172, Villa La Angostura, Neuquén* ☎ *2944/494–411.*

6

GETTING HERE AND AROUND

Buses from Bariloche are fast and frequent, but a car is the best way to get around the area and visit the town, which is creeping slowly from Lago Correntoso to Puerto Manzano. Bicycles are often available in hotels or can be rented in town.

ESSENTIALS

Visitor and Tour Info Secretaría de Turismo y Cultura ✉ *Av. Arrayanes 9, Villa La Angostura, Neuquén* ☎ *2944/494–124* 🌐 *www.villalaangosturaturismo.blogspot.com.* **Villa La Angostura** ✉ *Av. Arrayanes 9, Villa La Angostura, Neuquén* ☎📠 *2944/494–124* 🌐 *www.villalaangostura.gov.ar.*

WHERE TO EAT

$$$$ ARGENTINE ✕ **Australis.** This is one of the best microbreweries in Patagonia. The excellent cuisine integrates beer, all the way through to dessert—a memorable flan is made with chocolate and a delicious stout. The restaurant will cook up your own freshly caught fish if you bring it in. ✉ *Av. Arrayanes 2490, Ruta 231, Km 60, Villa La Angostura, Neuquén* ☎ *2944/495–645* 🌐 *www.cerveceriaaustralis.com.ar* 💳 *No credit cards* ⏲ *closed May–June.*

$ ARGENTINE ✕ **La Casita de la Oma.** Between the bay and the main street, this teahouse, with its award-winning garden, serves homemade cakes, pies, and scones. Moist chocolate brownie cake with *dulce de leche* (sweet carmelized milk) is a winner, as is a pile of filo leaves with dulce de leche and meringue on top. Jars of jam line the shelves. ✉ *Cerro Inacayal 303, Villa La Angostura, Neuquén* ☎ *2544/494–602* ⏲ *Closed May.*

WHERE TO STAY

For expanded hotel reviews, visit Fodors.com.

SPORTS OPTIONS

Note that due to the 2011 eruption of the Puyehue volcano many outfitters have closed. Ash accumulation in the area has made outdoor adventures difficult for now, but be sure to check with your hotel for more information.

$$$$ **Costa Serena.** Every room at this complex in Puerto Manzano has a lake view; A-frame *cabañas* (cabins) with decks, kitchens, and outdoor barbecues sleep up to seven, while suites have huge wooden Jacuzzis with views to the water. **Pros:** good family reunion spot. **Cons:** far from town and tourist attractions. *Los Pinos 435, Puerto Manzano, Villa La Angostura, Neuquén 2944/475–203 www.costaserenavla.com.ar 7 rooms, 3 suites, 4 cabins In-hotel: restaurant, bar, pool, gym, spa, beach Breakfast.*

$$$$ Fodor'sChoice ★ **Hotel Correntoso.** You can see the fish jump from your bedroom window, your dining table, the glass-paneled deck, or from the refurbished 100-year-old fishing bar down by the lake. **Pros:** great location, food, spa; well-organized excursions. **Cons:** expensive. *RN231, Km 86, Puente Correntoso, Villa La Angostura, Neuquén 2944/15–619–728, 11/4803–0030 in Buenos Aires www.correntoso.com 49 In-hotel: restaurant, bar, pool, spa, children's programs.*

$$$$ Fodor'sChoice ★ **Puerto Sur.** Stone and wood merge throughout the angular space of this hotel in Puerto Manzano, which was built into the side of a hill, with views of the lake and mountains from enormous windows; every room has a lake view, Jacuzzi, and restrained modern art. **Pros:** quiet, secluded spot. **Cons:** far from town and tourist activities. *Los Pinos 221, Puerto Manzano, Villa La Angostura, Neuquén 2944/475–399 www.hosteriapuertosur.com.ar 7 rooms, 3 suites, 4 cabins In-hotel: restaurant, bar, pool, gym, spa, beach closed mid-May and June Breakfast.*

PARQUE NACIONAL NAHUEL HUAPI

Parque Nacional Nahuel Huapi. Created in 1934, the Parque Nacional Nahuel Huapi is Argentina's oldest national park. The park extends over 2 million acres along the eastern side of the Andes in the provinces of Neuquén and Río Negro, on the frontier with Chile. It contains the highest concentration of lakes in Argentina. The biggest is Lago Nahuel Huapi, an 897-square-km (346-square-miles) body of water whose seven long arms (the longest is 96 km [60 miles] long, 12 km [7 miles] wide) reach deep into forests of *coihué* (a native beech tree), *cyprés* (cypress), and *lenga* (deciduous beech) trees. Intensely blue across its vast expanse and aqua green in its shallow bays, the lake meanders into distant lagoons and misty inlets where the mountains, covered with vegetation at their base, rise straight up out of the water. Nearly every water sport invented and tours to islands and other lakes can be arranged through local travel agencies, tour offices, and hotels. Information offices throughout the park offer help in exploring the miles of mountain and woodland trails and the lakes.

DID YOU KNOW?

Church bells sounding in clear air, wide streets leading to lakefront vistas—Bariloche is hard to dislike.

Having landed in Bariloche, you can explore the park on an organized tour or on your own. Nearby excursions such as the Circuito Chico, Circuito Grande, a trip to Tronadór, or the ski area at Catedral can be done in a day. Since much of the park is covered by Nahuel Huapi Lake (it's 96 km [57 miles] long, covering 346 square miles), some of your exploration will be by boat to islands, down narrow fjords, or to distant shores on organized excursions. Small towns like Villa La Angostura and Villa Traful are excellent destinations for further explorations on foot or horseback to smaller lakes with their connecting streams, waterfalls, and surrounding forests and high peaks. Since most of the park is at a low elevation (under 6,000 feet), getting around in winter is not difficult—just cold. Fall foliage, long, warm summer days, and spring flowers are the rewards of other seasons. Park entry is 12 pesos. ✉ *Av. San Martín 24, San Carlos de Bariloche, Río Negro* 🌐 *www.nahuelhuapi.gov.ar*.

GETTING AROUND

The easy way to get around is to plan your days with a local tour operator or remis, or hire a rental car, mixing up excursions between land and lake. When planning all-day or overnight trips, remember that distances are long and unpaved roads slow you down.

ESSENTIALS

Visitor Info Intendencia del Parque Nacional Nahuel Huapi ✉ *Av. San Martín 24, at the Civic Center, Bariloche, Río Negro* ☎ *2944/423–111* 🌐 *www.parquesnacionales.gov.ar*.

EXPLORING

Isla Victoria. The most popular excursion on Lago Nahuel Huapi is the 30-minute boat ride from Puerto Pañuelo at Llao Llao to Isla Victoria, the largest island in the lake. A grove of redwoods transplanted from California thrives in the middle of the island. Walk on trails that lead to enchanting views of emerald bays and still lagoons. Then board the boat to sail on to the Parque Nacional los Arrayanes. Boats to Isla Victoria and Parque Nacional los Arrayanes leave from Puerto Pañuelo, on the Península Llao Llao. They run twice daily (more in high season), at 10 am and 2 pm. The earlier departure includes time for lunch on the island in a cafeteria-style restaurant. The later departure is a shorter trip. Boats are run by **Cau Cau** (✉ *Mitre 139, Bariloche* ☎ *2944/431–372* 🌐 *www.islavictoriayarrayanes.com*) and **Turisur** (✉ *Mitre 219, Bariloche* ☎ *2944/426–109* 🌐 *www.bariloche.com/turisur*). ✉ *Río Negro*.

Parque Nacional los Arrayanes. The Parque Nacional los Arrayanes protects Lago Nahuel Huapi's entire Quetrihue Peninsula and its unique forest of arrayanes, or myrtle trees. These trees absorb so much water through their thin skins that all other vegetation around them dies, leaving a barren forest of peeling cinnamon-color trunks. A one-hour stroll up and down wide wooden steps and walkways is a unique experience, as light filters through the twisted naked trunks, reflecting a weird red glow. You can make this excursion from the pier at Bahía Brava in Villa La Angostura (or by boat from Bariloche via Isla Victoria). In summer months you can walk (three hours) or ride a bike, after registering at

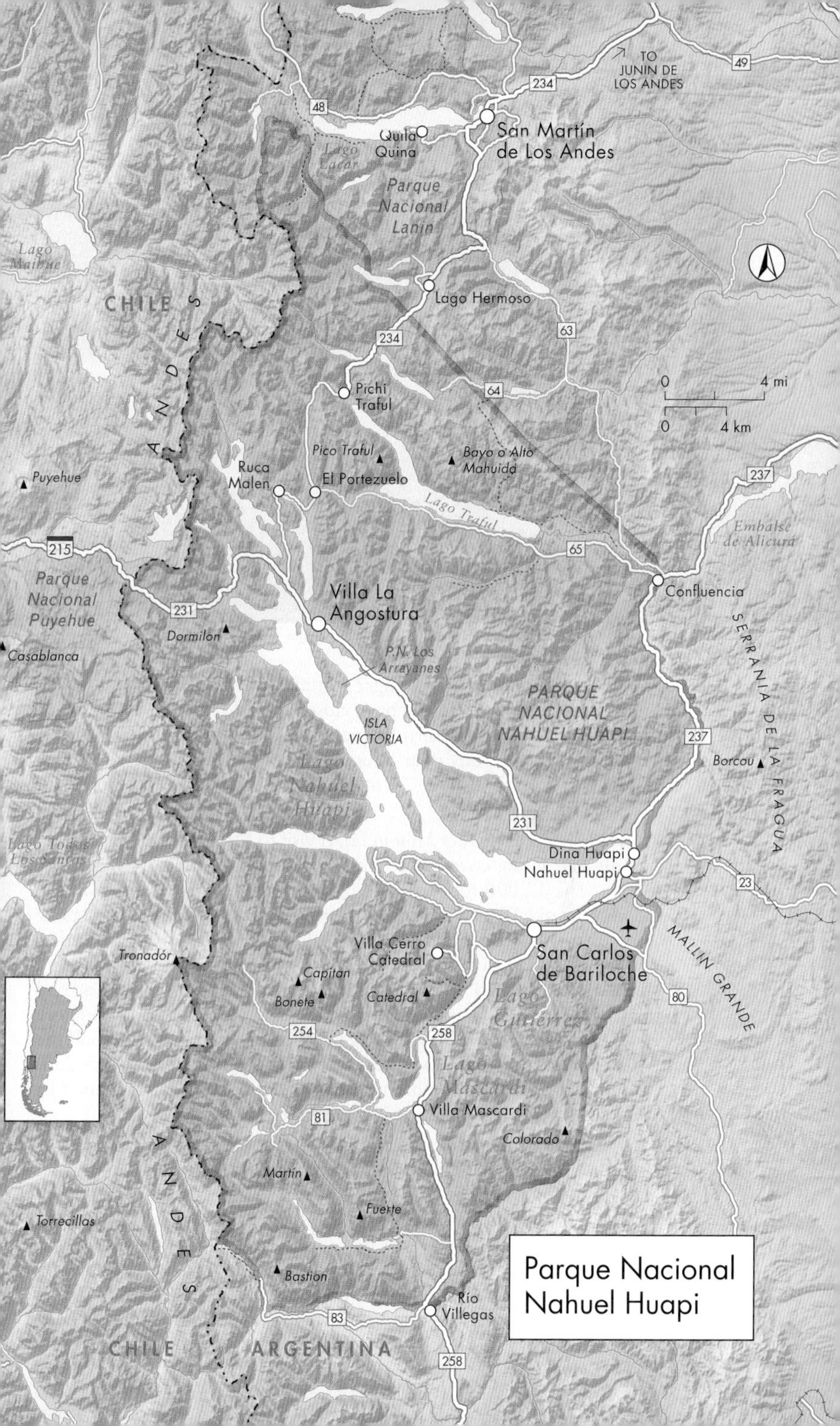

Parque Nacional
Nahuel Huapi
San Martín
de Los Andes
TO
JUNIN DE
LOS ANDES
49
234
48
Quila
Quina
Lago
Lacar
Parque
Nacional
Lanín
Lago
Maihue
CHILE
A N D E S
Lago Hermoso
63
234
Pichi
Traful
64
0
4 mi
0
4 km
Pico Traful
Bayo o Alto
Mahuida
Puyehue
Ruca
Malen
El Portezuelo
Lago Traful
237
Embalse
de Alicurá
215
65
Confluencia
Parque
Nacional
Puyehue
Villa La
Angostura
231
Dormilon
Casablanca
P.N. Los
Arrayanes
SERRANIA DE LA FRAGUA
PARQUE
NACIONAL
NAHUEL HUAPI
ISLA
VICTORIA
237
Borcou
Lago
Nahuel
Huapi
231
Lago Todos
Los Santos
Dina Huapi
Nahuel Huapi
23
San Carlos
de Bariloche
MALLIN GRANDE
Villa Cerro
Catedral
Tronadór
Capitan
Bonete
Catedral
Lago
Gutiérrez
80
254
258
Lago
Mascardi
Villa Mascardi
81
Colorado
Martín
Fuerte
Torrecillas
Bastion
Río
Villegas
83
CHILE
ARGENTINA
258

Take in the view of Lago Nahuel Huapi on your way to Villa La Angostura.

the *Guardaparque* office (ranger station) near the pier. Leave in the morning, as entrance to the park closes at 2 pm. A nice combination is to go by boat and return by bicycle (it's all downhill that way). If returning by boat, buy your return ticket at the pier before you leave. ✉ *12 km [7½ miles] along a trail from the Península Quetrihué, Río Negro* ☎ *2944/423–111*.

Monte Tronadór (*Thunder Mountain*). A visit to Monte Tronadór requires an all-day outing covering 170 km (105 miles) round-trip from Bariloche. The 12,000-foot extinct volcano, the highest mountain in the northern Lake District, straddles the frontier with Chile, with one peak on either side. Take Ruta 258 south along the shores of Lago Gutiérrez and Lago Mascardi. Between the two lakes the road crosses from the Atlantic to the Pacific watershed. At Km 35, turn off onto a road marked "Tronadór" and "Pampa Linda" and continue along the shore of Lago Mascardi, passing a village of the same name. Just beyond the village the road forks, and you continue on a gravel road, Ruta 254. Near the bridge the road branches left to Lago Hess and Cascada Los Alerces—a detour you might want to take on your way out.

As you bear right after crossing Los Rápidos Bridge, the road narrows to one direction only: it's important to remember this when you set out in the morning, as you can only go up the road before 2 pm and down it after 4 pm. The lake ends in a narrow arm (Brazo Tronadór) at the Hotel Tronadór, which has a dock for tours arriving by boat. The road then follows the Río Manso to **Pampa Linda,** which has a lodge, restaurant, park ranger's office, campsites, and the trailhead for the climb up to the Refugio Otto Meiling at the snow line. Guided horseback rides are organized at the lodge. The road ends 7 km (4½ miles) beyond Pampa Linda in a parking lot that was once at the tip of the receding **Glaciar Negro** (Black Glacier). As the glacier flows down from the mountain, the dirt and black sediment of its lateral moraines are ground up and cover the ice. At first glance it's hard to imagine the tons of ice that lie beneath its black cap. ✉ *Río Negro.*

WHERE TO STAY

For expanded hotel reviews, visit Fodors.com.

$$$$ **Isla Victoria Lodge.** The stone-and-wood structure on a cliff overlooking the lake and forests of coihues and cypresses, with its clean architecture and quiet interior of white walls, pine trim, leather upholstery, and fine Mapuche woven rugs, conveys a sense of peace and unity with the natural surroundings. **Pros:** price includes alcoholic drinks and on-site activities (including horseback riding); hiking trails. **Cons:** nightlife is relegated to stargazing. ✉ *IslaVictoria CC 26, Nahuel Huapi National Park, Río Negro* ☎ *11/43–949–605* 🌐 *www.maresur.com* *20 rooms, 2 suites* *In-room: safe, Internet, Wi-Fi. In-hotel: restaurant, bar, pool, spa, beach, water sports, some age restrictions* *All meals.*

6

SPORTS AND THE OUTDOORS

Intendencia del Parque Nacional Nahuel Huapi. For information on mountain climbing, trails, *refugios* (mountain huts), and campgrounds, visit the Intendencia del Parque Nacional Nahuel Huapi. ✉ *Av. San Martín 24, at the Civic Center, Bariloche, Río Negro* ☎ *2944/423–111* 🌐 *www.nahuelhuapi.gov.ar.*

HIKING

Nahuel Huapi National Park has many forest trails near Bariloche, El Bolsón, and Villa La Angostura. For day hikes in the forest along the shore of Nahuel Huapi Lake or to a nearby waterfall, search for trails along the Circuito Chico in the Parque Llao Llao. For altitude and grand panoramas, take the ski lift to the top of Cerro Catedral and follow the ridge trail to Refugio Frey, returning down to the base of the ski area.

West of Bariloche, turn right at Villa Mascardi onto the dirt road to Pampa Linda. From there you can hike a long day or overnight to Otto Meiling hut, or make shorter forays to the glacier or nearby waterfalls. A three-day trek will take you right past Tronadór and its glacier, along the Alerce River, and over the Paso de los Nubes (Clouds Pass) to Puerto Blest, returning to Bariloche by boat. Hiking guides can be recommended by local tour offices. For trail maps and information on all of the Lake District, look for the booklet (in Spanish) *Guía Sendas y Bosques* (Guide to Trails and Forests) sold at kiosks and bookstores.

Club Andino Bariloche. For ambitious treks, mountaineering, or use of mountain huts and climbing permits, contact Club Andino Bariloche. Click on the *mapas* link on the website. ✉ *20 de Febrero 30, Río Negro* ☎ *2944/422–266* 🌐 *www.clubandino.org.*

MOUNTAIN BIKING

The entire Nahuel Huapi National Park is ripe for all levels of mountain biking. Popular rides go from the parking lot at the Cerro Catedral ski area to Lago Gutiérrez and down from Cerro Otto. Local tour agencies can arrange guided tours by the hour or day and even international excursions to Chile. Rental agencies provide maps and suggestions and sometimes recommend guides.

Dirty Bikes. Dirty Bikes offers local day trips all over the Lake District, including long-distance trips to Chile and back, for all ages and abilities. ✉ *Vice Almirante O'Connor 681, Río Negro* ☎ *2944/425–616* 🌐 *www.dirtybikes.com.ar.*

La Bolsa del Deporte. This outfit rents and sells bikes. ✉ *Capraro 1081, Río Negro* ☎ *2944/433–111* 🌐 *www.labolsadeldeporte.com.ar.*

WHITE-WATER RAFTING

With all the interconnected lakes and rivers in the national park, there's everything from your basic family float down the swift-flowing, scenic Río Limay to a wild and exciting ride down Río Manso (Class II), which takes you 16 km (10 miles) in three hours. If you're really adventurous, you can take the Manso all the way to Chile (Class IV).

Aguas Blancas. Aguas Blancas specializes in the Manso River and offers an overnight trip to Chile with asado and return by horseback. They also run guided inflatable kayak trips. ✉ *Morales 564, Río Negro* ☎ *2944/432–799* 🌐 *aguasblancas.com.ar.*

Alunco. Alunco arranges rafting trips throughout the area. ✉ *Moreno 187, Río Negro* ☎ *2944/422–283* 🌐 *www.aluncoturismo.com.ar.*

Extremo Sur. Extremo Sur arranges trips on the Ríos Limay and Manso. ✉ *Morales 765, Río Negro* ☎ *2944/427–301* 🌐 *www.extremosur.com.*

IN AND AROUND EL BOLSÓN

EL BOLSÓN

131 km (80 miles) south of Bariloche via R40.

El Bolsón ("the purse") lies in a valley enclosed on either side by the jagged peaks of two mountain ranges. You catch your first glimpse of the valley about 66 km (41 miles) from Bariloche, with the glaciers of Perito Moreno and Hielo Azul (both more than 6,500 feet) on the horizon south and west. The spot was once a Mapuche settlement, then Chilean farmers came in the late 1800s in search of arable land. The town remained isolated until the 1930s, when a long, winding dirt road (often closed in winter) connected it to Bariloche. Attracted by the microclimate (about 7 degrees warmer than other Patagonian towns), young Argentineans, as well as immigrants from Europe, the Americas, and the Middle East contribute to the cultural identity of this community of about 11,000. The first in Argentina to declare their town a non-nuclear zone, they have preserved the purity of its air, water, and land. Red berry fruits thrive on hillsides and in backyard *chacras* (farms), and are canned and exported in large quantities as jams and

CLOSE UP

Beer Sampling

This region has long been the biggest producer of hops in Argentina, and with a local population dedicated to agricultural pursuits, it's logical that entrepreneurial *cervezarís artesanales* (artisanal breweries) would become a growing industry.

Cervezería El Bolsón. About 2 km (1 mile) north of town, Cervezería El Bolsón is the brewery that started the Patagonian "cerveza artesanal craze," and even if it's now the least artisanal of the bunch, it has become a local landmark. Every night from December through March, and Fridays and Saturdays for the rest of the year, the brewery's tasting room turns into a hopping bar and restaurant, where *picadas* (kind of like tapas), pizzas, sausages with sauerkraut, and a hearty goulash are listed on one side of the menu with suggested beers on the other. For instance, black beer is suggested with smoked meats; chocolate beer with dessert. There are 14 types of beer for you to taste, and descriptions of their ingredients are provided. A large campground is conveniently located by the river in back. There is now a second location (tap room and café) in town at the corner of San Martin and Juez Fernandez. It is called Cervezeria El Bolson Centro. ✉ *Ruta 258, Km 123.9, El Bolsón, Río Negro* ☎ *2944/492–595* 🌐 *www.cervezaselbolson.com.*

Otto Tipp. Otto Tipp was a German immigrant who opened the first local brewery in 1890. Beers here include the classic triumvirate of blonde, red, and black—plus non-alcoholic malt beer and a fruity wheat beer. You can watch beer being brewed and bottled from a bar stool. This brewery is four blocks from the tourist office. ✉ *Islas Malvinas at Roca, El Bolsón, Río Negro* ☎ *2944/493–700* ⏲ *Closed Mon.*

6

syrups. The exploding Patagonian microbrew beer industry is based on the largest crops of hops planted in Argentina.

GETTING AROUND

The main street, San Martín, has shops, restaurants, and some lodgings within a two- to three-block area. A grassy plaza next to the tourist office is the center of activities, with a crafts market on weekends and some weekdays. The sheer rock face of **Cerro Piltriquitrón** (from a Mapuche word meaning "hanging from the clouds") dominates the horizon on the southeast side of town. Trails along the Río Azul or to nearby waterfalls and mountaintops are a short taxi or bike ride from the plaza. In spring (late November–December) the roads are lined with ribbons of lupine in every shade of pink and purple imaginable. Berries are picked December through March. Summers are warm and lazy, and campgrounds at nearby lakes attract backpackers and families.

Huara Viajes y Turismo. A full-service travel and tour office, Huara Viajes y Turismo offers guided hiking, fishing, rafting, horseback, and mountain-bike trips. They also arrange day tours to Lago Puelo that include a boat trip. Rock climbing with rappels is offered on a multi-adventure trip near Lago Puelo. ✉ *Dorrego 410, El Bolsón, Río Negro* ☎ *2944/455–000* 🌐 *www.huaraviajesyturismo.com.ar.*

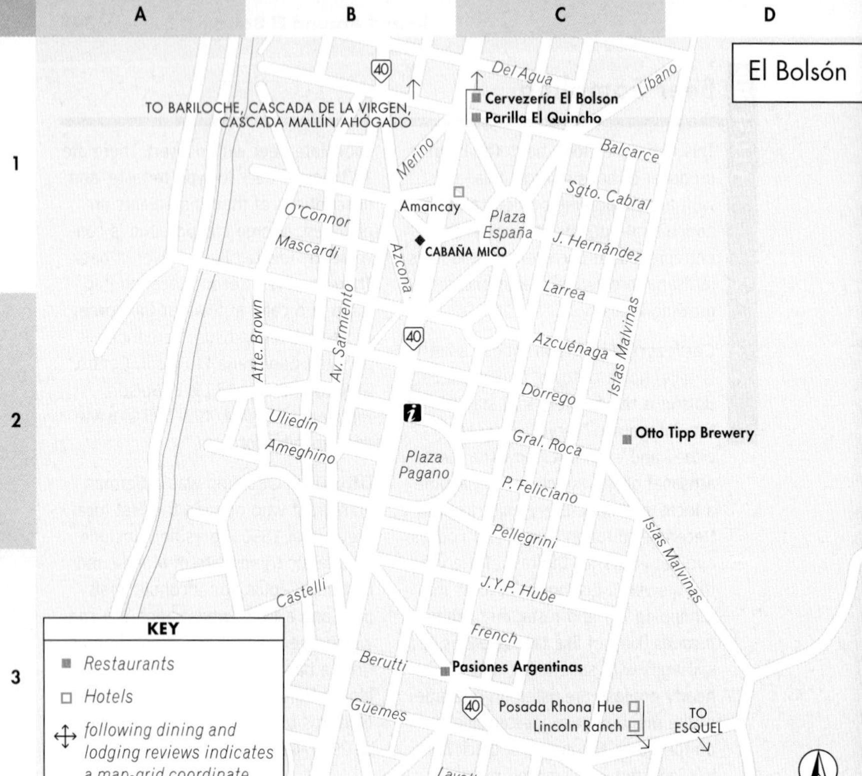

ESSENTIALS

Visitor and Tour Info Secretaría de Turismo ✉ *Plaza Pagano at Av. San Martín, El Bolsón, Río Negro* ☎ *2944/492–604, 2944/455–336* 🌐 *www.elbolson.gov.ar.*

EXPLORING

Bolsón International Jazz Festival. The Bolsón International Jazz Festival usually takes place in February (check online in advance) on the streets and in restaurants around town. The Fiesta Nacional de Lúpolo (National Hop Festival) is also celebrated in February. ✉ *El Bolsón, Río Negro* 🌐 *www.elbolsonjazz.com.ar.*

Bosque Tallado (*carved forest*). The Bosque Tallado, about 1 km (½ miles) from the base of Piltriquitrón, is a forest of dry beech trees (resulting from a fire in 1978) that have been carved over the years by 13 of Argentina's notable artists. Thirty-one monumental sculptures transform the dead forest into a living gallery. ✉ *El Bolsón, Río Negro.*

Cabaña Mico. Don't leave the area of Bolsón or El Hoyo (15 km south) without a jar of jam! You can try all the flavors at Cabaña Mico. Not to be outdone by the beer tasting next door at Otto Tipp, little pots of jam are lined up for sale on a long table with disposable sticks for tasting the 40 different flavors. ✉ *Islas Malvinas at Roca, El Bolsón, Río Negro* ☎ *2944/492–691* 🌐 *www.mico.com.ar.*

Cascada de la Virgen (*Waterfall of the Virgin*). The Cascada de la Virgen, 15 km (9 miles) north of El Bolsón, is most impressive in spring, when the runoff from the mountain falls in a series of three cascades visible from the road coming from Bariloche. Nearby is a campground (*2944/492–610 for information*) with cabins, grills, and a restaurant. ✉ *El Bolsón, Río Negro.*

CRAFTS FAIR

At the local **mercado artesanal** (artisanal crafts fair), which takes place on the main plaza on Tuesday, Thursday, Saturday, and Sunday from 10 to 5, local artisans sell ceramics, leather goods, wood handicrafts, objects made from bone and clay, and agricultural products—plus the famous local beers. El Bolsón is also known for its delicious small strawberries.

Cascada Mallín Ahogado (*Drowned Meadow Waterfall*). Four km (2.5 miles) north of El Bolsón on Ruta 258, the Cascada Mallín Ahogadomakes a great picnic spot. ✉ *El Bolsón, Río Negro.*

WHERE TO EAT

$$ ARGENTINE ✕ **Parrilla El Quincho.** About 10 minutes north of town, on the bank of the river Arroyo del Medio, this is the place to try *cordero patagónico al asador* (lamb roasted slowly on a metal cross over a fire), along with sizzling platters of beef. From El Bolsón, follow Ruta Nacional 40 north, and get off at the left exit for Catarata Mallín Ahogado. Follow that winding road north, then follow signs for El Quincho; you'll exit to the right after the Catarata exit (if you come to the Iaten K'aik museum, you've gone too far). ✉ *Mallín Ahogado, El Bolsón, Río Negro* ☎ *2944/492–870* ▭ *No credit cards* ⊙ *Closed in winter* ✥ *C1.*

$$ ECLECTIC ✕ **Pasiones Argentinas Resto Bar.** Paintings of passionate tango dancers enliven the brick walls of this popular restaurant near the Villa Turismo. Vegetarian dishes, pastas, pizzas, Asian, and even hamburgers fill the menu. Patagonian wine, local beer, Wi-Fi, and take-out food are added attractions. ✉ *Av. Belgrano at Berutti, El Bolsón, Río Negro* ☎ *2944/483–616* ▭ *No credit cards* ⊙ *Closed Mon.* ✥ *C3.*

WHERE TO STAY

The hotel selection in downtown El Bolsón is woefully inadequate. Numerous small guesthouses take small groups, and the Hotel Amancay is the only full-service hotel worth "recommending." About 2 km (1½ miles) south of town, off Avenida Belgrano, is **Villa Turismo,** a hillside community of cabins, bed-and-breakfasts, and small inns. Lodges in the surrounding mountains open for fishing season in summer (November–April) and close in winter (May–October).

For expanded hotel reviews, visit Fodors.com.

$ **Hotel Amancay.** A rose garden and masses of flowers greet you at the door of this yellow-stucco hotel three blocks from the center of town. **Pros:** walk to downtown restaurants; one of the best options in town; clean rooms. **Cons:** rooms and bathrooms are small and slightly rundown. ✉ *Av. San Martín 3207, El Bolsón, Río Negro* ☎ *2944/492–222* 🌐 *www.hotelamancaybolson.com.ar* *15 rooms* *In-hotel: parking* *Breakfast* ✥ *C1.*

6

DESTINATION HOTELS

Far from all the usual tourist sights, shops, and restaurants, usually on a dirt road and often with no real address, the Lake District's destination hotels are almost as soothing and inspiring as the very wilderness they're hidden in. Similar to the all-inclusive resort concept but without the resort-y feel, these hotels are focused on getting you as close to nature as possible. They often require a minimum stay of two or more nights—but this makes sense for guests, because getting to these places can be a production. Once you've arrived, the staff at these hotels will facilitate a relaxing nature-oriented stay where stargazing is the main evening event and hiking trails into the mountains are at your doorstep. Come with a group, as a couple, or with anyone you're eager to share some down time with.

If you're based in Bariloche, consider **Hosteria El Retorno, Hotel Tronadór, or Peuma Hue.** In Villa Traful, **Estancia Arroyo Verde** is a favorite destination hotel (though be sure to call in advance, due to its proximity to recent volcanic activity). The one with arguably the best location, though, is **Isla Victoria Lodge** in Nahuel Huapi National Park, right on Isla Victoria.

$$ **Lincoln Ranch.** Perched higher than all the other cabin complexes, these modern cottages have plenty of room and all the accoutrements of a vacation home. **Pros:** lots of space; easy walk up to Piltriquitrón. **Cons:** far from restaurants and downtown shops. ✉ *Villa Turismo, Subida Los Maitenes, El Bolsón, Río Negro* ☎ *2944/492–073* 🌐 *www.lincolnranch.com.ar* *10 1- and 2-bedroom cabins, 1 3-bedroom cabin* *In-hotel: pool, parking* ✣ *C3.*

$$ **Posada Rhona Hue.** Formerly the headquarters for a fruit and berry farm, this farmhouse has been converted by Anabella Gouchs into a B&B where every room is filled with an eclectic mixture of antiques and recycled objects used as furniture. **Pros:** country living; homemade jams and scones for breakfast; walking distance to Piltriquitrón. **Cons:** out of town; closed in winter except by special group requests. ✉ *Villa Turismo, Subida de Juan Marqués, El Bolsón, Río Negro* ☎ *2944/493–717* 🌐 *www.interpatagonia.com/rhonahue* *4 rooms, 1 apartment, 1 cabin* *In-hotel: pool, parking* *Closed in winter* *Breakfast* ✣ *C3.*

SPORTS AND THE OUTDOORS

HIKING

There are 10 *refugios* (mountain huts) with beds and meals in the mountains around Bolsón. A few easy hikes begin a short taxi ride from the center of town. The Río Azul (Blue River) drops down from the high mountains north of town and runs through the valley to Lago Puelo. Most of the hiking trails are in this area. To reach the Mirador Azul (5 km [3 miles] from the town center), ride or drive west on Azuénaga Street, cross the bridge over the River Quemquemtreu, and follow the signs. From here you can look down the valley to Lago Puelo and up at the snow-covered mountains to the west. A 6-km (4-mile) walk will take you to the **Cabeza del Indio** (Indian Head) and **Cascadas Escondidas**

Cerro Lindo, near El Bolsón, is a hiker's dream.

(Hidden Falls). A strenuous two-day trek to the **Hielo Azul** (Blue Glacier) climbs through forests to a refugio next to the glacier. Another overnight hike through the forest and past hidden lagoons is to the refugio by the glacier at **Cerro Lindo.** Easier to climb it than to say it, the summit of **Cerro Piltriquitrón** (pronounced pill-tree-quee-tron) offers stupendous views of lakes and mountains all around you, including Tronadór on the Chilean border near Bariloche. There's a refugio at the top with beds and meals.

HORSEBACK RIDING (CABALGATAS)

Riding a horse is a fun way to access most of the areas described in the hiking section, especially the area around **Cascada Mallín Ahogado,** or the Río Azul to the Azul Canyon or all the way to the glacier.

Cabalgatas El Azul ✉ *El Bolsón, Río Negro* ☎ *2944/483–590.*

Huara Viajes y Turismo ✉ *Dorrego 410, El Bolsón, Río Negro* ☎ *2944/455–000* 🌐 *www.huaraviajesyturismo.com.ar.*

MOUNTAIN BIKING

Hardy bikers ride all the way from Bariloche, enjoying the long descent into Bolsón. Once there, getting around is pretty easy, as there's not much traffic on the mostly flat dirt roads on the outskirts of town. Most of the waterfall walks and a long trail along the Azul River make pleasant day trips. Epuyén and Puelo lakes require more effort.

Huara Viajes y Turismo. For guided trips, contact Huara Viajes y Turismo. ✉ *Dorrego 410, El Bolsón, Río Negro* ☎ *2944/455–000* 🌐 *www.huaraviajesyturismo.com.ar.*

SKIING

Cerro Perito Moreno. The ski area at Cerro Perito Moreno, 25 km (15 miles) northwest of El Bolsón, is owned and operated by **Club Andino Piltriquitrón** (✉ *Sarmiento at Roca* ☎ *2944/492–600*), which also runs a restaurant at the base, where you can rent skis, snowboards, and sleds. The ski area is open from mid-June to mid-October and is used mainly by local families. Four short tows for beginners and one T-bar access the 750 meters (2,460 feet) of skiable terrain on east-facing slopes. Since storms approach from the west, snowfall can be minimal, so it's best to call the tourist office or Club Andino before you go. ✉ *El Bolsón, Río Negro.*

PARQUE NACIONAL LAGO PUELO

19 km (12 miles) south of El Bolsón on RN40 and RP16.

GETTING HERE AND AROUND

Parque Nacional Lago Puelo. Information is at the Parque Nacional Lago Puelo, and picnic and fishing supplies can be purchased at the roadside store, 4 km (2½ miles) before you reach the sandy beach at Lago Puelo. ✉ *Río Negro* ☎ *2944/499–183* 🌐 *www.lagopuelo.gov.ar.*

EXPLORING

Parque Nacional Lago Puelo. One of the smallest national parks in the southern Andes, Lago Puelo has the warmest water for swimming, the largest salmon (coming all the way from the Pacific Ocean), and many hiking possibilities—the most interesting of which are at the west end of the lake on the Chilean border. ✉ *11 km south of El Bolson on Ruta 16, Chubut* 🌐 *www.parquesnacionales.gov.ar.*

SPORTS AND THE OUTDOORS

BOAT EXCURSIONS

On Lago Puelo three launches, maintained by the Argentine navy, wait at the dock to take you on one- to three-hour excursions. The trip to El Turbio, an ancient settlement at the southern end of the lake on the Chilean border, is the longest. One side of the lake is inaccessible, as the Valdivian rain forest grows on steep rocky slopes right down into the water. Campgrounds are at the park entrance by the ranger's station, in a bay on the Brazo Occidental, and at the Turbio and Epuyén river outlets.

Juana de Arco. Juana de Arco is one of the local boat-tour operators. ✉ *Perito Moreno 1364, El Bolsón, Río Negro* ☎ *2944/498–946, 2944/15–633–838* 🌐 *www.interpatagonia.com/juanadearco.*

HIKING

Arriving at the water's edge, you have three trails to explore: one is an easy stroll in the woods on a wooden walkway; another involves a steep climb to an overlook; and the third is an all-day trek (eight hours round-trip) to **Los Hitos** on the Chilean border, where you can admire the rapids on the Puelo River. It's possible to camp there at **Arroyo Las Lagrimas** and continue on for five or six days across Chile to the Pacific Ocean. You can also take a boat to **El Turbio** at the other end of the lake, where a tough two- to three-day day trek climbs to Lago Esperanza. Another option would be to hike to El Turbio from **El Desemboque** on **Lago Epuyén.** For a guide, contact one of the tour offices in El Bolsón.

Patagonia

WORD OF MOUTH

"We drove out to Perito Moreno Glacier, and that first glimpse was just breathtaking . . . We spent the day on the walkways, listening to the ice cracking and roaring, watching it break off. I have never been so close to a glacier before and was amazed at the various hues of blue in the ice."

—colibri

WELCOME TO PATAGONIA

Torres del Paine, Chile

TOP REASONS TO GO

★ **Marine Life:** Península Valdés is home to breeding populations of sea lions, elephant seals, orcas, and the star of the local sea show, the southern right whale. Punta Tombo is the world's largest Magellanic penguin colony.

★ **Estancia Stay:** Visit an estancia, a working ranch where you can ride horses alongside tough-as-nails gaucho cowboys and dine on spit-roasted lamb under the stars.

★ **Glaciers and Mountains:** Set yourself opposite an impossibly massive wall of ice and contemplate the blue-green-turquoise spectrum trapped within. Meanwhile, stark granite peaks planted like spears in the Cordillera beckon extreme mountain climbers and casual trekkers alike.

★ **Brushing Up on Your Welsh:** In the largest Welsh colony outside Wales, the people of Gaiman have preserved their traditions and language. Gaiman's historic teahouses serve scones, cakes, and tarts from century-old recipes.

1 Puerto Madryn and Península Valdés. Puerto Madryn provides easy access to Península Valdés, one of the world's best places for marine wildlife viewing.

2 Trelew, Gaiman, and Punta Tombo. Gaiman and Trelew's teahouses and rose gardens date back to the original 19th-century Welsh settlers. Head south to Punta Tombo, the largest penguin rookery in South America.

3 Camarones and Bahía Bustamante. Called the Galapagos of the south, the wilderness of Camarones and Bahía Bustamante is like having a national park to yourself.

4 Sarmiento. This small, friendly town is a green oasis. There are stunning petrified forests nearby and a paleontology "park" with life-size dinosaur replicas.

5 El Calafate and the Parque Nacional los Glaciares. The wild Parque Nacional los Glaciares dramatically contrasts with nearby boomtown El Calafate. North is El Chaltén, base camp for hikes to Cerros Torre and Fitzroy.

6 Puerto Natales and Torres del Paine, Chile. Border town Puerto Natales is the last stop before one of the finest national parks in South America, Parque Nacional Torres del Paine.

7 Ushuaia and Tierra del Fuego. This rugged, windswept land straddles Chile and Argentina. Ushuaia, in Argentina, is the world's southernmost city.

outside El Chaltén, Argentina

GETTING ORIENTED

Most of Patagonia is windswept desert steppe inhabited by rabbits, sheep, guanacos, and a few hardy human beings. The population centers—and attractions—are either along the coast or in a narrow strip of barely fertile land that runs north to south along the base of the Andes mountain range, where massive glaciers spill into large turquoise lakes. In nearby Chile, Puerto Natales is the gateway town to Parque Nacional Torres del Paine. At the bottom end of the continent, separated by the Magellan Strait and split between Chile and Argentina, lies Tierra del Fuego. The resort town of Ushuaia ("westward-looking bay" in local Yamana dialect), Argentina, base camp for explorations of the Beagle Channel and the forested peaks of the Cordillera Darwin mountain range, is far and away the leading tourist attraction of the region.

Elephant seal, Península Valdés, Argentina

CALENDAR OF FAUNA ON PENINSULA VALDES

Although few wildlife-viewing experiences are as grandiose as seeing whales breach or witnessing orcas charge the beaches in a hunt for sea lions, there are numerous special moments throughout the yearly cycles of all Atlantic Patagonian fauna. Regardless of what time you visit, you'll be witnessing something memorable.

(above) Elephant seal bull with Snowy Sheathbill (top right) Dolphin Gull (bottom right) Southern Right Whale off Puerto Piramides

Since practically everyone who visits Península Valdés is here for the wildlife, any guide we recommend (⇨ *see Península Valdés Essentials section, below)* will know where to go for the best views of the wildlife that's most active. Renting a car is a possibility, but going with a guide service makes things easier—your guide will be able to navigate the unpaved roads while you scan the land and water for creatures.

Here is a Península Valdés wildlife primer to get you acquainted with what you'll see when.

WHEN TO GO

Birds: June–Dec.

Whales: June–Dec.

Dolphins: Dec.–Mar.

Elephant Seals: year round

Sea Lions: year round

Orcas: Sept.–Apr.

Penguins: Sept.–Mar.

SCOPE IT OUT

Consider purchasing or renting binoculars or a scope; your guide might provide them as part of the package.

LOOK TO THE WATER FOR . . .

Southern Right Whales. The first southern right whales arrive in Golfo Nuevo between the end of April and the beginning of May, and can be observed from beaches in and along Puerto Madryn as well as the Península Valdés. Your best chance of seeing them will be from a whale-watching point at Puerto Pirámides. These whales are between 36 and 59 feet long, and have several endearing behaviors such as "sailing," where they hold their fins up in the air, and when a mother uses her flippers to teach calves how to swim.

Elephant Seals. Elephant seals are larger mammals than sea lions, and have a different way of moving—using their flippers to waddle along on land, whereas sea lions use both front and back flippers to thrust themselves forward. Adult males can reach up to 6 meters (20 feet) in length and weigh up to 4 tons, and after four years develop a proboscis, or elephant-like appendage on their noses, which inflates to help produce sounds. The biggest elephant-seal colonies are in Península Valdés, at Punta Cantor and Punta Delgada.

Sea Lions. In January and February sea lions begin to form "harems," with each dominant male taking up to a dozen females. The fights to maintain these harems can be bloody and violent, and sometimes it's possible to witness an invading male drag off one of the females from the harem with his teeth. Most of the year, however, sea-lion colonies appear peaceful: the animals sun themselves or swim, and the pups are especially curious and playful. They can be observed year-round all along the Atlantic Coast. Summertime (which in the Southern Hemisphere begins on December 21) up until April is when sea lions and elephant seals are reproducing and raising pups.

Orcas. It's possible to see the black fins of orcas cutting through the water along the coastline, occasionally storming the beach in violent and spectacular chases. The best place to see orcas is at the extreme northern tip of Península Valdés, Punta Norte, in April.

LOOK TO THE AIR AND LAND FOR . . .

Seabirds. Among the many seabirds found in Patagonia—including dolphin gulls, kelp geese, southern giant petrels, rock and blue-eyed cormorants, snowy sheathbills, blackish oystercatchers, and steamer ducks—one species, the arctic tern, has the longest migration—it flies over 21,750 miles annually from the Arctic to Antarctics and back.

Penguins. Along Atlantic Patagonia—most notably Punta Tombo—there are large rookeries of Magellanic penguins, with up to 500,000 of these flightless birds. The males arrive from the sea each August. A month later the females arrive and the males begin fighting territorial battles. In October and into November the nesting pairs incubate the eggs. Once the chicks hatch in November, the parents make continual trips to the ocean for food. In January the chicks leave the nest, learning to swim in February. Their plumage matures throughout the fall, when the penguins begin migrating north to Brazil.

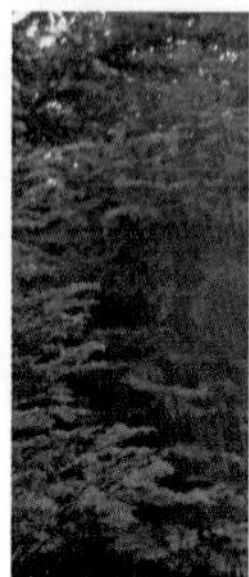

Updated by Amanda Barnes

Patagonia is a hybrid of the cultures of primarily European immigrants, who came here in the 19th century, and the cultures of the indigenous peoples, mainly the Tehuelche and Mapuche. The native Tehuelches fished and hunted the coast and pampas, and their spears and arrowheads are still found along riverbeds and beaches.

The first Spanish explorer, Hernando Magallanes, arrived in Golfo Nuevo in 1516, and was followed by several other Spanish expeditions throughout the 17th and 18th centuries. From 1826 to 1836 two English captains, Parker King, of the *Adventure,* and Robert Fitzroy, sailing the *Beagle,* made the first accurate nautical maps of the region. The indigenous populations are nearly all gone since the genocidal four-year military campaign (1879–83) led by General Roca and known euphemistically as the Conquest of the Desert.

Inland, a Welsh pioneer named Henry Jones explored the Chubut River valley in 1814. Fifty years later a small group of Welsh families—fleeing religious persecution in Great Britain—became the first Europeans to move to this area permanently, clearing the way for waves of Welsh immigrants that forged colonies in Gaiman, Trelew, Rawson, and Puerto Madryn. Beginning in the mid-19th century the Argentinian government courted settlers from all over Europe, including Italy, Spain, and Germany, as well as Boers from South Africa, offering land as a strategy for displacing indigenous populations and fortifying the young nation against neighboring Chile. These settlers adapted their agrarian traditions to the Patagonian terrain, planting windbreaks of Lombardy poplar along with fruit trees and flower gardens. They set up dairy farms and sheep ranches, and continued their cultural traditions and cuisine, such as Welsh tea, still found throughout Patagonia today.

Atlantic Patagonia is where the low windswept pampas meet the ocean. It's a land of immense panoramic horizons and a coastline of bays, inlets, and peninsulas teeming with seabirds and marine wildlife. The region is most famous for Península Valdés, a UNESCO Natural World Heritage Site where travelers can see southern right whales, orcas, southern elephant seals, and sea lions. There are seemingly endless dirt roads where you won't see another person or vehicle for hours, only guanacos, rheas, and other animals running across the steppe.

Farther south and inland to the Andes, the towns of El Calafate and El Chaltén come alive in summer (December–March) with the influx of visitors to the Parque Nacional los Glaciares, and climbers headed for Cerro Torre and Cerro Fitzroy. Imagine sailing across a blue lake full of icebergs, or traversing an advancing glacier in the shadow of the end of the Andes mountain range, watching a valley being formed before your eyes. A trip here is like a trip back to the Ice Age. It is that glacier, Perito Moreno, that is bringing tourists to this region in unprecedented numbers.

Experiencing Patagonia, however, still means crossing vast deserts to reach isolated population centers. It means taking deep breaths of mountain air and draughts of pure stream water in the shadow of dramatic snowcapped peaks. Most of all, it means being embraced by independent, pioneering souls beginning to understand the importance of tourism as traditional industries—wool, livestock, fishing, and oil—are drying up.

PATAGONIA PLANNER

WHEN TO GO

Late September to February—spring and summer in the Southern Hemisphere—is high season in Patagonia. Reservations are advised, especially September and October in Atlantic Patagonia and December–February in Southern Patagonia. Although the summer sun can be strong, the winds whistle year-round, so always bring extra layers and a windbreaker. In Atlantic Patagonia many properties close in April and May to prepare for the first whale-watchers in June and July. Southern Patagonia all but shuts down June–August.

GETTING HERE AND AROUND

AIR TRAVEL

Flying is the best way to reach Patagonia from Buenos Aires—flights from other parts of the country also go through here. The most popular route is between Aeroparque Jorge Newberry in Palermo, a short cab ride from downtown, and Trelew's tiny airport, which is the gateway to Atlantic Patagonia.

Aerolíneas Argentinas (🌐 *www.aerolineas.com.ar*) flies (along with its subsidiary Austral) several times daily between Buenos Aires and Trelew, Comodoro Rivadavia, or El Calafate and once or twice a day between Trelew and El Calafate and Ushuaia. LADE (Líneas Aéreas del Estado 🌐 *www.lade.com.ar*) connects Trelew and Comodoro Rivadavia to other parts of Patagonia, including Bariloche, El Calafate, and Ushuaia. Andes Líneas Aéreas (🌐 *www.andesonline.com*) has direct flights between Buenos Aires and Puerto Madryn three times per week. LAN (🌐 *www.lan.com*) also flies between Buenos Aires and Comodoro Rivadavia, Rio Gallegos, El Calafate, and Ushuaia a couple of times per week.

Although Aerolíneas Argentinas and Andes Líneas Aéreas offer cheaper tickets to Argentineans than to visitors, tickets with LADE and LAN are at one flat price regardless of nationality. The volcanic ash from the eruption in Chile in June 2011 continues to affect flights, so always check with operators before going to the airport. Strikes are also pretty common in Buenos Aires.

BUS TRAVEL

Comfortable overnight sleeper buses connect Patagonia to Buenos Aires (and other major cities). However, as getting to even the closest city in Atlantic Patagonia, Puerto Madryn, takes 20 hours, most travelers feel it's worth the price to fly. All the same, buses are a major form of transportation between destinations up to about 600 km (370 miles) apart. Don Otto (🌐 *www.donotto.com.ar*) is the most reliable carrier.

CAR TRAVEL

If you truly enjoy the call of the open road, there are few places that can rival the vast emptiness and jaw-dropping beauty of Patagonia. Be prepared for miles and miles of semi-desert steppes with no gas stations, towns, or even restrooms. Always carry plenty of water, snacks, a jack and tire-changing tools, with at least one spare. Take extra care when driving on *ripio* (gravel roads): it's easy to flip small cars at speeds over 80 kmh (55 mph). Fill your tank at every opportunity. If you're not driving, consider simply paying for a *remis* (car with driver) for day excursions.

RESTAURANTS

With so many miles of coastline, it's not surprising that Atlantic Patagonia is famous for its seafood, notably sole and salmon, *mejillones* (mussels), and *pulpo* (octopus). *Centolla* (king crab) is another specialty, especially south of Comodoro Rivadavia. Most restaurants are sit-down-and-take-your-time affairs that don't open for dinner until at least 8, and despite all the seafood on offer, steak still reigns supreme. The other carnivorous staple in the area is *cordero patagónico,* local lamb, usually served barbecued or stewed. Dining prices in most Patagonian cities rival those of upper-end Buenos Aires restaurants. Thankfully, so do the skills of local chefs, although expect more basic offerings of pizza, milanesas, and empanadas in smaller towns. Whenever possible, accompany your meal with a bottle of wine from one of the increasing number of Patagonian wineries.

Huge numbers of foreign visitors mean that vegetarian options are getting better; *woks de verdura* (vegetable stir-fries) are a newly ubiquitous option. Most cafés and bars serve quick bites known as *minutas.* The region is also famous for its stone fruits, which are used in various jams, preserves, sweets, and *alfajores* (a chocolate-covered sandwich of two cookies with jam in the middle). When in El Calafate, be sure to nibble on some calafate berries—legend has it if you eat them in El Calafate you are destined to return one day soon.

HOTELS

Although there are large, expensive hotels in Puerto Madryn, Trelew, and Comodoro Rivadavia, bed-and-breakfasts and other smaller *hosterías* offer the best deals and often the best lodging throughout the

CLOSE UP

Border Crossing

The border between Chile and Argentina is still strictly maintained, but crossing it doesn't present much difficulty beyond getting out your passport and waiting in a line to get the stamp. Most travelers end up crossing the border by bus, which means getting out of the vehicle for 30–45 minutes to go through the bureaucratic proceedings, then loading back in.

Crossing by car is also quite manageable (check with your car-rental company for restrictions on international travel). Chilean customs officers are extremely strict about bringing food into the country, especially compared to their Argentine counterparts.

region. Punta Arenas has many historic hotels offering luxurious amenities and fine service. A night or two in one of them should be part of your trip. Several good resorts and lodges skirt Puerto Natales or are within Parque Nacional Torres del Paine. The terms *hospedaje* and *hostal* are used interchangeably in the region, so don't make assumptions based on the name. Many *hostals* are fine hotels—not youth hostels with multiple beds—just very small. By contrast, some *hospedajes* are little more than a spare room in someone's home.

WHAT IT COSTS IN PESOS

	$	$$	$$$	$$$$
Restaurants	30 pesos and under	31 pesos–50 pesos	51 pesos–75 pesos	over 75 pesos
Hotels	300 pesos and under	301 pesos–500 pesos	501 pesos–800 pesos	over 800 pesos

Restaurant prices are based on the median main course price at dinner. Hotel prices are for two people in a standard double room in high season.

HEALTH AND SAFETY

Most mountains are not high enough to induce altitude sickness, but the weather can turn nasty very quickly. Sunglasses and sunscreen are essential. Although tap water is safe to drink throughout the region, most travelers still choose to drink bottled water. Do not approach or let your children approach sea lions, penguins, or any other animals, no matter how docile or curious they might seem.

Emergency Services Coast Guard ☎ *106.* **Fire** ☎ *100.* **Forest Fire** ☎ *103.* **Hospital** ☎ *107.* **Police** ☎ *101.*

PUERTO MADRYN AND PENÍNSULA VALDÉS

Visiting populations of whales, orcas, sea lions, elephant seals, and penguins all gather to breed or feed on or near the shores of this unique peninsula—at 132 feet below sea level, it's the lowest point on the South American continent. The wildlife isn't only water-based. Wandering the Patagonian scrub are guanacos, grey foxes, *maras* (Patagonian hares), skunks, armadillos, and rheas, while myriad bird species fill the air. There are also three inland salt lakes, and the curving gulf at Puerto Pirámides is one of the few places in Argentina where the sun sets over the water, not the land. With nature putting on such a generous display, it's not surprising that the 3,625-square-km (1,400-square-mile) peninsula has been designated a UNESCO World Heritage Site and is the main reason visitors come to Atlantic Patagonia.

Puerto Madryn is where you'll head first for organized excursions onto the peninsula. While a major part of the town's identity is as a staging ground for these trips, it's also well worth exploring and has an interesting history. The first economic boom came in 1886, when the Patagonian railroad was introduced, spurring port activities along with the salt and fishing industries. Although it isn't likely that the original Welsh settlers who arrived here in 1865 could have imagined just how much Puerto Madryn would evolve, a large part of the town's success is owed to their hardworking traditions, which continue with their descendants today. The anniversary of their arrival is celebrated every 28th of July here and in other Chubut towns. Only a statue—the Tehuelche Indian Monument—serves as a reminder of the indigenous people who once lived here and who helped the Welsh survive.

PUERTO MADRYN

67 km (41½ miles) north of Trelew; 450 km (279 miles) north of Comodoro Rivadavía; 104 km (64 miles) west of Puerto Pirámides.

Approaching from Ruta 3, it's hard to believe that the horizon-line of buildings perched just beyond the windswept dunes and badlands is the most successful of all coastal Patagonia settlements. But once you get past the outskirts of town and onto the wide coastal road known as the Rambla, the picture begins to change. Ranged along the clear and tranquil Golfo Nuevo are restaurants, cafés, dive shops, and hotels, all busy—but not yet overcrowded—with tourists from around the world.

Puerto Madryn is more a base for visiting nearby wildlife-watching sites like Península Valdés and Punta Tombo than a destination in its own right. The town's architecture is unremarkable, and beyond a walk along the coast there isn't much to do. Indeed, even the few museums serve mainly to introduce you to the fauna you'll see elsewhere. The exception is the very beginning of whale season (May–July), when the huge animals cavort right in the bay before heading north—you can even walk out alongside them on the pier. During these months it's worth the extra expense for a room with a sea view.

The many tour agencies and rental-car companies here make excursion planning easy. Aim to spend most of your time here on one- or

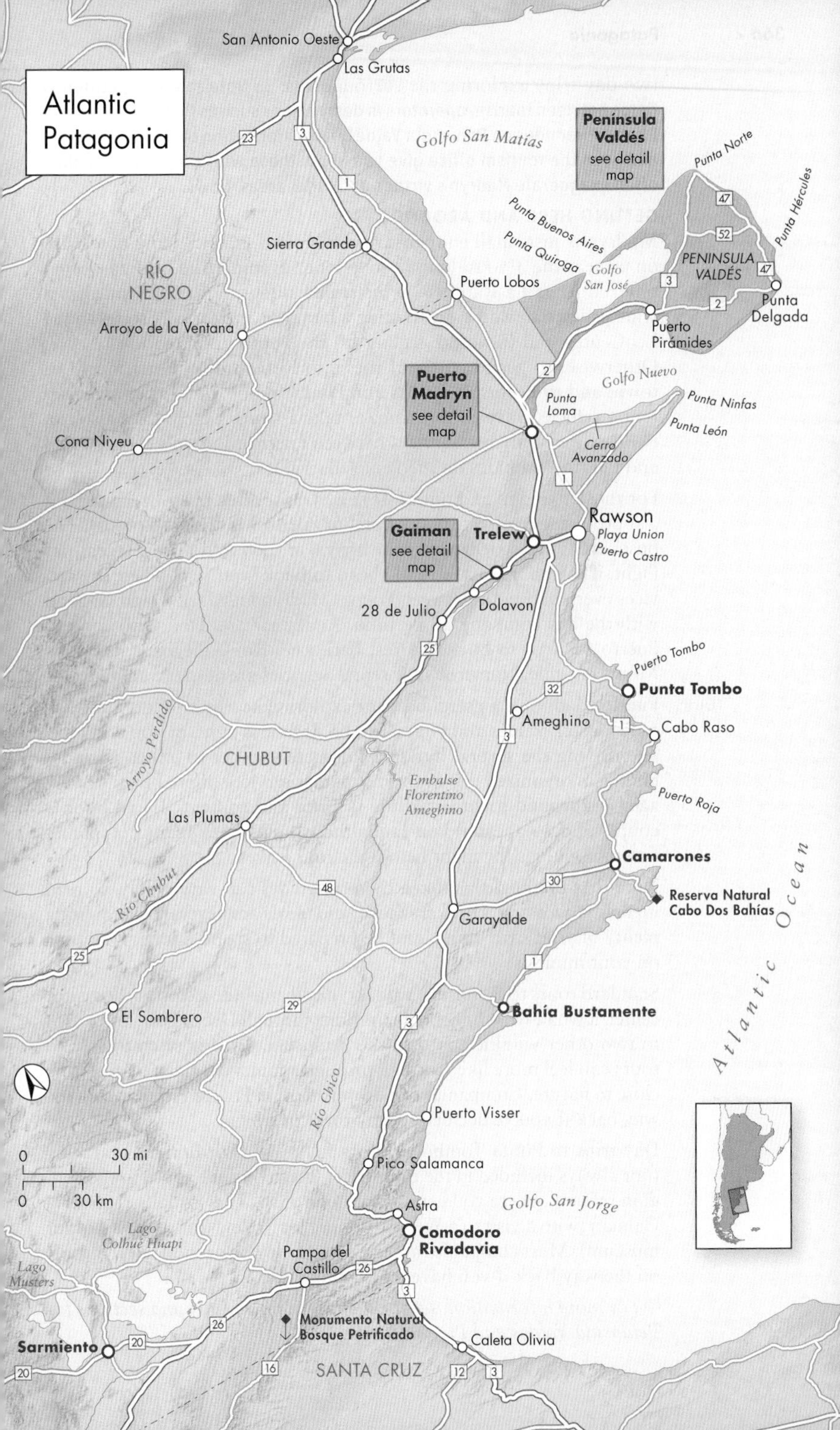

Atlantic Patagonia
San Antonio Oeste
Las Grutas
Golfo San Matías
Península Valdés see detail map
Punta Norte
Punta Hércules
Punta Buenos Aires
Punta Quiroga
Golfo San José
PENINSULA VALDÉS
Punta Delgada
Puerto Pirámides
Sierra Grande
Puerto Lobos
RÍO NEGRO
Arroyo de la Ventana
Golfo Nuevo
Punta Loma
Punta Ninfas
Punta León
Puerto Madryn see detail map
Cerro Avanzado
Cona Niyeu
Rawson
Playa Union
Puerto Castro
Gaiman see detail map
Trelew
Dolavon
28 de Julio
Puerto Tombo
Punta Tombo
Ameghino
Cabo Raso
Arroyo Perdido
CHUBUT
Embalse Florentino Ameghino
Puerto Roja
Las Plumas
Camarones
Reserva Natural Cabo Dos Bahías
Río Chubut
Garayalde
Atlantic Ocean
Bahía Bustamente
El Sombrero
Río Chico
Puerto Visser
Pico Salamanca
0 30 mi
0 30 km
Golfo San Jorge
Astra
Lago Colhué Huapi
Comodoro Rivadavia
Lago Musters
Pampa del Castillo
Monumento Natural Bosque Petrificado
Sarmiento
Caleta Olivia
SANTA CRUZ
23
3
1
47
52
2
32
25
30
48
29
26
20
16
12

two-day trips exploring the surroundings. ⚠ **Note that competition is fierce between tourism operators in destinations such as Puerto Madryn and Puerto Pirámides on Península Valdés. Take information that tour operators and even the tourism office give you about these with a grain of salt: they often exaggerate Madryn's virtues and other areas' flaws.**

GETTING HERE AND AROUND

Madryn is just small enough to walk around in, and many hotels are on or near the 3½-km-long (2-mile-long) Avenida Alte. Brown—often referred to as La Rambla—which runs alongside the bay and has a wide pedestrian walkway. Renting a bicycle is a great way to reach the EcoCentro and (if you're feeling fit) the Punta Loma nature reserve. Otherwise, to get to either of these, to El Doradillo beach north of town, and to Península Valdés and Punta Tombo you'll need to either rent a vehicle, travel with a tour, or take a *remis*. Mar y Valle also run two to three daily bus services between Puerto Madryn's bus terminal and Puerto Pirámides on the Península Valdés.

For those flying in and out of Trelew, Transportes Eben-Ezer operates a shuttle service direct to any hotel in Puerto Madryn (50 pesos). The buses are timed to leave after the arrival of each Aerolíneas Argentinas flight. They fill up fast, so call ahead to book your seat. There are services every half hour between Puerto Madryn and Trelew and Gaiman with the bus company 28 de Julio. Andesmar and Don Otto connect Puerto Madryn to Buenos Aires, Bariloche, Río Gallegos, and Puerto Montt in Chile. Numerous car rental agencies are along Avenida Roca.

TOURS Puerto Madryn is a useful base for exploring nearby wildlife sites such as Península Valdés and Punta Tombo. If time is tight, or you don't feel like driving the several hundred kilometers to get to either, consider taking an organized day tour. The regular services offered by the many agencies around town vary little in price and content. Try to book a couple of days ahead if you can, although mid-week many companies accept bookings the night before the tour leaves.

Note that the English spoken by most guides can vary wildly, so read up on the area first. Drinks, snacks, and meals are never included: bring plenty of your own along, and be prepared to spend a long, long time on your minibus.

Standard tours to Península Valdés typically include a stop at the visitor center, a whale-watching boat trip (June through December), and a visit to two other wildlife spots on the peninsula. Time is often tight, and tours can feel more like working through a fauna checklist than getting close to nature. Companies can drop you off in Puerto Pirámides on the way back if you've decided to stay there overnight.

Day trips to Punta Tombo stop off at Rawson for dolphin-watching (not always included in the tour price), then continue south to the penguin reserve, where you get a scant hour or so. They usually return via Gaiman (with a visit to a Welsh teahouse) or Trelew (to see the dinosaur museum). Most companies are happy to drop you at the Trelew airport on the way back if you have an evening flight.

⇨ *For more information, see the Getting Here and Around sections for Península Valdés and Punta Tombo.*

Continued on page 376

INTO THE WILD

by Tim Patterson

Patagonia will shatter your sense of scale. You will feel very small, surrounded by an epic expanse of mountains and plains, sea, and sky. Whether facing down an advancing wall of glacial ice, watching an ostrich-like rhea racing across the open steppe, or getting splashed by a breaching right whale off the Valdez Peninsula, prepare to gasp at the majesty of the Patagonian wild.

GLACIERS OF PATAGONIA

Cruise on Lago Argentino, Santa Cruz province, Glaciers National Park, Argentina

The Patagonia ice field covers much of the southern end of the Andean mountain range, straddling the Argentina–Chile border. The glaciers that spill off the high altitude ice field are basically rivers of slowly moving ice and snow that grind and push their way across the mountains, crushing soft rock and sculpting granite peaks.

Most of Patagonia's glaciers spill into lakes, rivers, or fjords. Chunks of ice calve off the face of the glacier into the water, a dramatic display of nature's power that you can view at several locations. The larger pieces of ice become icebergs that scud across the water surface like white sailboats blown by the wind.

TRAVEL SHRINKS

The link between high-impact activities—such as air travel—and climate change is clear, leading to a disturbing irony: the more people come to see the glaciers of Patagonia, the more carbon is released into the atmosphere, and the more the glaciers shrink.

WEATHER

Weather is unpredictable around glaciers: it's not uncommon to experience sunshine, rain, and snow squalls in a single afternoon.

ICE COLORS

Although clear days are best for panoramas, cloudy days bring out the translucent blue of the glacial ice, creating great opportunities for magical photographs. You'll also see black or gray streaks in the ice caused by sediment picked up by the glacier as it grinds down the mountain valley. When that sediment is deposited into lakes, it hangs suspended in the water, turning the lake a pale milky blue.

ENVIRONMENTAL CONCERN

There's no question that human-induced climate change is taking its toll on Patagonia's glaciers. Although the famous Perito Moreno glacier is still advancing, nearly all the others have shrunk in recent years, some dramatically. You can find out more about the effects of climate change and their impact on the glaciers at Calafate's new Gaciarium museum.

Right: Glacier Grey, Paine Circuit, Torres del Paine National Park, Chile

GLACIERS TO SEE

- Perito Moreno Glacier, Santa Cruz, Argentina
- Upsala Glacier, Santa Cruz, Argentina
- Martial Glacier, Tierra del Fuego, Argentina
- Serrano Glacier, Tierra del Fuego, Chile
- O'Higgins Glacier, Southern Coast, Chile

FIRE AND ICE: MOUNTAINS OF PATAGONIA

A trekker takes in the view of Cerro Torre (left) and Fitz Roy in Los Glaciares National Park, Patagonia.

In Patagonia, mountains mean the Andes, a relatively young range but a precocious one that stretches for more than 4,000 miles. The Patagonian Andes are of special interest to geologists, who study how fire, water, and ice have shaped the mountains into their present form.

CREATION

Plate tectonics are the most fundamental factor in the formation of the southern Andes, with the oceanic Nazca plate slipping beneath the continental South American plate and forcing the peaks skyward. Volcanic activity is a symptom of this dynamic process, and there are several active volcanoes on the Chilean side of the range.

GLACIAL IMPRINT

Glacial activity has also played an important role in chiseling the most iconic Patagonian peaks. The spires that form the distinctive skylines of Torres del Paine and the Fitzroy range are solid columns that were created when rising glaciers ripped away weaker rock, leaving only hard granite skeletons that stand rigid at the edge of the ice fields.

MOUNTAIN HIGH BORDERS

Because the border between Chile and Argentina cuts through the most impenetrable reaches of the ice field, the actual border line is unclear in areas of the far south. Even in the more temperate north, border crossings are often located at mountain passes, and the officials who stamp visas seem more like mountain guides than bureaucrats.

MOUNTAINS OF THE SEA

Tierra del Fuego and the countless islands off the coast of southern Chile were once connected to the mainland. Over the years the sea swept into the valleys, isolated the peaks, and created an archipelago that, viewed on a map, looks as abstract as a Jackson Pollack painting. From the water these island mountains appear especially dramatic, misty pinnacles of rock and ice rising from the crashing sea.

Right: Mt. Fitzroy

PROMINENT PEAKS AND RANGES

- Mt. Fitzroy and Cerro Torre, Santa Cruz, Argentina
- Cuernos of Torres del Paine, Chile
- Beagle Channel Mountains, Tierra del Fuego, Chile/Argentina
- Cerro Piltriqitron, El Bolson, Argentina
- Osorno Volcano, Lake District, Chile

YAY, PINGÜINOS!

Magellanic Penguin walking to his nest in Peninsula Valdes

Everyone loves penguins. How could you not feel affection for such cute, curious, and loyal little creatures? On land, their awkward waddle is endearing, and you can get close enough to see the inquisitive gaze in their eyes as they turn their heads from side to side for a good look at you. In the water, penguins transform from goofballs into Olympic athletes, streaking through the waves and returning to the nest with mouthfuls of fish and squid for their chicks.

TYPES

Most of the penguins you'll see here are Magellanic penguins, black and white colored birds that gather in large breeding colonies on the beaches of Patagonia in the summer and retreat north to warmer climes during winter. Also keep an eye out for the red-beaked Gentoo penguins that nest among the Magellanics.

If your image of penguins is the large and colorful Emperor penguins of Antarctica that featured in the documentary *March of the Penguins*, you might be slightly underwhelmed by the little Magellanics. Adults stand about 30 inches tall and weigh between 15 and 20 pounds. What they lack in glamour, Patagonia's penguins make up in vanity—and numbers. Many breeding sites are home to tens of thousands of individuals, all preening and strutting as if they were about to walk the red carpet at the Academy Awards.

PENGUIN RELATIONS

Male and female penguins form monogamous pairs and share the task of raising the chicks, which hatch in small burrows that the parents return to year after year. If you sit and observe a pair of penguins for a little while you'll notice how affectionate they appear, grooming each other with their beaks and huddling together on the nest.

HUMAN CONTACT

Although penguins are not shy of humans who keep a respectful distance (about 8 feet is a good rule of thumb), the history of penguin-human relations is not entirely one of peaceful curiosity. Early pioneers and stranded sailors would raid penguin nests for food, and in modern times, oil spills have devastated penguin colonies in Patagonia.

Magellanic Penguins

WHERE & WHEN

The best time to see penguins is from November through February, which coincides with the best weather in coastal Patagonia. Some of the most convenient and impressive colonies to visit are:

- Punta Tombo, Chubut, Argentina
- Cabo Virgenes, Santa Cruz, Argentina
- Isla Madalena, Chile
- Martillo Island, Tierra del Fuego, Argentina
- Puerto San Julian, Santa Cruz, Argentina

IN THE SEA

The Patagonian coast teems with marine life, including numerous "charismatic megafauna" such as whales, dolphins, sea lions, and seals.

❶ Seals and Sea Lions

In the springtime massive elephant seals and southern sea lions drag themselves onto Patagonian beaches for mating season—hopefully out of range of hungry orcas. These giant pinnipeds form two groups in the breeding colonies. Big, tough alpha bulls have their own harems of breeding females and their young, while so-called bachelor males hang out nearby like freshman boys at a fraternity party, hoping to entice a stray female away from the alpha bull's harem.

❷ Orcas

Orcas aren't as common as dolphins, but you can spot them off the Valdez Peninsula, Argentina, hunting seals and sea lions along the shore. Sometimes hungry orcas will chase their prey a few feet too far and beach themselves above the tide line, where they perish of dehydration.

❸ Whales

The Valdez Peninsula is also one of the best places to observe right whales, gentle giants of the ocean. Although the name right whale derives from whalers who designated it as the "right" whale to kill, the right whale is now protected by both national legislation and international agreements.

❹ Dolphins

Dolphins are easy to spot on tours, because they're curious and swim up to the boat, sometimes even surfing the bow wake. Commerson's dolphins are a common species in coastal Argentina and the Straights of Magellan. Among the world's tiniest dolphins, their white and black coloring has earned them the nickname "skunk dolphin" and prompted comparisons with their distant cousins, orcas.

IN THE AIR

5

9

6

7

8

Patagonia is a twitcher's paradise. Even non-bird-lovers marvel at the colorful species that squawk, flutter, and soar through Patagonia's skies.

❺ Albatross

You can spot several species of albatross off the Patagonian coast, gliding on fixed wings above the waves. The albatross lives almost entirely at sea, touching down on land to breed and raise its young. Unless you're visiting Antarctica or the Falklands, your best bet for seeing an albatross is to take a cruise from Punta Arenas or Ushuaia.

❻ Andean Condor

You probably won't see a condor up close. They nest on high-altitude rock ledges and spend their days soaring in circles on high thermals, scanning mountain slopes and plains for carrion. With a wing span of up to 10 feet, however, the king of the Andean skies is impressive even when viewed from a distance. Condors live longer than almost any other bird. Some could qualify for Social Security.

❼ Magellanic Woodpecker

You can hear the distinctive rat-tat of this enormous woodpecker in nothofagus forests of Chilean Patagonia and parts of Argentina. Males have a bright red head and a black body, while females are almost entirely black.

❽ Rhea (Nandu)

No, it's not an ostrich. The rhea is an extremely large flightless bird that roams the Patagonian steppe. Although they're not normally aggressive, males have been known to charge humans who get too close to their partner's nests.

❾ Kelp Goose

As the name implies, kelp geese love kelp. In fact, kelp is the only thing they eat. The geese travel along the rocky shores of Tierra del Fuego in search of their favorite seaweed salad.

Restaurants ▼
Cantina El Náutico 1
El Vernardion Club Mar 2

Hotels ▼
Australis Yene Hue Hotel and Spa ... 1
Hostería Las Maras 3
Hotel Peninsula Valdés 2

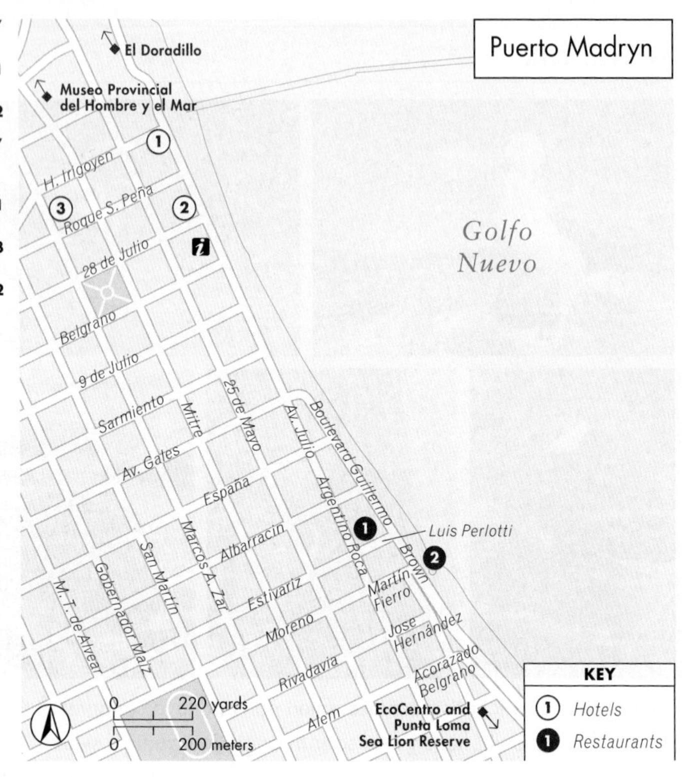

Botazzi is the only Madryn-based tour operator with its own whale-watching boats—its tours to Península Valdés are slightly more expensive than those of other companies, but it guarantees you 1½ hours on the water. Nievemar and Miras del Mar are two other reliable operators—the latter's Punta Tombo tours are particularly good value. If you're after a more personal experience, talk to Causana Viajes, who create custom special-interest trips.

ESSENTIALS

Bus Contacts 28 de Julio ✉ *Terminal de Ómnibus, Puerto Madryn, Chubut* ☎ *2965/472–056.* **Andesmar** ✉ *Terminal de Ómnibus, Puerto Madryn, Chubut* ☎ *2965/473–764* 🌐 *www.andesmar.com.* **Don Otto** ✉ *Terminal de Ómnibus, Puerto Madryn, Chubut* ☎ *2965/451–675* 🌐 *www.donotto.com.ar.* **Mar y Valle** ✉ *Terminal de Ómnibus, Puerto Madryn, Chubut* ☎ *2965/450–600.* **Transportes Eben-Ezer** ✉ *Puerto Madryn, Chubut* ☎ *2965/472–474.*

Currency Exchange Banco de la Nación ✉ *9 de Julio 127, Puerto Madryn, Chubut* ☎ *2965/474–466* 🌐 *www.bna.com.ar.* **Banco del Chubut** ✉ *25 de Mayo 154, Puerto Madryn, Chubut* ☎ *2965/471–250* 🌐 *www.bancochubut.com.ar.* **Thaler Cambio** ✉ *Av. Roca 497, Puerto Madryn, Chubut* ☎ *2965/455–858.*

Post Office Puerto Madryn ✉ *Belgrano at Maíz, Puerto Madryn, Chubut.*

Visitor Info Puerto Madryn ✉ *Av. Roca 223, Puerto Madryn, Chubut* ☎ *2965/453–504, 2965/456–067* 🌐 *www.madryn.gov.ar/turismo.*

Tour Info Bottazzi ✉ *Complejo La Torre, Martin Fierro 852 at Blvd. Brown, Puerto Madryn, Chubut* ☎ *2965/474–110* 🌐 *www.titobottazzi.com.* **Miras del Mar** ✉ *Moreno 316, Puerto Madryn, Chubut* ☎ *2965/474–316* 🌐 *www.mirasdelmar.com.* **Nievemar** ✉ *Av. Roca 493, Puerto Madryn, Chubut* ☎ *2965/455–544* 🌐 *www.nievemartours.com.ar.*

EXPLORING

EcoCentro. From its perch on a windswept outcrop 4 km (2½ miles) south of the town center, this museum and research center affords excellent views of Madryn's bays and desolate coastline. Inside, thoughtful, well-translated displays introduce you to the area's ocean fauna and seek to promote marine conservation. An invertebrates "touch pool" and a whale-sounds exhibit—which you reach by walking through a curtain imitating baleen plates—are especially good for kids. All the same, the exhibits are a little scanty to justify the astronomical entrance price. A slick gift shop and café are also on-site. ✉ *Julio Verne 3784, Puerto Madryn, Chubut* ☎ *2965/457–470* 🌐 *www.ecocentro.org.ar* *44 pesos* ⌚ *Jan. and Feb., daily 5–9; Mar. and July–Sept., Wed.–Mon. 3–7; Apr.–June, Wed.–Sun. 3–7; Oct.–Dec., Wed.–Mon. 3–8.*

El Doradillo. Following the coastal road 14 km (9 miles) north from Puerto Madryn brings you to this whale-watching spot. The ocean floor drops away steeply from the beach, so between the months of June and mid-December you can stand on the sand almost alongside southern right whales, usually mothers teaching their young to swim. During the rest of the year it's just a regular beach. It's a pleasant 1½ hours' bike ride from Puerto Madryn. Taxis charge about 150 pesos for the round-trip including a 45-minute stay. ✉ *Puerto Madryn, Chubut* *Free.*

Museo Provincial del Hombre y el Mar (Ciencias Naturales y Oceanografía). This whimsical collection of taxidermic animals, shells, skeletons, and engravings examines man's relationship with the sea. Housed in a restored 1915 building, the beautifully displayed exhibits evoke the marine myths of the Tehuelche, imagined European sea-monsters, the ideas of 19th-century naturalists, through to modern ecology. It's more about experience than explanation, so don't worry about the scarcity of English translations, although the excellent room on orca behavior is a welcome exception. Finish by looking out over the city and surrounding steppes from the tower. ✉ *Domecq García at José Menéndez, Puerto Madryn, Chubut* ☎ *2965/451–139* *6 pesos* ⌚ *Mar.–Nov., weekdays 9–7, weekends 3–7; Dec.–Feb., weekdays 9–8, weekends 4–8.*

Punta Loma Sea Lion Reserve. Some 600 South American sea lions lounge on the shore below a tall, crescent bluff at Punta Loma, 17 km (10½ miles) southeast of the city. Aim to visit during low tide. You can reach the reserve by car (follow signs toward Punta Ninfas); by bicycle, if the wind is not too strong; or by taxi—expect to pay about 150 pesos for the return trip including a 45-minute stay. ✉ *Puerto Madryn, Chubut* *35 pesos* ⌚ *Visit during low tide—check local paper or tourism office for tide schedule. Open 8–8.*

WHERE TO EAT

$$ SEAFOOD **Cantina El Náutico.** Photos of visiting Argentinean celebrities mingle with the marine-themed doodads that cover the walls at this firm local favorite. Run by three generations of a French Basque family, it specializes in simple fish and seafood dishes and homemade pasta, all served in huge portions. ✉ *Av. Roca 790, Puerto Madryn, Chubut* ☎ *2965/471–404.*

$$ ARGENTINE **Vernardino Club de Mar.** Set right on the beach, this bright, airy restaurant has one of the most pleasant locations in Puerto Madryn. If the wind allows, bag a terrace table at lunch, the perfect setting for a big bowl of calamari or one of their imaginative salads. Candles come out at night, together with more elaborate dishes like beef in a wild mushroom and beer reduction, or fresh-caught local salmon in a creamy mussel sauce. ✉ *Blvd. Brown 860, Puerto Madryn, Chubut* ☎ *2965/474–289* ▭ *No credit cards.*

LITERARY PATAGONIA

The British writer Bruce Chatwin achieved widespread acclaim with his work *In Patagonia* (1977), a lyrical journey many consider among the greatest travel books of all time, despite criticism related to Chatwin's embellishments. Much of Charles Darwin's classic *Voyage of the Beagle* (1839) takes place in Patagonia, where the young naturalist marveled at the region's stark geology during a boat trip up the Río Santa Cruz.

WHERE TO STAY

For expanded hotel reviews, visit Fodors.com.

$$$ **Australis Yene Hue Hotel and Spa.** This self-styled luxury hotel gets off to a good start with its cavernous lobby with cascading water garden and luminous breakfast room overlooking the bay; with their textured gray and yellow walls, boxy TV sets, and small beds, the rooms are rather less impressive, but at least they're spacious. **Pros:** the terrace pool, small gym, and spa make it the best-equipped hotel in Puerto Madryn. **Cons:** service is rough around the edges; bland rooms aren't up to the price. ✉ *Av. Roca 33, Puerto Madryn, Chubut* ☎ *2965/471–214* 🌐 *www.hotelesaustralis.com.ar* *71 rooms* *In-room: safe, Wi-Fi. In-hotel: bar, pool, gym, spa, business center* *Breakfast.*

$$ ★ **Hostería Las Maras.** Sofas, potted plants, warm lighting, and polished wooden tables bring a homey feel to the lobby of this small redbrick hotel; comfy beds with crisp white covers make the rooms just as snug, though consider the newly built superior doubles if you're after a bit more space. **Pros:** peaceful; home-away-from-home vibe. **Cons:** not on the waterfront. ✉ *Marcos A. Zar 64, Puerto Madryn, Chubut* ☎ *2965/453–215* 🌐 *www.hosterialasmaras.com.ar* *20 rooms* *In-room: no a/c, Wi-Fi. In-hotel: business center* *Breakfast.*

$$$ **Hotel Península Valdés.** The minimal gray-and-taupe lobby and slick, wooden-walled breakfast bar are the result of the gradual renovation of this well-established hotel; the renewal process has also reached the seventh-floor rooms, which have boxy hardwood furniture and an earthy color scheme. **Pros:** excellent service; disabled access. **Cons:** older rooms not worth the price; gym is tiny; cramped spaces. ✉ *Av. Roca 155, Puerto Madryn, Chubut* ☎ *2965/471–292* 🌐 *www.hotelpeninsula.com.ar*

Experienced divers might be lucky enough to swim near a right whale calf like the one in the foreground here.

76 rooms *In-room: safe. In-hotel: restaurant, bar, gym, business center* *Breakfast.*

SPORTS AND THE OUTDOORS

BICYCLING

Escuela Windsurf Na Praia. Cycling is a great way to reach El Doradillo and Punta Loma. You can rent mountain bikes by the hour or the day from Escuela Windsurf Na Praia, next to Vernadino Club Mar. *Av. Almte. Brown 860, Puerto Madryn, Chubut* *2965/455–633* *www.grupovds.com.ar.*

DIVING

Lobo Larsen. Dive shops line Puerto Madryn's beachfront, but you'd do well to detour a block inland to talk to Lobo Larsen. Their English-speaking dive masters offer snorkeling and introductory dives and courses to non-divers, and wreck and reef outings to certified divers. Best of all is the chance to dive or snorkel with sea lions who swim right up to you. *Av. Roca 885, Puerto Madryn, Chubut* *2965/470–277* *www.lobolarsen.com.*

KAYAKING AND WINDSURFING

Escuela Windsurf Na Praia. This outfit rents sea kayaks and Windsurfers, and runs guided nature-watching kayak tours to nearby bays. During their summer Sea School (*www.escueladelmar.com.ar*), local instructors work with children aged 6–14 on snorkeling, windsurfing, bait and lure fishing, basic nautical and fishing knots, and identification of local fauna, as well as offering motor and sailboat excursions. There is also a windsurfing school for adults. *Av. Almte. Brown 860, Puerto Madryn, Chubut* *2965/455–633* *www.grupovds.com.ar.*

PENÍNSULA VALDÉS

Fodor's Choice ★

Puerto Pirámides is 104 km (64 miles) northeast of Puerto Madryn.

The biggest attraction is the *ballena franca* (southern right whale) population, which feeds, mates, and gives birth here. The protected mammals attract more than 120,000 visitors every year from June, when they first arrive, through December. Especially during the peak season of September and October, people crowd into boats at Puerto Pirámides to observe at close range as the 30- to 35-ton whales breach and blast giant V-shaped spouts of water from their blowholes.

GETTING HERE AND AROUND

About 60 km (37 miles) northeast along the coast on Ruta 2 from Puerto Madryn, the land narrows to form an isthmus. A ranger's station here marks the entrance to the Península Valdés Area Natural Protegida (Protected Natural Area), where you pay a park entry fee of 70 pesos. A further 22 km (14 miles) down the road is the remodeled Centro de Visitantes Istmo Ameghino (Ameghino Isthmus Visitor Center). A series of rather dry displays provides a basic introduction to the marine, coastal, and continental flora and fauna ahead of you. More exciting are the complete skeleton of a southern right whale and the views over the isthmus from the lookout tower.

From the visitor center it's another 24 km (15 miles) to the junction leading to Puerto Pirámides, 2 km (1.2 miles) to the south. By following the road 5 km (3 miles) east you reach the start of the circuit of the interconnected 32- to 64-km (20- to 40-mile) dirt roads around the peninsula.

There are different ways to explore the peninsula. If you prefer natural surroundings to cityscapes and really want to see all the area has to offer, plan on spending at least a night or two here rather than using Puerto Madryn as your base. The accommodations in Puerto Pirámides easily rival those in town, and when the tour parties leave you get the rugged, windswept coastal landscape to yourself. Hearing whales splashing offshore at night is a particularly magical experience. By staying you also have time to do an additional whale-watching trip at sunset, and to go hiking, kayaking, or snorkeling with sea lions.

However, if your schedule is tight, consider one of the many organized day trips that operate out of Puerto Madryn. A minibus typically picks you up at your hotel around 8 am, stops briefly at the visitor center, then continues to Puerto Pirámides for whale-watching (June–December only) and lunch. During the afternoon you visit two other spots on the peninsula before returning to Puerto Madryn by about 7 pm. These tours are reasonably priced (at this writing, prices started at 300 pesos per person) and pack a lot in. However, you spend most of the day crammed in the minibus, don't get to visit the entire peninsula, and have little time to linger at wildlife spots.

To visit the peninsula more extensively at your own pace, you need to rent a car and stay overnight. Having your own wheels also gives you the freedom to stay in the beautiful but remote lodgings at Punta Delgada and Punta Norte. Bear in mind, though, that you'll have to drive several hundred kilometers on dirt and gravel roads in varying states of repair. Stock your vehicle well with drinks, snacks, and gas (the only station is at Puerto Pirámides), and don't try to overtake the tour buses: cars are much lighter, and flipping is unfortunately a common accident here. Economy vehicle rental starts at about 350 pesos per day; the nearest place to rent from is Puerto Madryn—there are numerous car rentals along Avenida Roca.

If all you want to do is whale-watch, you can reach Puerto Pirámides on the daily public bus service from Puerto Madryn run by Mar y Valle (in high season they shuttle back and forth three times a day). Tickets cost 24 pesos each way.

For the freedom of having your own car without the responsibility of driving, arrange for a remis (car and private driver). You can do this as a day trip from Puerto Madryn through most local tour operators (prices vary), or from Puerto Pirámides, if you're staying there, with El Gauchito. Expect to pay about 700 pesos for a full day (6 hours) exploring the peninsula.

Finally, you can combine some of the above approaches and get an overview of the peninsula on a tour, but then get off at Puerto Pirámides on the way back and stay overnight, do other excursions, and then return on the public bus.

7

ESSENTIALS

Bus Contacts Mar y Valle ✉ *Terminal de Ómnibus, Puerto Madryn, Chubut* ☎ *2965/450–600.*

Visitor and Tour Info Puerto Madryn ✉ *Av. Roca 223, Chubut* ☎ *2965/453–504, 2965/456–067* 🌐 *www.madryn.gov.ar/turismo.*

Remis Tours El Gauchito ✉ *Chubut* ☎ *2965/495–014.*

Tour Companies Bottazzi ✉ *Complejo La Torre, Blvd. Brown at Martín Fierro, Chubut* ☎ *2965/474–110* 🌐 *www.titobottazzi.com.* **Causana Viajes** ✉ *Mathews 1325, Chubut* ☎ *2965/452–769* 🌐 *www.causana.com.ar.* **Miras del Mar** ✉ *Moreno 316, Chubut* ☎ *2965/474–316* 🌐 *www.mirasdelmar.com.* **Nievemar** ✉ *Av. Roca 493, Chubut* ☎ *2965/455–544* 🌐 *www.nievemartours.com.ar.*

Visitor Info Centro de Visitantes Istmo Ameghino (Ameghino Isthmus Visitor Center) ✉ *At the entrance to the Peninsula, Chubut* ⏲ *Daily 8–8.*

EXPLORING

PUERTO PIRÁMIDES

The only settlement on Península Valdés is tiny Puerto Pirámides, which transforms into Argentina's whale-watching capital between June and December. The main street, Avenida de las Ballenas, runs parallel to the shore about 200 meters inland, and is lined with pretty tin-roofed buildings among dunes and scrubby flowers. Two streets run down from it to the sea; all the whale-watching operations are clustered around the first of these, known as *la primera bajada.*

For ecological reasons, only 350 people are allowed to live here permanently, but there is a good selection of hotels and restaurants. ■ **TIP→ Bring plenty of money with you, as the one ATM may be out of cash.** In addition to whale-watching and lounging around with a beer while

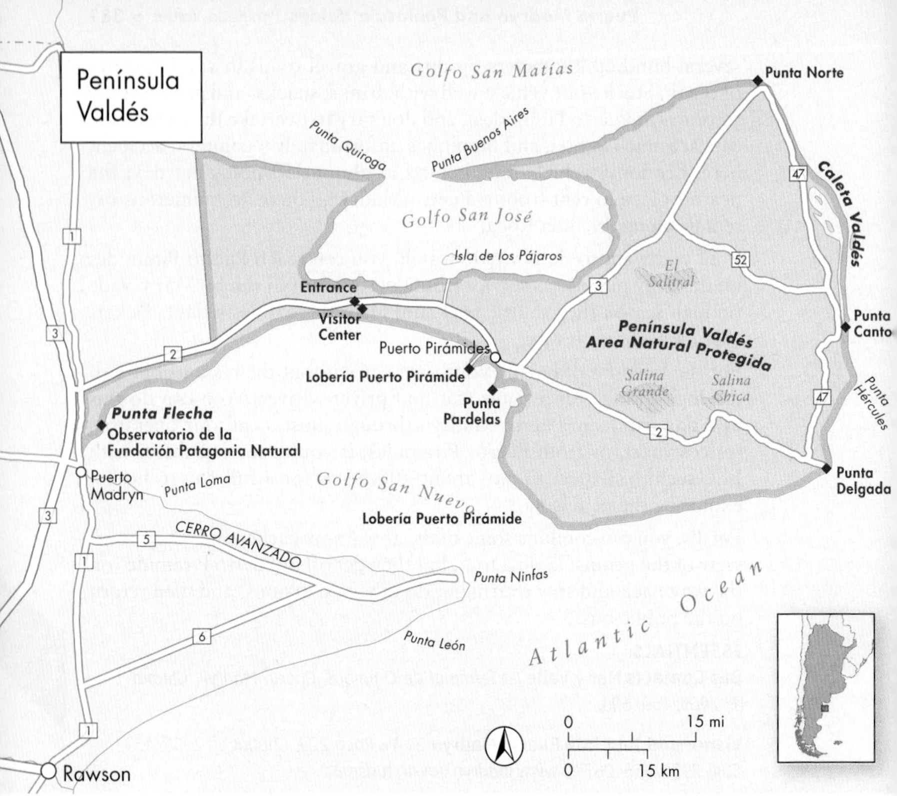

looking out on the pyramid-shaped cliffs that gave the town its name, activities include scuba diving or snorkeling with sea lions, kayaking, sand-boarding, and mountain-biking.

PUNTAS DELGADA, CANTOR, AND NORTE

Gravel-surfaced Ruta Provincial 2 continues 70 km (43 miles) east from Puerto Pirámides toward the edge of the peninsula. About halfway along are the **Salina Grande** and **Salina Chica**, two salt lakes you walk near. On the southeastern tip of Península Valdés lies **Punta Delgada**, marked by an old lighthouse. It now houses a luxury hotel: both the lighthouse and the surrounding beaches—home to a colony of elephant seals—are open only to hotel guests or those who dine at its restaurant.

Elephant seals also gather at **Punta Cantor**, a further 35 km (22 miles) north along the eastern coast of the island (on Ruta Provincial 47, though it's unmarked). A well-maintained cliff-side walkway leads you from the restrooms and restaurant near the road to a viewing area above the seals. The breeding season starts in August, when the males compete for beach space. Then the females arrive, form harems, give birth, and fatten up their cubs before heading out to sea in November. From Punta Cantor Ruta Provincial 52 crosses back across the peninsula, reconnecting with Ruta Provincial 3 to return to Puerto Pirámides. Alternatively, another 22 km (14 miles) north up the coast is **Caleta Valdés**, a long cove with turquoise waters beside which Magellanic penguins often gather.

The northeastern corner of the peninsula, **Punta Norte,** has the largest sea-lion settlement of all, and is also the best place to spot orcas in December. Magellanic penguins also roam the land from October through March. From Punta Norte Ruta Provincial 3 is an inland shortcut that heads straight back southwest to Pirámides, passing by **El Salitral,** the largest of the peninsula's three salt-lake ecosystems.

WHERE TO EAT

PUERTO PIRÁMIDES

For quick sandwiches or burgers before a whale-watching trip, try one of the snack bars that are interspersed with the tour operators on the Primera Bajada. All close at about 7 pm. Aside from the food joints on the main drag, check out the hotel restaurants for good options, too.

$$$ ARGENTINE **La Estación Pub.** The coolest bar in Pirámides is also the town's best seafood restaurant. Amid the nets and nautical gear hangs a motley collection of soccer-team flags, glam-rock posters, and LPs. Equally eye-catching are the tables—painted tomato-red, tangerine, or sea-green—and the menus, illustrated with pictures of David Bowie. As well as the requisite fish and steak dishes, offerings include a great range of pizzas and homemade pastas: try the garlicky mussel sauce. ✉ *Av. de las Ballenas s/n, Puerto Pirámides, Chubut* ☎ *2965/495–047* ⏲ *Closed Tues.*

7

WHERE TO STAY

For expanded hotel reviews, visit Fodors.com.

PUERTO PIRÁMIDES

$$ **Cabañas en el Mar.** Skip the aging A-frame cabins and try to book one of the apartments—their living rooms look down the street to the ocean and include fully equipped kitchens, making them popular with families and biologists here on extended stays. **Pros:** stylish; good value, especially for groups. **Cons:** located near all the whale-watching operators, so may be noisy during the day; cabins are much less attractive than apartments. ✉ *Av. de las Ballenas s/n, Puerto Pirámides, Chubut* ☎ *2965/495–049* 🌐 *www.piramides.net* *2 cabañas, 4 apartments* *In-room: a/c, kitchen, Wi-Fi.*

$$$ Fodor's Choice ★ **Hostería Ecológica del Nómade.** When you're staying in a wildlife reserve, taking care of Mother Nature seems only right; although this eco-friendly hotel uses solar panels and low-energy fittings and recycles its grey water, they haven't skimped on style or luxury. **Pros:** eco-awareness at no loss to comfort; detailed local information from staff and library of nature books; fabulous breakfasts. **Cons:** slightly removed from the restaurants on the main drag. ✉ *Av. de las Ballenas s/n, Puerto Pirámides, Chubut* ☎ *2695/495–044* 🌐 *www.eco-hosteria.com.ar* *8 rooms* *In-room: no TV, Wi-Fi* *Breakfast.*

$$$$ **Las Restingas.** The powder-blue clapboard facade of Puerto Pirámides's most upmarket hotel stretches along the beachfront: squint and you can see whales from the huge picture windows in the front-facing rooms and lobby lounge. **Pros:** excellent restaurant with a deck overlooking the sea; sea (and whale) views from some rooms. **Cons:** rooms facing the village are very overpriced; tiny bathrooms. ✉ *Primera Bajada*

CLOSE UP

General Julio Argentino Roca

Look at the street signs in any Patagonian city and you're sure to spot the name General Julio Argentino Roca. (To see what he looks like, whip out your wallet: he's riding along the 100-peso note, too). But look a little closer, and you may well find stickers or stencils changing the street's name to "Pueblos Originarios" (First Peoples).

The history books celebrate Roca as the man who "civilized" Patagonia and extended Argentine territory south, but the real story is much darker. In the late 1870s the bottom half of Argentina was still largely controlled by various indigenous peoples who resisted the European colonization of their territory. Funded by rich landowners from Buenos Aires anxious to extend their estates, war minister Roca led a series of brutal military attacks—euphemistically known as the Desert Campaigns—which led to the massacre of over a thousand Mapuche, Teheulche, and Ranquel warriors and the enslavement of countless indigenous women and children.

Despite countless attempts by indigenous rights groups to rename the streets and reprint the banknotes, for the time being these continue to honor the man behind the massacre.

at the beach, Puerto Pirámides, Chubut ☎ *2965/495–101* 🌐 *www.lasrestingas.com* *12 rooms* *In-hotel: restaurant, bar, pool, spa, beach, business center.*

PUNTA DELGADA

$$$$ ★ **Faro Punta Delgada.** This remote complex of buildings on the tip of Península Valdés once housed a navy station, post office, and a little school, as well as the *faro* (lighthouse); these days Punta Delgada offers luxuries that are simple and old-fashioned: comfortable beds with chintz covers, a pleasant pub with pool and darts, board games, and utter tranquillity under starry night skies. **Pros:** peaceful; private beaches afford great wildlife experiences; guided nature walks; fabulous food. **Cons:** rooms don't have water views; very isolated for some; busy with tour buses at midday. ✉ *Punta Delgada, Península Valdés, Punta Delgada, Chubut* ☎ *2965/458–444* 🌐 *www.puntadelgada.com* *27 rooms* *In-room: no a/c, no TV. In-hotel: restaurant, bar, beach* *Closed Apr.–June* *Multiple meal plans.*

SPORTS AND THE OUTDOORS

PUERTO PIRÁMIDES

From June to December the main attractions at Puerto Pirámides are whale-watching boat trips into the Golfo Nuevo to see southern right whales. Experienced captains pilot the boats between the huge mammals while bilingual guides tell you about their habits and habitats. Expect to use up lots of your camera memory as the graceful creatures dive, spout water, and salute you with their tails.

Most whale-watching companies operate several trips a day while the whales are in town, especially during the peak months of September and October. Standard daytime excursions last about 1¼ hours, and the price is set each year by the municipality (at this writing it was 260 pesos). Trips in smaller boats and longer tours are usually more expensive. Although no boat is allowed closer than 15 meters to the whales (the animals themselves sometimes break the rules by diving under your boat), you certainly feel closer from smaller vessels. On clear days the magical sunset tours are definitely worth paying extra for: you see the whales frolic as the sun sets over the water around them. It's best to call a day or two ahead to reserve, although many companies will fit you in if you show up on the day.

Hydrosport. Ecological commitment is the foremost priority at Hydrosport, a reliable, long-running operator with three different boat sizes. ✉ *Primera Bajada, Puerto Pirámides, Chubut* ☎ *2965/495–065* 🌐 *www.hydrosport.com.ar.*

Lobería Puerto Pirámides. Some 4 km (2½ miles) from Puerto Pirámides lies the Lobería Puerto Pirámides, a sea-lion colony which is also a great bird-watching spot. A signposted turnoff from the main road into town leads here, or you can follow the coastal path on foot. ✉ *Puerto Pirámides, Chubut.*

Patagonia Explorers. Kayaking in the Golfo Nuevo and the Golfo San Jose is offered by Patagonia Explorers, who also have English-speaking guides. ✉ *Av. de las Ballenas at Primera Bajada, Puerto Pirámides, Chubut* ☎ *2965/15–340–619* 🌐 *www.patagoniaexplorers.com.*

Southern Spirit. Southern Spirit uses large but fairly low boats that have an underwater sound-detection system so you can hear the sounds the whales make. They operate up to five 90-minute trips a day and don't charge more for the one at sunset. ✉ *Av. de las Ballenas at Primera Bajada, Puerto Pirámides, Chubut* ☎ *2965/15–572–551* 🌐 *www.southernspirit.com.ar.*

Tito Botazzi. Although trips tend to be more expensive with Tito Botazzi, they tend to be longer than other companies' and have excellent English-speaking guides. The sunset trips are on very small boats, and include wine and cheese in Hotel Las Restingas afterward. ✉ *Primera Bajada, Puerto Pirámides, Chubut* ☎ *2965/495–050* 🌐 *www.titobottazzi.com.*

TRELEW, GAIMAN, AND PUNTO TOMBO

When the Welsh settlers landed on the desertlike Patagonian coast in 1865, they realized they would need to move inland to find suitable land for farming. Some 25 km (15 miles) inland, in the fertile Chubut River valley, they founded Trelew and Gaiman. Both retain Welsh traditions to this day: Trelew holds an Eisteddfod (festival of Welsh poetry, song, and dance) each October, and Gaiman is the largest Welsh settlement outside of Wales.

With almost 100,000 inhabitants, Trelew is now a large city by Patagonian standards, and its airport is the gateway to Atlantic Patagonia. Beyond the excellent dinosaur museum, however, the dusty, windswept center is of little interest to tourists. With its teahouses, rose gardens, and chapels, Gaiman retains a country-town feel. Indeed, farms and stone-fruit orchards still fill the countryside surrounding it.

Trelew's Museo Paleontológico Egidio Feruglio, or Paleontology Museum, is bursting with fossil treasures.

On the coast 120 km (74 miles) south of Trelew lies the Punta Tombo penguin reserve, which you can easily visit on a day trip from Trelew, Gaiman, or Puerto Madryn.

TRELEW

11 km (6 miles) east of Gaiman; 250 km (155 miles) north of Camarones; 67 km (41½ miles) south of Puerto Madryn.

Trelew (pronounced Tre-*leh*-ew) is a commercial, industrial, and service hub that contains the region's main airport. Its biggest attractions are its paleontology museum and its proximity to the Punta Tombo reserve (though both can also be reached on day trips from Gaiman and Puerto Madryn). Otherwise, the city has little to recommend it: its mediocre hotels are notoriously overpriced, and aside from rental-car firms its tourism infrastructure is far less organized than Puerto Madryn's. If you come in the second half of October you can watch part of the Eisteddfod, a Welsh literary and music festival first held in Patagonia in 1875. Trelew was founded in 1886 as a result of the construction of the now-defunct Chubut railway line, which connected the Chubut River valley with the Atlantic coast. The town is named after its Welsh founder, Lewis Jones (*Tre* means "town" in Welsh, and *Lew* stands for Lewis), who fought to establish this railroad.

GETTING HERE AND AROUND

If you're driving, from the Ruta Nacional 3 take Ruta Nacional 25 to Avenida Fontana. The long-distance bus terminal is at Urquiza and Lewis Jones, along the Plaza Centenario. Most of what you'll visit is found in the half-dozen blocks between Plaza Centenario and Plaza Independencia, which is also where you'll find the tourist office.

ESSENTIALS

Bus Contacts Andesmar ✉ *Terminal de Ómnibus, Trelew, Chubut* ☎ *2965/433-535.* **Don Otto** ✉ *Terminal de Ómnibus, Trelew, Chubut* ☎ *2965/429-496.* **TAC** ✉ *Terminal de Ómnibus, Trelew, Chubut* ☎ *2965/439-207.*

Car Rental Hertz ✉ *Aeropuerto de Trelew, Trelew, Chubut* ☎ *2944/475-247* 🌐 *www.hertzargentina.com.ar.*

Currency Exchange Banco de la Nación ✉ *25 de Mayo, at Av. Fontana, Trelew, Chubut* ☎ *2965/449-100.*

Post Office Trelew ✉ *Mitre at 25 de Mayo, Trelew, Chubut.*

Visitor and Tour Info Tourist Office ✉ *Mitre 387, Trelew, Chubut* ☎📠 *2965/420-139* 🌐 *www.trelew.gov.ar.*

EXPLORING

Fodor's Choice ★ **Museo Paleontológico Egidio Feruglio (MEF).** Trelew's star attraction is the Museo Paleontológico Egidio Feruglio (MEF), where four hushed and darkened galleries of fossils both real and replica take you back in time. You start among the South American megafauna (giant armadillos and the like) that may have cohabited with the first humans here, then plunge back to a time before the Andes existed. Back then Patagonia was a subtropical rain forest filled with dinosaurs, including the largest creature to ever walk the earth: the 100-ton, 120-foot-long Argentinosaurus. Replicas of its massive leg bones are on display, along with countless other dino skeletons. Other highlights include a 290-million-year-old spider fossil with a 3-foot leg span and the 70-million-year-old petrified eggs of a Carnotaurus. The visit ends with a peek into the workshop where paleontologists study and preserve newly unearthed fossils. Tours in English are available—they're a good idea, as only the introductions to each room are translated. ✉ *Av. Fontana 140, Trelew, Chubut* ☎ *2965/432-100* 🌐 *www.mef.org.ar* *35 pesos* ⊙ *Apr.–Sept., weekdays 10–6, weekends 10–7; Oct.–Mar., daily 9–7.*

Museo Regional Pueblo de Luis (*Trelew Regional Museum*). Across the street from MEF is Trelew's old train station, which now contains a small museum of the town's history, the Museo Regional Pueblo de Luis. Photos, clothing, and objects from local houses, offices, and schools form the mishmash of displays on the European influence in the region, the indigenous populations of the area, and wildlife. ✉ *Av. 9 de Julio at Av. Fontana, Trelew, Chubut* ☎ *2965/424-062* *2 pesos* ⊙ *Weekdays 8–8, weekends 2–8.*

WHERE TO EAT AND STAY

For expanded hotel reviews, visit Fodors.com.

$$ ARGENTINE ★ ✕ **Miguel Angel.** With its paneled walls, sleek black tables, and vintage photos, this stylish Italo-Argentine restaurant is the happy exception to a dining scene that's as bleak as the steppes surrounding the town. Deferential waitstaff help you pick which of their pasta specialties to go for—options include squash ravioli in wild mushroom sauce, spinach and Parma ham agnolotti, or—most indulgent of all—stuffed gnocchi.

Lunching professionals come for the set menus, which often include thick steaks and roast potatoes. ✉ *Av. Fontana 246, Trelew, Chubut* ☎ *2965/430–403* ▭ *No credit cards* ⏲ *Closed Mon.*

$$$ CAFÉ ✕ **Touring Club.** Legend has it that Butch Cassidy and the Sundance Kid once stayed here—search long enough and you might find them among the old photos cluttering the walls. This cavernous old *confitería* (café) was founded in 1907, and became Chubut's first hotel in 1926. Its vintage tiles and molded ceiling don't seem to have changed much since, except that you can now use Wi-Fi from your scuffed table. The hotel's rooms are too shabby to recommend, but a toasted sandwich and a coffee or beer here is tantamount to a trip back in time. ✉ *Av. Fontana 240, Trelew, Chubut* ☎ *2965/433–997.*

$$ **Hotel Libertador.** This big hotel has definitely seen better days, though rooms are clean (if worn around the edges)—the faded bedcovers, textured wallpaper, and scuffed Formica furnishings of the standard rooms really aren't up to the price. **Pros:** on-site parking; amenable staff. **Cons:** only the superior rooms are worth the price. ✉ *Av. Rivadavía 31, Trelew, Chubut* ☎📠 *2965/420–220* *90 rooms* *In-room: no a/c, Wi-Fi. In-hotel: restaurant, parking* *Breakfast.*

$$$ **Rayentray.** The lobby's stained carpets, scuffed paneling, and cranky old elevator don't bode well at what is supposed to be Trelew's best hotel; indeed, the rooms are only slightly better. **Pros:** it's a block from Plaza Independencia. **Cons:** ridiculously overpriced. ✉ *San Martín 101, Trelew, Chubut* ☎ *2965/434–702* 🌐 *www.cadenarayentray.com.ar* *110 rooms* *In-room: Wi-Fi. In-hotel: restaurant, pool* *Breakfast.*

GAIMAN

17 km (10½ miles) west of Trelew.

The most Welsh of the Atlantic Patagonian settlements, Gaiman (pronounced *Guy*-mon) is a sleepy country town that is far more charming than nearby Trelew and Rawson. A small museum lovingly preserves the history of the Welsh colony, and many residents still speak Welsh (although day-to-day communication is now in Spanish). A connection to Wales continues with teachers, preachers, and visitors going back and forth frequently (often with copies of family trees in hand). Even the younger generation maintains an interest in the culture and language.

Perhaps the town's greatest draws are its five Welsh teahouses (*casas de té*)—Ty Gwyn, Plas-y-Coed, Ty Nain, Ty Cymraeg, and Ty Té Caerdydd. Each serves a similar set menu of tea and home-baked bread, scones, and a dazzling array of cakes made from family recipes, although the odd dulce de leche–filled concoction is testament to Argentine cultural imperatives. Most teahouses are open daily 3–8 and charge 60–90 pesos per person for tea (the spreads are generous enough to replace lunch or dinner, and you can usually take away a doggy bag of any cake you don't finish). Each establishment has its own family history and atmosphere, and there's healthy competition between them as to which is the most authentically Welsh.

Exploring ▼

Capilla Bathel . . . **4**

Capilla Vieja **3**

Parque Paleontológico Bryn Gwyn **2**

Museo Histórico Regional **1**

Hotels ▼

Hostería Yr Hen Ffordd **5**

Plas y Coed **1**

Posada los Mimbres **6**

Ty Gwyn **7**

Restaurants ▼

Cornel Wini **2**

Plas y Coed (teahouse) **1**

Ty Nain **4**

Ty Té Caerdydd (teahouse) **3**

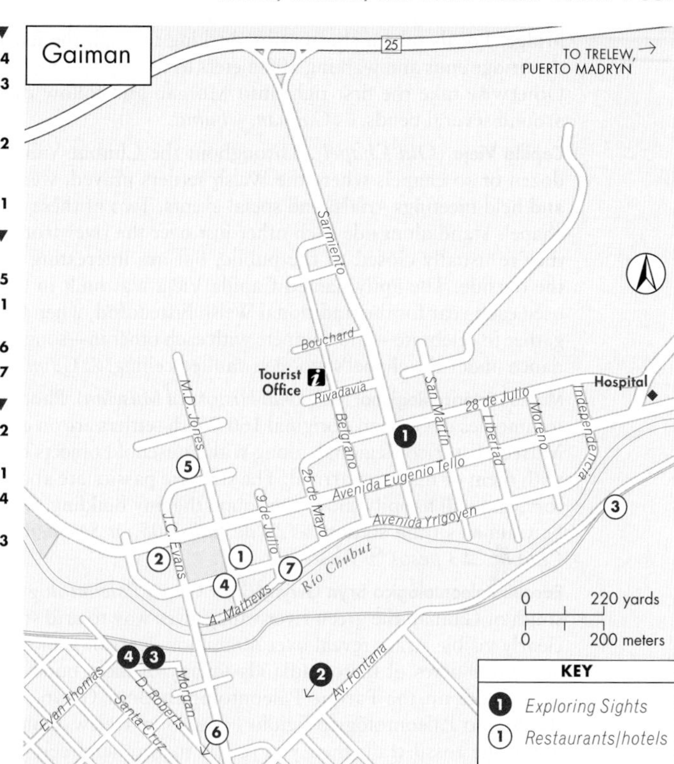

GETTING HERE AND AROUND

Gaiman is easily walkable: nearly all the teahouses and other attractions are within a five-block radius of the town square at Avenue Eugenio Tello and M.D. Jones. If you don't have a car, you can access the few sites outside of town—such as the Bryn Gwyn Paleontology Park—by taking an inexpensive remis from one of the *remiserías* on the square.

Although their English isn't great, the friendly young staff at the tourist office give enthusiastic advice on what to visit in Gaiman and hand out detailed maps of the town and its surroundings.

ESSENTIALS

Currency Exchange Banco del Chubut ✉ *J.C. Evans 115, Gaiman, Chubut* 🌐 *www.bancochubut.com.ar.*

Post Office Gaiman ✉ *J.C. Evans 114, Gaiman, Chubut.*

Visitor and Tour Info Tourist Office ✉ *Belgrano 574, at Rivadavía, Gaiman, Chubut* ☎ *2965/491–571* ⏲ *Mar.–Dec., weekdays 8–7, Sat. 9–7, Sun. 11–7; Jan. and Feb., weekdays 8–8, Sat. 9–8, Sun. 11–8.*

EXPLORING

Capilla Bethel. Capilla Bethel, next to Capilla Vieja, was built in 1914, and is used today by Protestants for Sunday service. To reach the chapels, walk south from the square on J. C. Evans and cross the pedestrian bridge. Locals take a shortcut by ducking through the fencing where the bridge ends and walking 100 meters to the right along the riverside. Otherwise take the first right into Morgan and follow the dirt road around several bends. ✉ *Gaiman, Chubut.*

Capilla Vieja (*Old Chapel*). Throughout the Chubut Valley are three dozen or so chapels where the Welsh settlers prayed, went to school, and held meetings, trials, and social events. Two of these simple brick chapels stand alongside each other just over the river from Gaiman—they're usually closed to the public, but are interesting to see from the outside. The aptly named Capilla Vieja was built in 1880, and is used each year for the traditional Welsh Eisteddfod, when townspeople gather to celebrate—and compete with each other in—song, poetry, and dance under the chapel's wooden vaulted ceiling. ✉ *Gaiman, Chubut.*

Museo Histórico Regional (*Regional Historical Museum*). Photographs and testimonies of Gaiman's original 160 Welsh settlers are on display in the Museo Histórico Regional, along with household objects they brought with them or made on arrival. The staff are passionate about their history, and will happily show you round the tiny building, which used to be Gaiman's train station. ✉ *28 de Julio 705, at Sarmiento, Gaiman, Chubut* 🎫 *3 pesos* ⏲ *Tues.–Sun. 3–7.*

Parque Paleontológico Bryn Gwyn (*Bryn Gwyn Paleontology Park*). Just south of Gaiman the green river valley gives way to arid steppes where clearly visible strata reveal over 40 million years of geological history. Some 600 acres of these badlands—many of them bursting with fossils—make up the Parque Paleontológico Bryn Gwyn, a branch of the Museo Paleontológico Egidio Feruglio in Trelew. Guides lead you along the fossil trail, then you're left to wander freely through the botanical gardens of native Patagonian plants. ✉ *8 km (5 miles) south of town, Gaiman, Chubut* ☎ *2965/432–100* 🌐 *www.mef.org.ar/mef/en/institucional/geoparque.php* 🎫 *10 pesos* ⏲ *Mar.–Sept., Tues.–Sun. 11–5; Oct.–Feb., Tues.–Sun. 10–6.*

WHERE TO EAT

$$ ARGENTINE ✕ **Cornel Wini.** For decades the Jones family, owners of this stately red-brick corner building, ran a hotel and bar (complete with a boxing ring in the basement) here, but switched to serving steaks, pizzas, and pasta. The decision has been a success: on weekends, locals from as far afield as Puerto Madryn pack themselves round the wooden tables of the bright, high-ceilinged dining room to devour their generous *parrilladas* (mixed grills). We love the presence of Gaiman's traditional dark fruit cake in the *Postre Wini*, in combination with ice cream, nuts, whipped cream, and liqueurs. ✉ *Av. Eugenio Tello 199, Gaiman, Chubut* ☎ *2965/491–397* ⏲ *Closed Tues.*

$$$ CAFÉ ★ ✕ **Ty Nain.** The matriarch who presides over the kitchen here, Mirna Jones, is a proud descendant of the first woman born in Gaiman. Her ivy-covered teahouse on the main square looks like a knickknack shop: it's stuffed with doodads and hung with crochet, and there are gramophones, carriage lamps, and antique radios on display above the four original chimneys, which date to 1890, although Formica paneling

CLOSE UP

Gaiman's Teahouses

There's an Alice in Wonderland effect as you nibble various cakes and look out on the vast Atlantic Patagonian steppe (which would make anyone feel small).

Gaiman's Welsh teahouses have been famous among travelers for decades. The first teahouse, Plas y Coed, opened in 1944, and figured in Bruce Chatwin's *In Patagonia.*

Each of Gaiman's teahouses serves up its own unique family recipes for all manner of baked goodies, including *torta galesa* (a rich dried-fruit cake), seasonal fruit tarts, buns and sponges, *torta de crema* (a rich baked cream cake), as well as homemade bread, scones, and jam. The tea is always served in big china pots dressed for the occasion in deliciously kitsch hand-knitted tea cozies to ensure your brew stays warm.

Just as the recipes and tastes differ slightly from teahouse to teahouse, so do their interiors. But common to all the teahouses are tapestries and ornamental tea towels, often inscribed with Welsh words and with intricate Celtic designs around the borders. Hanging from the walls—and often for sale, too—are heart-shaped wooden spoons with intricately carved handles. Known as love spoons, they're a Welsh tradition that dates to the 16th century: a young man would carve a spoon from a single piece of wood and give it to the girl he wished to marry.

Most of Gaiman's teahouses are owned and run by descendants of the original Welsh settlers, who are happy to recount their family history if you ask about it. There's a strong sense of appreciation for how easy things are today compared to just a couple of generations ago. Ana, of Plas y Coed, whose great-grandmother was featured in Bruce Chatwin's book, told us, "Imagine making everything from scratch and running this place without refrigerators."

There's an Alice in Wonderland effect as you nibble various cakes and look out on the vast Atlantic Patagonian steppe (which would make anyone feel small).

detracts slightly from the Old World style. ✉ *Hipólito Yrigoyen 283, Gaiman, Chubut* ☎ *2965/491–126* ▭ *No credit cards.*

$$$$ CAFÉ ★ ✕ **Ty Té Caerdydd.** A short way out of town lies Gaiman's largest teahouse, surrounded by cypress trees, sculpted gardens, and a giant tea pot. It stands apart from its rivals culturally, too: it's run by descendents of a Spanish family, which shows in the sprawling colonial-style architecture. Otherwise you'd never know they weren't Welsh, as they do the most impressive spread of traditional cakes in town. Better yet, this was where Princess Diana took her tea during her visit to Gaiman in the early 1990s (Scotland Yard liked the security of its rural location). The cup she used, numerous photos, and other memorabilia form a shrine-like display in her honor. ✉ *Finca 202, Zona de Chacras, Gaiman, Chubut* ☎ *2965/491–510.*

WHERE TO STAY

For expanded hotel reviews, visit Fodors.com.

$ **Hostería Yr Hen Ffordd.** Gaiman's best budget accommodation is this family-run B&B, where rooms are simple, but spacious and warm, with comfy beds, bright feather quilts, good bathrooms, and free Wi-Fi (quite a find in Gaiman). **Pros:** great breakfasts; friendly owners give spot-on advice on Gaiman's sights and restaurants. **Cons:** drab carpets detract from the century-old building's charm. ✉ *Michael Jones 342, Gaiman, Chubut* ☎ *2965/491–394* 🌐 *www.yrhenffordd.com.ar* *5 rooms* *In-room: no a/c, Wi-Fi* ▭ *No credit cards* *Breakfast.*

$ **Plas y Coed.** Gaiman's oldest teahouse has also been a bed-and-breakfast since 1997, and a stay here is rather like visiting with a favorite aunt: The rooms are simple but immaculate, and have polished wooden floors and pastel bedspreads, and there's a comfy lounge area for relaxing in. **Pros:** an inclusive, family atmosphere. **Cons:** not much room for groups larger than six. ✉ *M.D. Jones 123, Gaiman, Chubut* ☎ *2965/491–133* 🌐 *www.plasycoed.com.ar* *5 rooms* *In-room: no a/c. In-hotel: restaurant* ▭ *No credit cards* *Breakfast.*

$$$ ★ **Posada Los Mimbres.** Wandering the nature trail alongside the Chubut River is one of the joys of staying on this working farm; picking fruit from the orchard and helping at milking time are others. **Pros:** variety of rooms to choose from; the option of lunch and dinner mean you don't need to go back into town for meals; most ingredients are sourced from the farm; beautiful rural setting. **Cons:** isolated from town if you don't have a vehicle. ✉ *Chacra 211, Gaiman, Chubut* ☎ *2965/491–299* 🌐 *www.posadalosmimbres.com.ar* *6 rooms* *In-room: no a/c, no TV, Wi-Fi. In-hotel: restaurant, pool* ▭ *No credit cards* *Multiple meal plans.*

$ ★ **Ty Gwyn.** The soaring ceilings, wooden rafters, and cobbled white walls of this cavernous teahouse make it seem like you're eating in a medieval dining hall; an interior garden leads to the staircase that takes you to four lovely bedrooms with wood floors, heavy drapes, and dressers fashioned from antique sewing-machine tables. **Pros:** rooms overlook the river; generous breakfasts include fruit and eggs. **Cons:** cruise-ship groups arrive regularly in the high season. ✉ *Av. 9 de Julio 149, Gaiman, Chubut* ☎ *2965/491–009* 🌐 *www.cpatagonia.com/gaiman/ty-gwyn* *4 rooms* *In-hotel: restaurant* ▭ *No credit cards* *Breakfast.*

CLOSE UP

Pandas of the Sea

You've watched the whales, seen the seals, and admired the penguins. But how about *toninas* (dolphins)? The southern coast of Argentina is home to a particularly attractive species, *Cephalorhynchus Commersonii*, whose black-and-white coloring has earned them the nickname "pandas of the sea." **Toninas Adventure** (✉ *Av. Marcelino González at the docks, Puerto Rawson* ☎ *2965/498–372* 🌐 *www.enpuertorawson.com.ar/toninas* 🎫 *Boat-trip 120 pesos* ⏲ *9–6*), the only dolphin-watching enterprise in the area, operates hour-long boat trips from the port at Rawson. They guarantee sightings of their playful namesake creatures, who love to race alongside the boats in packs of three or four, regularly jumping up in perfect arcs. Puerto Rawson is on the coast 30 km (20 miles) east of Trelew, and is an easy detour on trips south to Punta Tombo or beyond. Most organized tours to Punta Tombo stop here.

PUNTA TOMBO

120 km (74 miles) south of Trelew; 105 km (65 miles) north of Camarones.

Fodor's Choice ★ **Área Natural Protegido Punta Tombo** (*Punta Tombo Protected Natural Area*). From the middle of September through March, up to half a million penguins live in the Área Natural Protegido Punta Tombo, the world's largest colony of Magellanic penguins and one of the most varied seabird rookeries. From the park entrance, a series of trails, boardwalks, and bridges lead you 3.5 km (2¼ miles) through the scrubby landscape where the penguins nest to the sea. The quizzical creatures seem unafraid of humans, and peer up at you from under the bushes where, between September and November, both males and females incubate eggs, often right beside the trail. Look for the bald vertical strips on the penguins' abdomens: they pluck out feathers so the eggs can sit warm against their skin. Come December, the ground is teeming with fluffy gray young, and the adult penguins waddle back and forth from the sea to feed them. Once you reach the rocky outcrops overlooking the water you'll see how graceful and powerful these creatures (who move so comically across the land) become when they enter the water. You may also spot guanacos, seals, and Patagonian hares in the reserve, as well as cormorants and a host of other seabirds.

The last 22 km (13½ miles) of the road from Trelew is fairly bumpy gravel. If you're not driving, you can easily reach Punta Tombo on a day tour from Trelew, Gaiman, or Puerto Madryn, although note that these often give you a scant 1½ hours in the reserve. A small restaurant next to the carpark serves good lamb empanadas and also has burgers, coffee, cakes, and cold beverages. ✉ *Punto Tombo, Chubut* 🎫 *35 pesos* ⏲ *8–8 (last entrance 6 pm).*

CAMARONES AND BAHÍA BUSTAMANTE

The few travelers willing to stray off Ruta Nacional 3 to follow gravel Ruta Provincial 1 along this stretch of Patagonia's coast will learn the meaning of "having the place to yourself." Expect to pass next to nobody as you travel from Puerto Madryn or Trelew to Camarones (passing Punta Tombo), and then from Camarones to Bahía Bustamante.

Dubbed "the Galapagos of the south," this area will seem like a desolate, inhospitable landscape to some. Yet the land is teeming with both continental and marine wildlife, not to mention the thousands of sheep and goats populating the vast estancias along the way. To others—those who crave open, uncrowded spaces—this area will seem like a paradise. With the exception of Península Valdés, nowhere else in the region yields such a dramatic sense of endless terrain.

The village of Camarones has basic lodging and dining facilities, Punta Tombo is only for viewing wildlife, and Bahía Bustamante is a private—by reservation only—"marine estancia." Each of these stops makes for a convenient, single-day drive, although if you're an experienced road-tripper you could do the whole stretch from Trelew to Bahía Bustamante in a day. If you take Ruta Provincial 1, expect to take at least 7 hours to do the roughly 350 km (218 miles). Via the faster but less scenic Ruta Nacional 3 it's 258 km (160 miles) direct to Bahía Bustamante without detouring to Camarones, which should take 3–4 hours.

CAMARONES

252 km (156 miles) south of Trelew; 105 km (65 miles) south of Punta Tombo; 258 km (160 miles) north of Comodoro Rivadavía.

After driving or riding for hours along the empty coastal road (or via Ruta Provincial 30 from Ruta 3), the tiny town of Camarones—a collection of brightly colored, tin-roofed buildings with scrollwork fascias, trim, and other curious architectural details—appears like an enchanted village. People here seem jovial and happy in their isolation. Most of the worries that plague the inhabitants of Argentina's big cities—crime, unemployment, pollution—simply don't exist here. The only controversy you may encounter is the battle between the town's two main industries, algae farming and salmon fishing: some species of algae here are invasive, and degrade the salmon's habitat.

The one main event each year is the Fiesta Nacional del Salmón (National Salmon Festival), celebrated in early February with fishing contests and the crowning of Miss Salmoncito (Little Miss Salmon). Other than that, the main attractions are the beautiful, empty beaches south of town and the Reserva Natural Cabo Dos Bahías.

GETTING HERE AND AROUND

Transportes El Ñandú connects Camarones to Trelew with bus service on Monday, Wednesday, and Friday, and ETAP runs services between Comodoro Rivadavía on Tuesdays and Thursdays. Rubén Catriel and Veroan provide remis services to local destinations, including Cabo Dos Bahías.

You're not the only visitor to Punta Tombo: guanacos might join you as you scope out the Magellanic penguins.

Most everything in Camarones is within four blocks of the main plaza, which slopes down to the waterfront and the *puerto*. The tourist office on Espero Street is open daily, and provides information on lodging and dining, and runs walking tours of the town's historical buildings.

ESSENTIALS

Bus Contacts ETAP ✉ *Camarones, Chubut* ☎ *297/489–3058.* **Transportes el Ñandú** ✉ *Camarones, Chubut* ☎ *2965/427–499 in Trelew.*

Currency Exchange Banco del Chubut ✉ *San Martín 570, Camarones, Chubut* ☎ *297/496–3050* 🌐 *www.bancochubut.com.ar.*

Post Office Camarones ✉ *Roca 100, Camarones, Chubut.*

Remises Veroan ✉ *Camarones, Chubut* ☎ *297/496–3007.*

Visitor and Tour Info Camarones ✉ *Belgrano at Estrada, Camarones, Chubut* ☎ *297/496–3013.*

EXPLORING

Reserva Natural Cabo Dos Bahías. Twenty-eight km (17½ miles) southeast of town, Reserva Natural Cabo Dos Bahías is a solitude-seeking nature-lover's paradise. Chances are you'll be the only humans wandering among the penguins, sea lions, birds, seals, guanacos, rheas, and foxes. ✉ *Camarones, Chubut.*

WHERE TO STAY

For expanded hotel reviews, visit Fodors.com.

$ **Indalo Inn.** The standard block construction and stuffed animals above the television in the dining room might not seem very inspiring, but the

Indalo has clean, comfortable rooms and pleasant little extras like a good wine selection and free Wi-Fi. **Pros:** friendly atmosphere. **Cons:** restaurant is hit-or-miss. ✉ *Av. Julio A. Roca at Sarmiento, Camarones, Chubut* ☎ *297/496–3004* 🌐 *www.indaloinn.com.ar* *15 rooms, 7 cabins* *In-room: Wi-Fi. In-hotel: restaurant* *Breakfast.*

RODS AND TANKS

Local companies **Expediciones Nauticas Patagonia Austral** (☎ *297/15–400–4844*) and **Rumbo Sur** (☎ *297/15–418–5567*) operate fishing excursions. Based in Rada Tilly, **La Naud Buceo** (☎ *2965/15–416–3427* 🌐 *www.lanaudbuceo.com*) runs diving trips to Cabo Dos Bahías.

SHOPPING

Casa Rabal. Right by the tourist office on the waterfront is Casa Rabal, one of the most amazing places to shop in all of Patagonia. Originally built in 1901, this dry goods store is one of the oldest in the area and has everything from locally made cheese to shoes to camping and fishing gear to drywall tools to diapers to bridles for your horse. ✉ *Camarones, Chubut.*

BAHÍA BUSTAMANTE

Fodor's Choice ★ *89 km (55 miles) south of Camarones; 180 km (110 miles) north of Comodoro Rivadavía; 250 km (155 miles) south of Trelew.*

Spending time in Bahía Bustamante is like having your own private Península Valdés. In 1953 it was founded by Lorenzo Soriano, who searched the Patagonian coastline for seaweed to use for extracting colloids. When he found this bay filled with seaweed he began, along with his sons, to create an entire town including a school, church, auto and boat garage, and housing for more than 400 people who worked harvesting these marine algae.

The operation slowed during the '90s, and nearly everyone moved away. In 2004, however, Lorenzo's grandson Matías returned to Bahía Bustamante and began renovating various houses and transforming the place into what he calls an "estancia marina," or marine ranch, with a special focus on ecological sensitivity, observation of marine and continental wildlife, and independence (producing all their own food and electricity). ■ **TIP→ Stays are available for individuals or small groups—only 20 people at a time can stay here—by reservation only.** Aim to stay for at least two or three nights to ensure that weather conditions allow you to take advantage of all the activities included. Even if you're flying rather than road-tripping south, this makes a great stopover between Buenos Aires and El Calafate or Ushuaia (you can fly in and out of Trelew).

GETTING HERE AND AROUND

Getting to Bahía Bustamante is an adventure. If you're driving from Camarones, continue south along the coastal Ruta Provincial 1 for approximately 85 km (52 miles). At the crossroads with Ruta Provincial 28, turn left toward Punto Visser (there's also a hand-painted sign to Bahía Bustamante). Continue for another 4 km (2½ miles), cross the small concrete bridge, and pass a sign that says Zona Alguera, Prohibido Pasar, and keep going until you reach the single-storey Administracion building. A quicker route to Bahía Bustamante from Trelew is via Ruta Nacional 3: after about 220 km (137 miles) turn left into Ruta Provincial 28, continue for 33 km (20 miles) to the intersection with Ruta Provincial 1, then follow the instructions above. Alternatively, the hotel can arrange private transfers from Puerto Madryn, Trelew, or Comodoro Rivadavía. All transport within Bahía Bustamante is handled by the staff.

WHERE TO STAY

For expanded hotel reviews, visit Fodors.com.

$$$$ **Bahía Bustamante.** Choose between six guesthouses right on the beach (food and activities included), or one of the simpler five guesthouses off the beach on an accommodation-only basis; each of the beach guesthouses includes twin bedrooms, a living room, a bathroom, and a kitchen. **Pros:** world-class cuisine and outdoor activities in a scenic wonderland; excursions are an adventure. **Cons:** this is remote territory, so come prepared for that. ✉ *RN3, Km 1674, Bahía Bustamante, Chubut* ☎ *11/5032–8677 reservations in Buenos Aires* 🌐 *www.bahiabustamante.com* *11 guesthouses* *In-room: no a/c, no TV. In-hotel: restaurant, beach* *Closed Apr.–Aug.* *All-inclusive.*

7

COMODORO RIVADAVÍA

1,854 km (1,149 miles) south of Buenos Aires; 1,726 km (1,070 miles) north of Ushuaia; 945 km (586 miles) north of Río Gallegos; 397 km (246 miles) south of Rawson.

Argentina's answer to Houston, Comodoro Rivadavía is the town that oil built. Unlike Houston, however, there's not much here apart from oil drilling. Argentina's first oil discovery was made here in 1907, during a desperate search for water because of a serious drought. It was an event that led to the formation of Yacimientos Petrolíferos Fiscales (YPF), among the world's first vertically integrated oil companies. After YPF's privatization in 1995, however, thousands were laid off, bringing hard times to Comodoro's 130,000 residents.

Surrounded by barren hills and sheer cliffs off the Golfo San Jorge, Comodoro looks dramatic from a distance. Up close, it's frayed around the edges. The charmless main commercial streets, where you'll find most restaurants and bars, are San Martín and Comodoro Rivadavía.

Because visiting oil workers occupy rooms for long periods of time, there is a nearly constant shortage of hotel rooms, so never show up here without an advance reservation.

WHERE TO EAT AND STAY

For expanded hotel reviews, visit Fodors.com.

$$$ SEAFOOD **Puerto Cangrejo.** The locals crowding the tables at this bustling, family-oriented restaurant are proof of its reputation as the best seafood spot in town. The best dishes are the starters: think oyster platters, a decadent bowl of calamari, or the *picada de mariscos*, a sampling of hot and cold shellfish dishes. Follow up with the *centolla* (king crab)

or stuffed salmon. ✉ *Av. Costanera 1051, Comodora Rivadavía, Chubut* ☎ *297/444–4590.*

$$$ **Austral Plaza Hotel.** Comodoro's smartest hotel is actually two hotels in one: the older, larger, but more modest Austral Express, and the newer Austral Plaza, a 42-room luxury hotel with marble floors, plush towels, and spacious rooms. **Pros:** excellent restaurant and dining room. **Cons:** gets booked up quickly; make reservations in advance. ✉ *Moreno 725, Comodora Rivadavía, Chubut* ☎ *297/447–2200* 🌐 *www.australhotel.com* *160 rooms* *In-room: no a/c, safe, Wi-Fi. In-hotel: restaurant, bar* *Breakfast.*

TO SPELUNK?

Unique in the region, **spelunking**, or cave exploration, is possible at the **Túnel de Sarasola**, a natural basalt tunnel 45 km (28 miles) west of Sarmiento. Agencia Santa Teresita (☎ *297/489-3238*) can arrange expeditions there.

SARMIENTO AND THE BOSQUE PETRIFICADO

150 km (94 miles) west of Comodoro Rivadavía.

Built in a fertile valley formed by the Río Senguer and its two interconnected lakes, Lago Musters and Lago Colhué Huapi, the Sarmiento area is a green oasis in the middle of the hard Patagonian steppe. The town itself—home to about 13,000 people—is relatively unattractive, but a visit here gives you a taste of what is undeniably and unpretentiously the "real Patagonia." Relatively few foreign travelers come here, even though the lakes and river, petrified forest, and paleontology park are great attractions, and the rolling farmland outside of town is truly striking, with its tall windbreaks of Lombardy poplars twisting in the strong wind.

GETTING HERE AND AROUND

There are several daily bus services between Sarmiento and Comodoro Rivadavía run by ETAP and Don Otto. The latter also has services to Esquel and Bariloche. Buses arrive at the bus station at 12 de Octubre and Avenida San Martín, which runs through the center of town.

Sarmiento is only 15 blocks long and eight blocks wide, and can be walked easily, but if you get tired or would like to arrange a trip outside of town, there are various *remiserías* along Avenida San Martín.

ESSENTIALS

Bus Contacts Don Otto ✉ *Terminal de Ómnibus, Sarmiento, Chubut* ☎ *297/489-4749* 🌐 *www.donotto.com.ar.* **ETAP** ✉ *Terminal de Ómnibus, Sarmiento, Chubut* ☎ *297/489-3058.*

Currency Exchange Banco de la Nación ✉ *España at Uruguay, Sarmiento, Chubut* ☎ *297/489-3127* 🌐 *www.bna.com.ar.*

Post Office Sarmiento ✉ *Ingeniero Coronel 317, Sarmiento, Chubut.*

Visitor and Tour Info Sarmiento ✉ *Av. Regimiento de Infanteria 25 at Pietrobelli, Sarmiento, Chubut* ☎ *297/489-8220* 🌐 *www.coloniasarmiento.gov.ar/turismo.*

EXPLORING

★ **Monumento Natural Bosque Petrificado Sarmiento** (*Sarmiento Petrified Forest Natural Monument*). Sarmiento is the jumping-off point for the Monumento Natural Bosque Petrificado Sarmiento, about 30 km (19 miles) from Sarmiento following Ruta 26 until you reach the access road on the right. Scattered along a vast and colorfully striated badlands are trunks of conifer and palm trees that were deposited here 75 million years ago when the area was a tropical river delta. Regardless of the time of year, bring a jacket. The wind cools you down quickly even in bright sunlight. If you don't have your own vehicle, book a remis from Sarmiento: most charge around 150 pesos for the return trip and an hour's waiting time. ✉ *30 km (19 miles) from Sarmiento following R26 until access road on the right, Sarmiento, Chubut* ☎ *297/489–8282* 🎫 *20 pesos* ⏲ *Apr.–Sept., daily 10–6; Oct.–Mar., daily 9–7.*

FAIR TIME!

One of the region's best local markets, Sarmiento's arts, crafts, and food fair is held every Saturday and Sunday from 9 to 8, year-round, right across from the tourism office at Avenida Regimiento de Infantería 25 and Pietrobelli. Here you can find jams, preserves, honey, woolen garments, and other crafts produced at local *chacras*.

Fodor's Choice ★ **Parque Paleontológico Valle de Los Gigantes** (*Valley of the Giants Paleontology Park*). Parque Paleontológico Valle de Los Gigantes has life-size and scientifically accurate replicas of a dozen different dinosaurs whose fossils were discovered in the region. Guided visits in English leave directly from the tourist office every hour on the hour—arrive 10 minutes ahead to get your ticket. ✉ *200 meters from the tourist office, Sarmiento, Chubut* ☎ *297/489–8220* 🎫 *8 pesos* ⏲ *Apr.–Nov., daily 11–5; Dec.–Mar., daily 9–8.*

While you're in the area, stop at **Lago Musters,** 7 km (4 miles) from Sarmiento, and **Lago Colhué Huapi,** a little farther on. At Lago Musters you can swim, and there's fishing year-round.

WHERE TO STAY

For expanded hotel reviews, visit Fodors.com.

$$ Fodor's Choice ★ **Hostería Labrador.** You get a taste of Patagonian country life when you stay on this working *chacra* (farm) as wife-and-husband team Ana Luisa Geritsen (who speaks Dutch and English) and Nicolás Ayling (who speaks English) welcome guests, tend the land, produce homemade fruit preserves and honey, and cook huge breakfasts for their guests. **Pros:** homey atmosphere; Nicolás can arrange local guided tours. **Cons:** far out of town—you need your own vehicle. ✉ *Ruta 20, 10 km (6 miles) from Sarmiento, 1 km (½ miles) before the Río Senguer, Sarmiento, Chubut* ☎ *2974/893–329* 🌐 *www.hosterialabrador.com.ar* *4 rooms* *In-room: no a/c, no TV* 🍽 *Breakfast.*

$ **Los Lagos.** This small, affordable hotel has updated carpets, furnishings, and bathrooms; the staff doesn't speak much English but they're friendly and helpful and there's a decent on-site restaurant. **Pros:** affordable; free Wi-Fi. **Cons:** can get hot in summer. ✉ *Av. Roca at Alberdi,*

Sarmiento, Chubut ☎ *2974/893–046* *20 rooms* *In-room: no a/c, Wi-Fi. In-hotel: restaurant* *No credit cards* *Breakfast.*

EL CALAFATE, EL CHALTÉN, AND PARQUE NACIONAL LOS GLACIARES

The Hielo Continental (Continental ice cap) spreads its icy mantle from the Pacific Ocean across Chile and the Andes into Argentina, covering an area of 21,700 square km (8,400 square miles). Approximately 1.5 million acres of it are contained within the Parque Nacional los Glaciares (Glaciers National Park), a UNESCO World Heritage site. The park extends along the Chilean border for 350 km (217 miles), and 40% of it is covered by ice fields that branch off into 47 glaciers feeding two enormous lakes—the 15,000-year-old **Lago Argentino** (Argentine Lake, the largest body of water in Argentina and the third-largest in South America) at the park's southern end, and **Lago Viedma** (Lake Viedma) at the northern end near **Cerro Fitzroy,** which rises 11,138 feet. Plan on a minimum of two to three days to see the glaciers and enjoy El Calafate—more if you plan to visit El Chaltén or any of the other lakes. Entrance to the southern section of the park, which includes Perito Moreno Glacier, costs 100 pesos.

EL CALAFATE

320 km (225 miles) north of Río Gallegos via R5; 253 km (157 miles) east of Río Turbio on Chilean border via R40; 213 km (123 miles) south of El Chaltén via R40.

Founded in 1927 as a frontier town, El Calafate is the base for excursions to the Parque Nacional los Glaciares, which was created in 1937 as a showcase for one of South America's most spectacular sights, the Perito Moreno Glacier. Because it's on the southern shore of Lago Argentino, the town enjoys a microclimate much milder than the rest of southern Patagonia.

To call El Calafate a boomtown would be a gross understatement. In the first decade of this millennium the town's population exploded from 4,000 to more than 25,000, and it shows no signs of slowing down; at every turn you'll see new construction. As a result, the downtown has a very new sheen to it, although most buildings are constructed of wood, with a rustic aesthetic that respects the majestic natural environment. One exception is the casino in the heart of downtown, the facade of which seems to mock the face of the Perito Moreno glacier. Farther out of the city is another glacier lookalike, the brand new Glaciarium museum, architecturally modeled on Perito Moreno and with Argentina's only ice bar. Now with a paved road between El Calafate and the glacier, the visitors continue to flock in to see the creaking ice sculptures. These visitors include luxury package tourists bound for the legendary Hostería Los Notros, backpackers over from Chile's Parque Nacional Torres del Paine, and *porteños* (from Buenes Aires) in town for a long weekend—including Argentina's President Cristina Fernández de Kirchner, who owns a vacation house and two hotels down here.

Near Los Glaciares National Park and El Calafate you'll find some of the most remote-feeling estancias in Argentina.

GETTING HERE AND AROUND

Daily flights from Buenos Aires, Ushuaia, and Río Gallegos, and direct flights from Bariloche transport tourists to El Calafate's 21st-century glass-and-steel airport with the promise of adventure and discovery in distant mountains and glaciers. El Calafate is so popular that the flights sell out weeks in advance, so don't plan on booking at the last minute.

If you can't get on a flight or are looking for a cheaper option, there are daily buses between El Calafate, El Chalten, Ushuaia, and Puerto Natales in Chile—all of which can be booked at the bus terminal. Calafate is also the starting (or finishing) point for the legendary Ruta 40 journey to Bariloche. If you can bear the bus travel for a few days, you'll pass some exceptional scenery, and most operators make stops at canyons, lakes, and the famous handprint-covered caves en route.

Driving from Río Gallegos takes about four hours across desolate plains enlivened by occasional sightings of a gaucho, his dogs, and a herd of sheep, and *ñandú* (rheas), shy llama-like guanacos, silver-gray foxes, and fleet-footed hares the size of small deer. Esperanza is the only gas, food, and bathroom stop halfway between the two towns.

Avenida del Libertador San Martín (known simply as Libertador) is El Calafate's main street, with tour offices, restaurants, and shops selling regional specialties, sportswear, camping and fishing equipment, and food.

A staircase ascends from the middle of Libertador to Avenida Julio Roca, where you'll find the bus terminal and a very busy Oficina de Turismo with a board listing available accommodations and campgrounds; you can also get brochures and maps, and there's a multilingual staff

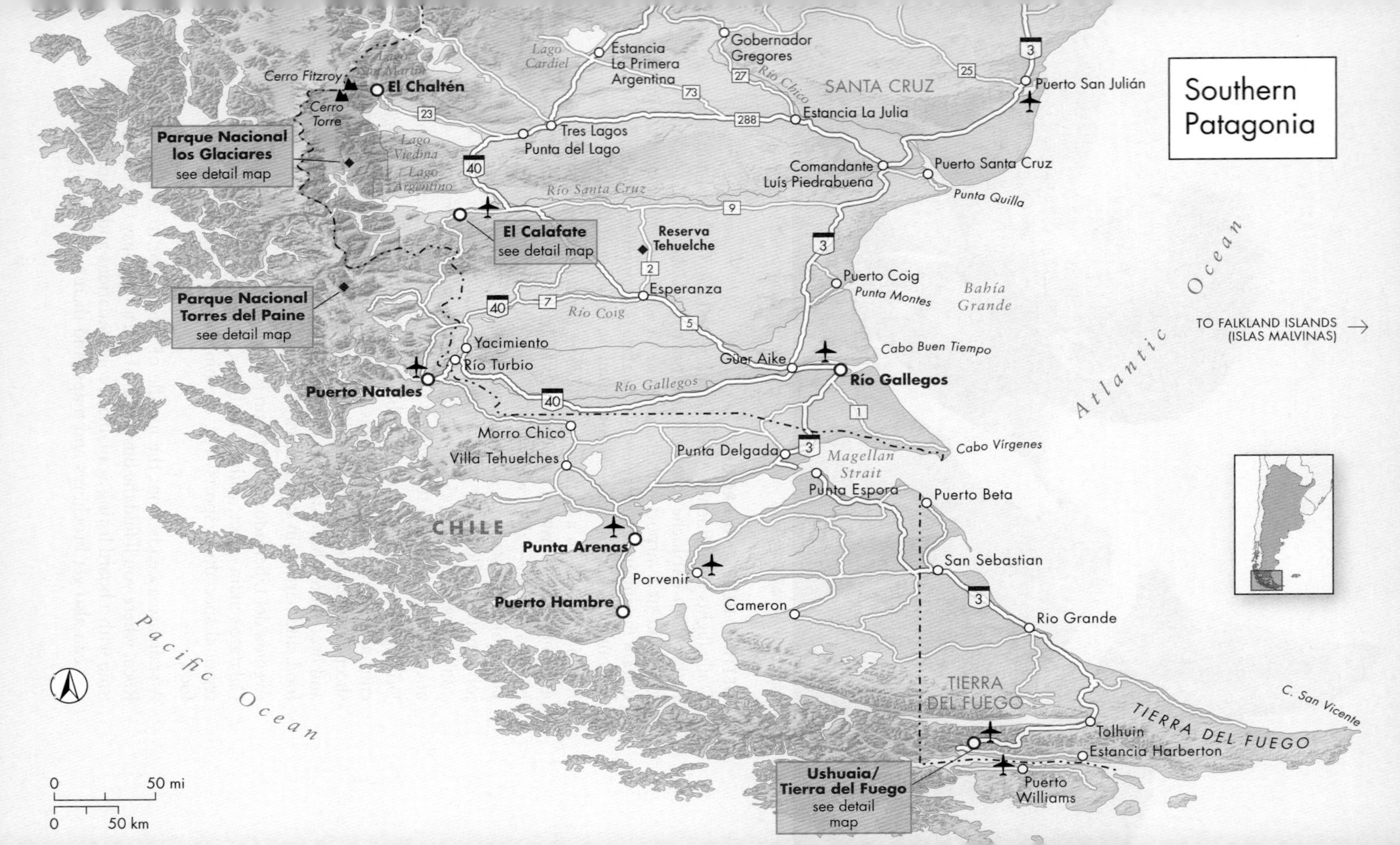
Southern Patagonia
Parque Nacional los Glaciares see detail map
Parque Nacional Torres del Paine see detail map
El Calafate see detail map
Ushuaia/ Tierra del Fuego see detail map
TO FALKLAND ISLANDS (ISLAS MALVINAS)
Atlantic Ocean
Pacific Ocean
SANTA CRUZ
CHILE
TIERRA DEL FUEGO
El Chaltén
Cerro Fitzroy
Cerro Torre
Lago San Martín
Lago Viedma
Lago Argentino
Lago Cardiel
Estancia La Primera Argentina
Gobernador Gregores
Río Chico
Estancia La Julia
Puerto San Julián
Tres Lagos
Punta del Lago
Comandante Luís Piedrabuena
Puerto Santa Cruz
Punta Quilla
Río Santa Cruz
Reserva Tehuelche
Esperanza
Puerto Coig
Punta Montes
Bahía Grande
Río Coig
Yacimiento
Río Turbio
Puerto Natales
Güer Aike
Cabo Buen Tiempo
Río Gallegos
Morro Chico
Villa Tehuelches
Punta Delgada
Cabo Vírgenes
Magellan Strait
Punta Espora
Puerto Beta
Punta Arenas
Porvenir
Puerto Hambre
Cameron
San Sebastian
Rio Grande
Tolhuin
Estancia Harberton
Puerto Williams
C. San Vicente
0 50 mi
0 50 km

CASH WOES

For a town that lives and dies on tourism, one of the most infuriating elements of the boom is the cash shortage that strikes El Calafate every weekend during high season. All the ATMs in town run out of money starting as early as Friday evening, and there's often no respite until midday Monday.

Long queues form along the main street in front of bank branches, and tempers fray. The shortage is compounded by tour companies who offer steep discounts for cash on combined glacier, ice-trekking, and estancia tours.

If credit-card service goes down (not an uncommon occurrence), tensions can boil over. Apart from stocking up during the week, the only way to ensure that you won't run out is to bring all the cash you'll need.

to help plan excursions. The tourism office has another location on the corner of Rosales and Libertador; both locations are open daily from 8 to 8. The Oficina Parques Nacionales, open weekdays 8–4, has information on the Parque Nacional los Glaciares, including the glaciers, area history, hiking trails, and flora and fauna.

TIMING

During the long summer days between December and February (when the sun sets around 10 pm), and during Easter vacation, tens of thousands of visitors come from all corners of the world and fill the hotels and restaurants. This is the area's high season, so make reservations well in advance. October, November, March, and April are less crowded and less expensive periods to visit. March through May can be rainy and cool, but it's also less windy and often quite pleasant. The only bad time to visit is winter, particularly June, July, and August, when many of the hotels and tour agencies are closed.

ESSENTIALS

Bus Contacts **Bus Sur** ✉ *El Calafate, Santa Cruz* ☎ *2966/442–765, 2902/491–631 in El Calafate.* **Cal Tur** ✉ *Terminal Ómnibus, El Calafate, Santa Cruz* ☎ *2962/492–217* ✉ *Av. Libertador 1080, El Calafate, Santa Cruz* ☎. **Interlagos** ✉ *Bus terminal, El Calafate, Santa Cruz* ☎ *2902/491–179.* **TAQSA** ✉ *Bus terminal, El Calafate, Santa Cruz* ☎ *2902/491–843* 🌐 *www.taqsa.com.ar.* **Turismo Zaahj** ✉ *Bus terminal, El Calafate, Santa Cruz* ☎ *2902/491–631* 🌐 *www.turismozaahj.co.cl.*

Currency Exchange **Casa de Cambio Thaler** ✉ *Av. del Libertador 963, El Calafate, Santa Cruz* ☎ *2902/493–245.*

Medical Assistance **Farmacia El Calafate** ✉ *Av. Libertador 1192, El Calafate, Santa Cruz* ☎ *2902/491–407.* **Hospital Distrital** ✉ *Av. Roca 1487, El Calafate, Santa Cruz* ☎ *2902/491–001.*

Post Office **El Calafate** ✉ *Av. Libertador 1133, El Calafate, Santa Cruz.*

Remis **El Calafate** ✉ *Av. Roca 1004, El Calafate, Santa Cruz* ☎ *2902/492–005.*

Rental Cars **ServiCar** ✉ *Av. Libertador 695, El Calafate, Santa Cruz* ☎ *2902/492–541.*

WORD OF MOUTH

"I was on a guided hike on top of Perito Moreno Glacier. An unforgettable experience, I was able to see unparalleled views of the Chilean Andes while climbing over ice ridges, drinking fresh glacial water, and just enjoying the natural world as I've never seen it before." —Anna Hainze, Fodors.com member

Visitor and Tour Info Oficina de Turismo ✉ *Rosales at Libertador, El Calafate, Santa Cruz* ☎ *2902/491–090* 🌐 *www.elcalafate.gov.ar* ✉ *Bus terminal, El Calafate, Santa Cruz.* **Oficina Parques Nacionales** ✉ *Av. Libertador 1302, El Calafate, Santa Cruz* ☎ *2902/491–005.*

EXPLORING

Glaciarium. This new glacier museum gives you an entertaining and educational walk through the formation and life of glaciers in the world (and in particular in Patagonia), the effects of climate change, as well as temporary art exhibitions. A 3-D film about the national park and plenty of brightly lit displays along with the stark glacier-shaped architecture give it a modern appeal. Don't miss out on the Glaciobar—the first ice bar in Argentina—where you can don thermal suits, boots, and gloves and drink a few cocktails in below-zero temperatures. Your whiskey on the rocks will be served with none other than 200-year-old glacier ice from Perito Moreno! ✉ *Ruta 7, Km 6, El Calafate, Santa Cruz* ✢ *Arrive by taxi (35 pesos each way), one hour walking, or by the shuttle service from the tourism office leaving every hour (25 pesos return)* ☎ *2902/497–912* 💳 *Museum 80 pesos (visit takes 1–2 hours); bar 70 pesos for 25 mins with free bar drinks* ⌚ *9–8 daily, shorter opening hours in winter.*

Glaciar Perito Moreno. The Glaciar Perito Moreno lies 80 km (50 miles) away on Ruta 11, and the road has now been entirely paved. From the park entrance the road winds through hills and forests of lenga and ñire trees, until all at once the glacier comes into full view. Descending like a long white tongue through distant mountains, it ends abruptly in a translucent azure wall 5 km (3 miles) wide and 240 feet high at the edge of frosty green Lago Argentino.

Although it's possible to rent a car and go on your own (which can give you a rewarding advantage of avoiding large tourist groups), virtually everyone visits the park on a day trip booked through one of the many travel agents in El Calafate. The most basic tours start at 100 pesos for the round-trip and take you to see the glacier from a viewing area composed of a series of platforms wrapped around the point of the Península de Magallanes. The platforms, which offer perhaps the most impressive view of the glacier, allow you to wander back and forth, looking across the Canal de los Tempanos (Iceberg Channel). Here you listen and wait for nature's number-one ice show—first, a cracking sound, followed by tons of ice breaking away and falling with a thunderous crash into the lake. As the glacier creeps across this narrow channel and meets the land on the other side, an ice dam sometimes builds up between the inlet of Brazo Rico on the left and the rest of the lake on the right. As the pressure on the dam increases, everyone waits for the day it will rupture again. The last time was in July 2008, when the whole thing collapsed in a series of explosions, heard as far away as El Calafate, that sent huge waves across the lake.

In recent years the surge in the number of visitors to Glaciar Perito Moreno has created a crowded scene that is not always conducive to reflective encounters with nature's majesty. Although the glacier remains spectacular, savvy travelers would do well to minimize time at

7

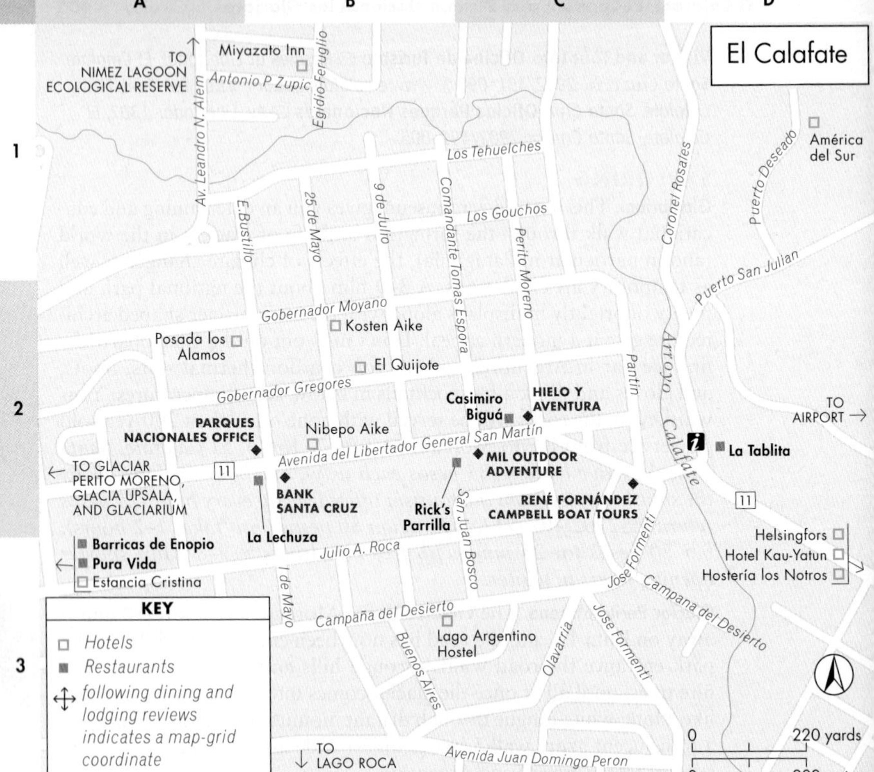

the madhouse that the viewing area becomes at midday in high season, and instead encounter the glacier by boat or on a mini-trekking excursion. Better yet, rent a car and get an early start to beat the tour buses, or visit Perito Moreno in the off-season when a spectacular rupture is just as likely as in midsummer and you won't have to crane over other people's heads to see it. ⊠ *El Calafate, Santa Cruz.*

Glaciar Upsala. Glaciar Upsala, the largest glacier in South America, is 55 km (35 miles) long and 10 km (6 miles) wide, and accessible only by boat. Daily cruises depart from Puerto Banderas (40 km [25 miles] west of El Calafate via Ruta 11) for the 2½-hour trip. Dodging floating icebergs (*tempanos*), some as large as a small island, the boats maneuver as close as they dare to the wall of ice that rises from the aqua-green water of Lago Argentino. The seven glaciers that feed the lake deposit their debris into the runoff, causing the water to cloud with minerals ground to fine powder by the glacier's moraine (the accumulation of earth and stones left by the glacier). Condors and black-chested buzzard eagles build their nests in the rocky cliffs above the lake. When the boat stops for lunch at Onelli Bay, don't miss the walk behind the restaurant into a wild landscape of small glaciers and milky rivers carrying chunks of ice from four glaciers into Lago Onelli. Glaciar Upsala has diminished in size in recent years. ⊠ *El Calafate, Santa Cruz.*

VISITING LAGO ROCA

Lago Roca. Lago Roca is a little-visited lake located inside the National Park just south of Brazo Rico, 46 km (29 miles) from El Calafate. This area receives about five times as much annual precipitation as El Calafate, creating a relatively lush climate of green meadows by the lakeshore, where locals come to picnic and cast for trophy rainbow and lake trout. Don't miss a hike into the hills behind Lago Roca—the view of dark-blue Lago Roca backed by a pale-green inlet of Lago Argentino with the Perito Moreno glacier and jagged snowcapped peaks beyond is truly outstanding. ✉ *El Calafate, Santa Cruz.*

Camping Lago Roca. There are gorgeous campsites, simple cabins, fishing-tackle rentals, hot showers, and a basic restaurant at Camping Lago Roca. Make reservations in advance if visiting over the Christmas holidays; at other times the campground is seldom crowded. For more comfortable accommodations, you can arrange to stay at the Nibepo Aike Estancia at the western end of Lago Roca, about 5 km (3 miles) past the campground. The National Park entrance fee is only collected on the road to Perito Moreno Glacier or at Puerto Banderas, where cruises depart, so admission to the Lago Roca corner of the park is free. ✉ *El Calafate, Santa Cruz* ☎ *2902/499–500* 🌐 *www.losglaciares.com/campinglagoroca* ⏲ *Closed May–Sept.*

7

Nimez Lagoon Ecological Reserve. The Nimez Lagoon Ecological Reserve is a marshy area on the shore of Lago Argentino just a short walk from downtown El Calafate. It's home to many species of waterfowl, including black-necked swans, buff-necked ibises, southern lapwings, and flamingos. Road construction along its edge and the rapidly advancing town threaten to stifle this avian oasis, but it's still a haven for birdwatchers and a relaxing walk in the early morning or late afternoon. Strolling along footpaths among grazing horses and flocks of birds may not be as intense an experience as, say, trekking on a glacier, but a trip to the lagoon provides a good sense of the local landscape. During high season the nature reserve is open from 8 am until 9 pm. Don't forget your binoculars and a telephoto lens. ✉ *1 km (½ miles) north of downtown, just off Av. Alem, El Calafate, Santa Cruz* ☎ *2902/495–536* 🎟 *25 pesos.*

WHERE TO EAT

$$ ECLECTIC ✕ **Barricas de Enopio.** The emphasis at this restaurant-bar is on the extensive wine list and great cheeses that accompany each glass. The flame grill used to barbecue *cordero* (lamb) and other Patagonian standards also doubles as a pizza oven, with thin crusts to savor. The menu also includes eclectic dishes such as pasta stuffed with venison or wild boar. The space is chic, casual, and cozy, with natural-cotton curtains and tablecloths, handmade lamps, and Tehuelche influences. This restaurant offers great value in a town where that's a rapidly diminishing commodity, but it's a bit of a walk from downtown. ✉ *Av. Libertador 1610, El Calafate, Santa Cruz* ☎ *2902/493–414* 🌐 *www.barricasdeenopio.com.ar* ✣ *A3.*

$$$ ARGENTINE ✕ **Casimiro Biguá.** This restaurant and wine bar boasts a hipper-than-thou interior and an inventive menu serving such delights as Patagonian lamb with *calafate* sauce (calafate is a local wild berry). The **Casimiro Biguá Parrilla,** down the street from the main restaurant, has a similar trendy feel. You can recognize the parrilla by the *cordero al asador* (spit-roasted lamb) displayed in the window. A third branch, also on Libertador, offers Italian dishes in a less formal setting. ✉ *Av. Libertador 963, El Calafate, Santa Cruz* ☎ *2902/492–590* 🌐 *www.casimirobigua.com* ✥ *C2.*

$$$$ PIZZA ✕ **La Lechuza.** This bustling joint is known for having some of the best pizza in town. The brick oven and thin crust make for a more authentic, Italian-style taste and texture than at most spots. Their empanadas are among the best in town—pick up a few and you have the perfect pastry pick-me-up during a long day's exploring. With two other branches on the main strip, the secret is out, but stick with the original pizzeria, as the locals do. If it's not crowded, you're in the wrong one. ✉ *Av. Libertador at 1 de Mayo, El Calafate, Santa Cruz* ☎ *2902/491–610* ✥ *B2.*

$$$ ARGENTINE Fodor's Choice ★ ✕ **La Tablita.** It's a couple of extra blocks from downtown and across a little white bridge, but this parrilla is where the locals go for a special night out. You can watch your food as it's cooking: Patagonian lamb and beef ribs roast gaucho-style on frames hanging over a circular asador, and an enormous grill along the back wall is full of steaks, chorizos, and *morcilla* (blood sausage) being cooked to perfection. The whole place is filled with a warm, delicious glow. The enormous *parrillada* for two is a great way to sample it all, and the wine list is well priced and well chosen. It's slightly more expensive than other parrillas in the center of town, but has a classier atmosphere that will make you want to linger for dessert, if you have room. ✉ *Coronel Rosales 28, El Calafate, Santa Cruz* ☎ *2902/491–065* 🌐 *www.interpatagonia.com/latablita* ✥ *D2.*

$$$ ARGENTINE ✕ **Pura Vida.** Bohemian music and earth tones mix with down-home cooking at this romantic, vegetarian-friendly restaurant several blocks from downtown. You'll be surrounded by funky artwork, couples whispering over candlelight, and laid-back but efficient staff as you try to decide which big-enough-to-share dish you'll order and work your way through a great dome of steaming bread on a platter with lashings of butter. Choose between soups, curries, and bakes; the beef stew served inside a *calabaza* (pumpkin) is the signature dish. The cooking isn't quite up to the rest of the restaurant's charms, and the wine list is thin, but Pura Vida is more than the sum of its parts, attracting a curious blend of diners with an almost mystical allure. ✉ *Av. Libertador 1876, El Calafate, Santa Cruz* ☎ *2902/493–356* ✥ *A3.*

$$$$ ARGENTINE ★ ✕ **Rick's Parrilla.** The lighting is too bright, the decor mixes utilitarian blandness with hokey equine touches, and the waiters are gruff. But this all-you-can-eat, *tenedor libre* restaurant has stayed incredibly popular for a reason. The bold canary yellow building on El Calafate's main street happens to be the center of the local social scene, but everyone comes here for the meat. Prime cuts, cooked expertly, run the gamut of traditional Patagonian lamb, steak, chicken breast, *morcilla* blood sausage, and even obscure offal selections for more adventurous diners.

A waiter asks for your favorites, and they come in waves, all for 85 pesos per person. Salads are unspectacular, but the trio of traditional sauces that come with all Argentine parrilla are top notch. Try the fancier restaurants around town if bells and whistles are a must, but you won't find better barbecue. ✉ *Av. Libertador 1091, El Calafate, Santa Cruz* ☎ *2902/492–148* ⊕ *C2.*

WHERE TO STAY

For expanded hotel reviews, visit Fodors.com.

$ **América del Sur.** This hostel is regularly rated among the ten best in South America, with good reason: Dorm and private rooms are all spotlessly clean, well laid out, and have underfloor heating. **Pros:** great views; super-friendly staff; nightly barbeques. **Cons:** an uphill hike from downtown. ✉ *Puerto Deseado, El Calafate, Santa Cruz* ☎ *2902/493–525* ⊕ *www.americahostel.com.ar* *20 rooms* *In-room: no TV. In-hotel: restaurant, bar* ⊕ *D1.*

$$$ **El Quijote.** Sun shines through picture windows onto polished slate floors in an expansive, modern lobby filled with ferns and palms—it's an incongruous but welcoming atmosphere; the quirkiness of this renovated hotel continues with a breakfast room modeled on a '50s-style U.S. diner; understated nods to Cervantes include miniature windmills and suits of armor. **Pros:** central location; attentive staff; large and welcoming lobby; funky dining room; roomy baths. **Cons:** thin walls; uncreative room decor; prices have leaped in recent years. ✉ *Gregores 1155, El Calafate, Santa Cruz* ☎ *2902/491–017* *www.quijotehotel.com.ar* *119 rooms* *In-room: safe. In-hotel: bar* *Closed May to Sept.* *Breakfast* ⊕ *B2.*

$$$$ ★ **Estancia Cristina.** Boarding a catamaran for the four-hour journey across Lago Argentina, you pass a field of giant icebergs in front of the Upsala Glacier—as spectacular as Perito Moreno, minus the crowds—then disembark at Punta Bandera for a short drive up to the three guest lodges, their stark green roofs mirroring the mountain ridges beyond. **Pros:** combines a glacier visit with a stay in a genuine estancia; gourmet packed lunches; knowledgeable guides; incredible mountain views from comfortable, well-appointed rooms. **Cons:** long boat journey to get here; chefs try too hard at dinner; pricey for a one-night stay. ✉ *Punta Bandera, El Calafate, Santa Cruz* *9 de Julio 69, El Calafate, Santa Cruz 9405* ☎ *2902/491–133* ⊕ *www.estanciacristina.com* *12 rooms* *In-room: safe, no TV. In-hotel: restaurant, bar* *Closed from May to mid-Sept.* *All-inclusive* ⊕ *A3.*

$$$$ Fodor's Choice ★ **Helsingfors.** If we could recommend only one property in southern Patagonia, it would be Estancia Helsingfors, a luxurious converted ranch-house with an absolutely spectacular location in the middle of the National Park on the shore of Lago Viedma. **Pros:** unique location; wonderful staff; comfy atmosphere; beautiful blue lake. **Cons:** three hours by dirt road from El Calafate; very remote. ✉ *Lago Viedma, three hours by dirt road from El Calafate, El Calafate, Santa Cruz* *Cordoba 827, piso 11, Buenos Aires, Santa Cruz 1961* ☎ *11/4315–1222 in Buenos Aires* ⊕ *www.helsingfors.com.ar* *9 rooms, maximum of 20 guests* *In-room: no TV. In-hotel: restaurant* *Closed May–Sept.* ⊕ *D3.*

$$$$ **Hostería los Notros.** Weathered wood buildings cling to the mountainside that overlooks the Perito Moreno Glacier as it descends into Lago Argentino; this luxurious inn is designed to exploit its unique position fronting one of the world's natural wonders, and lies 73 km (45 miles) west of El Calafate. **Pros:** unique location; great food; totally luxurious. **Cons:** very expensive; crowds bound for Perito Moreno can detract from the secluded atmosphere. ✉ *9405 El Calafate, Santa Cruz* ☎ *11/4813–7285 in Buenos Aires, 2902/499–510 in El Calafate* ⊕ *www.losnotros.com* *44 rooms* *In-room: no TV. In-hotel: restaurant, bar* *Closed June–mid-Sept.; standard rooms not available in May or Sept.* *All meals* ✣ *D3.*

$$$ Fodor's Choice ★ **Hotel Kau-Yatun.** From the homemade chocolates and flower bouquets that appear in the rooms each evening to the sweeping backyard complete with swing sets for the kids, every detail of this converted ranch property is tailored to thoughtful hospitality. **Pros:** great food; utmost care put into the details; central location. **Cons:** water pressure is only adequate. ✉ *25 de Mayo, El Calafate, Santa Cruz* ☎ *2902/491–059* ⊕ *www.kauyatun.com* *44 rooms* *In-room: Wi-Fi. In-hotel: restaurant, bar* *Breakfast* ✣ *D3.*

$$$$ **Kosten Aike.** Lined with wooden balconies, high beamed ceilings, and a slate floor, this hotel is a paragon of Andean Patagonian architecture. **Pros:** large rooms; central location; great views from the spa; good value at this price point. **Cons:** dining room decor is uninspired. ✉ *G. Moyano 1243, at 25 de Mayo, El Calafate, Santa Cruz* ☎ *2902/492–424, 11/4811–1314 in Buenos Aires* ⊕ *www.kostenaike.com.ar* *78 rooms, 2 suites* *In-hotel: restaurant, bar, gym, business center* *Closed May–Sept.* *Breakfast* ✣ *B2.*

$ **Lago Argentino Hostel.** Just around the corner from the bus terminal, this chilled-out hostel is operated by the same family that runs the popular Pura Vida restaurant; the atmosphere is cozy and eclectic, the rooms and public spaces are painted in a kaleidoscope of rustic bold primary colors. **Pros:** convenient location; pleasant garden; variety of room choices. **Cons:** earplugs recommended in the open-plan dorm rooms; mattresses and pillows could be thicker. ✉ *Campaña del Desierto 1050, El Calafate, Santa Cruz* ☎ *2902/491–423* ⊕ *www.interpatagonia.com/lagoargentino* *8 rooms* *In-hotel: laundry facilities* ✣ *B3.*

$$ **Miyazato Inn.** Jorge Miyasato and his wife Elizabeth have brought the flawless hospitality of a traditional Japanese country inn to El Calafate; each of the five rooms has hardwood floors, comfortable twin beds, and rice paper lampshades, and a sun-drenched dining area sits just off the lobby/lounge. **Pros:** clean and homey; outstanding value; owners offer a human touch. **Cons:** a noisier neighborhood just out of the center. ✉ *Egidio Feruglio 150, El Calafate, Santa Cruz* ☎ *2902/491–953* ⊕ *www.interpatagonia.com/miyazatoinn* *5 rooms* *Breakfast* ✣ *B1.*

$$$$ **Nibepo Aike.** This lovely estancia is an hour and half from El Calafate in a bucolic valley overlooking Lago Roca and backed by snowcapped mountain peaks; sheep, horses, and cows graze among purple lupine flowers, and friendly gauchos give horse-racing and sheep-shearing demonstrations. **Pros:** spectacular scenery; yummy food; welcoming

"We walked from our hotel in the center of town to the Laguna Nimez Reserve. Wild horses grazed lazily amid the white wildflowers. It was a magical moment... So unexpected!" —Lois Zebelman, Fodors.com member

staff. **Cons:** an hour by dirt road from downtown; two night minimum stay; no Wi-Fi. ✉ *For reservations: Av. Libertador 1215, El Calafate, Santa Cruz* ☎ *2902/492–797 reservations* 🌐 *www.nibepoaike.com.ar* *10 rooms* *In-room: no TV. In-hotel: restaurant* ⏲ *Closed May–Sept.* ✣ *B2.*

$$$$ **Posada los Alamos.** Surrounded by tall, leafy alamo trees and constructed of brick and dark *quebracho* (ironwood), this enormous complex incorporates a country manor house, half a dozen convention rooms, a spa, indoor swimming pool, and mini-golf course to offer all the trappings of a top-notch hotel. **Pros:** modern and distinctive reception and public areas, beautiful gardens. **Cons:** it's easy to get lost in the maze of corridors; rooms are indifferently furnished; overly formal staff. ✉ *Moyano at Bustillo, El Calafate, Santa Cruz* ☎ *2902/491–144* 🌐 *www.posadalosalamos.com* *144 rooms* *In-hotel: restaurant, bar, golf course, pool, gym, spa, business center* *Breakfast* ✣ *A2.*

SPORTS AND THE OUTDOORS

BOAT TOURS

The two most popular scenic boat rides in the Parque Nacional los Glaciares are the hour-long **Safari Náutico,** in which your boat cruises a few meters away from the face of the Glaciar Perito Moreno, and the full-day **Upsala Glacier Tour,** in which you navigate around a more extensive selection of glaciers, including Upsala and Onelli, and sections of Lago Argentino that are inaccessible by land. The Safari Náutico costs 100 pesos, not including transportation from El Calafate. The first boat starts the 45-minute round trip at 10 am and the last departs at 3:30 pm. The all-day Upsala tour costs 300 pesos.

Solo Patagonia. Solo Patagonia is a new tour operator in town and has taken over an established tour company and remains one of the only offering boat tours to Spegazzini and Upsala glaciers. ✉ *Av. Libertador 867, El Calafate, Santa Cruz* ☎ *2902/491–155* 🌐 *www.solopatagonia.com.*

HIKING

Although it's possible to find trails along the shore of Lago Argentino and in the hills south and west of town, these hikes traverse a rather barren landscape and are not terribly interesting. The mountain peaks and forests are in the park, an hour by car from El Calafate. If you want to lace up your boots in your hotel, walk outside and hit the trail, go to El Chaltén—it's a much better base than El Calafate for hikes in the national park. Good hiking trails are accessible from the camping areas and cabins by Lago Roca, 50 km (31 miles) from El Calafate.

ESTANCIAS TURÍSTICAS

Provincial Tourist Office. *Estancias Turísticas* (tourist ranches) are ideal for a combination of horseback riding, ranch activities, and local excursions. Information on all the estancias can be obtained from Estancias de Santa Cruz is in Buenos Aires at the Provincial tourist office. ✉ *Reconquista 642, El Calafate, Santa Cruz* ☎ *11/5237–4043* 🌐 *www.estanciasdesantacruz.com.*

HORSEBACK RIDING AND ESTANCIAS

Alta Vista. Convenient to El Calafate, Alta Vista is a solid choice for the standard estancia activities (horses, sheep, asados) and offers good guidance for local hikes. ✉ *33 km [20 miles] from El Calafate on Ruta 15, El Calafate, Santa Cruz* ☎ *2902/499–902* 🌐 *www.hosteriaaltavista.com.ar.*

Estancia El Galpón del Glaciar. Estancia El Galpón del Glaciar welcomes guests overnight or for the day—for a horseback ride, bird-watching, or an afternoon program that includes a demonstration of sheep dogs working, a walk to the lake with a naturalist, sheep-shearing, and dinner in the former sheep-shearing barn served right off the asador by knife-wielding gauchos. ✉ *Ruta 11, Km 22, El Calafate, Santa Cruz* ☎📠 *2902/497–793, 11/5217–6719* 🌐 *www.elgalpondelglaciar.com.ar.*

Estancia Maria Elisa. Estancia Maria Elisa is an upscale choice among estancias in Santa Cruz. ✉ *50 km from Calafate on Ruta 40, El Calafate, Santa Cruz* ☎📠 *2902/492–583* 🌐 *www.estanciamariaelisa.com.ar.*

Gustavo Holzmann. Anything from a short day ride along Lago Argentino to a weeklong camping excursion in and around the glaciers can be arranged in El Calafate by Gustavo Holzmann or through the tourist office. ✉ *Av. Libertador 4315, El Calafate, Santa Cruz* ☎ *2902/493–278* 🌐 *www.cabalgataenpatagonia.com.*

Nibepo Aike. A good estancia to consider if you want to stay close to El Calafate is Nibepo Aike. ✉ *53 km [31 miles] from El Calafate near Lago Roca on Ruta 15, El Calafate, Santa Cruz* ☎ *2902/492–797* 🌐 *www.nibepoaike.com.ar.*

Parque Nacional los Glaciares
Laguna del Desierto
Lago San Martín
Parque Nacional Bernardo O'Higgins
Pier Giorgio
Cerro Fitzroy 11,286 ft.
Cerro Torre 10,174 ft.
Chorillo del Salta
Adela Sur
El Chalten
MESETA DEL QUEMADO
Cordón
Pana
Congrejo
CHILE
Dos Cuernos
Dos Cumbres
Padre De Agostini
Huemul
San Jose Ranch
MESETA CHICA
MESETA DEL VIENTO
23
Los Alamos Ranch
MESETA BASALTICA
Glaciar Viedma
Viedma Glacier Ice Trekking
Puntudo
CORDILLERA DE LOS ANDES
PARQUE NACIONAL LOS GLACIARES
Mascarello
Lago Viedma
Helsingfors (Hotel)
Pico Negro
Norte
21
40
Mesón
Las Tetas o Dos Picos
La Leona
Glaciar Upsala
Planchón
Estación Astronómica Austral
Murallón
69
Pintado
Guardaparque
Estación Cristina (Hotel)
Loyola o Mirador
Río La Leona
ARGENTINA
Bertrand
Agassiz
Castillo
Horqueta
Lago Onelli
Onelli
19
Brazo Norte
San Ernesto Ranch
Spegazzini Glacier
Peineta
Puesto la Diana
Lago Argentino
PENÍNSULA AVELLANEDA
Boat Tours to Upsala
Charles Fuhr
Cueva del Gualicho
Punta Bandera
Mayo Sound
SIERRA CATTLE
Frías
El Calafate
Tempanos Canal
Mayo Glaciar
Negro
15
SIERRA BUENOS AIRES
60
Perito Moreno Glacier Ice Trekking
Estancia Los Notros
Glaciar Perito Moreno
Brazo Rico
Río Bote
Lago Roca (w/camping)
Mt. Peritrobelli
Mesa de Truco
CORCÓN DE LOS CRISTALES
Cervantes
Brazo Sur
Centinela o Alfiler
SIERRA BAGUALES
Adriana
Verlika
Parque Nacional Bernardo O'higgins
CHILE
Lago Dickson
10 mi
10 km
Mt. Stokes
Parque Nacional Torres Del Paine
SIERRA CONTRERAS

Great views of Cerro Fitzroy seem to wait at every bend in the trail in Parque Nacional Los Glaciares.

ICE TREKKING

★ **Hielo y Aventura.** A two-hour mini-trek on the Perito Moreno Glacier involves a transfer from El Calafate to Brazo Rico by bus and a short lake crossing to a dock and refugio, where you set off with a guide, put crampons over your shoes, and walk across a stable portion of the glacier, scaling ridges of ice, and ducking through bright-blue ice tunnels. It is one of the most unusual experiences in Argentina. The entire outing lasts about five hours. Hotels arrange mini-treks through Hielo y Aventura, which also organizes much longer, more difficult trips of eight hours to a week to other glaciers; you can arrange the trek directly through their office in downtown El Calafate. Mini-trekking currently runs about 540 pesos for the day, but prices are marching relentlessly higher. Hielo y Aventura also runs a longer "Big Ice" trek that traverses a much more extensive area of the glacier and costs 770 pesos. If you're between the ages of 18 and 40 and want a more extreme experience, Big Ice is highly recommended. ✉ *Av. Libertador 935, El Calafate, Santa Cruz* ☎ *2902/492–205* 🌐 *www.hieloyaventura.com.*

LAND ROVER EXCURSIONS

MIL Outdoor Adventure. If pedaling uphill sounds like too much work, check out the Land Rover expeditions offered by MIL Outdoor Adventure. These trips use large tour trucks to follow dirt tracks into the hills above town for stunning views of Lago Argentino. On a clear day, you can even see the peaks of Cerro Torre and Cerro Fitzroy on the horizon. MIL's Land Rovers are converted to run on vegetable oil, so environmentalists can enjoy bouncing up the trail with a clean conscience. ✉ *Av. Libertador 1033, El Calafate, Santa Cruz* ☎ *2902/491–446* 🌐 *www.miloutdoor.com.*

MOUNTAIN BIKING

Alquiler de Bicicletas. Mountain biking is popular along the dirt roads and mountain paths that lead to the lakes, glaciers, and ranches. Rent bikes and get information at Alquiler de Bicicletas. ✉ *HLS, Moreno 65, El Calafate, Santa Cruz* ☎ *2902/493–806.*

EL CHALTÉN

222 km (138 miles) north of El Calafate (35 km [22 miles] east on R11 to R40, then north on R40 to R23 north).

Founded in 1985, El Chaltén is Argentina's newest town, and it's growing at an astounding rate. Originally just a few shacks and lodges built near the entrance to Los Glaciares National Park, the town is starting to fill a steep-walled valley in front of Cerro Torre and Mt. Fitzroy, two of the most impressive peaks in Argentina. Famous for the exploits of rock climbers who started their pilgrimage to climb some of the most difficult rock walls in the world in the 1950s, the range is now drawing hikers whose more earthbound ambitions run to dazzling mountain scenery and unscripted encounters with wildlife including condors, Patagonian parrots, red-crested woodpeckers, and the *huemul*, an endangered deer species.

GETTING HERE AND AROUND

The four-hour car or bus trip to El Chaltén from El Calafate makes staying at least one night here a good idea. The only gas, food, and restroom facilities en route are at La Leona, a historically significant ranch 110 km (68 miles) from El Calafate where Butch Cassidy and the Sundance Kid once hid from the long arm of the law.

Before you cross the bridge into town over Río Fitzroy, stop at the Parque Nacional office. It's extremely well organized and staffed by bilingual rangers who can help you plan your mountain treks and point you to accommodation and restaurants in town. It's an essential stop; orientation talks are given in coordination with arriving buses, which automatically stop here before continuing on to the bus depot.

There's only one ATM in town (it's in the bus station), and it's in high demand; because of servicing schedules, on the weekend El Chaltén runs into the same cash availability problems that El Calafate does, though on a smaller scale. ⚠ **During the week, stockpile the cash you'll need for the weekend, or bring it with you if you're arriving between mid-day Friday and mid-day Monday.**

ESSENTIALS

Visitor Info Parque Nacional Office ✉ *El Chaltén, Santa Cruz* ☎ *2962/493–004.*

EXPLORING

Cerro Torre and Cerro Fitzroy. You don't need a guide to do the classic treks to Cerro Torre and Cerro Fitzroy, each about 6 to 8 hours round-trip out of El Chaltén. If your legs feel up to it the day you do the Fitzroy walk, tack on an hour of steep switchbacks to Mirador Tres Lagos, the lookout with the best views of Mt. Fitzroy and its glacial lakes. Both

7

routes, plus the Mirador and various side trails, can be combined in a two or three day trip. ✉ *El Chaltén, Santa Cruz.*

Chorillo del Salta (*Trickling Falls*). The Chorillo del Salta is a waterfall just 4 km (2.5 miles) north of town on the road to Lago del Desierto. The falls are no Iguazú, but the area is extremely pleasant and sheltered from the wind. A short hike uphill leads to secluded river pools and sun-splashed rocks where locals enjoy picnics on their days off. If you don't feel up to a more ambitious hike, the short stroll to the falls is an excellent way to spend the better part of an afternoon. Pack a bottle of wine and a sandwich and enjoy the solitude. ✉ *El Chaltén, Santa Cruz.*

Laguna del Desierto (*Lake of the Desert*). The Laguna del Desierto—a lovely lake surrounded by lush forest, complete with orchids and mossy trees—is 37 km (23 miles) north of El Chaltén on Ruta 23, a dirt road. Hotels in El Chaltén can arrange a trip for about 150 pesos for the day. Locals recommend visiting Lago del Desierto on a rainy day, when more ambitious hikes are not an option and the dripping green misty forest is extra mysterious. ✉ *El Chaltén, Santa Cruz.*

WHERE TO EAT AND STAY

For expanded hotel reviews, visit Fodors.com.

$$$ ARGENTINE ✕ **Aonikenk.** In a dark wooden dining hall you'll share hearty steaks, warming soups, and wine poured from penguin-shaped ceramic jugs, in a family restaurant that includes a hostel upstairs. It's rustic, and the food is not spectacular, but you can't beat the friendly atmosphere in what is easily El Chaltén's largest and most popular restaurant. It's also the only one that's consistently open for lunch and dinner in the off-season. ✉ *Av. M.M. de Güemes 23, El Chaltén, Santa Cruz* ☎ *2962/493–070* ▭ *No credit cards.*

$$ ARGENTINE ★ ✕ **La Cerveceria.** While El Chaltén is still building all it needs to become a fully fledged town, it already has a successful microbrewery. The owners of this restaurant and bar pride themselves on handmade beers, with the stout or *negra* not to be missed. They call the place a "Hausbrauerei," but it's not just the hops bringing in the crowds: they also cook up delicious soups, snacks, empanadas, and stew. The *locro,* a hearty traditional northern Argentine stew, is some of the best you'll find in southern Argentina. ✉ *San Martin 320, El Chaltén, Santa Cruz* ☎ *2962/493–109* ▭ *No credit cards* ⌚ *Closed during off-season May–Oct.*

$ 🏨 **Nothofagus.** A simple B&B off the main road, Nothafagus is named after the southern beech tree, and the lodge has a rough-hewn, woody feel with exposed beams and leaves stamped into the lampshades. **Pros:** great views; bright and sunny breakfast room. **Cons:** staff energy too low for some; spartan rooms and bathrooms, some of which are shared. ✉ *Hensen, at Riquelme, El Chaltén, Santa Cruz* ☎ *2962/493–087* 🌐 *www.nothofagusbb.com.ar* ⇨ *9 rooms* 👍 *In-room: no TV* ▭ *No credit cards* 🍽 *Breakfast.*

$$$ ★ 🏨 **Posada Lunajuim.** A traditional A-frame roof keeps the lid on a funky, modern lodge filled with contemporary artwork, exposed brick masonry, and a spacious lounge and dining room complete with a roaring fireplace and a library stacked with an intriguing mix of travel

books. **Pros:** you could spend all day in the common areas; staff and owners are pleasantly energetic and will make you a packed lunch for hikes. **Cons:** not all rooms have views; baths are quite small; a little pricey compared to the rest of town. ✉ *Trevisan 45, El Chaltén, Santa Cruz* ☎ *2962/493047* 🌐 *www.posadalunajuim.com.ar* *26 rooms* *In-room: safe, Wi-Fi. In-hotel: restaurant, bar* *Breakfast.*

SPORTS AND THE OUTDOORS

El Chaltén owes its existence to those who wanted a base for trekking into this corner of Los Glaciares National Park, specifically Cerro Torre and Cerro Fitzroy. It's no surprise that nearly everyone who comes here considers hiking up to those two mountains to be the main event—though the locro and microbrews at the end of the day are a plus.

HIKING

Both long and short hikes on well-trodden trails lead to lakes, glaciers, and stunning viewpoints. There are two main hikes, one to the base of Cerro Fitzroy, the other to a windswept glacial lake at the base of Cerro Torre. Both hikes climb into the hills above town, and excellent views start after only about an hour on either trail. The six-hour round-trip hike to the base camp for Cerro Torre at Laguna Torre has (weather permitting) dramatic views of Torres Standhart, Adelas, Grande, and Solo.

Trails start in town and are very well marked, so if you stick to the main path there is little danger of getting lost. Just be careful of high winds and exposed rocks that can get slippery in bad weather. The eight-hour hike to the base camp for Cerro Fitzroy passes Laguna Capri and ends at Laguna de los Tres, where you can enjoy an utterly spectacular view of the granite tower. If you only have time for one ambitious hike, this is probably the best choice, though the last kilometer of trail is very steep. At campsites in the hills above town hardy souls can pitch a tent for the night and enjoy sunset and dawn views of the mountain peaks. Ask about current camping regulations and advisories at the National Park office before setting off with a tent in your rucksack. Finally, use latrines where provided, and under no circumstance should you ever think about starting a fire—a large section of forest near Cerro Torre was devastated several years ago when a foolish hiker tried to dispose of toilet paper with a match.

MOUNTAIN CLIMBING

Casa de Guias. A guide is required if you want to enter the ice field, or trek on any of the glaciers in Los Glaciares National Park. Casa de Guias is a group of professional, multilingual guides who offer fully equipped multiday treks covering all the classic routes in the national park, and longer trips exploring the ice field that can last more than a week. They even offer a taste of big wall climbing on one of the spires in the Fitzroy range. ✉ *Av. San Martin 310, El Chaltén, Santa Cruz* ☎ *2962/493–118* 🌐 *www.casadeguias.com.ar.*

7

Picadas, or light snacks, reach a new level of delicious after an excursion in the wilds of Patagonia; a selection may include peanuts, pistacios, marinated baby onions, or a local cheese.

PUERTO NATALES, CHILE

242 km (150 miles) northwest of Punta Arenas.

Puerto Natales, Chile has become the main base for exploring a number of southern Patagonia's top attractions, including Parque Nacional Torres del Paine and Parque Nacional Bernardo O'Higgins. Please note, if calling outside of Chile, you will require the international dialing code (+56). From within Chile you need to add 0 before dialing any local code.

The land around Puerto Natales originally held very little interest for Spanish explorers in search of riches. A not-so-warm welcome from the indigenous peoples encouraged them to continue up the coast, leaving only a name for the channel running through it: Seno Última Esperanza (Last Hope Sound).

The town of Puerto Natales wasn't founded until 1911, becoming a community of fading fishing and meatpacking enterprises with some 20,000 friendly residents. Now as a launching point for many touristic sites, it has recently seen a large increase in tourism and development. A lot of tourism is also generated by the scenic **Navimag cruise** that makes four-day journeys between here and Puerto Montt, to the north of Chile.

While there are fewer hotels and restaurants to choose from than in Punta Arenas, the town has added a string of hip eateries, cafés, and boutique hotels in recent years, and is starting to challenge the more staid larger city as a hub for exploring the entire region.

Serious hikers often come to this area and use Puerto Natales as their base for hiking the classic "W" or circuit treks in **Torres del Paine,** which take between four days and a week to complete. Others choose to spend a couple of nights in one of the park's luxury hotels and take in the sights during day hikes.

If you have less time, however, it's quite possible to spend just one day touring the park, as many people do, with Puerto Natales as your starting point. In that case, rather than drive, you'll want to book a one-day Torres del Paine tour with one of the many tour operators in Natales. Most tours pick you up at your hotel between 8 and 9 am and follow the same route, visiting several lakes and mountain vistas, seeing Lago Grey and its glacier, and stopping for lunch in Hostería Lago Grey or one of the other hotels inside the park. These tours return around sunset.

Argentina's magnificent **Perito Moreno Glacier,** near El Calafate, can be visited on a popular (but extremely long) one-day tour, leaving at the crack of dawn and returning late at night—don't forget your passport. It's a four-hour-plus trip in each direction. (Some tours sensibly include overnights in El Calafate.)

GETTING HERE AND AROUND

Puerto Natales centers on the Plaza de Armas, a lovely, well-landscaped sanctuary. A few blocks west of the plaza on Avenida Bulnes you'll find the small Museo Historico Municipal. On a clear day, an early morning walk along Avenida Pedro Montt, which follows the shoreline of the Seno Última Esperanza (or Canal Señoret, as it's called on some maps), can be a soul-cleansing experience. The rising sun gradually casts a glow on the mountain peaks to the west.

ESSENTIALS

Bus Contacts Buses Fernández ✉ *Eleuterio Ramirez 399, Puerto Natales, Chile* ☎ *61/411–111* 🌐 *www.busesfernandez.com.*

Internet Cafés The Net House ✉ *Bulnes 499, Puerto Natales, Chile* ☎ *61/411–472.*

Rental Cars Avis ✉ *Eberhard 577, Puerto Natales, Chile* ☎ *61/614–388.*

Visitor and Tour Info Tourism Kiosk. At the time of writing, the tourism office is undergoing a refurbishment. A makeshift tourism kiosk has been opened in Plaza de Armas in the meantime. ✉ *Plaza de Armas, Puerto Natales, Chile.*

EXPLORING

Iglesia Parroquial. Across from the Plaza de Armas is the squat little Iglesia Parroquial. The ornate altarpiece in this church depicts the town's founders, indigenous peoples, and the Virgin Mary all in front of the Torres del Paine. ✉ *Puerto Natales, Chile.*

Museo Historico Municipal. A highlight in the small but interesting Museo Historico Municipal is a room filled with antique prints of Aonikenk and Kaweshkar indigenous peoples. Another room is devoted to the exploits of Hermann Eberhard, a German explorer considered the region's first settler. Check out his celebrated collapsible boat. In an adjacent room you will find some vestiges of the old Bories sheep plant, which processed over 300,000 sheep a year. ✉ *Av. Bulnes 285, Puerto Natales, Chile* ☎ *61/411–263* 🎫 *1,000 pesos* ⏲ *Weekdays 8:30–12:30 and weekends 2:30–6.*

Monumento Natural Cueva de Milodón. In 1896, Hermann Eberhard stumbled upon a gaping cave that extended 200 meters (650 feet) into the earth. Venturing inside, he discovered the bones and dried pieces of hide (with deep red fur) of an animal he could not identify. It was later determined that what Eberhard had discovered were the extraordinarily well-preserved remains of a prehistoric herbivorous mammal, *mylodon darwini,* about twice the height of a man, which they called a *milodón.* The discovery of a stone wall in the cave, and of neatly cut grass stalks in the animal's feces led researchers to conclude that 10,000 years ago a group of Tehuelche Indians captured this beast. The cave is at the Monumento Natural Cueva de Milodón. The cathedral-sized space was carved out of a solid rock wall by rising waters. It was the final destination for Bruce Chatwin in research for his book *In Patagonia*, but its dusty floor and barren walls are unspectacular, and the tacky life-size fiberglass model at the cave mouth is useful only as a reference to the size of the gigantic animal that lived here. ✉ *5 km (3 miles) off Ruta 9 signpost, 28 km (17 miles) northwest of Puerto Natales, Puerto Natales, Chile* ☎ *No phone* 🎫 *3,000 pesos* ⏲ *Summer, daily 8 am–6 pm.*

Plaza de Armas. A few blocks east of the waterfront overlooking Seno Última Esperanza is the not-quite-central Plaza de Armas. An incongruous railway engine sits prominently in the middle of the square. ✉ *Arturo Prat at Eberhard, Puerto Natales, Chile.*

NEED A BREAK?

El Living. When you've just gotten back from trekking the Torres del Paine and had your first hot shower in a week, sometimes you just want a place to relax that feels like home. El Living couldn't be better named. It feels like a living room, albeit one that's sitting in a bohemian loft in SoHo. The British owners have littered their couches with fashion, rock-climbing, and gossip magazines, and they offer gluten-free vegetarian and vegan dishes at the base of a continent that rarely caters to people who don't eat meat. Homemade pumpkin and ginger soup, kidney bean–pumpkin bake, vegetarian curries, and toasted banana and honey sandwiches are typical hipster comfort food. They're also delicious, especially washed down with *jugo de frambuesa* (fresh raspberry juice). There's no pressure to eat and leave; you could find yourself whiling away the rest of your afternoon, and coming back the next morning for breakfast. You'll find it in the Plaza de Correo on Arturo Prat, just next door to Asador Patagónico. ✉ *Arturo Prat 156, Puerto Natales, Chile* ☎ *61/411–140* 🌐 *www.el-living.com* ⏲ *11–11, closed in winter.*

WHERE TO EAT

$$$$ CHILEAN ★ **Asador Patagónico.** This bright spot in the Puerto Natales dining scene is zealous about meat. So zealous, in fact, that there's no seafood on the menu. Incredible care is taken with the excellent *lomo* and other grilled steaks, as well as the steak carpaccio starter. Though the wine list is serious, the atmosphere is less so—the place used to be a pharmacy, and much of the furniture is still labeled with the remedies (*catgut crin* anyone?) they once contained. There's good music, dim lighting, an open fire, and a friendly buzz; wear removable layers since it can get warm when the grill is cranking. *Prat 158, Puerto Natales, Chile* *61/413–553* *Closed Apr.–Sept.*

$$$$ CAFÉ **Café Melissa.** Excellent espresso and mountainous burgers are the pride of this unpretentious café, which also serves pastries and cakes baked on the premises. In the heart of downtown, this is a popular meeting place for residents and visitors, and there's Internet access and decent Wi-Fi. You can impress the locals and stun fellow travelers by ordering a *Fanschop*—a mix of beer and Fanta that many Chileans apparently enjoy. The café stays open through the afternoon lull until 10 pm. *Blanco Encalada 258, Puerto Natales, Chile* *61/415–679* *No credit cards* *10–10 Mon.–Sat., closed in winter.*

$$$$ SEAFOOD **Mama Rosa.** You'll watch the wind whip the Seno Última Esperanza from a comfortable lounge in front of the fireplace at this ultra-modern café. Complete with Apple Internet terminals and friendly English-speaking staff, this café has been recently converted from a seafood restaurant, and is now making the most of its corner location as part of the boutique Indigo Hotel. Marine fossils collected from the fjord, piles of *National Geographic* and *Outside* magazines, a range of herbal teas, lunch specials like crab ravioli, and delicate desserts served in gigantic portions make this the ideal place for a long lunch. Try the scrumptious carrot cake. *Ladrilleros 105, Puerto Natales, Chile* *61/413–609* *www.indigopatagonia.com* *Closed in winter; months vary.*

$$$$ CHILEAN **Restaurant Última Esperanza.** Named for the strait on which Puerto Natales is located, it is perhaps your last chance to try Patagonian seafood classics in a town being overrun by hip eateries. This traditional restaurant is well known for attentive, if formal service, and top-quality dishes from chefs Miguel Risco and Manuel Marín. Poached conger eel in shellfish sauce, king crab stew, and *cordero* (lamb) are specialties—delicious dishes served with plenty of flavor and little fuss. The room is big and impersonal, and for this reason alone the restaurant is perhaps losing ground to new arrivals more focused on atmosphere and comfort. *Av. Eberhard 354, Puerto Natales, Chile* *61/413–626.*

WHERE TO STAY

For expanded hotel reviews, visit Fodors.com.

$$$$ **Hostal Lady Florence Dixie.** Named after an aristocratic English immigrant and tireless traveler, this long-established hotel with an alpine-inspired facade is on the town's main street; its bright, spacious upstairs lounge is a great people-watching perch. **Pros:** very convenient location; friendly owner; relaxed atmosphere. **Cons:** not quite the boutique hotel

7

it purports to be; rooms have a dowdy feel in a town that's rapidly modernizing. ✉ *Av. Bulnes 655, Puerto Natales, Chile* ☎ *61/411–158* *19 rooms* *In-hotel: business center* *Breakfast.*

$$$$ **Hotel CostAustralis.** Designed by a local architect, this venerable three-story hotel is one of the most distinctive buildings in Puerto Natales; its peaked, turreted roof dominates the waterfront, and 40 new rooms were added in 2009. **Pros:** great views from bay-facing rooms; good restaurant; courteous and professional staff; startlingly low off-season rates. **Cons:** rooms are somewhat bland; endless corridors a little impersonal. ✉ *Av. Pedro Montt 262, at Av. Bulnes, Puerto Natales, Chile* ☎ *61/412–000* 🌐 *www.hoteles-australis.com* *105 rooms, 5 suites* *In-room: safe. In-hotel: restaurant, bar, business center* *Breakfast.*

$$$$ **Hotel Martín Gusinde.** Part of Chile's modern AustroHoteles chain, this intimate inn has retained an aura of sophistication even as it has grown to accommodate the surge in visitors to Puerto Natales. **Pros:** atmosphere is urbane. **Cons:** staff language barrier; seedy casino neighbor; absence of baths in this style of hotel is a mystery. ✉ *Carlos Bories 278, Puerto Natales, Chile* ☎ *61/412–770* 🌐 *www.hotelmartingusinde.com* *28 rooms* *In-room: safe. In-hotel: restaurant, bar* *Breakfast.*

$$$$ ★ **Indigo Patagonia Hotel & Spa.** Chilean architect Sebastian Irarrazabel was given free rein by a multi-national trio of owners to redesign this building along a nautical theme; inside, a maze of gangplanks, ramps, and staircases shoot out across cavernous open spaces, minimalist wood panels line walls and ceilings, and water burbles down a waterfall that borders the central walkway. **Pros:** steeped in ultramodern luxury; at the forefront of Puerto Natales's efforts to attract the hip young traveler market; rooftop spa; great views. **Cons:** so ultramodern it might be cloying if it's not your aesthetic; standard rooms do not have bathtubs (though the showers are excellent). ✉ *Ladrilleros 105, Puerto Natales, Chile* ☎ *61/413–609* 🌐 *www.indigopatagonia.com* *29 rooms* *In-room: no TV. In-hotel: restaurant, bar, spa.*

OUTSIDE TOWN

Several lodges have been constructed on a bluff overlooking the Seno Última Esperanza, about a mile outside of town. The views at these hotels are spectacular, with broad panoramas with unforgettable sunsets. It's too far to walk to town comfortably (about 20 minutes), but there is dependable taxi service for 10 pesos.

$$$$ **Altiplanico Sur.** This is the Patagonian representative of the Altiplanico line of thoughtfully designed eco-hotels, and nature takes center stage: the hotel blends so seamlessly with its surroundings, it's almost subterranean. **Pros:** couldn't be closer to nature; stellar views of the fjords and mountains, even from a low vantage point. **Cons:** staff speaks little or no English; long walk into town and there's no shuttle bus; few technological accoutrements. ✉ *Ruta 9 Norte, Km 1.5, Huerto 282, Puerto Natales, Chile* ☎ *61/412–525* 🌐 *www.altiplanico.cl* *22 rooms* *In-room: safe, no TV, Wi-Fi. In-hotel: restaurant.*

$$$$ Fodor's Choice ★ **Remota.** For most guests the Remota experience begins with the safari-esque transfer from Punta Arenas Airport, during which the driver stops to point out animals and other items of interest; on arrival, you meet what seems like the entire staff, check into your ultramodern

room, have a drink from a top-shelf open bar, and run off to the open-air Jacuzzis and impossibly serene infinity pool. **Pros:** after a few days the staff feels like family; restaurant uses the freshest locally sourced ingredients; becoming more flexible about minimum length of stay. **Cons:** all-inclusiveness discourages sampling local restaurants; views not as good as those from hotels inside Torres Del Paine National Park. ✉ *Ruta 9 Norte, Km 1.5, Huerto 279, Puerto Natales, Chile* ☎ *61/414–040* 🌐 *www.remota.cl* *72 rooms* *In-room: safe, no TV. In-hotel: restaurant, bar, pool, spa* *All-inclusive.*

$$$$ **Weskar Patagonian Lodge.** Weskar stands for "hill" in the language of the indigenous Kaweskar, to whom owner Juan José Pantoja, a marine biologist, pays homage in creating and maintaining this cozy lodge, which is high on a ridge overlooking the Última Esperanza fjord. **Pros:** great views from your room; helpful staff; cozy log-cabin decor. **Cons:** restaurant is a little overpriced; from the dining room you can really hear the wind when it's howling; bathrooms are so-so. ✉ *Ruta 9 Norte, Km 1, Puerto Natales, Chile* ☎ *61/414–168* 🌐 *www.weskar.cl* *21 rooms* *In-room: safe, no TV, Wi-Fi. In-hotel: restaurant, bar, spa* *Breakfast.*

PARQUE NACIONAL TORRES DEL PAINE, CHILE

80 km (50 miles) northwest of Puerto Natales.

ESSENTIALS

Visitor Information CONAF. CONAF, the national forestry service, has an office at the northern end of Lago del Toro with a scale model of the park, and numerous exhibits (some in English) about the flora and fauna. ✉ *CONAF station in southern section of the park past Hotel Explora, Chile* ☎ *61/691–931* 🌐 *www.conaf.cl* *Summer 15,000 pesos, winter 8,000 pesos* *Ranger station: Nov.–Feb., daily 8–8; Mar.–Oct., daily 8–5:30* *Punta Arenas Branch, Av. Bulnes 0309, Punta Arenas, Chile* ☎ *61/238–581* *Puerto Natales Branch, Baquedano 847, Chile* ☎ *61/411-438.*

EXPLORING

Fodor's Choice ★ **Parque Nacional Torres del Paine.** A raging inferno broke out in the Parque Nacional Torres del Paine on February 17, 2005, when a Czech trekker's gas camp stove was accidentally knocked over. At the time, he was camped in an unauthorized campsite in an area intended for grazing. The park's famous winds fanned the flames for more than a month, as 800 firefighters from Chile and Argentina tried to rein it in. According to reports by CONAF, the fire consumed 13,880 hectares, equivalent to 7% of the park. The tourist later apologized in an interview with *El Mercurio* newspaper, was fined $200 by authorities, and donated another $1,000 to the restoration fund. "What happened changed my life . . . I'll never forget the flames. I would like to express my most profound regret to the Chilean people for the damage caused." The Czech government has also taken responsibility for its citizen's mistake by donating 1 million dollars and recently planting 120,000 lenga trees. The main rehabilitation project was completed in 2010. CONAF asks that visitors respect the camping zones and the indications of park staff.

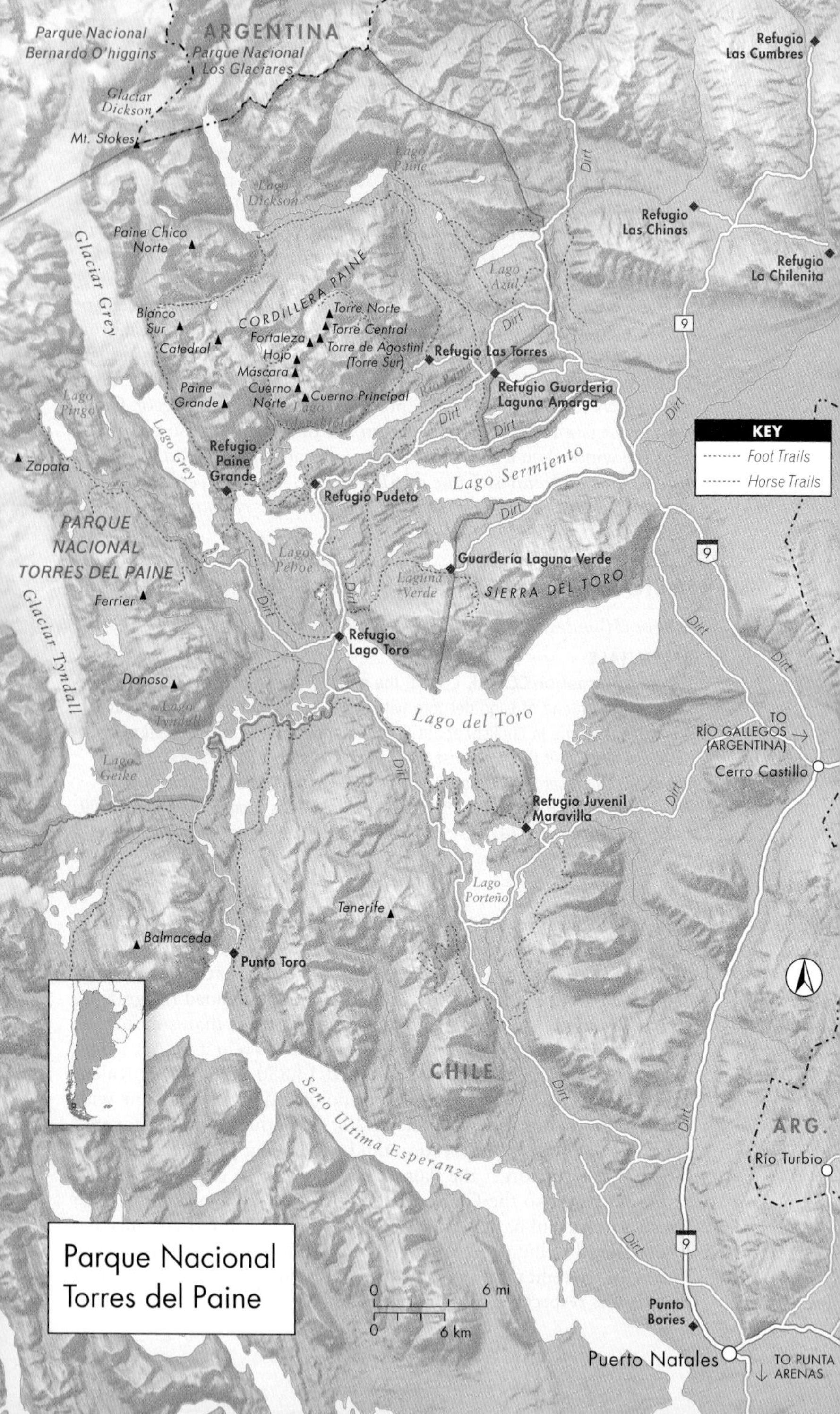
Parque Nacional Torres del Paine
ARGENTINA
Parque Nacional Bernardo O'higgins
Parque Nacional Los Glaciares
Glaciar Dickson
Mt. Stokes
Lago Dickson
Lago Paine
Refugio Las Cumbres
Refugio Las Chinas
Refugio La Chilenita
Paine Chico Norte
Glaciar Grey
CORDILLERA PAINE
Lago Azul
Blanco Sur
Catedral
Torre Norte
Torre Central
Fortaleza
Hojo
Torre de Agostini (Torre Sur)
Máscara
Cuerno Norte
Cuerno Principal
Paine Grande
Refugio Las Torres
Refugio Guarderia Laguna Amarga
Río Paine
Lago Pingo
Lago Grey
Refugio Paine Grande
Refugio Pudeto
Lago Sermiento
Zapata
PARQUE NACIONAL TORRES DEL PAINE
Lago Pehoe
Guardería Laguna Verde
Laguna Verde
SIERRA DEL TORO
Ferrier
Glaciar Tyndall
Refugio Lago Toro
Donoso
Lago Tyndall
Lago del Toro
Lago Geike
TO RÍO GALLEGOS (ARGENTINA)
Cerro Castillo
Refugio Juvenil Maravilla
Lago Porteño
Tenerife
Balmaceda
Punto Toro
CHILE
Seno Ultima Esperanza
ARG.
Río Turbio
Punto Bories
Puerto Natales
TO PUNTA ARENAS
Dirt
9
KEY
Foot Trails
Horse Trails
0 6 mi
0 6 km

The institution posts a series of recommendations for camping, and on how to prevent future disasters, on its web page.

About 12 million years ago, lava flows pushed up through the thick sedimentary crust that covered the southwestern coast of South America, cooling to form a granite mass. Glaciers then swept through the region, grinding away all but the twisted ash-gray spire, the "towers" of Paine (pronounced "pie-nay"; it's the old Tehuelche word for "blue"), which rise over the landscape to create one of the world's most beautiful natural phenomena, now the Parque Nacional Torres del Paine. The park was established in 1959. Snow and rock formations dazzle at every turn of road, and the sunset views are spectacular. The 2,420-square-km (934-square-mile) park's most astonishing attractions are its lakes of turquoise, aquamarine, and emerald waters; and the Cuernos del Paine ("Paine Horns"), the geological showpiece of the immense granite massif.

Another draw is the park's unusual wildlife. Creatures like the guanaco (a larger, woollier version of the llama) and the *ñandú* (a rhea, like a small ostrich) abound. They are acclimated to visitors, and don't seem to be bothered by approaching cars and people with cameras. Predators like the gray fox make less-frequent appearances. You may also spot the dramatic aerobatics of falcons and the graceful soaring of endangered condors. The beautiful puma, celebrated in a National Geographic video filmed here, is especially elusive, but sightings have grown more common. Pumas follow the guanaco herds and eat an estimated 40% of their young, so don't dress as one.

7

The vast majority of visitors come during the summer months of January and February, which means the trails can get congested. Early spring, when wildflowers add flashes of color to the meadows, is an ideal time to visit because the crowds have not yet arrived. In summer, the winds can be incredibly fierce. During the wintertime of June to September, the days are sunnier yet colder (averaging around freezing) and shorter, but the winds all but disappear. The park is open all year, and trails are almost always accessible. Storms can hit without warning, so be prepared for sudden rain or snow. The sight of the Paine peaks in clear weather is stunning; if you have any flexibility in your itinerary, visit the park on the first clear day. ✉ *Chile.*

EXPLORING THE PARK

There are three entrances to the park: Laguna Amarga (all bus arrivals), Lago Sarmiento, and Laguna Azul. You are required to sign in when you arrive, and pay your entrance fee (150 pesos in high season). *Guardaparques* (park rangers) staff six stations around the reserve, and can provide a map and up-to-the-day information about the state of various trails. A regular minivan service connects Laguna Amarga with the Hosteria Las Torres, 7 km (4½ miles) to the west, for 10 pesos. Alternatively, you can walk approximately two hours before reaching the starting point of the hiking circuits.

Although considerable walking is necessary to take full advantage of Parque Nacional Torres del Paine, you need not be a hard-core trekker. Many people choose to hike the **"W" route,** which takes four days,

DID YOU KNOW?

Kayaking can be a great way to get up close and personal to icebergs in glacial lakes, such as this one in Lago Grey. Just be sure to listen to your guide's instructions and do what she or he says; if the ice is large enough, it can shift in ways that send an unexpected edge of ice thrusting upward from below the surface—and, if you're too close, right into your kayak.

but others prefer to stay in one of the comfortable lodges and hit the trails in the morning or afternoon. **Glaciar Grey,** with its fragmented icebergs, makes a rewarding and easy hike; equally rewarding is the spectacular boat or kayak ride across the lake, past icebergs, and up to the glacier, which leaves from Hostería Lago Grey *(⇨ below)*. Another great excursion is the 900-meter (3,000-foot) ascent to the sensational views from **Mirador Las Torres,** four hours one way from Hostería Las Torres *(⇨ below)*. Even if you're not staying at the Hostería, you can arrange a morning drop-off there, and a late-afternoon pickup, so that you can see the Mirador while still keeping your base in Puerto Natales or elsewhere in the park; alternatively, you can drive to the Hostería and park there for the day.

If you do the "W," you'll begin (or end, if you reverse the route) at Laguna Amarga and continue to Mirador Las Torres and Los Cuernos, then continue along a breathtaking path up Valle Frances to its awe-inspiring and fiendishly windy lookout (hold on to your hat!) and finally Lago Grey. The W runs for 100 kilometers (62 miles), but always follows clearly marked paths, with gradual climbs and descents at relatively low altitude. The challenge comes from the weather. Winds whip up to 90 mph, and a clear sky can suddenly darken with storm clouds, producing rain, hail or snow in a matter of minutes. An even more ambitious route is the "Circuito," which essentially leads around the entire park and takes from a week to 10 days. Along the way some people sleep at the dozen or so humble *refugios* (shelters) evenly spaced along the trail, and many others bring their own tents.

EN ROUTE

Erratic Rock. For anyone seriously contemplating trekking the W or the full Circuit around Torres Del Paine, the Erratic Rock hostel in Puerto Natales offers a free seminar on how best to make the journey. Rustyn Mesdag, the hostel's Oregonian co-owner is a rambunctious, opinionated guide who gives the not-to-be-missed "Three O'clock Talk" describing all the routes, tips, and tricks you need to complete one of South America's most challenging treks. His hour-long presentation to a room full of eager hikers starts promptly at 3 pm every day of the high season, and is full of advice on camping, equipment, food, and provisions, including the latest reports on weather and trail conditions inside the park. It's a great introduction to possible trekking partners, as CONAF doesn't allow you to complete the walk on your own. The irrepressible Mr. Mesdag also publishes the ubiquitous Black Sheep newspaper in English. ✉ *Baquedano 719, Chile* ☎ *61/414–317* 🌐 *www.erraticrock.com.*

Driving is an easy way to enjoy the park: a new road cuts the distance to Puerto Natales from a meandering 140 km (87 miles) to a more direct 80 km (50 miles). Inside the national park more than 100 km (62 miles) of roads leading to the most popular sites are safe and well maintained, though unpaved. ■ **TIP→ If you stick to the road, you won't need a 4WD.**

You can also hire horses from the Hosteria Las Torres and trek to the Torres, the Cuernos, or along the shore of Lago Nordenskjold (which offers the finest views in the park, as the lake's waters reflect the chiseled massif). The hotel offers tours demanding various levels of expertise (prices start at 250 pesos). Alternatively, many Puerto Natales–based operators offer multi-day horseback tours. Water transport is also available, with numerous tour operators offering sailboat, kayak, and inflatable Zodiac speedboat options along the Río Serrano (prices start around 500 pesos for the Zodiac trips) toward the Paine massif and the southern ice field. Additionally, the Hostería Lago Grey operates the *Grey II,* a large catamaran making a three-hour return trip twice daily to Glaciar Grey, at 10 am and 3 pm, as well as dinghy runs down the Pingo and Grey rivers. Another boat runs between Refugio Pudeto and Refugio Lago Pehoé.

WHERE TO STAY

For expanded hotel reviews, visit Fodors.com.

$$$$ **Hostería Lago Grey.** The panoramic view from the restaurant and bar, past the lake dappled with floating icebergs to the glacier beyond, is worth the journey here; however, that doesn't change the fact that this older hotel is almost scandalously overpriced and not very attractive, with plain, dark rooms (only a few of which have a view). **Pros:** great views and comfortable seating in the well-stocked bar; location; heated bathroom floors; some rooms have a view—be sure to ask for one. **Cons:** thin walls in summer camp cottages; staggering price; staff speaks very little English. ✉ *Lago Grey, Chile* ☎ 🖷 *61/712–100* 🌐 *www.lagogrey.com* *60 rooms* *In-room: safe, no TV, Wi-Fi. In-hotel: restaurant, bar* 🍽 *Breakfast.*

$$$$ **Hosteria Tyndall.** A boat ferries you from the end of the road the few minutes around the meandering bends of the Serrano River to this wooden lodge, often surrounded by flocks of snow geese and other wild birds; inside, the simple rooms in the main building are small but cute and spotless, with attractive wood paneling. **Pros:** cheaper lodging and dining options than other places in the park; great views to Los Cuernos (the Horns) on a clear day. **Cons:** hallways are poorly lit; the lodge itself can get noisy. ✉ *Lago Tyndall, Chile* ☎ 🖷 *61/614–682* 🌐 *www.hosteriatyndall.com* *36 rooms, 6 cottages* *In-room: no TV. In-hotel: restaurant, bar* 🍽 *Multiple meal plans.*

$$$$ Fodor's Choice ★ **Hotel Explora – Salto Chico.** Next to a gently babbling waterfall on the southeast corner of Lago Pehoé, this lodge is one of the most luxurious—and most expensive—in Chile; outside, the shimmering lake is offset by tiny rocky islets, and although there may be some debate about the aesthetics of the hotel's low-slung minimalist exterior, the interior is impeccable, with a Scandinavian style using local woods throughout. **Pros:** the grande dame of Patagonian hospitality and one of the best hotels in the whole country; heart-stopping views from the center of the national park. **Cons:** a bank breaker; not a stunning building from the outside. ✉ *Lago Pehoé, Parque Nacional Torres Del Paine, Chile* *Américo Vespucio Sur 80, Piso 5, Santiago, Chile 8320000* ☎ *2/206–6060 in Santiago* 🖷 *2/395–2580 in Lake Pehoe* 🌐 *www.explora.com* *49 rooms* *In-room: no TV. In-hotel: restaurant, bar, pool, gym, business center* 🍽 *All-inclusive.*

$$$$ **Hotel Río Serrano.** What used to be a fairly humble posada has completed a successful transformation into a grand hotel; the main draw is the views from rooms on the third floor, taking in the whole Torres Del Paine mountain range, with the Serrano River and a wind-stunted forest in the foreground (these spectacular vistas are worth the significant added expense, especially if you can snag a room with a balcony). **Pros:** eager staff; impressive public areas; a stunning location with all-encompassing views. **Cons:** it's enormous, so guided tours can be a bit chaotic when the hotel's near capacity; still ironing out the kinks; rooms are tight on space. ✉ *Lago Toro, Chile* ☎ *61/410–684 for reservations (Puerto Natales)* 🌐 *www.hotelrioserrano.cl* *95 rooms* *In-room: no TV. In-hotel: restaurant, bar, golf course, business center* *Multiple meal plans.*

$$$$ ★ **Las Torres Patagonia.** Owned by one of the earliest families to settle in what became the park, Las Torres has a long history, and is the closest hotel to the main trails into the heart of the Torres Del Paine massif; originally an estancia, then a popular hosteria, the facility upgraded to a three-night-minimum, all-food-and-excursion-inclusive resort, in the style of Hotel Explora. **Pros:** friendly and efficient; homey atmosphere; couldn't be closer to the mountains. **Cons:** not cheap and prices keep rising; may be closer to the mountains, but the views are more sweeping at Explora or Rio Serrano. ✉ *Lago Amarga, Chile* ☎ *61/360–364* 🌐 *www.lastorres.com* *84 rooms* *In-room: no TV. In-hotel: restaurant, bar, spa* *Multiple meal plans.*

7

USHUAIA AND TIERRA DEL FUEGO

Tierra del Fuego, a more or less triangular island separated from the southernmost tip of the South American mainland by the twists and bends of the Estrecho de Magallanes, is indeed a world unto itself. The vast plains on its northern reaches are dotted with trees bent low by the savage winds that frequently lash the coast. The mountains that rise in the south are equally forbidding, traversed by huge glaciers slowly making their way to the sea.

The first European to set foot on this island was Spanish explorer Hernando de Magallanes, who sailed here in 1520. The smoke that he saw coming from the fires lighted by the native peoples prompted him to call it Tierra del Humo (Land of Smoke). King Charles V of Spain, disliking that name, rechristened it Tierra del Fuego, or Land of Fire.

Tierra del Fuego is split in half. The island's northernmost tip, well within Chilean territory, is its closest point to the continent. The only town of any size here is Porvenir. Its southern extremity, part of Argentina, points out into the Atlantic toward the Falkland Islands. Here you'll find Ushuaia, the main destination, on the shores of the Canal Beagle. Farther south is Cape Horn, the southernmost point of land before Antarctica (still a good 500 miles across the brutal Drake Passage).

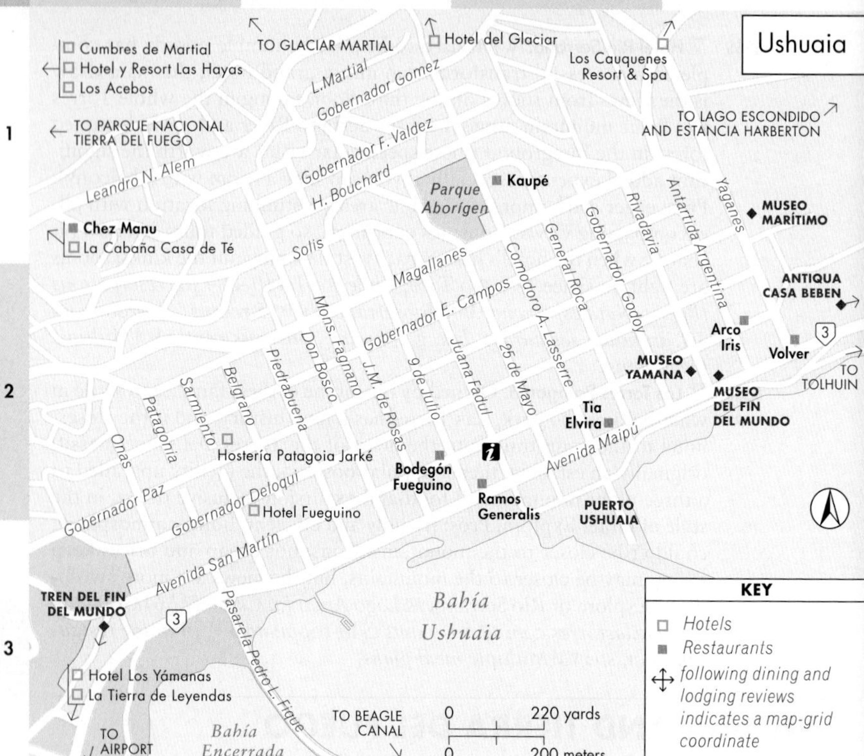

USHUAIA

230 km (143 miles) south of Río Grande; 596 km (370 miles) south of Río Gallegos; 914 km (567 miles) south of El Calafate; 3,580 km (2,212 miles) south of Buenos Aires.

At 55 degrees latitude south, Ushuaia (pronounced oo-swy-ah) is closer to the South Pole than to Argentina's northern border with Bolivia. It is the capital and tourism base for Tierra del Fuego, the island at the southernmost tip of Argentina.

Although its stark physical beauty is striking, Tierra del Fuego's historical allure is based more on its mythical past than on rugged reality. The island was inhabited for 6,000 years by Yámana, Haush, Selk'nam, and Alakaluf Indians. But in 1902 Argentina, eager to populate Patagonia to bolster its territorial claims, moved to initiate an Ushuaian penal colony, establishing the permanent settlement of its most southern territories and, by implication, everything in between.

When the prison closed in 1947, Ushuaia had a population of about 3,000, made up mainly of former inmates and prison staff. Today the Indians of Darwin's "missing link" theory are long gone—wiped out by diseases brought by settlers, and by indifference to their plight—and the 60,000 residents of Ushuaia are hitching their star to tourism. The city rightly (if perhaps too loudly) promotes itself as the southernmost city in the world (Puerto Williams, a few miles south on the Chilean side of the Beagle Channel, is a small town). You can make your way to the tourism office to get your clichéd, but oh-so-necessary, "Southernmost City in the World" passport stamp. Ushuaia feels like a frontier boomtown, at heart still a rugged, weather-beaten fishing village, but exhibiting the frayed edges of a city that quadrupled in size in the '70s and '80s. Unpaved portions of Ruta 3, the last stretch of the Pan-American Highway, which connects Alaska to Tierra del Fuego, are finally being paved. The summer months—December through March—draw more than 120,000 visitors, and dozens of cruise ships. The city is trying to extend those visits with events like March's Marathon at the End of the World.

A terrific trail winds through the town up to the Martial Glacier, where a ski lift can help cut down a steep kilometer of your journey. The chaotic and contradictory urban landscape includes a handful of luxury hotels amid the concrete of public housing projects. Scores of "sled houses" (wooden shacks) sit precariously on upright piers, ready for speedy displacement to a different site. But there are also many small, picturesque homes with tiny, carefully tended gardens. Many of the newer homes are built in a Swiss-chalet style, reinforcing the idea that this is a town into which tourism has breathed new life. At the same time, the weather-worn pastel colors that dominate the town's landscape remind you that Ushuaia was once just a tiny fishing village, snuggled at the end of the Earth.

As you stand on the banks of the Canal Beagle (Beagle Channel) near Ushuaia, the spirit of the farthest corner of the world takes hold. What stands out is the light: at sundown the landscape is cast in a subdued, sensual tone; everything feels closer, softer, and more human in dimension despite the vastness of the setting. The snowcapped mountains reflect the setting sun back onto a stream rolling into the channel, as nearby peaks echo their image—on a windless day—in the still waters.

Above the city rise the last mountains of the Andean Cordillera, and just south and west of Ushuaia they finally vanish into the often-stormy sea. Snow whitens the peaks well into summer. Nature is the principal attraction here, with trekking, fishing, horseback riding, and sailing among the most rewarding activities, especially in the Parque Nacional Tierra del Fuego (Tierra del Fuego National Park).

As Ushuaia converts to a tourism-based economy, the city is seeking ways to utilize its 3,000 hotel rooms in the lonely winter season. Though most international tourists stay home to enjoy their own summer, the adventurous have the place to themselves for snowmobiling, dog sledding, and skiing at Cerro Castor.

GETTING HERE AND AROUND

Arriving by air is the preferred option. Ushuaia's Aeropuerto Internacional Malvinas Argentinas (✉ *Peninsula de Ushuaia* ☎ *2901/431–232*) is 5 km (3 miles) from town, and is served daily by flights to and from Buenos Aires, Río Gallegos, El Calafate, Trelew, and Comodoro Rivadavía.

Crab really is king in Tierra del Fuego; king crab, or *centolla*, is delicious and readily available.

There are also flights to Santiago via Punta Arenas in Chile. A taxi into town costs about 25 pesos.

Arriving by road on the Ruta Nacional 3 involves Argentine and Chilean immigrations/customs, a ferry crossing, and a lot of time. Buses to and from Punta Arenas make the trip five days a week in summer, four in winter. Daily buses to Rio Gallegos leave in the pre-dawn hours, and multiple border crossings mean an all-day journey. Check prices on the 55-minute flight, which can be a much better value. There is no central bus terminal, just individual companies.

There is no regular passenger transport (besides cruises) by sea.

ESSENTIALS

Bus Services Tecni-Austral ✉ *Roca 157, Ushuaia, Tierra del Fuego* ☎ *2901/431–408.*

Postal Services Ushuaia Post Office ✉ *San Martin at Gob Godoy, Ushuaia, Tierra del Fuego.*

Visitor Information Tierra del Fuego Tourism Institute ✉ *Maipú 505, Ushuaia, Tierra del Fuego* ☎ *2901/421–423.* **Ushuaia Tourist Office** ✉ *Av. San Martín 674, Ushuaia, Tierra del Fuego* ☎ *2901/432–000* 🌐 *www.e-ushuaia.com* 🕓 *Weekdays 9–10, weekends 9–8.*

EXPLORING

Antigua Casa Beben (*Old Beben House*). One of Ushuaia's original houses, this long served as the city's social center. Built between 1911 and 1913 by Fortunato Beben, it's said he ordered the house through a Swiss catalog. In the 1980s the Beben family donated the house to the city to avoid demolition. It was moved to its current location along the coast and restored, and is now a cultural center with art exhibits. ✉ *Maipú at Pluschow, Ushuaia, Tierra del Fuego* ☎ *2901/431–386* *Free* ⏲ *Daily 10–8; 10–6 in winter.*

Fodor's Choice ★ **Museo Marítimo** (*Maritime Museum*). Part of the original penal colony, the Presidio building was built to hold political prisoners, murderous estancia owners, street orphans, and a variety of Buenos Aires' most violent criminals. Some even claim that singer Carlos Gardel landed in one of the cells for the petty crimes of his misspent youth. In its day it held 600 inmates in 380 cells. Today it's on the grounds of Ushuaia's naval base and holds the Museo Marítimo, which starts with exhibits on the canoe-making skills of the region's indigenous peoples, tracks the navigational history of Tierra del Fuego and Cape Horn and the Antarctic, and even has a display on other great jails of the world. You can enter cell blocks and read about the grisly crimes of the prisoners who lived in them and measure yourself against their eerie life-size plaster effigies. Of the five wings spreading out from the main guard house, one has been transformed into an art gallery and another has been kept untouched—and unheated. Bone chattering cold and bleak, bare walls powerfully evoke the desolation of a long sentence at the tip of the continent. Well-presented tours (in Spanish only) are conducted at 11:30 am, 4:30 pm, and 6:30 pm daily. ✉ *Gobernador Paz at Yaganes, Ushuaia, Tierra del Fuego* ☎ *2901/437–481* *70 pesos (valid for 2 days)* ⏲ *Daily 9–8 (summer), 10–8 (winter).*

Museo del Fin del Mundo (*End of the World Museum*). At the Museo del Fin del Mundo you can see a large taxidermied condor and other native birds, indigenous artifacts, maritime instruments, a reconstruction of an old Patagonian general store, and such seafaring-related objects as an impressive mermaid figurehead taken from the bowsprit of a galleon. There are also photographs and histories of El Presidio's original inmates, such as Simon Radowitzky, a Russian immigrant anarchist who received a life sentence for killing an Argentine police colonel. The museum is split across two buildings—the first, and original, is in the 1905 residence of a Fuegonian governor at Maipu 173. The newest museum building, opened in 2008, is farther down the road at Maipu 465, where you can see extended exhibitions of the same style. ✉ *Maipú 173, at Rivadavía, Ushuaia, Tierra del Fuego* ☎ *2901/421–863* *50 pesos (covers both museums)* ⏲ *Mon.–Sat., Oct.–Mar., 10–7; Apr.–Sept., noon–7.*

Museo Yamana. Tierra del Fuego was the last land mass in the world to be inhabited—it was not until 9,000 BC that the ancestors of those native coastal inhabitants, the Yamana, arrived. The Museo Yamana chronicles their lifestyle and history. The group was decimated in the late 19th century, mostly by European diseases. The bicentenary of Charles Darwin's birth passed with great fanfare in 2009, but his attitudes towards the indigenous people, dismissing them as "miserable, degraded savages" in *The Voyage of the Beagle*, are belied here by descriptions of the Yamana's incredible resourcefulness in surviving a bitter climate. Photographs and good English placards depict the Yamana's powerful, stocky build and bold body-paint; their use of seal fat to stay warm; their methods of carrying fire wherever they went, even in small canoes; and their way of hunting cormorants, which were killed with a bite through the neck. ✉ *Rivadavía 56, Ushuaia, Tierra del Fuego* ☎ *2901/422–874* 🌐 *www.tierradelfuego.org.ar/mundoyamana* 🎫 *25 pesos* ⏲ *Daily 10–8 (summer), 12–7 (winter).*

Tren del Fin del Mundo (*End of the World Train*). The Tren del Fin del Mundo is heavily promoted but a bit of a letdown. Purported to take you inside the Parque Nacional Tierra del Fuego, 12 km (7½ miles) away from town, you have to drive to get there, and it leaves visitors a long way short of the most spectacular scenery in the national park. The touristy 40-minute train ride's gimmick is a simulation of the trip El Presidio prisoners were forced to take into the forest to chop wood; but unlike them, you'll also get a good presentation of Ushuaia's history (in Spanish and English). The train departs daily at 9 am, noon, and 3 pm. One common way to do the trip is to hire a *remis* (car service) that will drop you at the station for a one-way train ride and pick you up at the other end, then drive you around the Parque Nacional for two or three hours of sightseeing (which is far more scenic than the train ride itself). ✉ *Ruta 3, Km 3042, Ushuaia, Tierra del Fuego* ☎ *2901/431–600* 🌐 *www.trendelfindelmundo.com.ar* 🎫 *240 pesos first-class ticket, 155 pesos tourist-class ticket, 85 pesos national park entrance fee.*

Canal Beagle. Several tour operators run trips along the Canal Beagle, on which you can get a startling close-up view of sea mammals and birds on **Isla de los Lobos, Isla de los Pájaros,** and near **Les Eclaireurs Lighthouse.** There are catamarans that make three-hour trips, generally leaving from the Tourist Pier at 3 pm, and motorboats and sailboats that leave twice a day, once at 9:30 am and once at 3 pm (trips depend on weather; few trips go in winter). Prices range start at 120 pesos; and some include hikes on the islands. Check with the tourist office for the latest details; you can also book through any of the local travel agencies. ✉ *Ushuaia, Tierra del Fuego.*

OFF THE BEATEN PATH

Tres Marias Excursions. Although there are a number of boat tours through the Canal Beagle, or around the bays to the Tierra del Fuego National Park, one offers an experience that will put you in the shoes of the earliest explorers to visit the far south. The operators of Tres Marias Excursions offer a half-day sailing trip to Island H, an outcrop in the middle of the channel, with cormorant colonies, families of snow geese, seaweed stands and a weather station that records the howling winds blowing in from the misnamed Pacific Ocean. The guides are skillful sailors and storytellers. On a gusty day you'll marvel at the hardiness of the Yamana people who survived frigid winters wearing little or no clothing, by setting fires behind natural and manmade windbreaks. You'll find the same plant and moss species that grow in the high Andes; they thrive here at sea level, because the conditions kill off less hardy, temperate species. On the way back you visit a sea lion colony, but won't soon forget arriving in Ushuaia under full sail as the late sun hits the mountains. At 300 pesos it's only a little more expensive, and a lot more adventurous, than the motorized alternatives touting for business at the dock. ✉ *Ushuaia, Tierra del Fuego* ☎ *2901/436–416* 🌐 *www.tresmariasweb.com.*

Lago Escondido (*Hidden Lake*). One good excursion in the area is to Lago Escondido and **Lago Fagnano** (Fagnano Lake). The Pan-American Highway out of Ushuaia goes through deciduous beech forests and past beavers' dams, peat bogs, and glaciers. The lakes have campsites and fishing and are good spots for a picnic or a hike. This can be done on your own or as a seven-hour trip, including lunch, booked through the local travel agencies (around 200 pesos standard tour, 400 pesos with lunch and 4x4). ✉ *Ushuaia, Tierra del Fuego.*

All Patagonia. One recommended operator for the Lago Escondido area, offering a comfortable bus, a bilingual guide, and lunch at Las Cotorras, is All Patagonia. ✉ *Juana Fadul 48, Ushuaia, Tierra del Fuego* ☎ *2901/433–622.*

Canal Fun. A rougher, more unconventional tour of the lake area goes to **Monte Olivia,** the tallest mountain along the Canal Beagle, rising 4,455 feet above sea level. You also pass the **Five Brothers Mountains** and go through the **Garibaldi Pass,** which begins at the Rancho Hambre, climbs into the mountain range, and ends with a spectacular view of Lago Escondido. From here you continue on to Lago Fagnano through the countryside past sawmills and lumber yards. To do this tour in a four-wheel-drive truck with an excellent bilingual guide, contact Canal Fun; you'll drive *through* Lago Fagnano (about 3 feet of water at this point) to a secluded cabin on the shore and have a delicious *asado,* complete with wine and dessert. In winter they can also organize tailor-made dog sledding and cross-country skiing trips. ✉ *9 de Julio 118, Ushuaia, Tierra del Fuego* ☎ *2901/437–395, 2901/435–777* 🌐 *www.canalfun.com.*

7

Estancia Harberton (*Harberton Ranch*). Estancia Harberton consists of 50,000 acres of coastal marshland and wooded hillsides. The property was a late-19th-century gift from the Argentine government to Reverend Thomas Bridges, who authored a Yamana–English dictionary and is considered the patriarch of Tierra del Fuego. His son Lucas wrote *The Uttermost Part of the Earth*, a memoir about his frontier childhood. Today the ranch is managed by Bridges's great-grandson, Thomas Goodall, and his American wife, Natalie, a scientist and author who has cooperated with the National Geographic Society on conservation projects and operates the impressive marine mammal museum, **Museo Acatushun** (🌐 *www.acatushun.com*). Most people visit as part of organized tours, but you'll be welcome if you arrive alone. They serve up a tasty tea in their home, the oldest building on the island. For safety reasons, exploration of the ranch can only be done on guided tours (45–90 minutes). Lodging is available, either in the Old Shepherd's House or the Old Cook's House (US$300 for a double, with breakfast). Additionally, you can arrange a three-course lunch at the ranch by calling two days ahead for a reservation. Most tours reach the estancia by boat, offering a rare opportunity to explore the **Isla Martillo** penguin colony, and a sea-lion refuge on **Isla de los Lobos** (Seal Island) along the way. ✉ *85 km (53 miles) east of Ushuaia, Ushuaia, Tierra del Fuego* ☎ *2901/422–742* 🌐 *www.estanciaharberton.com* 🎫 *45 pesos* ⏲ *Oct.–Apr. by tour only; daily 10–7, last tour 5:30.*

★ **Glaciar Martial.** If you've never butted heads with a glacier, and especially if you won't be covering El Calafate on your trip, then you should check out Glaciar Martial, in the mountain range just above Ushuaia. Named after Frenchman Luís F. Martial, a 19th-century scientist who wandered this way aboard the warship *Romanche* to observe the passing of planet Venus, the glacier is reached via a panoramic *aerosilla* (ski lift). Take the Camino al Glaciar (Glacier Road) 7 km (4 miles) out of town until it ends (this route is also served by the local tour companies). Even if you don't plan to hike to see the glacier, it's a great pleasure to ride the 15-minute lift, which is open daily 10–4:30, weather permitting (it's often closed from mid-May until August) and costs 25 pesos. If you're afraid of heights, you can instead enjoy a small nature trail here, and a teahouse. You can return on the lift, or continue on to the beginning of a 1-km (½-mile) trail that winds its way over lichen and shale straight up the mountain. After a steep, strenuous 90-minute hike, you can cool your heels in one of the many gurgling, icy rivulets that cascade down water-worn shale shoots or enjoy a picnic while you wait for sunset (you can walk all the way down if you want to linger until after the *aerosilla* closes). When the sun drops behind the glacier's jagged crown of peaks, brilliant rays beam over the mountain's crest, spilling a halo of gold-flecked light on the glacier, valley, and channel below. Moments like these are why this land is so magical. Note that temperatures drop dramatically after sunset, so come prepared with warm clothing. ✉ *Ushuaia, Tierra del Fuego.*

WHERE TO EAT

$$$$ ARGENTINE ✕ **Arco Iris.** This restaurant in the center of town is painted an unpromising hot pink but it's one of the finest and most popular of the good-value *tenedor libre* (all-you-can-eat) parrillas on the main strip—nobody orders à la carte. Skip the Italian buffet and Chinese offerings and fill up instead on the spit-roasted Patagonian lamb, grilled meats, and delicious *morcilla* (blood sausage). It's all you can eat for 85 pesos. Sit by the interior window towards the back where you see the *parrillero* artfully coordinate the flames and spits, and ask him to load your plate with the choicest cuts. ✉ *Av. San Martín 98, Ushuaia, Tierra del Fuego* ☎ *2901/431–306* ✥ *D2.*

$$$$ ARGENTINE ★ ✕ **Bodegón Fueguino.** A mustard-yellow pioneer house that lights up the main street, this traditional eatery is driven by its ebullient owner Sergio Otero, a constant presence bustling around the bench seating, making suggestions, and revving up his staff. Sample the *picada* plate (king crab rolls, Roma-style calamari, marinated rabbit) over an artisanal Beagle Beer—the dark version is the perfect balm on a cold windy day. Lamb dominates the mains, and the emphasis is on hearty rather than fashionable. Tables filled with locals and visitors make for a boisterous atmosphere. Don't worry about the no reservations policy as you won't have to wait long. ✉ *San Martin 859, Ushuaia, Tierra del Fuego* ☎ *2901/431–972* 🌐 *www.tierradehumos.com* ✍ *Reservations not accepted* ⏲ *Closed Mon.* ✥ *B2.*

$$$$ ARGENTINE Fodor'sChoice ★ ✕ **Chez Manu.** *Herbes de provence* in the greeting room, a tank of lively king crabs in the dining room: French chef Manu Herbin gives local seafood a French touch that both diversifies the Argentine gastronomy and creates some of Ushuaia's most memorable meals. Perched a couple

Can't beat the view in Ushuaia, the world's southernmost city.

of miles above town across the street from the Hotel Glaciar, the restaurant has stunning views of the Beagle Channel. The first-rate wine list includes Patagonian selections, while all dishes are created entirely with ingredients from Tierra del Fuego. Don't miss the baby scallops with a fondue of pulses, or the *centolla* (king crab) au gratin. ✉ *Camino Luís Martial 2135, Ushuaia, Tierra del Fuego* ☎ *2901/432–253* 🌐 *www.chezmanu.com* ✣ *A1.*

$$$$ ARGENTINE ★ ✕ **Kaupé.** The white picket fence, manicured lawns, and planter boxes play up the fact that this out-of-the-way restaurant used to be a family home. Inside, polished wooden floors, picture windows, and tables covered in wine glasses offer a sophisticated dining experience with an intimate touch. The star ingredient is centolla, best presented as chowder with spinach. This restaurant is on a steep ridge above town and offers spectacular views, and they're only a little bit spoiled by the radio antenna sticking up from the empty plot next door. Still, it's seafood served with panache and warmth in a dining room that belies the status quo of the kitschy restaurants near the waterfront. But it can be hard to find; even taxi drivers get lost in the warren of streets above town. ✉ *Roca 470, Ushuaia, Tierra del Fuego* ☎ *2901/422–704* 🌐 *www.kaupe.com.ar* ✍ *Reservations essential* ⏲ *Closed Sun.* ✣ *C1.*

$$$ ARGENTINE ✕ **La Cabaña Casa de Té.** This impeccably maintained riverside cottage is nestled in a verdant stand of lenga trees, overlooks the Beagle Channel, and provides a warm, cozy spot for tea or snacks before or after a hike to the Martial Glacier (it's conveniently located at the end of the Martial road that leads up from Ushuaia, tucked in behind the ski lift). An afternoon tea with all the trimmings costs 90 pesos, fondues are a specialty at lunchtime, and at 8 pm the menu shifts to pricier dinner fare

with dishes like salmon in wine sauce. ✉ *Camino Luís Martial 3560, Ushuaia, Tierra del Fuego* ☎ *2901/434–699* ⊕ *A1.*

$$$ ARGENTINE ✕ **Ramos Generales.** Entering this café on the waterfront puts you in mind of a general store from the earliest frontier years of Ushuaia. As you walk from room to room admiring the relics (like the hand-cranked Victrola phonograph), the hubbub around the bar reminds you that a warehouse like this was not just a store to pick up supplies; it was also a place for isolated pioneers to socialize and gather all the latest news from the port. Burgers and picada platters are uninspiring; choose fresh baked bread or scrumptious lemon croissants instead, and try the *submarino*—a mug of hot milk in which you plunge a bar of dark chocolate (goes well with a panini). ✉ *Maípu 749, Ushuaia, Tierra del Fuego* ☎ *2901/424–317* 🌐 *www.ramosgeneralesushuaia.com* ⊕ *C2.*

$$$$ ARGENTINE ✕ **Tia Elvira.** On the street that runs right along the Beagle Channel, Tia Elvira is an excellent place to sample the local catch. Garlicky shellfish appetizers and centolla are delicious; even more memorable is the tender *merluza negra* (black sea bass). The room is decked out with nautical knickknacks that may seem on the tacky side for such a pricey place. The service is friendly and familial. ✉ *Maipú 349, Ushuaia, Tierra del Fuego* ☎ *2901/424–725* ⊗ *Closed Sun. and July* ⊕ *C2.*

$$$$ ARGENTINE ✕ **Volver.** A giant king crab sign beckons you into this red-tin-walled restaurant, although the maritime bric-a-brac hanging from the ceiling can be a little distracting. The name means "return" and it succeeds in getting repeat visits on the strength of its seafood. Newspapers from the 1930s line the walls in this century-old home; the service is friendly and relaxed. The culinary highlight is the centolla, which comes served with a choice of five different sauces. This is among the best places to try Tierra del Fuego's signature dish. ✉ *Maipú 37, Ushuaia, Tierra del Fuego* ☎ *2901/423–977* ⊗ *Closed Mon. and Sun. lunch* ⊕ *D2.*

WHERE TO STAY

For expanded hotel reviews, visit Fodors.com.

Choosing a place to stay depends in part on whether you want to spend the night in town, several miles west towards the national park, or uphill in the hotels above town. Las Hayas Resort, Hotel Glaciar, Cumbres de Martial, and Los Yámanas have stunning views, but require a taxi ride or the various complimentary shuttle services to reach Ushuaia.

$$$$ ★ **Cumbres de Martial.** This charming complex of cabins and bungalows, painted a deep berry purple, is high above Ushuaia in the woods at the base of the ski lift to the Martial glacier; each spacious room has an extremely comfortable bed and a small wooden deck with terrific views down to the Beagle Channel. **Pros:** easy access to the glacier and nature trails; stunning views of the Beagle Channel; romantic cabins; spa. **Cons:** you need to cab it to and from town; few restaurant options within walking distance. ✉ *Camino Luís Martial 3560, Ushuaia, Tierra del Fuego* ☎ *2901/424–779* 🌐 *www.cumbresdelmartial.com.ar* *6 rooms, 4 cabins* *In-room: safe. In-hotel: restaurant, bar, spa* ⊗ *Closed Apr. and May* *Breakfast* ⊕ *A1.*

$$$$ **Hostería Patagonia Jarké.** Jarké means "spark" in a local native language, and this B&B is a bright, electric addition to Ushuaia; the

three-story lodge cantilevers down a hillside on a dead-end street in the heart of town. **Pros:** feels like home; warm, welcoming rooms with decent views. **Cons:** steep walk home; recent jump in prices has made it less-than-stellar value; can't compete with the views from the larger hotels farther uphill. ✉ *Sarmiento 310, at G. Paz, Ushuaia, Tierra del Fuego* ☎ *2901/437–245* 🌐 *www.hosteriapatagoniaj.com* *15 rooms* *In-room: safe, Wi-Fi. In-hotel: bar* *Breakfast* ✣ *A2.*

$$$$ **Hotel del Glaciar.** Just above the Las Hayas hotel in the Martial Mountains, this hotel has commanding views of Ushuaia and the Beagle Channel; inside, rooms are bright, clean, and very comfortable but sparsely decorated. **Pros:** old-style colonial atmosphere sets it apart from the modern behemoths on the mountain; all rooms have great views, either to the mountains behind or (for slightly more money) to the Beagle Channel. **Cons:** feels very big; staff not the friendliest in town; some of the wood panels on the outer walls are starting to show their age; late check-in (4 pm) and early check-out (10 am). ✉ *Camino Glaciar Martial 2355, Km 3.5, Ushuaia, Tierra del Fuego* ☎ *2901/430–640* 🌐 *www.hoteldelglaciar.com* *127 rooms* *In-room: safe. In-hotel: restaurant, bar, gym, business center* *Breakfast* ✣ *B1.*

$$$$ ★ **Hotel Fueguino.** A gleaming ultramodern edifice in downtown Ushuaia, the Fueguino boasts all the modern amenities: a conference center; a gym with the latest fitness machines; a spa; shuttle service; outgoing, professional, multilingual staff; and what might be the best Wi-Fi signal in town. **Pros:** ultramodern excess; super central. **Cons:** shambolic huts overrun with barking dogs just over the road; everything in the lobby is silver. ✉ *Gobernador Deloqui 1282, Ushuaia, Tierra del Fuego* ☎ *2901/424–894* 🌐 *www.fueguinohotel.com* *53 rooms* *In-room: safe. In-hotel: restaurant, bar, gym, spa, business center* *Breakfast* ✣ *B2.*

$$$$ **Hotel Los Yámanas.** This cozy hotel 4 km (2½ miles) from the center of town is named after the local tribe and offers a rustic mountain aesthetic. **Pros:** top-notch gym; some stunning views from rooms; sauna is lovely. **Cons:** questionable taste in lobby decoration. ✉ *Costa de los Yamanas 2850, Km 4, Ushuaia, Tierra del Fuego* ☎ *2901/446–809* 🌐 *www.hotelyamanas.com.ar* *41 rooms* *In-room: safe, Wi-Fi. In-hotel: restaurant, bar, pool, gym* *Breakfast* ✣ *A3.*

$$$$ Fodor's Choice ★ **Hotel y Resort Las Hayas.** Las Hayas is in the wooded foothills of the Andes, overlooking the town and channel below; ask for a canal view and, since the rooms are all decorated differently and idiosyncratically, sample a variety before settling in. **Pros:** good restaurant; charming staff and managers speak English; frequent shuttles into town; awesome spa. **Cons:** decor doesn't suit everyone; wall prints can be distracting. ✉ *Camino Luís Martial 1650, Km 3, Ushuaia, Tierra del Fuego* ☎ *2901/430–710, 11/4393–4750 in Buenos Aires* 🌐 *www.lashayashotel.com* *86 rooms* *In-room: safe, Wi-Fi. In-hotel: restaurant, bar, pool, gym, spa, business center* *Breakfast* ✣ *A1.*

$$$$ ★ **La Tierra de Leyendas.** "The Land of Legends" is a honeymooners' delight; it sweeps up awards often, meaning the secret's out, but this adorable B&B run by Sebastian and Maria still bears their personal touch down to the family photos on the walls. **Pros:** an extraordinarily

7

quaint find for western Ushuaia; enthusiastic, personal and attentive service; all seven rooms have views. **Cons:** the street name is no joke, it's insanely windy; the immediate surroundings are a bit barren; need to book a month or more in advance. ✉ *Tierra de Vientos 2448, Ushuaia, Tierra del Fuego* ☎ *2901/446–565* 🌐 *www.tierradeleyendas.com.ar* *7 rooms* *In-room: safe, Wi-Fi. In-hotel: restaurant* *Breakfast* *A1.*

$$$$ **Los Acebos.** From the owners of Las Hayas (just around the corner on the winding mountain road), Los Acebos is a modern hotel on a forested ridge with a commanding view over the Beagle Channel; spacious and super-clean rooms feature the same iconoclastic decor as Las Hayas, including the trademark fabric-padded walls, only this time with a '60s-style color scheme. **Pros:** great price for spacious and super-clean rooms; expansive views of the channel from the restaurant; staff good with children. **Cons:** a tad out of the way for a spa-less facility. ✉ *Luis F. Martial 1911, Ushuaia, Tierra del Fuego* ☎ *2901/424–234, 11/4393–4750 (reservations from Buenos Aires office)* 🌐 *www.losacebos.com.ar* *60 rooms* *In-room: safe. In-hotel: restaurant, gym, laundry facilities, parking* *A1.*

$$$$ **Los Cauquenes Resort and Spa.** This resort hotel is more of a gated campus, with a series of buildings and cabanas right on the shore of the Beagle Channel about 8 km (5 miles) west of town; privileged beach access and sparse development in the Barrio Bahía Cauquén means a nature hike starts right outside your room. **Pros:** luxurious spa offers comprehensive range of treatments and massages; specials on romantic getaways. **Cons:** no air-conditioning in rooms; thin walls can make for noisy nights. ✉ *De la Ermita 3462, Barrio Bahía Cauquén, Ushuaia, Tierra del Fuego* ☎ *2901/441–300* 🌐 *www.loscauquenesushuaia.com.ar* *54 rooms, 4 cabanas* *In-room: safe, Wi-Fi. In-hotel: restaurant, bar, pool, gym, spa, parking* *D1.*

NIGHTLIFE

Ushuaia has a lively nightlife in summer, with its casino, discos, and intimate cafés all close to each other.

Bar Ideal. This cozy and historic bar and café opens from 10 am onwards. ✉ *San Martín 393, at Roca, Ushuaia, Tierra del Fuego* ☎ *2901/437–860* 🌐 *www.elbarideal.com.*

Cine Packewaia. A huge corrugated iron barn that looks like an aircraft hangar, Cine Packewaia is right next to the Presidio and Maritime Museum. It shows first-run Hollywood movies three times a night, including a midnight screening. ✉ *Cpto. Naval A. Bernadi, Ushuaia, Tierra del Fuego* ☎ *2901/436–050* 🌐 *www.cinepackewaia.com* *20 pesos.*

El Náutico. The biggest and most popular pub, El Náutico attracts a young crowd with disco and techno music. ✉ *Maipú 1210, Ushuaia, Tierra del Fuego* ☎ *2901/430–415* 🌐 *www.nauticodiscopub.com* *Closed Sun.–Thurs.*

Kaitek Lounge Bar. This is the place to dance to pop music until 6 am. Open Friday and Saturday starting at midnight. ✉ *Antartida Argentina 239, Ushuaia, Tierra del Fuego* ☎ *2901/431–723.*

Tante Sara. Tante Sara is a popular café-bar with a casual, old-world feel, in the heart of town, where locals kick back with a book or a beer (they pour Beagle, the local artisanal brew). During the day it's one of the few eateries to defy the 3–6 pm siesta and stays open late. Their other branch, at San Martin 771, closes at 8:30 pm. ✉ *San Martín 701, Ushuaia, Tierra del Fuego* ☎ *2901/433–710* 🌐 *www.cafebartantesara.com.ar.*

SHOPPING

★ **Boutique del Libro–Antartida y Patagonia.** Part of a bookstore chain, this branch specializes in Patagonian and polar exploration. Along with dozens of maps and picture books, postcards, and posters, it offers adventure classics detailing every Southern expedition from Darwin's Voyage of the Beagle to Ernest Shackleton's incredible journeys of Antarctic survival. While books in English are hard to come by in the rest of Argentina, here you're spoiled for choice, and the Antarctica trip logbooks on sale at the counter might inspire you to extend your travel further south. ✉ *25 de Mayo 62, Ushuaia, Tierra del Fuego* ☎ *2901/432–117.*

Laguna Negra. If you can't get to South America's chocolate capital Bariloche, you'll find some of the best sweets in Argentina at this boutique/café in the center of town. Planks of homemade chocolate include coconut crunches, fudges, and brittles, along with Tierra del Fuego's best selection of artisanal beers, chutneys, and spices. In the small coffee shop at the back, drop a glorious slab of dark chocolate into a mug of piping hot milk—one of the best *submarinos* in town. Locals pop in for a quick cup of hot chocolate at all hours, even as other cafés close for the lull between 3 and 8 in the evening. If you get hooked, there's another branch on the main street of El Calafate. ✉ *San Martin 513, Ushuaia, Tierra del Fuego* ☎ *02901/431–144* 🌐 *www.lagunanegra.com.ar* ⏲ *9–9.*

PARQUE NACIONAL TIERRA DEL FUEGO

★ **Parque Nacional Tierra del Fuego.** The pristine park, 21 km (13 miles) west of Ushuaia, offers a chance to wander through peat bogs, stumble upon hidden lakes, trek through native *canelo, lenga,* and wild cherry forests, and experience the wonders of wind-whipped Tierra del Fuego's rich flora and fauna. Everywhere, lichens line the trunks of the ubiquitous lenga trees, and "chinese lantern" parasites hang from the branches.

Everywhere, too, you'll see the results of government folly, *castoreros* (beaver dams) and lodges. Fifty beaver couples were first brought in from Canada in 1948 so that they would breed and create a fur industry. In the years since, without any predators, the beaver population has exploded to plague proportions (more than 100,000) and now represents a major threat to the forests, as the dams flood the roots of the trees; you can see their effects on parched dead trees on the lake's edge. Believe it or not, the government used to pay hunters a bounty for each beaver they killed (they had to show a tail and head as proof). To make matters worse, the government, after creating the beaver problem, introduced weasels to kill the beavers, but the weasels killed birds instead; they then introduced foxes to kill the beavers and weasels, but they also killed the birds. With eradication efforts failing, some tour

The banner tree, or *Tuta complementaria*, is whipped by Patagonian winds from the time it's a mere shoot; the result has a banner-like effect, hence the name.

operators have accepted them as a permanent presence and now offer beaver-viewing trips.

Visits to the park, which is tucked up against the Chilean border, are commonly arranged through tour companies. Trips range from bus tours to horseback riding to more adventurous excursions, such as canoe trips across Lapataia Bay. Entrance to the park is 85 pesos.

Transportes Kaupen (☎ *2901/434–015*) is one of several private bus companies that travel through the park making several stops; you can get off the bus, explore the park, and then wait for the next bus to come by or trek to the next stop (the service only operates in summer). Another option is to drive to the park on Ruta 3 (take it until it ends and you see the famous sign indicating the end of the Pan-American Highway, which starts 17,848 km [11,065 miles] away in Alaska, and ends here). If you don't have a car, you can also hire a private *remis* to spend a few hours driving through the park, including the Pan-American terminus, and perhaps combining the excursion with the Tren del Fin del Mundo. Trail and camping information is available at the park-entrance ranger station or at the Ushuaia tourist office. At the park entrance is a gleaming restaurant and teahouse set amid the hills, **Patagonia Mia** (✉ *Ruta 3, Entrada Parque Nacional* 🌐 *www.patagoniamia.com*); it's a great place to stop for tea or coffee, or a full meal of roast lamb or Fuegian seafood. A nice excursion in the park is by boat from lovely **Bahía Ensenada** to **Isla Redonda,** a wildlife refuge where you can follow a footpath to the western side and see a wonderful view of the Canal Beagle. This is included on some of the day tours; it's harder to arrange on your own, but you can contact the tourist office to try. While on Isla

Redonda you can send a postcard and get your passport stamped at the world's southernmost post office. You can also see the Ensenada bay and island (from afar) from a point on the shore that is reachable by car.

Other highlights of the park include the spectacular mountain-ringed lake, **Lago Roca,** as well as **Laguna Verde,** a lagoon whose green color comes from algae at its bottom. Much of the park is closed from roughly June through September, when the descent to Bahía Ensenada is blocked by up to 6 feet of snow. Even in May and October, chains for your car are a good idea. No hotels are within the park—the only one burned down in the 1980s, and you can see its carcass as you drive by—but there are three simple camping areas around Lago Roca. Tours to the park are run by **All Patagonia** (✉ *Juana Fadul 26* ☎ *2901/433–622 or 2901/430–725*). ✉ *Tierra del Fuego* 🎫 *85 pesos.*

EN ROUTE

If you're in Ushuaia in the days leading up to New Year's Eve, drop in on **La Pista del Andino** campsite, on the edge of town. You'll be dwarfed by a mad mix of four-wheel drives, enormous customized German trucks, and worn-out bicycles with beaten panniers. It's a tradition among overland explorers to spend Christmas and New Year in the southernmost city in the world, and this turns out to be one of the most unusual "motorhog" celebrations around. Their routes zigzag across South America and are often painted on the sides of their vehicles—which have been known to be equipped with everything from rooftop tents to a satellite dish. Travelers share stories of crossing places like Siberia or northern Africa, and if you're lucky you'll encounter some who've ridden, driven, or pedaled the Pan-American Highway all the way from Alaska down to Ushuaia, a 17,000-mile journey that takes years to complete.

7

SPORTS AND THE OUTDOORS

FISHING

The rivers of Tierra del Fuego are home to trophy-size freshwater trout—including browns, rainbows, and brooks. Both fly- and spin-casting are available. The fishing season runs November–April; license fees range from 360 pesos per week to 420 pesos per season for nonresidents. Fishing expeditions are organized by the various local companies.

Asociación de Caza y Pesca. Founded in 1959, the Asociación de Caza y Pesca is the principal hunting and fishing organization in the city. ✉ *Av. Maipú 822, Tierra del Fuego* ☎ *2901/423–168.*

Rumbo Sur. Rumbo Sur is the city's oldest travel agency and can assist in setting up fishing trips. ✉ *Av. San Martín 350, Tierra del Fuego* ☎ *2901/421–139* 🌐 *www.rumbosur.com.ar.*

Wind Fly. Wind Fly is dedicated exclusively to fishing, and offers classes and arranges trips. ✉ *Av. 25 de Mayo 155, Tierra del Fuego* ☎ *2901/431–713, 2901/1544–9116* 🌐 *www.windflyushuaia.com.ar.*

MOUNTAIN BIKING

A mountain bike is an excellent mode of transport in Ushuaia, giving you the freedom to roam without the rental-car price tag. Good mountain bikes normally cost about 60 pesos a half day, or 90 pesos a full day. Guided tours are about the same price.

Ushuaia Extreme. You can rent bikes or do a tour with Ushuaia Extreme. ✉ *Gob. Paz 301, Tierra del Fuego* ☎ *2901/619–507* 🌐 *www.patagoniabiketour.com.*

All Patagonia. Guided bicycle tours (including rides through the national park) are organized by All Patagonia. ✉ *Fadul 26, Tierra del Fuego* ☎ *2901/430–725.*

Rumbo Sur. Rumbo Sur is the city's biggest travel agency and can arrange trips. ✉ *San Martín 350, Tierra del Fuego* ☎ *2901/421–139* 🌐 *www.rumbosur.com.ar.*

SCENIC FLIGHTS

The gorgeous scenery and island topography of the area is readily appreciated on a Cessna tour.

Aeroclub Ushuaia. Aeroclub Ushuaia offers half-hour and hour-long trips. The half-hour flight (340 pesos per passenger; 400 pesos for one passenger alone) with a local pilot takes you over Ushuaia, Tierra del Fuego National Park, and the Beagle Channel with views of area glaciers, waterfalls, and snowcapped islands south to Cape Horn. A 60-minute flight (575 pesos per passenger; 725 pesos, for one passenger alone) crosses the Andes to the Escondida and Fagnano lakes. ✉ *Antiguo Aeropuerto, Tierra del Fuego* ☎ *2901/421–717* 🌐 *www.aeroclubushuaia.org.ar.*

Heli-Ushuaia. Heli-Ushuaia offers 15-minute flights over the city for a minimum of two people for US$150 each and hour-long trips if you've got money to burn. ✉ *Antiguo Aeropuerto, Tierra del Fuego* ☎ *2901/444–444* 🌐 *www.heliushuaia.com.ar.*

SKIING

Canopy Ushuaia. Canopy Ushuaia are located at the Martial Glaciar and offer skiing in winter, or canopy lines in the summer. ✉ *Tierra del Fuego* ☎ *2901/1550–3767* 🌐 *www.canopyushuaia.com.ar.*

Cerro Castor. For downhill (or *alpino*) skiers, Club Andino has bulldozed a couple of short, flat runs directly above Ushuaia. The newest downhill ski area, Cerro Castor, is 26 km (17 miles) northeast of Ushuaia on Ruta 3, and has 26 trails and four high-speed ski lifts. More than half the trails are at the beginner level, with the rest as intermediate and expert trails, but none of this terrain is very challenging for an experienced skier. You can rent skis and snowboards and take ski lessons. ✉ *Tierra del Fuego* ☎ *2901/422–244* 🌐 *www.cerrocastor.com.*

Club Andino. Ushuaia is the cross-country skiing (*esqui de fondo* in Spanish) center of South America, thanks to enthusiastic Club Andino members who took to the sport in the 1980s and made the forested hills of a high valley about 20 minutes from town a favorite destination for skiers. It's a magnet for international ski teams who come from Europe to train in the northern summer. ✉ *Fadul 50, Tierra del Fuego* ☎ *2901/422–335.*

Haruwen. Haruwen, Hostería Los Cotorras, and Hostería Tierra Mayor are three places where you can ride in dog-pulled sleds, rent skis, go cross-country skiing, get lessons, and eat; contact the Ushuaia tourist office for more information. ✉ *Tierra del Fuego* ☎ *2901/421–306.*

Tour Operators

Outfitter	Telephone	Website	Activities Offered	Regions Covered
Abercrombie & Kent	630/954-2944 or 800/5540-7016	www.abercrombiekent.com	Bicycling, Coastal and Lake Cruises, Cultural Tours, Hiking, Horseback Riding, Natural History, Trekking	Antarctica, Argentine Patagonia, Chilean Patagonia, Lake District, Tierra del Fuego
Adventure Center	510/654-1879 or 800/227-8747	www.adventurecenter.com	Bicycling, Coastal and Lake Cruises, Cultural Tours, Hiking, Horseback Riding, Natural History, Running, Trekking	Antarctica, Argentine Patagonia, Atlantic Coast, Chilean Patagonia, Lake District, Tierra del Fuego
Adventure Life	406/541-2677 or 800/344-6118	www.adventure-life.com	Bicycling, Coastal and Lake Cruises, Cultural Tours, Hiking, Horseback Riding, Kayaking, Natural History, Rafting, Running, Trekking	Antarctica, Argentine Patagonia, Atlantic Coast, Chilean Patagonia, Lake District, Tierra del Fuego
Alpine Ascents International	206/378-1927	www.AlpineAscents.com	Climbing, Hiking, Mountaineering	Lake District, Antarctica
Andes Adventures	310/395-5265 or 800/289-9470	www.andesadventures.com	Hiking, Trekking	Argentine Patagonia, Chilean Patagonia, Tierra del Fuego
Australian & Amazonian Adventures	512/443-5393 or 800/232-5658	www.amazonadventures.com	Bicycling, Coastal and Lake Cruises, Cultural Tours, Hiking, Horseback Riding, Kayaking, Natural History, Rafting, Running, Trekking	Argentine Patagonia, Atlantic Coast, Chilean Patagonia, Argentina, Tierra del Fuego
Big Five Tours & Expeditions	772/287-7995 or 800/244-3483	www.bigfive.com	Bicycling, Coastal and Lake Cruises, Cultural Tours, Hiking, Horseback Riding, Natural History, Running, Trekking	Argentine Patagonia, Atlantic Coast, Chilean Patagonia, Tierra del Fuego
Boojum Expeditions	406/587-0125 or 800/287-0125	www.boojum.com	Horseback Riding	Bariloche
Country Walkers	802/244-1387 or 800/464-9225	www.countrywalkers.com	Hiking, Running, Trekking	Atlantic Coast
Earth River Expeditions	800/643-2784	www.earthriver.com	Rafting, Kayaking	Chilean Patagonia
ElderTreks	416/588-5000 or 800/741-7956	www.eldertreks.com	Hiking, Running, Trekking	Argentine Patagonia, Atlantic Coast, Chilean Patagonia, Tierra del Fuego

7

Tour Operators

Outfitter	Telephone	Website	Activities Offered	Regions Covered
Equitours	307/455-3363 or 800/545-0019	www.equitours.com	Horseback Riding	Argentine Patagonia, Chilean Patagonia, Cordoba
Experience Plus!	800/685-4565	www.ExperiencePlus.com	Bicycling	Lake District
Explora	866/750-6699	www.explora.com	Cultural Tours, Hiking, Natural History, Running, Trekking	Argentine Patagonia, Chilean Patagonia
FishQuest	706/896-1403 or 888/891-3474	www.fishquest.com	Fishing	Argentine Patagonia, Chilean Patagonia, Lake District
Fly Fishing And	406/425-9452	www.flyfishingand.com	Fishing	Argentine Patagonia, Lake District
G.A.P. Adventures	416/260-0999 or 800/708-7761	www.gapadventures.com	Bicycling, Coastal and Lake Cruises, Cultural Tours, Hiking, Horseback Riding, Natural History, Running, Trekking	Antarctica, Argentine Patagonia, Atlantic Coast, Chilean Patagonia, Lake District, Tierra del Fuego
Geographic Expeditions	415/922-0448 or 800/777-8183	www.geoex.com	Cultural Tours, Hiking, Natural History, Running, Trekking	Argentine Patagonia, Atlantic Coast, Chilean Patagonia, Tierra del Fuego
Global Vision	888/653-6028	www.gviusa.com	Kayaking, Mountaineering	Chilean Patagonia
Hidden Trails	604/323-1141 or 888/987-2457	www.hiddentrails.com	Horseback Riding	Argentine Patagonia, Chilean Patagonia, Lake District
Inca	510/420-1550	www.inca1.com	Cultural Tours, Coastal and Lake Cruises, Hiking, Natural History, Running	Antarctica, Argentine Patagonia
International Expeditions	205/428-1700 or 800/234-9620	www.ietravel.com	Cultural Tours, Coastal and Lake Cruises, Hiking, Natural History, Running	Antarctica, Chilean Patagonia
Joseph Van Os Photo Safaris	206/463-5383	www.photosafaris.com	Photo Safaris	Antarctica, Argentine Patagonia, Chilean Patagonia, Lake District
Journeys International	734/665-4407 or 800/255-8735	www.journeys-intl.com	Birdwatching, Coastal and Lake Cruises, Cultural Tours, Natural History	Argentine Patagonia, Atlantic Coast, Lake District, Tierra del Fuego
Kaiyote Tours	970/556-6103	www.kaiyotetours.com	Birdwatching	Atlantic Coast

Tour Operators

Outfitter	Telephone	Website	Activities Offered	Regions Covered
KE Adventure Travel	866/869-3625	www.kladventure.com	Hiking, Mountaineering, Natural History, Running, Skiing, Trekking	Antarctica, Argentine Patagonia, Chilean Patagonia, Lake District, Tierra del Fuego
Ladatco Tours	800/327-6162	www.ladatco.com	Bicycling, Coastal and Lake Cruises, Cultural Tours, Hiking, Horseback Riding, Natural History, Running, Trekking	Argentine Patagonia, Atlantic Coast, Chilean Patagonia, Lake District, Tierra del Fuego
Lindblad Expeditions	212/765-7740 or 800/397-3348	www.expeditions.com	Coastal and Lake Cruises, Photo Safaris	Antarctica
Liz Caskey Culinary & Wine Experiences	56/2-632-1511 or 904/687-0340	www.lizcaskey.com	Cultural Tours	Argentine Patagonia, Atlantic Coast, Chilean Patagonia
Mountain Madness	206/937-8389 or 800/328-5925	www.mountainmadness.com	Mountaineering, Trekking	Antarctica, Northwest Argentina
Mountain Travel Sobek	510/594-6000 or 888/831-7526	www.mtsobek.com	Cultural Tours, Hiking, Horseback Riding, Natural History, Running, Trekking	Argentine Patagonia, Atlantic Coast, Chilean Patagonia, Lake District, Tierra del Fuego
Myths and Mountains	775/832-5454 or 800/670-6984	www.mythsandmountains.com	Cultural Tours, Hiking, Natural History, Running	Argentine Patagonia, Chilean Patagonia, Lake District, Tierra del Fuego
Nature Expeditions International	954/693-8852 or 800/869-0639	www.naturexp.com	Cultural Tours, Hiking, Horseback Riding, Kayaking, Natural History, Rafting, Running, Trekking	Argentine Patagonia, Lake District
Off the Beaten Path	800/445-2995	www.offthebeatenpath.com	Cultural Tours, Fly Fishing, Hiking, Natural History, Running	Argentine Patagonia, Lake District
PanAmerican Travel Services	800/364-4359	www.panamtours.com	Bicycling, Coastal and Lake Cruises, Cultural Tours, Hiking, Horseback Riding, Natural History, Running, Trekking	Antarctica, Argentine Patagonia, Atlantic Coast, Chilean Patagonia, Lake District, Tierra del Fuego
Patagonia Travel Company	29/44-15-584-784	www.patagoniatravelco.com	Bicycling, Canoeing, Hiking, Horseback Riding, Kayaking, Mountaineering, Natural History, Rafting, Running, Trekking	Argentine Patagonia, Los Glaciares National Park, Tierra del Fuego
PowderQuest Tours	206/203-6065 or 888/565-7158	www.powderquest.com	Skiing	Argentine Patagonia, Chilean Patagonia, Lake District

Tour Operators

Outfitter	Telephone	Website	Activities Offered	Regions Covered
Quark Expeditions	888/892-0334	www.quarkexpeditions.com	Coastal and Lake Cruises, Natural History	Antarctica
Rod & Reel Adventures	541/349-0777 or 800/356-6982	www.rodreeladventures.com	Fishing	Chilean Patagonia, Tierra del Fuego
Snoventures	801/938-4806	www.snoventures.com	Skiing	Argentine Patagonia, Chilean Patagonia, Lake District
Southwind Adventures	303/972-0701 or 800/377-9463	www.southwindadventures.com	Coastal and Lake Cruises, Cultural Tours, Hiking, Horseback Riding, Natural History, Running, Trekking	Argentine Patagonia, Chilean Patagonia, Lake District
The World Outdoors	303/413-0938 or 800/488-8483	www.theworldoutdoors.com	Hiking, Natural History, Running, Trekking	Argentine Patagonia, Chilean Patagonia, Lake District
Tours International	281/293-0809	www.toursinternational.com	Cultural Tours, Hiking, Mountaineering, Natural History, Running, Skiing, Trekking	Antarctica, Argentine Patagonia, Atlantic Coast, Chilean Patagonia, Lake District, Tierra del Fuego
Travcoa	949/476-2800 or 800/992-2003	www.travcoa.com	Cultural Tours, Hiking, Natural History, Running	Antarctica, Argentine Patagonia
Victor Emanuel Nature Tours	512/328-5221 or 800/328-8368	www.ventbird.com	Birdwatching	Antarctica, Argentine Patagonia, Chilean Patagonia, Lake District, Tierra del Fuego
Wilderness Travel	510/558-2488 or 800/368-2794	www.wildernesstravel.com	Coastal and Lake Cruises, Cultural Tours, Hiking, Natural History, Running	Antarctica, Argentine Patagonia, Chilean Patagonia, Tierra del Fuego
Wildland Adventures	206/365-0686 or 800/345-4453	www.wildland.com	Coastal and Lake Cruises, Cultural Tours, Hiking, Natural History	Argentine Patagonia, Chilean Patagonia
Wild Wings	0117/965-333	www.wildwings.co.uk	Birdwatching	Antarctica
WINGS	520/320-9868 or 888/293-6443	www.wingsbirds.com	Birdwatching	Argentine Patagonia, Lake District, Tierra del Fuego
World Expeditions	800/567-2216	www.worldexpeditions.com	Cultural Tours, Hiking, Mountaineering, Natural History, Running, Trekking	Argentine Patagonia, Lake District, Tierra del Fuego
Zegrahm & Eco Expeditions	206/285-4000 or 800/628-8747	www.zeco.com	Coastal and Lake Cruises, Natural History	Antarctica

UNDERSTANDING ARGENTINA

SPANISH VOCABULARY

MENU GUIDE

SPANISH VOCABULARY

	ENGLISH	SPANISH	PRONUNCIATION
BASICS			
	Yes/no	Sí/no	see/noh
	Please	Por favor	por fah-vor
	Thank you (very much)	(Muchas) gracias	(**moo**-chas) **grah**-see-ass
	You're welcome	De nada	deh **nah**-da
	Excuse me	Con permiso	con pehr-**mee**-so
	Pardon me	¿Perdón?	pehr-**don**
	Could you tell me...?	¿Podría decirme...?	po-**dree**-ah deh-**seer**-me
	I'm sorry	Lo siento/Perdón	lo see-**en**-to/pehr-**don**
	Hello!/Hi!	¡Hola!	**o**-la
	Good morning!	¡Buen día!	bwen **dee**-a
	Good afternoon!	¡Buenas tardes!	**bwen**-as **tar**-des
	Good evening/Good night!	¡Buenas noches!	**bwen**-as **no**-ches
	Goodbye!	¡Chau!/¡Adiós!	chow/a-dee-**os**
NUMBERS			
	0	Cero	seh-ro
	1	Un, uno	oon, **oo**-no
	2	Dos	doss
	3	Tres	tress
	4	Cuatro	**kwah**-troh
	5	Cinco	**sin**-koh
	6	Seis	**say**-iss
	7	Siete	see-**yet**-eh
	8	Ocho	och-oh
	9	Nueve	nweh-veh
	10	Diez	dee-**ess**
DAYS OF THE WEEK			
	Sunday	domingo	doh-**ming**-oh
	Monday	lunes	**loo**-ness

ENGLISH	SPANISH	PRONUNCIATION
Tuesday	martes	**mar**-tess
Wednesday	miércoles	mee-**er**-koh-less
Thursday	jueves	**hweh**-vess
Friday	viernes	vee-**er**-ness
Saturday	sábado	**sah**-bad-oh

USEFUL PHRASES

Do you speak English?	¿Habla usted inglés? / ¿Hablás inglés?	**ab**-la oo-**sted** ing-**less** / **ab**-las ing-**less**
I don't speak Spanish	No hablo castellano	No **ab**-loh cas-**teh**-sha-no
I don't understand	No entiendo	No en-tee-**en**-doh
I understand	Entiendo	en-tee-**en**-doh
I don't know	No sé	No seh
What's your name?	¿Cómo se llama usted? / ¿Cómo te llamás?	ko-mo seh **shah**-mah oo-**sted** / ko-mo teh **shah**-mass
My name is...	Me llamo...	meh **shah**-moh...
What time is it?	¿Qué hora es?	keh **o**-rah ess
It's one o'clock	Es la una	ess la **oo**-na
It's two/three/four... o'clock	Son las dos/ tres/cuatro	son lass doss/tress/ **kwah**-troh
Yes, please/	Si, gracias.	see, **grah**-see-ass
No, thank you	No, gracias.	noh, **grah**-see-ass
How?	¿Cómo?	**ko**-mo
When?	¿Cuándo?	kwan-doh
Tonight	Esta noche	**ess**-tah **noch**-eh
What?	¿Qué?	Keh
What is this?	¿Qué es esto?	keh ess **ess**-toh
Why?	¿Por qué?	por keh
Who?	¿Quién?	kee-**yen**
Telephone	teléfono	tel-**eff**-on-oh
I am ill	Estoy enfermo(a)	ess-**toy** en-**fer**-moh(mah)

ENGLISH	SPANISH	PRONUNCIATION
Please call a doctor	Por favor, llame a un médico	Por fah-**vor**, **shah**-meh a oon **meh**-dik-oh
Help!	¡Auxilio!	owk-**see**-lee-oh
Fire!	¡Incendio!	in-**sen**-dee-oh
Look out!	¡Cuidado!	kwee-**dah**-doh

OUT AND ABOUT

ENGLISH	SPANISH	PRONUNCIATION
Where is...?	¿Dónde está...?	**don**-deh ess-**tah**...
the train station	la estación de tren	la ess-tah-see-**on** deh tren
the subway station	la estación de subte	la ess-tah-see-**on** deh **soob**-teh
the bus stop	la parada del colectivo	la pah-**rah**-dah del col-ek-**tee**-voh
the post office	el correo	el cor-**reh**-yoh
the bank	el banco	el **ban**-koh
the hotel	el hotel	el oh-**tel**
the museum	el museo	el moo-**seh**-yoh
the hospital	el hospital	el oss-pee-**tal**
the elevator	el ascensor	el ass-**en**-sor
the bathroom	el baño	el **ban**-yoh
Left/right	izquierda/derecha	iss-kee-**er**-dah/ deh-**rech**-ah
Straight ahead	derecho	deh-**rech**-oh
Avenue	avenida	av-en-**ee**-dah
City street	calle	**cah**-sheh
Highway	carretera/ruta	cah-ret-**eh**-rah
Restaurant	restaurante/restorán	rest-ow-**ran**-teh/ rest-oh-**ran**
Main square	plaza principal	**plass**-ah prin-see-**pal**
Market	mercado	mer-**kah**-do
Neighborhood	barrio	**bah**-ree-oh

MENU GUIDE

With so much meat on the menu, you'll need to know how to order it: *jugoso* (juicy) means medium rare, *vuelta y vuelta* (flipped back and forth) means rare, and *vivo por adentro* (alive inside) is barely warm in the middle. Argentineans like their meat *bien cocido* (well cooked).

aceite de olivo: olive oil

alfajores: Argentine cookies, usually made with dulce de leche and often covered with chocolate, though there are hundreds of varieties

arroz: rice

bife de lomo: filet mignon

bife de chorizo: like a New York strip steak, but double the size (not to be confused with *chorizo,* which is a type of sausage)

budín de pan: Argentine version of bread pudding

cabrito: roasted kid

cafecito: espresso

café con leche: coffee with milk

centolla: King crab, a Patagonian specialty

chimichurri: a sauce of oil, garlic, and salt, served with meat

chinchulines: small intestines

chorizo: thick, spicy pork-and-beef sausages, usually served with bread (*choripan*)

churros: baton-shaped donuts for dipping in hot chocolate

ciervo: venison

chivito: kid

cordero: lamb

cortado: coffee "cut" with a drop of milk

dulce de leche: a sweet caramel concoction made from milk and served on pancakes, in pastries, on cookies, and on ice cream

empanadas: pockets stuffed with meat—usually beef—chicken, or cheese

ensalada de fruta: fruit salad (sometimes fresh, sometimes canned)

estofado: beef stew

facturas: small pastries

huevos: eggs

humitas: steamed cornhusks wrapped around cornmeal and cheese

jamón: ham

lechón: roast suckling pig

lengua: tongue

licuado: milk shake

locro: local stew, usually made with hominy and beans, that's cooked slowly with meat and vegetables; common in northern Argentina

medialuna: croissant

mejillones: mussels

merluza: hake

milanesa: breaded meat cutlet, usually veal, pounded thin and fried; served as a main course or in a sandwich with lettuce, tomato, ham, cheese, and egg

milanesa a la napolitana: a breaded veal cutlet with melted mozzarella cheese and tomato sauce

mollejas: sweetbreads; the thymus glands, usually of the cow but also can be of the lamb or the goat

morcilla: blood sausage

pejerrey: a kind of mackerel

pollo: chicken

provoleta: grilled provolone cheese sprinkled with olive oil and oregano

puchero: boiled meat and vegetables; like pot-au-feu

queso: cheese

salchichas: long, thin sausages

sambayon: an alcohol-infused custard

tamales: ground corn stuffed with meat, cheese, or other fillings and tied up in a corn husk

tenedor libre: all-you-can-eat meat and salad bar

tinto: red wine

trucha: trout

Travel Smart Argentina

WORD OF MOUTH

"There is a money shortage in Argentina. It was a problem in Buenos Aires but was really an issue in Mendoza with people lining up around the block to get cash. Even the ATMs run out, so make sure you get enough cash, best early in the day and early in the week. There is also a shortage of coins. We went into the casino and asked them to exchange some US$ for pesos. They were happy to do it and gave a good rate with no ATM fees or line-ups!"

—sbackus

www.fodors.com/community

GETTING HERE AND AROUND

Argentina measures around 3,650 km (2,268 miles) from tip to tail, and many of its attractions are hundreds of miles apart. Carefully planning how you get around will save lots of time and money.

Buenos Aires lies about two-thirds of the way up Argentina's eastern side, on the banks of the Río de la Plata. It's the country's capital and its main transport hub. A well-developed network of long-distance buses connects it with cities all over Argentina; buses also operate between many cities without passing through Buenos Aires.

TRAVEL TIMES FROM BUENOS AIRES		
TO	BY AIR	BY BUS
San Antonio de Areco	n/a	2 hours
Atlantic Coast	1 hour	5–6 hours
Córdoba	1¼ hours	9–11 hours
Mendoza	1¾ hours	12–14 hours
Puerto Iguazú	1¾ hours	16–19 hours
Salta	2¼ hours	18–21 hours
Bariloche	2¼ hours	21–23 hours
El Calafate	3¼ hours	40 hours

Three of the country's main draws are around 1,000 km (621 miles) from Buenos Aires as the crow flies: Puerto Iguazú, the base for exploring Iguazú Falls, in northeastern Misiones Province; Salta, the gateway to the Andean Northwest; and Mendoza, in the wine region, near the Chilean border. Slightly farther, this time southwest of Buenos Aires, is Bariloche, the hub for the Lake District of northern Patagonia. The hub of southern Patagonia is El Calafate, close to the Perito Moreno glacier, a whopping 2,068 km (1,285 miles) southwest of Buenos Aires.

Flying within the country makes sense given these huge distances. That said, domestic flights are expensive, and at this writing flight delays of two to six hours are regular occurrences. As a result, many visitors opt for the more reliable overnight sleeper buses for trips of up to 1,000 km (621 miles; around 12 hours).

AIR TRAVEL

TO ARGENTINA

There are direct daily services between Buenos Aires and several North American cities, New York and Miami being primary departure points. Many airlines fly to Buenos Aires via Santiago de Chile or São Paulo in Brazil, which adds only a little to your trip time.

Aerolíneas Argentinas, the flagship airline, operates direct flights between Buenos Aires and Miami. Since its renationalization in 2008, Aerolíneas's reputation for chronic delays has greatly improved, although strikes do still ground services.

Chilean airline LAN is the Aerolíneas's biggest local competition. LAN flies direct from Buenos Aires to Miami, and, via Santiago de Chile or Lima to JFK, Dallas, San Francisco, and Los Angeles. LAN also allows you to bypass Buenos Aires by flying into Mendoza and Córdoba from JFK and Miami, both via Santiago de Chile.

There are direct flights from Atlanta on Delta. American has nonstop service from JFK, Miami, and Dallas. United flies from JFK via Washington, D.C. Continental connects Buenos Aires nonstop with Houston and Washington, D.C.

Flying times to Buenos Aires are 11–12 hours from New York, 9 hours from Miami, 10½ hours from Dallas or Houston, and 13–14 hours from Los Angeles, via Santiago de Chile.

WITHIN ARGENTINA

Most domestic flights operate from Buenos Aires, so to fly from the extreme south of the country to the extreme north, you often have to change planes here.

Aerolíneas Argentinas and its partner Austral operate flights from Buenos Aires to more Argentine cities than any other airline, including daily services (often more than one) to Puerto Iguazú, Salta, Mendoza, Córdoba, Bariloche, Ushuaia, and El Calafate. LAN also flies to these cities. Andes Líneas Aéreas operates flights between Buenos Aires and Salta, Jujuy, Córdoba, Puerto Madryn, and Bariloche, and sometimes runs direct services between Puerto Iguazú and Salta and Córdoba, bypassing Buenos Aires.

AIR PASSES

Aerolíneas Argentinas operates two coupon-based air passes. You do not need to fly in and out of the continent with Aerolíneas to be eligible for either, but you must purchase your pass before you arrive.

The South American pass enables you to visit Argentina and a minimum of two of the other countries in the region Aerolíneas flies to (Brazil, Chile, Colombia, Paraguay, Peru, Uruguay, and Venezuela). With the Visit Argentina Pass, you can travel to between three and twelve destinations within Argentina. Both passes use one coupon for each flight you take, but the catch is that many routes only operate from Buenos Aires, so you often have to return there. If you want to visit El Calafate and Iguazú with the Visit Argentina Pass, for example, you would need to buy four coupons. Three coupons (the minimum purchase) cost $579 before tax for either pass, though this is reduced to $479 on the Visit Argentina pass if you fly in and out of the continent on Aerolíneas. Taxes vary according to your destinations.

If you plan to take at least three flights within Argentina or South America in general, you might save money with Visit South America pass run by the OneWorld Alliance (which LAN is part of). Flights are categorized by mileage; segments (both domestic and international) start at $200.

AEROLÍNEAS ARGENTINAS

Ongoing industrial disputes and internal changes were taking place at Aerolíneas Argentinas when this book went to press. Be sure to check the carrier's flights and offerings in advance, as they are subject to change.

Airline Contacts Aerolíneas Argentinas *www.aerolineas.com.ar.* **American Airlines** *www.aa.com.* **Continental Airlines** *www.continental.com.* **Delta Airlines** *www.delta.com.* **LAN** *www.lan.com.* **United Airlines** *www.united.com.*

Airlines and Airports Airline and Airport Links.com *www.airlineandairportlinks.com.*

Airline Security Issues Transportation Security Administration *www.tsa.gov.*

Air Passes South American Pass *800/333-0276 Aerolíneas Argentinas* *www.aerolineas.com.ar.* **Visit South America Pass** *866/435-9526 LAN* *www.oneworld.com.*

AIRPORTS

Airports in Argentina are mostly small, well maintained, and easy to get around. Security at most isn't as stringent as it is in the States—computers stay in cases, shoes stay on your feet, and there are no random searches.

BUENOS AIRES

Buenos Aires' Aeropuerto Internacional de Ezeiza Ministro Pistarini (EZE)—known as Ezeiza—is 35 km (22 miles) southwest of and a 45-minute drive from city center. It's served by a variety of international airlines, along with domestic airlines running international routes.

Aerolíneas Argentinas and its partner Austral operate out of the older Terminal B. All other airlines are based at Terminal A, a pleasant, glass-sided building. A covered walkway connects the two terminals. Each terminal has a few small snack bars, a small range of shops, a public phone center with Internet services, and a tourist information booth. The ATM, 24-hour luggage storage, and car-rental agencies are in Terminal A.

⚠ **Avoid changing money in the luggage reclaim area. By far the best exchange rates are at the small Banco de la Nación in the Terminal A arrivals area; it's open round the clock.**

Most domestic flights operate out of Aeroparque Jorge Newbery (AEP). It's next to the Río de la Plata in northeast Palermo, about 8 km (5 miles) north of the city center. Both it and Ezeiza are run by the private company Aeropuertos Argentinos 2000.

ELSEWHERE IN ARGENTINA

Several other airports in Argentina are technically international, but only because they have a few flights to neighboring countries; most flights are domestic.

Aeropuerto Internacional de Puerto Iguazú (IGR) is close to Iguazú Falls; it's 20 km (12 miles) from Puerto Iguazú and 10 km (6 miles) from the park entrance. The northwest is served by Salta's Aeropuerto Internacional Martín Miguel de Güemes (SLA), 7 km (4½ miles) west of the city of Salta.

The airport for the wine region and western Argentina is Aeropuerto Internacional de Mendoza Francisco Gabrieli (MDZ), usually known as El Plumerillo. It's 10 km (6 miles) north of Mendoza. Northern Patagonia's hub is Bariloche, 13 km (8 miles) west of which is the Aeropuerto Internacional San Carlos de Bariloche Teniente Luis Candelaria (BRC), known as the Aeropuerto de Bariloche. The gateway to southern Patagonia is Aeropuerto Internacional de El Calafate Comandante Armando Tola (ECA), 18 km (11 miles) east of El Calafate itself.

Airport Information Aeroparque Jorge Newbery ✉ *Buenos Aires* ☎ *11/5480–6111* 🌐 *www.aa2000.com.ar.* **Aeropuerto Internacional de Ezeiza Ministro Pistarini** ☎ *11/5480–2500* 🌐 *www.aa2000.com.ar.* **Aeropuertos Argentinos 2000** ☎ *11/5480–6111* 🌐 *www.aa2000.com.ar.*

BOAT TRAVEL

There are frequent ferry services across the Río de la Plata between Buenos Aires and the Uruguayan cities of Colonia and Montevideo. The best-value services are the Colonia Express catamarans, which take an hour or less to Colonia and three hours to Montevideo. Full-price round-trip tickets cost 280 and 380 pesos, respectively, but are often reduced to less than half that if you book online. Buquebus operates similar services on high-speed ferries (round-trip tickets cost 450 pesos to Colonia and 800 pesos to Montevideo), but there are substantial off-peak and mid-week discounts.

The two companies also sell packages that include bus tickets to La Paloma, Montevideo, and Punta del Este on services direct from Colonia's ferry terminal. You can order tickets by phone or online. Buquebus leaves from a terminal at the northern end of Puerto Madero. The Colonia Express terminal is on Avenida Pedro de Mendoza (the extension of Av. Huergo) at 20 de Septiembre, south of Puerto Madero. It's best reached by taxi.

Contacts Buquebus ☎ *11/4316–6500* 🌐 *www.buquebus.com.* **Colonia Express** ☎ *11/4317–4100 English operator* 🌐 *www.coloniaexpress.com.*

BUS TRAVEL

Frequent, comfortable, and dependable long-distance buses connect Buenos Aires with cities all over Argentina and with neighboring countries. Bus travel can be substantially cheaper than flying, and far less prone to delays. Both locals and visitors often choose overnight sleeper services for trips up to 12 hours long.

Most bus companies have online timetables; some allow you to buy tickets online or by phone. Websites also list *puntos de venta* (sales offices), and you can usually buy tickets at the terminal as well, right up until departure time. Many now accept credit cards; even so, take enough cash to cover the fare. In January, February, and July, buy your ticket as far in advance as possible—a week or more, at least—and arrive at the terminal extra early.

Most long-distance buses leave Buenos Aires from the Terminal de Ómnibus de Retiro, which is often referred to as the Terminal de Retiro or simply Retiro. Ramps and stairs from the street lead you to a huge concourse where buses leave from more than 60 numbered platforms. There are restrooms, restaurants, public phones, lockers, news kiosks, and a tourist office on this floor.

You buy tickets from the *boleterías* (ticket offices) on the upper level; there are also two ATMs here. Each company has its own ticket booth; they're arranged in zones according to the destinations served, which makes price comparisons easy. The terminal's comprehensive Spanish-language website lists bus companies by destination, including their phone number and ticket booth location. *(See individual chapters for information about local bus stations.)* Keep your wits about you in the terminal: pickpockets and bag-snatchers often prey on distracted travelers.

Long-distance buses have toilets, air-conditioning, videos, and snacks. The most basic service is *semi-cama,* which has minimally reclining seats and often takes a little longer than more luxurious services. It's worth paying the bit extra for *coche cama (also* called *ejecutivo),* which has large, business-class-style seats and, sometimes, pillows and blankets. The best rides of all are on the fully reclining seats of *cama suite* services, where fully recline-able seats are often contained in their own little booth.

On services between nearby towns you can usually choose between regular buses (*común*) and air-conditioned or heated services with reclining seats (*diferencial*). The companies that run local services rarely have websites—you buy tickets direct from the bus station.

Contact Terminal de Ómnibus Retiro ✉ *Av. Antártida Argentina at Av. Ramos Mejía, Retiro, Buenos Aires* ☎ *11/4310–0700* 🌐 *www.tebasa.com.ar.*

CAR TAVEL

Argentina's long highways and fabulous scenery make it a great place for road trips. However, if you're only going to be staying in Buenos Aires and other big cities, renting a car isn't particularly useful; stick with a *remis* (hired car) or taxi; remises can be hired to take you around the countryside, too.

GASOLINE

Gas stations *(estaciones de servicio) are* in and near most towns and along major highways. Most are open 24 hours and include full service, convenience stores, and sometimes ATMs. In rural areas, stations have small shops and toilets but are few and far between and have reduced hours.

On long trips, fill your tank whenever you can, even if you've still got gas left, as the next station could be a long way away (signs at stations often tell you how far). Attendants always pump the gas and don't expect a tip, though most locals add a few pesos for a full tank. Credit cards often aren't accepted—look for signs saying *tarjetas de crédito suspendidas* (no credit cards) or *solo efectivo* (cash only).

The major service stations are YPF, Shell, Petrobras, and Esso. Locals say that YPF gas is the highest quality. It also tends to be the cheapest. Prices are often higher in the north of Argentina. South of an imaginary line between Bariloche and Puerto Madryn, gas is heavily subsidized and costs roughly half what it does elsewhere. There are three grades of unleaded fuels, as well as diesel and biodiesel. GNC is compressed natural gas, an alternative fuel. Stations with GNC signs may sell only this, or both this and regular gas.

PARKING

On-street parking is limited in big cities. Some have meter systems or tickets that you buy from kiosks and display on the dashboard. In meter-free spots there's often an informal "caretaker" who guides you into your spot and charges 2–5 pesos to watch your car, which you pay when you leave.

Car theft is common, so many agencies insist that you park rental cars in a guarded lot. Many hotels have their own lots, and there are plenty in major cities: look for a circular blue sign with a white "E" (for *estacionamiento* [parking]). In downtown Buenos Aires, expect to pay 12–15 pesos per hour, or 42 pesos for 12 hours. Rates are much lower elsewhere. Illegally parked cars are towed only from restricted parking areas in city centers. Getting your car back is a bureaucratic nightmare and costs around 200 pesos.

ROAD CONDITIONS

City streets are notorious for potholes, uneven surfaces, and poorly marked lanes and turnoffs. Many major cities have a one-way system whereby parallel streets run in opposite directions: never going the wrong way along a street is one of the few rules that Argentinians abide by. Where there are no traffic lights at an intersection, you give way to drivers coming from the right, but have priority over those coming from the left.

Two kinds of roads connect major cities: *autopistas* (two- or three-lane freeways) and *rutas* (single- or dual-carriageways) or *rutas nacionales* (main "national routes," usually indicated with an "RN" before the route number). Both types of roads are subject to regular tolls. Autopistas are well maintained, but the state of rutas varies hugely. In more remote locations even rutas that look like major highways on maps may be narrow roads with no central division. Always travel with a map, as signposts for turnoffs are scarce.

Night driving can be hazardous: some highways and routes are poorly lighted, routes sometimes cut through the center of towns, cattle often get onto the roads, and in rural areas *rastreros* (old farm trucks) seldom have all their lights working. Outside of the city of Buenos Aires, be especially watchful at traffic lights, as crossing on red lights at night is common practice. Beware of *guardaganados* (cattle guards). They're often raised so that your car flies into the air if speeding. A useful road-trip website is 🌐 *www.ruta0.com*, which calculates distances and tolls between places and offers several route options. There are basic maps and some highway-condition reports (in Spanish) on the website of the Dirección Nacional de Vialidad (National Highway Authority).

Information Dirección Nacional de Vialidad ☎ *11/4343–8520* 🌐 *www.vialidad.gov.ar.*

ROADSIDE EMERGENCIES

All rental-car agencies have an emergency help line in case of breakdowns or accidents—some services take longer than others to arrive. The best roadside assistance is usually that of the Automóvil Club Argentina (ACA), which sends mechanics and tow trucks to members traveling anywhere in the country. The ACA also offers free roadside assistance to members of North American clubs and automobile associations. However, bear in mind when you call for assistance that most operators only speak Spanish.

If you have an accident on the highway, stay by your vehicle until the police arrive, which could take a while, depending on where you are. If your car is stolen, you should report it to the closest police station.

Contacts American Automobile Association (*AAA*) ☎ *800/564–6222* 🌐 *www.aaa.com.* **Automóvil Club Argentino** (*ACA*) ☎ *11/4808–4000, 800/777–2894 emergencies* 🌐 *www.aca.org.ar.* **Police** ☎ *101.*

RULES OF THE ROAD

You drive on the right in Argentina, as in the United States. Seatbelts are required by law for front-seat passengers. You must use your headlights on highways at all times. The use of cellular phones while driving is forbidden, and turning left on two-way avenues is prohibited unless there's a left-turn signal; there are no right turns on red. Traffic lights turn yellow before they turn red, but also before turning green, which is interpreted by drivers as an extra margin to get through the intersection, so take precautions.

The legal blood-alcohol limit is 500 mg of alcohol per liter of blood, but in practice breathalyzing is common only in Buenos Aires and along the highways of the Atlantic coast during January and February. In towns and cities a 40-kph (25-mph) speed limit applies on streets and a 60-kph (37-mph) limit is in effect on avenues. On *autopistas* (freeways) the limit is 130 kph (80 mph), and on *rutas* (highways) it ranges between 100 kph (62 mph) and 120 kph (75 mph). On smaller roads and highways out of town it's 80 kph (50 mph). However, locals take speed-limit signs, the ban on driving with cell phones, and drunk driving lightly, so drive very defensively indeed.

Police tend to be forgiving of foreigners' driving faults and often waive tickets and fines when they see your passport. If you do get a traffic ticket, don't argue. Most tickets aren't payable on the spot, but some police officers offer "reduced" on-the-spot fines in lieu of a ticket: it's bribery, and you'd do best to insist on receiving the proper ticket.

In Buenos Aires, buses and taxis have exclusive lanes on major avenues. On other streets they often drive as though they have priority, and it's good to defer to them for your own safety.

If you experience a small accident, jot down the other driver's information and supply your own, then go to the nearest police station in the area to file a report. Contact your rental agency immediately.

Paved highways run from Argentina to the Chilean, Bolivian, Paraguayan, and Brazilian borders. If you do cross the border by land you'll be required to present your passport, documentation of car ownership, and insurance paperwork at immigration and customs checkpoints. It's also common for cars and bags to be searched for contraband, such as food, livestock, and drugs.

RENTAL CARS

Daily rates range from 280 pesos to 750 pesos, depending on the type of car and the distance you plan to travel. This generally includes tax and 200 free km (125 free miles) daily. Note that most cars have manual transmissions, so if you need an automatic, request one in advance.

Reputable firms don't rent to drivers under 21, and drivers under 23 often have to pay a daily surcharge. Children's car seats are not compulsory, but are available for about 30–40 pesos per day. Some agencies charge a 10% surcharge for picking up a car from the airport.

Collision damage waiver (CDW) is mandatory and is usually included in standard rental prices. However, you're still responsible for a deductible fee (known locally as a *franquicia* or *deducible*)—a maximum amount that you'll have to pay if damage occurs. The amount of this deductible is generally around 3,000 pesos for a car, and can be much higher for a four-wheel-drive vehicle. You can reduce the figure substantially or altogether by paying an insurance premium (usually 30–60 pesos per day); some companies have lower deductibles than others.

In general, you cannot cross the border in a rental car. Many rental companies don't insure you on unpaved roads. Discuss your itinerary with the agent to be certain you're always covered.

Rental Agencies **Alamo** ☎ *810/999–25266, 11/4322–3320 in Buenos Aires* 🌐 *www.alamo.com.* **Avis** ☎ *810/9991–2847, 11/4326–5542 in Buenos Aires* 🌐 *www.avis.com.* **Budget** ☎ *810/999–2834, 11/4326–3825 in Buenos Aires* 🌐 *www.budget.com.ar.* **Dollar** ☎ *800/555–3655, 11/4315–1670 in Buenos Aires* 🌐 *www.dollar.com.ar.* **Hertz** ☎ *810/222–43789, 11/4816–8001 in Buenos Aires* 🌐 *www.hertz.com.*

ESSENTIALS

ACCOMMODATIONS

Booming visitor numbers have sparked the construction of dozens of properties, and healthy competition is keeping most prices reasonable and quality high. There's variety, too.

Nearly all hotels—even hostels—include breakfast in the room price, but not all include the 21% tax in their quoted rates. Prices are also linked to municipality-run rating systems, which are based on a checklist of amenities (often outdated) rather than detailed evaluation. You can get wildly different things for your money, so do your homework. In destinations popular with locals, room prices soar in high season (usually January, February, and July), and some establishments won't take bookings for less than seven days. In the off-season the same places can be a steal.

APARTMENT AND HOUSE RENTALS

There are hundreds of furnished rentals available by the day, week, or month in Buenos Aires and other cities. Reputable local reservations services ApartmentsBA.com, ByT Argentina, and Buenos Aires Habitat have large online databases.

When choosing your rental, remember that air-conditioning is a must between December and March. Always check exact street locations on a map, as listings sometimes exaggerate a property's proximity to particular neighborhoods, landmarks, or subway stations. Likewise, apartments are often more worn than they appear in gleaming website photos.

Most online apartment agencies act as intermediaries between you and the owner: an English-speaking representative meets you at the apartment, you sign a contract, pay the owner, and are given the keys. You pay for your entire stay up front, and usually have to pay a deposit equivalent to a week's rent, which is returned when you leave. Note that though you give a credit card number to secure your reservation, actual payment is nearly always in cash only. Read cancellation policies carefully: many agencies don't refund if you're not happy with your apartment choice.

Local Rental Agents **ApartmentsBA.com** ☎ *11/5254–0100 in Buenos Aires, 646/827–8796 in the U.S.* 🌐 *www.apartmentsba.com.* **Buenos Aires Habitat** ☎ *305/735–2223 in U.S., 11/4815–8662 in Buenos Aires* 🌐 *www.buenosaireshabitat.com.* **ByT Argentina** ☎ *11/4876–5000* 🌐 *www.bytargentina.com.*

ESTANCIAS

You get a taste of Argentine country life—including home-cooked meals and horseback riding—when you stay at a ranch. Estancias Travel and Estancias Argentinas are two good booking services, but you usually get better rates if you call the estancia directly.

When booking, ask specifically about what activities and drinks are included in rates, and bear in mind that many establishments only accept cash payments. Be sure to factor in travel times and costs when planning your stay: remoter locations may only be reachable by private transport, often at a hefty cost.

Estancia Reservations **Estancias Argentinas** ☎ *11/4343–2366* 🌐 *www.estanciasargentinas.com.* **Estancias Travel** ☎ *11/5236–1054* 🌐 *www.estanciastravel.com.*

COMMUNICATIONS

INTERNET

Inexpensive Internet access is widely available in Buenos Aires. Both budget establishments and top-end hotels tend to have free Wi-Fi, though connection quality varies hugely. Some hotels also have Internet access through room televisions and many also have a PC in the lobby for guests to use.

If you're traveling without a laptop, look for a *ciber* (Internet café) or *locutorios* (telephone and Internet centers). Expect to pay between 5 and 8 pesos per hour to surf the Web. Broadband connections are common.

In Buenos Aires many bars and restaurants have free Wi-Fi—look for stickers on their windows. In general, these are open networks and you don't need to ask for a password to use them. You can also find Wi-Fi in many hotel lobbies, libraries, business and event centers, some airports, and in public spaces—piggybacking is common practice.

PHONES

The country code for Argentina is 54. To call landlines in Argentina from the United States, dial the international access code (011) followed by the country code (54), the two- to four-digit area code without the initial 0, then the five- to nine-digit phone number. For example, to call the Buenos Aires number 011/4123–4567, you would dial 011–54–11–4123–4567.

Any number that is prefixed by a 15 is a cell-phone number. To call cell phones from the United States, dial the international access code (011) followed by the country code (54), Argentina's cell-phone code (9), the area code without the initial 0, then the seven- or eight-digit cell-phone number without the initial 15. For example, to call the Buenos Aires cell phone (011) 15/5123–4567, you would dial 011–54–9–11–5123–4567.

CALLING WITHIN ARGENTINA

Argentina's phone service is run by the duopoly of Telecom and Telefónica. Telecom does the northern half of Argentina (including the northern half of the city of Buenos Aires) and Telefónica does the south. However, both companies operate public phones and phone centers throughout Argentina, called *locutorios* or *telecentros*.

Service is efficient, and direct dialing—both long-distance and international—is universal. You can make local and long-distance calls from your hotel (usually with a surcharge) and from any public phone or locutorio. Public phones aren't abundant, and are often broken; all accept coins. Phone cards can be used from both public and private phones by calling a free access number and entering the card code number.

At locutorios, ask the receptionist for *una cabina* (a booth), make as many local, long-distance, or international calls as you like (a small LCD display tracks how much you've spent), then pay as you leave. There's no charge if you don't get through. Note that many locutorios don't allow you to call free numbers, so you can't use prepaid calling cards from them.

All of Argentina's area codes are prefixed with a 0, which you need to include when dialing another area within Argentina. You don't need to dial the area code to call a local number. Confusingly, area codes and phone numbers don't all have the same number of digits. The area code for Buenos Aires is 011, and phone numbers have 8 digits. Area codes for the rest of the country have three or four digits, and start with 02 (the southern provinces) or 03 (the northern provinces); phone numbers have six or seven digits.

For local directory assistance (in Spanish), dial 110. Local calls cost 23 centavos for two minutes at peak time (weekdays 8–8 and Saturday 8–1) or four minutes the rest of the time. Long-distance calls cost 57 centavos per *ficha* (unit)—the farther the distance, the less time each unit lasts. For example, 57 centavos lasts about two minutes to places less than 55 km (35 miles) away, but only half a minute to somewhere more than 250 km (155 miles) away.

To make international calls from Argentina, dial 00, then the country code, area code, and number. The country code for the United States is 1.

CALLING CARDS

You can use prepaid calling cards (*tarjetas prepagas*) to make local and international calls from public phones, but not locutorios. All cards come with a scratch-off panel, which reveals a PIN. You dial a free access number, the PIN, and the number you wish to call.

Many *kioscos* (convenience stores) and small supermarkets sell a variety of prepaid calling cards: specify it's for *llamadas internacionales* (international calls), and compare each card's per-minute rates to the country you want to call. Many cost as little as 9 centavos per minute for calls to the United States. Telecom and Telefónica also sell prepaid 5-, 10-, and 20-peso calling cards from kioscos and locutorios. They're called Tarjeta Países and Geo Destinos, respectively. Calls to the United States cost 19 centavos per minute using both.

Calling Card Information Telecom ☎ *0800/888–0112* 🌐 *www.telecom.com.ar.* **Telefónica** ☎ *0800/333–4004* 🌐 *www.telefonica.com.ar.*

MOBILE PHONES

All cell phones are GSM 850/1900 Mhz. If you have an unlocked dual-band GSM phone from North America and intend to call local numbers, buy a prepaid Argentine SIM card on arrival—rates will be cheaper than using your U.S. network or renting a phone. Alternatively, buy a basic pay-as-you-go handset and SIM card (*tarjeta SIM*) for about 200 pesos.

Cell numbers here use a local area code, then the cell-phone prefix (15), then a seven- or eight-digit number. To call a cell in the same area as you, dial 15 and the number. To call a cell in a different area, dial the area code, including the initial 0, then 15, then the number.

Local charges for calling a cell phone from a landline depend on things like the company and time of day, but most cost between 50 centavos and 1.50 pesos per minute. In general, you only pay for outgoing calls from cell phones, which cost between 50 centavos and 2 pesos a minute. Calls from pay-as-you-go phones are the most expensive and calls to phones from the same company as yours are usually cheaper. The exception is for calls to a cell phone from a pay phone—both caller and recipient are charged; so if the number you're calling has no credit, you can't get through. Most locutorios allow the caller to pay the entire cost of calls to cell phones—look for signs saying *llamadas a celulares sin crédito* (calls to cell phones with no credit).

There are three main phone companies in Argentina: Movistar (owned by Telefónica), Claro, and Personal. Their prices are similar, but Claro is said to be cheapest, Movistar has the most users and best coverage, and Personal is the least popular service, so cards can be harder to find. You can buy a SIM card from any of the companies' offices and sales stands, which are easy to find all over the country. Top up credit by purchasing pay-as-you-go cards (*tarjetas de celular*), available from kioscos, locutorios, supermarkets, and gas stations or by *carga virtual* (virtual top-ups) at kioscos and locutorios, where sales clerks add credit to your line number (which you write down for them) while you wait. You can rent a cell—including smartphones—at the airport from Phonerental. A basic handset is free for the first week and costs 20 pesos a week thereafter. Outgoing local calls cost about 3.50 pesos a minute, but you pay 2.40 pesos per minute to receive both local and international calls. For very short stays, however, renting can be a good value.

Contacts Cellular Abroad ☎ *800/287–5072* 🌐 *www.cellularabroad.com.* **Claro** 🌐 *www.claro.com.ar.* **Mobal** ☎ *888/888–9162* 🌐 *www.mobalrental.com.* **Movistar** 🌐 *www.movistar.com.ar.* **Personal** 🌐 *www.personal.com.ar.* **Phonerental** ☎ *11/4311–2933* 🌐 *www.phonerental.com.ar.* **Planet Fone** ☎ *888/988–4777* 🌐 *www.planetfone.com.*

CUSTOMS AND DUTIES

Customs uses a random inspection system that requires you to push a button at the inspection bay—if a green light appears, you walk through; if a red light appears, your bags are X-rayed (and very occasionally opened). Officially, foreign tourists are allowed to bring $300 worth of alcohol, tobacco, and perfume into the country duty-free. You are also allowed another $300 worth of purchases from the duty-free shops that most of Argentina's international airports have after you land. In practice, however, most officials wave foreigners through customs controls and are rarely interested in alcohol or tobacco. Personal clothing and effects are admitted duty-free, provided they have been used, as are personal jewelry and professional equipment. Fishing gear and skis present no problems.

If you enter the country by bus from Bolivia, Brazil, or Paraguay, you, your bags, and the vehicle may be subject to lengthy searches by officials looking for drugs and smuggled goods.

Argentina has strict regulations designed to prevent the illicit trafficking of antiques, fossils, and other items of cultural and historical importance. For more information, contact the Dirección Nacional de Patrimonio y Museos (National Heritage and Museums Board).

Information in Argentina Dirección Nacional de Patrimonio y Museos ☎ *11/4381–6656* 🌐 *www.cultura.gov.ar.*

U.S. Information U.S. Customs and Border Protection 🌐 *www.cbp.gov.*

ELECTRICITY

The electrical current is 220 volts, 50 cycles alternating current (AC), so most North American appliances can't be used without a transformer. Older wall outlets take continental-type plugs, with two round prongs, whereas newer buildings take plugs with three flat, angled prongs or two flat prongs set at a "v" angle.

Brief power outages (and surges when the power comes back) are fairly regular occurrences, especially outside of Buenos Aires, so it's a good idea to use a surge-protector with your laptop.

EMERGENCIES

In a medical emergency, taking a taxi to the nearest hospital—drivers usually know where to go—can be quicker than waiting for an ambulance. If you do call an ambulance, it will take you to the nearest hospital—possibly a public one that may well look run-down; don't worry, though, as the medical care will be excellent. Alternatively, you can call a private hospital directly.

For theft, wallet loss, small road accidents, and minor emergencies, contact the nearest police station. Expect all dealings with the police to be a lengthy, bureaucratic business—it's probably only worth bothering if you need the report for insurance claims.

American Embassy American Embassy ✉ *Av. Colombia 4300, Palermo, Buenos Aires* ☎ *11/5777–4354, 11/5777–4873 after hours* 🌐 *argentina.usembassy.gov.*

General Contacts All Buenos Aires Emergency Services ☎ *911.* **Ambulance and Medical** ☎ *107.* **Fire** ☎ *100.* **Police** ☎ *101.*

HEALTH

MEDICAL CONCERNS

No vaccinations are required for travel to Argentina. However, the Centers for Disease Control (CDC) recommend vaccinations against hepatitis A and B and typhoid for all travelers. A yellow fever vaccine is also advisable if you're traveling to Iguazú. Each year there are cases of cholera in northern Argentina, mostly in the indigenous communities near the Bolivian border; your best protection is to avoid eating raw seafood.

Malaria is a threat only in low-lying rural areas near the borders of Bolivia and

LOCAL DO'S AND TABOOS

CUSTOMS OF THE COUNTRY

Welcoming and helpful, Argentinians are a pleasure to travel among. City dwellers here have more in common with, say, the Spanish or Italians, than other Latin Americans. However, although cultural differences between here and North America are small, they're still palpable.

Outside Buenos Aires, siestas are still sacrosanct: most shops and museums close between 1 and 4 or 5 pm. Locals are usually fashionably late for all social events—don't be offended if someone keeps you waiting over half an hour for a lunch or dinner date. However, tardiness is frowned upon in the business world.

Fiercely animated discussions are a national pastime, and locals relish probing controversial issues like politics and religion, as well as soccer and their friends' personal lives. Political correctness isn't a valued trait, and just about everything and everyone—except mothers—is a potential target for playful mockery. Locals are often disparaging about their country's shortcomings, but Argentina-bashing is a privilege reserved for Argentinians. That said, some anti-American feeling—both serious and jokey—permeates most of society. You'll earn more friends by taking it in your stride.

Sadly, the attitudes of many Argentinians toward foreigners vary greatly according to origin and race. White Europeans and North Americans are held in far greater esteem than, say, Peruvians or Bolivians. Racist reactions—anything from insults or name-calling to giving short shrift—to Asian, black, or Native American people are, unfortunately, not unusual. Although there's little you can do about this in day-to-day dealings, Argentina does have an antidiscrimination body, Institución Nacional contra la Discriminación, la Xenofobia y el Racismo (INADI; 🌐 *www.inadi.gov.ar*) that you can contact if you're the victim of serious discrimination.

GREETINGS

Argentinians have no qualms about getting physical, and the way they greet each other reflects this. One kiss on the right cheek is the customary greeting between both male and female friends. Women also greet strangers in this way, although men—especially older men—often shake hands the first time they meet someone. Other than that, handshaking is seen as very cold and formal.

When you leave a party it's normal to say good-bye to everyone in the room (or, if you're in a restaurant, to everyone at your table), which means kissing everyone once again. Unlike other Latin Americans, porteños use the formal "you" form, *usted,* only with people much older than they or in very formal situations, and the casual greeting *¡Hola!* often replaces *buen día, buenas tardes,* and *buenas noches.* In small towns, formal greetings and the use of *usted* are much more widespread.

LANGUAGE

Argentina's official language is Spanish, known locally as *castellano* (rather than *español*). It differs from other varieties of Spanish in its use of *vos* (instead of *tú*) for the informal "you" form, and there are lots of small vocabulary differences, especially for everyday things like food. Porteño intonation is rather singsong, and sounds more like Italian than Mexican or peninsular Spanish. And, like Italians, porteños supplement their words with lots and lots of gesturing. Another peculiarity is pronouncing the letters "y" and "ll" as a "sh" sound. Elsewhere these same letters are pronounced "y" or "j" and "ly". In the northern half of Argentina, the typical Spanish "r" is trilled much more softly.

In hotels, restaurants, and shops that cater to visitors, many people speak at least some English. All the same, attempts to speak Spanish are usually appreciated. Basic courtesies like *buen día* (good morning) or *buenas tardes* (good afternoon), and *por favor* (please) and *gracias* (thank you) are a good place to start. Even if your language skills are basic and phrasebook-bound, locals generally make an effort to understand you. If people don't know the answer to a question, such as a request for directions, they'll tell you so. ■**TIP→ Buenos Aires' official tourism body runs a free, 24-hour tourist-assistance hotline with English-speaking operators, 0800/999–2838.**

OUT ON THE TOWN

A firm nod of the head or raised eyebrow usually gets waiters' attention; "*disculpa*" (excuse me) also does the trick. You can ask your waiter for *la cuenta* (the check) or make a signing gesture in the air from afar.

Alcohol—especially wine and beer—is a big part of life in Argentina. Local women generally drink less than their foreign counterparts, but there are no taboos about this. Social events usually end in general tipsiness rather than all-out drunkenness, which is seen as a rather tasteless foreign habit.

Smoking is very common in Argentina, but anti-smoking legislation introduced in Buenos Aires in 2006 has banned smoking in all but the largest cafés and restaurants (which have to have extractor fans and designated smoking areas). Outside the city you still get smoke with your steak. Most larger restaurants offer no-smoking sections (*no fumadores*), but make sure to ask before you are seated. Smoking is prohibited on public transport and in government offices, banks, and cinemas.

Public displays of affection between heterosexual couples attract little attention in most parts of the country. Although same-sex marriage is now legal throughout Argentina, beyond downtown Buenos Aires same-sex couples may attract hostile reactions.

All locals make an effort to look nice—though not necessarily formal—for dinner out. Older couples get very dressed up for the theater; younger women usually put on high heels and makeup for clubbing.

If you're invited to someone's home for dinner, a bottle of good Argentine wine, a shop-bought cake or dessert, or chocolates are all good gifts to take the hosts.

SIGHTSEEING

You can dress pretty much as you like in Buenos Aires: skimpy clothing causes no offense.

Argentinian men almost always allow women to go through doors and to board buses and elevators first, often with exaggerated ceremony. Far from finding this sexist, local women take it as a God-given right. Frustratingly, there's no local rule about standing on one side of escalators to allow people to pass you.

Despite bus drivers' best efforts, locals are often reluctant to move to the back of buses. Pregnant women, the elderly, and those with disabilities have priority on the front seats of city buses, and you should offer them your seat if these are already taken.

Children and adults selling pens, notepads, or sheets of stickers are regular fixtures on urban public transport. Some children also hand out tiny greeting cards in exchange for coins. The standard procedure is to accept the merchandise or cards as the vendor moves up the carriage, then either return the item (saying *no, gracias*) or give them money when they return.

Most Argentinians are hardened jaywalkers, but given how reckless local driving can be, you'd do well to cross at corners and wait for pedestrian lights.

Paraguay. In 2009 outbreaks of dengue fever (another mosquito-borne disease) were widespread in northern Argentina, especially in Misiones province (where Iguazú Falls is), though public health campaigns reduced this in 2010. All the same, cases are regularly reported as far south as Buenos Aires. The best preventive measure against both dengue and malaria is to cover your arms and legs, use a good mosquito repellent containing DEET, and stay inside at dusk.

American trypanosomiasis, or Chagas' disease, is present in remote rural areas. The CDC recommends chloroquine as a preventive antimalarial for adults and infants in Argentina. To be effective, the weekly doses must start a week before you travel and continue four weeks after your return. There is no preventive medication for dengue or Chagas'. Children traveling to Argentina should have current inoculations against measles, mumps, rubella, and polio.

In most urban areas in Argentina, including Buenos Aires, people drink tap water and eat uncooked fruits and vegetables. However, if you're prone to tummy trouble, stick to bottled water. Take standard flu-avoidance precautions such as handwashing and cough-covering, and consider contacting your doctor for a flu shot if you're traveling during the austral winter; Argentina was hit hard by the H1N1 outbreak of 2009.

OTHER ISSUES

Apunamiento, or altitude sickness, which results in shortness of breath and headaches, may be a problem when you visit high altitudes in the Andes. To remedy any discomfort, walk slowly, eat lightly, and drink plenty of fluids (avoid alcohol). In northwestern Argentina, coca leaves are widely available (don't worry, it's totally legal). Follow the locals' example and chew a wad mixed with a dab of bicarbonate of soda on hiking trips: it does wonders for altitude problems. You can also order tea made from coca leaves (*mate de coca*), which has the same effect.

If you experience an extended period of nausea, dehydration, dizziness, or severe headache or weakness while in a high-altitude area, seek medical attention. Dehydration, sunstroke, frostbite, and heatstroke are all dangers of outdoor recreation at high altitudes. Awareness and caution are the best preventive measures.

The sun is a significant health hazard, especially in southern Patagonia, where the ozone layer is said to be thinning. Stay out of the sun at midday and wear plenty of good-quality sunblock. A limited selection is available in most supermarkets and pharmacies, but if you use high SPF factors or have sensitive skin, bring your favorite brands with you. A hat and decent sunglasses are also essential.

Health Warnings National Centers for Disease Control & Prevention 🌐 *www.cdc.gov/travel.* **World Health Organization** (*WHO*). 🌐 *www.who.int.*

HEALTH CARE

Argentina has free national health care that also provides foreigners with free outpatient care. Although the medical practitioners working at *hospitales públicos* (public hospitals) are first-rate, the institutions themselves are often underfunded: bed space and basic supplies are at a minimum, and except in emergencies you should consider leaving these resources for the people who really need them. World-class private clinics and hospitals are plentiful, and consultation and treatment fees are low compared to those in North America. Still, it's good to have some kind of medical insurance.

In nonemergency situations you'll be seen much quicker at a private clinic or hospital, and overnight stays are more comfortable. Many doctors at private hospitals speak at least some English. Note that only cities have hospitals; smaller towns may have a *sala de primeros auxilios* (first-aid post).

MEDICAL INSURANCE AND ASSISTANCE

Consider buying trip insurance with medical-only coverage. Neither Medicare nor some private insurers cover medical expenses anywhere outside of the United States. Medical-only policies typically reimburse you for medical care (excluding that related to preexisting conditions) and hospitalization abroad, and provide for evacuation. You still have to pay the bills and await reimbursement from the insurer.

Another option is to sign up with a medical-evacuation assistance company. Membership gets you doctor referrals, emergency evacuation or repatriation, 24-hour hotlines for medical consultation, and other assistance. International SOS and AirMed International provide evacuation services and medical referrals. MedjetAssist offers medical evacuation.

Medical Assistance Companies AirMed International *www.airmed.com.* **Medjet-Assist** *www.medjetassist.com.*

Medical-Only Insurers International Medical Group *800/628–4664* *www.imglobal.com.* **International SOS** *www.internationalsos.com.* **Wallach & Company** *800/237–6615, 540/687–3166* *www.wallach.com.*

OVER-THE-COUNTER REMEDIES

Towns and cities have a 24-hour pharmacy system: each night there's one *farmacia de turno* (on-duty pharmacy) for prescriptions and emergency supplies.

In Argentina, *farmacias* (pharmacies) carry painkillers, first-aid supplies, contraceptives, diarrhea treatments, and a range of other over-the-counter treatments, including drugs that would require a prescription in the United States (many antibiotics, for example). Note that acetaminophen—or Tylenol—is known as *paracetamol* in Spanish. If you think you'll need to have prescriptions filled while you're in Argentina, be sure to have your doctor write down the generic name of the drug, not just the brand name. Farmacity is a supermarket-style drugstore chain with stores all over Buenos Aires and some in Córdoba, Mendoza, and Salta.

HOLIDAYS

January through March is summer holiday season for Argentinians. Winter holidays fall toward the end of July and beginning of August. Most public holidays are celebrated on their actual date, except August 17, October 12, and November 20, which move to the following Monday. When public holidays fall on a Thursday or Tuesday, the following Friday or preceding Monday, respectively, is also declared a holiday, creating a four-day weekend known as a *feriado puente*.

Año Nuevo (New Year's Day), January 1. Carnaval (Carnival), Monday and Tuesday six weeks before Easter. **Día Nacional de la Memoria por la Verdad y la Justicia** (National Memorial Day for Truth and Justice; commemoration of the start of the 1976–82 dictatorship), March 24. **Día del Veterano y de los Caídos en la Guerra de Malvinas** (Malvinas Veterans' Day), April 2. **Semana Santa** (Easter Week), March or April. **Día del Trabajador** (Labor Day), May 1. **Primer Gobierno Patrio** (First National Government, Anniversary of the 1810 Revolution), May 25. **Día de la Bandera** (Flag Day), June 20. **Día de la Independencia** (Independence Day), July 9. **Paso a la Inmortalidad del General José de San Martín** (Anniversary of General José de San Martín's Death), August 17. **Día del Respeto a la Diversidad Cultural** (Day of Respect for Cultural Diversity), October 12. **Día de la Soberanía Nacional** (National Sovereignty Day; Anniversary of the Battle of Vuelta de Obligado), November 20. **Inmaculada Concepción de María** (Immaculate Conception), December 8. **Christmas,** December 25.

MAIL

Correo Argentino, the mail service, has an office in most towns or city neighborhoods; some *locutorios* (phone centers) serve as collection points and sell stamps. Mail delivery isn't dependable: it can take 6 to 21 days for standard letters and postcards to get to the United States. Regular airmail letters cost 9 pesos for up to 20 grams.

If you want to be sure something will arrive, send it by *correo certificado* (registered mail), which costs 26 pesos for international letters up to 20 grams. Postboxes are dark blue and yellow, but there are very few that are not directly outside—or even inside—post offices. Valuable items are best sent with express services like DHL, UPS, or FedEx—delivery within one to two days for a 5-kilogram (11-pound) package starts at about 800 pesos.

Argentina's post-code system is based on a four-digit code. Each province is assigned a letter (the city of Buenos Aires is "C," for instance) that goes before the number code, and each city block is identified by three letters afterward (such as ABD). In practice, however, only big cities use these complete postal codes (which look like C1234ABD; the rest of Argentina uses the basic number code (1234, for example).

Contacts Correo Argentino *www.correoargentino.com.ar.* **DHL** *www.dhl.com.* **Federal Express** *www.fedex.com.* **UPS** *www.ups.com.*

MONEY

Although prices in Argentina have been steadily rising, traveling here is still a reasonable value if you're coming from a country with a strong currency. Eating out is affordable, as are mid range hotels. Prices are usually significantly lower outside Buenos Aires and other large cities. Room rates at first-class hotels all over the country approach those in the United States, however.

ITEM	AVERAGE COST
Cup of coffee and three medialunas (croissants)	10–13 pesos
Glass of wine	18–25 pesos
Liter bottle of local beer at a bar	18–24 pesos
Steak and fries in a cheap restaurant	25–35 pesos
One-mile taxi ride in Buenos Aires	5.60 pesos
Museum admission	Free–15 pesos

You can plan your trip around ATMs—cash is king for day-to-day dealings. Always withdraw more cash well before your current supplies run out, particularly in small towns with few ATMs, as these often run out of money, especially over weekends or during holiday season. U.S. dollars can be changed at any bank and are often accepted as payment in clothing and souvenir stores and supermarkets. Note that there's a perennial shortage of change in Argentina. Hundred-peso bills can be hard to get rid of, so ask for 10s, 20s, and 50s when you change money and withdraw from ATMs. Traveler's checks are useful only as an emergency reserve.

You can usually pay by credit card in top-end restaurants, hotels, and stores; the latter sometimes charge a small surcharge for using credit cards. Even stores displaying stickers from different card companies may suddenly stop accepting them: look out for signs reading *tarjetas de crédito suspendidas* (credit card purchases temporarily unavailable). Outside of big cities, plastic is less widely accepted.

Visa is the most widely accepted credit card, followed closely by MasterCard. American Express is also accepted in hotels and restaurants, but Diners Club and Discover might not even be recognized. If possible, bring more than one credit card, as some establishments accept only one type. You usually have to produce photo ID—preferably a passport, but otherwise a driver's license—when making credit card purchases.

Nonchain stores often display two prices for goods: *precio de lista* (the standard price, valid if you pay by credit card) and a discounted price if you pay in *efectivo* (cash). Many travel services and even some hotels also offer cash discounts—it's always worth asking about.

Prices throughout this guide are given for adults. Substantially reduced fees are almost always available for children, students, and senior citizens.

ATMS AND BANKS

ATMs, called *cajeros automáticos*, are found all over Buenos Aires. There are two main systems. Banelco, indicated by a burgundy-color sign with white lettering, is used by Banco Francés, HSBC, Banco Galicia, Banco Santander, and Banco Patagonia. Link, recognizable by a green-and-yellow sign, is the system used by Banco Provincia and Banco de la Nación, among others. Cards on the Cirrus and Plus networks can be used on both networks.

Many banks have daily withdrawal limits of 1,000 pesos or less. Sometimes ATMs will impose unexpectedly low withdrawal limits (say, 300 pesos) on international cards—this is more common on Banelco than Link machines. You can get around it by requesting a further transaction before the machine returns your card. **TIP→ Breaking large bills can be tricky, so try to withdraw change (for example, 490 pesos, rather than 500).** Make withdrawals from ATMs in daylight, rather than at night.

ATM Locations Banelco *www.banelco.com.ar.* **Link** *www.redlink.com.ar.*

CURRENCY AND EXCHANGE

Argentina's currency is the peso, which equals 100 centavos. Bills come in denominations of 100 (violet), 50 (navy blue), 20 (red), 10 (ocher), 5 (green), and 2 (blue) pesos. Coins are in denominations of 1 peso (a heavy bimetallic coin); and 50, 25, 10, and 5 centavos. U.S. dollars are widely accepted in big-city stores, supermarkets, and at hotels and top-end restaurants (usually at a slightly worse exchange rate than you'd get at a bank). You always receive change in pesos, even when you pay with U.S. dollars. Taxi drivers may accept dollars, but it's not the norm.

At this writing, the exchange rate is 4.25 pesos to the U.S. dollar. You can change dollars at most banks (between 10 am and 3 pm), at a *casa de cambio* (money changer), or at your hotel. All currency exchange involves fees, but as a rule banks charge the least and hotels the most. You need to show your passport to complete the transaction. **TIP→ You may not be able to change currency in rural areas at all, so don't leave major cities without adequate amounts of pesos in small denominations.**

Exchange-Rate Information Oanda.com *www.oanda.com.* **XE.com** *www.xe.com.*

PACKING

Argentinian city dwellers are an appearance-conscious bunch who choose fashion over comfort any day. Though locals are stylish, they're usually fairly casual. Your nicer jeans or khakis, capri pants, skirts, and dress shorts are perfect for urban sightseeing. Combine them with stylish walking shoes or leather flats; sneakers are fine if they're out-about-town and hip. In summer many local women seem to live in nice flip-flops or sandals. With the exception of truly posh establishments, a dirty look is usually the only punishment restaurants give the underdressed; refusing entry is almost unheard-of. A jacket and tie or stylish dress are necessary only if you plan on some seriously fine dining.

In most smaller towns and villages dress is more practical and sometimes more conservative. Wherever you go in the country, take good-quality sunglasses, sunblock, and a cap or hat: the sun can be strong. A good insect repellent is useful in Buenos Aires in the summer and invaluable in Iguazú year-round.

Temperatures rarely drop below freezing in the northern half of Argentina, including Buenos Aires, but a heavier coat or jacket is still a must in winter. Temperatures drop dramatically at night in the high-altitude towns of the northwest, so bring a jacket even in summer. Proper cold-weather gear is essential for visiting southern Patagonia year-round.

Pharmacies in major cities stock a good range of toiletries, including some international brands, and hygiene products (note that only no-applicator tampons are available, however). Pharmacies, supermarkets, and kiosks sell condoms (*preservativos*), and oral contraceptive pills are available over the counter.

Toilet paper is rare in public restrooms, but you can buy pocket packs of tissues (known as *pañuelos descartables* or by their brand name, *Carilinas*) in kiosks. Antibacterial wipes and alcohol gel, available in pharmacies, can make bathroom trips more pleasant in remote areas.

PASSPORTS

Argentina operates a reciprocal entry fee scheme for citizens of countries that charge Argentinians for visas. This includes U.S. citizens, who must pay $140 on entering Argentina and carry a passport valid for at least six months. At this writing, the fee was only being charged to passengers arriving on international flights at Ezeiza and Jorge Newbery airports. You only need pay it once every ten years, and you can re-enter the country as many times as you like during that period for stays of up to 90 days—you'll receive a tourist visa stamp on your passport each time you arrive. Check the Visa Center website for up-to-date information about visa requirements.

If you need to stay longer, you can apply for a 90-day extension (*prórroga*) to your tourist visa at the Dirección Nacional de Migraciones (National Directorate for Migrations). The process takes a morning and costs about 300 pesos. Alternatively, you can exit the country (by taking a boat trip to Uruguay from Buenos Aires, or crossing into Brazil near Iguazú, for example); upon reentering Argentina, your passport will be stamped allowing an additional 90 days. Overstaying your tourist visa is illegal, and incurs a fine of 300 pesos, which you must pay at the Dirección Nacional de Migraciones before leaving Argentina. Once you have done so, you must leave the country within ten days. You should carry your passport or other photo ID with you at all times: you need it to make credit-card purchases, change money, and send parcels, as well as in the unlikely event that the police stop you.

Officially, children visiting Argentina with only one parent do not need a signed and notarized permission-to-travel letter from the other parent to visit Argentina. However, as Argentinian citizens *are* required to have such documentation, it's worth carrying a letter just in case laws change or border officials get confused. Single Parent Travel is a useful online resource that provides advice and downloadable sample permission letters.

For information on passport and visa requirements to visit the Brazilian side of Iguazú Falls, see the Planner pages at the start of Chapter 3, Side Trips from Buenos Aires.

Contacts Dirección Nacional de Migraciones ✉ *Av. Antártida Argentina 1355, Buenos Aires* ☎ *11/4317–0237* 🌐 *www.migraciones.gov.ar.* **Embassy of Argentina** 🌐 *www.embassyofargentina.us.* **Single Parent Travel** 🌐 *www.singleparenttravel.net.*

U.S. Passport Information U.S. Department of State ☎ *877/487–2778* 🌐 *travel.state.gov/passport.*

SAFETY

CRIME

When it comes to avoiding petty crime, attitude is essential: strive to look aware and purposeful at all times. Don't wear any jewelry you're not willing to lose. Even imitation jewelry and small items can attract attention and are best left behind. Keep a very firm hold of purses and cameras when out and about, and keep them on your lap in restaurants, not dangling off the back of your chair.

Always remain alert for pickpockets. Try to keep your cash and credit cards in different places about your person (and always leave one card at your hotel, if possible), so that if one gets stolen you can fall back on the other. Tickets and other valuables are best left in hotel safes. Avoid carrying large sums of money around, but always keep enough to have something to hand over if you do get mugged. Another time-honored tactic is to keep a dummy wallet (an old one containing an expired credit card and a small amount of cash) in your pocket, with your real cash in an inside or vest pocket: if your "wallet" gets stolen you have little to lose.

Women can expect pointed looks, the occasional *piropo* (a flirtatious remark, usually alluding to some physical aspect), and some advances. These catcalls rarely escalate into actual physical harassment—the best reaction is to make like local women and ignore them; reply only if you're really confident with Spanish curse words. Going to a bar alone will be seen as an open invitation for attention. If you're heading out for the night, it's wise to take a taxi.

There's usually a notable police presence in areas popular with tourists, such as San Telmo and Palermo in Buenos Aires. This seems to deter potential pickpockets and hustlers somewhat. However, Argentinians have little faith in their police forces: many officers are corrupt and involved in protection rackets or dealing in stolen goods. At best, the police are well meaning but under-equipped, so don't count on them to come to your rescue in a difficult situation. Reporting crimes is usually ineffectual, and is worth the time it takes only if you need the report for insurance.

The most important advice we can give you is to not put up a struggle in the unlikely event that you are mugged or robbed. Nearly all physical attacks on tourists are the direct result of their resisting would-be pickpockets or muggers. Comply with demands, hand over your stuff, and try to get the situation over with as quickly as possible—then let your travel insurance take care of it.

PROTESTS

Argentinians like to speak their minds, and there has been a huge increase in strikes and street protests. Protesters frequently block streets and squares in downtown Buenos Aires, causing major traffic jams. Some are protesting government policies, others may be showing support for these. Either way, trigger-happy local police have historically proved themselves more of a worry than the demonstrators, but though protests are usually peaceful, exercise caution if you happen across one.

SCAMS

Beware scams such as a kindly passer-by offering to help you clean the mustard/ketchup/cream that has somehow appeared on your clothes: while your attention is occupied, an accomplice picks your pocket or snatches your bag.

Taxi drivers in big cities are usually honest, but occasionally they decide to take people for a ride, literally. All official cabs have meters, so make sure this is turned on. Some scam artists have hidden switches that make the meter tick over more quickly, but simply driving a circuitous route is a more common ploy. It helps to have an idea where you're going and how long it will take. Local lore says that if hailing taxis on the street, those with lights on top (usually labeled "Radio Taxi") are more trustworthy. Late at night, try to call for a cab—all hotels and restaurants, no matter how cheap, have a number and will usually call for you.

When asking for price quotes when shopping in touristy areas, always confirm whether the price is in dollars or pesos. Some salespeople, especially street vendors, have found that they can take advantage of confused tourists by charging dollars for goods that are actually priced in pesos. If you're in doubt about that beautiful leather coat, don't be shy about asking whether the number on the tag is in pesos or dollars.

Advisories and Other Information Transportation Security Administration (*TSA*). 🌐 *www.tsa.gov.* **U.S. Department of State** 🌐 *www.travel.state.gov.*

TAXES

Argentina has departure taxes of $29 on international flights, $17.50 on domestic flights over 300 km, and $12.90 for domestic flights under 300 km. These taxes are included in your ticket price when you fly from some airports, including Buenos Aires'. Otherwise you can pay by credit card or in cash at booths in airports in pesos, dollars, or euros. Hotel rooms carry a 21% tax. Cheaper hotels and hostels tend to include this in their quoted rates; more expensive hotels add it to your bill.

Argentina has 21% V.A.T. (known as IVA) on most consumer goods and services. The tax is usually included in the price of goods and noted on your receipt. You can get nearly all the IVA back on locally manufactured goods if you spend more than 70 pesos at stores displaying a Global Blue duty-free sign. You're given a Global Blue refund check to the value of the IVA, which you get stamped by customs at the airport, and can then cash in at the clearly signed tax refund booths. Allow an extra hour to get this done.

Tax refunds Global Blue ☎ *11/5238–1970* 🌐 *www.globalrefund.com.*

TIME

Argentina is three hours behind G.M.T., or three hours ahead of U.S. Central Standard Time. Although Argentina does not currently observe daylight saving, it has in the past, so double-check time differences when you travel.

Time-Zone Information Timeanddate.com 🌐 *www.timeanddate.com/worldclock.*

TIPPING

Propinas (tips) are a question of rewarding good service rather than an obligation. Restaurant bills—even those that have a *cubierto* (bread and service charge)—don't include gratuities; locals usually add 10%. Bellhops and maids expect tips only in the very expensive hotels, where a tip in dollars is appreciated. You can also give a small tip (10% or less) to tour guides. Porteños round off taxi fares, though some cabbies who frequent hotels popular with tourists seem to expect more. Tipping is a nice gesture with beauty and barbershop personnel—5%–10% is fine.

TIPPING GUIDELINES FOR ARGENTINA	
Bellhop at top-end hotels	$1–$5 per bag, depending on the level of the hotel
Hotel maid at top-end hotels	1$–$3 a day (either daily or at the end of your stay, in cash)
Hotel room-service waiter	$1 to $2 per delivery, even if a service charge has been added
Taxi driver	10%, or round up the fare to the next full peso amount
Tour guide	10% of the cost of the tour if service was good
Waiter	10%–15%, depending on service
Restroom attendants	Small change, such as 50¢ or 1 peso.

TRIP INSURANCE

Comprehensive trip insurance is valuable if you're booking a very expensive or complicated trip (particularly to an isolated region) or if you're booking far in advance. Comprehensive policies typically cover trip-cancellation and interruption, letting you cancel or cut your trip short because of a personal emergency, illness, or, in some cases, acts of terrorism in your destination. Such policies also cover evacuation and medical care. (For trips abroad you should at least have medical-only coverage; *for more information,* ⇨ *see Medical Insurance & Assistance under Health, above*). Some also cover you for trip delays because of bad weather or mechanical problems as well as for lost or delayed baggage.

Another type of coverage to look for is financial default—that is, when your trip is disrupted because a tour operator, airline, or cruise line goes out of business. Generally you must buy this when you book your trip or shortly thereafter, and it's available to you only if your operator isn't on a list of excluded companies.

Always read the fine print of your policy to make sure that you are covered for the risks that are of most concern to you. Compare several policies to make sure you're getting the best price and range of coverage available.

Insurance Comparison Sites **Insure My Trip.com** ☎ *800/487–4722* 🌐 *www.insuremytrip.com.* **Square Mouth.com** ☎ *800/240–0369, 727/564–9203* 🌐 *www.squaremouth.com.*

Comprehensive Travel Insurers **Access America** ☎ *800/284–8300* 🌐 *www.accessamerica.com.* **AIG Travel Guard** ☎ *800/826–4919* 🌐 *www.travelguard.com.* **CSA Travel Protection** ☎ *800/873–9855* 🌐 *www.csatravelprotection.com.* **HTH Worldwide** ☎ *610/254–8700* 🌐 *www.hthworldwide.com.* **Travel Insured International** ☎ *800/243–3174* 🌐 *www.travelinsured.com.* **Travelex Insurance** ☎ *800/228–9792* 🌐 *www.travelex-insurance.com.*

VISITOR INFORMATION

All major cities and most smaller tourist destinations have tourist offices that can provide information on accommodation and sightseeing and maps. The quality of these varies according to local funding, but employees are usually friendly and helpful. The city of Buenos Aires has tourist information booths around the city. Its extensive website includes downloadable maps, free MP3 walking tours, and insightful articles on porteño culture, though sadly the English translations of these are often hard to understand.

Each Argentine province also operates a tourist office in Buenos Aires, usually called the *Casa de [Province Name] en Buenos Aires*. The government umbrella organization for all regional and city-based tourist offices is the *Secretaría de Turismo* (Secretariat of Tourism). Their no-frills website has links and addresses to these offices, and lots of other practical information.

Limited tourist information is also available at Argentina's embassy and consulates in the United States.

Contacts **Argentina (Official Web Portal)** 🌐 *www.argentina.ar.* **Argentine Secretariat of Tourism** ☎ *800/555–0016 in Argentina* 🌐 *www.turismo.gov.ar.* **Dirección de Turismo del Gobierno de la Ciudad de Buenos Aires** (*Turismo Buenos Aires*). ☎ *0800/999–2838 in Argentina* 🌐 *www.bue.gov.ar.* **Embassy of Argentina** 🌐 *www.embassyofargentina.us.*

ONLINE RESOURCES

The like-minded travelers on Fodors.com are eager to answer questions and swap travel tales. The regional information and downloadable maps on slick government-run Argentina Travel website are a great pre-trip planning resource. Its sister site, 🌐 *Argentina.ar* has excellent general information on different aspects of Argentine culture, studying and investing in the country, and helpful travel tips. Welcome Argentina has good overviews of Argentina's different regions.

The website of the *Buenos Aires Herald*, the city's English-language daily, gives a conservative take on major local news stories. Brief but often amusing commentaries on local news and cultural events are at *The Argentine Post*. The website of English-language monthly newspaper

The Argentina Independent has traveler-oriented news and cultural information. *What's Up Buenos Aires is* a slick bilingual guide, run by American expats, to contemporary culture and partying in the city. The website of bimonthly English-language magazine *BA Insider* is packed with up-to-date listings on cultural activities such as language exchanges, writing workshops, and volunteering opportunities. It also has a wealth of information and resources aimed at long-term foreign visitors to Buenos Aires. More insider tips on expat life in Buenos Aires are at the BA Expats forum and Discover Buenos Aires.

The Museo Nacional de Bellas Artes contains the world's biggest collection of Argentine art, and has lots of background on Argentinian artists. Todo Tango is a comprehensive bilingual tango site with tango lyrics, history, and free downloads.

Bilingual Wines of Argentina is overflowing with information about Argentina's best tipple. Mate Argentino has everything you wanted to know about mate (a type of tea) but were afraid to ask, but in Spanish only. For insight into local cooking, restaurants, and ingredients, head to Saltshaker, the blog of American food writer Dan Perlman, and Buenos Aires Foodies.

All About Argentina Argentina (Official Web Portal) 🌐 *www.argentina.ar.* **Argentina Travel** 🌐 *www.argentina.travel.* **Argentine Secretariat of Tourism** 🌐 *www.turismo.gov.ar.* **Embassy of Argentina** 🌐 *www.embassyofargentina.us.* **Fodors.com** 🌐 *www.fodors.com/forums.* **Welcome Argentina** 🌐 *www.welcomeargentina.com.*

Culture and Entertainment Museo Nacional de Bellas Artes 🌐 *www.mnba.org.ar.* **Todo Tango** 🌐 *www.todotango.com.ar.* **What's Up Buenos Aires** 🌐 *www.whatsupbuenosaires.com.*

Food and Drink Argentine Wines 🌐 *www.argentinewines.com.* **Mate Argentino** 🌐 *www.mateargentino.com.* **Saltshaker** 🌐 *www.saltshaker.net.* **Wines of Argentina** 🌐 *www.winesofargentina.org.*

Media The Argentine Post 🌐 *www.argentinepost.com.* **The Argentina Independent** 🌐 *www.argentinaindependent.com.* **Buenos Aires Herald** 🌐 *www.buenosairesherald.com.*

Great Reads Sample the work of Argentina's greatest writers with Jorge Luis Borges' *Labyrinths: Selected Stories and Other Writings* and Julio Cortázar's *Blow Up: And Other Stories.* Bruce Chatwin's *In Patagonia* is the most classic piece of travel writing on Argentina. Delve deeper into the lives of two (in)famous Argentinians with Tomás Eloy Martínez's *Santa Evita,* a fictional look at Eva Perón's life and death, and Jon Lee Anderson's excellent biography *Che Guevara: A Revolutionary Life.*

On-screen Juan José Campanella's Oscar-winning thriller *The Secret in Their Eyes* is set in the politically troubled Buenos Aires of the early 1970s. A remorse-struck gaucho is the stormy star of Fernando Spiner's *Aballay*, an arty Argentine Western filmed in Tucumán province. A hapless traveling salesman is the unlikely hero of Carlos Sorín's Patagonian road movie *Intimate Stories.* Lucrecia Martel's *The Holy Girl* is an oppressive but brilliantly made film about a Catholic schoolgirl in Salta. Bariloche is the backdrop to Fabián Bielinsky's eerie psychological drama *The Aura.*

INDEX

A

B

Z

PHOTO CREDITS

1, Ignacio Alvarez/age fotostock. 3, ARCO/P. Wegner/age fotostock. **Chapter 1: Experience Argentina:** 6-7, Andrew Mirhej, fodors.com member. 8 (top), jd_miller, fodors.com member. 8 (center), M. Scanel, fodors.com member. 8 (bottom), Andrew Mirhej, fodors.com member. 12, Tony Morrison/South American Pictures. 13 (left), Jacynth Roode/iStockphoto. 13 (right), berhbs, fodors.com member. 14 (left), pdqu2, fodors.com member. 14 (top center), Tokyo Tanenhaus/Flickr. 14 (bottom center), feserc/Flickr. 14 (right), fortes/Flickr. 15 (left), iStockphoto. 15 (top center), Clive Ellston, fodors.com member. 15 (bottom center), rm/Shutterstock. 15 (right), iladm/Shutterstock. 16, Andy Christodolo/Cephas Picture Library/Alamy. 17, Popperphoto/Alamy. 18, Brand X Pictures. 19 (left), AFP PHOTO/ALI BURAFI/Newscom. 19 (right), Juanderlust, fodors.com member. 20, Diego_3336/Flickr. 21, MIMOHE/Shutterstock. 24, Galina Barskaya/Shutterstock. 26, Pablo Caridad/iStockphoto. 27 (left), Image Asset Management/age fotostock. 27 (right), José Francisco Ruiz/age fotostock. 28 (left), Eduardo M. Rivero/age fotostock. 28 (bottom right), Jordi Camí/age fotostock. 29 (right), Apeiron-Photo/Alamy. 30 (left and top right), A.H.C./age fotostock. 30 (bottom right), Pictorial Press Ltd/Alamy. 31 (left), Archivo Gráfico de Clarín (Argentina)/Wikimedia Commons/Public domain. 31 (top right), Tramonto/age fotostock. 31(bottom right), Griffiths911/wikipedia.org. 32 (left), Christopher Pillitz/Alamy. 32 (top right), Nikada/iStockphoto. 32 (bottom right), DYN/Getty Images/Newscom. 33 (top), Roberto Fiadone/wikipedia.org. 33 (bottom left), wikipedia.org. **Chapter 2: Buenos Aires:** 35, Dan Leffel/age fotostock. 36, Christine Yuan, fodors.com member. 37 (top), EL UNIVERSAL/Newscom. 37 (bottom), Seamus, fodors.com member. 38, caron malecki, fodors.com member. 43, lilap/Flickr. 44, blmurch/Flickr. 50-51, iStockphoto. 57, James Wong, fodors.com member. 58, Alfredo Maiquez/age fotostock. 61, Alvaro Leiva/age fotostock. 65, Dan DeLuca/wikipedia.org. 66, caron malecki, fodors.com member. 69, giulio andreini/age fotostock. 73, wabauer, fodors.com member. 74, Beth/Queen/ZUMA Press/Newscom. 76, Jose Fuste Raga/age fotostock. 78, Wim Wiskerke/Alamy. 82, Church of emacs/wikipedia.org. 89, Martin Byrne, fodors.com member. 94, GUY Christian/age fotostock. 100 (top and bottom right), The Leading Hotels of the World. 100 (bottom left), Algodon Mansion. 101 (top), Hyatt Hotels. 101 (bottom left), Fabrice Rambert/Sofitel. 101 (bottom right), CasaCalma Hotel. 104, Christopher Pillitz/Alamy. 106, 2litros > raimundo illanes/Flickr. 109, Ernesto Ríos Lanz/age fotostock. 110, wikipedia.org. 111, eyalos.com/Shutterstock. 112 (top), *Picture Contact/Alamy*. 112 (2nd from top), *Christina Wilson/Alamy*. 112 (3rd from top), *Michel Friang/Alamy*. 112 (bottom), *Jason Howe/South American Pictures*. 113 (top), Archivo General de la Nación/wikipedia.org. 113 (bottom), Danita Delimont/Alamy. 114, christina wilson/Alamy. 121, Jon Hicks/Alamy. 126, Pablo Abuliak. **Chapter 3: Side Trips:** 129, David Lyons/Alamy. 130, Dario Diament/Shutterstock. 131 (top), Woodward Chile/Flickr. 131 (bottom), Carla Antonini/Wikimedia Commons. 132, Pablodda/Flickr. 136, Alberto/Flickr. 146-147, *Jeremy Hoare/Alamy*. 148, *Chris Sharp/South American Pictures*. 149, *Pablo D. Flores*. 150, *Jeremy Hoare/Alamy*. 151, *SuperStock*. 152 (top), *Hughes/age fotostock*. 152 (bottom), *Johannes Odland/Shutterstock*. 156, ricald/Flickr. 163, Ken Welsh/age fotostock. 164, Gerad Coles/iStockphoto. 165, Sue Cunningham Photographic/Alamy. 166-67, Fritz Poelking/age fotostock. 166 (inset), Albasmalko/wikipedia.org. 167 (inset), flavia bottazzini/iStockphoto. 168, travelstock44/Alamy. 169, vittorio sciosia/age fotostock. **Chapter 4: The Northwest:** 173, Fabian von Poser/age fotostock. 174, JOSE ALBERTO TEJO/Shutterstock. 175 (top), Colman Lerner Gerardo/Shutterstock. 175 (bottom), Alicia Nijdam/Flickr. 176, Ignacio Alvarez/age fotostock. 177 (top), B. Hennings, Nürnberg, Germany/wikipedia.org. 177 (bottom), Alicia Nijdam/wikipedia.org. 178, Guerretto/Flickr. 186, Ignacio Alvarez/age fotostock. 190-91, Wolfgang Herzog/age fotostock. 192, WYSOCKI Pawel/age fotostock. 193 (top), Walter Bibikow/age fotostock. 193 (bottom), borderlys/Flickr. 194-95, ARCO/Therin-Weise/age fotostock. 196 (top), Clive Ellston, fodors.com member. 196 (bottom), Joris Van Ostaeyen/iStockphoto. 197 (top), Lee Torrens/Shutterstock. 197 (bottom), Humawaka/wikipedia.org. 198, Ignacio Alvarez/age fotostock. 200, Clive Ellston, fodors.com member. 204, Angel Manzano/age fotostock. 210, Nacho Calonge/age fotostock. 215, ARCO/Stengert, N/age fotostock. 220, GM Photo Images/Alamy. 225, Heeb Christian/age fotostock. **Chapter 5: Wine Regions:** 229, David Noton Photography/Alamy. 230, CASA DEL VISITANTE Familia Zuccardi, Mendoza. 231 (top), iStockphoto. 231 (bottom), dubonnet, fodors.com member. 232, Jason Maehl/Shutterstock. 233 (top), José Carlos Pires Pereira/iStockphoto. 233 (bottom), fainmen/Flickr. 234, CASA DEL VISITANTE Familia Zuccardi, Mendoza. 243, Heeb Christian/age fotostock. 250-51, Cephas Picture Library/Alamy. 253, Yadid Levy/age fotostock. 258, Luc./Flickr. 264-65, Bon Appetit/Alamy. 264 (bottom), Dizzy/Alamy. 266 (top), Douglas Peebles/Stock Connection/Aurora Photos. 266 (2nd from top), Clay McLachlan/Aurora Photos. 266 (3rd from top), WinePix/Alamy. 266 (bottom), Karen Ward/South American Pictures. 267 (top), Pablo Abuliak. 267 (2nd from top), John and Brenda Davenport, fodors.com member. 267 (3rd from top), Pablo Abuliak. 267 (bottom), matetic.com. 269 (top), Pablo Abuliak. 269 (center), CASA DEL VISITANTE Familia Zuccardi, Mendoza. 269 (bottom),

Mark Surman/Flickr. 270, Tony Morrison/South American Pictures. 280, Pablo Abuliak. 291, Andre Charland from Canada/wikipedia.org. 298, Jason Maehl/Shutterstock. **Chapter 6: The Lake District:** 303, Arco Images GmbH/Alamy. 304 (top), rm/Shutterstock. 304 (center), Sam Chadwick/Shutterstock. 304 (bottom), Rafael Franceschini/Shutterstock. 305 (top), ricardo.martins/Flickr. 305 (bottom), JOSE ALBERTO TEJO/Shutterstock. 306, FLPA/Krystyna Szuleck/age fotostock. 307 (top), Greg Cooper/iStockphoto. 307 (bottom), wikipedia.org. 308, HappyTrvlr, fodors.com member. 309 (top), Josh Roe, fodors.com member. 309 (bottom), ArielMartin/Shutterstock. 310, Alfonsitomaria/wikipedia.org, 319, Yadid Levy/age fotostock. 321, Walter Bibikow/age fotostock. 328-29, hdcaplan, fodors.com member. 332-33, Diana Proemm/age fotostock. 334, Karl Weatherly/age fotostock. 336, David Kleyn/Alamy. 340, Jason Friend/Alamy. 343, Walter Bibikow/age fotostock. 346, Heeb Christian/age fotostock. 353, ImageState/Alamy. **Chapter 7: Patagonia:** 355, R. Matina/age fotostock. 356, David Thyberg/Shutterstock. 357 (top), Gerad Coles/iStockphoto. 357 (bottom), Pablo H Caridad/Shutterstock. 358, A Maywald/age fotostock. 359 (top), Eduardo Rivero/Shutterstock. 359 (bottom), Pablo H Caridad/Shutterstock. 360, Karen Coleman, fodors.com member. 367, Gareth McCormack/Alamy. 368, WYSOCKI Pawel/age fotostock. 369, Gareth McCormack/Alamy. 370, Colin Monteath/age fotostock. 371, Galen Rowell/Mountain Light/Alamy. 372 (top), Jan Baks/Alamy. 372 (bottom), Heeb Christian/age fotostock. 373, Peter Essick/Aurora Photos. 374 (left), Laura Hart/Shutterstock. 374 (top center), Michael S. Nolan/age fotostock. 374 (top right), jan.kneschke/Flickr. 374 (bottom right), ARCO/P. Wegner/age fotostock. 375 (top left), Danita Delimont/Alamy. 375 (bottom left), Derek Dammann/iStockphoto. 375 (bottom center), iStockphoto. 375 (top right), David R. Frazier Photolibrary, Inc./Alamy. 375 (bottom right), David Ryan/Alamy. 379, Michael S. Nolan/age fotostock. 386, Juan Carlos Muñoz/age fotostock. 391, paul bridgewater - www.londonmusicphotographer.com/Flickr. 395, Heeb Christian/age fotostock. 401, Raymond Forbes/age fotostock. 404, Anna Hainze, fodors.com member. 411, Lois Zebelman, fodors.com member. 414, Tony West/Alamy. 418, Michele Molinari/Alamy. 426, Marco Simoni/age fotostock. 432, Colin Monteath/age fotostock. 437, Dave Houser/age fotostock. 442, Danny Aeberhard/South American Pictures.

NOTES

ABOUT OUR WRITERS

After working as a journalist at British newspapers, **Amanda Barnes** left her job on the editor desk three years ago and headed to South America in search of sunshine, a real-life Borges fantasy, and mastering the art of a good *asado*. When she isn't trotting around on travel assignments Amanda is based at the heart of Argentine wine country, in Mendoza, where she is editor of *Wine Republic* magazine and writes for numerous international travel and wine publications. For this edition she updated the Patagonia chapter.

In 2009, with no Spanish ability and no real plan, **Cathy Brown** bought one way tickets to Buenos Aires for her family. The stunning landscapes and the warm, laid-back culture have since convinced her to make Argentina home. After a year in Patagonia, she moved to the Mendoza area, where she enjoys year-round sunshine, long siestas, and endless Malbec wine. Cathy is a hitchhiking, backpacking gypsy at heart who has curiously found herself an unlikely specialist in the luxury travel market niche, regularly writing and reviewing for *Luxury Latin America*. For this guide, she updated the Wine Regions chapter.

Karina Martinez-Carter lives in Buenos Aires, the city she moved to after graduating college in 2010. She contributes regularly to BBC Travel and also has written for *The Atlantic, The Huffington Post,* and *Time Out Buenos Aires,* among other publications. Karina updated the Buenos Aires Where to Stay section for this edition.

A British journalist working on the *Buenos Aires Herald*'s economy desk, **Sorrel Moseley-Williams** first visited Argentina as a year-abroad student in 1998 and has been in a long-term relationship with the country since 2006. She contributes to *Time Out Buenos Aires, The Real Argentina, Wallpaper*, DK Eyewitness Argentina, Screen International,* and *ON Mag* (in Spanish), and writes the weekly Wining On food and drink column found on *www.sorrelmw.com*. She updated the Northwest chapter and the Buenos Aires After Dark and Shopping sections for this edition.

Victoria Patience first came to Argentina to spend a year studying Latin American literature. Eleven years later, she still hasn't managed to leave. She lives in Buenos Aires province with her Argentinean husband, daughter, dogs, and cats. She is a freelance contributor to many Fodor's guidebooks and also runs her own editing and translation company, Nativa Wordcraft. Victoria updated the Experience and Travel Smart chapters, as well as the Buenos Aires Neighborhoods and Tango sections and portions of the Side Trips chapter.

Dan Perlman is a trained chef and sommelier, and an internationally published food, wine, and travel writer with some 30 years' experience under his whisk and pen. Currently he's living and working in Buenos Aires, where he runs the wildly popular Casa SaltShaker underground restaurant. Dan updated the Buenos Aires Where to Eat section.

Jessica Pollack, a Buenos Aires–based writer, updated portions of the Side Trips chapter for this edition.

Brian Stevenson came to Argentina in the mid 1990s while working as a river expedition leader for the adventure travel company Mountain Travel Sobek. He's made a number of return trips to travel and to work as a guide and outdoor photographer. He is currently writing and photographing a guidebook to skiing and snowboarding in Argentina and Chile that will be published in early 2013. He updated the Lake District Chapter for this edition.